KU-863-499

ED DOUGLAS

Himalaya

VINTAGE

3 5 7 9 10 8 6 4

Vintage is part of the Penguin Random House group of companies
whose addresses can be found at global.penguinrandomhouse.com

Penguin
Random House
UK

Copyright © Ed Douglas 2020

Ed Douglas has asserted his right to be identified as the
author of this Work in accordance with the Copyright,
Designs and Patents Act 1988

First published in Vintage in 2021
First published in hardback by Bodley Head in 2020

penguin.co.uk/vintage

A CIP catalogue record for this book is available
from the British Library

ISBN 9781784704483 (B format)

Printed and bound in Great Britain by Clays Ltd, Elcograf S.p.A.

The authorised representative in the EEA is Penguin Random House
Ireland, Morrison Chambers, 32 Nassau Street, Dublin D02 YH68.

Penguin Random House is committed to a sustainable future
for our business, our readers and our planet. This book is
made from Forest Stewardship Council® certified paper.

MIX
Paper from
responsible sources
FSC
www.fsc.org
FSC® C018179

Birth, sickness, ageing and death flow ever onward, a river without ford or bridge ... Have you prepared yourself a boat?

Dampa Sangye (died 1117)

This is a land of hearsay and rumour:
If you dig down and look, you'll find nothing
But hearsay and rumour
Heaped up beneath every home,
So this is a land of hearsay and rumour,
A country standing on hearsay and rumour,
A country that has risen up on hearsay and rumour ...

Bhupi Sherchan (1935–1989)

For Himalayan people, wherever

Contents

List of Maps

I

Pilgrims

The Earth asked Vishnu, 'Why do you come in the form of mountains and not in your own form?' Vishnu replied: 'The pleasure that exists in mountains is greater than that of animate beings, for they feel no heat, nor cold, nor pain, nor anger, nor fear, nor pleasure. We three gods as mountains will reside in the earth for the benefit of mankind.'

In the late summer of 1995 I flew to India for my first experience of climbing in the Himalaya. The monsoon was still strong and in those days, a quarter of a century ago, parts of Delhi flooded more readily; many lower-lying streets were submerged in brown water. It was still raining as we drove north in a bus, stopping for a night in Rishikesh on the banks of the swollen Ganges. The Beatles studied transcendental meditation here in 1968 with the Maharishi Mahesh Yogi, turning on millions of young Westerners to eastern spiritual practices. 'After I had taken LSD,' George Harrison recalled, 'a lingering thought stayed with me, and the thought was "the yogis of the Himalayas". ... That was part of the reason I went to India. Ravi [Shankar] and the sitar were excuses; although they were a very important part of it, it was a search for a spiritual connection.' It occurred to me only much later that I had been lifted into the mountains on the last gasp of the same cultural tide, upstairs in my suburban bedroom in the early 1980s, listening to old Bob Dylan records and reading stories of my climbing heroes high in the faraway, mythical Himalaya.

Next day we reached the mountains, half-submerged in a torrential downpour. The roads ran with water; mist clung to rock faces that overhung the roof of the bus. Heavy cloud shrouded the peaks. A mile or so from the village of Gangotri, in what was then part of Uttar Pradesh, the bus stopped abruptly. Huge granite boulders had tumbled down from a cliff above, loosened by the rain. It would take explosives and bulldozers to clear the way. For now, this was the end of the road. We peered up at the unstable slope wondering about the next rock fall, anxious to get going and out of the way. A number of lean and eager men surrounded the bus, grinning wildly, dressed in thin cotton shorts and shirts and holding plastic sheeting around their shoulders, their only protection against the rain. A price was agreed and our gear continued into the village on their backs. We followed, sheltering under umbrellas. It was as though I'd found a door marked 'adventure' and stepped through it.

The scale of the Himalaya is disorienting: not simply muscular but steroidal. On that first expedition, the intensity of the mountains felt overwhelming, even oppressive. Everything was bigger than I had experienced before: the peaks themselves, the rivers, the rock falls, the avalanches, the glaciers, the legends and myths. From the plains of India, the range was like a white wall, a castle of impossible dreams, a rampart separating South and Central Asia, China from India. The clash of their competing interests in the mountains on their respective borders has usually been at the expense of the people who live there, with China now occupying Tibet. In 1962, the world's two most populous nations had even gone to war in the Himalaya.

There are few places in the world where geography inspires the human imagination to such a degree. There are longer mountain ranges: the Andes are the longest at seven thousand kilometres. But there are none higher. The Himalaya are themselves part of a vast highland region that runs in a crescent for four thousand kilometres from Kyrgyzstan in the west to Myanmar in the east and includes the Pamir, Hindu Kush and Karakoram ranges. Around four hundred mountains on earth exceed 7,000 metres and they're all located here, including the magical fourteen that top 8,000.

The Himalaya range itself makes up the eastern two-thirds of this region, an area of 600,000 square kilometres between the Indus in the west and the Brahmaputra in the east, at the same latitudes as the Middle East, North Africa, Texas and northern Mexico. The range is anchored at either end by two great mountains, Nanga Parbat in Pakistan and Namche Barwa where Tibet's great river the Yarlung Tsangpo bends sharply south to become India's Brahmaputra. The region includes part of the high plateau of Tibet, the highest and largest plateau on earth, five times the size of France and with an average altitude of 4,500 metres: the roof of the world.

The Himalaya's diversity is astonishing and multifaceted. The western portion, including the Indian regions of Ladakh and Zanskar, are semi-desert, dry and cold for much of the year. The eastern end, the watershed of the Brahmaputra, includes some of the wettest places on earth, with precipitation in excess of ten metres a year. Nowhere is this heterogeneity more marked that in the Himalaya's vertical relief. For every kilometre you climb, average temperatures drop by more than six degrees Celsius. Altitude in this regard mimics latitude, meaning that with a few kilometres of altitude gain, you can travel the equivalent of thousands of kilometres in latitude, from the tropics to the polar ice caps. The amount of ice locked away in the glaciers of the Himalaya and Karakoram, now melting rapidly as the climate heats up, has prompted geographers to call the region the Third Pole.

Altitude, climate and scale are only the start. Like light scattering through a crystal, the complex, three-dimensional shapes made by the mountains have immense implications for their natural diversity and the human populations that inhabit them. Many with no knowledge of the Himalaya assume the mountains are a natural wilderness, but they support a population of around fifty million, no less diverse than the landscapes they live in, a place where three of the world's great religions – Hinduism, Islam and Buddhism – converge. Each Himalayan valley's human history is intimately connected to its geography. Slopes that catch the sun or else are sheltered from the wind are more hospitable to life than neighbouring aspects that don't. At a glance, you can see the difference between, for example, a shadowy gorge and a flat, sunlit piece of ground tucked in the lee of a ridgeline. The sheer scale of this landscape has an unusually intense impact on human activity, and ultimately physiology. Until very recently, the only way to get around was on foot or on the back of an animal. It's quite something to greet the day in a village on a ridgeline in the middle hills of the Himalaya and look across a valley to the neighbouring village and know it will take most of the day to reach it, plunging thousands of feet down to the river below in the shadow of morning and then labouring up the opposite slope in the hot afternoon sun. Like every-where else, water is of greatest concern, a life-giver and life-taker, but

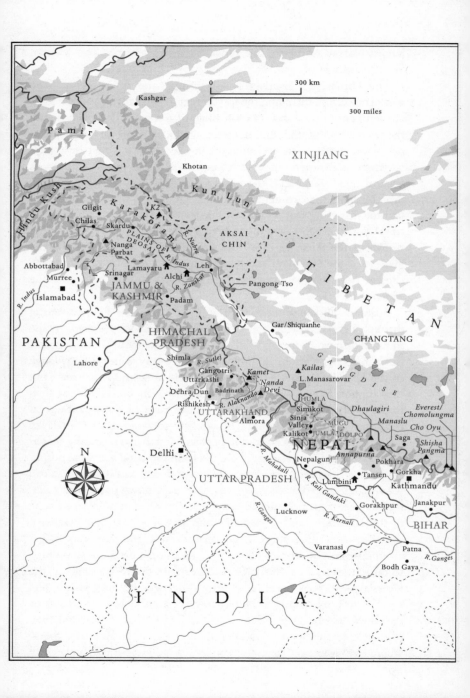

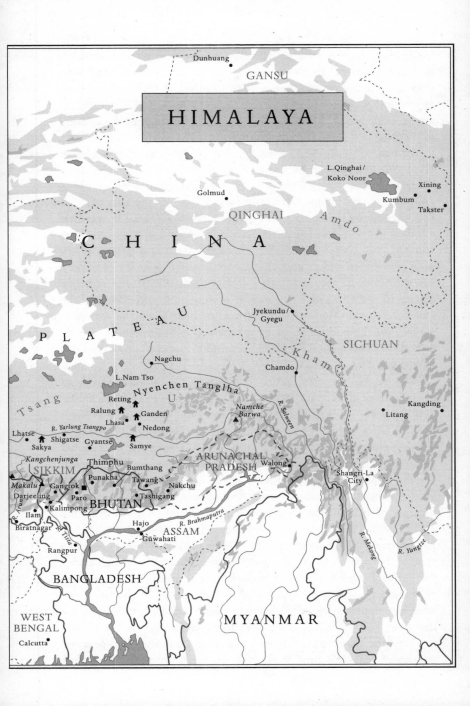

in the Himalaya it is architect as well, carving through the mountains, first as glaciers of ice then raging torrents of meltwater and rain, ripping them up, washing them away. Climbing is hard and unnecessary, a strange luxury. Mountains are places for gods, not people. Rivers are for both and of far more consequence and interest to those living in mountains than to those who merely visit them.

We had come to the Garhwal region of the Indian Himalaya to climb Shivling, a chipped tooth of white and gold that pierces the deepening blue of high altitude above the Gangotri glacier: ravishing and austere. For many climbers, not just me, it's the sort of peak that provokes a yearning that's actually physical. Since it was first climbed in the 1970s, some of the world's best mountaineers have climbed new routes on Shivling's steepest faces and ridges. When seen marked altogether on a photograph these lines look like spider's silk anchored to the mountain's fabric. Each thin strand contains stories of suffering and endurance, imagination and courage, the stuff of legend. Many of the mountains near it on the Gangotri glacier also have these lines of ascent and contain similar stories, passed on in books and films that in turn bring more climbers to this valley: pilgrims of a sort.

Yet whatever Gangotri means to climbers, it is sacred to hundreds of millions of Indians for something else. The glacier's hollow snout, now receding quickly, is known as Gaumukh, meaning 'the cow's mouth', from which flows a milky stream: the source of the Ganges. The towering shape of Shivling is located at the centre of a sacred geography first mapped out in the epic Sanskrit poem the *Mahabharata*, which lies near the heart of Hindu culture and whose origins stretch back almost three thousand years. As it starts its 2,500 km journey to the Bay of Bengal, the river is called Bhagirathi. According to the *Mahabharata*, the mythical figure Bhagiratha, after whom the river is named, prayed for a thousand years for its waters to flow in order to expiate the sins of sixty thousand relatives who had perished under the curse of a great sage they had wrongly accused. Yet the goddess of the river, Ganga, remained in the heavens, at the centre of the universe, 'the still point of the turning world', unwilling to leave. Only the great god Shiva had the power to make her go, so Bhagiratha followed the command of Shiva's counterpart, Brahma, to pray for one more year, this time living only on air. Only then was Ganga forced from heaven, rushing to earth on the *jata*, the matted dreadlocks of Shiva's head, bringing life-giving water to the plains of India.

This story in the *Mahabharata* is told to five brothers, the Pandavas, who really are on a pilgrimage. Like us, they were outsiders, spiritual explorers in an otherworldly part of India known as Devbhumi, land of the gods, far from the political frenzy of court life. Hinduism's founding texts, the *Veda*, are actually centuries older still, and their geographical references, to the Himalaya or anywhere else, are thin on the ground. (In fact, their cultural focus is further west, between the Indus and Sutlej rivers.) But by the time of the *Mahabharata*, a poem that looks back to a lost age of heroic kings, Hinduism and the Indo-Aryan culture that produced it had firmly rooted itself around the Ganges. In the *Mahabharata*, the extreme landscape of the Himalaya, where the Ganges finds its source, is being drawn inside the narrative of Hinduism's established and expanding culture.

The word 'Himalaya', Sanskrit for 'abode of snow', features regularly in the poem, although there are other names for the mountains too: Shivalaya, the 'abode of Shiva', Himachal, or 'mountains of snow', and Himavant, the 'mountain king' who was father of Ganga. In India the word is used for the entire chain of mountains but in Nepal, where it is simply Himal, the name refers to a discrete group of mountains within that chain. The pronunciation of Himalaya has proved slippery, though. In Europe and North America stress now goes on the third syllable, but in Sanskrit it goes on the second. And languages that developed from Sanskrit – Hindi, Urdu, Nepali – all deal with the word slightly differently.

During the mid 1920s this vexed question troubled a senior Indian civil servant called Geoffrey Corbett. From his office window in the hill-town of Simla, looking up from government papers on India's commerce and industry, Corbett could see the Himalaya. Corbett had been a climber since he was a boy and would spend his leave exploring the mountains. Already a member of the famous Alpine Club, the first mountaineering club founded in 1857, he thought of founding a Himalayan Club; it wasn't a new idea, but Corbett had the contacts and became the first honorary secretary. Yet how to say their name? Given that Corbett chaired meetings with officials from all over India, he paused in the middle of a discussion and asked them. He got a different answer from each linguistic background: Hindi, Urdu and

Bengali. He put the matter to the languages adviser at army head-quarters. The adviser concluded that Tibetans as well as Hindi and Urdu-speaking Indians stressed the first 'a' as long, especially Urdu speakers. The other syllables were up for grabs. In Nepal, it was simply Himal. In Hindi, it was more like Himalay. For India's Muslim population it was Himaliya, a pronunciation declared defective since 'Muhammadans' were not the original inhabitants. The adviser suggested a stress mark on the first 'a' to guide English speakers: Himàlaya. Corbett also asked a friend, Brijlal Nehru, cousin of India's first prime minister after independence. Their final conclusion was: 'Hi' as in 'him', 'ma' as in 'father', and 'la' and 'ya' as in the French word 'le'. He summarised his findings in a paper published in the *Himalayan Journal* for 1929. 'The common Anglicised pronunciation is Himalaya. But in recent years there has been a tendency among superior folk to say Himaiiya or Himaliya.' The modern usage of 'Himalayas' is jarring to my ear, despite the instinctive English habit to pluralise Hindi words that are already plural: think 'pyjamas' and 'chapatis'. Call it snobbery, but this book sticks with Himalaya.

The *Mahabharata* and the other great Sanskrit epic the *Ramayana* are collectively known as the *Itihasa*, a Sanskrit word meaning 'history'. Many scholars have peered through the mythological fog and tried to snatch at concrete details. For though the *Mahabharata* is not really history, it's also not *not* history. For the five Pandava brothers, kings from the plains, as for the Indian civil servant Sir Geoffrey Corbett, the Himalaya performed two contrasting roles: as a place of spiritual retreat and separation from the world, but also a meeting ground, where radically different cultures met and traded on a long-established network of high mountain trails. The compilers of the *Mahabharata* – unified into the mythological figure of Vyasa, the Homer of ancient India – not only had a considerable geographical knowledge of this part of the Himalaya but also had knowledge of its different ethnic groups. Yet even two thousand years ago, the Himalaya represented nature untamed by humans: dark forests and raging rivers, a place for wild animals, tigers and bears. They were a place for 'wild men' too, who didn't plough like the people of civilised nations.

In his monumental *Himalayan Gazetteer*, the Victorian-era Irish civil servant Edwin Atkinson described how Hindu migrants settling in these mountains 'leavened the manners and observances of the rough indigenous population'. That process of civilising mountain people fitted Atkinson's narrative in which the British Empire was doing something similar, even as its wildness drew imperial adventurers to the forests and snowy wastes of the frontier. Rudyard Kipling chased that idea in his 1898 poem 'The Explorer':

> Something hidden. Go and find it. Go and look behind the Ranges—
> Something lost behind the Ranges. Lost and waiting for you. Go!

Mountains have always been places for lowlanders to exercise their imaginations: full of demons or else sublime and adventurous. The abode of snow has offered a vast white screen on which to project the fantasies of all comers: exiled kings, foreign imperialists, spiritual seekers, self-important explorers, archaeologists, missionaries, spies, mapmakers, artists, hippies – and climbers. The Himalaya are shrouded in their stories, like monsoon clouds: stories of secret knowledge and new horizons, about somewhere at the end of things, somewhere beyond. These myths hardly ever recognised the complexity and rich-ness of the cultures that developed there over millennia, as varied as the mountains that shaped them. Those cultures were either ignored or appropriated by outsiders looking to profit. That tension, between myth and reality, still tears at the Himalaya today. How these stories were made and then remade is one of the themes of this book.

*

By morning the rain had stopped. Cloud was lifting from the earth like smoke. Ganga was thundering through her narrow valley, a broiling mass of water, thick with sediment, her roar underpinned with the more solid – and ominous – rumble of huge boulders being swept downstream with the force of water. The sound was a powerful reminder that the Himalaya are being washed away only marginally more slowly than they are being raised into the sky. We instinctively think of mountains as eternal, but they're not. They are falling to bits and being remade like the rest of nature – like us.

A few of us decided to take our umbrellas and visit the small temple in the centre of the village, to receive a blessing from the priest. Leaning out from the incense-rich shrine, he smeared a mark on our foreheads, right between our eyes, known as a *tilaka*. The temple was quiet, the crowds put off by the risks of the monsoon season. Normally, the village of Gangotri is thronged with pilgrims, especially in the two months before the rains start in July. Gangotri is one of a series of four pilgrimage sites in the region known as the Chhota Char Dham, that are visited as a circuit, Gangotri most usually being visited second. The other three are Yamunotri, source of the Yamuna river; Kedarnath, whose temple is dedicated to Shiva; and Badrinath, the holiest of all, its temple to the god Vishnu situated on the banks of the Alaknanda river, which later joins the Bhagirathi to become the Ganges. According to the *Mahabharata*, it was here at Badrinath that the god Krishna stood, on one foot, arms raised, for a hundred years, 'living on the wind'.

If you want to imagine the spot where a demigod like Bhagiratha might seek the assistance of Shiva, then our base camp below Shivling – Shiva's Lingam, 'phallic symbol' of his divine creative force – would come close. The place was called Tapovan, literally 'forest of austerity', although there were only scrubby trees in the thin air at 4,400 metres. Tapovan is a term from the *Mahabharata*, denoting a place of spiritual practice. Every summer, a few yogis make the trek to meditate below the mountain. While there are many Tapovans, this one is famous, thanks to one of the world's most beautiful mountains soaring over-head and the source of the Ganges a short distance below. When we put up our tents, planning to stay for a few weeks, three yogis were still in residence, living, like Bhagiratha, on fresh air, plus a handful of rice, sleeping in a rough stone shelter.

At night, the skin of our tents froze, the mountain spectral in the moonlight. By day, we narrowed our eyes against the fierce sun of altitude, rubbing cream into our faces. A sadhu, an ascetic, would sit in its warm brightness, cross-legged on a flat piece of granite with the mountain above him, naked except for a small pouch of cloth at his waist, hollow-chested, head piled with his own version of Shiva's dreadlocks, eyes closed in contemplation. He and I were both devotees. We were both enduring physical discomfort, both searching for some-thing, although I could see the sadhu knew his metaphysical road better than I knew mine. I had no idea as I sharpened my crampons and packed my rucksack that I was starting a long climb towards a better understanding of these mountains.

Where did mythology end and reality begin? How and where did the mountaineering stories of my youth fit into the broader history of the Himalaya? Climbers spend more time around government bureaucrats in the Himalaya than anywhere else in the world. But how did those governments come into being? How did the curious patchwork of nations that make up the Himalaya fall into place? Why was the Himalaya not all in either India or China? From the outside looking in, it occurred to me that while there were many Western books published on Himalayan geography, historians tended to break the region down into polities. That approach ignored the Himalayan region's sense of itself: its shared culture and experience, a coherence ordinarily overlooked in Western accounts. Why was it that stories about climbing Everest were far more common than stories about the people who lived in its shadow? As though Scotland was being judged on its golf courses. What of Himalayan art and philosophy, politics and intrigue? My own narrow perspective shattered into a million ways of seeing. I wanted to reconcile what had brought me to the Himalaya with what I found there. I returned again and again, not just as a climber, but as a journalist and writer, always with questions. Yet every time I felt I was getting close to the top, the prize I thought I was reaching for receded again into the distance. Every time I changed my viewpoint, new horizons opened out, new summits beckoned. It was often an uncomfortable experience, and not just physically. The scars of colonialism reach high into the mountains, even in those regions that remained nominally independent. And I became acutely aware that climbing mountains was self-indulgence compared to the physical and psychological hardships many faced as a fact of life.

The yogis and seekers we met on the way to the mountain seemed part of an eternal India, mystical and otherworldly, beyond the usual constraints of history. But just as I had been drawn there by stories of adventure, my own sacred texts, and by the example of my heroes, the ascetics and renunciates also had their inspiration; the minds of others had compelled them to come too. Tapovan is famous for its association with the Hindu saint Sri Swami Tapovanam ('Sri' being an honorific, and 'Swami' meaning guru, or teacher, literally 'he who is with himself'). Born Chippukutty Nair in 1889 to an aristocratic family in Kerala in southern India, Tapovanam went against his father's dream that he become an important figure in the government and quit school, where he felt constrained by its limited spiritual outlook and the prospect of a dry, predictable career. After his father's death, when Swami Tapovanam was still in his early twenties, he remained in Kerala, a poet and part of the local literary scene, until his brother had finished school. Then he left home for ever, following his dream of living the simplest life possible in that part of the Himalaya consecrated in the books he studied.

The winters he spent in Rishikesh, the summers in the high mountains, anxious about bears in the forest but entranced with the landscape. Tapovan, above the treeline, where snow leopards roamed at night, was one of his favourite places to meditate. 'My heart was filled with wonder and pleasure as I sat watching the golden-hued, rocky peaks called Sivalinga and Bhageerathi Parvat, rising on either bank, the long ranges of snow-clad mountains on both sides, dazzling in their silver radiance.' The intense pleasure he took from his experience of the natural world shines through his writings. People flocked to hear him speak and several wealthy patrons offered to build him ashrams, but he preferred the forest and left the world as simply as he had lived in it, unlike the Beatles' guru Maharishi Mahesh Yogi, who died a reclusive billionaire in the Netherlands, giving interviews by video link, too frightened of infection to meet journalists in person.

Swami Tapovanam felt another strong link to this sacred part of the Himalaya. East of Gangotri and his favourite meditation spots, on the other side of Shivling, are the Alaknanda valley and the the temple of Badrinath, greatest of the four pilgrimage sites on the Chhota Char Dham. According to the *Mahabharata*, it was from Badrinath that the Pandavas began their final, fatal expedition: the *Swargarohini*, the ascent to heaven. For Swami Tapovanam, sitting in this Hindu temple was like coming home. The head priest there is by tradition a Keralan, and the two could converse together in their mother tongue, Malayalam, in which Tapovanam had written his poetry as a young man. The tradition of a Keralan priest lies in the temple's founding legend. Badrinath had once been the site of a Buddhist temple but legend tells how the Keralan spiritual philosopher Adi Sankara, living some time in the eighth century, found a black stone known as a *shaligram* – a fossilised shell representing Vishnu – in the Alaknanda river and used it to claim this auspicious place for Hinduism.

This was at a time when Hinduism was resurgent and Buddhism in retreat. The details of Adi Sankara's life are disputed. There are more than a dozen hagiographies. We're not even sure when he lived. Like Swami Tapovanam, who took immense pride in sharing the same language and culture as his spiritual inspiration, Sankara was a sann-yasi, an ascetic, living simply among the power places of India, and from the same tradition of Hinduism known as Advaita Vedanta. His philosophical difference with Buddhism centred on the fundamental conception of the soul. In Buddhism, such a thing is illusion. For Sankara it was real. For ordinary mortals, contemplating the cosmos from the roof of the world, the idea that your core self might survive physical death seems more comforting than the cessation of a mirage.

The story of Adi Sankara shows how the Himalaya was a contested space in the first millennium, just as it was a thousand years later as the British Empire spread. Sankara lived after 543 CE and the fall of the Gupta dynasty, India's golden age, an era of immense cultural and intellectual achievement, and religious tolerance too. Thereafter northern India had fractured into smaller kingdoms; competing narra-tives laid claim to places, like Badrinath, that were spiritually significant. The arrival of Islam in the subcontinent during the twelfth century only added to the pressure. Many of Sankara's hagiographies were written during the fourteenth century as Muslim influence expanded. New political and religious interests pushed aside existing powers like tectonic plates, driving populations to seek refuge, often in the moun-tains, their backs against the highest wall on earth. Some of those refugees built new dynasties; others fossilised, preserving fragments of near-forgotten cultures that had elsewhere disappeared. The moun-tains could be a refuge or a trap, and sometimes both.

Until India's border war with China in 1962, there were few motor-able roads high in the mountains, meaning that pilgrims were required to make an arduous trek at altitudes up to four thousand metres above sea level. The need to hire porters made it expensive, prohibiting many from making the journey. A woman who could afford it might hire a porter to carry her in a basket on his back, or else hire four to carry her on their shoulders in a more dignified sedan chair. Pilgrims were required to pay in advance, and there were dark stories of women being tipped out into the river, out of sight of the village, so porters could maximise profits in the short season. Poor sanitation and huge numbers meant dozens of deaths each year from dysentery. Lower down, in the forest, malaria took its toll. The country above these pilgrim towns, fresher and cleaner, remained largely the preserve of sannyasi and yogis prepared to endure the hardship of cold nights and thin air, living on milk from the goatherds that graze their flocks there in the summer months. After the war, India invested heavily in its Himalayan road network, changing the region for ever and opening the Chhota Char Dham to mass tourism. Hundreds of thousands of Hindus now visit each year and the government is planning to upgrade its infrastructure to bring even more. Gangotri and the other sites have become part of the restatement of India's Hindu culture and a reinforcement of its nationalist origins.

The concept of mountains as places of perfection in an imperfect world is a powerful trope in India, just as it was for a Western climber like me with a head full of Romantic ideas of the wild. In the age of Kali, the modern age of strife and noise, middle-class Indians increasingly view mountains as places to escape the petty compromises of day-to-day life and live more simply. The *Puranas*, a sprawling multi-volume cosmic encyclopaedia written largely, but not exclusively, in the first centuries of the first millennium, has a great deal to say about the sacred geography of this spiritual wellspring. According to the *Puranas*, in these valleys are spirits, *gandharvas*, both good and ill, half animal or bird, enchanting the gods with their singing, as well as nature spirits, *yaksha*, mercurial, sometimes lecherous protectors of the trees and the wealth of the earth, and their cousins, the *rakshasa*, eating raw human flesh, born from the breath of Brahma. These mountains are the region of Swarga, or paradise, the home of the righteous. 'Here there is no sorrow, nor weariness, nor anxiety, nor hunger, nor apprehension; the inhabitants are exempt from all infirmity and pain, and live in uninterrupted enjoyment for ten or twelve thousand years.' At the centre of this cosmic landscape, we are told, is the mountain Meru, in the shape of a lotus seed, like an inverted, rounded cone, on its summit the city of Brahma, among its petals the abode of the gods, and projecting from its base, like the filaments of a lotus, many mountains. Meru is often taken to be Mount Kailas, high on the Tibetan plateau, poised between the Himalaya to the south and the Kun Lun mountain range to the north. The myth of Shangri-La

– a hidden, paradisal realm located in the Himalaya – was the concoction of an English novelist, but it has its origins in texts like these.

In my long trek to understand the Himalaya, however imperfectly, such mythology was a frequent stumbling block. How did it relate to the Himalayan world as it appeared to me, one of economic disadvantage, self-reliance and cultural complexity? Most ordinary people were focussed on survival and a better future for their kids, not sublime landscapes or perspectives on the infinite. And yet it was the latter that sold the place to tourists like me. There was no shortage of Himalayan voices, but these voices were often drowned out, displaced by those outsiders who thought their ideas about the Himalaya were more urgent or important. Himalayan people had even adopted these interpretations about their home in the mountains and then sold them back to the people who held them. There is an elegant illustration of this, one that mixes religion, commerce and colonialism, bridging the gap between the cosmic and the quotidian.

Among the *Puranas* is another work called the *Manasakhanda*, one that is often cited when describing the Kailas region, partly because it has more useful information about the pilgrimage sites in this part of the Himalaya than any other text, but also because it's so charming. Its chief focus is the segment stretching south from Mount Kailas and the sacred waters of Lake Manasarovar nearby. One story tells how Dattatreya, an ascetic who has renounced the world and now lives among the mountains, goes to Kashi, the city of light, more familiar in Europe as Varanasi. Here he talks with Dhanvantari, prince of Kashi. The pair are also both gods: the ascetic being an incarnation of Vishnu while the prince is god of *ayurveda* or health. The two discuss *tirtha*, or sites of pilgrimage, and the ascetic tells the prince at length about the wonders he has seen in Himachal. 'He who thinks of Himachal, though he may not behold them, is greater than he who performs all worship in Kashi,' he says. 'In a hundred ages of the gods, I could not tell thee of the glories of Himachal ... As the dew is dried up by the first rays of the sun, so are the sins of man by the sight of holy Himachal.'

It's a beautiful text and much quoted not only in modern travel books but more scholarly works too. Yet its origins are surprising. Those familiar with the King James Version of the Bible may hear its echo in these words, which are not a translation of the *Manasakhanda* but a précis, made in the middle of the nineteenth century by a British colonial official called John Strachey, who spent part of his early career as a district officer in the far north of India, bordering Tibet. While investigating the finances of pilgrimage centres in his local area, Kumaon, John Strachey came to know a pandit, or scholar, called Rudrapatta Pant, who showed him the text of the *Manasakhanda*, which was used by pilgrims as a kind of spiritual travel guide. Strachey translated passages from it into English. Many British colonial officials leavened their bureaucratic duties with more congenial subjects; Strachey's was literature. Thus, when he submitted his notes on the economic value of pilgrimages for publication in Edwin Atkinson's *Himalayan Gazetteer*, he included his own version of the *Manasakhanda*, based on Pant's translation but revised from within his own literary and religious tradition, that of the Church of England.

So much for the translation. What of the original text? Beneath its soaring imagery, there are interesting clues as to its origins. It contains, for example, no mention of Gangotri and Gaumukh, among the most sacred sites in the region, but ones that are strongly associated with Shiva. Then there is its linking of the goddess Ganga not with Shiva, as in the *Mahabharata*, but with Vishnu. These changes and omissions characterise the *Manasakhanda* as a Vaishnavite text, belonging to that strand of Hinduism that has Vishnu as supreme lord: an unusual perspective in the Himalaya, which is more often Shaivite. It is also notable that the recommended pilgrimage sites featured in the *Manasakhanda* were all in Kumaon, with none at all in neighbouring Garhwal. What might explain these biases?

For centuries through the medieval period, the Chand dynasty ruled Kumaon, fighting a series of intense wars in the seventeenth century against the neighbouring kingdom of Garhwal. Some of the finest temples in the capital of Almora were built to celebrate Kumaon victories. By the mid eighteenth century, around the time Strachey and Atkinson believed the *Manasakhanda* was most likely written, both Kumaon and Garhwal had been taken over by the Rohilla, a group of Muslim Pashtun who had migrated from Afghanistan in the service of the Mughal emperors to settle in northern India. This region was in turn absorbed by the punchy new state of Gorkha, now Nepal, and then, twenty years later, when the British went to war with Nepal, by the East India Company. While the British restored the western part of Garhwal to Sudarshan Khan, son of the last king, the eastern part was merged with Kumaon and kept under direct rule of the British, where it would remain until 1947. Among the chief differences between Kumaon and the princely state of Garhwal was taxation. Revenues in Garhwal went to Sudarshan Khan. In Kumaon they went to the British. So it was at the least a fortunate coincidence that the *Manasakhanda*, a text which pilgrims would look to for travel guidance, effectively directed its readers to sites exclusively in Kumaon, where their taxes would end up in British coffers, while reinforcing the area's Vaishnavite tradition. In other words, pandits in Almora, wishing to re-establish religious control after Muslim occupation and the tyranny of the Gorkhas, could not have had a more useful document, one that both suited the interests of the new occupying force but also let them go about their sacred business. And so a text that seems, at first glance, to be a simple expression of the eternal, unchanging appeal of the high Himalaya turns out to be a highly political document in a constantly shifting world of briefly held allegiances. That doesn't make the words any less beautiful or, for the millions who have seen a Himalayan dawn, less true, but it does show how the Himalayan world has been simplified and glossed for the benefit of outsiders.

*

The near-paradox of the eternal mountains as political fault-line is no less relevant now. Himalayan communities still struggle to maintain their identity in the face of competing strategic interests from Delhi or Beijing. Not long after our expedition to Shivling, this corner of India became its twenty-seventh state, a combination of the old Himalayan kingdoms of Garhwal and Kumaon breaking off from the larger state of Uttar Pradesh. Locals favoured the name Uttarakhand for their new home, a term used for the region in the *Puranas*; the Hindu nationalist BJP government in Delhi insisted on Uttaranchal, a 'saffronised' Hindu nationalist alternative that seemed less separatist. It was finally changed to Uttarakhand in 2007, three years after the BJP lost power.

Tensions like those in Garhwal and Kumaon have existed across the Himalaya throughout history and no more so than today. On the far side of Nepal, a longstanding campaign to create another new state, called Gorkhaland, based on the hill station of Darjeeling in West Bengal, sees regular outbreaks of violence, most recently in 2017. From Kashmir in the west to Arunachal Pradesh in the east and Tibet to the north, the needs of locals are often at odds with the strategic interests of wealthier regions far away, and centres of power that in the past wanted Himalayan gold or musk now want hydroelectricity or border security. These days, rather than powerful armies, cultural identity, often in the form of religion and language, and protest are the favoured tools with which to defend those interests.

The Himalaya's complex and uncertain political future lies in its heterogeneous past: so many voices, so many traditions trying to be heard. And that rich and fragmented history is a consequence of the region's astounding geography. It is impossible to understand one without the other. Extreme environments prompt unusual strategies for survival, and almost nowhere else is that relationship between geography and culture so starkly obvious than in the world's highest mountains. As a mountaineer, the resourcefulness I've seen among local people in meeting the hardships of their day-to-day lives makes what most of us do there seem laughable. It is only by holding in the imagination an impression of the scale and challenges of the world's highest mountains that their incredible human stories can be fully grasped. But how? And where to start?

2

Origins

From Tapovan, where sannyasi reach out to touch the mind of Brahma, you can turn your back on Shivling and look north across the Gangotri glacier to a towering line of peaks – the Bhagirathi range – framed against the indigo sky. Most impressive of all is the vast south wall of Bhagirathi III, around two kilometres high, a sumptuous vertical granite cliff capped with crumbling black shale. During our expedition in 1995, Bhagirathi III looked to me like the fragment of a colossal chessboard, black on white. I was intrigued at this contrast between the granite, which was much lighter in colour than granites I knew elsewhere, and the black shale above. Granites in the Himalaya are unusually pale, known as leucogranites, *leuko* being Greek for white. Their geochemistry is unusual: tourmaline, red garnet, much white mica and less black. I didn't know it then, but there in front of me was a snapshot from a continuing process millions of years in the making – and unmaking – of the greatest mountains on earth.

A few years before I climbed Shivling, a geologist called Mike Searle, now a world expert on the formation of the Himalaya, arrived at Tapovan with the ambition of climbing a new route on the mountain, not just for fun, but because it seemed the most effective way of collecting granite samples from different altitudes. Searle was trying to answer an obvious question that proved surprisingly difficult: when did the mountains of the Himalaya reach their current elevations of up to seven and eight thousand metres? By collecting samples and studying elements locked inside minerals within the granite, Searle and his colleagues could produce a plausible timescale of when and at what depth in the earth's crust the granite first melted and then cooled as it was exhumed by uplift and erosion on the surface.

The route he and his climbing partner Tony Rex chose was great for collecting samples but unnervingly dangerous, exposed as it was to avalanches rushing down the mountain's north-west face. On their second day the weather turned and they found themselves trapped in a bitter storm. That night there was nowhere even to sit down and so they just stood there, jacket hoods cinched tight, buffeted by wind and spindrift, waiting for dawn. In the middle of the night they heard a loud crack above them, like an explosion, followed almost immediately by an immense rock fall. There was no longer any question of going to the summit. They now had to abseil a near-vertical kilometre and a half down to the flat glacier below, collecting samples of granite as they went. (For obvious reasons, this was always going to be done on descent.) Slowly their rucksacks filled with heavy rocks and when they stopped to brew some tea, they agreed it would be much easier to put all the rock samples in one rucksack and then drop it down the mountain. What could possibly go wrong? They watched the rucksack gather speed, before it hit a rock sticking out of the snow slope and burst, showering the mountain with rock samples, each in its own annotated plastic bag. They spent the next three hours climbing down and collecting as many as they could find.

To date the rocks back in the laboratory, Searle and his colleagues measured the radioactive decay of two different isotopes of uranium, a technique only developed in the 1980s. This showed the granite he had collected from near the summit crystallised from molten magma twenty-three million years ago. Tests also showed that Searle's samples had been exhumed rapidly from the time when they solidified to around fourteen million years ago, when their 'exhumation' slowed markedly. Erosion then accelerated at the start of the Quaternary glaciations about two and a half million years ago, which resulted in the landscape I was looking at across the Gangotri glacier. The black shale this molten granite had intruded was sedimentary and much older: from the Palaeozoic Era, around five hundred million years ago. Where the granite and shales had met, chunks of the original rock, called 'country' rock, had been ripped out by the liquid granite and then frozen in place as it cooled. Searle and his team used their results to suggest a model of orogeny – mountain-building – in the Himalaya that reached its peak between twenty and twenty-three million years ago. Their next task was to collect granite samples from other locations to see if their model worked across the entire Himalaya range.

I had read about Searle's adventures and we had friends in common. One told me how Mike had filled a barrel with rock samples at the end of a remote valley in the Karakoram, north of the western end of the Himalaya, and hired a porter to carry them back to the roadhead, several days' hard trekking down a glacier heaped with rubble. The porter, not unreasonably, wondered why anyone would want rocks from the far end of the glacier, when there were lots of perfectly good ones much closer to home. So he emptied the barrel Mike had given him, refilling it when they arrived. Mike, my friend told me, took the news philosophically.

I heard this story camped in the Gangdise mountains, a hundred kilometres or so north of the main Himalayan chain, high on the Tibetan plateau. Later in that same trip, sitting in the garden of a hotel in Nepal's capital, Kathmandu, my friend spotted Mike who was just back from another research trip. We asked him about the landscape of the Gangdise, which is such a contrast to the crammed chaos of the Himalaya: huge peaks at a distance from each other, like galleons afloat the vast brown plateau of Tibet. For the next half hour, Mike spoke clearly and simply about the origins of the Himalaya, how they had formed and the impact on what had been the south coast of Asia, when the high country we had stood on overlooked the shrinking Tethys Sea that in the Mesozoic Era separated the continents of Gondwana and Laurasia. The scale of time and space was inconceivable to me, unimaginable, and yet Mike seemed to watch the surface of the earth crease and buckle over millions of years under the gaze of his mind's eye. It seemed a story as fantastical as Hindu myths of earth's creation.

Our understanding of how mountains form is surprisingly recent. Long after the mountains had been mapped, we knew more about the geology of the moon than how the Himalaya formed. When Mike Searle was a student in the 1970s, the idea of plate tectonics, of land masses moving across the earth, had only recently become mainstream. Its parent theory, the idea of continental drift, had been posited in 1912 by the German meteorologist and geophysicist Alfred Wegener. Until then, geologists believed the earth's major geological features had been fixed when the molten surface of the planet cooled. Early attempts on Everest offered some clues. Alexander Heron produced the mountain's first geological map after the reconnaissance of 1921. Geologists Noel Odell in 1924 and Lawrence Wager in 1933 both collected sedimentary limestone from near the summit. It was clear the top of Everest had once been at the bottom of an ocean. How this ocean floor came to be nine kilometres above the surface of the earth was, before plate tectonics, less obvious. Seeing the conformity of Everest's summit rocks, all three assumed they had been pushed upwards but how that happened remained unproven.

When Wegener died of exposure on the Greenland ice cap in 1930, his theory had supporters, like the British geologist Arthur Holmes, who theorised that convection deep in the earth might drive the continents across its surface. But the majority opinion was against Wegener, sometimes bitterly so: it became a battle between the 'drifters' and the 'fixists'. After the Second World War, the scientific case for Wegener's idea of whole continents splitting apart and colliding began to build. Mountain ranges were discovered in the deep ocean, where magma had welled up through cracks in the ocean floor and then crystallised. Magnetometers designed to detect submarines were used to survey the seabed, where basalt rocks recorded the earth's polarity at the moment of their formation. The surveys showed this variation in black and white stripes, like a zebra's, as the earth's polarity flipped periodically from north to south and back again. This was clinching evidence that the ocean's floor was spreading apart. The continents really were on the move. Wegener's idea was proved correct, if not in every detail. You can trace on a map India's northward drift in the sequence of volcanoes that stretch from Réunion, east of Madagascar in the Indian Ocean, via the Chagos and the Maldives to the Western Ghats, east of Mumbai. A 'hot spot' anomaly deep in the earth's mantle where Réunion is currently located created all these volcanoes, each in turn cooling as it drifted away to the north.

There aren't any fossils of sea creatures younger than fifty million years in the Himalaya. This suggests that the collision of India with Asia that produced the mountains occurred around this time. That makes the Himalaya a youthful range in comparison to its near neighbours. Metamorphic rocks in the Hindu Kush, for example, are three times older, suggesting a much earlier process of mountain building. As the youngest and highest mountain range in the world, the

Himalaya was the obvious place to study how continental plates collide. By calibrating magnetic anomaly stripes recorded in the Indian Ocean, geologists reconstructed how in the last one hundred and twenty million years India rifted from Antarctica and drifted north, following the breakup of the huge supercontinent Gondwana in the Southern Hemisphere.

Over tens of millions of years the Tethys Sea narrowed and then almost entirely disappeared. The Persian Gulf remains as a tiny vestige of this ancient ocean, an elderly neighbour to the much younger Red Sea, which is widening by a centimetre every year. As India and Asia closed together, at latitudes around the equator, the Tethys seabed was lifted up into the sky. Most of it has long since eroded away; only smashed up fragments remain in the Himalaya. But in Oman in eastern Arabia, where the Tethys has yet to close, these formations, known as ophiolites, remain intact. It was here that Mike Searle began his research career, as though marching back in time to the dawn of the mountains he spent his life studying.

Following the initial collision, India ploughed on northwards, folding the surface like the crushed bonnet of a geological car wreck. The Indian plate plunged underneath Asia. Volcanic activity along the former coastline of Asia fizzled out as the cold Indian plate slid beneath it. And it's still going, converging at around fifty-five millimetres per year, rotating very slightly anticlockwise. Eight hundred kilometres of the Indian plate has already disappeared under Asia. The earth's crust under Tibet doubled in thickness to seventy or eighty kilometres as it was jacked up into the air, creating a desert plateau with an average altitude of five thousand metres. India's lithosphere, that is the crust and upper mantle, extends under the Tibetan plateau north of Everest by more than three hundred kilometres.

The plateau itself is far drier than the southern side of the mountains. The Himalaya may be the abode of snow, but there's remarkably little of it north of the mountains. There's good reason most of the Himalayan population lives south of the range in the wetter middle hills. Ngari Prefecture in western Tibet receives less than seven centimetres of precipitation a year; Arunachal Pradesh, on the southern slopes of the eastern Himalaya, is the second wettest state in India, getting on average three metres of rain a year. As a consequence, erosion rates are low in Tibet and the uppermost layer of rock remains intact, so studying formations beneath it is difficult. In the Karakoram to the north-west, by contrast, far greater rates of erosion have exposed their structure in the most dramatic mountain landscapes in the world. The Tibetan plateau itself is being extruded east, towards south-east China, creating rift valleys between the mountains.

Where tectonic plates meet is termed the suture line. Around the thousand-year-old Lamayuru monastery in Ladakh, the sparsely populated region to the west between Kashmir and Tibet, you can see the suture of Asia and India clearly in the surface rocks. To those armed with a little knowledge, formations like these are among the greatest wonders of the Himalaya. The degree of folding you see exposed in the Himalaya is testament to the planetary scale of the forces at work. Most mountains flatten out when viewed from the International Space Station at an altitude of around four hundred kilometres. The Himalaya do not: the mountains form a vast crescent, the biggest of big bananas, between the near-sea-level plains of India and the gigantic high plateau of Tibet, corrugated with the ceaseless impact of numberless glaciers and rivers, grinding and washing the mountains away.

The Himalayan suture line extends east for some 2,400 kilometres from near where the Indus turns south around Nanga Parbat, ninth highest peak in the world and four hundred kilometres north-east of Islamabad, to where the Brahmaputra, called the Yarlung Tsangpo in Tibet, turns south around Namcha Barwa, due east of Tibet's capital Lhasa. These points, like brackets or quotation marks, are termed syntaxes. While the length of the Himalaya records a head-on collision between India and Asia, south to north, at these corners, the squeeze comes from every angle. As a consequence, the massif of Nanga Parbat is currently rising faster than anywhere else on earth; the presence of so many warm springs in the region shows how rapidly the hot lower crust is being lifted. Rocks here are the youngest in the Himalaya, formed deep in the earth and then elevated with astonishing speed to the surface and on up to the highest altitudes. Geologists working on Nanga Parbat have found migmatites, a kind of partially melted gneiss that formed only a million years ago at depths of between ten and twenty kilometres. These migmatites are now found at altitudes up to eight kilometres. That means they have been exhumed at around eleven to thirteen millimetres each year, the fastest rate ever recorded on the planet. The story at Namcha Barwa, the eastern anchor of the Himalaya, is similar, although geological mapping here is more challenging. The topography is extreme: deep gorges thick with jungle. Data collected along the fabled Yarlung Tsangpo gorge, so remote it was only fully explored in the twentieth century, suggests the mountain-building process is only a little slower than at Nanga Parbat.

The granite I could see from Tapovan told another part of the story that is equally staggering. As the India plate dived under Asia and melted, some of its molten core was squeezed back southwards into the weakness between the two plates, what's called a mid-crustal channel, under the immense weight of the crust above, like an elephant sitting on a tube of toothpaste. In places, this ductile granite was able to balloon into colossal formations, like the one I could see on Bhagirathi. The south-west face of Everest is the upper boundary of this mid-crustal channel. The lower part is gneiss and granite rocks that were molten as recently as fourteen million years ago, squeezed under sedimentary rock twenty times its age, much of which has now eroded away. Where the ductile granite met the limestone, the country rock metamorphosed into marble, a feature on Everest known as the Yellow Band.

The sedimentary rocks at the summit of Everest are layers of lime mudstones. The famous features of the mountain that so obsessed the British expeditions of the 1920s and 1930s, particularly the Second Step, are limestone crags standing proud of the shale beneath. In 1964 the Swiss geologist Augusto Gansser published *Geology of the Himalaya*, which included an image of the stem of a fossilised crinoid or sea lily collected by the first Swiss climbers to reach the top in 1956. (Gansser had travelled the length of the Indian Himalaya two decades previously as part of Arnold Heim's Swiss scientific expedition; the pair coined the phrase Main Central Thrust for the core of metamorphic rock extruding south across the length of the Himalayan arc. Gansser also crossed the Nepali border without permission into Tibet and made a circumambulation of Kailas, dressed as a pilgrim, noting its geology as he travelled. Before setting out, a monk gave him a bag of small pills that would cure any illness he might encounter. It was these pills, Gansser liked to joke, that were the source of his longevity. He died in 2012 aged a hundred and one.)

Gansser's image of the fossilised sea lily proved the top of Everest to be the remains of an ancient ocean floor, which makes the human experience of standing on it all the more extraordinary. Lawrence Wager, who also collected rocks in 1933 during a brave attempt at the top, was in the 1950s head of the geology department at Oxford. He judged his samples were formed at the end of the Carboniferous, around three hundred million years ago. Their age is now more firmly fixed in the Ordovician, making them more than four hundred and forty million years old.

Deep time is hard for the human mind to conceive but the radically different ages of rocks on Everest, and the processes that put them there, tear at our instinct to regard mountains as unchanging. The truth is the Himalaya are being made and unmade constantly. Mike Searle and his team discovered that rocks high on the Karakoram peak of Masherbrum had been formed at depths of about thirty-five kilometres, meaning everything above those rocks had been eroded away: fractured, split, gouged, scraped, crushed and washed downstream towards the sea. A quarter of the rock sediment washed into the world's oceans comes from the Himalaya. It arrives in the Bay of Bengal at a rate of a billion tonnes a year, settling on the seabed to form what is known as a submarine fan. The Bengal Fan, the largest such feature in the world, extends three thousand kilometres south into the Indian Ocean and spreads to a width of fourteen hundred. Off the coast of Calcutta it reaches a thickness of eighteen kilometres. With that sort of pressure, the rocks at the bottom are themselves metamorphosing, and so gravity and time spin the wheel of the planet's making.

*

For humans encountering the Himalaya, the very greatest of its impacts is climatic. Stand on the summit of a high mountain along the chain and, if it's clear, you can look north towards the arid brown of the Tibetan plateau. Then, having turned ninety degrees in either direction, you take in an apparently endless sequence of ridgelines, each of them marking the limit of another river that has carved it out. On one side a desert, on the other some of the wettest places on earth. The contrast is startling, the explanation even more so. As the Tibetan plateau was lifted into the atmosphere, there was less air to interrupt the heat of the sun. As a consequence, the plateau gets hotter than land at sea level; it acts like a vast hot plate that through convection pumps the air above it into the upper troposphere. This in turn draws in a warm, moist wind from the Indian Ocean: the South Asian monsoon. As this air reaches the Himalaya, it rises and cools and its moisture precipitates. It is the action of all that water falling as rain and snow on the south side of the mountains, unable to cross the barrier of the mountains to the north, that has created landscapes so vastly different.

At times the monsoon falters: there is evidence that the population centre around the fortress of Tsaparang in western Tibet failed in the early seventeenth century as the monsoon weakened, drying up fields that were once fertile. The reasons for this are as yet poorly understood but monsoons also weakened in the 1980s and scientists were able to correlate this to a cooling of the Tibetan plateau. The impact of all that hot air rising from the plateau on the jet stream and the global climate is not yet fully understood. There has until recently been a vacuum of data from the region but in recent years Chinese researchers have placed sensors even the plateau's remoter corners to measure heat rising from all types of land surface. It's hoped that more and better data will improve monsoon climate models, and with better forecasting comes the possibility of saving lives.

Not only does the monsoon intimately affect the hundreds of millions of people who live in its shadow, the rise of Tibet may have impacted the earth's climate as a whole. When the monsoon began isn't certain, but it strengthened markedly seven million years ago, again connected to the rise in altitude of the Tibetan plateau. The palaeoclimatologists Maureen Raymo and William Ruddiman and oceanographer Philip Froelich have linked this increase in rainfall to an increase in chemical weathering, which occurs when carbon dioxide dissolved in rainwater reacts with minerals in the rock, locking it out of the atmosphere. Their theory suggests this process increases during periods of mountain building, because more material is being eroded into rivers. The higher the Tibetan plateau rose, the more rain fell, increasing erosion rates and speeding up the process of chemical weathering. As more carbon dioxide was locked away, the planet cooled, leading to the Pleistocene ice ages that so markedly shaped human history. It is a controversial theory, but there is tantalising evidence supporting it. Climate scientists use the ratio between two oxygen isotopes captured in marine limestone as a proxy for temperature: the greater the ratio the cooler the planet. There is a marked correlation between the timing of this global cooling and the rise of the Himalaya. The Tibetan plateau continues to impact global weather systems; Xiangde Xu from the Chinese Academy of Meteorological Sciences has reported that not only does the Tibetan plateau affect rainfall in China but there is a correlation between greater snowfall on the plateau and warmer Canadian winters.

The combination of rainfall and elevation in the Himalaya is reflected in the immense river systems that drain the mountains. It is not the mountains that frame human activity in the Himalaya: it is the rivers. The three great rivers of East Asia – the Salween, the Mekong and Asia's longest, the Yangtze – all rise close together on the eastern end of the Tibetan plateau. No wonder bridge-builders have been so admired here. Some of the greatest rivers predate the Himalaya's rise, including the Indus and the Yarlung Tsangpo–Brahmaputra. Others began with the mountains, including the Ganges and the great river systems of Nepal. These have eroded deep into the mountains, in places right across their axis. The head of the Arun river in Nepal has cut through east of Makalu, the world's fifth highest mountain, to within just ten kilometres of the Yarlung Tsangpo. As the process continues, the Arun will 'capture' the Yarlung Tsangpo and the headwaters of this great river will subsequently flow through Nepal.

It is the combination of altitude and climate that makes the Himalaya so formidable and so formidably diverse. At its narrowest the distance between the plains, or terai, to the south of the mountains and the Tibetan plateau is around a hundred and fifty kilometres. Within that distance the gain in altitude is as much as eight kilometres. Remember that with every kilometre gained in altitude there is a drop in temperature of more than six degrees Celsius. Altitude acts in a similar way to latitude, meaning that in the briefest distance you can move through a wide range of ecosystems: subtropical broadleaf forests in the Siwalik foothills, mixed temperate forests of oak and rhododendron in the middle hills, firs and pines at higher altitudes. Juniper has been found growing in Bhutan at over 4,700 metres, but for the most part the trees thin much lower. Pastureland above the tree line can extend well over five thousand metres. Above that, you are in an ecosystem more akin to the Arctic.

Thanks to altitude, the biodiversity of the Himalaya is astonishing, especially in the eastern part of the range where the monsoon is so strong: eastern Nepal, Sikkim, Bhutan and the Indian state of Arunachal Pradesh. Sikkim, only a little bigger than Delaware, or the English county of Cumbria, has six hundred and fifty different species of orchid. Nepal has a similar number of butterfly species, roughly the same as the whole of the United States, a country more than sixty times its size. At high altitude across the Himalaya are blue sheep, musk deer, red pandas, wolves and snow leopards. In the middle hills I've seen leopards, Himalayan bears and langurs, black faces fringed with white fur. In the southern subtropical foothills are tigers, Asian rhinos and wild elephants. In the rivers are dolphins and gharial, a species of crocodile. There are poisonous snakes too, vipers and cobras, another significant risk to life and a major cultural trope on either side and at either end of the mountains in the form of *nagas*, serpent spirits. Hunting and foraging have been a fact of life for many Himalayan ethnic groups for millennia and even now there is still one group, the Raute, who remain hunter-gatherers. The forests and mountainsides are not just a larder or a place to find building materials: they are a treasure trove of medicinal plants. One of the best-known trades in the Himalaya is in *yartsa gunbu*, meaning 'winter worm, summer grass' in Tibetan, a caterpillar infected with a fungus that grows like a plant and is worth its weight in silver on the Chinese market.

The natural hazards of such a rapid rise in elevation are complex and unpredictable: floods, earthquakes and landslides, but also less obvious dangers, such as glacial lakes draining almost instantly and catastrophically. The most famous example of this was a lake of ten square kilometres near Mount Machhapuchhre in the Annapurna region, which collapsed in the mid sixteenth century, sending a wall of water and five cubic kilometres of debris into the Pokhara valley. These events, called Glacial Lake Outburst Floods, are of great concern today as climate change prompts glacial retreat. Landslides also cause flooding, as they did most notably in early 1841, when a mountain spur on the west side of Nanga Parbat detached and fell into the Indus, creating a dam. A lake quickly formed, and the king of Gilgit, Karim Khan, sent notes written on birch bark and floated downstream, warning that a flood was imminent. When the dam broke in June, a huge wall of water swept down the Indus destroying hundreds of villages and killing thousands of people and their animals. A Sikh army camped near the river outside Attock in northern Punjab was engulfed and five hundred men died in an instant. A survivor, a *zamindar* or commander, described it thus: 'As a woman with a wet towel sweeps away a legion of ants, so the river blotted out the army of the Raja.' The waters at Attock rose fourteen metres above the normal summer flood level. And while exceptional in its scale, the 1841 disaster was far from unique: Henry Strachey, older brother of John, heard of a similar event in 1835. Floods caused in this way continue to kill along the length of the range.

Earthquakes have been a regular disruptive force throughout Himalayan history. They are mentioned in the *Mahabharata* and later Buddhist texts. We know a major earthquake in 1255 rocked Nepal's Kathmandu valley. Even so, despite an extensive literature of historical annals, there is a dearth of accounts. We know there was a series of earthquakes in the sixteenth century, including one in Kumaon in 1505, but it was only in the colonial period that systematic records began to be kept. One of the most important accounts, for its detail and insights, is from 1897, when Richard Dixon Oldham of the Geological Survey of India witnessed an earthquake of magnitude 8.7 in Assam. A fault on the northern side of the Shillong plateau was displaced by as much as sixteen metres and the northern part of the plateau was lifted instantly into the air by eleven metres. Loss of life was surprisingly low, but houses were destroyed across an area three times the size of England.

Geologists call mountains high-energy environments and the immense physical and natural diversity in the Himalaya is reflected in a high-energy human population. Because differences in climate and environment come thick and fast as you move across terrain, the cultural habits that have arisen in response to those differences are intensely focussed. While the monsoon is the region's major weather system, local climate, even from one side of a valley to the other, can be astonishingly different; a south-facing slope can have a growing season of a month longer. Himalayan people understand very well the French concept of *terroir*. This diversity is reflected in language: there are more than seventy distinct languages and dialects in Nepal alone. Yet despite this localism, people have always been on the move in the Himalaya. Across the mountains, traders have exchanged Tibetan salt for Indian grain for millennia, a trade only recently disrupted by the arrival of roads. The seasonal migration of herders taking animals to high pasture is another practice that has endured. Population growth and urbanisation is changing the region's human face faster than ever, and politics with it. Climate change is having a greater impact here than almost anywhere else. Yet, as we shall now see, the adaptations people have made to thrive in this extreme environment not only reach the roots of their culture, they also extend to their genetic code, creating a human suture line unlike almost anything else in human history.

3

The First Explorers

On the outskirts of the Chinese city of Shenzhen, just north of Hong Kong, is a former shoe factory eight storeys high that now hosts one of the defining industries of the twenty-first century: genetics. BGI, formerly known as the Beijing Genomics Institute, moved here from the capital in 2007 after it fell out with its masters at the Chinese Academy of Sciences. With one foot in academia and the other in business, it was too strange for the conservative capital: a mixture of state-owned and private enterprise. Yet the company is now the biggest player in the world of genetic sequencing, gobbling up American competitors and employing four thousand people. Those eight storeys are full of DNA sequencing machines and the data farm required to harvest the colossal amounts of information produced. Apart from human beings, including the first full sequencing of an Asian, BGI has sequenced all kinds of things: strains of rice, the cucumber, the chickpea, the giant panda, the Arabian camel, the yak and forty types of silkworm, the latter to protect China's all-important silk industry. It has also sequenced the DNA of Tibetans.

The indigenous people of the Tibetan plateau are of immense interest to geneticists and evolutionary biologists because of their unique adaptation to the physiological challenges of living permanently at altitudes of over four thousand metres with only half the oxygen of sea level. A few other populations around the world have adapted genetically to this challenge: there are two in the uplands of Ethiopia. But no population has done it quite like Tibetans and other ethnic groups with Tibetan heritage, such as the Sherpa of Nepal. Those of us born at normal altitudes, when confronted with the task of surviving on half the air, produce a cascade of physiological responses, starting with increased breathing and a faster heart rate.

Over time, the blood thickens with extra haemoglobin in red blood cells. Whether this is what we mean by acclimatisation, or is actually a problematic by-product, is a matter of debate for some researchers. Haemoglobin makes your blood sticky, causing stroke; long-term elevation can lead to chronic illness and heart attack. Tibetans manage to function perfectly well at altitude with haemoglobin levels that are sometimes lower than lowland populations. Their respiration and heart rates are also similar.

Modern genetics and the mapping of the human genome have allowed us to at least start to unpick the complex interactions and adaptations that make Tibetans so successful at altitude, from how blood vessels function in their muscles to changes in the upper respiratory tract that lets Tibetan noses breathe more easily in the thin, dry air of high altitude. Researchers from the University of Queensland in Australia and Wenzhou Medical University found nine separate genetic differences between Tibetans and lowland populations, including genes connected with haemoglobin levels and the immune system.

The most critical issue is reproduction. You can only pass on your genes if your children survive. I once met a newly born infant in the arms of his mother in a yak-hair tent at over four and a half thousand metres in the middle of the Tibetan plateau. It was a humbling experience. There was no hospital within eighty kilometres and no midwife either. The little boy's mother had relied on her mother to help her with childbirth, but his rude health was also a product of natural selection. Tibetan women have evolved larger uterine arteries to maintain a healthy flow of oxygen to the growing foetus. Tibetan babies are born at the same weight as lowland babies but are able to extract more oxygen from the air. The birth weight of lowland babies born at altitude reduces by a hundred grams for every thousand metres of height gained. Tibetan mothers also have genetic differences that allow them to produce more folates, an essential B-vitamin, when they're pregnant.

These discoveries deepen our understanding of history too. The ability of one group of people rather than another to thrive at high altitude is one of the organising principles in the story of the Himalaya. Trekking up valleys on the south side of the range into the high mountains, you come across an obvious ethnic switch between people

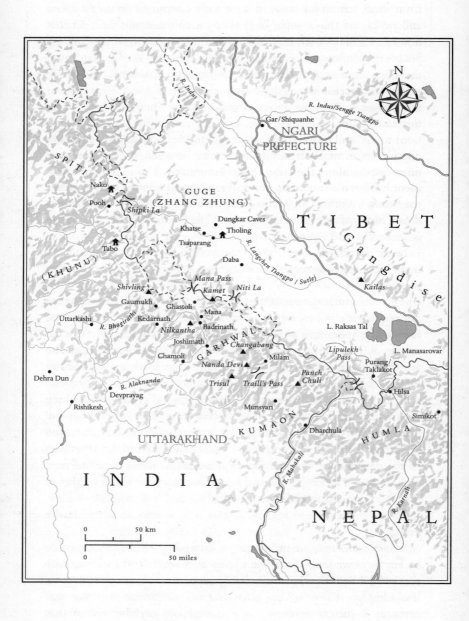

from the southern lowlands of the subcontinent and South East Asia and people of the Tibetan high plateau, an invisible threshold that hovers at around 3,500 metres. North of this genetic suture line are people most often and loosely termed Bhotias, people of Bod or Bhot, the Tibetan name for Tibet. (The etymology of 'Tibet' is uncertain; one theory has it as a Turkic corruption of *tu phod*, a term from north-eastern Tibet for upper Tibet.) South of this line, and east on the lowlands of China, are populations that lack the genetic adaptations to live and thrive comfortably at altitude. Yet this differentiation doesn't quite match any modern border between states; those run most usually along the crest of the mountains. This ethnic misalignment has been a source of political tension in recent centuries. After the Second World War, newly communist China briefly laid claim to those parts of the Himalaya with Tibetan populations that were governed by India and Nepal.

Not surprisingly, given the current political context in which Tibet is such contested territory, research into the origins of the Tibetan people is dangerous ground; it's hard to imagine a more controversial context in which to pursue research. In 2010, the highly regarded journal *Science* published research that claimed to have found the fastest known example of human evolution in the shape of the Tibetan people. The research was then reported in newspapers around the world. The lead authors, Xin Yi and Jian Wang, both worked for the Beijing Genomics Institute. The paper claimed that the specific genetic differences between Tibetans and Han Chinese occurred only three thousand years ago. The previous fastest known genetic change had been tolerance for lactose among northern Europeans some 7,500 years ago. For those pushing a nationalist narrative making Tibet part of the Chinese motherland the implication of this research seemed obvious: the Tibetan people were an offshoot of the Han population that split within the timeframe of recorded history. To archaeologists, the claim made little or no sense. Mark Aldenderfer, an expert in the prehistory of Tibet at the University of California, Merced told the *New York Times* that the time frame proposed was 'simply not tenable by anything we know from the historical, archaeological or linguistic record'. While the archaeological picture on the Tibetan plateau is far less complete than on the south side of the Himalaya, there was certainly sufficient evidence to challenge directly the notion that continuous human habitation was as young as the scientists at the Beijing Genomics Institute claimed.

Apart from altitude, a key factor in the peopling of Tibet was climate. Around fifty thousand years ago, the Tibetan plateau was dry and cold: vegetation would have been sparse and the mountains heavily glaciated. Then the climate improved with a rise in rainfall and an increase in temperature. Flourishing grasslands encouraged an expansion in the range and numbers of ungulates native to the plateau: wild yaks; *chiru*, the Tibetan antelope; *khyang*, the wild ass; and species of wild sheep. This warmer and wetter period extended north of the plateau to the Taklamakan and Gobi deserts, making migration from the north more likely. Evidence for this includes stone tools found at around 3,100 metres in the Tsaidam basin, an extensive shelf on the north-eastern corner of the plateau, dated at over thirty thousand years old. Closer to the Himalayan chain, eighty kilometres north of Lhasa, is Chusang, a late Palaeolithic site discovered in 1995. At an altitude of 4,200 metres, a series of nineteen human hand and footprints have been preserved in travertine, a sedimentary rock that forms from mineral deposits around hot springs. All the prints were made at the same time when the travertine was still a soft, calcite mud: a snapshot of a family group perhaps, since some of the prints are small enough to be made by children. All sorts of people declare themselves to be explorers; this band, you feel, really were. They faced all the problems of the early European and Asian explorers – the cold, the thin air and brutal wind – but without their technologies or scientific knowledge.

Quartz in these travertine deposits can be dated with some accuracy, and these prints are believed to be around twenty thousand years old. At other sites across the Tibetan plateau, stone tools have been found which, while they cannot be dated, are believed to be even older than the Chusang prints. It was clear that what was known about early Tibet from an archaeological record dating back at least twenty thousand years didn't match claims from geneticists about a much more recent divergence from China's population. Could they be different groups of people? Perhaps the warmer and wetter climate these early settlers enjoyed grew colder and more arid as the last 'ice age', more accurately the Last Glacial Maximum, approached twenty thousand years ago. Perhaps whoever it was living on the plateau had migrated or died, to be replaced by new migrants from China as the plateau warmed again some ten thousand years ago.

In the last few years, this fragmentary picture has filled out considerably, with new and more robust genetic research filling in many gaps, supported by new archaeological discoveries, particularly at the oldest site found so far, on the banks of the Salween river in southeast Tibet. Here stone tools and animal remains have been dated to between thirty-one and thirty-eight thousand years ago. Not only does this new work support the idea that Tibetans have been settled on the plateau for tens of thousands of years, it also fits new genetic evidence that their presence was continuous, despite the worsening climate of the last glacial period. This evidence has some startling implications for our species as a whole.

In 2014, BGI published new research on genetic sequences of Tibetans they had looked at previously, this time comparing them with the same sequences from a wide range of modern and archaic humans. The results were startling. A sequence they had previously identified as significantly different from those of lowlander populations was found in only one other sample: that of the archaic human species dubbed Denisovan. Until recently, we had only the little finger bone of one individual of this hominin, found in a cave in the Altai mountains of Siberia. The bone belonged to a girl who lived 41,000 years ago, when different human subspecies lived side by side. Sequencing her genome has shown that Denisovans had interbred with Neanderthals. Now it appeared modern humans had as well. In 2019, anthropologist Jean-Jacques Hublin from the Max Planck Institute at Leipzig published a paper on a second Denisovan find: a jawbone found in a cave in Gansu province, placing Denisovans on the Tibetan plateau itself.

In September 2016, a team from the Shanghai Institutes for Biological Sciences published research that made a broader and deeper analysis of Tibetan DNA. They were the first researchers to sequence the entire genome of a Tibetan, in fact thirty-eight of them, including Sherpas. They then compared the results with the entire genomes of Han Chinese and with available genetic data from other modern and archaic humans. Their results showed that around six per cent of the Tibetan gene pool was composed of archaic sequences, including the Denisovan DNA found previously. That's substantially more than the

percentage of Neanderthal DNA in modern Europeans. They also
found a segment that connected Tibetans to a modern human population living in Siberia 45,000 years ago, the so-called Ust'-Ishim man,
whose fossilised thighbone gave up sufficient genetic material for the
genome to be sequenced. As it turns out, Tibetans have more genetic
material in common with Ust'-Ishim than any other modern population, including modern Siberians. They concluded that the earliest
Tibetan settlers carried the genes of all three hominins, that Tibetans
had arrived on the plateau between sixty-two and thirty-eight thousand
years ago, but that the bulk of their genes was far more modern,
around twelve to ten thousand years old, as the last glacial period
ended.

The complexity of these discoveries has allowed a fuller, though
far from complete, story of the settlement of the Tibetan plateau to
emerge. Having migrated from North Asia and settled on the plateau
during the Palaeolithic, Tibet's human population, surviving at high
altitude for hundreds of generations, faced twenty thousand years ago
the brutal prospect of a cooling climate. It was once thought the
plateau was covered in ice during the Last Glacial Maximum but this
is now discounted. While the plateau has an average altitude of over
four and a half kilometres, there are many places less exposed and
somewhat lower in altitude where populations could survive, such as
the big river valleys. No doubt many groups migrated or died out,
but some remained in these sheltered sanctuaries. When the climate
became warmer and less arid again, plant and animal species extended
their range once more across the plateau. Neolithic populations,
speaking proto-Tibeto-Burmese languages, migrated from the upper
Yangtze river in modern Sichuan and from the more northerly province of Gansu onto the Tibetan plateau where they encountered small
indigenous bands with a very particular genetic inheritance. Far greater
in number, these new arrivals interbred with the existing population
and acquired those genes that conferred the biggest advantage: the
ability to live and successfully reproduce in a hypoxic environment.

Western writers are sometimes guilty of romanticising the links
between Tibetan culture and the physical environment, but it's true
to say that Tibet's high altitude has had a profound impact not just on
Tibetan physiology but on its history too. Until the twentieth century,
when China used modern warfare, technology and infrastructure to

extend its reach permanently to the northern edge of the Himalaya, the genetic adaptation to altitude Tibetans enjoyed was their greatest defence. Tibet experienced invasions from lowlanders over the centuries, but maintaining a permanent presence required more resources from the invaders than the rewards justified; the hardships of life at high altitude were too unpalatable. In the course of Tibetan history, several foreign armies would struggle to feed themselves.

What Tibet had to offer could be acquired more easily through trade, which was vibrant and transformative. Culture and ideas, Buddhism for example, could and did flow uphill to high altitude. The notion of a mythical, isolated Tibet is just that: a myth. As historian Sam van Schaik wrote, Tibet has been 'deeply involved with other cultures throughout its history'. For actual living people, though, such involvement was harder. Permanent occupation by a lowland population, specifically Han Chinese, has required modern obstetrics and a determined, often ruthless political will. Even now, the infant mortality rate for Han Chinese here is three times the rate for Tibetans.

If the Tibetan genome tells an eloquent story, the archaeological record of how Tibet emerged from the last 'ice age' ten thousand years ago is sparse. Almost all the earliest sites whose age have been measured date from around five thousand years ago, mostly along the eastern margins of the plateau but some in what would become the first crucible of historic Tibetan identity, the Yarlung Tsangpo valley, very much in the Himalayan region. Before that, there are little more than hints, assemblages of stone tools that suggest cultural differences, particularly between south Tibet and the arid, rolling hills of the Chang Tang in the north, where people have historically and through necessity been more nomadic. The idea of different cultures on the plateau is important. In the popular imagination, Tibet and Buddhism are synonymous. The Dalai Lama's high profile in exile and his place at the centre of Tibetan identity make that assumption inevitable. But Buddhism wasn't first established in Tibet until the seventh and eighth centuries, long after Christianity arrived in Europe and more than a thousand years after the Buddha lived. It was draped, like sheer fabric, over the complex and varied cultures that had developed and endured for centuries. With Buddhism came literacy; before Buddhism there was no Tibetan script. This watershed moment has dominated not just Western understanding of Tibet but

Tibet's sense of itself: creating a narrative from a voiceless world requires considerable ingenuity.

The earliest known Neolithic culture on the Tibetan plateau is found at its easternmost edge near Chamdo, third largest city in the Tibet Autonomous Region and close to the border with China's Sichuan province. Kharub, often Sinicised to Karou, is a collection of domestic residences representing several periods of occupation between six and four thousand years ago. The later structures excavated at Kharub look, at least from the interpretation of Chinese archaeologists, remarkably similar to a vernacular still common throughout rural Tibet. The site is on a bench above the Dza Chu river, which becomes the Mekong, at around 3,100 metres. As well as remains of wild goats and deer and evidence of foraging, there's evidence that millet was cultivated at Kharub and that people there experimented to achieve the best yields in the thin air of high altitude, where it's possible to grow only a narrow selection of cereal crops. There's evidence too of domesticated pigs.

Another site further west, Chugong, on the north side of Lhasa's Kyi Chu valley, is up to four thousand years old and also shows evidence of animal husbandry, including yak, which evolved, like Tibetans themselves, to prosper at high altitude. Yaks are a totemic creature in Tibetan culture, but until Chugong the first evidence of them in this area came from much later, in a document from the Western Zhou dynasty dating from 850 BCE. Tibetans learned to use every part of the yak productively, as Inuit do the seal, its bones carved into buttons or combs, the characteristic yak belly fringe providing the best hair for tent ropes. Yak tails were of particular value and were traded cross the Himalaya and far beyond. Roman women were using yak-hair flywhisks at the time of the Emperor Domitian in the first century. In south-western Tibet, the *Mahabharata* describes trade from Tibet in gold and precious stones; it's inconceivable that goods and technologies didn't travel the other way, into Tibet from neighbouring regions on the other side of the Himalaya: Kinnaur and Garhwal, and across Ladakh to the plateau. This region of Tibet acquired domesticated crops in this way, especially wheat, barley and peas, but the archaeology here is even scarcer than in the east. In north-western Tibet, archaeological finds suggest the influence of pre-Scythian tribes, the culture of the steppe extending to the plateau, of which more later.

A huge number and variety of objects were recovered from Kharub, ceramic bowls and jars with geometric patterns, polished stone and exquisite bone tools: awls and needles, weaving tools and combs. There were plenty of decorative objects too, including jade pins, shells and perforated stone jewellery. These and artefacts from Chugong are on display at the Tibet Museum in Lhasa. One of the exhibits from Kharub stopped me in my tracks when I saw it for myself: a series of nine semi-precious stones strung together and featuring a malachite pendant. There was also a polished cylindrical bead of turquoise, and another of what looked like jade, perhaps from ancient mines in the Tarim basin. There was no interpretation on the exhibit but what it illustrated was obvious: cultural continuity between the ancient past and the present. In the seventh century, for example, according to Chinese chronicles, the rank of Tibetan ministers could be judged from their insignia: different-sized beads hanging from string at their shoulders. The most precious, more than gold or silver, was turquoise. Nothing has changed. The fragments in the museum echo a motif and style that fills the shop windows of jewellery stores in modern Lhasa. Plenty of cultures revisit prehistoric art for inspiration; in Tibet it never went away.

As with writing, Buddhism marked a watershed in Tibet's artistic traditions. When we think of Tibetan art, it's most probably the complex and beautiful murals and elegant statuary of Tibetan Buddhism, which date back as far as the eighth century. This tradition drew its aesthetic from India, particularly from the Buddhist centres of the Pala dynasty in Bengal and Kashmir. Its arrival in Tibet reflected a sea change in religious practice and political power. What preceded it was radically different: the art of the people, not religious specialists, reflecting a kind of everyday spiritual awareness that mediated the worlds of hunting and pastoralism. Its inspirations were local gods and the rituals of the passing seasons.

Tibet's rock art offers the most immediate insights into this preliterate culture. The museum has plenty of examples on display. The most popular figurative subjects, commonly painted in red ochre, or *tsak*, were wild animals, particularly ungulates: yaks, complete with belly fringe, and deer, the two most commonly featured species and both widely present as keystones in the shamanistic spirit world that predated Buddhism. Predators also featured: tigers and lions. The

natural world is a central theme, as you would expect when survival
depends on it. There are pictographs of hunters on horseback drawing
bows, sitting on saddles that are similar in style to ones still used on
the Tibetan plateau, although stirrups arrived only with the Turkic
tribes in the fifth century.

Cosmological symbols are also common: the sun and moon, but
also the swastika in both its clockwise and counterclockwise form,
which appeared in the Indus valley fifteen hundred years before the
Buddha was born. Many of these symbols were absorbed into Tibetan
Buddhism, just as animistic totems were into the early Christian
church. They feature in *thangkas*, Buddhist religious paintings, alongside *srungma*, protective spirits that are distinctive to Tibetan Buddhism.
The meaning of this iconography evolved as Tibet itself changed but
the process of recruiting to Buddhism the symbols and rituals of a
pre-existing system of belief is clear. Some aspects were undoubtedly
lost, though: pre-Buddhist imagery sometimes shows arrows jutting
from the flanks of wild yaks, not a scene repeated in Buddhist iconography, with hunting frowned upon. Others may be rooted in this
preliterate art, for example gods riding on yaks. The discovery of the
earliest *thangkas* painted with red ochre in the Mogao Caves on the
Silk Road hints at the continuity from Tibet's preliterate view of the
universe to a wholly new one based on Buddhist philosophy. The old
world was full of demons and visions; the new was austere and
thoughtful. Tension between them has remained a constant and often
creative dynamic in Tibetan culture and religious practice ever since.

*

Documents found in the Mogao Caves, the Caves of the Thousand
Buddhas, dominate our understanding of early Tibetan history, like a
welcome landmark emerging from the mist. The caves are near
Dunhuang, far to the north of the Himalaya, on the edge of the Gobi
desert in what is now Gansu province. Dunhuang was a Han dynasty
garrison that became a supply point for camel trains on the Silk Road,
a junction between its northern and southern routes, and a crossroads
for travellers between Mongolia and India. It was a Buddhist city by
the fourth century, with a population of tens of thousands, when the
first caves were dug at Mogao, elaborately painted with visual aids to

meditation and paid for by wealthy patrons. The site was a major Chinese Buddhist centre during the Tang dynasty, at its height in the eighth and ninth centuries, by which time hundreds of caves had been dug and decorated; its Buddhist priests escaped persecution after the Tang turned against foreign religions in the 840s only because the city was by then a possession of the Tibetan Empire. As Islam conquered much of Central Asia, the caves were abandoned. When the Yuan dynasty, patrons of Tibetan Buddhism, collapsed in the fourteenth century, the city itself went into decline. Growth in sea trade had fatally weakened the Silk Roads, until President Xi Jinping revived the idea in the twenty-first century.

Even after much of the complex was abandoned, though, Mogao remained a site of worship. In the late nineteenth century, Wang Yuanlu, an itinerant Taoist monk from Shanxi province, settled there and became the site's unofficial guardian, raising money for restoration. In 1900, as workmen he'd hired were clearing sand from the entrance to one cave they discovered a hidden door to another. This cave was filled with thousands of ancient documents, the youngest of which dated from the early eleventh century. Excavated as a memorial chapel for a monk called Hongbian who died in the ninth century, it is now better known as the Library Cave. The reason it was walled off with documents hidden inside has intrigued scholars. One explanation is that this was an attempt to hide them from invaders at the time of the defeat of the nearby Buddhist Khotan kingdom in 1006 at the hands of the Muslim Karakhanids. ('We came down on them like a flood,' wrote the Turkic scholar Mahmud al-Kashgari. 'We went out among their cities, / We tore down the idol-temples, / We shat on the Buddha's head!') Khotan had been a Buddhist kingdom for more than a thousand years, dating back to the time of the Indian Buddhist emperor Ashok and the Greeks in Central Asia. By the end of the eleventh century, Khotanese had been almost entirely replaced by the Turkic language of their conquerors. When Marco Polo visited in the late thirteenth century, he reported that all Khotan's inhabitants were Muslim.

Wang Yuanglu made repeated attempts to interest local Chinese authorities in his discovery but various officials who saw documents from the Library Cave failed to understand their significance. In 1907, the Hungarian-born British archaeologist and explorer Aurel Stein visited Dunhuang with his capable interpreter and secretary Jiang Xiaowan. Stein's description of the cave hints at the riches inside: he estimated 230 bundles of Chinese scrolls and 80 Tibetan bundles, each containing around a dozen scrolls. He counted eleven large volumes of Tibetan *pothi*-style books, narrowly rectangular in shape and loosely bound, between traditional wooden covers. The pile of manuscripts and scrolls was ten feet high and occupied a space of five hundred square feet. The papers had no catalogue and were often scrambled together.

Stein paid Wang Yuanglu to let him take away 'over thirty compact bundles of scrolls' and various other miscellaneous bundles. The books he left, guessing they were reiterations of just one or two *sutras*, or scriptures. The following year the French scholar Paul Pelliot arrived at Dunhuang to pick over what Stein had left. Pelliot could read classical Chinese and other Central Asian languages and was thus able to make a fast and detailed assessment of what remained. (He was also a student of the Sanskrit scholar Sylvain Lévi, a crucial figure in Himalayan antiquity.) Even then the treasures of the Library Cave weren't exhausted. Japanese travellers bought more in 1911 and Aurel Stein returned in 1914 to buy what Wang Yuanglu promised was the last of the treasures. Stein suspected the monk was lying and he was right: a few months later the Russian archaeologist Sergei Oldenburg bought a large number of Chinese and Tibetan scrolls, now in St Petersburg. Oldenburg, whose friendship with Lenin's brother protected him after the Russian Revolution, founded an authoritative index of Buddhist texts that continues today. There was still a mass of documents left behind, many in Tibetan, and the great majority of these are now in Dunhuang Museum, rivalling the British and French collections in terms of size; these and other collections are now coordinated through the International Dunhuang Project.

Buddhist texts of comparable importance were discovered at other sites, but Dunhuang was among the most important discoveries of ancient texts anywhere in the world. They transformed our understanding of Asian religions. Most of the fifty thousand manuscripts are in Chinese, but other languages are present, including Tibetan, Uighur, Sanskrit and Khotanese, the latter hardly known until the Library Cave's discovery. Most of the material is Buddhist, and includes canonical works, like the famous Diamond Sutra from 868, the earliest printed book for which we have a date, now in the British Library. The Diamond Sutra is part of the *Prajnaparamita*, a Sanskrit term meaning 'perfection of wisdom'. Its Sanskrit title is *Vajracchedika*, which literally means 'diamond cutter' or 'thunderbolt cutter', a metaphor for its value as a tool in reaching central truths within Buddhist philosophy: the self as illusion and liberation from attachment. The Dunhuang texts aren't confined to Buddhism, however. There is a manual for the ancient game of Go, musical scores, works on mathematics and astronomy, texts from other religions, including Christianity (the so-called Jesus Sutras), and Manichaeanism, treatises on medicine and Chinese pharmacology, as well as texts on Tibet's history.

The Dunhuang documents also include material on the esoteric tantric Buddhism so popular in Tibet towards the end of the first millennium, material until recently overlooked in comparison to other treasures from the Library Cave. Tantric Buddhism, Vajrayana in Sanskrit, emerged in northern India in the early medieval period, practised by *mahasiddha*, 'great adepts', spiritual practitioners who pioneered a faster route to enlightenment by quitting their monasteries and sacred vows to live in caves and forests, like Hindu sannyasi, or renunciates, but also behaving in ways anathema to the philosophical elites they left behind, having sex, drinking alcohol and eating meat. Only by experiencing the actuality of ordinary life could its emptiness be properly understood. The Tibetan Buddhist scholar Robert Thurman has described these adepts as 'psychonauts', explorers of the furthest reaches not of the world but of the mind.

The Western imagination is transfixed with the sexual aspects of tantric practice, but while it's there, it is only a fragment from a much wider system of teaching. The eleventh century Bengali *mahasiddha* Tilopa, having been thrown out of his monastery, made his money grinding sesame seeds for their oil – *til* is Sanskrit for oil – and worked as a bouncer and procurer for a prostitute. Later, however, Tilopa became an itinerant and highly admired teacher, whose students included Naropa, among the founders of the Kagyu school of Tibetan Buddhism, an umbrella term covering a range of tantric teachings. As characters, *mahasiddha* were wildly romantic, growing their hair long and abandoning the distant austerity of more conventional practitioners. They rose to prominence during the Pala dynasty, the last Buddhist empire to rule a large part of India, but they also shared with Hindu Shaivites (followers of Shiva) some of their spiritual profile and practices. This confluence of the faster-running tributaries of Buddhism and Hinduism remains a major cultural feature of the Newari community in Kathmandu, that city's human core: intense, mystical, sometimes dark. Centuries after Buddhism had faded in India, Tibetan scholars would still be trying to figure out what tantric practice really implied.

Piecing together the emergence of the Tibetan state, a process that began in the seventh century, is far from simple. When the British diplomat Charles Bell published one of the first Western accounts of early Tibetan history in 1924, he drew in particular on the *Blue Annals*, completed in 1476, centuries after the events they described. And as Bell himself observed, Tibetan historiography was usually more concerned with the progress of religion and its institutions, not the rise and fall of rival political factions or economic development. Following the *dharma* or spiritual path of Buddhism has been a largely cohesive force on the plateau of Tibet for a thousand years but it wasn't inevitable, even if those Tibetan histories make it seem so. What we do know is that a dynasty emerged from Tibet's Yarlung valley in the seventh century that dominates the historical landscape, and it was largely in the wake of its emergence that, over the next two centuries, Buddhism took root. Remarkably, what began as illiterate animist clans making fragmentary appearances in Chinese chronicles, feuding in a remote backwater, became, within a few generations, an empire that stretched from the Pamir mountains in the far west to northern Myanmar in the east, and from the Gobi in the north to Nepal in the south, with a brief occupation of China's Tang dynasty capital at Chang'an. This stratospheric rise of the Yarlung dynasty transformed Tibetan culture and gave Tibet its own alphabet; only then was the way opened to its future as a holy land, where Buddhism prospered even as it dwindled in India, in the face of expansionist Islam and resurgent Hinduism.

Two key sources found at Dunhuang transformed our understanding of this critical period, as Tibet emerged on the world stage. The *Tibetan Annals*, originally one scroll, now held in two portions in London and Paris, covers the early reign of Songtsen Gampo, 'Songtsen the Wise', the first Tibetan emperor, recording important events and genealogies, including clan affiliations, from the middle of the seventh century to the year 764, when the fragments Stein and Pelliot brought back to Europe end. The second document is known as the *Old Tibetan Chronicle*, a potent blend of narrative, songs and various lists that tells the story of the Tibetan emperors from their mythical beginnings, through the reign of Songtsen Gampo, and on into the ninth century. The list of emperors named ends with U Dumtsen, also known as Langdarma, an equivocal figure in the Tibetan imagination, as someone who attempted to suppress Buddhism. The chronicle was most likely composed in the ninth century, although the Hungarian scholar Géza Uray believed the manuscript, written on chopped-up segments of a Chinese scroll, had been rearranged later for political reasons. The discovery of these sources gave scholars a powerful new vantage point from which to view Tibet's emergence as a major power in Central Asia, one not so cluttered with Tibet's later religious sense of itself. Charles Bell, for example, followed Tibet's later medieval histories in regarding Songtsen Gampo as an ardent supporter of Buddhism, a young king converted by his foreign wives who ordered monasteries built across the land. He is known as the first of the three 'dharma kings', and regarded as an emanation of Tibet's protective deity Avalokitesvara, Chenrezig in Tibetan, the Buddha of compassion. But there is no mention in either the *Old Tibetan Chronicle* or the *Tibetan Annals* of Songtsen Gampo having been a Buddhist at all.

Songtsen was born a tsenpo – a king – and a *lhase*, or divine son, thirty-third in a line of kings whose origins are lost in time and whose gods are largely forgotten. The first of them was Nyatri Tsenpo, dropped to earth on Yarlha Shampo, a sacred mountain in the Yarlung valley, on the end of a sky-cord that drew him back to heaven when his time came. The Tibetan calendar and Losar, the New Year, are said to have begun with his reign. An ancient fortress called Yumbu Lhakang that stands on a cliff above the Yarlung valley is traditionally associated with Nyatri. It is certainly old, a narrow white tower, windowless at the bottom, overlooking the fields that sustained its inhabitants. The chronicles tell how this sequence of kings lost its divinity through the foolish behaviour of the tsenpo Drigum who turned clan chiefs first against each other and then against himself. The sky-cord was severed forever and Drigum was buried in the ground. No one, including the great Dalai Lamas, ruled all Tibet without managing the concerns of the clans.

Songtsen himself died in 649 and the account of his funeral offers clues to the nomadic origins of the Yarlung kings, hinting at influences from neither India nor China but the steppe. Herodotus had heard how the Scythians lacerated their bodies as part of their mourning; Tibetan nobles did the same, painting their faces with ochre and cutting off their hair. Echoes of the steppe accompanied Songtsen to his burial place, shaped like a nomad's tent. Like the nearby Turkic peoples, the Tibetans believed their king lived on inside his tomb, surrounded with his things from life, seated in his copper coffin, his old servants close at hand, those who had sworn allegiance raising a stone pillar and swearing an oath.

If his death was rooted in the past, Songtsen's life transformed that of the plateau. His father Namri Lontsen had extended their clan's power, forging links with other clans, expanding their control into central Tibet. During his reign, Namri had sent ambassadors to the Chinese court and made alliances with the powers that surrounded him: Zhang Zhung to the west and to the north-east a confederacy of tribes known as the Azha in Tibetan, and Tuyuhun to the Chinese, expert horse-breeders inhabiting what would become part of the Tibetan province of Amdo. This region was of much more concern to China, then emerging from chaos under the new Tang dynasty. To the south, across the mountains in the fertile valley of Kathmandu, was the Licchavi king, Amshuverma, controlling an important trans-Himalayan trade route and building a fabulous palace with the proceeds. The people he ruled were already famous for their metal-work. Beyond Amshuverma was the Indian king Harsha, who, aged just sixteen, had inherited the throne from his murdered brother, avenging his death and creating an empire.

Songtsen would do something similar. After his father was poisoned, he inherited the title of tsenpo aged just thirteen. Reacting to the loss of a strong leader, the affiliated clans rose up. Songtsen responded quickly, capturing and executing the man who had killed his father and putting down the insurrection against his family. Where his father had been content to secure treaties, Songtsen wanted absolute control. He subjugated the west and in 634 sent envoys to the Chinese court. Songtsen's reputation as a capable and bellicose military leader had gone before him, so the Chinese reciprocated quickly, being preoccupied with better known rivals, the Turks and the Azha to the north.

China's experienced emperor Taizong saw potential in recruiting Songtsen as an ally against the Azha. The Tibetans were delighted; such diplomatic respect raised their status.

Knowing that Taizong had promised Chinese noblewomen as brides to the rulers of the Turks and the Azha, Songtsen sent another envoy to Taizong requesting the same. It was an astute act of statecraft on both sides, a mark of respect to the rising Tibetan king, but also an obligation to the Chinese emperor. At first the Chinese agreed, but at the insistence of the Azha ruler, Murong Nuohebo, who happened to be at court, the offer was withdrawn. Songtsen was furious and immediately launched a powerful attack on the Azha, his army reinforced with troops from his recent conquests in the west, scattering his enemies. Within a few years, Tibet would add this vast region to its empire. Songtsen then continued to the frontier with China at Sungchou, modern Songpan, some three hundred kilometres north of Chengdu, and sent gifts to the emperor, saying he had come for his princess. Without waiting for a reply, he then attacked the city.

What happened next depends on whose annals you read. The Tang chroniclers claim a Chinese general drove Songtsen back. Tibetan chroniclers suggest the tsenpo withdrew his army in the face of a larger force and continued harrying Taizong's armies. The latter seems more plausible. If Songtsen had been defeated, as the Tang claimed, they would not have so readily entertained Songtsen's renewed demand for a bride. In 641 he sent his shrewdest counsellor, Gar Tongtsen, to the Tang capital at Chang'an, the city of perpetual peace, to negotiate the marriage. Chang'an was then the greatest city in the world, with a population of a million inside its city walls and two million outside. Chang'an had scores of Buddhist and Taoist temples, but it was ecumenical and tolerant, with Nestorian Christian churches and Zoroastrian temples as well. There were pleasure gardens with a lake you could boat on and festivals to entertain the people. Taizong had recently built a palace in his hunting park north of the city. There was a fascination too for the exotic: Turkic styles were then all the rage. People from all over the known world came to Chang'an, Japanese pilgrims and Jewish traders. The city brimmed with self-confidence. Its famous markets, at the end of the Silk Roads, sold everything anyone wanted.

Given the wealth on display at court and the disdain Chinese elites expressed towards 'barbarians', and that by force of circumstance Gar Tongtsen was illiterate, it says a great deal that Songtsen's ambassador impressed Taizong. There is an image of their encounter, the original painted by the government official Yan Liben, hanging in the Palace Museum in Beijing. Gar is shown in red and gold Chinese silks, hands pressed together, in front of Taizong, who is being carried on an open sedan chair by nine servant women, all identical. Even if Gar impressed Taizong, the power dynamic Yan Liben conveys is clear: Gar is a supplicant from a weaker power. Later Tibetan histories expanded on his reputation for cleverness, how he outfoxed the Chinese to bring home not just Songtsen's bride but one for himself as well. Gar Tongtsen's wiliness appeals to Tibetans, who have often relied on their wits to overcome such a vast numerical disadvantage. ('There is no disputing the matter of numbers,' Gar Tongtsen's son once told an arrogant Chinese general. 'But many small birds are the food of a single hawk, and many small fish are the food of a single otter.')

The girl Gar brought home was a young teenage princess called Wencheng, not Taizong's daughter, but a relative from a junior noble family. The annals suggest she was intended for Songtsen's son and heir, and it was only because his son died young that Songtsen married her himself. In doing so, he achieved a peace that lasted for a decade or more after his death in 649. Among the gifts Wencheng brought with her was a statue of the Buddha, the first recorded in Tibet, although there were most probably Buddhists in Tibet already. Her story is used in modern Chinese schools as a clumsy illustration of China's deep-rooted connection to Tibet, a big uncle guiding a little nephew, with Tibet a tributary of the motherland. The reality was very different: these were powerfully different cultures, from how they conceived the world to what they ate and how they drank their tea. Songtsen is often credited as introducing Tibet to its favourite beverage, but recent archaeological discoveries suggest tea had been in Tibet for centuries before his reign. This might explain how wholly different its preparation is from tea drunk in China: salt and butter are blended into it, and the tea itself arrives in a dried, brick form, useful for nomadic lifestyles.

Even so, as its empire grew, Tibet's interactions with China changed its culture. This shift is neatly illustrated in the change of name of

Songtsen's new capital, from Rasa, meaning 'walled place', to Lhasa: 'place of the gods'. Like elite families across Central Asia, Tibetan aristocrats sent their sons to Chang'an to be educated and to see what the rest of the world had to offer; they returned with new ideas and tastes. Through his ambassador Gar, Songtsen asked Taizong for silk-worms and the techniques for making wine. Most importantly, under-standing very well the power of the written word, he asked for artisans to teach Tibet how to make paper and ink. That allowed government to be regularised and properly constituted. The very existence of the annals at Dunhuang illustrates the impact the Chinese had on the Tibetan elite, which absorbed the Chinese habit of recording itself, an interesting contrast to the subcontinent, where literature was more metaphysical.

For historians, Tang records and Tibetan manuscripts from Dunhuang are powerful documentary sources. Yet their focus on matters of state and military rivalry make it easy to underplay the immense cultural influence from the south side of the Himalaya, which was closer than China and a longstanding source of trade and cultural contact. Throughout the 630s, the king of the Kathmandu valley (in modern-day Nepal), Narendradeva, a descendant of the Licchavi king Amshuverma, took refuge in Lhasa to escape a coup, and spent several years there plotting his return. Part of the legend of Songtsen's reign is that he had not one but two foreign wives, the first of them being a Nepali bride, a daughter of Amshuverma, the princess Bhrikuti. According to legend, like Wencheng she also brought a statue of the Buddha to the marriage. Many scholars have doubted her existence – there is no mention of her in the Dunhuang manu-scripts – but another marriage into an important neighbouring elite is entirely plausible. It's certainly the case that Narendradeva, who wore an amulet of the Buddha, returned to Kathmandu with support from Tibetan troops, which is why, the Tang recorded, he was subject to Lhasa. The impact of these Licchavi nobles on the Tibetan court hasn't left the same record as China did, but it must still have been significant. Amshuverma had worked on a Sanskrit grammar, according to the famous Chinese Buddhist monk and traveller Xuanzang. That must have interested Songtsen. When it came to inventing a script for his language, Songtsen would turn to Sanskrit, much as a medieval European scholar would turn to Latin. There is a story that Songtsen, after many previous attempts, commissioned a young man from the Tonmi clan to travel to India and study writing with a famous Brahmin. The teacher's initial scepticism was overturned by the diligence of his student, so much so that he awarded the young man the nickname Sambhota: 'the good Tibetan'. Whether or not it's true, Songtsen's commitment to literacy and its impact on Tibetan culture were both impressive and profound. Decades later a Chinese minister described Tibetans as 'intelligent and sharp, and untiring in their love of study'. It was meant as a warning.

A few years after Songtsen's death, the statue of Buddha that Wencheng had brought from China was moved from its original temple to a new site, one that would eventually become the spiritual heart of Lhasa and by extension Tibet, known as the Jokhang, the 'house of the statue', and more commonly in Tibet as the Tsuglakhang. Walking round the temple today, following the devotional circuit known as the Barkhor, the sacred smell of juniper incense in the air, alongside hundreds of Tibetans, many counting off their *mala*, or prayer beads, a few spinning prayer wheels, the hum of mantras on their lips, is a humbling reminder of the many centuries of shared spiritual effort. Yet Buddhism had some way to go in the late seventh century before it became the spiritual practice of ordinary people, and not just foreign princesses and well-travelled nobles.

When Songtsen died, his grandson, the next tsenpo, was still a small child. So his chief minister Gar became regent and proved no less capable in charge than he had serving Songtsen, using the invention of writing to get a firmer administrative grip on the empire and relying on his sons as military leaders. The Chinese emperor Taizong had died in the same year as Songtsen, and the Tang's hold on the city-states of the Silk Road had weakened. The revenues and opportunities the Silk Road offered were impossible to resist. When the Tibetans came down from their high plateau to lay siege to Khotan, the city was as famous for its intellectual openness as it was for its devotion to Buddhism. None of that impressed Tibet's warriors, in their leather scale armour, faces painted with red ochre; as far as the cosmopolitan people of Khotan was concerned, their sole motivation was money. They seemed determined to humiliate Buddhism, not adopt it. Khotan's religious freedoms suffered miserably under the Tibetan army's occupation.

Buddhism's reputation within Tibet fluctuated after Gar's regency ended and the tsenpos reasserted their power. In 710, another Chinese princess, Jincheng, arrived in Lhasa to marry the young tsenpo Tride Tsugtsen, then only a boy and in the control of his mother, who ruled as proxy. Jincheng was a devout Buddhist and used her influence to support her faith; she was known as a temple-builder. The Tang had by now reasserted its control of the Silk Roads, and after a wave of anti-Buddhist purges, refugees began arriving in Lhasa seeking her protection. This she happily gave; as numbers swelled, so resentment rose among the indigenous population. When an epidemic broke out – probably smallpox – killing many Tibetans and the princess herself, it was easy to pin it on the foreign religion. The message was clear: don't meddle with the old ways. Attitudes at court hardened; Buddhism was banned.

Like many new states experiencing rapid change, Tibet struggled to balance notions of traditional identity with ideas from the wider world it now inhabited. Inevitably, factions arose. Those aristocrats that had built links with Buddhist institutions in China chafed at the reactionary tilt of the tsenpo and his ministers. The state itself was under pressure. A treaty of convenience with Arab forces in Central Asia had compensated for the loss of the Silk Roads to some extent, but Tibet needed trade to finance its security. Tride Tsugtsen grew old: his nickname was Me Agstom, or 'bearded grandfather'. His death, however, was at the hands of hired assassins, in the year 755. At the end of that year, the brilliant Tang general An Lushan launched a rebellion against the emperor Xuanzong, a rebellion that ultimately failed but which weakened the Tang dynasty. For the next few years, the new tsenpo, Trisong Detsen, watched as the tide of Chinese power consumed itself and ebbed away. The Tang dynasty, which had prom- ised to 'swallow the peoples of the four directions', stripped its best troops from recently established garrisons in north-east Tibet. The way was open for Trisong Detsen to send his troops back onto the Silk Roads.

When the city of Dunhuang fell, having held out against a Tibetan siege for more than a decade, the Tang were forced to acknowledge it could no longer control its borders with Tibet. In 763, Tibetan troops briefly occupied the Tang capital Chang'an, and although they soon withdrew, their presence nearby was a constant threat. China made deals with the Uighurs in the north and the Arab Abbasid Caliphate to the west, relieving pressure on their borders and at some cost to the Tibetans. But the complex power structure in Central Asia had shifted for good. In the early 820s, China and Tibet signed a peace treaty recorded in a famous stele that still stands in front of the Jokhang. Despite modern Chinese propaganda, it was a treaty made between equals. It would be almost a thousand years before China was able to reassert control in Central Asia.

Tibet's political fortunes soared under Trisong Detsen. The *Old Tibetan Chronicle* records: 'Externally, they expanded the kingdom in all four directions; internally, welfare was abundant and undiminished.' Yet it is his religious leadership for which modern Tibetans so warmly remember him today. He is the second of the 'dharma kings', and comfortably the most important. While later Tibetan histories some-times conflict with the Dunhuang manuscripts, to the advantage of the Buddhist establishment, there is much more accord when it comes to Trisong Detsen. The success of Tibetan Buddhism – and the reason why most people in the West know something of it, even while they have never heard of the Tibetan Empire – is rooted in Trisong Detsen's determined patronage, though admittedly it was only achieved on the back of Tibet's political success and access to international trade. It was an investment that paid off in unexpected ways. Although the Tibetan Empire would collapse four decades after Trisong Detsen's death, his spiritual legacy has endured, against the odds, for far longer.

*

Tibetan Buddhist historians wrote from the perspective of their reli-gion being an inevitable spiritual destiny, but there was nothing certain about it. Before Trisong Detsen, Buddhism had been one of several competing options for the spiritual future of Tibet. The Tibetan elite was well aware of Islam. While seeking Arab support against their enemies in the early 700s, Tibet had requested an Islamic scholar be sent to instruct them on this new religion. A golden Buddha was sent to Mecca, although it was melted down for coins soon after. The Tibetans also knew about Christianity, Zoroastrianism, Manichaeism and its prophet Mani, and Chinese philosophies like Taoism and Confucianism. In the minds of their rivals the Chinese, meanwhile, they were barbarians, people who worshipped spirits in the earth and air and gods of war that needed placating: fearsome warriors but little else. Tang records describe them as mostly nomads, their way of life savage, covered in filth, never bathing or washing their hair.

As an ambitious man, and one exposed to the sophistication of Chinese culture, Trisong Detsen set about adding some philosophical breadth and depth to Tibetan society. Whatever his personal spiritual beliefs, of which we know little, Buddhism was the obvious candidate: it was already present and acknowledged at court and as an institutional model it was the most completely understood. Islam and Christianity were too exotic, Taoism too Chinese, and Manichaeism, as far as Trisong Detsen was concerned, flat-out fraudulent. Buddhism was truly international. It had adherents among the nomad tribes of the north, in the hot flatlands on the south side of the mountains, and in the Tibetan Empire's vassal state of Nepal, or Balpo as the Tibetans knew it. It was in Buddhism's intellectual heartland of Kashmir as well as the Chinese imperial capital of Chang'an, and in the cities of the Silk Road. Tibet could either retreat into itself or go out and meet the world around it. Trisong Detsen chose the latter.

Before Trisong Detsen, the introduction of Buddhism had been piecemeal, episodic and often inspired by foreigners like the Chinese princesses. This time, once the tsenpo committed, its spread was systematic, ambitious and farsighted. Foreigners, inevitably, still played a central role. The greatest teachers were from the Buddhist universities and monasteries in India, and among students of Zen in China. Yet their presence at court was problematic and created suspicion. A Tibetan nobleman called Selnang, from the Ba clan, was a key figure in recruiting foreign scholars. His role is described in the *Testament of Ba*, a document that describes the establishment of Buddhism in Tibet and the founding of Samye monastery, the first of the great monastic institutions that would direct Tibet's story for the next thousand years. Fragments from an early version of this story were found in the Dunhuang Caves dating from the ninth or tenth century. They reveal a process that was fraught with tension.

Selnang travelled to Nepal and brought back an eminent scholar called Santarakshita, abbot of Nalanda, the Buddhist monastery or *mahavihara* in what is now the Indian state of Bihar, a little south of Kathmandu. In later versions, the abbot is politely quizzed about the teachings of Buddha. In the earliest version he is imprisoned in the Jokhang until the Tibetan court can be reassured that Santarakshita wasn't about to cast a spell over them. That done, plans for a great monastery, modelled on Nalanda's neighbour Odantapuri, were laid, but a series of natural disasters reawakened local fears of foreign gods. Santarakshita was sent away and only recalled when nerves were calmed. This time he brought with him a tantric master. Padmasambhava was born in the Swat valley, west of the Indus, now part of Pakistan but then a Buddhist centre. The foundation myth of Samye monastery tells how Padmasambhava identified and then drove out the demons blocking the spread of the *dharma*. The story can be read as a metaphor, naming and disempowering the spirit enemies of Trisong's progressive vision; it is also the foundation story for Tibet's powerful Nechung Oracle, a protective spirit still consulted by the Dalai Lama. Padmasambhava was a fiery and unwelcome presence at court, and he was encouraged to leave once he'd worked his magic, yet in time he would become immensely popular, a folklore hero, known as Guru Rinpoche, the 'precious teacher'.

The temple of Samye was designed in the shape of a mandala, literally a circle, but meaning a geometric metaphysical diagram, reflecting the four cardinal points of the universe with Mount Meru at its centre, a design from the heart of Indian Vedic cosmography. The temple at the centre had three storeys, the first in Indian style, the second Chinese and the third modelled on the temples of Khotan, a statement of Tibet's cosmopolitan intent. Samye still stands, and its original layout is preserved, although war, earthquake, fire and the destruction inflicted in the 1960s and '70s under China's rule during its Cultural Revolution have all taken their toll on the buildings. It became the foundation stone of the Nyingma school of Tibetan Buddhism, the oldest of the four great schools, Nyingma meaning 'old ones', with Guru Rinpoche a founder of the tradition but its origins a fusion of Tibet's indigenous religion and Buddhist philosophy.

Samye would be the location for one of the great dramas of Trisong's reign, an encounter between two competing visions of Buddha's teaching. Just as he had brought Santarakshita, Selnang also brought Zen monks to Tibet. The two traditions clashed over how best to transcend the earthly cycle of suffering and achieve enlightenment. The Indian sutra tradition took a gradualist approach, conceptualising the path to nirvana in day-to-day practice, sutra meaning 'discourse'. Zen promised a more dynamic, immediate route to non-being, regarding the step-by-step approach as pedantic, unworthy of a brilliant, incisive mind. Trisong decided the two sides should meet at Samye in debate. He called on Kamashila, a student of Santarakshita, to present the sutra approach. A monk called Moheyan offered the Zen perspective but Kamashila outfoxed him, won the argument and as a consequence Tibetan Buddhism became rooted in the Indian tradition, and Zen faded from view. Although some scholars doubt such a pivotal debate took place, the story reflects a broader struggle for ascendancy between the different schools of Tibet's Buddhist missionaries.

When it came to Buddhist scriptures, however, there was no competition. The thousands of sutras and their commentaries were to be found in monasteries and universities across the Himalaya in India. Trisong embarked on a hugely ambitious and wildly expensive process of bringing translators from India and Nepal to work with Tibetan scholars who had learned Sanskrit. Terms that simply didn't exist in Tibetan had to be created; the language itself grew and morphed as it swallowed a religious culture whole. This work more than anything rooted Buddhism sufficiently well for it to survive the Tibetan Empire's later collapse and the fall of its divine emperors. Trisong's legacy lit a flame, turning Tibet into a spiritual beacon, a process instigated and funded by an empire that soon after disappeared from view. When that happened, the flame of Buddhism guttered but was not extinguished. It was nourished back to life not in Lhasa, the city of the gods, but in a now obscure corner of western Tibet, in the northern shadow of the Himalaya, by a long-forgotten empire whose last embers were the first glimpse any European had of the Tibetan world.

4

Lost Kingdoms

As you leave the scruffy frontier town of Saga, seven hundred kilometres west of the capital Lhasa, Tibet dries up like a husk. Travelling the same latitudes as Algeria, you pass sand dunes within sight of white summits. The light at dawn is sumptuous, turning the lower hills the colour of honey and caramel, but it's hard to imagine anything living in such austerity. Then you spot wild asses, *khyang* in Tibetan, cropping the meagre white grass struggling out of the stony ground. The air is thin at fifteen thousand feet; everything feels closer, yet the vast scale of the landscape reduces you. It's easy to see why a philosophy stressing the illusory nature of an individual consciousness, as Buddhism does, might prosper here.

The road west follows the broad valley of the Yarlung Tsangpo river, which becomes the Brahmaputra when it reaches India, one of the four great rivers of Asia that have their source in western Tibet. To the north are the mountains of the Lungkar Shan, a range that contrasts sharply with those to the south: isolated snowy peaks overlooking broad valleys where nomads watch year by year as the glaciers that feed their pasturelands wither and die in the face of climate change. The Chinese carved a militarily strategic road along this ancient route in the 1950s; it stretches two thousand kilometres between the Tibetan town of Lhatse in the east and the far western province of Xinjiang, crossing the disputed Aksai Chin region along the way. Now tarmacked, the G219 is one of the most spectacular drives on earth.

At Punsum, the road passes a line of three rounded hillocks topped with prayer flags fluttering in the wind. Ancient trade routes turn south from here to cross high passes into far western Nepal. Then the road climbs towards a pass more than 5,200 metres high, the

Mayum La ('la' means 'mountain pass'), on one of the world's great watersheds, between the Tsangpo flowing east and three other great rivers: the Indus, Sutlej and Karnali.

Late in 1715, Ippolito Desideri and Manuel Freyre, two Jesuit missionaries, were likely the first Europeans to cross this pass, travelling in the opposite direction: they were on their way from Ladakh in the far west to Lhasa, journeying under the protection of a widowed Tatar noblewoman returning to the capital. Escaping what he called the 'Great Desert' of Tibet was a relief for Desideri, a formidable scholar cruelly prohibited from publishing by his own church. A few days before, he had set eyes on 'a mountain of excessive height and great circumference, always enveloped in cloud, covered with snow and ice, and most horrible, barren and steep, and bitterly cold'. This was Kailas. Staring at this dazzling peak, without any protection for his eyes, had left him blind, the pain alleviated, at his hostess' recommendation, by rubbing snow in his eyes. The party rested beneath the mountain on the shores of Lake Manasarovar before continuing onto the Mayum La, Desideri speculating shrewdly on the identity of the great rivers whose sources surround the mountain that had temporarily blinded him. So it was that Europeans discovered the axis of the world.

Manasarovar is Sanskrit, meaning 'the mind's waters', the mind in question being Brahma's, primal lord of creation in the Hindu tradition. According to legend the lake was placed there to give the followers of Shiva, god of creative destruction meditating atop Kailas, sacred waters with which to refresh their souls. Drink from them and after death you will join him. One of several Tibetan names for the lake is Mapham-pa, the 'unconquerable one', denoting the place where Buddha's mother bathed before dreaming of him entering her womb, from the right side, in the form of a white elephant. The lake's ninety-kilometre shoreline is a place of pilgrimage not just for Hindus and Buddhists but Jains and followers of Bon, Tibet's second-most popular faith. More material narratives are now elbowing some room, too. Where the G219 passes the lake's northernmost shore, there is a new visitor centre fringed with mobile phone towers. A large advertising hoarding features the Chinese president Xi Jinping and a slogan in Mandarin: 'Don't depend on the sky, don't depend on the earth, depend on ourselves to get rid of poverty.'

A few kilometres further west, a spur road leads to Darchen, the starting point for a ritual circuit, *kora* in Tibetan, of Kailas itself. Darchen was until fifty years ago a small hamlet; thirty stone houses were reported here at the turn of the twentieth century by a visiting Japanese monk. During the Cultural Revolution of the mid 1960s the mountain was almost abandoned but in recent years Beijing has invested heavily in infrastructure, cashing in on a boom in religious tourism, especially among Indians who don't bother much with acclimatisation, crossing the border in dangerous and sometimes fatal haste to visit the most sacred mountain and lake in the world. A busy main street is flanked with bleak hotels and solar-powered streetlights, seasonal restaurants and souvenir shops. The trail around Kailas itself is marred with garbage and human waste but the peak rises above it all: exquisitely proportioned, a near-perfect cone of searing brilliance. The meaning of the name Kailas is contested, but the Sanskrit word *kelasa*, meaning 'crystal', seems appropriate.

For all its desolate beauty, Kailas, like Jerusalem, is a crowded spiritual space. The trail around it is punctuated everywhere with shrines and monasteries of many religions and sects. However, it is the Kagyu school of Tibetan Buddhism, which, as we saw in the last chapter, emerged in the eleventh century through *mahasiddha* like Naropa, that dominates Kailas, thanks to a fabled struggle that took place here between an eleventh-century Kagyu poet and yogi, Milarepa, and the champion of the Bon faith, Naro Bonchung. At stake, according to legend, was the spiritual future of Tibet.

Milarepa's battle with Naro Bonchung is related in a biography written several hundred years later, in the fifteenth century, by a Kagyu monk named Tsangnyon Heruka, who wore his hair long and drank from a *kapala*, or skull-cup. His name translates as the 'madman of Tsang', the region of central Tibet he was born in, but his madness was far from pathological. The *nyon-pa*, the mad or wild ones, practised what might be called 'crazy wisdom', wandering as beggars and meditating far from the controlled environment of a monastery. They broke their vows of celibacy, grew their hair and drank alcohol, spiritual vagabonds whose public displays of wild, aberrant behaviour seemed uncontrolled but were part of a disciplined spiritual practice characteristic of the Kagyu lineage. It was a restatement of the concepts that had inspired the Kagyu school in the first place. Milarepa appealed to Tsangnyon because of the way he lived and the things he did, but also because Milarepa was part of the founding lineage of the deeply tantric Kagyu order: there is a direct line of teachers and students that links him with the Indian tantric adept, Tilopa himself.

Tsangnyong's biography of Milarepa was one of the first books printed in Tibet using wood blocks and was an instant hit. At every turn, Bonchung is thwarted by Milarepa. When Bonchung breaks a rock with magic, Milarepa cuts it in two with a yogic stare. Having seen his best efforts easily surpassed, the Bon priest acknowledges Milarepa's superiority but then gambles everything on a final race to the summit. Milarepa's followers wake early to witness Naro Bonchung sitting astride his magical flying drum, playing on a trumpet made from a human thighbone and dressed in a green cloak. Milarepa is dozing, unconcerned as those around him panic. He merely makes a sign towards his rival that pins him in a holding pattern around the mountain. Then, as the first rays of the sun touch the summit, he clicks his fingers and is instantly transported there. Relic traces of this cosmic encounter are still visible to the faithful on their ritual circuit of the mountain. Thanks to Milarepa's victory, it was the Kagyu school that controlled the spiritually prestigious Kailas region. Milarepa's life story is still popular, translated for today's generation into manga comics and movies; he's often pictured with green skin, from drinking too much nettle soup. But this fantastical legend also has a historical backdrop, one that raises fundamental questions: about what Tibet's cultural and spiritual world looked like before the arrival of Buddhism; how that preliterate world was absorbed into the new Tibet; and how regional politics would impact on the new state religion.

*

Kailas has another name that is older than the rest: Tisé. Its meaning is obscure but its etymology lies rooted in another language altogether, that of the Zhang Zhung culture, also written as Shangshung. This language used to be described as Indo-European, as opposed to Tibeto-Burmese, but even that broad categorisation has since been called into question. There are simply not enough written examples to be defini-tive. Five texts that may yet prove to be Zhang Zhung have emerged from the Library Cave near Dunhuang but the fragments we have aren't sufficient to reconstruct its origins. Some scholars have claimed Zhang Zhung is related to ancient languages spoken in Indian Himalayan districts like Lahaul and Spiti, immediately on the other side of the Himalaya. Others argue the language of the Zhang Zhung originated in the Chinese and Tibetan borderlands far to the north-east some time in the Neolithic, thousands of years before the great castles, temples and tombs that characterise the later culture were built in the first millennium. This group migrated west, it is argued, in response to a worsening climate of lower rainfall and desertification, forcing people to adopt nomadic practices to survive. Only now is the archaeological work underway that may answer the mystery of the lost kingdom of Zhang Zhung and deepen our understanding of the exceptional bond Tibetans have with their landscape.

In 1962, in his landmark work *Tibetan Civilisation*, the historian Rolf Alfred Stein recounted how the growing kingdom of Songtsen Gampo, expanding west in the seventh century into the upper Yarlung Tsangpo valley, 'encountered a distinctly foreign nation – Shangshung with its capital Khyunglung'. He described Zhang Zhung as the home of Bon, 'a religion adopted by Tibetans before Buddhism'. That begged several questions Stein couldn't answer. Just how 'foreign' were the Zhang Zhung? Had they originated in the same place as Tibetans? Stein also found it hard to picture Zhang Zhung as an organised state. Yet the first wife of the powerful king Songtsen Gampo, long before the Chinese princess Wencheng and his many other wives, had been the daughter of Zhang Zhung's king. In return, Gampo had offered his own sister, forming a double bridal alliance between the rulers. Given how shrewd he was in his dealings elsewhere, especially with the Tang, it's unlikely Songtsen would have wasted the political advantages of his sister's marriage on an inconsequential band of nomads.

We also know, however, that the marriage was not a success. Songtsen's sister is identified in Dunhuang texts dating from the mid ninth century as Sadmarkar. In some of the earliest Tibetan lyrics we have, written from her point of view, she bemoans her situation:

> The place that it's my fate to inhabit
> Is this Silver Castle of Khyunglung.
> Others say:
> 'Seen from the outside, it's cliffs and ravines,

> But seen from inside, it's gold and jewels.'
> But when I'm standing in front of it,
> It rises up tall and grey.

She acted as a spy for her brother for a few years of isolated misery until Songtsen sent an army to ambush and kill the king of Zhang Zhung as he travelled with his men north-east towards Amdo: his dynasty then swallowed the vast territory of western Tibet whole. In this way Songtsen the king became an emperor.

Historians writing about Tibet's emergence have generally focussed on the arrival of major powers that would dominate future relationships: those from China, from the subcontinent, and nomadic tribes from the steppe. Zhang Zhung has been a footnote, one of many lost Himalayan kingdoms whose very obscurity has bred a kind of esoteric intrigue. It is also associated with Shambhala, the mythical lost kingdom that appears in Hinduism and is mentioned in the *Kalachakra*, perhaps the best-known and most complex tantric practice in Tibetan Buddhism. Yet modern scholarship suggests that Zhang Zhung played a significant role in early central Asian history, a potential rival to the emerging Yarlung valley kingdom and a culture whose origins stretched back well over a thousand years before Tibet's 'dharma kings' ended its power in the seventh and eighth centuries.

In the modern era, driving west from Kailas on the G219, one looks out toward a Hindu and largely Muslim world – to the northern Indian states of Uttarakhand, Himachal Pradesh and Jammu and Kashmir, and beyond to northern Pakistan, Afghanistan and Iran – seen from one that is Buddhist. During the putative thousand years of the Zhang Zhung kingdom, that world was widely Buddhist: the vast Iron-Age Maurya dynasty whose most famous ruler was Ashoka, a Buddhist convert; the Graeco-Buddhist zenith of the Gandhara Empire in northern Pakistan; the Central Asian Kushan Empire which in the first century broke like a wave around the bulwark of the Himalaya much as Islam and the British would later. At the time of Zhang Zhung's fall, Kashmir remained a major centre of Buddhist culture. Given that the Tang dynasty to the north and the Newars of Kathmandu (not to be confused with the modern-day term, Nepalis) to the south-east were also Buddhist, western Tibet can be seen as encircled by what had become an international religion practised by

Asia's elite, which is why a newly ambitious Asian polity like Tibet wanted to adopt Buddhism for itself.

In conquering Zhang Zhung and taking control of the Silk Roads, the Tibetans plugged into the seventh century's information highway, carrying goods and ideas between China, Persia and the Christian kingdoms of the eastern Mediterranean. (It's worth remembering that the people most commonly found along its length were refugees.) Alongside the dominant Buddhist narrative already familiar to Tibetans, they were exposed to new faiths, such as Christianity. The presence along the Silk Roads of the Church of the East, known, somewhat pejoratively, as the Nestorians, would feed into European fantasies about Tibet a thousand years later. Yet, even though Buddhism was adopted among the Tibetan elite, it had not yet taken root outside of the court. Tibet's indigenous gods still held sway.

The lost world of Zhang Zhung is a good place to look for clues about those gods, and modern archaeology is discovering plenty of them. Rolf Stein may have argued that Zhang Zhung was just a lofty desert bridge spanning the eastern and western parts of the Tibetan Empire, but new evidence shows that before Tibet took control, Zhang Zhung was a substantial kingdom at the confluence of intersecting long-distance trade routes, a conduit for ideas and cultures from beyond the plateau. In turn, Zhang Zhung had plenty to offer: gold, salt and musk, as well as medicinal plants. Artefacts found in Zhang Zhung cemeteries at Guge in western Tibet have been shown to originate in northern India and beyond, showing that trade was crossing the main Himalayan chain as well as moving east and west. The chance discovery of a tomb in 2006 that contained silk from the Han dynasty shows this trade extended northwards too. In 2016, Chinese archaeologists announced they had found the chemical traces of tea in another tomb in western Tibet dating back to 200 CE, firmly in the Zhang Zhung period, revising our notion of the arrival of tea in Tibet by some five hundred years. The archaeologists speculated that a side shoot of the Silk Roads had run across central Tibet, a notion that chimes with modern China's 'belt and road' initiative. It seems no less likely that tea arrived from the Silk Roads on a prehistoric north–south trade route.

Our knowledge of Zhang Zhung remains both tantalising and frustrating. In 1933, a group of scholars led by the celebrated Italian

Tibetologist Giuseppe Tucci visited the village of Khyunglung, at the head of the Sutlej valley, recording a number of sacred buildings as well as residential areas. They judged these ruins to be the location of Khyunglung Ngulkhar, the 'horned eagle valley silver citadel' mentioned in sacred Bon texts and in manuscripts recovered from the caves near Dunhuang. The horned eagle or *khyung* is a central motif in Zhang Zhung culture, later conflated with the more familiar snake-eating Hindu deity Garuda. Until quite recently, these remains were the only known centre of Zhang Zhung culture, but that picture is now filling out. American and Chinese archaeologists Mark Aldenderfer and Huo Wei excavated several buildings in Dindun, a village of semi-subterranean houses with two cemeteries dated to between 400 BCE and 100 BCE. Chinese archaeologists led by Dr Tong Tau have identified a major site at Khardong fifteen kilometres or so upstream from the village of Khyunglung and close to the tombs at Gurgyam where the Han Dynasty silk was found. This substantial settlement, Dr Tong believes, is a far more likely location for the capital of the Zhang Zhung kingdom. Khardong is also close to a major Zhang Zhung cemetery at Chunak where excavations have revealed items from all over Asia, including bronze mirrors similar to examples found on the Eurasian steppe and a gold mask linked with similar objects in northern India and Nepal.

Despite all this new material, there is still much to learn. It's not clear, for example, whether Zhang Zhung was simply the name given to a far more complex and varied political entity or if it referred, perhaps, to the culture from which that entity grew. The oldest Tibetan texts, dating roughly from the early ninth century, refer to this region more commonly by other names such as Mrayul Thangyye or Tod. We know Zhang Zhung neighboured another kingdom to the east, known as Sumpa, which had some cultural features in common but lacked others. It's also likely that Sumpa was overshadowed, even controlled by Zhang Zhung, suggesting a wide sphere of influence. Yet the wild country north and north-west of Kailas and Khyunglung is so vast that much remains to be discovered and studied.

The independent archaeologist John Vincent Bellezza has travelled more widely in this region than any academic before him, recording hundreds of sites, from citadels occupying high ground to temples and tombs; he has also documented 'warrens' of small windowless rooms whose architecture contrasts markedly with that of prehistoric eastern Tibet. These are among the highest dwellings constructed in human history. Bellezza has drawn particular attention to the practice of raising stones upright at tombs, often configured in haunting rows in the middle of the plateau or else in mortuary buildings. The most dramatic site is at Yul Khambu where Bellezza saw thousands of these standing stones between three inches and eight feet in height. Nowhere else in Tibet was this done, not even in the neighbouring kingdom of Sumpa, suggesting some kind of cultural watershed. It is perhaps too early to assign these practices to the Zhang Zhung but it's clear that a very particular kind of culture developed high in the western plateau. They have more in common with cultures in north Asian locations like southern Siberia, the Pamirs and Mongolia than anything in central Tibet or further east.

This pattern is repeated in the stunning rock art discovered all over the upper reaches of northern Tibet, much of it concerned with hunting game and located at rock shelters found in old encampments. There are also images here of the *khyung*, the horned eagle so closely associated with the Zhang Zhung. Among more symbolic images, the swastika is a favourite emblem, apotropaic protection to ward off evil spirits and assure long life; the Tibetan for swastika, a Sanskrit term, is *yungdrung* meaning both 'unborn' and 'undying'. It's a symbol that could have arrived via the Indus valley or else from the semi-nomadic tribes of central Asia, even Mongolia. Both the clockwise and counterclockwise versions appear: it was only later that these were divided along sectarian lines, the clockwise being associated with Buddhism, anticlockwise with Bon.

So what exactly was the religious tradition that predated Buddhism's arrival? The meaning of the word *bon* in the context of Tibetan religion is complex, even controversial. Bon is used routinely to indicate a wide range of non-Buddhist Tibetan religious practices over the ages, both before and after Tibet's conversion. The Milarepa saga, for example, is the moment when a landscape sacred to Bon was appropriated for the *dharma*, the Buddhist spiritual path. Before Buddhism, a supernatural world of spirits and demons was negotiated by *bonpo*, local shamans involved in rites of propitiation and healing. Such rites, rooted in a harsh natural world that both nurtured and threatened those who relied on it, varied widely across the plateau, and yet were merged together in the popular imagination following the adoption of Buddhism. The indigenous religion, the *mi cho* or religion of men, responded by reformulating itself, adopting many of Buddhism's key features, including the role of the lama (the Tibetan translation of guru, or teacher), and ideas of enlightenment, and developing a sacred literature that retrospectively pushed its origins backwards through time, beyond those of Gautama Buddha. This retrofitted sacred narrative became the religion now practised as Bon, but its rites and beliefs are profoundly different to those old ways practised in Zhang Zhung and elsewhere in Tibet.

Under the surface of both this reformulated Bon and Buddhism itself it's possible still to trace the shape of Tibet's original spiritual landscape. Bon absorbed the ideas of the elite's new religion while keeping its indigenous roots. At the same time, Buddhism, like Christianity in Europe, adapted itself to animist practices that were millennia old. As a result, there is still a myriad of powerful spiritual and cultural tropes that suffuse contemporary Tibetan culture predating the arrival of Buddhism. One example are *zi* beads, also spelled *dzi*, patterned agates characterised by lines and dots that form propitious geometric patterns. These have been found in many parts of Asia including Persia and India, but it's among Tibetan peoples throughout the Himalaya that they have held their fascination – and immense value. The most coveted *zi* have nine dots or 'eyes', *mi* in Tibetan, nine being a sacred number in Bon. Even in Giuseppe Tucci's day, those of highest quality were too expensive for him to afford. The origins and even the manufacture of these prized antiques is something of a mystery but it's now widely accepted that far from being imports, the finest examples originated in Tibet. That Dr Tong and his team of Chinese archaeologists should find them in graves at Chunak is no surprise: the Zhang Zhung kingdom has been mooted as a putative origin for the most precious of these sacred beads.

Another lucky charm that has in recent decades seen its value soar is the assortment of copper alloy amulets called *thokchak*, meaning 'the first metal'. Tang chroniclers acknowledged the excellence of Tibetan metalworkers, whose chain mail was of the highest quality: the elegance of these amulets also attests to that. Some were functional objects, like buttons or clasps; others were more obviously symbolic. Some of the finest that Tucci included in his influential book

Transhimalaya were from western Tibet: beautiful representations of the motif so closely associated with Zhang Zhung, the *khyung* or horned eagle, in some examples looking like a yak's head on a bird's body. Like the standing stones of north-western Tibet, many *thokchak* speak to the influence of nomads from the Eurasian steppe, echoing the stunning metalwork of the Scythians. The influence of India and China on the Himalaya is well documented; this northern strand has yet to be fully assimilated into our understanding.

The amalgam of indigenous local spirits, with all the richness of their mythologies embroidered into the landscape, and Buddhism, with its moral austerities and political muscle, could provoke conflict: over the killing of animals for meat for example, or drinking alcohol. But the interaction of the two would come to form a culture both unique in the world and rewardingly complex. Nowhere was that more true than here, in western Tibet, which played a critical role in the centuries-long struggle to establish Buddhism in Tibet, in what is known to Tibetans as *chidar*, translated as the 'second diffusion'.

At the centre of this resurgence was another lost kingdom, one that sprang up from the ashes of the collapsed Tibetan Empire in the tenth century in the Sutlej valley, a few kilometres downstream of the abandoned capital of the Zhang Zhung. This was Guge and its influence on the future of a renascent Buddhist Tibet would be immense.

*

On the Indian side of the border with western Tibet, buried in the mountains just south of where the mighty Sutlej meets the Spiti river, is a village called Pooh. Here there is a pillar of stone from around the late tenth century carved with the birth name of the king who would spark Tibet's Buddhist revival: Khorre, better known by his spiritual name La Lama Yeshe O. This pillar marked the fringes of Yeshe O's kingdom, a sphere of influence that extended west as far as Baltistan in Pakistan's Karakoram mountains and Ladakh, the 'Little Tibet' within India's modern border, and east to parts of what is now north-western Nepal, as well as to the northern fringes of the Indian Himalaya. It was called Ngari Khorsum, 'the three circuits of Ngari', Ngari likely being a reference to Kailas but implying western Tibet.

This forgotten empire would mark a revival in the Yarlung dynasty from which Yeshe O sprang, the glory days of the great dharma kings Songtsen Gampo and Trisong Detsen.

In the middle of the ninth century Tibet had collapsed into chaos and clan rivalry. In 848, on the Silk Road, Dunhuang fell once more to the Chinese. Monasticism in central Tibet failed; the tombs of the Yarlung dynasty were robbed and desecrated. And so a branch of the family, still devoutly Buddhist, headed west, carving out a new kingdom with its capital at Purang, close to the border of modern north-west Nepal, where the town is known as Taklakot. The family controlled a large swathe of the western Himalaya: Ladakh and Zanskar, Spiti and the upper Sutlej valley. Yeshe O lived between 947 and 1024. He inherited a polity based on the Sutlej valley, the kingdom of Guge, ruling with his brother, a Buddhist monk who took charge of spiritual affairs. Their goals were political survival and spiritual renewal, working together to recreate the visionary world of their great predecessor Trisong Detsen from two centuries before. They made Buddhism their state religion, and in doing so, some scholars argue, provided a model for the synthesis of religious and political power under the Dalai Lamas.

The wider population supported religious institutions with produce and land; in return they were compensated when children joined the clergy and were given education and military training, the latter a pressing need in the face of Islam's rapid progress through Central Asia. Yeshe O repressed or co-opted pre-Buddhist cults that would have been familiar to the Zhang Zhung. In the village of Pekar, located near Pooh in the Sutlej valley, but on the northern side of the Himalaya, Yeshe O suborned the local deity, a mythical warrior called Pehar whose origin was likely Central Asian and part of the narrative of the powerful local clan. Pehar's new role was to control opposing demons, a tutelary spirit for the new 'faith' of Buddhism, a role depicted in astonishing and near-contemporaneous temple paintings in what are known as the Caves of Bliss, some thirty kilometres north of Yeshe O's new capital at Tholing. The depiction of Pehar making an oath of protection to the *dharma* was in effect to show the old gods making a similar oath to the new king.

What constituted the true path of Buddhism obsessed Yeshe O. Central Tibet, as we have seen, had become an unruly spiritual frontier, where Indian tantric Buddhism was proving wildly popular, a school known in Tibet as Vajrayana, the thunderbolt vehicle, with its esoteric teachings and challenging ideas. Some practitioners took tantric visualisations about killing animals and even humans or taboo-breaking sexual behaviour literally. That was not what Yeshe O had in mind for Guge. He wanted a return to the supposed purity of Trisong Detsen, not modern heresies. To recapture that essence, he recreated another worthy aspect of Trisong Detsen's legacy: translation. And to that end he sent twenty-one bright young men to Kashmir, still a centre of Buddhist learning in India, to bring back sacred texts to be translated from Sanskrit to Tibetan, and in doing so herald an age of spiritual renewal.

Such translators, *lotsawa* in Tibetan, are venerated in Buddhism, since the act of translation requires a profound understanding of the texts. The greatest of these at Yeshe O's court was Rinchen Zangpo. He was born in 958 in Ngari, possibly in the village of Reni, also in the Sutlej valley, which in Tibetan is called the Langchen Tsangpo. As a two-year-old he was seen tracing Sanskrit letters in the dirt and despite his parents not being Buddhist was ordained as a monk at just thirteen. He spent many years in India studying tantric and non-tantric Buddhist texts in Sanskrit. When Rinchen Zangpo finally returned, he came to the attention of Yeshe O, according to legend, after winning a duel of magic with a charismatic trickster, whom Rinchen Zangpo swiftly exposed as a fake. How many of the stories that surround him are true isn't so important; they simply illustrate that Rinchen Zangpo was a man of preternatural gifts dedicated to the true path of the *dharma* in a world where everyone and his yak thinks they're a spiritual master. Yeshe O made him court chaplain and set Rinchen Zangpo to work translating Sanskrit texts, later sending him back to Kashmir, this time in some style, to gather more. The influx of this new scholarship, funded by Guge's access to gold mines in the Indus valley and the musk trade with the Arab world, informed and developed Tibet's understanding of Buddhism.

Rinchen Zangpo was also charged with recruiting artists for the substantial building programme Yeshe O initiated. In 996 he laid the foundations for four great temples: Tholing at the centre, Tabo to the west on the Spiti river, Nyarma to the north in Ladakh and Khorchag to the east, close to the former capital of Purang. Tholing was the mother temple, known as the Tsuglakhang, and among the cultural apogees of Tibetan art. It was from Tholing, as Giuseppe Tucci wrote following his visit in 1933, that 'a crowd, today almost unknown, of thinkers and ascetics shed over the whole of Tibet a spiritual light which is not yet extinguished'. A British trade representative called Gerard Mackworth-Young who visited before the Great War captured the immense drama of Tholing's location:

> The riverbed is here a scorching waste of rocks and dust about a mile wide ... The monastery of Tholing stands opposite, on a shelf overlooking the Sutlej. Its long crimson walls, set off by a few brilliant poplars in full leaf, its rows of white pure stupas, Buddhism's signature hemispherical structure, high above, its gold roof sparkling in the haze, struck just that crowning note of unreality which the whole scene demanded.

Mackworth-Young's vision is no longer there. Almost all of what time had spared of Guge's early artistic glories was destroyed during the Cultural Revolution, robbing the world of the brilliance of this remote Buddhist renaissance. Among the very few survivors are temple caves in the Khartse valley, where Rinchen Zangpo died a venerated figure in his nineties, decorated with exquisite illustrations of the *lotsawa* and his king, Yeshe O, both men painted with immense skill in the fourteenth century: their collaboration had transformed western Tibet and their legacy survived in the unique development of Tibet as a nation governed through the prism of spiritual faith.

For most of the eleventh century, Yeshe O's successors maintained Guge's spiritual vision and extended its political control, reuniting the various parts of the family's kingdom from the capital Tholing. Most importantly, at least for the future of Buddhism in Tibet, when Yeshe O abdicated in favour of his nephew Changchub O, the new king made it a priority to persuade the dazzling Buddhist scholar Atisa Dipamkara to visit Guge. By now the Karakhanid Turks had spread east along the Silk Roads, converting its Buddhist centres to Islam and, so the legend has it, taking Yeshe O hostage. Rather than use his gold to pay off the Turks, Changchub spent it instead – at his uncle's request – in prising Atisa away from his monastic university. This was Vikramasila, located in what is now the Indian state of Bihar but was

then the Pala Empire, which stretched the length of the southern
limit of the Himalaya – the final major Buddhist polity on the subcontinent.

Atisa's arrival would be critical in the emergence of Tibet's monastic
tradition. One of many Indian scholars at work in Tibet in this period,
he remains, like Guru Rinpoche, venerated for his role in establishing
the nation's spiritual identity, known by his Tibetan name Jowo Je.
Born in 982 to a noble family, most probably in Bikrampur in modern
Bangladesh, he was called Candragarbha before he arrived in Guge,
where Changchub O hailed him as Atisa, meaning 'lord'. By then, the
year 1042, Atisa was widely regarded as one of the finest Buddhist
scholars in the world, having spent a dozen years teaching in Sumatra
before burnishing his reputation at Vikramasila. He was impressed by
the Tibetan students he encountered there, sent to India from Guge
to deepen their learning. The head of his institution was reluctant to
lose his best teacher to 'that yak pen' of Tibet, making him promise
to return in three years. Instead, Atisa would spend the remaining
thirteen years of his life there.

While living at Tholing, Atisa wrote his greatest work, *A Lamp for
the Path to Enlightenment*, and dedicated it to Changchub O. It was
written in response to the Guge kingdom's uncertainty about tantric
practice. How should its complexities be reconciled? How did it relate
to established methods? How should its shocking imagery be inter-
preted? Atisa's great gifts, as related in Tibetan religious histories, were
his depth of understanding and his humility in illustrating it. In Tholing
he encountered the great translator Rinchen Zangpo, then in his mid
eighties; it was he who had recommended Atisa be brought to Tibet.
Despite being the older man, it was Rinchen Zangpo who learned
more from the encounter, Atisa showing him how to break through
the surface of the multifarious tantras to reach their single unified
root.

After three years in Tholing, Atisa left with a group of his students
for central Tibet and the border with Nepal, heading for home as he
had promised. When they were delayed on the way, an argument
broke out among his followers about which direction Atisa should
take. Nagtso, the Tibetan translator who had persuaded him to come
on Changchub's behalf, thought Atisa should honour his promise to
return. Another student, Dromton, who came to Guge to hear Atisa

teach, persuaded him instead to come home with him to central Tibet, where monks from the north-eastern region of Amdo had been reformulating monasteries after Tibet's dark ages. Discovering the library at Samye, with its huge resource of Sanskrit texts, Atisa understood the depth to which Buddhism had penetrated Tibet: it was too good an opportunity to miss. Over his lifetime, he wrote and translated more than two hundred books.

When Atisa died near Lhasa in 1054, his student Dromton established a new monastery at Reting to continue his teaching, which became known as the Kadam school, *ka* meaning 'scripture' and *dam* meaning 'precept'. The Kadam-pa (-pa being a suffix that means 'people') were known for their asceticism and intellectual rigour, and their legacy is found not just at Reting but in the cave frescoes in Guge. In time, the Kadam school would evolve into a new school of Tibetan Buddhism, the Geluk, that of the Dalai Lamas. It was through Atisa and Dromton in the eleventh century that Avalokitesvara, *bodhisattva* (meaning 'enlightenment seeker') of compassion, became a protective spirit of Tibet, known there as Chenrezig, and that the Dalai Lamas would come to be regarded as incarnations of Chenrezig, thus making the Dalai Lamas an indivisible part of Tibetan identity.

*

Despite its long dedication to the *dharma*, there would be no lasting monastic legacy in Guge. When Giuseppe Tucci arrived in 1933, Guge was desolate, the few inhabitants barely conscious of the great glories that had existed in their midst. In the 1100s, Turkic raiders overran the Guge kingdom, which fractured once more into its constituent parts. Its former capital Purang alone seems to have escaped the chaos, expanding into the north-western districts of Nepal. It was a monastic order from central Tibet, the Kagyu, that eventually established itself in the west, captured in legend with Milarepa's famous triumph at Kailas. In the thirteenth century, Tholing's holiest temple, the Tsuglakhang, was donated to the Kagyu, who renovated it in their central Tibetan style while keeping some of the Kashmiri aesthetic that had been the hallmark of Guge in its glory days.

When the Mongols arrived in the thirteenth century a different Buddhist lineage became pre-eminent: the Sakya, the only major school

in Buddhism that is hereditary. As Mongol influence on Tibet faded
in the fourteenth century, Guge enjoyed a magnificent renaissance.
During this period, the reformist followers of the new Geluk school
were invited to Guge, a natural fit for them given their origins in
Atisa's teachings. Tholing remained a great spiritual centre but Guge's
capital now moved elsewhere, to an astonishing palace fortress called
Tsaparang. The openness to new ideas that had characterised Guge's
first golden age would be repeated in the second. And it was this
willingness to engage with outside influences that explains in part
how western Tibet experienced a concerted effort to be converted by
a religion almost wholly foreign to it: Christianity.

Tibet's elite must have been aware of Christ before Buddhism
became the established religion. By the 700s, followers of the heretic
archbishop of Constantinople Nestorius, having broken with Rome
in the 420s, had established themselves among the Christians of Persia
and expanded along the Silk Road, where Syriac was then the lingua
franca, and into China. They flourished under the Tang dynasty; a
famous Nestorian stele erected in 781 in Chang'an (now Xi'an) quotes
the imperial edict from 635 that authorised Christ's teaching: 'The way
has no unchanging name, sages have no unchanging method.' The
missionary who won that concession to preach the Gospel, Alopen,
is named on the stele, and out of this striking example of Chinese
ecumenical curiosity came the so-called Jesus Sutras discovered in the
Dunhuang caves, a blend of Buddhist, Christian and Taoist philosophy,
connecting the Buddhist concept of *sunyata*, loosely translated as
'emptiness', with Christian negative theology, the mystical 'unknowa-
bility' of God's nature. The Nestorian patriarch in 781 was Timothy
I, born in modern Iraq and elected in Baghdad; a great supporter of
missionary work, he wrote that there were Christians in Tibet and
intended to appoint a bishop there. Indeed, hints of Christian worship
from this period have been found inside Tibet, but if it was practised,
it didn't gain a foothold. The stele at Chang'an was buried as Christianity
was suppressed in China: Buddhism was the only 'foreign' religion
permitted.

That there were many Christians in the further reaches of Asia,
marooned behind a Muslim curtain, was well known in Europe if
poorly understood. Concocted versions of a letter supposedly written
to the Byzantine emperor Manuel I by the Christian Prester John,

'supreme ruler of the Three Indies', circulated in the courts of Europe in the latter part of the twelfth century. The letters supposedly described Prester John's homeland, a place of immense wealth and no disease, blending familiar images of Eden with fantastical creatures and men from the works of Herodotus. What prompted most interest was Prester John's offer to use his army to liberate Jerusalem, this in the aftermath of the failed second crusade. Although a forgery, the letter was set in a geographical context that had a foot in reality. Scholars have linked the myth with the military conquest in 1141 of the Seljuk Turks by the Central Asian Kara-Khitan tribe. Though largely Buddhist, their number included many Christians.

Such legends coincided with a growing appetite for travel writing. In the late thirteenth century Marco Polo satisfied that market at both ends of the Silk Roads, entertaining Kublai Khan with exotic yarns about Europe before returning to Italy to do the same about the Mongol emperor. An earlier traveller than Polo, the Franciscan William of Rubruck, published *Itinerarium*, a memoir of his mission for Louis IX in 1254, undertaken reluctantly, to deliver a letter to Kublai's predecessor Mongke Khan at his capital of Karakorum. He was shocked at Mongke's courtly entertainment: a three-way religious debate between Muslims, Buddhists and Nestorians. The notion of religious tolerance was unbearable to Rubruck, yet he gives us the first European reference to the sacred Sanskrit phrase *om mani padme hum*: most usually translated as 'hail to the jewel in the lotus', although its true meaning is both complicated and contested.

From the start, Europe's discovery of Tibet was enmeshed with missionary intent. It was Franciscan friars who brought Europe many of the first descriptions of the country. In 1245 Giovanni da Pian del Carpine, a companion of St Francis of Assisi, was the first European to report back on the Mongol court in his *Ystoria Mongalorum*, having been sent east by the pope in the aftermath of the Mongol invasion of Europe. Like Marco Polo he noticed the Tibetans there, an intrinsic element in the spiritual life of the elite, and described aspects of their lives, including *jhator*, usually described in the West as sky burial, although not a term from Tibetan, the ritual dismemberment of the dead for consumption by carrion. (The origins of this practice are obscure but some have seen links with Persian Zorastrianism, from a common route in Central Asia. Tibetan kings were buried; lamas were cremated and their ashes incorporated into sacred architecture.) Another Franciscan, Odorico Mattiussi, better known as Odoric of Pordenone, included a whole chapter on Tibet in his account of visiting China in the 1320s: 'Concerning the Realm of Tibet Where Dwelleth the Pope of the Idolators'. Odoric's claim to have visited Tibet may be true, but much of his material was clearly gleaned from encountering Tibetans outside the country, and the suggestion he visited Lhasa is widely discounted.

It was the Jesuits, however, with their pragmatic zeal, who really got stuck in towards the end of the sixteenth century. Jesuits at the Mughal court of the emperor Akbar were well aware of Tibet. Rodolfo Acquaviva, shortly before he was butchered in Goa during the Cuncolim Revolt, wrote of the land of 'Bottan', meaning Tibet, beyond the Himalaya in 1582. In the *Mongolicae legationis commentarius* of 1591, Rodolfo's companion Antonio Monserrate wrote of lost vestiges of Christianity hidden in the remote valleys of the Himalaya where priests read from the scriptures and distributed the bread and wine, although he discounts the possibility that these were Tibetans, whom he describes as being governed by magicians. Jesuits discovered the existence of Lake Manasarovar and of a city nearby: Monserrate's book is accompanied with a crude map showing the lake with the legend *Hic dicuntur Christiani habitare*: 'here there are Christians said to be living.'

It would be easy to overstate the scale of the Jesuit interest in the lost world of Prester John. Tibet was mostly a footnote to their main concerns: China, Japan and India. In 1596 Matteo Ricci, leader of the Jesuit mission to China, did call for an exploration of the lands between the Mughal and Manchu empires. And Monserrate's description of a lost Christian congregation living in the Himalaya certainly inspired the Portuguese António de Andrade, head of the Jesuit mission in the Indian city of Agra. Andrade joined a party of Hindu pilgrims to Badrinath, in the modern Indian state of Uttarakhand, travelling with his fellow priest Manuel Marques up the Alaknanda river towards the Tibetan border. Leaving Marques behind, Andrade followed the valley, travelling in the shadow of the mountain Kamet, only twenty-five kilometres north of Badrinath, to reach the Mana Pass at 5,600 metres. Suffering from snowblindness and the 'noxious vapours' Andrade believed were the source of his altitude sickness, he saw before him the high barren plateau of Tibet: the first European to describe the wearying reality of Himalayan travel. He must have thought himself in some sort of purgatory.

Andrade returned to Badrinath and after a month retraced his steps, this time with his companion Marques, entering Tibet to witness the dying embers of the Guge kingdom. Much of its power had by now drifted east to Lhasa and west to a resurgent Ladakh. The king of Guge was nevertheless open to the idea of Christianity. It was possible, Andrade argued, that *bodhisattvas* might have arisen in the West. And since truth could not harm truth, why shouldn't he preach the gospel in Guge and challenge the teachings of Buddha? Andrade returned home and in 1625, with permission and funds from his superior in Goa, established a chapel at the palace fortress of Tsaparang, the astonishing citadel and monastic complex in the Sutlej valley. A small number of priests struggled to keep the mission going through the late 1620s and their accounts provide valuable insights into the religious and economic life of Guge. Andrade was intrigued at how closely the Tibetan monastic orders resembled Christian ones. Yet their efforts were in vain. In 1630, Tsaparang fell to the great Ladakhi king Sengge Namgyal. He enslaved the few hundred converts the Jesuits had made including two of the priests: it took a concerted diplomatic effort to extract them from his palace at Leh. The kingdom of Guge now began its swift and final decline into the obscurity Tucci witnessed in 1933. Climatologists have recently discovered that the monsoon weakened considerably in the early seventeenth century, plunging western Tibet into a period of desertification, suggesting Guge's failure was as much a consequence of climate change as invasion. The last king of Guge died in 1676. When the East India Company became aware of western Tibet and its lucrative wool trade into Kashmir, that trade was controlled through Leh in Ladakh. The ancient Guge kingdom had faded into near-oblivion.

*

Jesuit attempts to convert Tibet might have come to nothing, but there was a curious legacy. In February 1627, two more missionaries, Estêvão Cacella and João Cabral, became the first Europeans to enter Bhutan, where they were soon robbed and thrown in prison. They

did, however, encounter the first king of Bhutan, the Kagyu monk
Ngawang Namgyal, and following Antonio Monserrate's lead, asked
about neighbouring regions in hopes of locating any lost communities
of Christians. They were told about Shambhala, which they mistook
as being Cathay, whose location was a question of burning geographical interest to Jesuit missionaries across Asia. (Was Cathay the same
as China? Or somewhere else?) So it was that their account of their
journey included the first reference from a European to the mythical
paradise of Shambhala, its origins in the half-forgotten shamanic past
of western Tibet.

This lost world of perfection, such an obvious parallel to Eden, and
the tenuous linking of Christianity and Buddhism, would become a
compelling subject to adventurous spiritual seekers in the late nineteenth century. Switched on to Tibet by growing academic and philosophical interest in Buddhism – Hegel was fascinated by the notion
of emptiness – new-age mystics climbed on board the bandwagon,
including the Theosophist Helena Blavatsky, whose concocted band
of enlightened beings, the Masters of the Ancient Wisdom, she claimed
to have met in Tibet. All these disparate strands coalesced in James
Hilton's 1933 novel *Lost Horizon*, whose exotic setting is the hidden
world of Shangri-La where moral and spiritual perfection endure: for
some in the West it's an idea that almost defines the Himalaya.

Hilton's hero Conway and three companions are kidnapped on
board an aircraft, which crash-lands near the remote monastery of
Shangri-La. Its mysterious head 'lama' is in reality a Christian
missionary priest who arrived in the early eighteenth century and has
achieved immense longevity. The setting, a lost world of moral purity,
is largely emblematic. Hilton's novel has little to do with the reality
of Tibet and more to do with its reputation as somewhere unexplored.
None of the central characters are Tibetans: they are almost exclusively
cast as servants and characterised as noble savages. Almost nothing
of Tibetan culture emerges from its pages. In the monastery's library,
Conway finds some of the books Hilton drew on in his research in
the British Library, including Andrade's account of Tsaparang and the
lost kingdom of Guge. The sacred mountain Hilton locates near
Shangri-La bears close comparison to Kailas. But the mystical order
who inhabit the monastery echo Theosophist fantasies. *Lost Horizon*
is not about Tibet at all; its themes are moral exhaustion after one

world war and anxiety about the next, and a critique of consumerism. Yet the notion of a hidden sanctuary promising spiritual refreshment and healing resonates in Tibetan culture, represented in the idea of *beyul*, sacred valleys whose secret locations are concealed in texts waiting to be read by spiritual masters. There's a need for Eden, or Shambhala, in all of us.

The fictional Shangri-La's status as a refuge from modernity's consumerist values didn't stop the Chinese government renaming Zhongdian, a small town two thousand kilometres east of Tsaparang in Yunnan province, as Shangri-La City. They spent $200m on this spiritual Disneyworld, building an airport and other infrastructure in the lush and forested mountains of south-west China. The palace fortress of Tsaparang, on the other hand, stands aloof in its arid, remote valley, dramatic testament to the true story of Tibet. The sacred sites in nearby Tholing are being slowly restored, although to what standard is hard to say. The temple complex still feels like a broken fossil from a lost epoch. The village itself has become a garrison town for the People's Liberation Army, forward post for the latest dynasty controlling the ancient network of trade routes across the Himalaya.

5

The Architects of Xanadu

It had been a glittering autumn's day in Kathmandu. The usual layer of smog was gone, unveiling the city's mountainous backdrop in adamantine clarity: Ganesh to the north-west, the snow pyramid of Langtang Lirung to the north and to the north-east the white diamond of Dorje Lhakpa, all of them seven kilometres or so above sea level and seeming so close I felt I could touch them. From Ratna Park in the middle of town, a place ordinarily cloaked in fumes, I'd even spotted the distant shark's fin of the world's highest mountain: Chomolungma.

Older inhabitants must have thought of their youth, when the city was more often like this, before everything changed. In the span of a generation, from the 1980s onwards, hundreds of thousands of migrants from all over Nepal had moved into the city, drawn by economic necessity, or as refugees from the Maoist insurgency that had plunged the nation into war. Modest Kathmandu had become one of the fastest-growing cities in South Asia. New neighbourhoods of dismal concrete sprang up, turning the valley from green to grey. A city that for much of its history was concerned with ritual pollution became swamped with the real thing: plastics, fumes and filthy rivers.

These days, tourists are often in a rush to escape Kathmandu. In the popular imagination, the Himalaya are a place for adventure, of wild new horizons, not urban sprawl. And yet even now the valley's ancient cities remain among the most elegant and richly complex achievements in human history, not just for the breathtaking quality of their architecture and decorative arts, but for the ways of living that evolved alongside the built environment. Despite the impacts of mass production and global communication, these exquisite urban centres remain so culturally compelling and intricate that the city itself becomes a narcotic. You can lose yourself here, following the arc of festivals as the weeks tick by, finding something new and beautiful to ponder on every walk through the narrow streets. A place where, as the scholar Giuseppe Tucci put it, 'all the terror, the anguish and the hope of India are expressed with a frankness that approaches exultation'.

Now it was dusk, and light on the distant snows was darkening from pink to indigo. Among the temples and palaces of Patan, south of the Bagmati river, a large crowd was gathered around a *dabali*, a raised platform, where a dancer in a white lion-mask was menacing a stout fellow wearing a silver crown and armed with what looked like a papier-mâché mace. Red scraps of cloth tied at the lion's wrists and elbows streamed from his arms as he whirled around the dais, making him a blur of extravagant fabric, the long mane that reached down to the small of his back catching the light from braziers at all four corners of the stage. Every so often the lion performed a stunt, leaping into the air and gathering his legs underneath him, or spinning round nimbly, or else pawing the air with imaginary claws, and every time he did so the children watching shrieked with excitement, their squeals competing with the raucous noise of clashing cymbals and parping trumpets. As the lion skipped and prowled, the king waggled his cudgel and backed away, legs wide apart, feet turned out, weighed down with garlands of marigolds, awaiting his fate.

This was the Kartik Naach, or Kartik dances, Kartik being the month in the Hindu calendar when they're held. The story is drawn from the *Puranas* and tells how Narasimha, an avatar of Vishnu whose name translates as 'man-lion', overcomes the *asura* or demon, Hiranyakashipu, who has been persecuting his followers. Hiranyakashipu is angry because an avatar of Vishnu has killed his brother. He wants revenge. Hiranyakashipu goes through great austerities so Brahma will protect him with magical powers: no man or animal can harm him. Yet even as he wages war, he can't dissuade his own son, the saintly Prahlada, from his devotion to Vishnu. So Hiranyakashipu resolves to have him killed in a sequence of outlandish assassination attempts. Prahlada's virtue saves him every time. Hiranyakashipu then mocks his son. Pointing to a pillar of stone, he asks if Vishnu exists even in this lump of rock. But when he hits the pillar with his mace, Narasimha emerges and because he is half man and half animal, neither wholly one nor

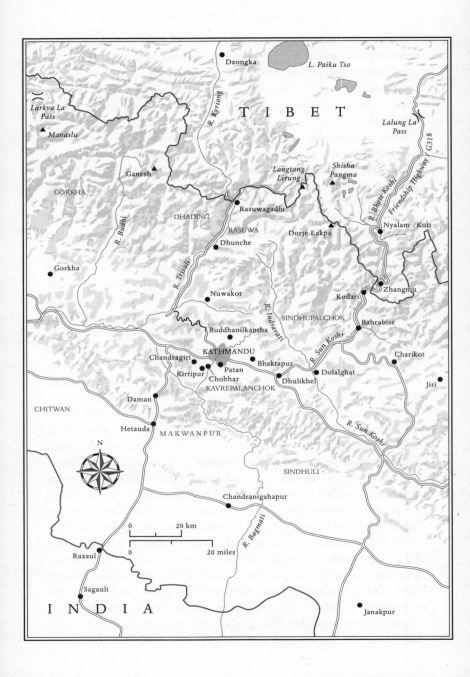

the other, the man-lion poses a fatal threat. In the story, Narasimha eviscerates Hiranyakashipu. As the dance reached this climax in the story, Narasimha simply touched the demon on the chest, who fainted dead away, born aloft like a crowd-surfing rock star while spectators held up their smartphones to share the triumph of good over evil on social media.

There are far older and more famous festivals in the Kathmandu valley. The chariot procession that each spring carries the god Bunga Dyah, giver of rain, around the streets of Patan under the auspicious gaze of Patan's Kumari, or living goddess, is well over a thousand years old and means a great deal more to the original Newari popu-lation of the city. (Sacred to Buddhists and Hindus, Bunga Dyah is for some synonymous with Avalokitesvara, the *bodhisattva* of compassion known in Tibet as Chenrezig.) The Kartik dances on the other hand began during the reign of Siddhi Narasimha Malla, king of Patan, in the mid seventeenth century, a few years before the first Europeans reached the city. Across the border in Tibet, the Guge kingdom was in its final death spiral; in Lhasa the fifth Dalai Lama and his powerful proxy Sonam Rabten were exerting control for the Geluk school of Tibetan Buddhism after decades of sectarian and regional conflict. This was good news for the Malla kings who ruled the Kathmandu valley: during the rule of the 'Great Fifth', as the Dalai Lama became known, they were given the job of minting Tibet's currency, a lucra-tive industry that bankrolled the chief and hugely expensive preoc-cupation of Kathmandu's Malla kings: competition with each other, often expressed in the extravagance of their architecture, and their decorative and performance arts.

Although there were a thousand years between the deep-rooted people's festival for Bunga Dyah and the courtly theatre of the Kartik dances, both were built on Kathmandu's unique collection of advan-tages, beginning with its propitious location, nestling in mountains at 1,400 metres, and its generous climate. The month of Kartik runs from late October to late November. The weather is fine but not yet too cold. It's an auspicious month, the start of the wedding season, right after the hugely popular festival of Dasain. In mythology, the eleventh day of Kartik is when Vishnu awakes from his four-month yogic doze to marry his bride Laksmi. There's no better time to tie the knot.

As Kartik wears on, the temperature drops and you're grateful at night for a fire. Until the jungles of northern India were cleared, the cold temperatures also put an end to the deadly malaria season. Known as *aul* in Nepal, malaria didn't just affect the plains. As the British resident Brian Hodgson wrote in the mid nineteenth century: 'No elevation short of 3,000 to 4,000 feet above the sea suffices to rid the atmosphere of the low Himalaya from malaria.' Villagers would build their farmhouses above this line so they could escape the mosquitos, walking down to their lower fields in the morning. Climate change seems to be raising the mosquito's ceiling, creating new problems in remote villages. There's an argument that Nepal's history has been shaped as much by the mosquito as by any great king.

The valley's original inhabitants, arriving in the first millennium BCE, a shadowy group called the Kirata who spoke a Tibeto-Burmese language from which Newari developed, must have pinched themselves at their good fortune: a largely flat valley with some of the most fertile soil in the region and above the malaria line. The valley's location had another benefit. It was conveniently close to the high mountains and developing trade routes into Tibet. Merchants and pilgrims would wait until the cold season to cross the malaria-infested jungle. By then it was also winter in the high mountains, where snowfall and low temperatures posed a different kind of fatal hazard. So they would wait for spring in the Kathmandu valley, where there was sufficient food, for the passes to clear and Tibetan traders to come down from the plateau, or else to continue their own journey. The seventh-century traveller and Buddhist monk Xuanzang, who travelled to Indian Buddhist sites seeking inspiration, was among the first to record how trade funded the valley's complex religious life, with Buddhist and Hindu institutions coexisting side by side.

Trade was already well established by the time the first literate dynasty established itself in Kathmandu, early in the fifth century. The Licchavi were an offshoot of a long-established polity based at the ancient city of Vaishali, across the Ganges from Patna in north-east India. This was the dynasty that Songtsen Gampo had known as a vassal state to the emergent Tibetan Empire. The Licchavi period coincided with the Gupta Empire in India, centuries of immense artistic achievement, which reached their apogee in Kathmandu from the late fifth to early seventh centuries: stone sculpture from this period remains unsurpassed. The Licchavi founded many of Kathmandu's most sacred temples on sites that were already revered: the great Buddhist stupa at Swayambhu, the Shaivite Pashupatinath beside the Bagmati river, and Changu Narayan, a temple to Vishnu with the valley's oldest inscription, dating from the fifth century. At Budhanilakantha, on the northern rim of the Kathmandu valley, is a colossal seventh-century statue of Vishnu in his incarnation as Narayan: asleep in a sunken pond, resting on the endless loops of a *naga*, or snake spirit, in the shape of a cobra whose hooded heads shade him as he sleeps. The pond represents the primordial cosmic ocean. When he awakes, Vishnu will take his place in heaven in a universe created by Brahma, himself born from a lotus that grew from Vishnu's navel as he slept. The god Shiva provides the predominant Hindu narrative strand in the Himalaya, and his incarnations dominate the Kathmandu valley, but Vishnu's royal influence also stretches back deep into the city's past; as the story of the Kartik dances shows, Vishnu was central to the Malla kings. Those who replaced them, the now defunct Shah dynasty, last kings of Nepal, regarded themselves as incarnations of Vishnu.

When the Buddhist Pala dynasty emerged in the late eighth century, the Licchavis still controlled the valley but were beginning their decline. The rulers that followed had links to the Pala Empire and the Buddhist universities – Nalanda, Vikramasila and Odantapuri – in what is now the Indian state of Bihar. (The name 'Bihar' derives from the Sanskrit and Pali term *vihara*, literally 'abode' but meaning monastery.) From this world the tantric influences that are the hallmark of Newari culture emerged; the teacher Atisa, who as we saw in the last chapter brought this late Indian Buddhist renaissance to Tibet, was ordained at Nalanda and received his most important teaching at Vikramasila. Under the Pala, new artistic traditions developed, stunning images in bronze and gold, a cultural explosion that filled Kathmandu with tantric gurus, drawing students from Tibet. The artisans were monks themselves, and from the tenth century, as Tibet took up the rage for tantric Buddhism, their work was in high demand there as well. Around the time of the Norman Conquest in England, something extraordinary happened in the heart of the Himalaya, a combination of bold, dangerous philosophy and exquisite art. As the writer and long-time resident of Kathmandu Thomas Bell put it: 'The rise of tantrism in medieval Kathmandu turned the city into a magical garden.' And the ideas and psychological insights that grew in that Indian garden were soon transplanted to the high plateau of Tibet beyond the Himalaya.

It was a final flourish from Indian Buddhism. The Pala Empire in Bengal, already in decline in western India during the mid ninth century, found itself under increasing pressure from a resurgent Hinduism and the kingdoms that supported it. Islam had displaced Buddhism from Afghanistan and Pakistan by the early eleventh century, although Buddhism hung on in Kashmir until the fourteenth. Its large monastic institutions grew distant from the lay population, weakening their connection to ordinary people. To their eyes, tantric Buddhism looked pretty much the same as the Hindu version. Then, in around 1193, the Persian warlord Ikhtiyar al-Din Muhammad Khalji swept across Bihar and this gradual decline became annihilation. Monks and nuns were put to the sword, gold icons looted and religious books burned. Buddhism was essentially scraped off northern India, its followers scattered, many of them taking refuge at Kathmandu. (Ikhtiyar al-Din soon overreached himself attempting to invade Tibet and lost his army; he was assassinated not long after.)

This culture, swept away on the tide of history from the very places where Buddha had preached, now found refuge in the mountains, where it not only survived but enjoyed a period of artistic and architectural achievement. Kathmandu's valley in the mountains was strategic enough to get rich but obscure enough to escape fatal predation as successive waves of invaders swept across the plains of India. In this way, Nepal, meaning the valley of Kathmandu, held a peculiarly important position in Asian history, a crossroads where South, Central and East Asian religious and artistic influences met, coalesced and survived, a living reminder of a half-forgotten world, the key to a secret history that would remain hidden from Europeans even after they discovered the city.

The cultural brilliance of medieval Kathmandu was not lost on the rest of Asia, however. Soon after its emergence, it would find new expression in the court of a new force that had torn through all of Asia and into Europe: the Mongols.

★

Just as Buddhism, fading from India, flourished in Kathmandu, so it also gained new impetus in Tibet. In the west, we have seen, the Guge kingdom had sponsored a Buddhist cultural revival, drawing from Kashmiri influences and teachers like Atisa. Central Tibet, meanwhile, became a spiritual laboratory for tantric practices from northern India and the Pala Empire, via trade routes that passed through the Kathmandu valley. A famous example of a tantric 'wild one' prompting an entire lineage is Marpa Lotsawa, Marpa the translator, born into a landowning Tibetan family but too restless to settle to life as a farmer. He travelled to Nalanda in India to study with the great teacher Naropa (who in turn had studied with Tilopa) and brought home new tantric mantras that he would practise on behalf of the laity in return for gold, which in turn funded return trips to India for more study. Gold mining was intense in eleventh century Tibet and gold fuelled the dissemination of Buddhism, trickling south through Kathmandu to India as spiritual energy flowed the other way. Marpa's student was the charismatic Milarepa, and their lineage became the Kagyu sect of Tibetan Buddhism, Kagyu meaning 'whispered transmission'.

Some feared that the huge popular success of tantric teachings and their wilder interpretations threatened to corrupt their meaning into little more than magical spells used for personal gain. Konchok Gyalpo was one such, born into the aristocratic Khon family. A contemporary of Milarepa, he founded a new Buddhist centre at Sakya, thirteen kilometres south-west of Shigatse in southern Tibet, beginning another Tibetan Buddhist lineage that survives today, the third of the four great schools of Tibetan Buddhism and the only one whose spiritual leader is drawn from within the same family. The Sakya would prosper in the fragmented world of Tibet in the early part of the second millennium, but largely through the intervention of foreign powers.

It was another version of Tibetan Buddhism, however, that would intially influence the Mongols, one that sprang from the Tangut people. Known to themselves and Tibetans as the Minyak, they had been pushed out of the rolling grasslands of north-eastern Tibet during the time of the Tibetan Empire to the Ordos region near the Yellow river. Now, in the eleventh century, they were building their own centre of power and moved back into Tibet, taking the Tibetan plateau city of Xining. As the Tibetan emperors had done, they translated Buddhist scriptures into their own language. In doing so they developed a new kind of relationship with Tibetan teachers, particularly from the Kagyu lineage, who travelled to the powerful Tangut court. In 1227, the Mongols' devastating forces swept down and utterly destroyed the Tangut capital Xingqing. Despite this, they saw value in continuing the ruler-priest relationship the Tangut had pioneered between themselves and Tibetan monks, as it offered an effective way to control the high and exposed Tibetan plateau at arm's length, without committing resources that might be used more profitably elsewhere.

By the mid thirteenth century, Tibet had largely been absorbed into the Mongol Empire under Mongke Khan, the fourth *khagan*, or 'emperor', beginning a period of Mongol influence in Tibet that would last until the eighteenth century. Mongke gave his patronage to the Kagyu lineage, although the leader of the empire's Buddhists came from Kashmir. But the Sakya lineage also had influence among some of the Mongol elite and in 1258, Kublai Khan, under the influence of his wife Chabi, acknowledged Drogon Chogyal Phagpa, leader of the Sakya-pa, as his tantric guru, essentially converting to Tibetan Buddhism. Mongke died in 1259 and, after a civil war with their younger brother Ariq Boke, Kublai was elected the fifth *khagan* in May 1260. At the end of that year Phagpa became Kublai's *kuoshi*, a kind of state religious instructor, cementing the idea of a ruler–priest relationship between Mongols and Tibetans, a conscious attempt by Kublai to move away from the Mongol reputation as nomadic raiders. A Tibetan would now lead the empire's Buddhists, or at least that portion that Kublai retained in the new Yuan dynasty he formally proclaimed in 1271, and which ruled China and its wider region for the next century. Phagpa and the Sakya also became the controlling power in Tibet, to the disadvantage of the Kagyu, although they continued to have support from the Mongol Il-Khanate in the west, ruled by Hulagu, another of Kublai's brothers.

To cement this new synthesis of religious and political power, Kublai commissioned a stupa dedicated to Phagpa's predecessor and uncle, the great Buddhist scholar Sakya Pandita. A previous Mongol lord, Godan, had tried to use Sakya Pandita as a proxy to control all the Tibetans, an effort that was largely ignored. Now, thanks to Kublai, the Sakya really were in charge. To build the stupa, Phagpa needed artisans capable of something exceptional to symbolise this new relationship with the Mongols. Such skills were absent from Tibet and so he looked across the Himalaya. India had been the wellspring of Buddhism in Tibet from the time of the emperors almost five hundred years earlier, but the rise of Islam had largely extinguished that source. The great university at Nalanda, where Marpa had studied tantric Buddhism, had been razed to the ground. So Phagpa looked to the Kathmandu valley, where Buddhism and its art continued to flourish, and its famous Newari craftsmen, who had made such an influential cultural impact during the era of the tsenpo emperors, when craftsmen from the Kathmandu valley had helped adorn the Jokhang temple in Lhasa.

A well-known legend tells how Phagpa sent a request to Jayabhima Deva Malla, among the first of the Malla dynasty that ruled the valley from the early thirteenth century. ('Malla' means wrestler. A dynasty of that name in north-eastern India features in the *Mahabharata*. The Mallas of the Kathmandu valley weren't the only ones to borrow that mythical prestige, which can be confusing.) Phagpa wanted a hundred artisans to build the Khagan's stupa. He clearly didn't need that many men for just one stupa; this was a wholesale acquisition of the Himalayan artistic tradition that gave Tibetan Buddhism its distinctive visual imagery. Chinese artists didn't have the knowledge to produce the Tibetan Buddhist iconography Phagpa required, the myriad tantric deities in all their manifestations. In hiring artisans from Kathmandu, Phagpa was bringing a kind of iconographic legitimacy to the new relationship between the Sakya lineage and Kublai Khan.

As it happened, the king in Kathmandu could only muster eighty artisans. The earthquake of 1255, estimated to have killed thirty thousand people, a third of the valley's population, must have had a devastating impact on the city, limiting the skilled labour Jayabhima Deva had to spare, even for a Mongol emperor. Meeting the workers personally before they left for Tibet, the king asked them to choose one of their number as leader. The only one prepared to take on the responsibility was a young man still in his mid teens, an artist of genius called Arniko. He admitted his youth but claimed he was 'old in mind'. It was the start of a journey that would lift him to the highest levels of Kublai's court and earn him a fortune. It was Arniko who would be responsible for the spiritual iconography that gave the Yuan court its religious authority.

Tradition holds that Arniko was born in the city of Patan, perhaps because it enjoyed the greatest artistic reputation, but the little we know about him comes from the chronicles of the Yuan dynasty where he made his name, rather than from his birthplace. Even his name is debated: in China it was written as Anige. The best source we have is his epigraph, written by a Chinese court official called Cheng Jufu. Yuan chroniclers claimed he came from royal stock, but since he married a Mongol princess, that was more likely a piece of expeditious social retrofitting. Rather like the hagiographies of Buddhist saints, the stories around Arniko are of a preternaturally gifted and serious-minded child. The epigraph tells us that even as a three-year-old, Arniko would be looking around the temple during religious ceremonies and passing judgment on the architecture. At school, he memorised complex sutras on the arts at one sitting, like Mozart absorbing every aspect of music he'd never heard before. By the time he left for Tibet he was an expert in painting, carving and casting images. Starting in 1261, he led a group of Newari artisans in building a golden stupa that Kublai commissioned for the Sakya monastery in central Tibet, a complex that was then rapidly evolving as Sakya power within Tibet grew. The stupa was built in the monastery's main hall, and although it no longer exists, the legacy of Arniko's Newari artisans can be traced in stunning murals at Shalu monastery neaer Shigatse, the languid, elliptical shapes an echo of the last Pala Empire on the roof of the world.

Arniko did such a good job that Phagpa insisted he visit Kublai Khan's capital Dadu (modern Beijing) at the end of 1262. His introduction to Kublai was recorded. The Khagan looked at him for a while before asking if he was afraid 'to come to the big country?' Arniko's reply was politically shrewd for a teenager.

The sage regards people in all directions as his sons. When a son comes to his father, what is there to fear?

—Why do you come?

—My family has been living in the west for generations. I took the imperial edict to build the stupa in Tibet for two years. I saw constant wars, and wish your majesty could pacify there. I come for sentient beings.

The emperor tested the young Newari with a challenge: to restore a damaged bronze statue the court's artists had judged beyond repair, a task he eventually accomplished although it took three years. Kublai was delighted and over the next decade Arniko worked his way up to become supervisor for all classes of artisans, thousands of them, responsible for a huge expansion of state-sponsored art that Kublai eventually curtailed because it was so expensive. Arniko was responsible for the religious imagery, imperial portraits and other court projects, seals and insignia, a kind of branding that defined the regime's character, its strong links between the Sakya preceptor and the *khagan*'s sovereignty. The Mongol lords liked the golden images of Buddha, but they left the complex philosophy to their Tibetan priests. When Kublai went to war, Phagpa gave his blessing and Arniko created a mural featuring the fierce tantric protector deity Mahakala to make the enterprise auspicious.

Arniko's most famous achievement was the White Stupa in Beijing, which still stands, having been singled out for protection by Communist China's first premier, Zhou Enlai, some years before the Cultural Revolution. It is a curious combination of Pala, Newari and Chinese styles, a consequence perhaps of its architect's cosmopolitan life. Around it he designed a temple so vast it took fifty-eight thousand trees to complete, the most expensive building project of Kublai's reign but destroyed in a fire in 1368. Arniko is also associated with the Sarira Pagoda, another white stupa fifty-two metres high, at the Buddhist centre of Wutaishan in Shanxi province, sacred home of the *bodhisattva* Manjushri, completed in 1301 some years after Kublai's death. By then Arniko had already built another commission at Wutaishan for Kublai's successor Temur: the Wangsheng Youguosi, or Temple of Myriad Saints Safeguarding the State, which proved to be one of the most expensive and complicated buildings the Yuan dynasy built and is sadly no longer extant. Controversial at court, the project nevertheless brought its Newari architect huge riches. Kublai had rewarded him with jade and gold belts, dozens of expensive robes, fur coats and hats, chariots and horses; for this latest triumph Temur's mother rewarded him with almost half a ton of silver. Kublai made sure Arniko's Newari wife was brought from Kathmandu and he married several times more, including his Mongolian princess. He took on a Chinese soubriquet, Xixuan, meaning 'western studio', a reference to his house in western Dadu as well as his distant origins and artistic school. He died in 1306 a wealthy man with huge landholdings and thousands of serfs, not the first and certainly not the last migrant from Nepal hoping to exploit his talents in a foreign land.

When Kublai died, Arniko produced portraits of his old patron and his favourite wife Chabi, who had died a few years earlier. She had been a great supporter of the Mongol court's Tibetan influence but later, as some believe, converted to Christianity like her mother-in-law. Always cosmopolitan, she was a restraining influence on Kublai, mindful of maintaining respectful relations with the *khagan*'s mostly Chinese subjects. The art historian Anning Jing has argued that these portraits are those now hanging in the National Palace Museum in Taipei, showing Kublai Khan in his more corpulent middle years and Chabi in her remarkably tall Mongolian headdress, known in Chinese as a *gugu*. The technique expressed in these paintings suggests an artist trained in the Himalaya, not China.

*

Echoes of Arniko's creative world resonated in Europe, most famously in *The Travels of Marco Polo*, which included a description of Shangdu, the summer palace of the Mongol emperor Kublai Khan; Arniko was not its chief architect, but he had made his contribution. 'There is at this place a very fine marble palace, the rooms of which are all gilt and painted with figures of men and beasts and birds, and with a variety of trees and flowers, all executed with such exquisite art that you regard them with delight and astonishment.' Polo's book was for centuries one of the few available sources on Central Asia. The Elizabethan travel writer Samuel Purchas drew on it for his *Purchas, his Pilgrimage*: a geo-religious encyclopaedia he collated and published in 1613. Purchas himself never travelled more than three hundred or so kilometres from his native Essex, taking inspiration instead from the seafarers he met there. He also inherited the papers of Richard Hakluyt, chaplain to Robert Cecil, secretary of state to Elizabeth I and James I. Hakluyt wrote widely on exploration and voyages of discovery, and was an adviser to the East India Company, founded in 1600.

It was Purchas' book that Samuel Taylor Coleridge had open on his chest when he fell into a vision-filled sleep at his rented cottage in the Somerset village of Nether Stowey, having taken grains of opium to alleviate a bout of dysentery. Coleridge understood very well the impact opium had on his imagination. 'I should much wish,' he wrote in a letter to Robert Southey during that period, 'like the Indian Vishna, to float about along an infinite ocean cradled in the flower of the Lotos, & wake once in a million years for a few minutes – just to know I was going to sleep a million years more.'

Purchas' version of Polo's story opens with the phrase: '*In Xamdu did Cublai Can* build a *stately* Palace, encompassing *sixteene miles* of plaine *ground* with a wall, wherein are *fertile* Meddowes, pleasant Springs . . . ' The Khan, Purchas wrote, spent his summers in a 'sumptuous house of *pleasure*' that could be dismantled and moved around: deluxe nomadism. Coleridge borrowed the first sentence, added an extra syllable to give 'Xanadu', turned the 'house of pleasure' into a 'stately pleasure dome' and swapped the prosaic 'build' for 'decree': much more the style of a Mongol Khan. The poem 'Kubla Khan' is not of course about the Mongols: it's about the human imagination in the act of creation, Coleridge sculpting a dream and offering it to the reader. He did have ideas about the real Kublai Khan, describing him in a letter as 'the greatest Prince in Peoples, Cities & Kingdoms that ever was in the World'. But for Coleridge Kublai was simply the most powerful and exotic leader he could imagine, an Oriental barbarian beyond even the remotest outcasts of the Bible. European Romanticism fed on such stories of exotic fantasy and lost utopias, and colonial conquest made 'the Orient' a rich vein of material. Such imaginings had a pervasive influence on European perspectives of the East. Coleridge does at least allow Kublai Khan a sensuous creativity at odds with his barbarian reputation, reflecting the Mongol's patronage of the arts and his intellectual curiosity. And somewhere in that world view, unknown to Purchas or Coleridge, were cultural flavours brought across the Himalaya from Kathmandu.

The first Europeans to visit the city were seventeenth century Jesuit missionaries, among them Johann Grueber, born in the Austrian city of Linz in 1623. Having served for several years as a mathematics assistant at the Qing imperial court, he was summoned back to Rome in 1661. The sea route was closed, thanks to a hostile Dutch navy, so with his Belgian companion Albert d'Orville, Grueber made a daring journey from Beijing to Goa in south-western India through Tibet and Nepal. Setting out he travelled first west to Xining, where he joined a merchant's caravan to Lhasa, passing along the northern shore of the vast lake of Kokonor before turning south-west, indulging his passion for drawing as he went. Grueber was the first European to reach Lhasa, where he spent a month or so waiting for another merchant's caravan to cross the Himalaya. While he waited, he sketched the locals and tried to meet the fifth Dalai Lama, Ngawang Lobsang Gyatso, the Great Fifth. As a Jesuit unwilling to kneel before an idolater, the audience was denied. Grueber sketched him anyway, from a portrait hung at the gate of the Dalai Lama's new palace, which he called the 'Burg Beitala': known to us as the Potala.

Grueber's onward journey south to Kathmandu took him towards Shigatse and the monastery of Tashilhunpo, seat of another great Buddhist lineage, the Panchen Lamas. He was not the first Jesuit to visit. The Portuguese João Cabral, who entered Tibet from Bengal with Estêvão Cacella, escaped imprisonment in Bhutan and fled to Shigatse in 1628. There he sought permission from the 'petty kings' to the south of the Himalaya to enter Nepal. Sadly, Cabral's letter to his superiors in Rome about his experiences in Kathmandu is lost, so Grueber's accounts are the first European perspective we have on the city. Their experiences would later feed into a monumental effort to collate knowledge about China and its environs by the Jesuit polymath Athanasius Kircher, among the most famous European intellectuals of his day. Thus it was a Jesuit perspective that coloured Europe's first view of the Himalaya's greatest city.

Grueber and d'Orville reached the Kathmandu valley early in 1662. Before them was a territory half the size of New York City containing three competing kingdoms: on the north side of the Bagmati river, Kathmandu itself, known also as Kantipur, *kanti* meaning 'lustrous'; Patan, also known as Lalitpur, 'the beautiful city'; and Bhaktapur on the eastern side of the valley, the 'city of devotees', known also as Bhadgaon. Each of these three towns had – and has – names in Newari, the Tibeto-Burmese language of the valley's original urban dwellers: Yambu for Kathmandu, Yala for Patan and Khwopa for Bhaktapur. Despite recent decades of mass migration, Newars still form almost a third of the wider urban population of modern Kathmandu.

Siddhi Narasimha Malla, the Patan king who had instituted the Kartik dances twenty years earlier, had only just died and Grueber, as he wrote in a letter to his superiors in Austria, discovered the valley of 'Nekbal' in a state of war. The king of Kathmandu, Pratap Malla, was testing the resolve of the new king of Patan, Srinivasa, Siddhi Narasimha's son. The two men had a grandfather in common, the last king to rule both Kathmandu and Patan. Such Lilliputian squabbles must have baffled a veteran of the Qing court like Grueber, who was anyway more interested in Christian souls than the family quarrels of obscure Himalayan kings. To that end, he presented Pratap with an ingratiating gift: a small telescope, a slice of Europe's emerging technological revolution that would drive the Enlightenment. Pratap put the telescope to his eye and saw the troops of Srinivasa leap into focus, apparently within touching distance. 'Let us march against them!' Pratap cried. He was so delighted with the telescope and other 'mathematical instruments' Grueber left behind that he promised to build the Austrian a house and allow him to teach the gospel if he agreed to return.

Pratap's shift in perspective as he held the telescope to his eye is somehow emblematic of the Malla dynasty's self-absorption, cupped in the palm of their fertile valley at 1,400 metres. The magical telescope had brought his fixation even closer, much to his delight. What happened beyond the ring of mountains was only of marginal importance: a point of view that endured long after the Malla kings fell from power. The vigorous new dynasties that replaced them would also fall under the valley's spell. It was such a fascinating world, why go elsewhere? When Grueber did leave Kathmandu he trekked some sixty kilometres to the town of Hetauda, then on the fringes of the tiny hill kingdom of Makwanpur. In Makwanpur he saw a customhouse, evidence of the mighty Mughal Empire to the south, to which the kings of the Kathmandu valley paid tribute each year: treasure and elephants. In this way, the Malla kings kept the world at a distance, unless an alliance with rulers outside offered advantage to one of the kingdoms in the endless skirmishes with their neighbours. That habit would be at least part of their undoing. The business of the world was becoming more insistent: they couldn't keep it out for ever.

Almost sixty years later, in 1721, the Jesuit missionary Ippolito Desideri was ordered back to India when a rival monastic order, the Capuchins, took over the Catholic mission in Lhasa. He stopped off in Kathmandu on his way south to Goa and witnessed a similar confrontation to the one Grueber had seen:

> Whether caused by compassion for all living creatures or by lack of courage, [Newari] behaviour in war is most ridiculous and fantastic. When two armies meet they launch every sort of abuse at one another, and if few shots are fired, and no one is hurt, the attacked army retires to a fortress, of which there are many, resembling our country dovecotes.

This was not altogether sneering: the dovecotes of Italian architect Andrea Palladio, which it's reasonable to suspect he had in mind, were exquisite.

> But if a man is killed or wounded, the army which has suffered begs for peace, and sends a dishevelled and half-clothed woman, who weeps, beats her breast and implores mercy, the cessation of such carnage, and such shedding of human blood. The victorious army then dictates terms to the vanquished and war ends.

Such choreographed posturing was simply another example of the Malla dynasty's chief concern: art in all its forms. From *pyakha*, ritual dance-dramas like the Kartik Naach, to protracted and dramatic festivals, to the architecture of palaces and temples, to the exquisite Newari painting, metalwork and wood carving produced in the valley's workshops, the Malla kingdoms are a good illustration of what the anthropologist Clifford Geertz termed the theatre state, where expression of power through art and spectacle is not merely a means to an end, a kind of propaganda, but the purpose of that power and the source of its renewal. This theatrical statecraft reached its zenith in the mid seventeenth century and Pratap Malla was among its most successful practitioners. Nor was he shy in saying so. He transformed both Kathmandu's Durbar Square and the palace complex of Hanuman Dhoka. Under the icon of the monkey-faced god Hanuman outside its main entrance he commanded a new inscription to be added, identifying himself as: 'King of Kings, Chief of Nepal, extremely clever, Chief of all Kings, Twice Illustrious Great King, Poet Laureate, Enthroned Lord Jaya Pratap Malla.' Inside the palace is an impressive stone carving of Narasimha in the act of disembowelling the demon Hiranyakashipu, his eyes and teeth picked out in silver.

Having mocked Newars for the ineffectual theatricality of their soldiery, Desideri also condemned them for their preference for sly assassination. 'Nearly all bear deceit written on their faces.' He thought them 'unstable, turbulent and traitorous', a harsh assessment from a man born in the medieval Tuscan city of Pistoia, only a few kilometres from Florence, another city-state built on trade, finance, religion, art and brutal political feuding. Perhaps it was the introspection of the valley that left Desideri unimpressed. He had visited the former Mughal capital Agra on his way to Tibet, and seen the architectural glories of that empire. Perhaps he lacked the artistic imagination to make sense of the Kathmandu valley's unique cultural achievement. Newars were, he admitted, 'intelligent, and very industrious, clever at engraving and melting metal', but his only comment on the hundreds of temples he saw was that they were 'generally small'.

Those temples told a rich story of the deep cultural bonds between central Tibet and Kathmandu winding their way back and forth across the high mountain passes. Desideri missed it, but his predecessor João Cabral, writing a century earlier, read the architecture more carefully. In a letter to his superior Alberto Latertius, stationed on the Malabar coast of India, he described the Tibetans he encountered in Shigatse, their wealth and the 'great fields of wheat, and I never saw land that looked more like the Alemtejo in Portugal.' He explained also that the Tibetans 'have the same pagodas as the kingdom of Nepal and some of Bengal. Only in the superstition of castes and eating habits, which they do not hold, are they different.' Thus Cabral sketched out the centuries-old transmission of tantric Buddhist culture from the Pala dynasty of Bengal through Kathmandu to Tibet.

Desideri, by contrast, had little interest in material things. His focus was Tibetan Buddhism. It annoyed him that Athanasius Kircher was still peddling the idea of Tibetan Buddhism's links to Christianity in his immense work *China Illustrata*. Desideri had actually been there and studied the issue: he knew Kircher was wrong. Reincarnation fascinated Desideri, who referred to it as 'metempsychosis', a term popularised by Pythagoras, and he noticed that Newars believed in it 'to an even greater extent than the Thibettans'. Yet while priests in Italy could also be scientists, the gurus he met in Kathmandu seemed to Desideri merely irrational. 'They are very superstitious in all things, futile observers, and utter heathens.'

★

Kircher once wrote that 'the sun never sets on the actions of the Society of Jesus', so wide was its geographical spread. Something similar was said of the British Empire, which arrived on the fringes of the Himalaya in the second half of the eighteenth century. The first Briton to visit Kathmandu was Captain William Kirkpatrick, not a priest but an emissary of the East India Company, who arrived in early 1793. His mission had failed before it began: Kirkpatrick was there to mediate in a trade war that had erupted between Nepal's new Gorkha dynasty and Tibet in 1788. When Gorkhali troops crossed the mountains to loot Tibetan monasteries, including Tashilhunpo, the Dalai Lama appealed for help to the Qing dynasty and the Qianlong emperor, who sent a large Chinese army to clear them out. Having come within around thirty kilometres of Kathmandu, the Chinese, overextended and suffering heavy casualties, withdrew, signing a treaty with the Gorkhali regent that settled the affair (see Chapter Eight). Kirkpatrick was no longer required. The Gorkhalis, who had wanted military support from the East India Company, were bitter about the British sitting on their hands and weren't disposed to greet Kirkpatrick warmly. There was little for him to do but be a tourist for a week before he went back to Calcutta.

Kirkpatrick made the most of it. Arriving at Chandragiri, on the western rim of the encircling mountains, he described the Kathmandu valley as 'beautifully and thickly dotted with villages and abundantly chequered with rich fields', like an English country gentleman looking down on an estate he might wish to acquire. Kirkpatrick *was* a gentleman but had been born illegitimate into a family with plantations in the Carolinas, a family now looking for a fresh colonial start in the wake of the American Revolutionary War. Where better to boost one's social status than India? (His third daughter Julia would marry into the influential Strachey family, making him the great-grandfather of Lytton Strachey. His grandsons were the same Strachey brothers that explored Kailas.) Kirkpatrick had orders from his masters in Calcutta to make maps, observe military capability and take note of commercial opportunities: pashmina wool, salt, elephants and yak tails, as popular as flywhisks in the British Empire as they had been in the Roman. (They were also used as beards in Chinese opera.)

Kirkpatrick was fluent in Persian, intellectually curious but most of all practical. If the Jesuit Desideri was gripped by metaphysical concepts, Kirkpatrick admired useful things. This was how European knowledge of Nepal accreted, on the scaffold of each traveller's particular perspective. Kirkpatrick published the first illustration of the Nepali blade known as the *khukuri* in the book he wrote about his journey.

> [I]t is in felling small trees or shrubs, and lopping the branches of others for this purpose, that the dagger, or knife worn by every Nepaulian, called Khookheri, is chiefly employed; it is also of very great use, as I repeatedly experienced, in clearing away the road when obstructed by the low hanging boughs of trees, and other similar impediments.

Knives were of obvious appeal to a military man, but he also took a close interest in building materials, noticing the elegance and complexity of Nepali bricks:

> Nepaul in general is remarkable for the excellence of its bricks and tiles, but those of Bhatgong [Bhaktapur] are commonly allowed to be very far preferable to the rest. Certain it is, they surpass any I ever met in India, but it is not equally certain from whence their excellence proceeds. Some of those whom I questioned on the subject, referred it to the nature of the earth used in making them, and some to the water in tempering them; while others affirmed it to arise purely from a particular mode of burning them.

In studying bricks, Kirkpatrick had zeroed in on one of the key architectural motifs characterising Newari architecture, something that reached to the heart of a culture Europeans were struggling to understand. He arrived at the moment when the artistic and architectural glory days of Newari craftsmen were starting their decline, with the Malla kings gone from power. His question, 'from whence their excellence proceeds', was profound, if unconsciously so. The immediate answer was all the factors he suggested: knowing where to find the best and different types of rich alluvial clay and the knack of firing them evenly. The city's founding legend, as described in the *Swayambhu Purana*, gives a clue to this clay's origins. It speaks of a lake that once filled the valley, teeming with *naga* or snakes, still a ubiquitous motif in the valley. The *bodhisattva* Manjushri came south from the mountains and cleft the valley's southern rim, draining the water and leaving exposed the rich earth that gives the valley's bricks their lustrous warmth: the architectural equivalent of a hug. There is a seamless flow between the clay of the fields and the walls of old Newari houses, harmonising with the intricately carved wooden windows and window screens, called *tiki jhya*, the struts, pillars and doors that complete Newari houses and temples. A signature detail of Newari building was a style of brick called *dachi-apa*, with the ends angled inward slightly toward the interior-facing side so that so that nothing prevents the exterior face, dipped in red clay slip before firing, from being flush with its neighbours. It's a beautiful effect and seals the building's façade against heavy monsoon rain, protecting the soft mortar beneath. There were no schools or manuals to follow in building such houses: just timeworn technologies, evolved over centuries. Nowadays the mortar is sticky yellow clay, but historically it was called *silay* and included all kinds of gloop: *surkhi*, or brick dust, lime and ghee (clarified butter), even molasses.

Typically this elegant exterior façade would be matched with an interior wall of more conventional bricks; the gap between them was filled with rubble and clay. A wooden frame added strength to the structure. The overall effect of the soft mortar and wooden support is a defence against the regular seismic challenge of living in a planetary crumple zone. Yet if the earthquake is big enough, this style of building will come down. The stage on which the Kartik dances take place today stands in front of the sixteenth century Char Narayan temple in Patan, or at least it did. During the earthquake that struck Kathmandu in 2015, the two-tiered pagoda-style building was reduced to rubble. More recently, the Kartik Naach has taken place against a backdrop of empty space surrounded by a high metal fence. At least the temple's materials, including its icons and carved roof struts were recovered, and safely stored before they were looted. The temple would soon be reconstructed, which is more than can be said for many of the private Newari houses that fell in the same tragic event.

Plenty of traditional Newari houses have gone anyway, torn down and replaced with a style of house familiar all over Asia: reinforced concrete beams and pillars, shuttered with modern bricks. The contrast with traditional building methods couldn't be more obvious. The old social networks that organised these neighbourhoods for centuries, the *guthis*, are the merest shadow of their former selves. Yet the modern buildings still occupy the same footprint that buildings have occupied for centuries and with the same arrangement of storeys, with the kitchen and prayer room on the top floor. When Newars speak of a house, they often mean the site it stands on, not the building itself. Families built on four sides around a courtyard, or *chok*, the focal point for daily life and festivals alike. The interior square is somewhere to dry grain, hang washing and look out for each other's kids as they play. Each courtyard will have a shrine or *chaitya*, in its Nepali form an elegant diminutive stupa, spiritual power points along with the water supply and electricity. Every day starts before dawn with the sound of bells being rung and the smell of incense as the city wakes up and makes an offering, rice and a smear of vermilion on an icon. Doors and thresholds in particular are focal points: during the monsoon, for example, at the festival of Nag Panchami, pictures of snakes are pasted above doorways alongside magical mantras to ward them off. These are intimate spaces; people live so close that every argument is heard, every joke shared. You could not design a more fertile environment for gossip and rumour. Seeking privacy, and a dependable water supply, wealthier families have moved out to the suburbs. And these days there are usually a couple of motorbikes parked next to the shrine. But even now the pattern of life goes on in broadly similar terms as it did when Kirkpatrick took his tour, albeit with only a tiny fraction of the squalor and disease he witnessed. 'The hamlets and villages in these mountainous tracts exhibited, at a distance, an appearance highly romantic,' he wrote, touching on his era's zeitgeist, its taste for the sublime, although 'on a nearer view this delusion vanished, and the most prominent picture that remained displayed the squalidness of poverty, and the miseries of distress.'

The religious ambition of Jesuit missionaries and the Orientalist view of Romanticism gave way eventually to proper academic study of Kathmandu's complex but aesthetically rewarding interplay of cultural genius and Himalayan politics. Even then, European prejudice could get in the way. Born in 1841 Gustave Le Bon was an early anthropologist who read Darwin and decided there was a correlation between cranium size and intelligence, an evolutionary explanation for European 'superiority'. The theory won him a prize from the French Academy of Sciences. He developed a portable cephalometer for measuring the skulls of different ethnic groups he met in the field and for the rest of his long and eclectic career, the idea that culture was somehow a consequence of race was never far from his thoughts.

In the 1880s the French government commissioned Le Bon to travel though the subcontinent and report back on the cultures he found there. Thus he became one of the first Frenchmen to visit Kathmandu, more or less closed to foreigners beyond the few British servants of the Raj then stationed there. He arrived in 1885, first visiting Kathmandu and then the ancient Buddhist stupa at Swayambhunath, the most sacred site in the valley for Buddhist Newars. Nothing, with the possible exception of Coleridge's poem, had quite prepared him for what he experienced at Patan, as he walked among the temples and palaces:

> I doubt that an opium-eater has ever dreamt, in his wildest dreams, of
> a more fantastic architecture than the one of this strange city. Although
> I have visited Europe, from London to Moscow and the whole of the
> classic Orient, from Morocco to Egypt and Palestine, I had until then
> never seen a more striking scene than the main street in Patan.

Le Bon was strong on theorising and opinion but often in too much of a hurry for the detailed work that underpinned proper scholarship. While in Kathmandu, he took lots of photographs and dashed off a travelogue about Nepal's ancient past. Then he moved on to fresh intellectual pastures: the psychology of crowds. Having witnessed the Paris Commune as a young man, he developed an aversion to socialism and a fascination for how humans behave in large groups. His groundbreaking book on the subject, *Psychologie des Foules*, was an instant bestseller, influencing everyone from the public relations guru Edward Bernays to Benito Mussolini.

Sylvain Lévi would prove a much more reliable scholar. Born in Paris in 1863, the son of a cap-maker, by the age of twenty he was studying Sanskrit at the Sorbonne under the brilliant Indologist Abel Bergaigne and tutoring the children of France's chief rabbi Zadoc

Kahn. Five years later, when Bergaigne died in a hiking accident in the French Alps, Lévi took his place. One of his chief concerns as a scholar was how Indian Buddhism had shaped the cultures of Asia. Lévi believed that in Kathmandu he would find examples of Indian art that had disappeared from the rest of the subcontinent: 'India in the making', as he put it, a living fossil from which he could extrapolate whole worlds that had faded elsewhere to extinction. In 1898 he arrived in Kathmandu, fuming that the local population was 'absolutely, totally, radically ignorant', and lecturing to them from their own temples in perfect Sanskrit. When the priest at the temple of Changu Narayan refused him admittance, he had the maharaja lend him four soldiers to trace an important inscription from the fifth century, pinning down details of the Licchavi dynasty's rise to power. Marshalling all that he had learned, Lévi was able to write a three-volume history of Nepal, producing a sweeping narrative that has underpinned Nepal's historiography ever since.

When Lévi returned to France, he got a letter from Gustave Le Bon, who had maintained his interest in Nepal and was asking to meet. Lévi wasn't keen. He had bitter memories of Le Bon, who had sought his help in securing a grant from the government for a book of his Kathmandu photographs. Having pocketed the cash, Le Bon had then publicly dismissed Lévi's work on the impact of Ancient Greek culture on India, despite not knowing the first thing about it. Lévi wrote back that Le Bon, a photograph man, would find his manuscripts and inscriptions too boring. He then invoked his meticulous and open-minded Sanskrit teacher, Abel Bergaigne, telling Le Bon how he shared Bergaigne's 'wonderful incomprehension' of India, a sly dig at Le Bon's grandiose complacency.

This wasn't merely a spat between academics. Ancient Indian culture carried a contemporary political edge in an era when spurious racial theories were held by leading intellectuals. The eighteenth-century discovery of a proto-language, Indo-European, common to ancient languages like Latin and Sanskrit, not only galvanised academic interest but also inspired dangerous ideas. Racial theorists came up with a common human ancestor so superior that their culture spread throughout Asia and Europe: an Aryan master-race. The publication of Eugène Burnouf's *Introduction to the History of Indian Buddhism*, the most influential book on Buddhism in the nineteenth century, gave similar prominence to fringe ideas, such as those of Helena Blavatsky's Theosophists, involving the lost wisdom of ancient non-Christian philosophies. Burnouf's own cousin Émile, another Sanskrit scholar, was one of those who argued for the existence of an Aryan master-race, believing not only that Jesus was an Aryan, but that the swastika was a symbol of this ancient race's fire-altars, a notion that appealed to the Nazis.

Gustave Le Bon wasn't so extreme, but he was cut from the same cloth, and Lévi knew it. As a Jew, he could see where such talk was headed. In 1925, eight years before Adolf Hitler came to power and ten years before his own death, he told an interviewer of his enduring debt to his old teacher Abel Bergaigne:

> if you write four lines about my work I would like at least three of them to be about Bergaigne. It was he, after [Eugène] Burnouf, who put Vedic studies in the path, which they have followed ever since. The Germans, assured of their antiquity and purity of their race, proclaimed themselves the direct heirs of the ancient civilizations of India ... Bergaigne was the first to cause this fiction to crumble.

Lévi would remain a committed defender of Jewish rights for the rest of his life, denouncing antisemitism in a speech at the Trocadéro Palace in Paris in the aftermath of Hitler's rise to power in 1933.

After the Second World War, as Nepal became accessible and began to develop a modern economy, interest in and knowledge of Kathmandu's architectural heritage deepened and broadened but followed in essence the lead of Lévi's formative narrative. A notable example was the work of Mary Slusser, who arrived as the wife of an American aid worker and then spent decades in a systematic study of the valley's cultural heritage, culminating in groundbreaking books, *Nepal Mandala* and *The Antiquity of Nepalese Wood Carving*. At the same time, the Kathmandu valley's rapid development raised concerns that its unique architectural legacy would be swept aside. Bhaktapur's main temple and palace complex was the subject of a visionary and brilliantly led conservation effort and is now a hugely popular stop for tourists exploring the valley, which means it can at times feel rather selfconsciously like heritage. Götz Hagmüller and Niels Gutschow, both long-time residents of the town, were among several influential

Austrian and German conservation architects to work in the city. Hagmüller later led the restoration of Keshav Narayan Chowk, an eighteenth-century palace in Patan Durbar Square, which now houses the Patan Museum, among the finest in South Asia, housing some of the best examples of Newari art. Another Austrian architect working on the project, Thomas Schrom, persuaded Patan's authorities to close the square with its palaces and temples to motorised vehicles, turning one of the glories of world architecture into a haven from the city's manic traffic and a window onto the labyrinthine complexities of the religious culture that produced it.

6

The Rise of Gorkha

If you want to tune in to the mood of a nation, look to its statues. For example, in March 2015 students launched a successful campaign to remove the 1934 bronze of the imperialist Cecil Rhodes from the University of Cape Town, a campaign that spread to universities around the world, including Rhodes' alma mater, Oxford. In the summer of 2017, a white-supremacist rally marched through the city of Charlottesville, Virginia, protesting against the removal of a statue of the Confederate general Robert E Lee. One of them drove his car at speed into a group of counter-protestors, killing the 32-year-old anti-racism activist Heather Heyer. In India, in early 2018, prime minister Narendra Modi appealed for calm after a flurry of statue vandalism. An image of Vladimir Lenin, widely admired among Indian communists, was destroyed in the north-eastern state of Tripura. In retaliation a bust of the famous Hindu nationalist Syama Prasad Mukherjee was destroyed in the communist stronghold of Kolkata.

The infant republic of Nepal had its own statue moment in September 2017, although in this case it was a statue going up, not coming down, that prompted debate. With great fanfare, Bidya Devi Bhandari, modern Nepal's second ever president and the first woman to hold the post, unveiled a golden statue of Prithvi Narayan Shah, the founder of the modern state of Nepal. And yet, this took place less than a decade after the new republic got rid of the last Shah king, Gyanendra, thus terminating the dynasty that had sat on the throne for two hundred and fifty years. Ten years earlier, as the people struggled to drag democracy out from under Gyanendra's autocratic weight, Maoist cadres from the Young Communist League and other left-wing groups had got to work, systematically smashing up statues of kings.

One activist boasted that 'the vestiges of the Shah kings are being removed as the country is heading toward a republic'. It seemed then that monarchy would have no place whatsoever in the new Nepal.

Those intent on erasing the past didn't discriminate: all the recent members of the Shah dynasty suffered, irrespective of reputation. Mahendra, another autocrat, crowned in 1955, was considerably less popular than his father Tribhuvan, who had returned the family to power in 1951 after a century in which the Shah kings were mere figureheads. Nepal's leading university and national airport are still named after Tribhuvan: he had steered the country away from oppression and towards the light. It made little difference: images of both father and son were destroyed. Mahendra was the glowering type, inscrutable in his trademark dark glasses. In 1960, shortly after the UK government made him a British army field marshal, he threw Nepal's first democratically elected prime minister into jail. Mahendra's son Birendra, who inherited the throne in 1972, seemed milder but it still took almost two more decades before democracy was restored. In 2001, in the middle of the Maoist civil war, the crown prince Dipendra, drunk, stoned and angry, murdered his father and mother and seven other members of the royal family before turning the gun on himself. The crown went to Birendra's widely disliked brother Gyanendra and five years later the Shahs were out.

Maoist cadres didn't stop their destruction at Nepal's more recent kings. They also targeted Nepal's founding father Prithvi Narayan Shah, who completed his conquest of the Kathmandu valley in 1769, bringing the Malla era, with all its dances and temple building, to a close. In 2003, the Maoists blew up a statue of Prithvi at Nuwakot: a town of totemic importance in his story and the place of his death in 1775. In 2006, protestors attacked the most famous statue of him in the country, which stands on a tall plinth outside the government secretariat in the middle of Kathmandu. While they weren't able to bring it down, they did manage to damage it, removing his crown and sword. Afterwards it was shrouded from view, much as the statue of General Lee was in Charlottesville after the death of Heather Heyer. The new prime minister announced that National Unity Day, held on 11 January, Prithvi Narayan Shah's birthday, was henceforth cancelled. The following year, after the last Shah king had already been deposed, another image of Prithvi, this one in his hometown of Gorkha, the starting point of his brilliant career of conquest, was demolished on the orders of local Maoist leaders.

Some senior Maoists drew a comparison between their destruction of royal symbols and that following the French Revolution in 1789: scraping away the iconography of a repressive regime. Yet there was also an ethnic dimension to this hostility, tension that the Maoists had skilfully exploited during the war. Populations speaking Tibeto-Burmese languages, like Newars in the Kathmandu valley, and other ethnic groups throughout central and eastern Nepal – Gurung, Magar, Tamang and Rai – saw the collapse of the monarchy as a chance to overturn centuries of domination by a Hindu elite speaking an Indo-European language that had emerged in western Nepal a thousand years earlier. Originally it had been known as Khas *kura*, literally Khas 'word' or 'speech', Khas being the Indo-Aryan group that spoke it. As the Shahs took power, it became known as Gorkhali; this language is now modern Nepali, the region's lingua franca and the single most unifying cultural feature of the nation. Nepali is similar to Hindi, in the way that Italian and Spanish are alike. More than any other king, Prithvi Naryan Shah was emblematic of this Hindu Khas group; so that many from other ethnic groups who spoke different languages were delighted to see his dynasty gone and the restrictive caste system they embodied put into reverse. Throwing off this narrow interpretation of what being Nepali meant was a relief for those marginalised for so long.

Then, just at this moment, as Nepalis settled in without their kings, Prithvi Narayan Shah made a comeback. Khadga Prasad 'K P' Oli, a powerful nationalist, albeit from the main grouping of Nepal's communists, suggested boosting tourism by erecting a new statue of the nation's founding father at the top station of a cable car recently opened to the Kathmandu valley's rim at Chandragiri, a significant location in Prithvi Narayan Shah's story of conquest. A year later, in September 2017, the statue was ready to be inaugurated by Oli's old political ally and new president of Nepal, Bidya Devi Bhandari. On 11 January 2018, a decade after king Gyanendra was voted out of office, National Unity Day was also resurrected with support from across the political divide. A member of the ruling Nepali Congress told the newspapers: 'Prithvi Narayan Shah should not be punished for what his descendants did. He should be respected for giving us a sovereign and unified Nepal.'

The country's president and the Nepali Congress prime minister Sher Bahadur Deuba laid flowers at the statue that had been defaced a decade earlier. A leading diversity campaigner, Om Gurung, warned that 'by reviving Prithvi Narayan Shah's legacy, politicians have proved they love the status quo', the 'status quo' being the social and religious hierarchy the Shahs had embodied. And yet, when the nationalist-communist K P Oli replaced Deuba as prime minister shortly there-after, the Maoists entered into negotiations with his party, once their sworn enemies, for a merger: it was a stark indication of how compro-mised the Maoists, despite their talk of inclusivity, had become. Prithvi Narayan Shah had proved a more lasting influence on the people of Nepal than Chairman Mao.

What message were politicians recruiting from the life and times of Nepal's founding father? What did Prithvi's contested legacy reveal about a nation whose steep mountains and deep valleys create such cultural complexity? Teasing out the answers to these questions reveals the unique challenges of identity and politics in the Himalaya, a mountain range caught between the two most populous nations on earth: India and China. Those challenges obsessed Prithvi Narayan Shah. Only by sticking together, he believed, could the diverse people of Himalaya find enough space for their disparate cultures to survive, even though in practice he favoured some of those cultures more than others. ('It is merely a matter of interpretation,' the Nepali writer Kamal P Malla observed, 'whether one calls it a "vision" of unified Nepal or a vulture's gaze upon its prey.') In the modern world, with China's occupation of the Tibetan plateau and India's huge military presence in the Himalaya, it's a message that has more political potency than ever, one that modern kings and politicians alike have been swift to exploit.

*

The image of Prithvi Narayan Shah most familiar to Nepalis shows a richly dressed figure wearing an ornate *khukuri* (the traditional Nepali blade) at his chest and a crown dripping with jewels, topped off with feathers from a bird of paradise. This fabulous headgear was worn by all the modern Nepali kings; the artist and polymath Desmond Doig described it on Birendra's head at his coronation in 1975: 'No other crown could be so fantastically devised, so priceless. It is a glitter of closely set diamonds and pearls, hung with drop rubies and emeralds the size of plums and atop it, clasped by more diamonds, is a cascade of bird-of-paradise plumes.' (The crown hadn't been refurbished since Mahendra's coronation in 1956 and its feathers were droopy. Trade in bird of paradise feathers had been banned so the US government helped out with some fresh feathers confiscated from smugglers.)

Although he is depicted wearing it, this was never Prithvi Narayan Shah's crown. In fact there are almost no contemporary images of him at all; a bronze figure at Nuwakot, the town where he made his name, may or may not be Prithvi and shows him kneeling piously, hands together in prayer. The image Nepal has of him was painted by a twentieth-century artist called Amar Chitrakar, who started his career painting posters for Bollywood movies and moved on to state insignia: stamps, portraiture and statues. It was Amar Chitrakar who gave us the painting of Prithvi Narayan Shah that now hangs in Kathmandu's National History Museum; this is the image Nepalis have in their minds when they think of their founding father. It's the same image used for the statue in front of Nepal's government secretariat, the Singha Darbar, erected for National Unity Day in 1965, part of the autocratic king Mahendra's propaganda to legitimise his reactionary putsch and the termination of Nepal's first attempt at democracy. It's the same image used for the golden statue that now looks down over the Kathmandu valley from the cable car station at Chandragiri. Prithvi is evidently a warrior, but he is leaning on his sword and it's in his left hand. This image is about more than martial prowess. His right hand, his sword hand, is raised above his head, the index finger extended. It's tempting to see him as testing the political winds, but the message is clear: one nation, the Nepali equivalent of *e pluribus unum*. The implication is equally clear: we're complicated but we have to get over that. No wonder Prithvi Narayan Shah remains relevant more than two centuries after his death.

Prithvi was born in 1723 in the hilltop village of Gorkha, around a hundred kilometres north-west of Kathmandu, in a quietly grand Newari-style house perched on a ridge whose backdrop is Manaslu, eighth highest mountain in the world, some fifty-five kilometres to the north. It feels a remote spot for a man who forged a nation. He was the tenth king in his line, ruler of Gorkha, a small mountain state among a clutch of small mountain states known as the *Chaubisi rajya*, the 'twenty-four' kingdoms: a loose confederation often squabbling with itself. Further west, towards the western border of modern Nepal was another grouping of these minuscule polities, known as the *Baisi*, or the 'twenty-two'. About these we still know remarkably little, but this is where the modern state of Nepal's story starts, in the eleventh century, centuries before the birth of Prithvi Narayan Shah, with the rise of a near-forgotten empire.

Almost nothing was known about the Khasa kingdom before the twentieth century. It was understood that Gorkhali, or Khas *kura*, the language that became Nepali, arrived from the west, migrating with the Indo-Aryan people who spoke it. Chroniclers in Kathmandu also recorded, in the thirteenth century, how Khas-speaking raiders had suddenly appeared from the same direction. Even now, their origins aren't certain, but the Khas are particularly associated with Garhwal and Kumaon, Indian districts to the west of the modern border with western Nepal. For centuries they had been migrating east through the middle hills of the Himalaya, earning themselves the name *parbatiya*, meaning mountain dwellers. By the end of the first millennium they had reached the Karnali watershed in what is now Nepal and established a kingdom. It was here in 1956, at a village called Dullu, that Giuseppe Tucci, the Italian anthropologist who had recorded the remains of the Guge kingdom just to the north in Tibet, found ancient inscriptions they had left, half-buried in the ground. Local people had no idea where they had come from or what they meant. Brushing dirt from the lettering, Tucci was able to read them. 'Kings until now unknown,' he wrote, 'sang to us from the stones in the Sanskrit tongue the glories of their ancestors and their own deeds.'

What Tucci had found were the remnants of a highly decentralised polity often referred to as the Khasa Empire and to Tibetans as Yatse. (It's also known as the Malla kingdom, but to avoid confusion with the unrelated Malla dynasty in Kathmandu we'll ignore that.) Local chieftains were in day-to-day control but paid tribute to a dynasty founded by a king called Nagadeva. This lineage, at the zenith of its power, controlled a vast area, including Garhwal and Kumaon, and as far east as Gorkha. It was from the latter, under the leadership of

a chieftain named Jitarimalla, that they attacked Kathmandu. The
kings were Buddhist at the start, but as he recorded their religious
architecture Tucci realised this culture was not Tibetan but a distant
relic of the long-dead Mauryan Empire. If their rulers were Buddhist,
the ordinary Khas had a more egalitarian, animist spiritual framework.
Ancient shamanistic rites associated with the Khas divinity Masto are
still practised in western Nepal.

Early in their history, the Khasa kings moved up the Karnali valley
into western Tibet, attracted by its gold mines and the wool and salt
trade. As the Guge kingdom there weakened in the twelfth century,
raided by Turkic tribesmen from Central Asia, it also came under
Khas control. To boost trade, the Khas rulers invested in irrigation
systems to increase rice yields and pack-animal roads to boost trans-
Himalayan trade along the *uttar pata*, the northern route linking Nepal
and western Tibet to the Silk Roads. For a time they had their capital
up on the plateau at Purang, called Taklakot in Nepali, at an altitude
of well over four thousand metres. That proved too high and dusty
for southerners. So the main capital was shifted to the Sinja valley,
north-west of Jumla. (The early Nepali language is sometimes called
Sinjali.) This region was the focus for much of the Khas dynasty's
architectural effort. Recent excavations have uncovered the remains
of palaces and temples, as well as the capital's ancient settlement.
Archaeologists have also found underground pipes, testament to the
kingdom's technological skill in irrigation. Growing rice was central
to their success and their identity. How indigenous groups, often
Tibeto-Burmese in origin, regarded this influx of Khas migrants is
largely conjecture, but conflict wasn't inevitable. These existing groups
often relied on shifting cultivation and herding to survive; it's likely
the Khas exploited new ecological niches rather than displacing established populations. The consequence was that ethnic groups with very
different origins became enmeshed.

By the end of the fourteenth century, the Khas were well established
in Nepal but their empire was in fast decline. Nagadeva's dynasty
ended, replaced by the family of their chief ministers. The Tibetan
provinces were lost. What was left fractured, with new kingdoms
emerging in Garhwal and Kumaon. The region's progress subsided,
the stone steles and monuments the Khasa kings had built were half-
forgotten in the patchwork of isolated and impoverished statelets: the

Baisi, or 'twenty-two', and *Chaubisi rajya*, the 'twenty-four kingdoms', where the Shah dynasty would arise.

★

From the start of the thirteenth century, when the Muslim Delhi Sultanate conquered India, to the sixteenth century and the arrival of the Mughals, Hindu warrior clans known as Rajputs migrated, swords for hire, on the lookout for new opportunities. The Himalaya attracted its share of this migration. Sometimes the new arrivals were escaping Muslim control; often they were looking for new frontiers in the mountains to escape the more congested plains. Rajputs were from the Hindu *kshatriya* or warrior caste, men from the plains who regarded themselves as nature's rulers and looked down on the Khas *parbatiya*, the hill-men. They brought with them their religion, a more hierarchical Brahmanic Hinduism that was at odds with the looser, more shamanistic version practised by Khas and indigenous groups, like the Magars and Gurungs around Prithvi's hometown of Gorkha.

As long as their own practice wasn't contradicted, ordinary people were happy. On the other hand, local Khas chiefs and landowners were just as happy to adopt this more rigorous version of Hinduism: it gave them a better structure with which to secure their own personal power. The Khas elite acquired the caste of *kshatriya* themselves, Chhetri in Nepali, regarding themselves as 'twice-born', upper-caste Hindus, a process legitimised by Brahmin priests who in the process became society's regulators. As a ruler, the quality of your priest's learning was a reflection of your kingdom's status; Khas priests were widely regarded as ignorant and poorly educated: only Indian gurus would do.

The Scottish surgeon Francis Buchanan-Hamilton was in 1802 part of a diplomatic mission to Kathmandu, a posting he loathed, judging Nepalis 'such cursed liars'. Despite the prejudice, his account remains one of the most heavily quoted sources on the emergence of the modern state of Nepal. He saw clearly how its rulers were deepening the role of caste religion.

The ignorance of the Parbutty [*parbatiya*] Bramins, and their neglect of the rules of the sacred order in eating unclean things, seem early

to have disgusted the Gorca [Gorkha] Rajas, who have long employed
two families of Canogia [Kannauj in Uttar Pradesh] Brahmins to act
as hereditary Gurus ... When the power of Prithi Narain [Prithvi
Narayan] had extended to Nepal [meaning the Kathmandu valley], he
invited from Tiruhut [Tirhut, south of Kathmandu] a hundred families
of pure Brahmins, and settled on them lands of considerable value.

This was the process of Nepal's intense socio-religious stratification.
For a while, the boundaries remained fluid between Chhetri and
indigenous groups. But in the nineteenth century, long after Prithvi
Narayan Shah's reign, this process hardened, became codified and
deeply oppressive, condemning large parts of Nepal's population to
inescapable poverty, a wellspring for discontent that finally erupted in
the late twentieth century.

We tend to see cultures as accreting, like sedimentary rocks, but in
reality they metamorphose, under pressure to conform to the demands
of the world around them. This is what happened to the Shahs, a
family that were rising in power at this time and from which Prithvi
would emerge. The dynasty's origins are hazy, emerging from a
complicated ethnic and religious world that was up for grabs: the
dynasty's founding legends are designed to make the family more
appetising, sprinkle some Rajput spice over Prithvi's lineage and add
the flavours of aristocracy. For his part, Hamilton dismissed them as
Magars, indigenous hill-dwellers speaking not Khas but their own
Tibeto-Burmese language, as though there was something wrong with
that.

Besides the issue of rewriting its origins, the Shah story is also one
of younger sons: less entitled, more ambitious. Chronicles of their
dynasty record the *bartabhanda*, the taking of the sacred Brahmin
threads, of two Shah brothers, and of the younger becoming ruler of
the settlement of Nuwakot, on the banks of the Trisuli river. This
strategic town sits on the other side of the mountain ridge that encir-
cles Kathmandu. A few generations later, a younger son from this
Shah lineage returned west at the invitation of the people of Lamjung
to become their king. A younger son from this new lineage, Drubya
Shah, used his older brother's men to take over the neighbouring
village of Gorkha. The older brother, lord of Lamjung, expected the
prize to be handed over: it wasn't. Thus began a feud between the

two kingdoms that Prithvi Narayan would still be fighting generations later.

The kingdom of Gorkha under its new Shah rulers filled a bigger space than its territory, which barely stretched between the Marsyangdi and Trisuli rivers, an area smaller than Rhode Island or Kent. This was in large part because of an early seventeenth-century king called Ram Shah. He was a bullish leader, who acquired new territories and led raids into Tibet. But he is best remembered now for a series of administrative reforms that were so practically useful that his neighbours soon adopted them. Some were superficially mundane but significant in their impact: standardising weights and measures for example, of benefit to commerce and those most vulnerable to being short-changed. He boosted trade with his neighbours and bore down on the more predatory behaviour of money and commodity lenders, fixing interest rates. He valued environmental management too, ordering tree planting to secure a year-round water supply, prevent landslides and offer shade to the poor as they walked along the trails. He expedited justice and ruled that only the person who committed a crime should be punished, not the whole family. These judicial reforms in particular mean his name still has currency; there is a Nepali proverb that originated with Ram Shah: *nyaya napaya Gorkha janu*; if you want justice, go to Gorkha. In return for this levelling of the playing field, the elite families that supported him were entrenched in their positions of privilege.

Statecraft was a hallmark of Prithvi's reign as well, captured in his memoir, the *Divya Upadesh,* among the most important political statements in the history of modern Nepal. Another was failure: in particular the failure of his father Nara Bhupal to achieve his ambition of capturing the town of Nuwakot, recently brought under the control of the city of Kathmandu. Take Nuwakot, strategically positioned on one of two trade routes between the valley and Tibet, and an invader would open the way to conquering the valley itself. Nara Bhupal underestimated the task. Nuwakot was on the far bank of the Trisuli river and protected by a fort, *kot* being a fortified place in Nepali. When his favoured general judged the challenge too great for the limited Gorkhali force, Nara Bhupal replaced him with a Brahmin called Maheshwar Pant and, as his deputy, a Magar, Jayanta Rana. In 1737, when Prithvi was fourteen years old, these two led the attack on

Nuwakot but were beaten back. Nara Bhupal was devastated at the defeat and withdrew from his kingdom's affairs.

His wife Chandraprabha was made of sterner stuff. Although not Prithvi's mother, she began instructing the boy in his responsibilities, preparing him to rule. Prithvi married the first of his wives, the daughter of the king of the powerful Sen dynasty of nearby Makwanpur, a strategic alliance Nara Bhupal had brokered but which after the defeat at Nuwakot no longer interested him. A story from this wedding, well sourced, tells how Prithvi demanded he be allowed to take his bride Hemkarna straight home to Gorkha, as was the Gorkhali custom. The bride's family demanded to keep her, as was theirs. After an acrimonious dispute, with Prithvi threatening to cut his way out with his sword, the young prince was forced to leave without her. Here was a man quick to temper: advisers told him he had 'the voice to frighten elephants'. On the way home, he got his first sight of the Kathmandu valley, at Chandragiri where his golden statue now stands. His retinue pointed out its three cities: Bhaktapur, Patan and Kathmandu.

> The thought came to my heart that if I might be king of these three cities, why, let it be so. At this same time these two astrologers said to me, 'O King, your heart is melting with desire.' I was struck with wonder. How did they know my inmost thoughts and so speak to me? 'At the moment your gaze rested on Nepal you stroked your moustache and in your heart you longed to be king of Nepal, as it seemed to us.'

Experiencing for the first time the splendour of the three cities, comparing this to his own austere home at Gorkha and smarting at the humiliation of his father, it's hardly surprising that when Prithvi became king in 1742 at the age of nineteen, his first thought was to attack Nuwakot. Nation building was far from his thoughts in those days: he wanted to avenge a humiliation and take the valley's wealth. When his more cautious Magar lieutenant called a halt, he turned to his father's general Maheshwar Pant who crossed the Trisuli and launched an attack uphill towards the fort. The valley's Malla kings were for once united and well prepared: the Gorkhali troops were easily repulsed and had to burn the bridge as they retreated across the Trisuli to escape being destroyed. This antagonised his Magar

subjects, who pointed out that all their replacement had managed to
do was 'dry up a golden river', meaning set fire to the Trisuli bridge.
'Thereafter,' as the Nepali historian Mahesh Chandra Regmi put it,
'Prithvi Narayan Shah began to act prudently.' Despite his antipathy
towards the *parbatiya*, the Khas hill-men of Nepal, Francis Buchanan-
Hamilton had a grudging respect for Prithvi Narayan, 'a man of sound
judgement, and great enterprise', a man who understood how to use
the factionalism of the Kathmandu valley to his advantage. 'Sometimes
by force, but oftener by fraud and perfidy, he subjected most of the
country to an authority, which he maintained by the terror of his
cruelty.'

This reputation for cruelty is contentious. Hamilton had reason to
discredit him, beyond the racial prejudices of his time; Prithvi had
interrupted the business of his employer, the East India Company, a
corporation that readily suspended its humanity in pursuit of profit.
Nepali historians, notably the father of modern Nepali history
Baburam Acharya, defended Prithvi's excesses as necessary to maintain
unity in the face of external threats, particularly the British, although
when Prithvi came to power the British were barely on the horizon
as an influence on the Himalayan region. A famous early example of
someone who suffered 'the terror of his cruelty' was the former
Gorkha general Jayant Rana, who had fled to Kathmandu after the
first attempt to take Nuwakot. Before attacking the town again, Prithvi
tried to lure his father's general back to the Gorkha side: Jayant was
a valuable asset to Prithvi's enemies, Kathmandu's Malla kings, for
his knowledge of Gorkha's martial habits. Jayant told Prithvi he would
remain 'true to his salt', meaning his Kathmandu employer, and 'would
be true to this until death'. The challenge was accepted. When eventually Nuwakot fell to Prithvi in 1744, Jayant was flayed alive. Despite
this, in the context of his day, Prithvi's recorded acts of violence, with
rare and famous exceptions like this, seem typical.

If he could be impetuous when angry, and publicly humiliate his
rivals, Prithvi was more often shrewd and patient. What Hamilton
read as 'perfidy' was simply tactical awareness: Prithvi knew where
he was weak and how to use the advantages of the country. The
failure at Nuwakot had shown him the value of firearms, so he went
down to the plains and got firearms. He had his men trained in their
use and maintenance, although because procuring ammunition and

gunpowder was difficult, for both sides, they were used sparingly. Most fighting was done hand to hand, with *khukuris*, swords and spears. Throughout his reign, and particularly in the *Divya Upadesh*, Prithvi stressed the virtues of autarky, the reliance of the state on its own resources. When appointing key advisors he also exploited the political complexities of the elite families around him. He made the superbly capable Kalu Pande his *kazi*, or chief minister, and then had Pande's daughter marry into the rival Basnyet clan. 'I made a Pande the shield,' he boasted in his memoir, meaning the minister in charge of diplomacy, 'and a Basnyet the sword.'

Having reorganised his army and equipped himself with better counsel, Prithvi then shored up his rear flank. He signed treaties with Lamjung to halt their old feud and left troops under the command of trusted lieutenants to defend Gorkha from any threat of rebellion from the *Chaubisi*, should they take advantage while he was busy elsewhere. He made diplomatic overtures to the king of Bhaktapur, splitting the unity that had thwarted him before. Then he embarked on the Shah family's third attempt to take Nuwakot in seven years. Gorkha's tactics had so far proved inept, so Prithvi changed those too. Head-on assaults were foolish bravado: insurgency and tactical nous suited the country far better. Prithvi would make an art form of disinformation, of messing with his enemies' minds. In September 1744, when he moved on Nuwakot, his men went as farmers with the subterfuge of digging an irrigation-channel on Gorkha's side of the Trisuli river. Nuwakot's defenders were not expecting an attack during the tail of monsoon season.

With his men in place, Prithvi made his offer to the defiant Jayant Rana, who promptly rushed to Kathmandu for more troops, leaving his son Shankha Mani in charge. The valley was celebrating one of its main festivals, Indra Jatra, and the reaction was slow and insufficient. Prithvi divided his forces, sending Kalu Pande north to cross the Trisuli upstream of Nuwakot out of sight of the defenders to attack from the north-east, from high ground. The Newari troops, expecting an attack from the south, were disoriented and quickly routed. Shankha Mani exhorted his men to fight and moved to challenge Prithvi's younger brother Dal Mardan Shah, who, as the story goes, cut him down. Jayant Rana was at Belkot on the road back to Nuwakot when the news reached him and he prepared to counterattack. Prithvi knew that Nuwakot would not be safe with Jayant's large force positioned above the Trisuli river so he attacked at once, with substantial casualties on both sides, capturing Belkot as well as Nuwakot and fulfilling his promise to punish Jayant Rana.

The capture of Nuwakot would remain an important moment for Prithvi. The town was always close to his heart. Indeed, Prithvi Narayan Shah's troops didn't arrive on the edge of the Kathmandu valley out of nowhere, like some foreign marauding horde. The cultural and political connections between the belligerents were deep and broad. The Malla dynasties had often drawn on various groups over the centuries to bolster their position at times of crisis. Ram Shah, for example, the reforming king of Gorkha, did a deal with Siddhi Narasimha Malla, the king of Patan who instituted the Kartik dances, to provide successors for each other in case they died childless. There had been Khas populations in the Kathmandu valley for centuries by Prithvi's time; eventually the Khas language was included alongside Newari in court documents. And migration went both ways. Ram Shah had invited Newari merchants to set up shop in his kingdom to further trade. When Prithvi commissioned palace buildings in Nuwakot, they were built by Newari craftsmen in the Malla style. So while this was a struggle between competing states, at times it had the intimacy and bitterness of civil war.

After the fall of Nuwakot, it took Prithvi another twenty-five years to realise his boyhood ambition and capture the Kathmandu valley. It's tempting to ask what took him so long. Then again, considering the obstacles he faced, the more obvious question might be how he managed it at all. Others had tried before him and even succeeded temporarily: the Khasa Empire from western Nepal and then the first sultan of Bengal, the brilliant Muslim general Ilyas Shah, both occupied Kathmandu in the fourteenth century. But when Prithvi took the cities, he had laid the foundations over decades for something more permanent. The challenges he faced in doing so were as steep as the mountains around him, although he knew better than anyone how to take advantage of the terrain he had grown up in. Most importantly, he was limited in his resources. The mini-states of the Himalayan belt were not only constrained by geography, with hyper-local languages and cultures. They were also constrained economically. Indeed there were so many of these tiny kingdoms not because of political weakness but because of their limited economies. It was almost impossible for one of them to dominate another without becoming vulnerable themselves: there simply weren't the resources available.

To escape these limits, Prithvi had created a polity that can loosely be termed the agrarian-military complex. Ordinarily, a king would pay his generals in the rents he took from his people, taken in grain and produce; this was then shared among the troops. Prithvi Narayan paid his soldiers directly with assignments of land, making them personally invested in the success of their missions. (For Prithvi, 'soldiers are the very marrow of the king'.) Like a shark, therefore, the project needed to keep moving forward, or at least have the prospect of doing so. That required ever more land and the best of it was in the terai, the plains below the mountains. In absorbing hill-states with access to the terai, he created enough wealth to reward his troops, a strategy that would, as we shall see, ultimately lead to conflict with the British. By and large, as Prithvi expanded his kingdom, he left indigenous leaders in place and either co-opted or replaced their Rajput elites; these were assessed on their performance. It was a lean and hungry system of government but one that relied on a determined and competent leader at the centre. As the Indian civil servant and historian Henry Thoby Prinsep suggested, the British had relied on a similarly acquisitive but light-touch approach, 'which had gained for us the empire of Hindoostan'.

Capturing Nuwakot plugged Prithvi into a rich stream of Himalayan trade, but this did not, as he had hoped, make him wealthy enough to purchase the weapons necessary to storm the Kathmandu valley. The Tibetans were used to dealing with the Malla kings of Kathmandu, not an aggressive rustic upstart who didn't understand how things were done. Furthermore, Prithvi now ruled a confederation of small kingdoms acquired largely against their will; they had to be kept in line. Compared to Gorkha, the Malla kings were well funded and cosmopolitan, connected to a network of military support and allies, including the Mughals, from the plains. Autarky was not in their nature. Even though their trade with Tibet was interrupted, they still had a lot of capital assets. Much later, when the Gorkhali threat became critical, Jaya Prakash Malla, the only Malla king to understand the danger Kathmandu was facing, used the treasures of his city to pay for mercenaries to defend the kingdom.

The strategy Prithvi adopted was one of patience and caution, one that focussed on encircling and then strangling the valley's commerce, Kathmandu's lifeblood, while its rulers, like frogs in cold water, remained unaware of his endgame. The Malla kings thought they knew the Gorkhalis: just one more Khas group the Malla cities had been using in their struggles with each other for generations. They failed to understand the scale of Prithvi's ambition. One by one, over years, strategic points around the valley fell under Prithvi's control. It was a strategy that bears a striking resemblance to that of the Maoist insurgents in the late twentieth century, a smouldering conflict with little actual fighting. War burned limited resources: men and treasure. Gorkha didn't have enough of either.

Having taken control of Tibetan trade routes, Prithvi tried to increase his kingdom's wealth by capturing the source of Kathmandu's wealth: minting coins for Tibet. The Tibetans were having none of it; they only wanted coin from the source they recognised: the Malla treasuries. So Prithvi concentrated instead on creating a state of mind in his opponents, one of division and weakening resolve, before striking with a single fatal blow. His lieutenants were trustworthy and experienced, his men battle-hardened and tough. The Malla kings of the Kathmandu valley seemed to Prithvi decadent and effete, more interested in theatre than war. In the *Divya Upadesh*, he wrote of how life in the city could do that to you: 'This three-citied Nepal is a cold stone. It is great only in intrigue. With one who drinks water from cisterns, there is no wisdom; nor is there courage.' All he had to do was wait and let them defeat themselves.

Even then, Prithvi proved too hasty. When he did strike, thirteen years after taking Nuwakot, he discovered he had fatally underestimated the resolve of ordinary people to keep the Gorkhalis out of the Kathmandu valley. His target was the town of Kirtipur, which sits on the only significant hill wholly within the valley, overlooking the western approaches to its major cities. Taking these heights would be a major step in controlling the valley. In May 1757 he arrived at the village of Dahachok just below Chandragiri. It was a place he would later recommend as his capital, set apart, high above the intrigues and moral weakness of the valley. It was obvious to the Malla kings and their generals what would happen next. Prithvi's trusted counsellor and general Kalu Pande was the most senior among several advisers who recommended caution: the Malla kingdoms seemed unusually united and the valley's young men were well prepared to fight the Gorkhalis. Prithvi disagreed, arguing that the Malla forces would only grow stronger: they should attack now. He goaded Kalu Pande, rushing him into battle. Kalu lead twelve hundred Gorkhali troops toward Kirtipur, whose gates were closed to the invaders. The armies of the three cities, three thousand men in total, then attacked the Gorkhali forces from three sides, those from the city of Patan leading the charge. Kalu Pande was struck by an arrow and fell; his enemies leapt forward and cut off his head. The Gorkhalis around him, seeing their general killed, panicked. Prithvi himself barely escaped the battlefield, carried away in his palanquin to Nuwakot. Although their casualties had been far greater, the Malla kings were jubilant: they believed they had neutralised the threat of Prithvi Narayan Shah for good.

Yet while the Gorkhalis had suffered a setback, and Prithvi had to endure the personal misfortune of losing his most trusted general, they rebuilt their strength, returning to their earlier strategy of isolating the valley while keeping the various kingdoms around Gorkha under control. In 1759, the heights of Shivapuri on the northern rim of the Kathmandu valley fell to the Gorkhalis. In 1762, five years after the disaster at Kirtipur, Prithvi's troops easily took control of the main fort at Makwanpur, ruled by his wife's family, the Sen, which lay on Kathmandu's trade route with India; another stronghold at Sindhuli to the east soon followed. This brought more land on the terai to reward his troops.

Makwanpur had good relations with Mir Qasim Khan, nawab of Bengal, the viceroy of the Mughal emperor. Qasim's relationship with the East India Company, which had put him in power, was at this time fracturing badly; he had as a consequence been reforming his army at his new capital in Bihar. From Qasim's perspective, Makwanpur's capture by Gorkhali troops was an opportunity to help an ally and test his troops against what he thought were easy prey. It was a fatal error. The Gorkhali army, battle-hardened after decades of conflict, thrashed Qasim's soldiers and took their equipment: a clear signal to Prithvi's neighbours that here was a power to be respected.

Indeed, the world around the Himalaya had been changing dramatically in the years of Prithvi's rule. In 1739, Nader Shah, the Persian military genius, following the familiar route of Central Asian migrants and invaders through the Hindu Kush, had destroyed a Mughal army vastly superior in numbers, fragmenting an empire now in its death throes. Across the subcontinent smaller kingdoms emerged from the Mughal shadow and new leaders profited from the changing political landscape, helping re-establish a sense of organised Hindu identity, notably with the rise of the Maratha confederacy. Bands of sannyasi, in this period more swords for hire than godly ascetics, roamed Bengal, turning to banditry whenever necessary. The French and British, at war in Europe, fought for control of each other's trading interests. Robert Clive, an almost exact contemporary of Prithvi's, had led the East India Company's troops to victory at Plassey over the nawab of Bengal in 1757. When Prithvi started his campaign to conquer Kathmandu, the East India Company had been little more than a distant rumour. North of the Himalaya, meanwhile, the Manchu Qing Empire had established its influence in Tibet and Xinjiang. At the end of his life, Prithvi warned that 'This country is like a gourd between two rocks. Maintain a treaty of friendship with the emperor of China. Keep also a treaty of friendship with the emperor of the southern sea [the East India Company]. He has taken the plains.'

Boosted with the weaponry he had taken from Mir Qasim, Prithvi closed in on the Kathmandu valley. When Kirtipur fell at last, witnessed by Capuchin missionaries, the Gorkhalis punished at least some of its inhabitants for their defiance by cutting off their noses and lips. Some Nepali historians have disputed this, although Captain William Kirkpatrick encountered a few victims when he visited the valley three decades later. With his enemies at the gates, the raja of Kathmandu, Jaya Prakash Malla sent a desperate appeal to the East India Company's nearest agent at Bettiah, asking for help. The British had been paying close attention to the gold coming out of the Kathmandu valley: this gold was, in fact, Tibetan, part of the coinage arrangement with the Malla dynasty, but the British didn't know that. They were also interested in the magnificent stands of timber along their northern border and considered the cool hills of Nepal a possible outlet for British woollens, which weren't much in demand on the hot plains of India. The Company also judged Gorkha to be a brake on trade and had sympathy for Jaya's plight. So a substantial force was despatched to relieve Kathmandu under the command of a young captain called George Kinloch.

Kinloch's journal of this expedition languished half-forgotten in the papers of Robert Clive's secretary Henry Strachey, grandfather of the Stracheys who explored Kailas, until its rediscovery by Nepali historian Yogesh Raj. The story it contains is like something from the darker reaches of a Joseph Conrad novel. The envoys Jaya Prakash sent warned there was no time for delay, so Kinloch set off in August 1767, during the monsoon. In those days the plains were thinly populated and the jungles of Nepal barely at all. There was 'no trace of any living creature, except wild Elephants, Tigers and Bears which are here in large numbers'. Kinloch didn't have a map and often wasn't sure where he was. The mountains were like nothing that he'd seen before 'altho' I have cross'd the highest and wildest in the Highlands of Scotland'. The army's artillery was moving too slowly in the difficult terrain so Kinloch went ahead with an advance party that managed to take the fort at Sindhuli despite resolute defence by no more than eighty Gorkhalis. Mr Logan, the expedition surgeon, led the charge, losing a finger in the process; the Gorkhalis, Kinloch wrote, 'behaved like Brave and resolute Men'.

At every turn he found himself blocked or thwarted. The grain merchant contracted to supply the troops disappeared for a week and the army became trapped in heavy rain, starving and desperate, reduced to digging up roots in the jungle. By mid October, Kinloch was delirious, most probably with malaria. 'Sickness now rages and many die, so that my own Malady is heightened by the groans of many poor wretches around me.' After two weeks without proper food, he awoke at two in the morning, disturbed by a 'Very strange and sudden noise'. It was his sepoys, originally a Persian term, then used for Indian infantry serving in the Company's forces, taking up their arms as one body and disappearing into the blackness. 'It being the Dead of Night, and the matter carried this far with such secrecy, I had reason to apprehend the worst of Consequences and never doubted but it was general ...' At this point his journal ends, in mid sentence. Kinloch believed himself only two days from Kathmandu but there's no way of knowing if he was right. He made it back to Patna, although we don't know how, and died the following year of the illness he had acquired in the jungle, still arguing that the Company should try again.

The consequences of this forgotten humiliation were significant. Had Kinloch succeeded in bringing artillery to the valley he might well have stopped Prithvi's final victory. The Malla dynasties would have proved easier for the Company to deal with than the rugged opposition of the Gorkhalis, who now believed they had the measure of the British. Jaya Prakash himself died from a musket ball defending the durbar or palace, at Bhaktapur, where he had gone for protection after the city of Kathmandu fell. Patan too had fallen. Ranjit Malla, the last king of Bhaktapur, was sent into exile at Benares (Varanasi), supposedly composing a raga as he left the valley for the last time. 'How,' he asked, 'did I fail to comprehend the conspiracy of evil which brought this devastation on me?' The Shah dynasty took over the palaces of the Malla kings but Newari ateliers and artists found their new Gorkhali patrons not so interested in the politics of theatre. Prithvi, always the accountant, despised performance art as wasteful, warning against the corrupting influence of musicians from India. 'In rooms lined with paintings, they forget themselves in melodies woven on the drum and sitar. There is great pleasure in these melodies. But it drains your wealth.'

Having taken Kathmandu, Prithvi was content to let other generals continue the Gorkhali conquest of kingdoms to the east. His *vakil*, or envoys, were able to negotiate back the land-holdings Kinloch had snatched on the terai. Having been bitten once, the British weren't going to make the same mistake again. Following a failed monsoon in 1769, north-eastern India was plunged into famine, thanks in part to punitive taxes and grain monopolies imposed by the East India Company. Warren Hastings, the new governor of Bengal, concluded in his report of 1772 that up to a third of the population had died: ten million people. Prithvi watched this from his cool, green valley high in the mountains and pondered where the 'southern emperor' would strike next. 'He will realise that if Hindustan unites, it will be difficult, and so he will come seeking places for forts. Prepare forts, without burdening the people. Set traps in the trails. One day that force will come.' That day was soon at hand.

7

The High Road to Tibet

Tucked away in Britain's Royal Collection is an unusual painting done in Calcutta, now Kolkata, in the late eighteenth century. It is the work of Tilly Kettle, the first well-known English portrait artist to travel to India, and shows Tibet's Panchen Lama, second only to the Dalai Lama in the Geluk school of Tibetan Buddhism, sitting cross-legged on a dais. On the left of the picture, standing near a window looking on, is a young Scotsman in Bhutanese dress. Through the window is an idealised version of the Himalaya: the young man, we're being told, has just arrived from the other side of these high mountains. Two attendants, one dressed as a monk, stand either side of the lama. Another figure bows slightly as he presents the Panchen Lama with a white ceremonial scarf, a *kada*, signifying purity and compassion. Seated under the window are two further local men, relaxed and informal, puffing on long-stemmed tobacco pipes, rather unlikely in a Tibetan monastery. But while much in this painting is invented or stylised, its significance is unmistakeable: it represents the first meeting between political Europe, in the form of a representative of the East India Company, and one of the most powerful figures in the spiritual and temporal world of Tibet. It was an encounter of genuine warmth and personal friendship, but it came at a pivotal moment in Himalayan history, and marked a shift that would lead inexorably, if not inevitably, towards the invasion and occupation of Tibet by Chinese forces in 1950.

Tilly Kettle's painting was presented to George III, although it's unclear who did the presenting. It was probably not the Scotsman, whose name was George Bogle. At the time it was painted, most probably in 1775, Bogle was facing financial hardship, sending home as much money as he could to service his family's debts. It's more likely that Bogle's patron Warren Hastings, the embattled first governor general of India, acquired the picture. It was useful propaganda in his campaign to wrest back control of the Company's supreme council in Calcutta, snatched away from him with the passing of the Regulating Act of 1773: the British government's attempt to get a grip of the management of the East India Company and its spiralling debts.

Many have heard of the Boston Tea Party and the American War of Independence; few understand the links between these famous events and the financial woes of the East India Company. Its plight was exposed in 1772 when a London banker fled to France, having lost £300,000 shorting East India Company stock. This prompted a credit crunch, which meant the Company couldn't refinance its debt, ironically devastating its share price. To survive, the Company needed to sell its vast holdings of tea in London as quickly as possible. The Company wasn't allowed to sell tea direct to the American colonies and had to pay duty on it in London before selling it on to intermediaries. Such a large mark-up put the Company at a disadvantage; American consumers were more than happy to drink cheaper contraband tea smuggled in from Dutch wholesalers, who dealt with the Chinese through their colony at Batavia (today's Indonesian capital, Jakarta). To protect the nation's stake in the East India Company and keep it afloat, in May 1773 the British parliament passed the Tea Act, giving it the right to ship tea direct to America without paying duty in London first. This outraged legitimate tea merchants in Boston and other American cities and led to direct action – the so-called Tea Party – to prevent tea being unloaded.

Like a modern global bank, the East India Company had become too big to fail but was forced to pay a price for the government's continuing support: the Regulating Act, passed a month later. This was aimed squarely at the East India Company itself, an attempt to cut corruption, limit dividends and reorganise its dismal administration. In return, the Company's debts were refinanced. Warren Hastings was appointed governor general of not just Calcutta but all three presidencies in India, laying the foundation for British rule over the whole subcontinent. In the blink of an eye, India's fortunes had been made collateral to the East India Company's experiment in globalisation. Despite these reforms, the Company still had deep structural problems. Although it had a monopoly on British trade with China, the Company was restricted to one port, Canton, the modern city of Guangzhou, and found itself effectively shut out of Chinese markets and China's interior. All China wanted in return for its tea and silk was silver, creating a huge trade imbalance for the British. Any route to freer trade with China was worth considering, even one as remote as Tibet.

Bogle arrived in Calcutta as a writer, or clerk, in 1770 in the midst of the cataclysmic Bengal famine. He wrote to his brother of the nightmarish impact:

> There were men employed to pick up the Dead Bodies in the Streets, and throw them into the River, and from the 1st to the 9th of last Month no less than twelve Hundred Carcasses were found – in the streets of Calcutta – that had not died of Pestilence, or Sickness, but absolutely of Hunger.

The situation was even worse in Murshidabad, the once proud Mughal capital of Bengal, where as many as five hundred people a day were dying. The resident there reported cannibalism, something Bogle also mentioned in his letters, and an outbreak of smallpox that deepened the tragedy. Whole villages simply disappeared. The East India Company's response was to increase taxation to meet a drop in revenues, wealth that flowed abroad to pay shareholders in priority over preventing future disasters. There were allegations of famine profiteering by British employees of the Company acting in their own interest.

Until very recently, the *kada*, the ceremonial white scarf being offered to the Panchen Lama in Kettle's painting was captioned by the Royal Collection as a bolt of cloth, a sales sample meant to lever open the floodgates of trade between Bengal and Tibet, and ultimately China. The mistake was understandable. Bogle did travel to Tibet with samples – European cutlery, Bengali cloth, mirrors, clocks, glassware, a string of pearls (which was of particular interest to a great Tibetan lama), thermometers, telescopes and a toy that gave off a small electric shock – all part of the effort to open new markets and boost profits, a door-to-door salesman on the roof of the world. Hastings had also given him a shopping list, particularly for those goods that were easy to transport through the mountains: gold, precious stones, musk and less obvious items, like plants used to dye fabrics. This was supplemented by a second private request from Hastings to bring back shawl goats and a pair of yaks, 'cattle which bear what are called cowtails', meaning yak tails, fresh ripe walnuts and any other seeds that looked useful, 'ginseng especially'. In fact, Bogle should bring back anything that might persuade 'Persons of Taste in England' to open their purses, and anything else he judged of interest to the endlessly curious Hastings.

The Panchen Lama, whose name was Lobsang Palden Yeshe, was both a great religious leader and a shrewd politician: he understood very well the purpose of George Bogle's mission and the acquisitive nature of his employers. Bogle mentions this in his despatches, how the lama had been warned against allowing Bogle's visit, that the East India Company 'was like a great King and fond of War and Conquest, and as my Business and that of my People is to pray to God, I was afraid to admit any Fringies [from the Farsi *farangi*, meaning Franks, or Europeans] into the Country'. The lama's presentation of himself as a simple holy man with little experience of the world, a naïf who had never before seen a European, was cheerfully disingenuous. At the time of Bogle's visit, with the eighth Dalai Lama in Lhasa still a teenager, the Panchen Lama was the most powerful individual in Tibet.

*

Tilly Kettle's painting showed the Panchen Lama in yellow silk robes, a colour and fabric emblematic of the Chinese imperial court but also of the order of monks the lama belonged to, the Geluk, 'the virtuous school', for their strict monasticism, often referred to by Europeans as the 'yellow hats'; Bogle describes the Panchen Lama wearing 'a mitre-shaped cap of yellow broadcloth, with long bars lined with red satin'. The idea of a yellow hat had been borrowed from another Tibetan Buddhist school, long defunct, to give the Geluk-pa, the 'people of Geluk', their own identity as they established themselves in a crowded spiritual field. The depth of history behind these symbols and the political complexity they hinted at were almost wholly new to the British: how the Panchen Lama came to be the power that he was; the nature of his relationship with the centre at Lhasa; the rival factions that threatened him; the strangeness of reincarnation. It needed a sprightly mind to start unpicking this knot; luckily for the Company, it had Bogle.

By the time Europe – its missionaries, traders and explorers – first encountered Tibet in the seventeenth and eighteenth centuries, the Geluk-pa dominated its political scene. When foreign actors dealt with Tibet, they did so through the Geluk-pa. The order's colossal monastic institutions not only exerted political control but dominated the economy as well. Monasteries were significant businesses in their own right with aristocratic patrons adding lustre to their art and treasures. This was what Bogle witnessed. Yet the origins of the Geluk-pa were a far cry from the pomp and wealth on display at the Panchen Lama's monastic seat, Tashilhunpo, in the town of Shigatse.

During the thirteenth and fourteenth centuries, under the religious patronage of the Yuan dynasty, the Sakya school of Buddhism had dominated Tibet, eclipsing the other major lineages, the Nyingma and Kagyu. The Sakya was favoured by Kublai Khan, prompting the Sakya leader Phagpa to recruit Newari craftsmen from Kathmandu, including the famous Arniko. Then, as Mongol power fractured in the mid fourteenth century, central Tibet, meaning the provinces of U (including the city of Lhasa) and Tsang, became contested space. As the Yuan faded, and with it Sakya power, Changchub Gyaltsen, a young and charismatic Kagyu leader from the famous monastery of Phagmodru, 'sow's ferry crossing', rose to govern large parts of Tibet from his capital at Nedong, some hundred kilometres south-east of Lhasa, extending his influence to Kham in eastern Tibet and north-east to Amdo.

With the weight of their foreign overlord removed, many Tibetans looked back with pride to the era of the divine tsenpos, the empire and Tibet's adoption of Buddhism. Aiming to revive the spirit of Songtsen Gampo, Changchub and his immediate successors built new fortresses or *dzong* and encouraged a renaissance in Buddhist philosophy and translation, and tolerance also between different Buddhist schools. Among those who emerged from this period of spiritual freedom and renaissance was perhaps the single most influential Tibetan student of Buddhism in history: Tsongkhapa, 'the man from onion valley'. It was under his influence that the Geluk school was founded and rose to prominence, changing the course of Tibetan history.

Tsongkhapa's father Lubum Ge was Mongolian. His birth, in the Amdo town of Tsongkha in 1357, glittered with miraculous portents. Where a drop of blood from his umbilical cord fell to earth, a sandalwood tree emerged. His mother Shingza Acho later built a stupa here and in time the site became Kumbum monastery, among the most important in the Geluk tradition. Aged eight he became a novitiate monk and was given the name Lobsang Drakpa from his tutor Dondrub Rinchen, a master in important Buddhist tantras that would form the basis of the Geluk school and a student in the Kadam school of philosophy founded by Atisa, the translator Changchub O had brought to Tibet during the second diffusion. Aged sixteen, Tsongkhapa left for central Tibet, but he couldn't settle at one monastery; his restless intellect drove him from place to place in a wide-ranging exploration of Tibetan Buddhism's different strands. He met a Sakya monk, Rendawa, with the same questioning outlook, who tutored him through his exams and gave him the confidence to continue on his path. To thank him, Tsongkhapa wrote a short verse in his praise. Later Rendawa returned it, having crossed out his own name and replaced it with that of his former student. The verse became known as the 'Migtsema':

> Avalokitesvara, great treasure of non-objectifying compassion,
> Manjushri, master of stainless wisdom,
> Vajrapani, destroyer of the entire host of demons,
> Tsongkhapa, crown jewel of the sages of the land of snow …

Most important was Tsongkhapa's time at a small hermitage called Drowa Gon, near Lhodrak, one of the few Kadam temples that had not been absorbed by the Sakya; here he learned more of Atisa's teachings with its abbot, Drubchen Namkha Gyeltsen. Later, with his tutor Rendawa, he taught for three months at Reting, the original Kadam monastery founded by the followers of Atisa soon after his death. As his learning deepened, important themes emerged that would help define Geluk philosophy: an adherence to logic and the patient accumulation of knowledge being the groundwork for powerful, intuitive insight. Some of his views remain controversial even now, particularly his interpretation of *madhyamaka*, the 'middle way', which is central to Tibetan Buddhist philosophy. His most famous work, written in his mid forties while at Reting, was *The Great Treatise on the Stages of the Path to Enlightenment*.

Plagued from youth with a bad back, he found it increasingly difficult to travel and spent more and more time in Lhasa. By then his tutors had become his students and hundreds flocked to hear him speak about the *dharma*. In 1409, he instituted the Monlam Chenmo, or Great Prayer Festival, still celebrated around the time of the Tibetan New Year, or Losar. That same year, persuaded by his many followers to commission a permanent home, he founded Ganden monastery near Lhasa, Ganden meaning 'joyful'. Ganden was followed in 1416 by Drepung monastery and in 1419, the year of his death, Sera : these are the three great Geluk monastic establishments centred on Songtsen Gampo's ancient capital. Before then, Tibet's monastic strength had lain elsewhere; now Lhasa was the centre.

At first, Tsongkhapa's followers were known as Ganden-pa, people from Ganden, but the name Geluk-pa became popular after his death, meaning 'virtuous ones'. The behaviour of the *sangha*, meaning 'assembly', the monastic community, had been of intense importance to Tsongkhapa. He is sometimes compared to Martin Luther for his reforming zeal; he certainly adhered to vows of celibacy and abstention from drinking alcohol or eating meat, but he was more ecumenical than Luther. Most importantly, unlike earlier famous schools of Tibetan Buddhism, the Geluk emerged from within the Tibetan world and wasn't directly inspired or fed by scholars in the holy land of India, a Buddhist world that had by Tsongkhapa's time ceased to exist.

In his lifetime the monasteries founded in Tsongkhapa's name held a few hundred monks, but within a century Drepung alone had ten thousand and Sera something similar. Given the small Tibetan population, the size of these vast establishments was, according to some historians, a brake on Tibet's economic development. They were certainly a brake on population growth, but given the physical limits on Tibetan agriculture that was not necessarily a bad thing. The Geluk monasteries also came to dominate Tibetan politics, which entered a period of civil strife a few years after Tsongkhapa's death as the Phagmodru dynasty began to unravel. Clan rivalry between the provinces of U and Tsang spilled over into religious sectarianism. Gedun Drub, one of Tsongkhapa's younger students, took the new Geluk school to Tsang and founded a Geluk monastery at Shigatse:

Tashilhunpo. In this way he extended the influence of his order into a place with strong historical links to Sakya and older Kagyu schools: an outpost of the new Buddhist world founded at Lhasa. Here Gedun Drub remained, choosing to be reincarnated after death in the body of a young monk.

The role of reincarnation in Tibetan Buddhism's spiritual lineages can seem opaque and esoteric, although George Bogle took it in his stride. Reincarnation itself is of course part of Buddhism: the cycle of life, death and rebirth is part of the journey for all living things, returned to earth involuntarily as a consequence of negative emotions and actions, or *karma*. From around the twelfth century some great Buddhist teachers began choosing to return rather than going on to nirvana and the bliss of self-extinction. They did so, they said, for the benefit of all sentient beings. Such reincarnate lamas, or *tulku*, would predict the location of their rebirth and even their parents. In the thirteenth century, Rangjung Dorje, leader of the Karma Kagyu school, the largest within the Kagyu tradition, formalised this process, combining his choice of reincarnation with the lineage he led. This innovation would have a profound impact on Tibetan society, lifting Buddhist lineages, in theory if not in practice, beyond the reach of secular power. Religious authorities took charge of selecting and educating their next leader. In this way, they transmitted their particular philosophical strand to the leader of the next generation, who became a temporary host or platform for an enduring ideal.

The long-established aristocratic clans and the country's immense religious establishments had now become the two most powerful forces within Tibet, but finding a political structure that met the interests of both proved intractable. Eventually foreign powers were dragged back into the equation. In 1578, Gedun Drub's third reincarnation, a lama called Sonam Gyatso, accepted an invitation from the Mongol leader Altan Khan to renew the priest–patron relationship his forebear Kublai Khan had enjoyed with the Sakya. Altan Khan gave Sonam Gyatso the Mongolian name Dalai Lama, 'Dalai' being a translation of his ordination name 'Gyatso': meaning 'great ocean'. Sonam Gyatso respectfully backdated this new title to include his two previous incarnations and so as a consequence Gedun Drub was counted as the first Dalai Lama. The fourth Dalai Lama, Yonten Gyatso, conveniently reappeared in the body of a descendant of Altan Khan, but by then Mongol power had faltered and the Geluk-pa were under pressure. This foreign-born Dalai Lama, needing approval, persuaded the abbot of Tashilhunpo, Choekyi Gyaltsen to come to Drepung monastery in Lhasa, where the Dalai Lamas then had their seat. Choekyi Gyaltsen soon became deeply involved in the increasingly turbulent political situation across the region. Lhasa, part of U province, was now under the control of a king from Tsang called Karma Phuntsog Namgyal. His spiritual allegiance was to the rival Kagyu lineage the Karmapa; the Dalai Lama didn't have remotely the power he would come to acquire later.

In 1617 the fourth Dalai Lama died and for a while Choekyi Gyaltsen applied a brake to the search for his reincarnation. Two years later, the last vestiges of the Phagmodru regime in U collapsed as the Tsang laid siege to its capital at Nedong. Lacking the support and protection of the Phagmodru, Geluk monks and their Mongolian patrons became restless. To prevent violence, Choekyi allowed the search for the fifth Dalai Lama to proceed. A candidate had already been identified in secret, a boy who had attracted interest from several rival Buddhist schools because of his exceptional promise. And as he himself would later joke, the boy failed hopelessly in one of the crucial tasks that marked out a reincarnated lama: identifying the possessions of his predecessor. Yet this boy, the fifth Dalai Lama, ordained as Ngawang Lobsang Gyatso, would be the making of the lineage. It was the 'Great Fifth' who built the world famous Potala on the old site of Songtsen Gampo's palace, which still dominates the modern city of Lhasa. He also recognised Choekyi Gyaltsen as the Panchen Lama, 'Panchen' being a portmanteau word from *pandit* and *chenpo*, meaning 'great scholar'. This new lineage was retrospectively extended back to another of Tsongkhapa's students, Khedrup Je. This calculation made Choekyi the fourth Panchen Lama.

As a boy, the Dalai Lama's power rested with his regent Sonam Choephel, a senior monk from Ganden; more than anyone, Sonam Choephel was the architect of the Geluk's rise to power. Securing that power was Gushi Khan, a Khoshut Mongol leader from the tribe that had superseded Altan Khan's descendants and defeated rival Mongol supporters of the Karma Kagyu school. In 1642, civil strife ended, or at least paused, as Gushi Khan invested the fifth Dalai Lama with both temporal and spiritual control of Tibet at Tashilhunpo. The Karmapa,

1. A photograph of Everest, centre frame, taken looking south from Space Shuttle *Atlantis* in November 1994. The peak's vast east face is lit with morning sunlight while the north face remains deep in shadow.

2. A rock sample collected from the summit of Everest in 1956 showing fossilised fragments of a crinoid, or sea lily, proof that it had once been under the sea.

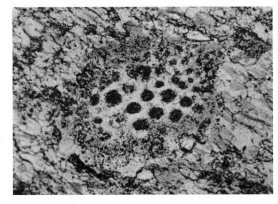

3. Part of the jawbone of what paleoanthropologists believe is a Denisovan hominin from the Middle Pleistocene, found on the Tibetan plateau in modern Gansu province. Genetic analysis suggests that the evolutionary adaptations of Tibetan peoples to the hypoxia of high altitude may have originated in Denisovan DNA.

4. The fortified palace of Yumbu Lhakang above the Yarlung Tsangpo river, a hundred miles south of Lhasa and the focus of the Yarlung dynasty. Most probably constructed in the late seventh century, it was badly damaged in the Cultural Revolution, the structure having since been restored.

5. The Diamond Sutra, the world's earliest printed book for which we have a date: May 868. It was found in the Mogao or 'Peerless' Caves near the city of Dunhuang in modern China's Gansu province. Tibetan manuscripts found in the caves transformed our understanding of early Tibetan history. The Diamond Sutra is among the most important scriptures for the Mahayana form of Buddhism practised in the Himalayan region.

6. Freddy Spencer Chapman's photograph of the Dalai Lama's palace, the Potala, taken in 1936 from the Chakpori monastery. Construction began in 1645, part of the Dalai Lama's effort to re-establish Lhasa as the capital of a reunified Tibetan nation. It was completed in 1694, twelve years after the Great Fifth's death.

7. A view of Jomolhari from the Tibetan plateau taken by Freddy Spencer Chapman as the British mission returned to India in 1937. This was the peak Sir William Jones had spotted from the plains of India in 1784, suggesting the Himalaya's immense altitude.

8. A photograph from the 1870s by the British photographers Bourne & Shepherd, of Kathmandu's Durbar Square.

9. Crowds gather in Kathmandu to celebrate the birthday of Prithvi Narayan Shah, founder of Nepal, born in Gorkha on 11 January 1723. This statue has also been the target of demonstrators protesting for ethnic minority rights.

10. Six furlongs to the mile: the first known map of the Kathmandu valley, drawn from surveys carried out by Charles Crawford, later surveyor general, who commanded the detachment accompanying the Knox mission of 1802.

11. Jung Bahadur with his senior queen Hiranyagarbha Devi, two daughters and attendants, photographed by Clarence Comyn Taylor, who had been badly wounded in 1857 and turned to political service, arriving in Kathmandu in 1863 as assistant resident. These were the first photographs of the valley, part of a wider British effort to document the peoples of India.

12. Christ Church in Simla, completed in 1857 and designed by John Theophilus Boileau of the Bengal Engineers. The Simla district Boileaugunj is named for him.

13. Born in County Sligo in 1821, Eliza Rosanna Gilbert spent her early years in India and later found fame as 'Lola Montez, the Spanish dancer'. She was the lover of Ludwig I of Bavaria, wielding great influence, and Jang Bahadur, de facto ruler of Nepal.

14. The Tibetan aristocrat Lungshar, left, with the four Tibetan boys sent to Rugby for education, Mondo, Ringang, Kyipup and Gongkar, after being presented to George V at Buckingham Palace in June 1913.

15. The viceroy of India Lord Curzon stands over the tiger he has just shot, during his visit to Nepal in early 1901, shortly before the coup that brought the more reliable Chandra Shamsher to power.

17. Sir Joseph Dalton Hooker, botanist and close friend of Charles Darwin, four years after his landmark three-year visit to the eastern Himalaya.

16. The young Chandra Shamsher, maharaja of Nepal from 1901 to 1929.

18. Reflecting the sudden influx of labour, a group of Nepalis and Bhotias in Darjeeling, photographed in the 1860s by Samuel Bourne, partner in the well-known Simla studio Bourne & Shepherd. 'Bhotia' was a colonial term used by the British as a catch-all for ethnic groups with their roots in Tibet living on the Indian side of the mountains.

19. The plant explorer William Purdom, dressed as a brigand, in Tibet in 1911.

20. Francis Younghusband in his greatcoat surrounded by staff officers on the bloody and quixotic British invasion of Tibet in 1904. Two future frontier cadre officers stand behind, Eric 'Hatter' Bailey with the cane and Frank O'Connor with hands in pockets.

21. Ugyen Wangchuk, governor of Trongsa in Bhutan. In 1907 he was crowned king with support from the British: reward for his support during their invasion of Tibet. Until this point, following defeat by the British and the Treaty of Sinchula in 1865, Bhutanese politics had been fractious. The photo was taken by John Claude White in 1905 as he invested Ugyen with the insignia of Knight Commander of the Order of the Indian Empire.

22. The political officer for Sikkim Charles Bell sits with Thubten Gyatso, the thirteenth Dalai Lama. Standing is Sidkeong Tulku Namgyal, crown prince of Sikkim. Educated at Pembroke College, Oxford, his reign was brief.

leader of the Karma Kagyu, had already fled into exile in Bhutan. The new government, known as the Ganden Phodrang, would govern Tibet until China's occupation in the 1950s. The impression many in the West have of the Tibetan state is that of the Phodrang, created under the fifth Dalai Lama's rule: it was during his lifetime that the first Jesuit missionaries arrived in Tibet. So central was the Great Fifth to Tibetan stability that when he died in 1682, his chief minister, or *desi*, Sangye Gyatso, kept the news secret for another fifteen years, while the succession was managed.

Sangye Gyatso proved a capable young man, acquiring Ngari in western Tibet, formerly the Guge kingdom, from its rulers in Ladakh, but his attempts to steer Tibet into the future came unstuck. Gushi Khan's grandson Lajang attempted to reassert Mongol control of Tibet and captured the sixth Dalai Lama, using artillery against Drepung monastery in the process. (Sangye Gyatso himself was decapitated, not by Lajang but by one of Lajang's wives, a Tibetan noblewoman. Gyatso had, the story goes, offered her as a wager over a game of chess and lost.) When the sixth Dalai Lama died in 1706 on his way into exile, Lajang tried to replace him with a monk of a similar age, widely believed to be his own son. He also behaved warmly towards the newly arrived Christian missionaries in Lhasa, including the Jesuit Ippolito Desideri, who believed Lajang might be converted. The missionaries would bear witness to the catastrophe that followed.

The Geluk monasteries of Lhasa turned against Lajang. Someone who treated the lineage of the Dalai Lama so casually and flirted with a foreign religion couldn't possibly be in charge. They welcomed, initially at least, the interest of a rival band of Mongols, the Dzungar, followers of the Geluk school, who fell on Tibet with astonishing ferocity, reigniting sectarian violence and pitching the country into chaos. Lajang was murdered attempting to escape and many Nyingma monasteries were destroyed. Only with the intervention of a powerful new dynasty in China opposed to the Dzungars was order restored.

While the Great Fifth ruled in Lhasa, the Manchu dynasty, the 'Great Qing', had been rising in China, a process completed during the long reign of the Kangxi emperor, each of the dynasty holding their own imperial name. The Qing were not Han Chinese, but part of a tribal confederation from Manchuria in northern China, descended from the Jurchen, closely related to other northern Asian populations, including the Mongols. Lajang Khan had been a proxy of the Kangxi emperor, who had watched in horror as Lajang mismanaged the situation before the Dzungar, his Mongol enemies, set fire to Tibet. He ordered a Qing army to restore order and drive out the Mongols. The Qing then reordered the government, in the process absorbing some portions of historical Tibet into the Qing Empire. (This included parts of Amdo: the rhubarb trade, centred on modern Gansu, was of particular interest to the Qing.)

Unluckily for Tibet's new government, the Kangxi emperor died in 1722 and Tibet was plunged once again into sectarian war. Opposing sides used alliances with competing Mongol factions and the Qing Empire to snatch advantage. The Qing saw the Panchen Lama as a useful counterweight to the immense power of the Dalai Lama and tried to set him up in his own semi-independent polity: the origin of China's particular interest in Tashilhunpo. Only in 1751, little more than two decades before the East India Company sent George Bogle to Tibet, was the situation finally settled. The Qing constituted a new government comprising a cabinet, or *kashag*, of four ministers, with the Dalai Lama as head of state. Two Qing officials, known as ambans, were charged with maintaining Qing imperial interests.

This was the world of the sixth Panchen Lama, Lobsang Palden Yeshe, one of deep divisions only recently healed and a new foreign overlord to consider. The Qing were deeply suspicious of Europe's rising power and the Geluk remembered the threat missionaries had presented during the rule of Lajang Khan. Tibet was acutely conscious of the dangers of inviting further foreign intervention. Bogle would witness how China kept an arm's length control of its western frontiers. The Panchen Lama himself understood the importance of intelligence, keeping abreast of any threat to Tibet's fragile peace. He managed a complex network of traders and informants who kept him apprised not only of Qing court politics but the world on the other side of the mountains, in the holy land of India, where a new, foreign mercantile power had risen. Among them was Purangir, the man who had led Bogle into his presence and most probably the figure offering a scarf to the lama in Tilly Kettle's painting.

In Europe, it is still the first Europeans who travelled through the Himalaya who are given recognition for their sense of adventure and courage. Yet more often than not they relied heavily on the knowledge and negotiating skills of others, travellers speaking several languages whose agendas were consequently concealed from their immediate employers. Purangir was just such a man. Fluent in Mongolian and Tibetan, among other languages, he spent his life travelling the length and breadth of Asia for masters of different faiths, including several assignments for the East India Company, juggling competing interests, seeing everything but giving little away: part monk, part spy, part trader.

Purangir, then in his mid twenties, was a *gosain*, a sannyasi or monk ordained into the monastic orders known as the Dasnami, associated with Adi Sankara, the Keralan who had returned Garhwal to Hinduism centuries before. Dasnami means 'ten names', or 'ten schools': Purangir was a *giri*, meaning a member of the 'mountain' school, and ordained at Joshimath, close to Badrinath, northernmost of the four *maths*, or monasteries, that Adi Sankar founded. In the sixteenth century, sannyasi had been organised into bands of warrior-monks to defend Hinduism against the Mughals, groups that had in Bogle's day degenerated into gangs of bandits available for hire: Jaya Prakash Malla, for example, had hired six hundred of them to stave off the Gorkhalis as they closed in on Kathmandu.

These gangs plagued everyone, from Prithvi Narayan Shah to the East India Company, hiding out in the jungles of the terai before making raids. As we shall see, sannyasi almost killed the Bengal surveyor James Rennell in 1766 on the fringes of the Bhutanese Himalaya. Famine had brought fresh raids from these gangs, so much so that Hastings banned them from the Company's territory. Sannyasi could be men of integrity and learning, like Purangir, but it's also possible the *gosain*'s status – and the fierce reputation that accompanied it – protected Bogle on his journey through the same country where Rennell was attacked.

Gosain were required in theory either to be resident in their monastery or else on the road, travelling as mendicant pilgrims. The freedom of movement such holy men enjoyed, slipping easily between different cultures, presented huge opportunities for trade and the acquisition of valuable information. By the eighteenth century, they had come to dominate trade across northern India in valuable commodities like silk and precious stones, using their monastic bases as trading houses and diversifying into money lending and land ownership. They were particularly strong at Benares on the Ganges. Tibetan gold and musk, as well as pilgrimage sites like Kailas, drew *gosain* across the Himalaya, trading coral and pearls in return. Purangir's currency was information, gathered as he travelled through the mountains: a walking encyclopaedia and a soul of discretion. His relationship with the Panchen Lama was especially close. There were spiritual synergies between Tibetan Buddhism and Hindu monks like Purangir, a shared knowledge of tantric practice, and the Panchen Lama built a refuge for them at Tashilhunpo. For the lama, India was the holy land but like many Tibetans he feared the heat and disease, especially smallpox, to which north Asians were susceptible. The knowledge Purangir imported was worth the expense.

In the spring of 1774, Purangir, accompanied by the Panchen Lama's Tibetan servant Pema, delivered a letter from the Panchen Lama to Warren Hastings at Calcutta. It was written in Persian, the diplomatic language of northern India, and accompanied with gifts: Tibetan woollen cloth, gold, both dust and ingots, and musk. The subject of the letter was military action taken by the British to expel Bhutanese fighters from the small Indian state of Cooch Behar in the foothills of the eastern Himalaya. The Bhutanese believed they had the right to appoint Cooch Behar's ruler: its ousted raja Dharendra Narayan, still a minor, thought otherwise and had sought help from the East India Company to regain his throne. Warren Hastings, sensing an opportunity, had offered to get rid of the Bhutanese, if the raja paid the cost of doing so. He also demanded half the king's revenues for the Company's continuing protection. The raja had no choice but to agree; Cooch Behar essentially gave up its sovereignty. To stop the British, the *desi*, or political leader of Bhutan, a man called Zhidar, sought help from Prithvi Narayan Shah in Kathmandu and from Assam to the east. Before help could arrive a small British force had been despatched, and while its commander and many of his troops succumbed to malaria in the jungles of the terai, the Bhutanese were driven back. In the wake of this setback, Zhidar had been ousted. (His use of forced labour and diplomatic overtures to the Qing emperor had already offended the ordinary Bhutanese.) He went into exile at Tashilhunpo, seat of the Panchen Lama, who was now offering to mediate in the dispute, so recently and decisively concluded, on behalf of the Bhutanese who, he claimed, in a considerable stretch of the facts, were Tibetan subjects. In this way, the Company tripped over the interests of Tibet, just as they had a few years earlier with the abortive Kinloch expedition to Nepal.

This letter was an unexpected but welcome opportunity for Warren Hastings. As a young man he had been the protégé of Robert Clive, whose victory at Plassey had secured the Company's future in India. Like Bogle, Hastings had started as a clerk, in 1750, a diligent worker who mastered Urdu and Persian in his spare time. His appreciation and understanding of Indian politics and culture had been put to good use in expanding the Company's influence. (Early in his career he had been appalled at the corruption and greed he had witnessed in his fellow officers. Yet thirteen years after Bogle returned from Tibet, Hastings would be subject to one of the most extraordinary trials in British history, prosecuted by the philosopher Edmund Burke and playwright Richard Sheridan for similar misconduct in what became a public airing of Britain's conduct in India.) In the mid 1770s, Hastings was in his mid forties, slight, almost ascetic, dome-headed in Tilly Kettle's portrait of him, magisterially powerful but fizzing too, always curious about his sphere of influence. On the day in late March 1774 that Purangir arrived in his office with the letter from the Panchen Lama, Hastings had his council's approval for a mission to Tibet. Given British ignorance of the Himalaya (was Bhutan another name for Tibet?) a dependable but open and quick-witted young man was required to lead the mission, someone intellectually dynamic, like Hastings himself, but also an adventurer who could charm his way out of trouble: such was Bogle.

Hastings had a soft spot for young Scots, but there were plenty of other reasons to like George. The historian Kate Teltscher described him as 'playful, penetrating, self-deprecating and shrewd', qualities that shine through his account of his Tibetan adventure. This wasn't published until a century after his journey, when his descendants handed over a box brimming with papers to the honorary secretary of the Royal Geographical Society, Clements Markham. Hastings had sent a copy of Bogle's manuscript to his friend Samuel Johnson, after Johnson sent Hastings *A Journey to the Western Islands of Scotland*, but somewhat undersold it as a mere curiosity. Bogle's rich story lay among Johnson's papers, apparently ignored. The Highlander spirit touched both accounts, although Bogle proved far more curious and tolerant of mountain culture than Johnson.

Bogle's father was the wealthy Glasgow merchant George Bogle of Daldowie, one of the Tobacco Lords who made their fortunes during the city's heyday as an elegant commercial centre with comparatively fast links to the American colonies. His education included six months studying logic at Edinburgh University, aged fourteen, before a long apprenticeship in the family business, now run by his elder brother Robert. The family had powerful connections, such as Henry Dundas, Tory politician, pillar of the Scottish Enlightenment and supporter of British influence in India. Jobs in the East India Company were hazardous, as the rapidly filling cemetery at Calcutta showed: around half of those who arrived in Bengal died there. Yet a position with the Company was a golden opportunity for younger sons to get rich quick. That possibility would soon become an issue for the whole Bogle family. After George had been in Calcutta for two years, the same credit crunch that tipped the East India Company towards disaster also ruined the family firm. Bogle's brother Robert was plunged into despair and attempted suicide. (A servant grabbed his shirt tails as he threw himself out of an upstairs window.) Having recovered the balance of his mind, he took action to secure their ageing father's grand house at Daldowie and turned to his younger brother as the best hope of clearing the family's debts. It was now critical to his family's fortunes that George's career was a success.

Bogle won promotions and came to the attention of Warren Hastings, who made him his private secretary. He also fell in with some of the shadier characters then operating in India, living for a time with Lauchlin Macleane, commissary general of the army, a fraudulent speculator whose connections had got him a post in India to clear his mountainous debts. Macleane dazzled those he met with his charm, including Hastings, whose self-absorption left him vulnerable to conmen. Macleane fled India following the Regulating Act of 1773, before his schemes were rumbled. That Bogle navigated such murky terrain with his reputation intact spoke to his affable nature and sharp intelligence. He wrote to his brother Robert that the shameless could prosper in India in ways they wouldn't dare try in Europe:

'several People keep the best Company, and are exceedingly well regarded, who are great Rogues, not only from Suspicion, but even by their own Confession.' Macleane wanted George as his deputy, but Hastings wouldn't let his young protégé go. The decision saved Bogle from the darker corners of the Company's corruption and put him on the high road to Bhutan.

His journey to the mountains in 1774 started at the worst time of year, in the heat of the pre-monsoon, but Bogle proved a doughty and observant traveller. With him went a retinue of more than sixty servants, and a fellow Scotsman, Alexander Hamilton, a tall and robust doctor whose physical presence rather overshadowed the spry Bogle. George kept copious notes, partly at the insistence of Hastings, with the possibility of a book in both their minds. John Hawkesworth's edited version of Captain James Cook's journals from the voyage of the *Endeavour* had proved a racy and contentious sensation. Enlightenment philosophers fed on such tales of exploration as illustrations of their theories about human nature. Bogle's journey offered to fill in a similar blank on the map and might be similarly rewarded. 'As none of the Company's Servants, and I might almost say no European, had ever visited the Country which I was about to enter,' he wrote to his father, 'I was equally in the Dark as to the Road, the Climate or the People.' Tibet, however, was not Australia, and when Bogle finally reached the plateau he would discover the wonders of Europe he brought with him were more familiar than he supposed. The Jesuits had already attuned Tibetans to western philosophy.

Having travelled north across the plains, Bogle arrived at the borders of mountainous Bhutan. Plans conceived in Calcutta had not prepared him for the scale of the Himalaya, or of their suddenness. 'It is impossible to conceive any change of country more abrupt or any contrast more striking.' Everything that caught his eye was noted: the kinds of crops that grew in the fecund climate of Bhutan, the height of waterfalls, vernacular architecture. 'The earth produces its fruits with an ease almost spontaneous, and every puddle is full of fish.' He made his own contribution, planting potatoes to assess their viability on his return. With his eye unclouded by the accounts of other travellers, the image he presents is fresh and almost innocent: 'At the place where the road crosses the mountain, standards or banners are set up, of white cloth, with sentences written upon them. They denote some-thing religious and are common at the tops of hills.' Bogle was looking at 'wind horses', prayer flags printed with the mantra *om mani padme hum*, familiar to any tourist who has trekked in the Himalaya.

Bogle took careful note of any infrastructure for possible military advantage, but he didn't have to be a soldier to realise how difficult fighting would be in these mountains: 'What a Road for Troops,' he wrote in his diary. He made a detailed description of the stunning iron suspension bridge at Chukha, in south-west Bhutan, without apparently knowing that it was one of scores of similar structures attributed to the fifteenth century Tibetan Tangtong Gyalpo, known as the Chakzampa, the 'iron-chain man', a pioneering civil engineer and blacksmith who built dozens of suspension bridges across the Himalaya. Tangtong would have been remarkable for his civil engi-neering alone, but was also a great spiritual adept. He was another *nyon-pa*, a wild one, known as Lungton Nyonpa, 'wild man of the empty valley', a name he used to sign his works, cultivating a myth-ical status like that of the poet Milarepa. Like Milarepa he encapsulates something paradoxical in the Tibetan Buddhist soul: that the illusion of an individual consciousness could be so persuasively real. The bridges he built were as much illustrations of his psychological exper-tise as they were practically useful: ferries and bridges are frequent metaphors in Tibetan Buddhist teaching.

The Panchen Lama's letter had not been an invitation to visit Tibet: Warren Hastings had simply read it that way. So a few days before reaching Tashichho Dzong, residence of the *Druk desi*, Bhutan's prime minister, near the modern capital Thimphu, Bogle found himself in a diplomatic impasse. Another letter from the Panchen Lama inter-cepted him saying it wasn't possible for the British to visit Tibet: the country was subject to China and he needed the emperor's permission to let in a foreigner. That would take a year. A second letter, to Purangir, warned that a smallpox epidemic was raging and the Panchen Lama had withdrawn from Tashilhunpo to a more isolated monastery: it wasn't convenient. Bogle read these excuses as pretexts; he refused to accept the letters or the gifts that accompanied them. Doing so would mean an admission of defeat and a swift return to Calcutta: not the required outcome for a man anxious about his prospects. Sensing that he must put a diplomatic shoulder to the door of Tibet, he despatched Purangir, an enthusiastic supporter of their mission, to visit the Panchen Lama and clear the way.

As he waited for a response, Bogle had time to learn a little about life in Bhutan.

> The more I see of the Bhutanese, the more I am pleased with them. The common people are good-humoured, downright [meaning straight-forward], and I think, thoroughly trusty. The statesmen have some of the art which belongs to their profession. They are the best-built race of men I ever saw; many of them very handsome, with complexions as fair as the French.

Unlike the Jesuits and Capuchins who had visited Bhutan and Tibet, interest in Buddhism among the British diplomats who visited in the late eighteenth and nineteenth was limited. Like the missionaries, Bogle recognised similarities between Tibetan monks and their Roman Catholic counterparts and the institutions they served. But as a Presbyterian, such religiosity left him indifferent: the long cere-monies he felt obliged to attend bored him rigid. Yet religion, and religious division, lay at the core of the relationship between Tibet and Bhutan.

The Bhutanese elites Bogle now met could trace their lineage back almost two hundred years to aristocratic families in Tibet and the exile of their founding spiritual and political leader Ngawang Namgyal. He had been recognised as the eighteenth reincarnated leader of the Druk lineage at Ralung monastery, just north of the Bhutanese border in Tibet, Druk being a branch of the Kagyu school that started with Marpa Lotsawa in the eleventh century. The ruler of Tibet's Tsang province, the most powerful political figure at that time in Tibet, favoured another candidate. Fearing arrest, Namgyal escaped into the remote and defensible mountains to the south and set about estab-lishing a new kingdom that would eventually encompass modern Bhutan. In his mid twenties and under continuous existential threat from successive Tsang princes, Namgyal, who became known as Shabdrung, meaning 'at the feet of', set about carving out a new semi-theocratic state. In 1621, he founded Chagri monastery high in the Thimphu valley, where he felt sufficiently secure to embark on a three-year retreat. He brought the first known Europeans to visit

Bhutan, the Jesuit missionaries Estêvão Cacella and João Cabral, to this monastery in 1627. Cacella wrote to his masters:

> For two months we accompanied the King through these and other mountains until we reached his house which is situated in the mountain where he went on retreat; he keeps no more than his lamas with him because the place cannot hold more people as in order to build a house one would have to cut many rocks and work very hard to level some space in that very steep mountain; he had chosen that place to protect himself from a King who lives some eight days distance from here, Demba Cemba [Karma Tenkyong], the most important king of Bhotanta [Tibet].

In fact, the main concern of this important king, Karma Tenkyong, lay elsewhere: the Tsang's struggle with the Geluk-pa and their Mongol supporters. Bhutan was a side issue. But the Tsang-pa still made repeated efforts to crush Namgyal's new state. To defend themselves, Namgyal's followers built impressive monastic castles – *dzong* – to defend their new kingdom from its enemies. The most impressive was at Simtokha, completed in 1629, which dominated a strategic crossroads and the approach to the capital. This was the site of the so-called Battle of the Five Lamas in 1634, when disgruntled local religious leaders combined with Tsang military force to storm the castle. The story goes that the *dzong*'s gunpowder store exploded unexpectedly, destroying the invaders. In the aftermath, Namgyal was able to establish a new legal code, the *Tsa Yig Chenmo*, a monastic form of constitution that bound leading landowners to his new Druk state. Bhutan's tight cultural homogeneity springs from this period: Bhutan's name for itself is Drukyul, or Druk country, and the state supports the Druk school financially. Some rival schools were banned, including the lineage the bridge-builder Tangtong had founded there. As the new and rising power of the Geluk strengthened its grip on Tibet from the mid seventeenth century, that school too was forbidden. When Ngawang Namgyal died in 1651, the news was kept secret for fifty-four years: the state was too vulnerable to admit the loss of its inspirational leader. Handing on his powers to a similarly capable leader proved impossible. Yet splitting up his different roles ensured two hundred years of factionalism and infighting.

Bogle witnessed an explosive illustration of this as the rivalry between Bhutan's exiled political leader Zhidar and the new *desi*, Kunga Rinchen, was fought out in front of him. A conspiracy to reinstate Zhidar was discovered and his supporters fled to the *dzong* at Simtokha. Stationed a few kilometres south, Bogle watched from his window as the fighting ebbed and flowed. Many of the soldiers were local villagers and although their weaponry was antiquated – cane helmets and shields – it was effective. Their firearms were antiques but the Bhutanese also used six-foot bows with iron-tipped arrows, sometimes coated in poison. Hamilton was kept busy patching up the wounded. Eventually Kunga Rinchen won control, burning rebel villages and cutting off supplies to Simtokha. The rebels fled over the mountains to Tibet.

A day later Bogle and Hamilton set out to follow them for their audience with the Panchen Lama, who despite warnings from Lhasa was sympathetic to Purangir's arguments. The young Dalai Lama's regent might technically be in charge, but the Panchen Lama was the most senior monk in Tibet and had a personal connection with the Qianlong emperor. He would listen to the British. It was now mid October and the first snows of winter coated the tops of the foothills, but in less than a month the two Scotsmen were face to face with the Panchen Lama. In Kettle's painting the Lama is imagined as a compact figure, neat and composed. The reality was more corpulent and jovial. 'His complexion,' Bogle wrote,

is fairer than that of most of the Tibetans, and his arms are as white as those of a European; his hair, which is jet black, is cut very short; his beard and whiskers never above a month long; his eyes are small and black. The expression of his countenance is smiling and good-humoured. His father was a Tibetan; his mother a near relation of the Rajahs of Ladak. From her he learned the Hindustani language, of which he has a moderate knowledge, and is fond of speaking it. His disposition is open, candid, and generous. He is extremely merry and entertaining in conversation, and tells a pleasant story with a great deal of humour and action. I endeavoured to find out, in his character, those defects which are inseparable from humanity, but he is so universally beloved that I had no success, and not a man could find in his heart to speak ill of him.

Bogle found himself no less a subject of interest, with crowds coming to look at him 'as people go to look at the lions in the Tower'. The Panchen Lama offered to have them removed, but Bogle demurred, acknowledging that he was just as interested in them. He was a close observer of human behaviour, watching how the lama gave his blessing to the crowds that gathered at his throne. Aristocrats and *gyelong*, or senior monks, received his bare hand on their heads. Nuns and regular laymen had a cloth interposed between their heads and his hand. The riff-raff were touched as he passed them with a tassel he held in his hand. Bogle noticed too the Panchen Lama's generosity. Around a hundred and fifty *gosain* were lodged with him, some on business, others on 'pilgrimage', although Bogle noticed these Hindu pilgrims seemed most interested in their monthly allowance of tea, butter and flour, as well as cash. These 'Gentoo fakirs' were, in Bogle's estimation, 'a very worthless set of people, devoid of principle'. He speculated on the Panchen Lama's tolerance. 'This charity to the pilgrims flows, I imagine,' Bogle wrote, 'partly from the generosity of the Lama's temper, partly from the desire of acquiring information, and satisfying his curiosity about Hindustan, the school of the religion of Tibet.'

Bogle comes across as down-to-earth, amiable and pragmatic; he was culturally open and while he greeted the Panchen Lama in European dress, he soon adopted Tibetan clothing and habits. The metaphysical complexities of the Panchen Lama's philosophy, however, were not for him. 'The religion of the Lamas is somehow connected with that of the Hindus, though I will not pretend to say how.' While acutely observant of religious ritual and social structure, the history of the Panchen Lama's religious order was of subordinate interest to the matter at hand: trade. The recent political history of Tibet was of crucial importance to his mission and Bogle would later explain to his masters in Calcutta how it was that China had two political agents, the ambans, stationed in Lhasa: 'About seventy years ago, the Emperor of China acquired the sovereignty of Tibet, in the way that sovereignties are generally acquired, by interfering in the quarrels between two contending parties.' It was, Bogle knew, a trick the British had mastered in India.

If the authorities in Lhasa had the Chinese ambans looking over their shoulder, there was a similar distrust in Tibet of the new power to the south. 'In former times,' Bogle reported, when Europeans were settled in Hindustan merely as merchants, there would have been no difficulty in establishing factories and freedom of trade; but the power and elevation to which the English have now risen render them the objects of jealousy to all their neighbours. The opposition which was made to my proceeding into Tibet, as well as the many difficulties I had to encounter in the execution of my commission, arose from this source. The government at Lhasa considered me as sent to explore the country, which the ambition of the English might afterwards prompt them to invade, and their superiority in arms render their attempt successful.

On the other hand, it would have been foolish not to engage with an emerging power in the holy land of India. Furthermore, the new Gorkha regime in Kathmandu had upended centuries of trade and useful relations. Newari art and architecture had adorned the Himalayan Buddhist world for centuries. Good relations with the powerful rival of this unwelcome new neighbour were desirable. The Panchen Lama also showed great interest in establishing a centre for pilgrims in Bengal, re-establishing a connection with Tibet's spiritual roots centuries after the fall of Bengal's Pala dynasty.

There was another aspect to Bogle's journey to Tibet that is easy to overlook in the broader narrative of trade and diplomacy. He liked Tibet and he liked Tibetans. 'In their private character they are decent and exemplary, and, if I may judge of others by one under whose roof I lived, they are humane, charitable, and intelligent.' During his mission Bogle had been anxious to get back to Calcutta but once there he found he missed the Panchen Lama. Bogle performed kindnesses for him from afar, having his watches mended and sending him chess sets. He wrote his book, drifting a little, and then settled into a dull posting as a revenue collector. Diplomacy with Tibet rested now on the capable shoulders of Purangir, who in 1776 oversaw the building of a pilgrim and trade house for the Panchen Lama at Howrah near Calcutta, on the shores of the Hooghly river: the Bhot Bhawan, the 'Tibet mansion', a refuge for Tibetan pilgrims visiting the sacred sites of the Buddha's life. Hastings might have failed to open a trade route with Tibet, but the Panchen Lama had got his listening post in India.

Diplomacy would be the Panchen Lama's undoing. In the decade before Bogle's visit, the Qianlong emperor had commissioned a temple at the Manchu summer capital of Chengde, in Hebei province north-east of Beijing, to celebrate his sixtieth birthday in 1771. Called the Putuo Zhongcheng, it was modelled on the Potala, the Dalai Lama's palace in Lhasa, an architectural expression of Qing solidarity with (and superiority to) its minorities. Summoned a decade later to Chengde for the Qianlong emperor's seventieth-birthday celebrations, the Panchen Lama faced a dilemma: risk a perilous journey and the dangers of smallpox or pass up a golden diplomatic opportunity. There would be a strong Mongol presence at the party, an opportunity too good to miss. Purangir went with him, meeting the Panchen Lama en route at the Geluk monastery of Kumbum. Purangir later told the British that the Panchen Lama had indeed mentioned the matter of trade between the East India Company and China to the Qing emperor, but the Company only had his word for it. By then the Panchen Lama had succumbed to smallpox, the disease he knew was waiting for him. He faced death, in the Tibetan Buddhist way, sitting propped against a wall, cross-legged, meditating his way towards the 'light of the void'. Purangir was among the few close followers with him at the end.

Four months later, early in 1781, George Bogle, wholly ignorant of his Tibetan friend's death, himself drowned, aged thirty-four, while taking his daily bath in a Calcutta water tank. 'Sunk beneath the water,' wrote Kate Teltscher, 'were Bogle's charm and penetration, his curiosity and ambition, his talent for friendship and diplomatic flair.' He was buried beneath a massive sarcophagus in Calcutta's South Park Street Cemetery and then largely forgotten until Clements Markham, who ran the geographical section at the India Office, discovered Bogle's book in his grandfather's papers, his grandfather having been a secretary to Warren Hastings. Its publication in 1876 allowed Bogle a little of the fame the Scotsman undoubtedly deserved, albeit posthumously, as did his companion Alexander Hamilton, who died four years before Bogle of fever in the malarial foothills of Cooch Behar.

★

The yaks Hastings wanted Bogle to bring back from Tibet did arrive in Calcutta but not until years later, with the second diplomatic mission to Tibet in 1783, led by Samuel Turner. Only the male survived to make the long journey to Britain, where George Stubbs painted him in a work titled 'The Yak of Tartary'. The yak was stuffed after death and appeared as an exhibit in the Crystal Palace. Turner's account of his journey, published in 1798 after he returned to Britain, caused a minor literary sensation. Tibet became what we might now call a meme: Turner's audience with the young Panchen Lama, the reincarnate of the man Bogle had known, was particularly affecting to a British audience. The Irish poet and lyricist Thomas Moore – 'Melody' Moore, friend of Byron – wrote a piece of froth about the boy, 'The Little Grand Lama':

> In Thibet once there reign'd, we're told,
> A little Lama, one year old –
> Rais'd to the throne, that realm to bless,
> Just when his little Holiness
> Had cut – as near as can be reckon'd –
> Some say his *first* tooth, some his *second*.

Thus was one of the most enigmatic, complex and culturally rich spiritual and philosophical traditions the world has known bowdlerised for the entertainment of the British public. Some of that twee naïvety suffuses Rudyard Kipling's Tibetan character in *Kim*: the Teshoo Lama, the name borrowed from the title of Turner's account.

There was a coda to Bogle's journey to Tibet. In 1948 a woman called Nora Heathcote, outraged at seeing George Bogle described in the *Sunday Times* as being an Englishman, wrote to the paper to correct their mistake and to claim descent from him through a Tibetan lady said to be the sister of the Panchen Lama, a woman named in the family's papers as Tichan, perhaps a corruption of the Tibetan name Dechen. Clements Markham, in his 1876 edition of Bogle's book, mentioned two daughters, Martha and Mary, who were put on board a ship to Britain after Bogle's death so they could be raised by his family. Whether these were daughters of a Tibetan princess or a Bengali common-law wife is uncertain. Bogle certainly had an affair in Tibet, because his travelling companion, the doctor Alexander Hamilton, was prescribing him a mercury ointment on the trek home, commonly used for venereal disease. The British diplomat and Tibet scholar Hugh Richardson had a correspondence with Nora Heathcote, who was born in 1876, and disentangled the complex family history of the Bogle family. There were likely sons as well as daughters, and while he discounted the idea that 'Tichan' was the sister of the Panchen Lama, he thought it probable that Bogle had a child with a Tibetan woman, and that some Himalayan blood still ran in Scottish veins.

Although, like so many of his colleagues and friends, Bogle died a young man, and the fame he might have enjoyed went to Samuel Turner, Bogle's diplomatic efforts in establishing trade links with Tibet were successful, if short-lived. Throughout the 1780s, relations between Bengal and Tibet continued to prosper and trade increased. Purangir returned to Tibet with Turner's mission and again without British supervision in 1785. He described commerce at Tashilhunpo as flourishing, with Indian merchants making huge profits on the advantageous exchange rate available to them in Tibet. This happy state of affairs might have continued but for the bitter trade war that was about to break out between Nepal and Tibet. Purangir spent more and more time at Bhot Bhawan, the temple at Howrah, where he perished in 1795, confronting robbers who had broken in: the *gosain* was buried in the garden.

Samuel Turner, leader of the second Tibet mission, shared Bogle's love of the Himalaya. He took with him a surveyor and artist called Samuel Davis, whose watercolours of Bhutan offer an elegant insight into a world that had barely changed since Cabral's visit in the early 1600s and wouldn't much until the arrival of tourism in the 1970s. His own portrayal of the Bhutanese, 'strangers to extortion, cruelty, and bloodshed', is similarly positive. Then something changed; the British hardened their minds against the cultures around them. The botanist William Griffith, medical officer on the Bhutan trade mission of 1837, offered a wholly different view of the Bhutanese: 'they shewed themselves to be ignorant, greedy barbarians, such as should be punished first, and commanded afterwards'. Shortly before the British invaded Bhutan in 1864, Ashley Eden, who had travelled there the year before as special envoy, described the people as 'an idle race, indifferent to everything except fighting and killing one another'. The enchantment George Bogle had experienced in Tibet, the 'fairy dream' as he called it, faded to nothing, replaced with the cold, hard calculation of commerce.

8

Trade Wars

The remote frontier settlement of Rasuwagadhi lies on the border between Nepal and Tibet, at an altitude of 1,800 metres. Immediately beneath it is the Trisuli river, called the Kyirong in Tibet; to its west is the Himalayan giant Langtang Lirung: on a clear autumn morning, it's this mountain, over sixty kilometres away, that dominates the Kathmandu valley's northern skyline. Nearby is the Tibetan peak of Shisha Pangma, fourteenth highest mountain in the world. A rail link between such a remote high place and India's network on the plains at near sea-level may seem fanciful but that is exactly what is currently proposed: a branch line on Chinese President Xi Jinping's global plan to recreate the Silk Roads. 'We hope,' China's senior diplomat Wang Yi said in 2018, 'that such cooperation can contribute to the development and prosperity of all three countries. Personally I have a dream, to travel to China from Nepal across the Himalayas in a modern train, enjoying the scenic beauty.' This growth in traffic will change the Himalaya for ever, perhaps to the disappointment of romantics, and certainly at some environmental cost. But the potential for economic development in an impoverished region makes such schemes almost inevitable.

Already, China has built a high-speed rail link to Shigatse, the seat of the Panchen Lama, some three hundred kilometres from Rasuwagadhi, whisking Chinese tourists to the monastery of Tashilhunpo, these days a nexus in China's influence on Tibetan Buddhism. A new road and dry port facility has already been built in the narrow Kyirong valley at the border. Damaged by the 2015 earthquake that struck Nepal, it was repaired and reopened two years later. More recently, China and Nepal have agreed that the railway to Shigatse will be extended to Kathmandu through the Kyirong, among the most beautiful and sacred valleys of Tibet.

Exploiting the tension caused in Delhi by its closer ties with China, Nepal has also signed a deal with India to connect Kathmandu with the subcontinent's extensive rail network. Nepal already has access to India's railways. Less than thirty kilometres up the line from Sagauli Junction is the border crossing between the frontier towns of Raxaul, on the Indian side, and Birgunj, now the second-largest city on Nepal's terai. At the start of the twentieth century, Birgunj was little more than a handful of villages but its location, directly between Kathmandu and British India, made it the obvious place to build a customs post. The town's significance grew in 1927 when the British completed a narrow-gauge railway into Nepal, improving connectivity between an ally who had sacrificed its sons during the Great War and markets south of the border. Although much of that line is now defunct, the section at the border has recently been upgraded to the modern Indian network's broad gauge, linking Indian Raxaul to Nepali Birgunj's new container storage facility. Many obstacles lie in the path of both these schemes. But even if they don't come to fruition, there is already a strong economic and political argument to re-energise the ancient trade route that once linked India to the Tibetan plateau. Whether China will permit this ancient road's other role of cultural artery, drawing the lifeblood of Indian creativity onto the Tibetan plateau, is another matter.

Across the Himalayan belt, since before recorded history, pilgrims, artisans and above all traders travelled the high country north to the Silk Roads of Central Asia and south to the plains of India, using those Himalayan valleys and gorges that were amenable to pack animals, their belongings and goods carried by yaks at altitude and mules, or else on the backs of human porters. Much of the conflict and political tension in the Himalaya coalesced around these lucrative pinch points, the narrow 'money rivers' of this wild, remote country. The British historian John Pemble has described such trade in the eastern Himalaya as 'a feeble trickle' and 'a peddling business in luxury goods, carried on mainly at the behest of the wealthy and curious'. In the context of nineteenth-century global trade, this is arguably true; the East India Company was initially curious about grabbing a share of this trade but concluded it wasn't worth the trouble, finally prefer-

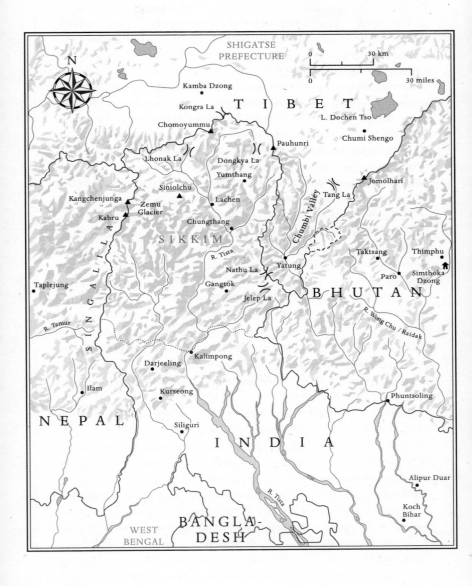

ring instead to use the mountains as a protective barrier. Yet the wealth this 'peddling' generated underpinned the spectacular artistic legacy of Himalayan centres like the Kathmandu and Yarlung Tsangpo valleys. Trade also funded an immense cultural transfer, the importation of Buddhism to the Tibetan plateau and along with it Indian and Chinese art and technology. In the western Himalaya, there was also huge trade in what was called shawl wool or cashmere, since Kashmir is where Europeans first encountered it, more commonly now pashmina, Persian for 'woolen'. The best source for this was the Chang Tang of Ngari Khorsum, the high country north of the old Guge kingdom where nomads with terrifying mastiffs drove goats and sheep to wool marts with close access to Himalayan trading routes, particularly at Gartok, west of Kailas. The Indus and Sutlej rivers offered ready access to Ladakh and Kashmir in the west and Indian hill-states to the south, where the people of Lahaul in particular dominated the trade, taking shares in the immense flocks on the high plateau.

Alongside this international exchange is a quieter story: most Himalayan trade routes and the products that were carried along them were local and of negligible value to the wider economy: grains, foodstuffs and salt, breeding animals, medicinal herbs. It might not have looked valuable to the wider world, but this trade also formed the bedrock of a vibrant and complex cultural exchange that characterises the Himalaya no less than grand temples or exquisite statues. If you measure success in turnover, then you could perhaps judge this Himalayan trade as trivial: in terms of the societies it fostered, it was vital.

The fault line in this web of ethnicity and trade was always between ethnic Tibetan populations, genetically adapted to life at high altitude, and those from the south; to paraphrase the Italian anthropologist Giuseppe Tucci, the 'rice–lama line', between rice-growers from the south and Tibetan Buddhists from the north. Growing food at altitude is difficult and limited to particular crops, and so the risks inherent to trade become more worthwhile. For most of Himalayan history, traders could make a small fortune in the space of a few harvests. Trade also encouraged a more cosmopolitan outlook; hospitality in a tough environment like the Himalaya is not desirable, it's essential. The anthropologist Christoph von Fürer-Haimendorf described 'a system of hospitality ideally suited to the needs of long-distance traders not only in need of shelter in an inclement climate but dependent for their business on relationships of personal trust established and strengthened by occasions for conviviality'. It was on the trade routes of the eastern Himalaya that the Sherpa reputation for hospitality was born.

In the modern era, China's occupation of Tibet in the 1950s casually brushed away most of this delicate web from its high, dusty corner, a loss the wider world hardly noticed. Many of the customary local trade routes, which had existed long before nation states, were abruptly closed. The borderlands of the Himalaya turned from a space into a line: something fluid and magical turned to stone. On top of that, the human 'boundary', the 'rice–lama line' between those adapted to altitude and those not, was offset from the political boundary, which ran along the crest of the mountains. As a consequence, large popu- lations of ethnic Tibetans, such as the Sherpa, people who had since time immemorial relied on freedom of movement, were trapped on the wrong side of a new and seemingly arbitrary line, more or less cut off from their root. The consequences were predictably distressing, and not just materially: Tibetans, with their strong nomadic tradition, like to travel. Even in remote Tibetan villages, it was once common- place to find individuals who had crossed the length and narrow breadth of the Himalaya. Now they travel to India to study or for an audience with the Dalai Lama, and often at great personal cost in terms of harassment and worse from China's security forces.

Inside Nepal, the results were equally dramatic but also intriguing, sometimes prompting a realignment of identity to suit the new prevailing conditions. In the early 1970s, little more than a decade after the Dalai Lama's flight from Tibet prompted the hardening of the border, Fürer-Haimendorf met ethnic Tibetans living in the old Nepali frontier village of Mugu, far to the west of Kathmandu, part of what had once been the medieval Khasa kingdom centred in the Sinja valley. This group had been trading from here across the border into 'official' Tibet for centuries; their distant ancestors helped build the Buddhist monastery in the Limi valley to the west. Now they were presenting themselves as Chhetri, a Hindu caste, turning their Tibetan faces away from the high plateau towards the more Hindu-oriented middle hills where they were now confined. (On the flip side, the Tibetan diaspora, which China's occupation created, led to a spiritual resurgence in

Buddhism south of the Himalaya wherever exiled Tibetans found sanctuary, a resurgence that sparked interest from foreign tourists, spreading that resurgence even further.)

While much Himalayan trade was for centuries local and small-scale, some was of immense value and sometimes extraordinarily distant. It was this trade that underpinned the artistic brilliance of Kathmandu and attracted the attention of the East India Company. We have already seen how gold financed the expansion of the Tibetan Empire and the acquisition and translation of Buddhist texts. ('Like a spring of precious gold bursting out upon the ground,' wrote the eleventh-century tantric master Nirupa, 'all the learned Indians come to Tibet.') Trade in rhubarb, prized in Chinese medicine, flourished on the Silk Roads in the first millennium; Marco Polo saw it growing in its native habitat, on the north-east fringes of the Tibetan plateau. As we have seen, more unusual items, like yak tails, used as flywhisks in Indian temples, were recorded in ancient Rome. But the most important luxury product was musk: glandular secretions from deer used in the manufacture of perfume and traditional medicine. This is still one of the most expensive animal products anywhere in the world, to the detriment of modern musk deer. In antiquity its value was astronomical.

★

As early as the ninth century, Arab doctors were writing in praise of Tibetan musk, on sale in the souks of Mecca. The smell of it was so strong that when ships arrived at the old port of Basra, in modern-day Iraq, customs officials knew if musk was on board. It had been exported to the Middle East since at least the third century, long before the rise of Islam, but its role in Islamic culture undoubtedly boosted trade. When Arab and Persian poets wanted to evoke the fragrance of their beloved, they turned to musk. In Shiraz during the tenth century the Persian author al-Tha'alibi described a debate at court in which one contestant, the globetrotter Abu Dulaf, made his selection for the finest products and services available to mankind through the munificence of Allah: silks from China; Kyrgyz squirrel fur; Greek eunuchs; slave girls from Bukhara; concubines from Samarkand: 'may he let me eat the apples of Syria, the fresh dates of Iraq, the bananas of the

Yemen, the nuts of India ... And may He let me breathe the musk of Tibet.'

Tibetan musk, and that of Kashmir, was prized over its Chinese competition, in part because of the Himalayan aromatic herbs, including spikenard, which the musk deer browsed. Tibet was also closer to the Middle East, and Tibetan merchants had the habit of leaving the musk pod unadulterated. Chinese producers would open them to add other materials, and traders weren't averse to passing off the inferior Chinese version as Tibetan, a process made easier because Tibetan traders didn't travel far beyond their plateau: musk was sold on to traders operating along the fringes of the Himalaya. The Sogdians were the great trading group of the Silk Road, and letters in their language from the fourth century, recovered from the Dunhuang Caves, mention musk acquired from the Tibetan borderlands of modern Gansu. There are documentary traces of its journey through Central Asia to the Arab port of Daybul on the Indus delta in modern Pakistan, from where it was distributed throughout the Arab world.

Jewish merchants also had a significant role in the musk trade. The Sephardi traveller Benjamin of Tudela travelled throughout the Middle East in the second half of the twelfth century and wrote a book about his experiences, a century before Marco Polo. He too writes of Tibetan musk, the first European reference. Translated later from Hebrew into Latin for the European market, *The Travels of Benjamin* became another tributary feeding the stream of travel compendia that permeated Western scholarship.

There are fewer literary clues about the musk trade at the start of its journey, in the Himalaya, although deer have a spiritually symbolic presence. There is a story from a Tibetan hagiography about the *mahasiddha* Padampa Sangye, a contemporary of Milarepa from the eleventh century, born in southern India but closely associated with the Tingri region of Tibet, close to Everest. It tells how he built his monastery around a stone thrown by the Buddha to indicate where his teachings would flourish north of the mountains. Padampa Sangye found the stone at Tingri with musk deer circling around it, and then dissolving *into* it. The potent medical properties of musk are associated with Padampa's teaching.

Another reference, this one in the *Blue Annals*, written in the fifteenth century, captures an illuminating example of how trade and tantric

teaching collided to transform Tibet in the eleventh century. Kor
Nirupa, quoted above, was born in 1062, an inauspicious year, as the
fifth son, an inauspicious number, and sent off to Lhasa to be a monk.
(His sister threw a handful of dirt after him as he left, a sign of ostra-
cism.) In Lhasa he met two students of Atisa, the great Indian scholar,
who had died a few years before. One of them was a Newar,
Anutapagupta, who taught him Sanskrit for a year and then sent him
off to collect a book from the widow of a translator. Nirupa, still only
nine years old, ended up working at a gold mine, where his belongings were stolen. So he cast a magic spell, a move very much from
pre-Buddhist Tibet, and discovered enough gold to meet his obligation
to the Newar. Not long after, his father died and he went home to
pay his respects, where he dug up a chunk of turquoise his sister had
hidden. This he sold for a weight of gold, 'one roll of gold embroidered silk and musk worth one golden *zho*', around five grams. With
this he set off for Kathmandu with his two friends, to be initiated into
the mysteries of tantric Buddhism.

Arab sources give us clues about the species of deer involved – the
favoured animal, they reported, was small and lived in forests, presumably at lower altitudes – and how it was collected. The ninth-century
geographer Ahmad al-Ya'qubi, in the *Kitab al-Buldan*, the Book of
Lands, born at the time of Tibet's tsenpo emperors, centuries before
Benjamin of Tudela, wrote that

> it was well known that the origin of musk was in Tibet and elsewhere.
> The local traders there build something like a little tower, which has
> the height of a forearm. The animal in whose navel the musk is
> produced comes and scratches its navel on this tower so that the navel
> falls off [meaning the musk gland]. The traders go there at a certain
> time of year, which is known to them and gather the navels freely.
> When they bring it to Tibet, they have to pay tax on it.

*

We know just how important the duties paid on musk were thanks
to the extraordinary records of an Armenian merchant called
Hovhannes Joughayetsi, who spent five years living in Lhasa from
1686. This was only twenty-five years after the Jesuits Johann Grueber

and Albert d'Orville, commonly regarded as the first Europeans to reach the Tibetan capital. Their interest was theological: their mission to save souls. Hovhannes went to make money. Both wrote about their experiences, but Hovhannes's account was simply that: his accounts. There are precious few references to the colour or drama of the road he travelled, no burning zeal to save souls. When Hovhannes mentions God, it's to ask his protection from bandits, not to speculate on the metaphysics of tantric Buddhism. When he arrives in Lhasa, he is required to pay duty on the goods he has imported, totalling eleven and a half kilos of silver, a handy revenue stream for the government. A rupee at this time was worth around eleven grams of silver; Hovhannes was paying his servant forty rupees a year, less than half a kilo. For every litre of musk he bought, he had to pay the Tibetan treasury thirty-eight grams of silver.

What an Armenian was doing in Lhasa in the 1680s is another matter. In the early seventeenth century, the region that is modern-day Armenia was split between Persia and its bitter rival the Ottoman Empire. In 1604, Persia's Safavid leader Shah Abbas invaded western Armenia and then withdrew, burning towns and villages as he went, bringing home with him a huge population of Armenians. The peasantry was put to work growing silk; the merchant classes, well known for their commercial acumen, were set up in Nor Jougha, a suburb of the Shah's extraordinary new capital at Isfahan in central Persia, tasked with building trade networks across Asia and the Middle East. Armenian merchants were known as *khoja*, a respected class of Christians in the eyes of Islam, part of the religiously tolerant world Shah Abbas encouraged. In 1683, two such merchants hired Hovhannes to trade for them in India. They would get three-quarters of the profit, Hovhannes the rest. Their range of operations was impressive, extending all the way from Western Europe to the Levant and into East Asia. When he left Nor Jougha for India, Hovhannes carried with him hundreds of yards of red and green English broadcloth to sell.

For reasons unknown, the accounts ledger Hovhannes kept while living in Lhasa surfaced in Lisbon. It's possible he died there after returning to Europe. It lays out the Armenian's profit and loss in painstaking detail, necessarily so since his well-being relied on its accuracy. Hovhannes had studied all aspects of trade in Isfahan, from foreign weights and measures, to taxation law and accountancy, so he knew that if he didn't provide an exact reckoning of how he'd spent his masters' money as soon as he got home he could be jailed and whipped every day for a year. His understandable attention to detail offers a dry but hugely revealing insight into the complex world of Himalayan trade, the sophisticated financial instruments it relied on, how important it was to the local economy and just how international the Himalaya has been for much of its history.

In the late seventeenth century, trade in much of the subcontinent was still regulated by the Mughals, and although Agra was no longer their capital, it remained a crucial hub with a thriving Armenian population that worshipped at their Orthodox church. Hovhannes based himself here for more than two years, travelling around India, buying goods and then selling them on. In 1684 for example, he bought two tons of indigo at Khurja, weighed, pleasingly, in *charms*, and travelled to the Gujarati port of Surat in Western India to ship a portion back to Isfahan and Basra in modern Iraq. Like all merchants, he relied on the sophisticated Mughal banking system that allowed large sums to be remitted across the trading network that he and his colleagues inhabited, a system that had impressed and inspired earlier European financiers.

By early 1686, Hovhannes had built up his own capital and signed an agreement establishing a new company with a partner from Shiraz to embark on a far more adventurous trading mission, to the country he described as Butand, meaning Bhot, or Tibet. He was still working for his masters in Isfahan, but now he had his own stake in the game. If Jesuit missionaries were bringing the word of God to the Buddhist holy land, Hovhannes used the new company's capital to take things to trade: amber and pearls, bolts of fabric and much more besides, goods worth over eight thousand rupees, equivalent to about ninety-four kilos of silver. He also hired servants to travel with him and bought gunpowder and bullets to protect them all on the road. He left Agra on 12 February 1686 for Shikohabad, in the modern state of Uttar Pradesh, named for the Mughal emperor Aurangzeb's brother, and there joined a caravan east to Patna, in Bihar on the south bank of the Ganges, with its important Armenian population, where he bought more cloth to trade.

The choice of route was revealing. Although he had contacts in Patna, Hovhannes also knew that war had badly affected trade in the western Himalaya in the early 1680s. The fifth Dalai Lama's government in Lhasa had sent an army to Ladakh in 1679, partly because Ladakh's Druk Kagyu Buddhists were giving support to their co-religionists in Bhutan, and partly to challenge Druk intolerance of Geluk monks. In response, the Ladakhis asked the Mughals, their new and powerful neighbours in Kashmir, to help them out with some military brawn under the leadership of the Mughal general Fidai Khan. At the most westerly point of the Tibetan plateau and bordering Muslim countries, Ladakh's Buddhists had faced the greatest challenge from Islam in the high Himalaya: their *chogyal*, or king, had recently promised to build the first mosque in the Ladakhi capital Leh to placate the Mughal emperor Aurangzeb. In response, the Tibetans allied with Dzungar Mongols to drive their common enemies back. A peace treaty was signed in 1684 but Ladakh paid a heavy price. The kingdom lost a huge amount of territory to Kashmiri Muslims, and trade in wool and goat's hair, around half the Ladakhi economy, became their opponent's monopoly. Significant numbers of Muslims relocated across the Zoji La, the pass linking Kashmir to Ladakh, to establish themselves at Leh and other major Ladakhi towns, marrying local women and altering Ladakh's demography for good. They came to dominate this western trade route all the way to Lhasa, where a sizable Kashmiri population also settled. The Jesuit Ippolito Desideri met Kashmiri merchants at Leh on his way to Lhasa in 1715. (They claimed he wasn't a priest at all but a wealthy foreign merchant carrying pearls, gems and other precious merchandise.) By the late nineteenth century, after Ladakh had been absorbed into Jammu and Kashmir, Leh had more than a hundred Kashmiri shops in the main bazaar, where caravans from all over Central Asia and the Himalaya converged.

In April 1686, Hovhannes journeyed north from Patna to reach the Kathmandu valley, having paid tax at the border to import his goods. For three months he rested in Bhaktapur, where the king Jitamitra Malla was adding to the city's architectural lustre, expanding and beautifying its palaces and temples – all paid for by currency trading with Tibet and duties from merchants like Hovhannes, who along with the usual bribes, was asked to hand over the English spyglass he carried with him. The Armenian took more than two months to reach Lhasa, travelling up the fast-flowing Bhote Kosi, the 'Tibet river', and across the mountains to Kuti, known now as Nyalam, where he kicked his heels until the local chief returned to seal the goods for onward travel. He visited Shigatse, seat of the fifth Panchen Lama, Lobsang Yeshe, who was becoming embroiled in the provincial wars that would plague Tibet in the early eighteenth century. When Hovhannes reached the capital in September, there to welcome him was a small Armenian merchant community largely overlooked by history. The Jesuits Grueber and d'Orville and those missionaries like Desideri that came after are the ones remembered: adventurous servants of God piercing the veil of a hidden world behind the mountains. Hovhannes was more of this world. He short-changed his servants, but not too badly, and wasn't averse to a little smuggling, avoiding duties on some of the precious stones he carried. As a non-Muslim in the Mughal Empire, he was required to pay a poll tax, called the *jizya*; this he dodged with a false certificate.

The Tibetan world Hovhannes encountered in Lhasa must have felt very different to that of the Christian missionaries who followed. He arrived four years after the fifth Dalai Lama's death, but before that fact had been made public or the Qing Kangxi emperor had been informed. During the almost five years he spent there, Hovhannes learned Tibetan and dealt with all the complexities of operating a business in a foreign country: adjusting to local customs, breathing the thin air, dealing with crooked officials, paying taxes and arguing his case in commercial disputes. Although he stayed put in the city, he used other Armenian and Tibetan merchants to trade for him in Xining, some eighteen hundred kilometres to the north-east, on the fringes of the Tibetan plateau, now the largest city in historical Tibet. He did deals with Newars living in Lhasa, and came into contact with merchants from other ethnic groups: more Kashmiris, known in Lhasa as Kachee, soon to build their first mosque in the city, and the Hindu *gosain* so familiar to George Bogle. With the money he made from selling the goods he brought from India, Hovhannes mostly bought musk, gold and tea. This had been traded for centuries via the so-called Tea Horse Road that linked Sichuan, immediately to the east of Tibet, with the plateau, with Tibetan ponies being sent in return to China. Musk was his most lucrative concern. By the time he left Lhasa in 1692, Hovhannes had bought almost half a metric tonne of the stuff, worth a fortune in the souks of the Middle East. The duties he owed the Tibetan treasury must have totalled tens of thousands of rupees.

★

Achieving such success had required a monumental effort of concentration. Lhasa was not an easy place to do business. Not only were
his partners and competitors trying to trick him, the government did
its best to extract as much of his profit as possible, using weights and
measures that cheated the merchants. Another scam to which
Hovhannes fell prey would ultimately become a cause of war between
Nepal and Tibet. Three days after he arrived in Lhasa, Hovhannes
was required to pay import duties on the goods he'd brought from
Patna, just as he had in Nepal. This was done in kind to a particular
value of silver and a promissory note given to the Armenian guaran-
teeing he would be reimbursed a proportion of this heavy tax in silver
coins. When they came, the coins were found to be impure: the silver
the Tibetan authorities were using was debased. Yet the purchase tax
Hovhannes paid on the musk he was buying had to be paid for in
pure silver. The Himalayan economy was becoming a clear illustration
of Gresham's law: bad money driving out good.

It was a system guaranteed to infuriate your trading partners, except
that Tibet was on the receiving end of the same scam: the Newari
kings who minted Tibet's coins were also at it. They had started
supplying Tibet with its coinage earlier in the seventeenth century
during the reign of the fifth Dalai Lama. Tibet would send pure silver
to be minted and the Newars would send back coins of the same
weight alloyed with a certain amount of copper; the balance of silver
was their profit. How closely they stuck to the agreed amount was
carefully scrutinised. The Tibetans experimented with minting their
own coins in the 1660s and 1680s, just before Hovhannes arrived, but
they remained reliant on the Kathmandu valley for their currency for
another hundred years. However, when the Gorkha raja Prithvi
Narayan Shah conquered the Kathmandu valley in 1767, eighty years
after Hovhannes returned there from Lhasa, Nepal's new ruler wanted
the Tibetans to phase out its compromised coins. 'Keep the mint pure,'
he told his people in his political testament, the *Divya Upadesh*. He
asked the Tibetans to replace their compromised coinage with his
dynasty's new and purer version, something the Tibetans were reluctant to do on the terms Prithvi was offering. Since the Qing Empire
was now backing the Tibetans, there was no way militarily that Prithvi

felt able to prosecute his aim. As a consequence, trade with Tibet collapsed.

Then, in 1775, while George Bogle was living at the Panchen Lama's seat of Tashilhunpo, news arrived there that 'the tyrannical and faithless' Gorkha king Prithvi Narayan Shah was dead. The Panchen Lama immediately wrote to Prithvi's successor in a bid to restore trading relations with Kathmandu.

> I have heard of the death of your father, Prithi Narayan. As this is the will of God you will not let your heart be cast down. You have now succeeded to the throne, and it is proper that you attend to the happiness of your people, and allow all merchants, as Hindus, Mussulmans, and the four castes, to go and come, and carry on their trade freely, which will tend to your advantage and to your good name. At present they are afraid of you, and no one will enter your country. Whatever has been the ancient custom let it be observed between you and me.

Those ancient customs would not be observed. On the contrary, trade continued to be a source of friction. The Gorkha regime that now controlled much of the southern Himalaya needed to fund its military, through a restoration of trade or else new conquests. That friction would in the late 1780s erupt into war between Nepal and Tibet, a war that would entangle China and the East India Company, and bring the full might of armies of the Qing Empire to the fringes of the Kathmandu valley.

★

When the mountain explorer H W Tilman visited Rasuwagadhi in 1949, a year before China invaded Tibet, he found a desolate spot: an old fort and a few soldiers on the Nepali side and on the Tibetan just a stone slab inscribed with some Chinese characters. Translated a few years later by a second traveller, Duncan Forbes, this turned out to be a marker post defining the border that had been erected, on 26 November 1792, after the 'victory over the Gorkhas accomplished by General Fu, the Great General for the Pacification of the West'. It commemorated the Qing victory on behalf of Tibet over the Nepalis, a consequence of these trade wars and achieved in the face of incredible physical challenges as the Qing crossed the towering mountains as 'though they were moving over a level plain'. The stone didn't lie: the Qing victory was a swaggering expression of Chinese power, but it came at great cost, absorbing such huge amounts of treasure that the Qing concluded that in future the same ends should be achieved through diplomacy rather than war. The question is: why did they bother in the first place?

Until the end of the eighteenth century, Himalayan geography limited economic opportunities and put a brake on the size and influence of the region's political structures. It was trade that connected the Himalaya's distinct cultural spheres of influence with the outside world. Otherwise, the Himalaya had been a bulwark around which the tides of history flowed; set against the hazards of the mountains, not least the thin air of the Tibetan plateau, the available rewards had not persuaded outsiders to stay for long. By the end of the eighteenth century, this was changing. Foreign colonial powers were extending their influence deep into the mountains.

Warren Hastings judged the trade routes of the eastern Himalaya to be a way for the East India Company to reach China, sending George Bogle off to explore the idea. In the long run it proved little more than romantic speculation: the Company would solve its trade imbalance with China by other means. New global trading patterns were emerging that would make the old caravans Hovhannes Joughayetsi knew seem a charming anachronism; the mountains would become simply the East India Company's northern wall against the Qing Empire. While the Himalaya was a region with its own identity, where influences arrived from all directions to create a distinct and remarkable culture, for the emerging global powers, it would be made into a buffer zone, somewhere on the margins, a useful space to absorb the shocks and tension of geopolitics formulated hundreds and even thousands of kilometres away. The diverse peoples of the Himalaya would find themselves, just as Prithvi Narayan Shah predicted, sandwiched between two giant competing interests. Himalayan trade might have been of critical importance to kings in Kathmandu or the abbots of Tibetan monasteries. It would be of only marginal interest to the region's new masters in Calcutta and Beijing.

Prithvi Narayan Shah had seen this future and tried to find a balance between fierce self-reliance and a need for trade. In the last years of his reign, his army, though tiny by Indian or European standards, almost tripled in size and was equipped with firearms and artillery. The cost of this expansion couldn't be met from productive farmland alone; only restoration in trade could ease the immense pressure on Nepal's exchequer. Prithvi was pragmatic enough to recognise this. 'Whatever his conduct as a conqueror,' wrote William Kirkpatrick, the East India Company man who arrived in Kathmandu in 1793 and reported so attentively on its brickwork, 'or however severe his nature may have been, he was not inattentive to the means of conciliating those on whose support he principally depended.' Although the Kinloch expedition of 1767 – when the British attempt to intervene against the Gorkhalis had ended in malaria for Kinloch and humiliation for the Company – had soured Prithvi's relations with the British and persuaded him to expel Kathmandu's Capuchin missionaries, Prithvi was prepared to patch up relations with Warren Hastings, who tacitly allowed Prithvi free rein to expand his kingdom eastwards, if it brought stability. Hastings wanted Gorkha's help in ending the predations of sannyasi bandits then plaguing Bengal.

Likewise, in his final letter to the Panchen Lama, a man with whom Prithvi had bitter differences, the king made an offer to restore trade through the Bhote Kosi and Kyirong valleys. As George Bogle observed, 'the wealth of Nepal', meaning its former trade with Tibet, had 'furnished the Gorkha Rajah with the means by which he rose'. However, Prithvi had 'neglected to cherish the source'. We have seen already how in his political memoir the *Divya Upadesh* Prithvi had preached the values of self-reliance and autarky. Kashmiri merchants and Indian *gosain* had been forced out of Kathmandu, either expelled directly or driven out by tariffs that had risen sharply to meet the Gorkhali regime's increased costs. Prithvi was now trying to recover his position. His advance east towards Sikkim, located between Nepal and Bhutan, also allowed Gorkha to exert pressure on another major trade route for Tibet, through the Tista valley to the Jelep La, a route of strategic interest to the British as well. Control Sikkim, Prithvi assumed, and the Tibetans would be forced to negotiate.

After the death of Prithvi Narayan in 1775, his successors in the Shah dynasty became more aggressive, constructing themselves as the dominant military power along the southern flank of the Himalaya. Gorkha swept up statelets and mini-kingdoms that had resisted Prithvi in the west and far west of modern Nepal: the Gandaki river basin and the old Khasa Empire of the Karnali valley. His eldest son and successor Pratap Singh and the sixth Panchen Lama together tried to re-establish the 'ancient custom' that had enriched both Kathmandu and central Tibet, as the Panchen Lama requested in his letter. The privileged position of Newari merchants in Lhasa was confirmed and Tibet agreed only to do business with Bengal through Kathmandu. That was also the hope of George Bogle, who told his masters in Calcutta:

> The opening of the road through Nepal, and obtaining the abolition of the duties and exactions which have lately been imposed on trade in that country, appears an object of great importance towards establishing a free communication between Bengal and Tibet. The death of Prithi Naraya, the late Rajah of Nepal, seems to afford a favourable opportunity of effecting this point.

The deaths of all three men – Pratap Singh, the Panchen Lama and Bogle – within the space of a few years meant it didn't work out that way. Since conquering Kathmandu, discipline among the Gorkhalis had begun to fracture. With Prithvi's death, intrigue and feuds began eating into the Gorkha regime's coherence. When Pratap Singh died aged twenty-six, only two years after his father, a power struggle began between his widow, acting as regent to their son, and Pratap's younger brother Bahadur Shah, particularly over territorial expansion. When the Panchen Lama died of smallpox at Chengde, and with his reincarnation still a child, Tibet's political centre of gravity moved firmly towards the Dalai Lama and the system of government imposed by the Qianlong emperor, whereby any policy developed in Lhasa had to meet the approval of the two Qing ambans stationed there. China was suspicious of foreign involvement in its sphere of influence, and the British, however much they wanted to improve trade with Tibet, were reluctant to antagonise their most important trading partner. Tibet continued to offer support to its tiny neighbour Sikkim, a Buddhist kingdom with an important trade route to Bengal, much to the annoyance of Nepal, which had only agreed to back away from occupying Sikkim in return for a monopoly on trade.

This fraught situation would have been explosive enough without the interventions of the abrasive Gorkhali regent Bahadur Shah, whose instinct was to act and whose goal was to expand as fast as possible the proto-empire he was building. Apart from the issue of debased coinage, the Gorkhalis chafed that the Tibetans were exploiting them, mixing dust with the salt they exported and imposing heavy import tariffs on Nepali flour. In early 1788, Bahadur infuriated Lhasa by appointing as head of Kathmandu's Tibetan affairs the Shamarpa, a dissident reincarnate lama (*tulku*) from the Karma Kagyu school, who had recently fled a dispute in Tibet over the property of his half-brother, the former Panchen Lama. Lacking the wiliness of Prithvi Narayan, the regent threatened to occupy Kuti and Kyirong, that is the two ancient trade routes into Tibet from Kathmandu, until his grievances were resolved. The Tibetans response was to shut the border, suggesting that 'if the Goorkha wished for war, he was welcome to advance.' The Gorkhalis appealed to the Chinese emperor but the ambans in Lhasa chose not to tell Beijing what was happening. In short order, thousands of Gorkhali troops were crossing into Tibet through Kyirong and Kuti, their objective the riches of Tashilhunpo monastery, seat of the Panchen Lamas.

The seventh Panchen Lama was still a boy, but his regent issued appeals for help to the Qing emperor and also to the governor general of the East India Company. From the latter, he also requested secrecy: Beijing would not appreciate Tibet turning to the region's other great power. The governor general was Lord Cornwallis, who ten years previously had been the commanding officer at Yorktown, where the British surrender set the stage for the loss of its American colonies. Not antagonising the Chinese was foremost in his mind during this crisis, lest something similar occur. At home, the impeachment of his predecessor Warren Hastings was underway, another unwelcome fate for Cornwallis to ponder. Concluding that Beijing would be infuriated at British interference, he told the Panchen Lama he would not offer any assistance. Nor did he agree to keep their correspondence a secret. The Company wanted the ear of the Qing emperor on the matter of its parlous trade imbalance and nothing must interfere with business.

For their part, the Chinese sent officials to investigate. The Tibetans were happy to fight but the Chinese weren't confident of military success. They pressed the Tibetans to negotiate, a difficult task with an occupying army threatening destruction. To the east, Gorkhali troops had also occupied Sikkim, taking control of the crucial Jelep La and the Chumbi valley beyond, cutting off a trade route they felt the Tibetans had opened against the spirit of their earlier agreement, breaking Nepal's monopoly. Thinking they could get better terms from Tibet with Qing mediation, the Gorkhalis negotiated what became known as the Kyirong Treaty, which granted territory, including the frontier town of Kuti, and commercial concessions; it also addressed directly the complex issue of Tibet's debased coinage. An exchange was agreed, one good coin for two bad, and an annual tribute of fifty thousand rupees a year, a phenomenal sum. The Gorkhalis could be forgiven for thinking they had won.

This generous settlement might have been a humiliation for the Qing emperor had his representatives been entirely open with him about its terms. They chose instead to be economical with the fine detail, telling Beijing that Nepal, not Tibet, would be paying a form of tribute and that their troops had returned home without the loss of a single Chinese soldier, both of which were only more or less true. When Gorkhali ambassadors visited Beijing in the autumn of 1789, Nepal's young king was honoured with a feudatory title and his regent, the pugnacious Bahadur Shah, became *kung*, or duke.

Then Lhasa began to wriggle on its expensive hook, stirring up trouble in far western Nepal and offering asylum to the deposed ruler of Jumla, one of the mini-kingdoms of far-western Nepal that had resisted the advance of the Gorkhalis. The Dalai Lama then told Kathmandu that further payments would be suspended. There were bad-tempered and fruitless negotiations at Kuti, where the divisive figure of the dissident Shamarpa led the Gorkhali side; soon after, thousands of Gorkhali soldiers were marching back into Tibet under the command of two of Nepal's most able generals, one of them Damodar Pande, son of Prithvi Narayan's favourite general Kalu Pande, who had died besieging Kirtipur. The Panchen Lama was whisked away to Lhasa under the protection of his regent and the Tibetans appealed once again to Beijing. When the Gorkhali force arrived at Shigatse, its leaders demanded gold and a hundred thousand rupees, and having been refused, they sacked the monastery of Tashilhunpo.

News of this latest humiliation revealed the true nature of the situation on the Qing Empire's western border. The official who had

promised the Qianlong emperor that the conflict had been resolved
committed suicide even before he could be summoned to the imperial
presence. The Qing ordered a punitive expedition under the command
of Fuk'anggan, the nephew of the empress, then in his late thirties
and with deep experience of quashing rebellions, having pacified
Sichuan and put down insurrection in Taiwan. Fuk'anggan led a huge
force, including ten thousand troops from the elite Eight Banners,
which he marched across the plateau from Qinghai in the depths of
winter. The Qianlong emperor also sent an envoy to Kathmandu,
demanding the return of the Tashilhunpo treasures and the surrender
of the Shamarpa to Tibetan custody. In Lhasa, Newari tradesmen,
whose business had suffered since the Gorkhalis took power in
Kathmandu, were encouraged by the Qing to travel home to Nepal
and stir up resentment there. One of them was detained at the Nepali
border and personally interrogated by the regent Bahadur Shah, who
learned that Fuk'anggan's army was bearing down on Nepal.

Not for the last time, a Nepali ruler now attempted to play their
giant neighbour to the north against the one from the south. Bahadur
sent a letter to the Chinese explaining his grievances but also warning
of British interest in Tibet. He also signed a commercial treaty with
the British, hoping this would bring with it their political and even
military support, a notion Calcutta didn't rush to contradict.
Fuk'anggan also wrote to the British, however, informing them of
Qing plans to invade Nepal, a move Bahadur had thought unlikely,
given the terrain. This was a sobering development. That said, should
China occupy Kathmandu, the Qing armies would be adjacent to the
East India Company's richest possessions, which might persuade the
British to Bahadur's side. But if Bahadur Shah genuinely thought the
British would help him in his hour of need, he would be disappointed.
The British were planning a major and costly diplomatic mission to
the Qing court, led by Lord Macartney, to raise British grievances over
trade. Nothing could jeopardise that.

Facing the might of Fuk'anggan's army on the plateau would have
been suicide, so the Gorkhali troops withdrew to the border where
they could more easily defend the approaches to Kathmandu in the
narrow river gorges cutting through the mountains. But the Gorkhali
force at Rasuwagadhi was outflanked by a brilliant piece of mountain
warfare. Fuk'anggan himself led three regiments to bridge the Lende

river, which meets the Kyirong near Rasuwa and forms the modern boundary between Tibet and Nepal. While the Gorkhali forces resisted this move, a second Chinese force crossed the river upstream and circled behind their enemy's position to attack them from above. The Gorkhalis were routed and only managed to stop the Qing army's advance thirty-five kilometres from Kathmandu at the Betrawati river, just north of Nuwakot. At this point Bahadur Shah appealed directly to the British for military aid, particularly artillery, but at the same time the Company received a letter from the Dalai Lama, requesting neutrality. Mindful of commerce, Lord Cornwallis offered to mediate, sending the young Scottish envoy Captain William Kirkpatrick to Kathmandu (where we met him in Chapter Five): a diplomatic way of sitting on his hands and hoping Nepal wasn't destroyed.

That the Gorkhali crown survived might seem surprising. The Qing's ambition had been to split Nepal apart and the Chinese certainly battled on, breaking through Gorkhali lines to reach Nuwakot. But the fighting season was almost over and the cost in material and men was steepening. Fuk'anggan's lines of communication were stretched. How would he resupply in the bitter winter months across the highest mountains on earth? How much was conquering Nepal really worth? Better to agree terms and head for home before the temperature fell. The scale of China's investment in its Nepali adventure was not immediately appreciated, either by the British or the Gorkhalis, but it was colossal and would not be repeated. Expensive wars and corruption at court were draining the treasury and the Qing would soon face expensive rebellions closer to home. The Qianlong emperor, whose armies had crushed enemies around the whole perimeter of the empire, abdicated in 1796; he warned his successor, the Jiaqing, to be wary of intervening in Gorkha affairs. It was advice the new emperor would follow.

The treaty the Chinese signed with Bahadur Shah seemed punitive enough: the loot from Tashilhunpo was handed back and tribute demanded; Nepal agreed to renounce any ambitions north of the Himalaya and to send ambassadors every five years under diplomatic conditions illustrating Nepal's junior status. In return China offered to help if Nepal should be invaded. Otherwise the status quo held. Nepal was free to resume its conquest of the west and negotiate on its own terms with its southern neighbour. Bahadur Shah had judged

Calcutta's hesitation in offering Nepal support as a form of betrayal, which is why William Kirkpatrick received such a chilly welcome when he arrived in Kathmandu in 1793. The Chinese were also bitter at the East India Company. Fuk'anggan believed incorrectly that Company sepoys had helped the Gorkhalis. When Lord Macartney's diplomatic mission to the Qing court eventually failed, he believed it was this imagined intervention that persuaded the Qianlong emperor to dismiss his embassy.

In the long run, it was arguably the Tibetans who lost most. While they got back the glories of Tashilhunpo, the political price was high. The Qing emperors had been forced to make several critical military interventions throughout the eighteenth century to prop up an often fractious and sectarian Tibetan government and keep dissidents from conspiring with those Mongol groups that remained a threat to China. Tibet hadn't just been protected: it was swallowed up. Dalai Lamas in the nineteenth century would be both short-lived and heavily controlled: Tibet's borders were maintained at the pleasure of the Qing dynasty. Only as the Qing fell in the twentieth century did the Dalai Lamas emerge again as great leaders.

*

The disaster at Rasuwagadhi and the terms of the treaty between Gorkha and China would lead almost inevitably to conflict with the East India Company. With Tibet so ruthlessly put off limits by the Qing, Nepal's expansionist ambitions were restricted to areas south of the Himalaya. The immediate loser was the Gorkhali regent Bahadur Shah. Under his rule, Nepal had expanded quickly; between the invasions of Tibet in 1788 and 1791, Gorkhali troops had moved into Kumaon, west of the Mahakali river. Now he had overreached. The king's courtiers, or *bharadar*, blamed him for recklessly endangering the regime. The king, Rana Bahadur, reached his majority soon after the Chinese invasion and sought to exert his authority. Bahadur Shah was murdered in 1797. Even so, the factionalism continued, drawing in Nepal's neighbours as competing interests conspired with one or other for advantage. Rana Bahadur, a capricious and debauched individual who borrowed huge sums from his courtiers, first abdicated in favour of his infant son and then in 1800 went into exile in Benares, under the control of the East India Company. The British were swift to exploit the worsening political situation in Nepal, signing a treaty with the Gorkha state in 1801 at Danapur, close to Patna, promising peace in return for trade relations and the establishment of a British residency in Kathmandu.

A large faction of the Gorkhali court was bitterly opposed to the presence of a British resident and appealed to the Qing, warning them that the British were using the exiled Rana Bahadur to extend their influence in Nepal and threaten the regime. Instead of intervening, the Chinese advised the Gorkhalis to get their ex-king back. Meanwhile, the governor general Richard Wellesley told the newly appointed British resident of Kathmandu Captain William Knox to 'direct your attention as to the means of opening a beneficial trade with the countries of Bootan and Tibet either directly with the Company's Provinces, or through the medium of the merchants of Nepal'. Knox's mission arrived in the spring of 1802 and for a time was tolerated, but at the end of the year power shifted again. Damodar Pande, the man who had led the attack against the Qing a decade earlier, was made chief minister. As a consequence, relations with Knox became increasingly sour and Wellesley recalled him. The Company had become preoccupied with fighting its second war with the Maratha confederacy in India; it had no wish to antagonise China on its far western marches. Trade with the Qing was much too important. Knox withdrew and in short order the trade agreement with Nepal was torn up. The exiled Gorkhali king Rana Bahadur was told to go home.

With him came an ambitious and capable minister called Bhimsen Thapa. Many already regarded Bhimsen as the controlling influence behind Rana Bahadur's actions. Francis Buchanan-Hamilton, who had been part of Knox's mission, described him as a

very vigorous rash young man, who, owing partly to the moderation of the Company's negociations [sic] with Rana Bahadur, by him attributed to fear, and partly to the hope of protection from the Chinese, seems to have beheld the British government with contempt.

Bhimsen promptly had Damodar Pande beheaded and took control of the king. The dynasty that Prithvi Narayan had built so ably a few decades before had become, and would remain for the next one hundred and fifty years, a token to be squabbled over.

Bhimsen would dominate Nepal's political scene for the next four decades, a brilliant tactician who learned from his mistakes, his greatest being to misread the British. With the failure of Knox's mission in 1804, which in some ways was merely a prologue to the Company's forthcoming war with Nepal, Bhimsen renewed Nepal's westward expansion, sending his father to occupy the still independent kingdom of Palpa and taking over the important trading town of Rerighat, now Ridi Bazar. That year the Gorkhali army also invaded Garhwal, the kingdom to the west of Kumaon. There was little prospect of trade being normalised with the Gorkhalis tightening their grip on the Himalaya.

In 1806, Rana Bahadur was murdered at the hands of his half-brother and Kathmandu was plunged into a brief period of extreme bloodletting: the Bhandarkhal massacre. Ninety-three people died, seventeen of them women, all of them in some way obstructive to the interests of Bhimsen Thapa, who emerged intact and in control. Nepal continued its conquests, absorbing territory between the Yamuna and Sutlej rivers.

To pay Gorkha's troops for this renewed aggression, Bhimsen nationalised land gifted to religious institutions, a risky move in an increasingly conservative Hindu polity. The reward was the Gorkha government taking an even firmer grip on the region at the expense of its neighbours. The East India Company looked on with growing concern. Francis Buchanan-Hamilton, who had been with Knox, observed how the Gorkhali conquests placed a chill over trade:

> besides the military point of view, they are desirous of having few passages as a point of economy in collecting the customs. Accordingly, so far as they can, they have stopt every pass, except that by Butaul [Butwal], which of course, has become a considerable mart, although most inconveniently situated.

There seemed little prospect of mutually beneficial trade with a neighbour so aggressively acquisitive and so resistant to outside influence. Something would have to change.

9

The Hard Road to Sagauli

In the post-monsoon season of 1819, the newest recruit to the Bengal Civil Service's Foreign and Political Department arrived at Delhi, en route to the Himalaya. Brian Houghton Hodgson was, in the words of his first biographer, a 'pretty boy' whose delicately pink cheeks made him seem younger than his eighteen years. The heat of Calcutta and a fragile constitution had almost ended his career before it had begun, but thanks to influential connections he was on his way to the cooler hills of Kumaon, newly under the control of the British.

Hodgson dutifully presented himself to the resident at Delhi, General Sir David Ochterlony, now sixty-one years of age, gammon-faced and white haired, the Company's oldest 'political' encountering its youngest. Ochterlony conducted his private life like a *nawab*, a 'white Mughal', promenading each afternoon on the banks of the Yamuna river with his *bibis*, his common-law local wives, each on their own elephant. Hodgson was unimpressed, noting 'the costly and pompous style then inseparable from our Indian embassies'. He was a product of Haileybury, a school established to train servants of empire who wouldn't indulge in that kind of thing. Ochterlony seemed to Hodgson the living representation of the dangers of 'going native'. Ironically, and in his own quiet way, Hodgson would himself become a late flowering of an orientalism already out of fashion: 'marrying' his own Muslim *bibi* and becoming a scholarly authority on the world he inhabited, a world that Ochterlony himself had conquered: the kingdom of Nepal.

The excesses and corruption of the East India Company had by the early nineteenth century created a new narrative among critics and political thinkers. In engaging and even identifying with Indian culture, they claimed, European Christian values had been subverted

and debauched. Historians and thinkers like James Mill, writing in
the *Edinburgh Review*, argued it was the moral duty of the East India
Company to civilise India, to break down its entrenched superstition,
not, as Sir William Jones had done at Fort William College, 'to
employ the lights of a people still semi-barbarous'. There was no
question of this being done with the democratic consent of the
Indian people: their 'moral and political situation' made that imprac-
tical. 'A simple form of arbitrary government tempered by European
honour and European intelligence is the only form which is now fit
for Hindustan.'

Ochterlony, born in Massachusetts to a Scottish father, had arrived
in India more than forty years earlier, when Warren Hastings was
governor general and Britain was consolidating its hard-won position
on the subcontinent. Commissioned into the Bengal Native Infantry,
he had fought as a subaltern in the Second Anglo-Mysore War, been
wounded, losing an eye, and then imprisoned, to be released only at
the end of hostilities. In 1803, and by then a major, he had commanded
a battalion in the Second Anglo-Maratha War. After the capture of
Delhi he was appointed resident at the Mughal court, and when
Yashwant Rao Holkar laid siege to its famous Red Fort to liberate the
Mughal emperor, Ochterlony was on the battlements directing its
successful defence. Later he was sacked as resident in favour of another
Scot, Archibald Seton, adding a streak of bitterness to a mercurial
temperament. In the flood of action Ochterlony was eager and
resourceful; thwarted, he could be sour.

In 1808, Ochterlony's career blossomed once again. He was
appointed agent for relations with the Sikh states under their capable
emperor Ranjit Singh, whose sphere of influence met the British along
the Sutlej river. The two men shared a common affliction: Ranjit Singh
had lost the sight of one eye during a childhood bout of smallpox.
'The natives have an idea that a person possessed of one eye only,
sees much farther than those who are blessed with two, and is better
able to conduct a difficult negociation,' wrote a correspondent for the
Asiatic Journal in 1835, ten years after Ochterlony's death.

It was generally supposed that he had been selected on account of the
necessity of sending some person able, from similar circumstances of
mental and bodily conformation, to cope with so subtle an adversary.

In doing so he burnished his reputation as a sharp-witted politician who could put himself in the mind of his indigenous adversaries.

Ochterlony's appointment also brought him into contact with the expanding Gorkhali regime. In the aftermath of the Qing victory at Rasuwagadhi in 1792 and the expulsion of the Knox mission from Kathmandu, Bhimsen Thapa renewed Gorkha's westward expansion by sending the king's army into Garhwal under the command of a distant cousin, an old warhorse called Amar Singh Thapa. To give thanks for his victories, Amar Singh built a temple for pilgrims at the holy mountain village of Gangotri. Yet the excesses of the Gorkhali occupation were notorious. The imposition of heavy taxes, demands for forced labour and violent abuses, including rape, in Gorkha's western provinces led to large-scale depopulation of the middle hills, despite exhortations of restraint from Kathmandu. Kumaon, which had been conquered many years before Garhwal, suffered longer; the British would use such behaviour to stir up resentment before their war with Nepal.

Four years later, Amar Singh's troops were still moving west beyond the Yamuna river towards the Sutlej and the borders of Ranjit Singh's Sikh Empire, gradually sweeping up the thirty or so tiny kingdoms and principalities crammed into a habitable area not much bigger than the English Lake District. Almost every valley in this rugged terrain had its own Rajput lineage: royal debris swept uphill centuries before on the rising tide of Muslim expansion. In theory their princes paid tribute to the Mughal court; in reality many of these mountain fiefdoms weren't worth the bother. To the Mughal emperors, these mountains were most useful as the source of their ice, brought down in the hot summer months, first by river and then on the backs of porters. However, Amar Singh Thapa's religious mentor and astrologer, Shiva Dat Rai, happened to come from one of these mini-kingdoms, a place called Bilaspur. (The late eighteenth-century traveller George Forster, the first Briton to traverse Central Asia, described Bilaspur as existing 'in a state of deep confusion and filth'.) Shiva Dat Rai now persuaded Amar Singh Thapa to attack Bilaspur's bitter enemies in neighbouring Hindur to the south. With that accomplished, Shiva Dat Rai urged the general to restore territories Bilaspur had lost on the west bank of the Sutlej and defeat the enterprising raja, Sansar Chand, who had taken them. This action brought the Gorkhali general Amar Singh

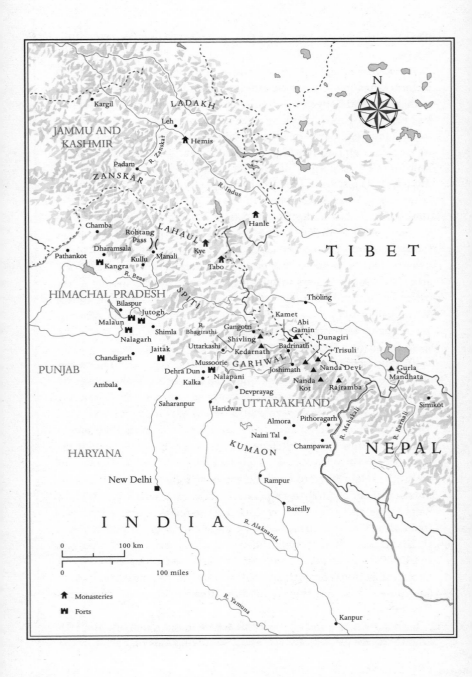

Thapa to the foot of the most famous stronghold in the Himalaya: Kangra.

Forts were a key feature of control in the Himalaya, at the heart of local kingdoms and principalities from Bhutan in the east to Ladakh in the west, and Kangra was among the most significant. The Mughals had kept a garrison there long after their power had faded elsewhere in the Himalaya. Now they were finally gone. If Bilaspur was a fossil of forgotten glories, the kingdom of Kangra was different: a larger, reinvigorated federation of smaller states occupying much of the modern Indian state of Himachal Pradesh. By the time of its confrontation with Amar Singh Thapa, Kangra had become a vibrant and cultured kingdom under its raja Sansar Chand, who had reclaimed his patrimony from the fading Mughals. With Kangra back in his family's control, Sansar Chand set about restoring the fortunes of his dynasty. Having done so, he was able to indulge his passion for the arts, establishing ateliers in his kingdom and commissioning a new palace at Sujanpur. Kangra was the crucible for what became known as the Pahari school, one of the great flowerings of Himalayan art. Yet in seizing territory from Bilaspur in 1805, Sansar Chand sowed the seeds of his own destruction.

To start with, things went well for Sansar Chand. He sent troops across the Sutlej to harry Amar Singh Thapa on his flank and stir up trouble among the mini-states the Gorkhali general had so recently conquered. Having dealt with that problem, Amar Singh's attack on Kangra itself spluttered to a halt. Rumours swirled in Kathmandu that Amar Singh was being dilatory in the siege; had he taken a bribe from Sansar Chand to allow supplies through? Bhimsen Thapa sent his brother Nain Singh to finish the job but he died during the assault. Bhimsen then decided to negotiate, and since Sansar Chand was a Rajput, sent two aristocrats to reach a settlement: Rudravir Shah and Dalbhanjan Pande, cousin to the recently executed Damodar. Amar Singh, a Khas hill-man, took the arrival of the aristocratic Rudravir and Dalbhanjan as a snub, so when they agreed to leave Kangra in return for an indemnity, Amar Singh accused the pair of taking a bribe themselves, poisoning their reputation at court. The siege of Kangra was renewed.

Both sides now courted the influence of Ranjit Singh and the Sikh Empire, where Ochterlony was establishing relations on behalf of the

British. Local hill-states, like Chamba and Turagarh, fed up with the rapacious nature of Gorkhali armies, began to withhold supplies from Amar Singh's troops, who became weakened from disease and hunger. Ranjit Singh finally intervened, driving the Gorkha army back across the Sutlej, but he took Kangra for himself. Sansar Chand would die a pensioner of the Sikhs, shorn of his kingdom; the Sutlej would remain the far western extent of the Gorkhali state.

Having ground to a halt at the Sutlej, conflict now flared up once more between the East India Company and the Gorkhas, but this time it wasn't trade that tipped the Company into attacking Nepal. Following the dismal results of their missions to Kathmandu, those of Kirkpatrick in 1793 and Knox in 1804, the British had been losing interest in Himalayan trade, which had anyway dried up in the east and in the west was jealously guarded by Ranjit Singh, who now controlled the Kashmiri wool trade. Rather, the issue that triggered war involved tax revenues: specifically revenues from twenty-two villages in the Butwal region north of the city of Gorakhpur, now in the Indian state of Uttar Pradesh and close to modern Nepal's southern border. The Gorkhas saw these as belonging to Palpa, which was now governed by Bhimsen Thapa's father. The Company regarded them as part of Awadh – then known as Oudh – which the British now controlled.

In arguing with the Gorkhalis about these villages, the British were caught between two ways of seeing themselves: as a commercial company, doing whatever was necessary to protect its balance sheet, in which case the figures at stake did not justify expensive conflict; or else as a government, with an obligation to protect the state's integrity, in which case the revenues ought to be protected as a matter of prin-ciple. But while the Company's governors at Calcutta might have fretted over the commercial opinion of the Court of Directors in London and whether conflict was actually worthwhile, Bhimsen Thapa in Kathmandu saw the British simply as acquisitive empire-builders, not unlike himself: the British would concede only if a greater prize could be offered. To his general Amar Singh Thapa, obsessing over his defeat by Ranjit Singh, it made perfect sense to approach the Company not as antagonists but as potential allies, joining forces to throw the Sikhs out of Kangra fort. The Gorkha regime clearly and presciently assumed that since the British would end up fighting the

Sikhs anyway they might as well get on with it. In the hope of bringing the British on side, Amar Singh handed back villages on the plains south of Hindur that he had grabbed from the British not long before. In 1808, and newly appointed agent for British relations with Ranjit Singh, Ochterlony found all this baffling: on the one hand being in conflict with the Ghorkas, on the other being courted by them. It was, he complained, 'very difficult to assign motives for the actions of men who seem hardly to possess the faculty of reason'.

If the Company was caught between two ways of seeing itself, then it also had two views of the world it administered, one Indian, the other European, a dichotomy that can be reduced to one word: maps. In the early nineteenth century the southern fringe of the Himalaya was a confusing place. The notion of spatial ownership, of chunks of land defined on maps of great accuracy, was still new in Britain but almost wholly foreign in India. Land ownership in the jungles and clearings of the terai was especially hazy, since this strip of territory, perhaps no more than thirty kilometres wide, had often acted as a buffer zone between rulers from the plains and from the hills. To the Nepalis, borders meant mountain ridges and river courses, not lines on a sheet of paper. Pre-colonial records were extensive, thanks to Mughal bureaucracy, but rather than define specific areas, these records documented territory in terms of lists of villages, with divisions and subdivisions, strips of information like DNA, which over time, also like DNA, mutated under the pressure of local politics and corrupt officials. The result was that patches of land could belong to a parent tax authority that was not contiguous and located many kilometres away. Colonial officials were often bamboozled by these taxation records, which came with no correlate maps and were riddled with inconsistencies and forgeries.

The Mughals had done things their way, and for a while the Company had adopted their practices, adding to the mountain of Mughal tax records. Yet in Europe accurate maps were transforming the very idea of land ownership, and would shortly do the same in India. From the British perspective, the tax revenues of these villages didn't mean much; increasingly, the issue was the need for a definitive border. The Company viewed the most logical place for that border as the line of hills that marked the beginning of the Himalaya. Bhimsen Thapa understood that if Gorkha capitulated in the dispute with the British over the twenty-two villages at Butwal, then in due course the Gorkhali regime could lose much of its territory along the Terai, the most productive land it held with which to pay its troops and maintain the regime. It was the very definition of an existential threat.

When Francis Rawdon-Hastings, then the Earl of Moira, arrived in India in October 1813 as the new governor general, he was determined to resolve this border dispute with Nepal one way or another. When negotiations fizzled out, he prepared a plan of attack, one that would return Ochterlony, now in his late fifties, to the battlefield. The campaign promised to be expensive but since the villages in question were, so far as Moira was concerned, part of Oudh, now Awadh, he had no compunction in getting Oudh's nominal ruler to pay for it. The Court of Directors in London signed their assent in February 1814, in plenty of time for the autumn fighting season. At the end of May, Gorkhali troops attacked a police post in Butwal, killing eighteen Company men, their chief officer tied to a tree and shot full of arrows. The Earl of Moira had his excuse for war.

*

By the time the British attacked, Bimsen Thapa had been the leading political figure in Nepal for almost a decade. Tall and spare, Bhimsen had refined features that hinted at Rajput blood, but his family's hillbilly status provoked sneers from those more confident of their breeding. Perhaps because of this, Bhimsen proved a ruthless political operator. In 1806, the year Amar Singh first attacked Kangra, Bhimsen had persuaded the king Rana Bahadur to marry Bhimsen's niece, Tripura Sundari Devi, daughter of his younger brother Nain Singh. Such blatant manoeuvring enraged Rana Bahadur's half-brother, Sher Bahadur. In an argument at court, he drew his sword and cut the king down. Rana Bahadur's bodyguard, Bal Singh Kunwar, Nain Singh's son-in-law, immediately drew his own sword and took revenge on Sher Bahadur: this was the prompt for the bloodletting dubbed the Bhandarkal massacre. It was typical of Bhimsen to use this slaughter as an opportunity, rounding up scores of enemies at court and having them executed for their role in this 'plot', their places taken by members of his own clan. Rana Bahadur's senior queen and his many concubines were forced to commit *sati*, self-immolating on funeral pyres, their screams drowned out by martial drums.

Tripura Sundari, so quickly married and widowed, was made regent to the new king, her stepson Girvan Yuddha Bikram, cementing the Thapa clan's total control of the monarchy. Tripura was herself only twelve years old but she would grow up to be a powerful woman in her own right. The book on women in Nepali politics has yet to be written, but Tripura's story deserves reassessment: the birth of Nepali literature, in recent decades a vibrant and distinctive voice, is often attributed to Bhanubhakta Acharya, a later nineteenth-century poet who translated the *Ramayana*, but Tripura Sundari also has a claim. Her personal artistic achievement was a translation of a section of the *Mahabharata* into Nepali, or Gorkhali as it was then known, in which the Raja Dharma, the 'path of a king', elucidates the duty and conduct for a warrior-caste ruler who had grabbed the reins of power and was feeling insecure about his social status. The unexpected death of her stepson Girvan soon after he achieved his majority meant she later had another spell as regent, until her own death from cholera in 1832, aged just thirty-eight. For as long as she lived, the nature of palace politics made Tripura an important ally for Bhimsen: it's no coincidence that his power began to ebb after her premature death.

*

As a ruthless and savvy operator who dominated this period, historians have sometimes assumed Bhimsen was overbearing, that the other *bharadar*, or nobles, shrank before him. Bhimsen could certainly be brutal, necessarily so given the context in which he sometimes operated. But his great skill was reading people, understanding the hopes and fears of those he relied upon for his position: the various brittle strands of the Shah dynasty, some of them teetering on madness; the other nobles, who were often agitating for his removal; and the army, which dominated the Gorkhali project and had to be kept on side. Bhimsen Thapa had no grand vision for Nepal beyond his own clan's political survival, but keeping the army focussed and happy implied a rolling programme of expansion: more soldiers meant more land with which to pay them and if that antagonised the British, then so be it. As tension with the British mounted in the spring of 1814, he reassured the teenage king Girvan by drawing to his attention a famous instance of successful resistance against the East India Company by the Maratha in 1805.

> The small fort at Bhurtpoor [Bharatpur] was the work of man, yet the English, being worsted before it, desisted from the attempt to conquer it; our hills and fastnesses are formed by the hand of God, and are impregnable. I therefore recommend the prosecution of hostilities. We can make peace afterwards on such terms as may suit our convenience.

In calling for resistance against the British, Bhimsen also pointed to the Gorkhali 'victory' over the Chinese, conveniently forgetting how close Nepal had come to a catastrophe only avoided because the Chinese were so far from home. The British were next door: more easily resupplied and reinforced. His attitude seems improbably cavalier for someone with such a reputation for political nous. So how did Bhimsen miscalculate so badly? The view of the first British resident of Kathmandu, William Knox, was that Bhimsen Thapa 'attributed to fear' the emollient approach the British had taken with his master Rana Bahadur. The way the British conducted themselves was alien to Bhimsen; for their part British diplomats in the early 1800s were exasperated at the difference in the way their Gorkhali colleagues behaved with them, in contrast to the deference they showed Qing officials, who had no trouble getting Nepal's cooperation. Nepali ambassadors, or *vakil*, had a clearer understanding of Chinese intentions from their regular diplomatic missions to pay tribute: hierarchies were clearly signalled in Chinese diplomatic etiquette. They found British manners more opaque and harder to interpret.

Bhimsen had seen the British at first hand when he served as bodyguard during Rana Bahadur's period of exile in Benares and regarded them as duplicitous. He had looked on with disgust as the East India Company kept the king dangling with a pension and the promise of support, no more than a useful bargaining chip that they exploited to increase their influence and get access for Knox's trade mission to Kathmandu. Once installed as resident, and under the terms of the 1801 treaty signed at Danapur, Knox demanded reimbursement for the huge debts Rana Bahadur had run up while in exile. Bhimsen noted the difference between the Company's image of itself as a model of

European progress and moral Christian authority, and its underhanded cynicism: subsidising the exiled king as he subverted his own family's power before demanding its money back once this was accomplished. Bhimsen knew his country had been played and hated the British for it, a loathing that would burn deep for decades.

Bhimsen had also taken careful note of the Company's military capability so when he seized power in 1806 to become Nepal's first *mukhtiyar*, or chief minister, he instituted a series of reforms to the Gorkhali military, introducing several organisational features he'd admired in the Bengal army. Even before that, Nepal's best troops had adopted uniforms in imitation of the Company's men: red jackets and white cross belts. They were drilled just as the Bengal army was, using English words of command. (This was why the Qing had suspected British involvement in the Gorkhali invasion of Tibet.) French mercenaries had earlier been hired to build up the Gorkhali artillery, casting guns and manufacturing gunpowder. Bhimsen Thapa continued this use of foreign military advisers; he hired British deserters to help train his troops and manufacture muskets. One of them, a man called Byrnes, was still a colonel of artillery in 1814 when war broke out with the East India Company. These British advisers even taught their Gorkhali students some English marching tunes, which they played on their fifes going into battle, much to the astonishment of their British opponents. They learned too from the Chinese, who in 1792 had used lightweight one-pounder artillery pieces made of leather that could be carried on the shoulder of one man: practical in the mountains, even if they burst after a few rounds.

The identity of those Gorkhali troops was also significant, having important implications for the future of the British in India and beyond. Officers were Khas Chhetris but ordinary soldiers were mostly Magars, along with some Gurungs, from Tibeto-Burmese ethnic backgrounds. They were superb soldiers: muscular, agreeable and without the religious observances that complicated more orthodox Hindu units. By contrast, most of their opponents in the Company's Bengal army were high-caste men from Awadh. Having grown up in the mountains, the Gorkhali troops had that rugged self-reliance so typical of mountain people, remaining cheerful despite the worst provocations of hunger and exhaustion. These were the men identified in the British imagination as 'Gurkhas', misreading what was in effect a political classification for an ethnic one. When the war between them was over, Ochterlony would offer incentives to prise some of these troops into his own service, and when he took Amar Singh's surrender in 1815, they signed an agreement that any troops in the service of Nepal who wished to join the British forces should be free to do so. This was the starting point for the famous Gurkha regiments that helped shape the British Empire. Some of those recruited by the British were indeed Gorkhali, Magars and Gurungs from regular Nepali regiments, but most were in fact irregular auxiliaries the Gorkhali army recruited in Garhwal and Kumaon to make up numbers.

Bhimsen's hatred of the British perhaps blinded him to the level of support he might actually get from beyond his own borders in Nepal's struggle with the East India Company. The Gorkhali regime, both before and after war with the British, sought common cause with other enemies of the Company, particularly the Maratha confederacy and the Sikh ruler Ranjit Singh, whose military capability was on a par with that of Gorkha. Although the Sikhs had routed the Gorkha army at Kangra, both sides could see advantages in joining forces against the British. But as things worked out, Ranjit's interest was half-hearted and the war would be lost before he could act. Even more important was the attitude of the Qing, whose air of invincibility had been dented following the so-called White Lotus rebellion, a guerilla insurgency against crippling tax rates. This had cost the life of the Manchu general Fuk'anggan, who had led the invasion of Nepal. The rebellion was overcome but the regime was struggling with deepening corruption and periods of famine. Despite this, when the Chinese insisted that Nepal's five-yearly embassy visit Beijing, Gorkha's envoys took the opportunity to press for China's support. They were advised to live in harmony. Even so, the possibility that the Qing would intervene in the event of an overwhelming defeat of Gorkha was perhaps the most potent brake on the Earl of Moira's ambitions.

The old warrior Ochterlony was convinced that the most immediate threat to the British in India was from the Gorkhali army, in particular his adversary Amar Singh Thapa. In 1813, Amar Singh's troops occupied four villages on the plains of Hindur, the small kingdom that Amar Singh had taken in 1805 during his drive west. The British believed these villages came under their protection, under the terms of a proclamation made in 1809. The governor general wrote to Girvan

Yuddha, the Gorkhali king, demanding his troops withdraw. The reply, essentially coming from Bhimsen Thapa, was a history lesson: 'As the Honourable Company have by the grace of God established their dominion in Hindoostan by the power of the sword, so have I by the same means acquired possession of the hills together with the lowlands dependent on the territories of former Rajahs.' Even so, 'in consideration of friendship', he issued orders to Amar Singh to withdraw.

Ochterlony had already begun gathering intelligence for a possible campaign in the west, so when Amar Singh, having withdrawn his soldiers from the plains, asked to meet him, he took the opportunity to 'skirt along the hills, or as near as the roads will admit', travelling east from the Sutlej river. Their meeting at Kalka was amicable but Amar Singh was still fixated on the fort at Kangra, believing that since the British would have to fight the Sikhs, they should join forces with Gorkha. Kangra was of no concern to the Company, Ochterlony told him. He made careful notes on Gorkhali fortifications, which he admired for their strength and ingenuity, and a map of his journey. He also drew on reports from other officers to produce a shrewd overview of Gorkhali troops in their western provinces, particularly their equipment and ethnic background, observations he reported to the governor general's office. This intelligence would stand him in good stead.

Provocation for war came not in the west, where Ochterlony would command a column, but in the east, where negotiations over the status of Butwal were breaking down. This was land that Bhimsen Thapa's father had acquired when he took Palpa, so the Gorkhalis had been collecting rents there for five years when a proxy for the Company, arguing that the land had belonged to the nawab of Oudh and was consequently his, attempted to seize the villages, killing a Gorkhali official. A commission was set up to look into the entire border issue, but before it convened, the Gorkhalis took more villages, bringing the total to twenty-two. The British commissioner, Captain Paris Bradshaw, issued an ultimatum, demanding the Gorkhalis withdrew.

Girvan Yuddha sought advice from his ministers and generals on the right course of action. Given what the governor general was proposing – establishing Company authority on the terai – the king posed a simple, rhetorical question: 'How then is my Raj to exist?' In that question lay the most persuasive explanation for Gorkha defiance. The economics hadn't changed. Nepal paid her soldiers through land, specifically through rents, known as *jagir*. Those who performed long service to the king might be rewarded with a piece of land in perpetuity, a kind of pension called *birta*. The regime had to grow to meet these commitments. Nepal couldn't afford to be pushed back from its most profitable gains, cultivated land on the terai, where there was also plenty of virgin jungle available to those with the necessary capital to clear it. To do so would fatally undermine the new nation's economic model. Gorkha leaders hoped that the virulent form of malaria known as *aul* that plagued the terai and had decimated the Kinloch expedition would stop the British. They ignored Paris Bradshaw's ultimatum.

The consequences of war against the British were obvious to the king's ministers. The myriad kingdoms across the southern Himalaya that the Gorkhalis had knitted into an empire could splinter again. Such petty states would be at the mercy of the great power to the south, precisely the outcome Prithvi Narayan Shah had feared. The British had the same idea, courting the various local chiefs the Gorkhas had ousted across the Himalaya. David Ochterlony believed these displaced and disgruntled rulers, 'ingrates' he judged them, weren't worth the bother; some local populations were no happier to see their old raja's return than they were the arrival of the Gorkhas. In the east, the *chogyal*, or king, of Sikkim offered support to the British in their fight against Gorkha but, as a British official put it, 'in so doing the most earnest and impressive entreaties were made that they might not be deceived, as the most inevitable destruction would attend them if they were', These stirrings of rebellion added to a growing anxiety among Gorkhali commanders. Amar Singh Thapa and the Gorkhali governor of Kumaon, Brahma Shah, no friend to each other, put their names to a letter warning of disaster. Both had spent years stamping Gorkhali control on the western provinces and knew how fragile the situation was.

The English, seeing their opportunity, have put themselves into an attitude of offence, and the conflict, if war now be undertaken, will be desperate. They will not rest satisfied without establishing their own power and authority, and will unite with the Hill Rajas, whom we have dispossessed. We have hitherto but hunted deer. If we engage in this war, we must prepare to fight tigers.

Amar Singh betrayed no hint of this concern in a letter he wrote to Ochterlony in the summer of 1814, warning the British that

the troops of the Goorkhas, resembling the waves of the ocean, whose chief employments are war and hostilities, will make the necessary preparations to prevent the usurpation of any one place.

Ultimately, both sides misread each other's 'red lines'. The British failed to understand how a border dispute might be judged an existential threat in Kathmandu and that any consequent war would be prosecuted wholeheartedly. They also misjudged the resilience and courage of the Gorkhali army. Public opinion in India held that the war would be short and that the raja of Nepal would quickly capitulate. The Earl of Moira entertained the idea this might happen before any shots were fired. Bhimsen Thapa, meanwhile, did not believe that the East India Company would mount a serious attack on Nepal. His mistake was failing to appreciate how the diplomatic twists and turns and bellicose posturing his government employed in its border dispute had stoked the Earl of Moira's own existential fears for the British in India: commercial prudence aside, the governor general could not be seen to vacillate.

The confidence of British officers was inversely proportional to their experience of Gorkhali military capabilities. The governor general was a bluff old soldier who planned thoroughly, but he didn't know mountains, concluding blithely that 'the difficulties of mountain warfare were greater on the defensive side'. He anticipated 'a brilliant and rapid termination of the war', conceding only that it needed to be 'rapid' because any failure would encourage the Sikhs and Marathas to exploit British vulnerability. Ochterlony had experience of Gorkhali troops and had personally met Amar Singh Thapa in 1813. His first view of the army had also been dismissive, 'ill-armed and undisciplined barbarians who effect [sic] a wretched imitation of the dress, accoutrements and constitution of a British native battalion'. The closer war came, however, the more he balanced his opinion. Like the general he was about to fight, Ochterlony was becoming increasingly sceptical about his prospects. True, 'Goorkha power must be completely over-thrown to avoid a constant source of trouble and expense,' but, as he wrote to his friend Charles Metcalfe, the young and capable colonial administrator who had taken over as resident in Delhi:

> To set off with the idea of overthrowing a long-established Government, and for such an unprofitable purpose, appears to me the most Quixotic and the most impolitic measure we have ever attempted – setting aside all the physical difficulties.

'Quixotic' and at times embarrassing: despite Amar Singh's respect for the Honourable Company's soldiery, there would shortly be moments of bloody incompetence.

*

The Company's army, the largest the British had put into the field in India thus far, was in the overall command of an officer of the regular British army rather than a Bengal Infantry man. This in itself created tension among the East India Company's own officers, demoralised from years of neglect. In the eighteenth century the Company's army had been the wonder of the colonial world but was now in urgent need of reform. Then there was the officer himself. Robert Rollo Gillespie, like Ochterlony recently promoted to major general, was the epitome of the imperialist adventurer. A hard-drinking gambler, a womaniser who in his youth fought duels, Gillespie was regularly in trouble with authority and always leading the attack. He was famous for his immediate and decisive response to the mutiny of sepoys at Vellore in 1806, the first significant uprising against British command by indigenous troops. The speed and aggression Gillespie had shown in coming to the aid of his fellow countrymen had made him a national hero.

Yet Gillespie's glory days were now in the past. As preparations were laid for war in the cooler post-monsoon season of 1814, Gillespie was facing another personal crisis, accused of corruption in his previous posting in Java by the founder of Singapore, Stamford Raffles. Worse, he had suffered head injuries fighting the Dutch and French at Fort Cornelis in Java three years before; the historian John Pemble thought it likely that when he took command against the Gorkhas he was not in his right mind. The diarist Lady Nugent, who spoke regularly with Gillespie when he arrived in India shortly before the Nepal war, believed his 'natural impetuosity and his extraordinary vanity and love of fame had led him into false ideas and errors that would embitter his future life'. His future life was not long. Gillespie's rage and impatience when besieging Gorkha troops inside the strategic fort of Nalapani at Khalanga prompted one of his famous charges, and he was shot through the heart by a sniper on 31 October. One witness wrote: 'General Gillespie was shot dead in the act of huzzaing to the men, waving his hat in his left hand and sword in his right hand; and yet not a man would follow him nor advance with them.' It was the first significant action of the war and the campaign's commanding officer was already dead. Many of the officers who served him were relieved. The Gorkhali troops were proving a brave and resolute enemy. Gillespie's body was preserved in spirits and transported to Calcutta for burial, where the joke was that he had been 'a pickle when alive, and a preserve when dead'. In Britain, predictably, he was hailed as a glorious hero.

The Nalapani fort held out for another month, a few hundred Gorkhalis facing thousands of better-equipped troops, benefitting from the determined leadership of Balbhadra Kunwar, Bhimsen Thapa's nephew, who consequently remains a national hero for at least some in Nepal. Courage and tactical nous were the Gorkhali advantages: disharmony and poor leadership the failings of the British. Both sides had over the course of the previous half-century been aggressively expansionist; both were defending hard-won colonial interests. Balbhadra's father, like so many of the wider Thapa clan, had been a colonial governor serving in various postings in the west and far west of Nepal's provinces.

The consequence was, as ever, a pitiful destruction of human life. Although stoutly defended, Nalapani was small and of mediocre construction: it left its occupants cruelly exposed. When the British captain Henry Sherwood stepped inside its ruins, he bore witness to a pathetic scene: 'Those who could in any way move had attempted to get out: but others were calling for water, and our officers were assisting, as well as they could, by pouring water out to them.' The fort's water supply had been cut, which ultimately had forced its abandonment; Balbhadra had escaped along with as many of his men as could still walk. 'Some of the poor creatures had lain there for three days with their limbs broken,' Sherwood continued. 'I shall never forget one young woman with a broken leg, lying among the dead.' He saw an injured Gorkha soldier 'making figures in the bloody dust with his fingers', out of his mind from a head-wound.

> The most affecting sight was two little girls, one about four years old, the other about one. Their father and mother had both been killed. They were both taken care of, but the elder screaming very much, fearing she should be separated from the younger. ... This day I saw the horrors of war; and indeed, horrible it is.

The Earl of Moira's plan for the war split Nepal into two, west and east of the Kali Gandaki, the deep river gorge roughly in the middle of the country. The army was deployed in four columns, two in either theatre. The larger of the two forces in the east was assigned the capture of the fort at Makwanpur, seizing the road to Kathmandu, a killer blow. A smaller force to its left would leave Gorakhpur for the disputed frontier lands of Butwal, drawing Gorkha opposition away from the main column and if the situation allowed capturing Tansen, the capital of the formerly independent state of Palpa, whose governor had been Bhimsen Thapa's father. He had died in the days leading up to the war and it was his grandson, Bhimsen Thapa's nephew, Ujir Singh Thapa, who led the Gorkhali defence in this sector. Facing him was Major General John Wood, whose vacillation and uncertainty before a fortification called Jitgadhi sent him back to Gorakhpur under pressure from a jubilant enemy force. When Wood asked that the bodies of the British dead be returned, Ujir Singh told him: 'Any attempt to commit unjust aggression on this powerful state will be severely punished by its gallant army.' It was a similar story for the main eastern force: hesitation, delay and a clumsy intervention by the Earl of Moira, who replaced his original commander, the hesitant Major General Bennet Marley, with someone even less incisive.

Of the four columns advancing on Nepal, it was that of the older and less favoured David Ochterlony, operating in the furthest west of the Gorkhali kingdom that coped best with the tactical demands of mountain warfare. His force, almost entirely native infantry and cavalry with some European artillery, was boosted with Sikh troops from rajas under the Company's protection, impressive men but unused to disciplined fighting. Given considerable discretion, Ochterlony chose to equip his force with heavy artillery even though the Earl of Moira had envisaged a fast-moving campaign with mobility as the key. Ochterlony was more patient, deciding that the enemy's reliance on forts justified his slow progress with heavy guns. So it proved. He used elephants to bring his artillery to where it could threaten the first fort at Nalagarh, and the garrison promptly surrendered. Trees were felled and roads cleared to bring these guns to the next objective, Ramgarh, where Amar Singh Thapa waited with the best of his army, behind stockades and well dug in. His troops proved far better and more resilient soldiers than the sepoys Ochterlony commanded. Ochterlony's masterstroke was to trick Amar Singh into moving his position, from Ramgarh, where he was largely impregnable, to Malaun, where the Gorkhali general had quartered his wife and young son – and his wealth too. As a consequence, the British took both locations, with almost no casualties.

Amar Singh was brave, but a poor tactician. After the death of Gillespie and the fall of Nalapani, he had told his son Ranjor Singh, commander of the Gorkhali troops in that sector, to withdraw from the superbly fortified town of Nahan in favour of a tiny fortress at Jaithak. The decision baffled Henry Sherwood, who wrote how the Gorkhas 'at one moment defend themselves well, not only with bravery but with judgement; and at another, neglect the commonest means of defence'. Nevertheless, taking Jaithak proved beyond Gillespie's successor, Gabriel Martindell. An attempt to storm it cost the British hundreds of casualties in one day, one of the dead being William Makepeace Thackeray's uncle Thomas, shot in the chest as he tried to withdraw with his men, having formed a square to delay the counter-attacking Nepalis. Only seven men in his command made it back alive. After that reverse, Martindell was poleaxed with indecision.

Two peripheral campaigns proved far more successful. In the east the British cooperated with the raja of Sikkim to push back the Gorkhas beyond the Mechi river. In the west a hastily concocted force under the command of William Gardner, many of them irregulars, including hundreds of mercenary Pathans from Afghanistan, managed to wrest the small town of Almora from the Gorkhali governor of Kumaon, Brahma Shah. This followed the death of his brother Hasti Dal, a revered and talismanic general, overhauled while trying to secure the Gorkhali lines of communication to the west. (One of the most effective reforms the Gorkhalis had instituted in their new empire was their official *hulak* postal system that kept Kathmandu apprised of events.) The Gorkhali forces, just like the British, also had to resupply their forces and the fall of Almora effectively cut Nepal off from Garhwal, where Ochterlony was fighting Amar Singh Thapa. A series of surrenders followed, and the dynamic shifted from which side would win to which faction in Kathmandu would emerge in control of a much-reduced Gorkha Empire. Brahma Shah told the British he wanted power returned to more aristocratic hands, dismissing the Thapa clan as Khas upstarts. Yet despite his personal responsibility in this calamity, Bhimsen Thapa would hold on to power.

*

In November 1814, in the early weeks of the war, Major Paris Bradshaw, who had previously been the boundary commissioner negotiating with Kathmandu and was now Major General Bennett Marley's political agent, was put in charge of concluding a peace treaty with the Gorkhalis. The draft he had made by the end of that month was signed more or less unchanged little more than a year later at Sagauli, on 2 December 1815. Before the war, Gorkha power had been at its zenith, stretching from the Tista river in the east, now in the Indian state of West Bengal, to the Sutlej in the west, in modern Himachal Pradesh. It had truly been a Himalayan empire. After the war, Nepal had lost a third of its territory, including the provinces of Garhwal and Kumaon as well as vast tracts of valuable land in the terai. The new boundaries were the Mahakali river in the west and the Mechi river in the east.

With the Gorkha threat neutralised, Ochterlony and Charles Metcalfe were already turning their attention to the Sikh Empire and the protection of the Company's flank east of the Sutlej. Yet even with the treaty agreed, Bhimsen Thapa still tried to wriggle off his hook, refusing to have it ratified, and the Company put Ochterlony in charge of a final – arguably unnecessary – campaign to force the issue, in February 1816 taking the fortress at Makwanpur, just a few days' march from Kathmandu. Necessary or not, during this interlude between the agreement of terms and the capitulation at Makwanpur, Bhimsen looked for help in his struggle against the British, to Ranjit Singh and other potential enemies in common. He also wrote to the Jiaqing emperor, accusing the East India Company of outrageous provocations and aggression, but the ambans in Lhasa refused to forward his letters to Beijing. Or at least, that's what they told Bhimsen Thapa.

In fact, the Qing had been paying close attention to events in Nepal. British success prompted the Jiaqing emperor into sending an army into Tibet. For several months in the summer of 1816, the Earl of Moira and his staff had to consider the threat of China's intervention. Now began a three-way game of diplomatic poker. China could ill afford another expensive war in order to reassert its control over Nepal, but wanted to maintain its status with Britain. From the British point of view, having just found out how much treasure fighting in the mountains could absorb, and having suffered several uncomfortable reverses, the last thing needed was an escalation of hostilities. There were plenty in Britain who wondered at the sense of fighting the Gorkhalis in the first place, not least the Duke of York, commander-in-chief of the British army, a man who knew a lot about cards and other games of chance. As it was, Bhimsen Thapa, who now held the worst hand, would play best. Knowing Britain was anxious about its relationship with China, he would exploit that apprehension to claw back some of his losses.

Under the terms of Sagauli, the British were entitled to have a diplomat resident at Kathmandu, and on 17 April 1816, the Gorkhali envoy Gajraj Mishra led the new acting resident, Lieutenant John Peter Boileau, through the streets of Kathmandu to the palace. Born in Dublin of Huguenot stock, Boileau had been stabbed in the thigh during fighting in late 1814 but had recovered to split his assailant's head in two. Now he was enforcing the governor general's terms for peace. Led up several flights of narrow stairs to the audience chamber, Boileau found the waiting courtiers framed by curtains of white muslin, shielding them from the hot sun. The king, Girvan Yuddha, now eighteen and in his majority, sat under a canopy suspended from four silver standards, but he rose and stepped down from his dais to greet the officer. Real power lay elsewhere in the room; the man Mishra introduced next was Bhimsen Thapa.

In presenting his credentials, Boileau made it clear that while the governor general looked forward to a new relationship with Nepal, the first task of the Gorkhali government was to implement the treaty they had just signed. Bhimsen was courteous, even animated, but impossible to read. No promises were made. Around him were the raja's *bharadar*, the nobility, all of them wondering, just like Boileau, what the chief minister's next move might be, none of them with a coherent plan to get rid of him.

The British, first in the shape of Boileau, then followed in late July by his permanent successor Edward Gardner, were anxious to prevent any confrontation with China. Bhimsen understood this very well, but his relations with the East India Company were only one part of a much more important issue: his own survival. Although he had told China the next British target was Tibet, Bhimsen knew the Qing would quickly conclude the British posed no further threat. Meanwhile, his enemies at court, principally the Pande family, were smarting from the humiliation of a heavy defeat. Acting tough against the British would take the pressure off from both angles, providing a display of strength for the Pandes to consider and a pretext for stoking Chinese anxieties, news of which would chasten the British. So Bhimsen stationed troops to keep watch on the resident and sent Amar Singh Thapa, shortly before the old general's death, for talks with Qing envoys close to the Tibetan border. Almost immediately, he began feeding information on these overtures to the resident who in turn had a detailed exchange with his masters in Calcutta, who were now contemplating another war with the remnants of the Maratha Empire. In this way, Bhimsen applied pressure on the Company's most sensitive nerve: China.

Everything now depended on relations with the Qing. If they demanded it, Gardner was to withdraw. Meanwhile the British hurried to reassure China that Nepal retained its independence and the East India Company had no designs on its territory. The Qing did in fact request Gardner be recalled, but the Earl of Moira, now titled the Marquess of Hastings following the war with Gorkha, finessed this by requesting the Chinese install their own resident, to keep an eye on what the restless Gorkhali army was up to. The Chinese demurred,

Gardner stayed put and Bhimsen Thapa could justifiably claim that he had managed to keep Nepal largely independent. His hand was strengthened when the young king died, reportedly in an outbreak of smallpox, in November 1816; as noted earlier, the king's young son was put in the care of Bhimsen's niece Tripura Sundari, who began her second term as regent.

The Marquess of Hastings soon realised that in making peace with Nepal, the East India Company had effectively become tax collector for the raja in Kathmandu: in the terms of Sagauli, the British had agreed to an indemnity, to be paid to the Gorkhali king as compensation for land on the terai seized during the fighting. The governor general now decided to give back this land: the very land and more besides that the British had gone to war over. The Victorian historian Edward Thornton claimed this decision 'converted the war into an idle but dismal farce', but given Nepal's relationship with China, and Britain's relationship with China, the governor general had little choice. The Company's limited room for manoeuvre also explains why the resident at Kathmandu fulfilled a very different and more limited role compared to residents stationed in other important locations on the Indian subcontinent: not so much a diplomat or negotiator, but an early-warning system of Gorkhali militarism.

To accommodate their resident, the king of Nepal had given the British a scrap of land more than three kilometres north of the palace, whose name in Nepali translates as the 'house of devils'. Plagued by fog in winter and mosquitoes in summer, Edward Gardner followed the governor general's policy of appeasement towards Nepal to the letter by doing absolutely nothing as politely as possible, a position he maintained for the next thirteen years until Calcutta antagonised him by cutting his salary, at which point he retired. His replacement was the pink-cheeked neophyte Ochterlony had met at Delhi ten years earlier: Brian Houghton Hodgson. His role would be far more active. Through timing, opportunity and inclination, Hodgson would put himself at the centre not only of court politics in Kathmandu, but also what might be termed Himalayan Studies: the region's ethnography and natural history, and Buddhism, just as Europe discovered it. As we shall see in the next chapter, he also forged relationships that would have a direct bearing on the future of the British Empire.

The impact of détente between Kathmandu and Calcutta on the people of Nepal was the most dismal consequence of the war. Gorkha's powerful army had not gone away and was agitating for revenge. There was no question of reforming how they were paid and no real interest on the part of Bhimsen Thapa in doing so. He was a pragmatist, anxious to keep the court and the army on side. His problem was that the same number of fish were now occupying a smaller pond. Senior officers took their salary as grain from farmers and sold it in India for cash, which was repatriated not to where it was earned but to Kathmandu. In this way, the wealth of the land was centralised on Nepal's capital and the ordinary people of Nepal suffered decades of little or no investment and no escape from a life of desperate toil. The situation was most keenly felt in those areas of modern Nepal, such as the far west, most recently gathered into the Gorkha Empire and regarded largely as spoils of war. These are still among the poorest parts of Nepal.

Over the next century and a half, the deadening hand of distant interests would hold back the people of the Himalaya. For the most part, assuming they toed a line drawn in Calcutta or Beijing, they were left to their own devices. Abetting this colonial indifference were ruling elites that failed, usually by omission, to develop the material lives of ordinary people. The historian Ludwig Stiller captured Nepal's stagnant drift in his book *The Silent Cry*. Prithvi Narayan Shah had believed his new nation walked on two legs, its military and its farmers, and that without a rich peasantry, the country would founder.

> Somewhere on the road of conquest, amid the crash of guns and the sweat of battle, these ideals were lost. The military had assumed the right to grow and to live at the expense of the farmers of Nepal, and all too many of the bharadars forgot the meaning of their title ('those who carry the burden of the nation') and demanded that the nation serve them.

The picture was different across the border in Kumaon, now under British control. In April 1816, Captain Felix Raper was in its capital Almora, a hundred and sixty kilometres or so west of the new border with Nepal, writing to a friend. Raper had, with permission from the Gorkha governor of Srinagar, explored the source of the Ganges nine

years earlier in the company of the Anglo-Indian adventurer Hyder
Jung Hearsey. It was a region he knew well. Now he predicted great
things for the town, which would become 'a fashionable resort in the
hot weather'. His guess proved correct. Before long the British had
built a sanatorium near Almora and the notion of the British hill
station was born. Mountain villages barely heard of before the Nepal
War became as famous as Calcutta: Mussoorie, close to the fortress
of Nalapani where the hot-headed gambler Gillespie perished; the
beautiful hamlet of Naini Tal; and Simla, which would become the
summer capital of the Raj, immortalised by Rudyard Kipling, hidden
in the mountains north of where Amar Singh Thapa had been outfoxed
by David Ochterlony. Leaving aside the impact hill stations had on
the life of the British up until their departure in 1947, they transformed
the economic prospects of the former colonies of Nepal, albeit under
British hegemony. Young men from poor villages in Nepal, Kumaon
and Garhwal would over time become an integral part of the Indian
army, protecting the Raj, a source of wealth and prestige for Britain
as it transformed itself, economically and culturally, into the wealthiest
nation on earth.

10

Mapping the Himalaya

In late 1774, the affable George Bogle was at Tashilhunpo monastery in Tibet, pressing the East India Company's trading interests with the Panchen Lama. Suspicion about his intentions and those of governor Warren Hastings, his master in Calcutta, ran deep. An unofficial envoy, a man Bogle called Chauduri, came to visit him, sent from Lhasa by the eighth Dalai Lama's regent. Bogle didn't like Chauduri much, commenting on the man's 'cringing humility', which he compared unfavourably with the 'plain and honest manners of the Tibetans'. Chauduri was not himself Tibetan but from Palpa, on the other side of the mountains, at that time one of the small independent hill-states yet to be absorbed into the Gorkha kingdom of Nepal. While he promised Bogle more than the Company desired, ultimately he delivered nothing; Bogle speculated that Chauduri was either a chancer out to gain advantage for himself or more probably someone sent to gather intelligence whom the regent in Lhasa could deny knowing, which he promptly did.

Whatever Chauduri's motives, his presence in Tibet is a reminder that far from being a blank on the map, southern Tibet was part of a Himalayan network of cultures linking two of the most populous regions on earth, India and China. The regent had in this instance used a 'Hindustani' to deflect British interest; at other times Tibetan officials relied on the presence of the Manchu ambans, ambassadors stationed in Lhasa to maintain the Qing Empire's influence on its western borders. We've already seen the value the Panchen Lama placed on trade and information, and his reliance on the *gosain* merchant Purangir as an intermediary. Bogle himself attested to the wealth of trade passing through the hands of Kashmiri merchants and Kalmuks from Siberia.

But Tibet's experience of the world extended far beyond its immediate neighbours. Although Bogle was the first European whom Lobsang Palden Yeshe, the sixth Panchen Lama, had met, the lama had a wide range of European objects in his possession: a French pocket compass and a *camera obscura* with scenes of London, for example. When the lama pointed out a similarity between the facial features of figures painted on a piece of Chinese porcelain and those of his Scottish guest, Bogle explained that the images of shepherdesses had in fact been copied by Chinese craftsmen from European art. This exchange of knowledge flowed both ways. Bogle was given instruction in Tibetan history and law, as well as more arcane subjects like cosmography. He was also presented with a map, a gift from the Panchen Lama himself; it was an almost casual offer but one resonant with significance. It also challenges western assumptions about what remote Tibet knew of the world beyond the mountains.

*

Bogle had crosed the Himalaya armed with the best knowledge then available to the East India Company about Tibet's geography, politics and culture, drawn from the work of Jean-Baptiste Du Halde, and accompanied by the *Nouvel atlas de la Chine, de la Tartarie chinoise et du Thibet*, published in 1737, the work of French cartographer Jean-Baptiste Bourguignon d'Anville. Neither man had even been to China, let alone Tibet: they drew on the researches of Jesuit missionaries trained as surveyors, who maintained the confidence of the otherwise anti-Christian Qing Kangxi emperor. The Jesuits were able to fix positions of longitude and latitude using astronomical measurements, a significant advance on Chinese techniques. The Kangxi emperor commissioned from them an atlas, a flowering of the French Académie Royale des Sciences in China. Though he restricted its use within his own kingdom to court officials, a copy was sent back to Europe, where it transformed western attitudes to China and the regions around it, including Korea, another kingdom 'forbidden' to Europeans.

Surveying for these Jesuit maps began in 1708 and the first of them were published in 1718, after a decade of surveying work. China's western tributary states were to be included but Tibet, then under the direct control of the Khoshut Khanate, was not part of the original project. The Kangxi emperor soon corrected the omission. In 1709 a Qing diplomatic official called Ho-shou, newly appointed to Lhasa, was given the extra responsibility of surveying Tibet. He took with him to his new posting some Chinese cartographers, according to Du Halde, 'to make a map of all the territories immediately subject to the Great Lama'. These territories were of political significance to the Kangxi emperor: this was during the period of rival Dalai Lamas, with a pretender under the control of the Khoshut leader Lajang Khan in Lhasa, while the seventh Dalai Lama Kelzang Gyatso, whom the Kangxi emperor, as well as most Tibetans, preferred, was based in Litang. Two years later their work was handed to the Jesuit cartographer Jean-Baptiste Régis in Beijing, but he thought it of poor quality and while it was used for early versions of the Chinese maps, the Jesuits lobbied for a better survey, one that relied on their more exact techniques. In 1717, the emperor finally gave permission for more work to be done.

Two Tibetan lamas educated in geometry and receiving instruction from the Jesuit Pierre Jartoux were despatched to do the job properly. With them travelled an official called Sengju from the *Lifanyuan*, or 'Court of Colonial Affairs', which mostly took care of matters related to Mongolia and Tibet. The survey team took compass bearings, measured distances and established their latitude using gnomons (shadow-casting devices), adding a scientific basis to long-established Chinese traditions in map making. They also collected coordinates of significant mountains and, the sources suggest, measured their altitude: all this a century before the great colonial project, the Survey of India, began its precise cartographic work in the Himalaya and overturned the widespread European belief that the Andes were the highest mountains on earth.

For the Qing Empire, cartographic information was strategically useful. At the end of the seventeenth century, in the north-east corner of the Tibetan plateau, the Kokonor, or 'blue sea', region (known afterwards as Qinghai) had come under Beijing's direct control. The route from the Qinghai city of Xining to Lhasa, some two thousand kilometres to the south, was well known to merchants and pilgrims, including the Armenian community then living in Tibet. Now the Qing armies, the Eight Banners, had a reliable map of the road; Lhasa was calculated to be twelve degrees west of Xining. If the Survey of India was part of a colonial project to strengthen political control by a distant elite, then so was Qing cartography a century before. When the entire project was completed, no country in Europe had better maps than China.

The Tibetan survey team reached as far west as Kailas but the catastrophic Dzungar Mongol invasion of Tibet in 1717 prompted them to withdraw swiftly and quietly to China, most probably via Sichuan, since the survey provided updated information on the road between Lhasa and the Sichuan town of Kangding, known as Tachienlu in those days or Dartsedu in Tibetan. Their information was passed to their instructor, Pierre Jartoux, and while the maps produced were not as reliable as those to districts under direct Qing control, they were a big improvement.

As far as the British were concerned, however, a serious omission was the map's vagueness on the source of the Ganges; the surveying lamas had been forced to rely on oral information from fellow monks about where the river rose. Despite this lacuna, the exchange of knowledge between China and the West was productive. According to the Jesuit Antoine Gaubil, one of the surveying lamas kept a journal of their travels. This was most likely a man called Zangbu Rabjamba, the latter name being an academic title that indicates he must have studied at one of the three main monasteries of central Tibet. We know that the same monk who kept the journal, soon after returning to Beijing, also translated a Chinese work on European astronomy, knowledge brought to the Qing by the Jesuits, into Tibetan. The contribution of Tibetans to the scientific understanding of their own country, the so-called 'Lama Survey', has faded from view, just as most of the Indian and Anglo-Indian surveyors working in the Himalaya a century later would also be left in obscurity.

The maps Bogle carried by Jean-Baptiste Du Halde and Jean-Baptiste Bourguignon d'Anville, based on those of their Jesuit predecessors, were as far as he was aware the most up-to-date of Tibet available, so he must have been surprised when the Panchen Lama casually offered him a better one. It was, Bogle wrote, 'a splendid Object', and acquiring it would no doubt earn him praise from his superiors in Calcutta. Yet he hesitated.

I considered that the Company could have no Interest in this Country but that of Commerce; and that to know a number of outlandish

Names, or to correct the Geography of Thibet, although a matter of great Curiosity, and extremely interesting to Geographers and Map-sellers, was of no use to my Constituents, or indeed to mankind in general, and that to this I might be sacrificing Objects of far greater Importance, by encreasing that Jealousy which had hitherto so cruelly thwarted me in all my Negotiations.

And so Bogle, despite the Panchen Lama's insistence, turned the offer down. When he saw his host's disappointment, he hastened to explain that he was much more interested in the culture of Tibet than its geography, which pleased the Panchen Lama so much that Bogle offered him an account of Europe, to satisfy the Panchen Lama's curiosity.

As the weeks passed, Bogle's affection for Tibet only deepened; he grew close to the Panchen Lama's family and began a love affair. The subject of the map was dropped, but there remains a tantalising question. There is no way of knowing what the map was that Bogle was shown, let alone who made it, but nothing available in Europe surpassed the Qing survey until the second half of the nineteenth century. If the Panchen Lama's map was indeed more comprehensive than the one Bogle had used, who had drawn it?

One of the contenders is the Italian Ippolito Desideri, among the first missionaries to reach Lhasa, arriving there in 1716, and the first to study properly the Tibetan language and religion. He was allowed a chapel in Sera monastery, where he studied Buddhism, and was still there in late 1717 when the Dzungar Mongols invaded and overthrew the Khoshut leader Lajang Khan. This was despite the arrival of Capuchin missionaries the autumn before, who insisted that the Vatican had made Tibet and Nepal the Capuchins' to convert and that the Jesuit Desideri should leave. After years of fruitless argument with Rome, Desideri did eventually return to India but there's no version of the map Bogle might have been shown in Desideri's papers.

Another possible source of the Panchen Lama's map is a man called Samuel van de Putte, whom Desideri encountered on his journey to Pondicherry in southern India, having been appointed to lead the Jesuit mission there. Stopping off at Patna, on the south bank of the Ganges, Desideri and van de Putte had what must have been a remarkable encounter: van de Putte, although born in the Netherlands, was fluent in Italian and had many stories to tell, being several years into an epic journey that would last most of his lifetime, one of the greatest journeys made in Asia by a European, and yet almost unknown.

*

Samuel van de Putte came from a family on the rise, his father Carel being a vice-admiral in the navy of Zeeland, a Dutch province predominantly below sea level, from the port of Vlissingen whose prosperity, then fading, had been built during the Netherlands' golden age of privateering. The epaulettes on his shoulders, won fighting the English in the Four Days' naval battle of 1666, gave Carel rights to *buiten-goederen*, booty that secured his financial future. Aged fifty, he married Johanna Biscop, from a solid middle-class family. They had five children in quick succession but within ten years both were dead. The young Samuel, born in 1690, moved with his sisters and brothers to live with their uncle, and the family house was sold. He graduated from the famous law school at Leiden and by 1715 was an alderman in his hometown. Inheriting a legacy from his parents, he found sufficient funds to buy back his childhood home. A sober life of prosperous Dutch rectitude awaited him. Perhaps that prospect goaded him to have an adventure; with Egmond van Nijenburg, a wealthy friend from university, Samuel embarked on the early eighteenth-century version of the grand tour.

The friends travelled through France and Venice and settled in Padua, where Samuel studied medicine, the subject that really inspired him, and learned Italian. In the university library he found a copy of *Giro del mondo*, the extraordinary travelogue of the Italian lawyer Giovanni Francesco Gemelli Careri, then still living in Naples. Thought by some at the time to be a fraud, it told an astonishing story of independent travel that circled the globe, done for its own sake, in a spirit of simple curiosity. Perhaps not surprisingly, the Jesuit missionaries Careri met in India had thought him a spy sent by the pope. Why else would anyone travel? The reason lay in the thwarting of Gemelli Careri's career because of his family's lack of nobility, something that may have resonated with Samuel. While his companion Egmond's father had been made a baron of the Holy Roman Empire, assuring Egmond's success, for Samuel, by contrast, a life of legal drudgery lay ahead. Perhaps that didn't seem as appealing after reading Gemelli Careri.

After Constantinople and a tour through the Holy Land, Egmond and Samuel reached Aleppo. Here they parted company. Egmond turned for home, slipping back into the privileged life he had left. Samuel joined a merchant's caravan and set out across the desert, along the Silk Road to Isfahan. He would be travelling with caravans almost constantly for the next three years, his journey pieced together from fragments, occasional obscure references in the official archives of merchants and missionaries. His father had bought shares in the Dutch East India Company (VOC), then the largest company in the world, and his younger brother Constantijn worked for them in Amsterdam; this gave Samuel a global assistance network. But when he passed through the company's station at Gamron (Bandar Abbas) in the Persian Gulf his request for assistance was refused: a wild, half-starved eccentric two years in the desert dressed like an Arab seemed a poor bet. His appearance at Gamron was reported to Batavia, the centre of VOC operations in Asia, and passed on to the Netherlands, where his brother intervened. An instruction was issued in October 1724 to stations throughout Asia to be prepared to help him. Before then, Samuel van de Putte had reached the VOC station at Cochin in southern India, a year after leaving Gamron, exhausted and riddled with illness.

The following summer he was in Patna, two hundred and fifty kilometres south of Kathmandu, having travelled overland to Pondicherry before sailing up the coast to Bengal, still under Mughal control. His motivation for travelling to the Himalaya is unclear. Gemelli Careri didn't go there, so perhaps he was looking to try something more original. Perhaps he had acquired a taste for wilder landscapes. In light of the choices he made later, Samuel van de Putte's life seems like a voyage of psychological exploration, a faint echo of the tantric *mahasiddha* who travelled the Himalaya centuries before. It seems unlikely that it was coincidence he met Desideri, who had with him the manuscript about Tibet he had been working on since he returned five years before, the manuscript that would be proscribed and archived on his return. Van de Putte read Desideri's work and made twenty pages of notes. He also followed Desideri's advice about travelling through Nepal to reach Tibet, the first Dutchman to do so, and the last for more than two hundred years.

Van de Putte would spend the next five years in Lhasa, staying for at least some of the time with the Capuchin missionaries still living there. He took a strong interest in Tibetan Buddhism, making friends with lamas. In 1731 he joined a group of them journeying to Beijing via Qinghai, before returning to Lhasa in 1736. This time he travelled through Sichuan and entered Tibet at Kham in the south-east, the first European to visit this part of Tibet. After another short stay, he returned to India through Ladakh. We know the route he took on these travels only because he explained it in a letter to the head of the Capuchin mission at Lhasa, Francesco Orazio della Penna. It's not that he didn't keep copious records. He had a perfect command of Tibetan and the knowledge he gathered was preserved in notes, diaries and maps. But when he died in 1745, aged fifty-five, at the Dutch East India Company headquarters of Batavia, he left instructions that everything he had amassed during his travels should be burned. An entire lifetime's travelling and knowledge went up in smoke: or at least, almost all of it.

It seems a baffling, acutely painful decision, but the man who carried out his wishes said that van de Putte had reached the conclusion his material wasn't sufficiently accurate to be worth publishing. A few papers escaped and these were returned to his family in the Netherlands: some notes, fragments of letters and sketch maps, one of which the geographer Clements Markham included in his compendium of early European exploration of Tibet, published in 1876, a sketch-map that subsequently disappeared. The French compass the Panchen Lama showed George Bogle a century before was most probably a relic of the survey carried out in 1708. It's possible the map he showed him was the work of Samuel van de Putte. Bogle called his predecessor the 'Marco Polo of the Lowlands', but though well meant, it's too glib a comparison. Marco Polo travelled for profit and wrote for profit too. Samuel van de Putte did neither, but his motivation and the true scope of the material he gathered will forever remain obscure.

*

Whoever produced the map the Panchen Lama showed George Bogle, it clearly resonated with the Tibetan, not as some foreign curio but as a meaningful document. He was a travel writer himself, at least in the sense that he was writing a kind of cosmological guidebook: *The*

Explanation of Shambhala and Narrative of the Holy Land, the holy land
in question being India, the source of Buddhism. Bogle himself would
end up as an informant for this book, which was completed in 1775,
the year he left Tibet, filling in details about the current rulers of the
holy land, who had so recently replaced the Mughals. After centuries
of retreat and dislocation, the Panchen Lama must have seen the
changing political scene in India as a possible source of optimism for
Buddhism in its place of birth.

The treatise was, amongst other things, an attempt to locate tantric
centres of practice, known as *pitha* in Sanskrit. In the Tibetan imagination, India had become something of a lost world, where sacred
places that had witnessed the Buddha's life were waiting to be redis-
covered, as though they remained current, despite the centuries that
had passed since Buddhism and its institutions had been razed and
swept away. Like other writers in the seventeenth century, the Panchen
Lama located Kushinagar, the place were Buddha achieved enlightenment, in the Assam village of Hajo, on the banks not of the Ganges
but the Brahmaputra, far from the sites in Bihar and Nepal that we
now associate with Buddhism, as though Jerusalem had moved to
Cairo. How this happened is an obscure but important story for our
understanding of how the lama viewed maps.

A resurgent Hindu Shaivite temple at Hajo began to attract Buddhist
pilgrims in the early seventeenth century, Shaivism being strongly
flavoured with tantrism. Assam was accessible to southern Tibet, since
the powerful Geluk state then ruling in Lhasa extended its control to
the old Monyul kingdom, part of the modern Indian Himalayan state
of Arunachal Pradesh, which borders Assam to the north. As more
and more pilgrims visited Hajo, mania built. A famous *terton*, or revealer
of secrets, Pagsam Yeshe, visited in the 1680s. When he reached Hajo,
thanks to a prophecy of the Guru Rinpoche, he discovered sacred
treasures, including part of the *bodh* tree where the Buddha achieved
enlightenment. He brought a branch of it back to Tibet. A few visitors
were sceptical, with one ascribing Hajo's fame to 'the crafty Indian
inhabitants there who live by means of deception'. But mostly the
narrative was accepted; here was a vibrant, living religious world located
in the mother country that reconnected Tibet to its spiritual origins.

When the Panchen Lama included Hajo in his treatise, its status as
the focus of the holy land was a matter of fact and would remain so

deep into the nineteenth century. He was simply following the example
of similar works from other respected Buddhist scholars before him.
One of them was Sangye Gyatso, the powerful regent who had kept
the death of the fifth Dalai Lama in 1682 a secret from his own people
and the Chinese emperor. He had a clear motivation to acknowledge
the pilgrimage site of Hajo, since the new Dalai Lama was from that
part of the world; in doing the same, the Panchen Lama was in good
historical company. What he wanted to know now, he told George
Bogle, was the location of Shambhala, the fabulous kingdom of purity
outlined in the *Kalachakra* teachings and the Hindu *Puranas*. Perhaps
Bogle would seek out that information from informed pandits when
he returned to Bengal?

When we think about maps, we think about useful accurate information that will take us where we want to go. We sometimes consider
them as cultural artefacts, but rarely, in the West, do we see them as
spiritually enriching. Yet the story of Hajo tells us a lot about what
mattered to Tibetans as they navigated their way through the complex
terrain of the Himalaya. Physical landscapes were simply starting points
for spiritual exploration, an idea shared by Buddhists across Asia. The
first Japanese map to depict the whole world was published at Kyoto
in 1710, the work of Buddhist priest Rokashi Hotan. Its central focus is
Asia with India, being the holy land, at its centre. Hotan drew on the
travels of the Chinese Buddhist pilgrim Xuanzang's travels in the
Himalaya and includes motifs typical of Buddhist cosmography.
Included on the map is the mythological Lake Anavatapta where the
Buddha was conceived, essentially Lake Manasarovar, along with the
four great rivers, the Karnali, Indus, Brahmaputra and Sutlej, flowing
from their respective heads: of a peacock, a lion, a horse, and an elephant.

The British geographer John Brian Harley wrote in 1989, in his
paper 'Deconstructing the Map', how western cartography can dull
our responses to the very different sorts of geographical information
available to someone like the Panchen Lama. The kind of maps we
are accustomed to, depicting in two dimensions a simplified, graphic
version of the world from a great height,

> tend to 'desocialise' the territory they represent. They foster the notion
> of a socially empty space. The abstract quality of the [Western-style]
> map . . . lessens the burden of conscience about people in the landscape.

Decisions about the exercise of power are removed from the realm of immediate face-to-face contacts.

Thus, when the Survey of India arrived in the late eighteenth century, there was already a great deal of knowledge available to it about Himalayan geography, principally from traders and pilgrims, and a map made using European methods from the early seventeenth century. And yet in the popular European imagination of the time, the geography of the Himalaya was often characterised as blank, somewhere to be filled in by courageous soldiers and explorers writing their own narratives. The reality was more like a palimpsest, some-where that was scraped clean before a new script could be written. 'We are about to walk off the map,' George Mallory would claim in 1921, on his way to Everest. But it wasn't true.

★

Following the Battle of Buxar in 1764 and Robert Clive's success in prising Bengal from the Mughal emperor, the British were anxious to get a clearer picture of the country they now governed. The artery of the Ganges was of greatest interest: was there a channel navigable for shipping north of Calcutta? To answer that question, the governor Henry Vansittart, despite grappling with a corrupt East India Company and its souring relationship with the nawab of Bengal, Mir Qasim, had just enough time before resigning to commission an enterprising young marine surveyor called James Rennell, the first truly great geographer the British produced.

A Devon man, born in December 1742, Rennell was four when his father, an artillery officer, died fighting France in the Low Countries. His mother had to sell the family home and Rennell was from the age of ten raised by the vicar of Chudleigh, where the boy was already drawing maps for fun. After a few years of grammar school, Rennell, barely thirteen, was commissioned midshipman on the Royal Navy frigate *Brilliant* and saw active service against the French during the Seven Years' War. He came out to India in 1760 and was seconded to the East India Company, working for the Scot Alexander Dalrymple as a marine surveyor, drawing charts and harbour plans. With the war over, and without connections, Rennell saw little future in the navy and switched permanently to the Company, where Vansittart found him. Aged just twenty-one, Rennell was put in charge of the survey of Bengal, a cornerstone of the future Survey of India. Knowing the Company's public reputation, he remained grateful for its investment in science, writing a quarter of a century later:

> Whatever charges may be imputable to the Managers for the Company, the neglect of useful Science, however, is not among the number. The employing of Geographers, and Surveying Pilots in India; and the providing of astronomical instruments, and the holding out of encouragement to such as should use them; indicate, at least, a spirit somewhat above the mere consideration of Gain.

To take up his post, Rennell was commissioned as an ensign in the Bengal engineers and in the autumn of 1764 he started work on the course of the Ganges. The manuscript he produced with his geographical and meteorological observations so impressed Vansittart that he got Rennell an income of a thousand pounds a year, a colossal amount compared to his navy salary; Rennell built a house at Dacca, now the Bangladeshi capital Dhaka, which became his base, making the first plan of the city. In 1766, he volunteered to accompany an old navy friend, now serving in a sepoy regiment, on a mission to drive out a band of sannyasi, who had looted a town on the borders of Bhutan. Here he first encountered the vast white wall of the Himalaya, which he called the Tartarian Mountains. In a village he called Deehoota, thought to be safe ground, Rennell's little band of officers was unexpectedly surrounded. The others cut their way to safety but Rennell was trapped, his pistol misfired and his Armenian assistant killed. Armed only with a short sword, Rennell retreated, so peppered with sabre cuts that the sannyasi thought him done for. He stumbled towards a detachment of troops rushing to his aid but collapsed before he reached them. His wounds were packed with crushed onions and he was laid in an open boat, which returned him in six days to Dhaka, more dead than alive. One of the blows left a wound a foot long that had cut his right shoulder blade and several ribs; Rennell never again had full use of his right arm, and lost the use of his left index finger too. Robert Clive, the new governor, recognised his sacrifice by appointing Rennell surveyor general and giving him a detachment of sepoys to protect him as he worked. He also cut Rennell's salary, under pressure from the Court of Directors to reduce costs.

Rennell spent seven years in the field on four separate, extended expeditions, his work completed, in the words of one biographer, 'at the point of a bayonet'. Surveying was and remained formidably dangerous. A leopard once mauled five of his men before he managed to drive a blade down its throat. He also suffered further ambushes. In late 1767, one of his sepoys was killed in an encounter with Bhutanese soldiers. Quite how far Rennell made it into Bhutan is a matter of some conjecture; he wrote home to Devon, shortly before this encounter, that 'I am now in the midst of my Journey to Thibet being got into a more Northern Climate and in the neighbourhood of the Mountains, I breathe a cool and healthy air.' It's certainly likely that he was ahead of Bogle in visiting the country.

In 1772 Rennell married Jane Thackeray, great-aunt of the novelist, and his long absences became increasingly burdensome. Successive bouts of malaria took their toll on his health and Rennell's old wounds plagued him. In late 1777, some eighteen years after arriving in India, and with the *Bengal Atlas* almost ready for publication, the couple embarked for London with a pension of six hundred pounds from a grateful East India Company. James Rennell had just turned thirty-five.

Rennell is remembered not only as one of the great authorities on Indian geography. He was, as his biographer Clements Markham judged him, 'an explorer both by sea and land, a map compiler, a physical geographer, a critical and comparative geographer, and a hydrographer'. Elected to the Royal Society in 1781 for his map of Bengal, he became a hub for further research and friends with many of the great scientific explorers of the age, like Sir Joseph Banks. Rennell's map of India was first published in 1782 and he continued to update it. Awarding him the Royal Society's Copley Medal in 1791, Banks said, 'I should rejoice could I say that Britons, fond as they are of being considered by surrounding nations as taking the lead in scientific improvements, could boast a general map of their island as well executed as Major Rennell's delineation of Bengal and Bahar [Bihar].'

This was no exaggeration, yet when it came to the Himalaya, on Rennell's horizon and in his notes as he worked his way across Bengal, he had no choice but to rely on the earlier work of Jesuit surveyors and mapmakers published in d'Anville's atlas. Rennell was full of praise for d'Anville. 'When it is considered that this excellent Geographer had scarcely any materials to work on for the inland parts of India but some vague itineraries, and books of travels, one is really astonished to find them so well described as they are.' Yet the Himalaya in both maps were necessarily hazy and incomplete. Rennell accurately located Kathmandu and the trading town of Kuti, across the border in Tibet, but the mountains of Nepal appear simply as a jagged crest with the legend: 'Snowy mountains supposed to be a ridge of the Emmodus of the Ancients', a name lifted from Ptolemy's map of the second century.

James Rennell had no compelling reason to be concerned with surveying the mountains to the north: Kinloch had led his nightmarish expedition into Nepal, to help Jaya Prakash Malla, raja of Kathmandu, to resist Prithvi Narayan Shah's forces, in the year Vansittart commissioned Rennell, but British entanglement with Nepal still lay decades in the future. So did the Sublime and later Romanticism, and the passion for mountain landscapes they both inspired. 'These are among the highest of the mountains of the old hemisphere,' he wrote in a footnote to his account of Indian geography.

> I was not able to determine their height, but it may in some measure
> be guessed by the circumstance of their rising considerably above the
> horizon, when viewed from the plains of Bengal, at the distance of 150
> miles.

That these were the tallest mountains in the 'old hemisphere' was not much of a boast: science had hitherto considered El Teide, the peak of Tenerife, the likeliest contender. It was calculated to be around 4,500 metres at the time, almost one thousand metres higher than its true altitude, an indication of the technical challenges surveyors then faced. And El Teide was relatively easy to measure, being visible from busy shipping lanes and, therefore, sea level. Remote mountains far from the ocean were a much greater challenge.

Another man who grasped the implication that the Himalaya were visible from such vast distances was the orientalist and philologist Sir William Jones. Regarded in Europe as one of the greatest minds of his age, he was called by Goethe 'a far-seeing man who seeks to connect the unknown to the known'. His father, also William, had been a talented mathematician from Anglesey, dubbed 'Longitude' Jones for his knowledge of navigation: he died aged sixty-nine when William was three. His mother, the remarkable Mary Nix Jones, poured everything into her son, taking work as a seamstress to pay his school fees at Harrow. Her sacrifice worked. Despite a radical political edge, by the autumn of 1784 William Jones was, like his father, a member of the Royal Society as well as being a judge at the High Court of Calcutta; earlier that year he had founded the Asiatic Society. On 5 October, Jones was at Bhagalpur on the Ganges, almost due south of Mount Everest. To the north-east, just after sunset, he saw the alpen-glow of a peak to the north-east he identified as 'Chumalary peak', Chomolhari or Jomolhari as it's spelled now. This mountain was well known on the plains, a familiar landmark dominating the ancient trade route between Sikkim and Tibet above the Chumbi valley. It is sacred too, particularly to the Kagyu schools of Tibetan Buddhism, being associated with the Tsering-ma: the five 'sisters of long life'. The Tsering-ma feature in myths surrounding the eleventh-century poet and yogi Milarepa and are protectors of the *dharma*; one of them, Miyo Langsangma, yellow in colour with a bowl of food in one hand and a mongoose in the other, rides a tigress. She has also been asso-ciated with another mountain: Chomolungma, or Mount Everest.

Jones was never afraid to speculate, and his vision of Jomolhari inspired his curiosity. His father had written a famous instruction manual on navigation, so while Jones was famous as a philologist and linguist rather than a surveyor or cartographer, the subject was both familiar and congenial to him. Jones had known both George Bogle and Samuel Turner in Calcutta; their information had given him a good idea of how wide the mountain range was. And thanks to the work of Rennell and others, he guessed Jomolhari 'must be at least 244 British miles' away from his position. In fact, as the crow flies, it is 228 miles (367 kilometres), but even so, that kind of distance had an obvious implication for Jones: these mountains were not only exceptionally high, there was 'abundant reason to think that we saw from Bhagilpoor the highest mountains in the world, without excepting the Andes'.

It was natural for Jones to think of the Andes. In the late 1730s, France's Académie des Sciences had launched an expedition to calculate

the length of a single degree of longitude at the equator, with a view
to solving the conundrum posed by Isaac Newton: whether the circumference of the earth was greatest at the equator or around the poles;
in essence, do we live on a grapefruit or an egg? The measurements
for this calculation were taken in the modern state of Ecuador, work
that eventually led to the metric system. The scientists, who included
two Spaniards, also measured the altitude of a huge volcano called
Chimborazo in the Andes, close to the city of Quito and just south
of the equator. The French mathematican Charles-Marie de La
Condamine arrived at an altitude of 6,274 metres; his Spanish counterpart Jorge Juan y Santacilia came up with 6,586 metres, a considerable difference. Later in the century, a five-year exploratory expedition
led by Alessandro Malaspina calculated Chimborazo's altitude at 6,352
metres. Alexander von Humboldt, having measured the peak himself
at 6,544 metres and attempted to climb it in 1802, spent a lot of time
trying to unpick the reasons for this disparity: differences in calculating
barometric pressure and the refraction of light through the atmosphere
were among the culprits. (The true figure is actually 6,263 metres.) In
other words, some of the best minds of the eighteenth century had
invested a lot of time thinking about the Andes, and educated opinion
accepted Chimborazo as the highest mountain in the world. As it
turns out, because the earth bulges at the equator, Chimborazo's
summit is indeed the furthest point from the planet's centre, Everest
being more than 3,100 kilometres further north at a latitude of almost
30° N. Yet in terms of its height above sea level Chimborazo is pretty
average fare by Himalayan standards. Jomolhari, the peak Jones was
looking at, is more than a kilometre higher.

Toppling the Andes would take decades, despite the gathering
weight of evidence. Sir William Jones died in 1794 and was buried in
the same Calcutta cemetery as George Bogle. At the time of his death,
he had been working on a monumental translation of Hindu law, a
task taken over by Henry Colebrooke, a civil servant and noted Sanskrit
scholar. In the mid 1790s, Colebrooke was an assistant revenue collector
at Purnia in northern Bihar. Like Jones, he made observations of the
mountains to the north, but from a position some 140 kilometres
closer, calculating an approximate altitude of twenty-six thousand feet,
or around eight thousand metres. This was of great interest to his
cousin Robert Colebrooke, who had just been appointed surveyor

general of Bengal, but was also a matter of frustration. The Himalaya were still at a great distance and any measurement made from the plains was burdened with conjecture and doubt.

An opportunity to take a closer look arrived in April 1802, when a young surveyor arrived in Kathmandu with the trade mission of Captain William Knox, sent under the terms of the 1801 treaty at Danapur. Captain Charles Crawford, the man who actually signed the document, commanded the military escort that travelled with Knox and the botanist-surgeon Francis Buchanan-Hamilton. During the eleven months the mission spent in Kathmandu, Crawford set about making a map of the Kathmandu valley. Drawn to a scale of one inch to a furlong (an eighth of a mile; so approximately 2.5 cm to just over 200 metres), the map not only offered an impressively accurate interpretation of the valley's geography, it was also a thing of beauty. Buchanan-Hamilton included a copy with his collection of herbarium specimens, elegant coloured illustrations and manuscripts that he gave to James Edward Smith, founder of the Linnaean Society: the root of botanical studies in Nepal. The map was sensitive military information but the botanist's patron was the governor general Richard Wellesley, who allowed Crawford to pass it on to Smith. Robert Colebrooke was also impressed with Crawford's work, finding it 'executed with particular neatness'; Crawford was promoted and given the job of surveying Bengal's northern frontier.

Crawford hadn't just surveyed the valley while he was in Kathmandu. He had taken a good look at the mountains to the north and was convinced they were of 'vast height'. He took bearings on all the most obvious peaks visible from more than one position, presumably Langtang Lirung and Dorje Lhakpa among them. Having ascertained his approximate altitude, taken bearings, allowed for refraction, computed distance and applied trigonometry, Crawford calculated the mountains to the north were between eleven and twenty thousand feet (3,350 to 6,100 metres) above his 'stations of observation'. Annoyingly, for Crawford and for us, he didn't forward his homework to Calcutta: the drawings and journal of his survey. Crawford later told Henry Colebrooke that his data were in England, but the documents have never surfaced and are often assumed to have been lost. There's no way to address the various questions his work raises. How did he know how far away the mountains were? How did he calculate his altitude in the valley? There were certainly techniques available to do this. The scientist Jean-André Deluc had calculated altitude from the boiling point of water in 1762. But there's no evidence Crawford did the same.

Even so, the young officer's story made an impact. The East India Company's rapid expansion at this time was bringing more and more territory within its orbit. The governor general Richard Wellesley, his commander-in-chief General Gerard Lake, and Wellesley's brother Arthur, the future Duke of Wellington, prospered against the Maratha Empire during the first years of the nineteenth century, bringing the upper portion of the Ganges within reach of British exploration for the first time. This provided a tantalising opportunity for Robert Colebrooke. James Rennell's map of the upper Ganges had been speculative, since the Tibetan surveyors working for the Jesuits hadn't gone there, simply passing on stories they heard. The river, Rennell wrote, was 'well known to derive' its source 'from the vast mountains of Thibet'. He showed it arriving in India via a subterranean tunnel and repeated the Hindu legend that the river emerged from a great rock called the 'cow's mouth'. Rennell and Colebrooke had clashed subsequently over Colebrooke's idea of building a canal in the lower reaches of the Ganges to solve the problem of its regularly shifting course; Rennell thought the plan unworkable and had warned the Company to leave well alone. Now there was an opportunity for Colebrooke to burnish his reputation as surveyor general and solve the puzzle of the source of the Ganges, something unknown to Rennell. 'An actual survey,' his cousin Henry wrote in the *Asiatic Journal*, in a sly dig at Colebrooke's predecessor,

> of the Ganges above *Haridwar* (where it enters the British territories,) to the farthest point to which it had been traced by *Hindu* pilgrims, and to its remotest accessible source, was an undertaking worthy of British enterprise.

Robert Colbrooke began his last journey in the autumn of 1807, taking with him his wife and the two eldest of their nine children, drifting up the Ganges in a country boat towards Kanpur. At night the family listened to the roar of tigers and by day they drew crowds of onlookers, who, in the words of historian John Keay, 'had not previously come across a European – let alone a breeding pair complete with offspring'. On the way to Kanpur they explored the Rapti river and the town of Gorakhpur, which is almost due south of the Annapurna range in Nepal. Here, surrounded by curious locals, Colebrooke took bearings on two peaks to the north, quite probably Annapurna itself and the other peak over eight thousand metres: Dhaulagiri. He calculated that each was 'more than five miles in perpendicular height above the level of the plain on which I stood'.

Having spent Christmas in Lucknow, Colebrooke's wife and children headed home and the surveyor spent the rest of the cold season in the jungles of Kumaon. This country was more hostile and so at Kanpur he had picked up a detachment of sepoys under the command of Lieutenant William Webb, only twenty-two but with some training in survey work. Then Colebrooke fell ill: malaria and dysentery. Like so many of the surveyors that came later to the fringes of the Himalaya, the jungle of the terai had undone him. At a place called Pilibhit, about fifty kilometres north-east of Bareilly and just off the south-west tip of modern Nepal, Colebrooke took another series of observations of the mountains but could no longer continue overland. He returned to Bareilly, charging Webb to continue his mission to find the source of the Ganges. By August, weakening fast, he was on board a boat to Bengal; he died a month later at Bhagalpur, where William Jones had years before observed Jomolhari, glowing in the evening light.

Webb was not alone in his mission to the source of the Ganges. Captain Felix Raper, a friend from his regiment, the 10th Bengal Native Infantry, came too, keeping a lively journal of their adventure. The third member of their party was very different, a near-mythical Anglo-Indian called Hyder Jung Hearsey. At just twenty-five he was already a hardened soldier, a mercenary named after the emperor Hyder Ali of Mysore, whom his father Andrew had been fighting shortly before Hyder was born in 1782. (His name is sometimes written as Hyder Young Hearsey.) The boy's grandfather and great-grandfather had been on the losing side at the Battle of Culloden, when the Jacobite rebellion was finally crushed, thereby forfeiting the family estates in Cumberland; something of the rebel stuck to Hyder too. His mother was Andrew Hearsey's Indian common-law wife, whose name is unknown. Andrew later married an Englishwoman, Charlotte Crane, while he was in Britain pursuing a legal case. While her children were able to find employment in the East India Company – Hyder's half-brother John had a distinguished military career, reaching the rank of general and fighting in the rebellion of 1857 – Hyder Hearsey, as an Anglo-Indian, was excluded. He got a little education at school in Woolwich but otherwise had to take his chances.

Aged sixteen, the year his father died, he had entered the service of Saadat Ali Khan, nawab of Oudh, but moved swiftly on to be a cadet in the army of the outlandish French mercenary Pierre Cuillier-Perron, the former sailor leading the charge for the Maratha confederacy that dominated much of India in the late eighteenth century. Aged just seventeen, Hyder distinguished himself in the siege of Agra, earning Perron's gratitude, but when the Frenchman began to see a chance to re-establish French power in India, many of his British and Anglo-Indian officers left him, Hyder Hearsey among them. Soon thereafter he found himself fighting his old commander in the service of the Irish mercenary George Thomas and, after Thomas' death, starting his own army, which Hearsey led in the service of the East India Company. He also married Zuhur-ul-Nissa, adopted daughter of the Mughal emperor Akbar II, an illustration of his upward mobility. His new bride had estates near Bareilly, recently ceded to the Company by the nawab of Oudh, which is where Colebrooke found this fiercely self-reliant 'rough diamond'. Needless to say, Webb and Raper didn't like him.

This trio arrived in Haridwar during the spring fair, which coincided in 1808 with the Kumbh Mela, the 'pitcher gathering', not the immense event it is today but still significant. Held every dozen years, this vast, broiling assembly of pilgrims rarely passed without violence or mishap. Many of the pilgrims were *gosain*, there to do business as well as bathe in the Ganges. The fair was an opportunity for darker habits too: hundreds of slaves were for sale, 'of both sexes, from three to thirty years of ages', forced down from the hills. By chance, the expedition met there the Gorkhali governor of Srinagar, Hasti Dal Chautariya, a corpulent, jovial man who had come down for the festival. (Hyder Hearsey and Hasti Dal would meet again a few years later on opposite sides in the Company's war with Gorkha: Hearsey led irregulars that would later become Gurkha regiments.) Hasti Dal was content for the British to continue upstream but soon afterwards he was replaced, and the new governor, Bhairav Thapa, wasn't so congenial: the British were forced to pay a vastly inflated price for porters to continue their journey, entering the rugged valley systems of the middle hills, 'a mighty maze without a plan', as the surveyor general of India John Hodgson termed it.

Raper's account of their journey is full of interest.

It is necessary for a person to place himself in our situation, before he can form a just conception of the scene. The depth of the valley below, the progressive elevation of the intermediate hills, and the majestic splendor of the 'cloud-capt' Himalaya, formed so grand a picture that the mind was impressed with a sensation of dread rather than of pleasure.

It was, Raper wrote, 'a sight the most sublime and awful that can be pictured to the imagination'. He was even more interested in people, paying close attention to the social differences between the people of the mountains and the plains.

We perceived a great difference in the manners of the people. They appeared to be much more civilized, and so far from exhibiting any signs of apprehension, they came running towards the road, to see us pass. The women even, did not shew that bashfulness and reserve, which females in *Hindostan* in general exhibit; but, mixing with the crowd, they made their comments with the greatest freedom. ... Their garments are made of coarse cloth; whereas those of the men are of thick blanket, manufactured from the wool and hair of the sheep and goats, which are of kinds peculiar to the hills. We could not help remarking, that, even in these unfrequented regions, the female mountaineers exhibited the general failing of the sex, having their necks, ears and noses, ornamented with rings and beads. When these are beyond their means, they substitute a wreath or bunch of flowers; for which purpose the white rose is chosen, both for its beauty and scent.

The trio did not make it quite to the source of the Ganges, reaching the confluence of the Bhagirathi with the Jadh Ganga, which rises in Tibet. By then they had done a lot more walking than they'd expected and the path ahead seemed even harder. Webb decided to send a local to scout out the terrain ahead and then report back. 'Captain Hearsay's

moonshee [munshi, meaning 'translator' and 'secretary'], a very intelligent man, was selected for that undertaking,' Raper wrote. 'To render
his observations more correct, he was provided with, and instructed
in the use of his compass.' Raper made careful notes of what he saw
of the Bhagirathi.

> From the appearance of the river itself, which becomes contracted in
> its stream, and from the stupendous height of the *Himálaya* mountains,
> whence it flows; there can be no doubt but its source is situated in the
> snow range; and any other hypothesis can scarcely be reconciled to
> hydrostatical principles. The pilgrims, and those people in the vicinity
> of this place, who gain a livelihood by bringing water from the spot,
> say that the road beyond *Gangotrí* is passable only for a few miles, when
> the current is entirely concealed under heaps of snow, which no trav-
> eller ever has or can surmount. With respect to the Cow's Mouth, we
> had the most convincing testimony to confirm us in the idea that its
> existence is entirely fabulous, and that it is found only in the *Hindù*
> book of faith.

It doesn't seem to have occurred to Webb or to Henry Colebrooke
that Gaumukh, 'the cow's mouth', might be of ice rather than rock;
it's also possible the mythological name for the source of the Ganges
was simply stuck to the actual place. The first Briton to reach Gangotri
was James Baillie Fraser, a Scottish travel writer who visited the
Gorkhali-built temple in June 1815, soon after the East India Company's
war with Nepal. He asked the temple priest about the cow's mouth
but the priest just laughed and said that 'most of those pilgrims who
came from the plains asked the same question.'

Webb and the others continued on to the Alaknanda valley and
the temple at Badrinath, then to the Tibetan village of Mana, where
the missionaries Andrade and Marques had hired guides to reach
Tsaparang some two centuries earlier. Webb was satisfied this river
was greater and reached deeper into the mountains than the
Bhagirathi and was consequently the true source of the Ganges.
Relieved that his assignment was a success, Webb turned for home.
Robert Colebrooke's cousin Henry was now president of the Asiatic
Society and it fell to him to prepare Raper's account for publication

in its journal of 1812. The report is remarkable for several reasons, not least the near-absence of Hyder Jung Hearsey. It seems safe to assume that his deep experience of the region and overall toughness could only have been an asset to the party; of that we hear almost nothing. The stony silence masked a bitter and convoluted dispute over the origin of a map Hearsey sent to James Rennell in late 1808. Hearsey was hoping it would prompt some compensation for him, given that Gorkhali soldiers had robbed the expedition on its way out of the mountains. He was instead accused of stealing the map from Webb and, given his reputation and skin colour, the allegation was believed. Hearsey had kept his own journal, which records the surveying work he did, and the map William Webb eventually sent to his superiors two years later wasn't remotely to the same standard as Hearsey's.

Henry Colebrooke was careful in his preface to Raper's article not to be too hasty in his judgment about the height of the Himalaya.

> Without however supposing the *Himálaya* to exceed the *Andes*, there is still room to argue, that an extensive range of mountains, which rears, high above the line of perpetual snow, in an almost tropical latitude, an uninterrupted chain of lofty peaks, is neither surpassed nor rivalled by any other chain of mountains but the *Cordillera* of the *Andes*.

In 1816 he revisited the subject in another article for the *Asiatic Journal*. By then William Webb had taken his own reading of Dhaulagiri and learned its name, something Robert Colebrooke had not managed, giving it a height of 26,862 feet (8,188 metres), only twenty metres off its current measured altitude. Meanwhile, two other surveyors, John Hodgson and James Herbert, had reached Gaumukh itself and seen the soaring spire of Shivling. Reviewing all the evidence gathered so far, Henry Colebrooke was much more definitive:

> I consider the evidence to be now sufficient to authorize an unreserved declaration of the opinion, that the *Himálaya* is the loftiest range of Alpine mountains which has been yet noticed, its most elevated peaks greatly exceeding the highest of the *Andes*.

Colebrooke's claim was sensational but met with a faint raspberry:
this was another tall tale from the subcontinent. How could he be so
sure? The anonymous author of a long and expert article in the influential *Quarterly Review* was deeply sceptical:

> we cannot help thinking that he has come to this conclusion rather
> hastily. We have not one word to offer against his calculations nor his
> formula: we have such an opinion of his accuracy, that we are willing
> to take the results on trust. All we mean to protest against is the insuf-
> ficiency of his facts to authorize the conclusion which he has drawn
> from them.

The reviewer zeroed in on Webb's measurement of Dhaulagiri as the
most convincing of his evidence and then argued just as convincingly
that given the distance from which his observations were taken the
possibility they were grossly inaccurate was too great to ignore. In a
nutshell, the science behind the measurements of the Andes was a
lot more convincing than Colebrooke's. Interest in funding further
work in measuring the Himalaya quickly faded after this sigh of indifference. William Webb, who in a harsh light appears something of a
duffer, had been close to the height of Dhaulagiri, but as much by
luck as by judgment. Passed over for promotion he quit the Company's
service. Budget cuts paused the Survey of India's work in the Himalaya
for a decade or so, and although the Anglo-Burmese war of 1824
allowed the Company access to the north-eastern parts of the
Himalaya – Richard Wilcox and James Burlton explored Assam and
the Brahmaputra valley in the late 1820s – surveyors didn't yet have
either the instruments or the mathematics to measure accurately the
height of the Himalaya.

Until the late eighteenth century, the precise altitude of where you
were standing hadn't worried anyone unduly. In 1818, two Scottish
brothers, Alexander and James Gerard, reached the upper slopes of a
mountain near the Shipki La, in the district of Kinnaur near where
the Sutlej emerges from Tibet, simply 'to see the barometer below
fifteen inches', thus setting what they believed was a world altitude
record. They suffered horribly from altitude sickness, comparing it to
'the sedative effect of intoxication'. The brothers told the world they
had gone higher than Alexander von Humboldt had on Chimborazo

in 1802, but the man himself was unimpressed: 'these mountain ascents, however they engage the curiosity of the public, are of very little scientific utility'. The relevance of altitude, on the other hand, was increasingly important, thanks in part to von Humboldt's own scientific vision. Wherever you were in the world, altitude affected the distribution of plants, just as latitude did: a compelling scientific reason for accurately measuring the height of mountains. As the botanist William Griffith, who went to Bhutan in 1837, pointed out: 'the Botanist who travels without the means of determining these points, destroys half the value of his collections'.

In a neat irony, the paper that followed Colebrooke's in the *Asiatic Journal* of 1816 was by a man whose work would ultimately provide the platform for accurately measuring the height of the Himalaya. For more than a decade William Lambton had been gradually travelling up the length of India from south to north, working in near-obscurity, triangulating a masterfully accurate sequence of positions: the 'Great Indian Arc of the Meridian'. A protégé of Arthur Wellesley, Lambton wasn't just a surveyor: he was a geodesist, measuring accurately the geometric shape of the earth, taking as his inspiration the Scottish surveyor William Roy, whose innovative spherical trigonometry proved the pivot between the approximate maps of the past and modern cartography. From 1818 onwards, the slow but steady continuation of Lambton's work, stetching over the next five decades, was known as the Great Trigonometrical Survey of India, or simply the Great Survey. It's hard now to appreciate the scale of what it achieved and at what human cost, like judging the miracle of an analogue telephone from the age of Google, but adding in the likely prospect of death. The geographer Clements Markham calculated that in the worst seasons of surveying along the frontier of Nepal, the number of dead, British and Indian, reached three figures. In the diagram of fixed positions that eventually emerged from the Great Survey in 1870, it is as if India has grown a spine of scaffolding with arms extended outwards to either side; it was from these arms that the true height of the Himalaya were finally measured. But no sooner had the survey been completed and marvelled at, than technology moved on and the scale of its enterprise was forgotten.

Lambton himself would die in the field, aged seventy, his more famous successor being George Everest, irascible where Lambton was self-effacing, but no less determined. His family came from Greenwich in east London, home of the prime meridian, and they pronounced their name Eve-rest; George would sharply correct anyone saying Ever-est. He was followed as surveyor general by Andrew Waugh, who, against protocol, appended his mentor's name to a mountain he himself observed in 1847, a mountain that had by 1850 been calculated as the highest yet measured, higher even than Kangchenjunga, so clearly seen from Darjeeling. It did not happen the way it is sometimes reported: of a computer (meaning in those days a *person* who computes) rushing into Waugh's office claiming he had discovered the highest point on earth. The work was a process of slow accretion, its conclusion not made public until 1856. Even then there was speculation that a new contender discovered in the neighbouring mountains of the Karakoram range, labelled K2 in the surveyor's scheme, might be bigger. Everest himself never saw his mountain; his interest in the Himalaya was largely confined to enjoying the fresh air at his home near the new hill station of Mussoorie. He also stuck to the Survey of India's rule of finding local names for whatever they measured. What he made of his name being applied to the world's highest mountain is not recorded.

At the time of Waugh's observation, Everest was back in England, hunting foxes in Leicestershire. Later in life he settled permanently in London, by then the imperial city of Victorian England. At the time of his birth in 1790 the Himalaya had been on the fringes of the East India Company's sphere of influence; Britain had been one among several competing powers. Now in Everest's old age the mountains were the northern limit of the British Raj, in its philosophy and culture a very different enterprise. As British India evolved, reflecting the technological progress of the Industrial Revolution, so the purposes of Himalayan geography shifted with it, becoming a finely calibrated tool of, as William Webb termed it, 'great practical utility'. And by then the political map of the Himalaya had been torn up and wholly redrawn.

II

The Tyrant and the Scholar

On the morning of 12 May 1857, a young army captain galloped into the Himalayan hill station of Simla with a telegram. The message had been sent from Delhi to the captain's father Sir Henry Barnard, commanding officer of the Sirhind division of the Bengal army stationed two hundred kilometres north of the city at Ambala. His son was now forwarding it to the commander-in-chief of the Indian army. The message, sent to Ambala on India's newly installed telegraph system, reported the opening shots in what British colonial powers would term the Indian or Sepoy Mutiny, and many Indians refer to as the First War of Independence. There had been no shortage of wars against British hegemony in South Asia, most recently the Anglo-Sikh conflicts of the 1840s. This was different. This was a rebellion from deep within, striking at the heart of the British security apparatus: the military and police. What began as a revolt among troops at the garrison town of Meerut, not far from the foothills of the mountains, soon spread south to Delhi and across the northern plains of India.

The commander-in-chief, General George Anson, tucked the telegram under his plate while he finished his breakfast in the cool of another Himalayan morning. Anson had little experience of the subcontinent. He had seen no fighting since Waterloo, when he was a young subaltern in the Guards, and had spent much of the interim as a member of parliament. He had a passion for horseracing and cards; his appointment the year before had been an unwelcome interruption. Being an officer in the Queen's service, Anson had little respect for the Indian army, which he regarded as ill disciplined; nor did he have much sympathy with the cultural concerns of Indian sepoys. Like many of the British troops under his command, he had come to the hills from Ambala to escape the heat of the Indian summer, which played havoc with his health, and at first was reluctant to move. He gave orders for arsenals to be secured and troops to move down from the mountains toward Delhi. Three days later, as the situation spiralled towards disaster, he was back in Ambala, complaining that the 'conduct of the Native Army has destroyed all confidence in any regiment'. He would be dead from cholera within a fortnight and by then India was ablaze.

In the town of Simla itself, news of mutinous 'native' troops soon spread panic: a microcosm of the wider crisis, just as the hill station itself was a microcosm of the British in India. Forty years earlier, Simla, the future summer capital of the Raj, had been a small mountain hamlet set in dense forest, a prize taken from the Gorkhas in 1815 and given to the maharaja of Patiala as reward for his support in the war against Nepal. The region had been studded with Gorkhali forts, including one at nearby Jutogh, and so the country became familiar to British officers and agents stationed nearby. Simla's rugged scenery combined contemporary romantic ideals of the sublime with relief from the often deadly hot summer months. The congenial political officer Charles Kennedy built the first 'pukka' house there and visiting friends began to acquire land so they could do the same. This started a small property boom. Sanatoria opened nearby. When the governor general Lord Amherst stayed in 1827, he set a fashion that turned Simla from a summer retreat into a bustling social whirl, 'the resort of the rich, the idle and the invalid', as the pleasingly waspish French botanist and traveller Victor Jacquemont described it in 1829.

A colonial community sprang up whose allegiance can be read in the names of the gimcrack houses they occupied: Richmond Villa, Woodbine Cottage, The Briars and Annandale View. In a letter to his wife Emily, the architect Edwin Lutyens caught Simla's surreal appearance: 'If one was told that monkeys had built it, one could only say, "What wonderful monkeys – they must be shot in case they do it again."' It was a world of amateur dramatics and archery on the lawn, but most of all Simla was gossip. 'Nowhere possibly in the world,' wrote a correspondent for the *Pioneer* newspaper later in the century, 'are the passions of human nature laid so open for dissection as they are in remote hill stations on the slopes of the eternal abodes of snow.' Servants of empire enjoyed lifestyles they couldn't possibly afford at home and their hours of leisure freed them to talk. Yet despite this liberation from domestic cares, they found that in Simla 'discontent breeds, and jealousy and scandal dominate. The smallness of society, eddying round in such a tiny backwater, makes for stagnation.'

In the late 1830s, just as the town hit its stride, a teenage bride born in Sligo on the west coast of Ireland arrived in Simla. Her beauty, enriched with a splash of Spanish genes, prompted lots of 'jealousy and scandal'. For now she was still Eliza James. Her stepfather, Simla's deputy adjutant general, had sent Eliza home to his relatives in Scotland to have the wild streak educated out of her. It didn't work. She eloped to India at fifteen with 'a sort of smart-looking man with bright waistcoats and bright teeth,' according to Emily Eden, the witty sister of the governor general Lord Auckland. He was twice her age but still an impoverished subaltern. '[Eliza] is very pretty,' Emily Eden thought,

> and a good little thing, but they are very poor, and she is very young and lively, and if she falls into bad hands, she would soon laugh herself into foolish scrapes. At present the wife and husband are very fond of each other, but a girl who marries at fifteen hardly knows what she likes.

When the couple returned to Calcutta, Eliza's 'bright waistcoat' abandoned her. On the boat back to Europe, once again on her own, she changed her name to Lola Montez, a self-styled Spanish dancer who would one day count Franz Liszt and Ludwig I of Bavaria among her lovers, as well as Jang Bahadur Rana, prime minister of Nepal.

The self-absorption of colonial life was no less pervasive among the men in Simla. The Irish journalist William Howard Russell, whose war reporting of the Crimea had made him famous, toured India in 1858 at the end of the rebellion and spent several weeks in the town, leaving an unflattering snapshot of the moments before dinner at the Simla Club:

> Servants are hurrying in to wait on the sahibs, who have come to dinner from distant bungalows. The clatter of plates and dishes proclaim that dinner is nearly ready. The British officers and civilians, in every style of Anglo-Indian costume, are propping up the walls of the sitting-room, waiting for the signal to fall on. The little party in the corner

have come down from the card-room, and it is whispered that old
Major Stager has won 700 rupees from young Cornet Griffin, since
tiff[in]; but Griffin can never pay unless he gets his Delhi prize-money
soon; and that little Shuffle, the Major's partner, who does not look
twenty yet, but who is well known as a cool hand, has extracted nearly
twice as much from that elderly civilian, who has come up with a liver
and full purse from the plains. The others are the soldierless officers
of ex-sepoy regiments, Queen's officers, civilians, doctors, invalids,
unemployed brigadiers, convalescents from wounds or illness in the
plains; and their talk is of sporting, balls, promotions, exchanges,
Europe, and a little politics, re-chauffé'd from the last *Overland Mail*;
but as a general rule, all serious questions are tabooed, and it is almost
amusing to observe the excessive *esprit de corps* which is one of the
excellences as [well as] one of the defects of the English character, and
which now breaks up the officers of the Queen's, of the Company's
service, and of the civil departments into separate knots.

Russell saw the anxieties of men whose prospects had been turned
upside down by the rebellion and the far-reaching reforms it provoked
as the East India Company was wound up and the Crown took control.
At its remove from the plains, Simla was full of people taking stock,
assessing their careers, calibrating their prestige, as well as recreating
the social patterns of British life in the Himalaya. The place itself,
which had its own rich, complex and indigenous story, was to its new
occupiers simply raw material to be acquired and improved, an appro-
priation reflected in the toponyms the British gave to Simla and the
mountains around it: Lord Bentinck's Nose, a hill on the town's north-
west horizon that was said to resemble that of the governor general
who did the land deal that secured the town for the British in the
1830s; Boileauganj, for the soldier and engineer John Theophilus
Boileau, who designed and in 1844 laid the cornerstone of Christ
Church, finally consecrated in 1857, bringing Anglicanism to the
Himalaya just in time for the greatest existential crisis the British had
faced in India for a century.

For the most part, from Meerut to Madras, British officials faced
rebellion with courage and determination. The judge at Fatehpur,
Robert Tucker, who had erected stone pillars near his bungalow
inscribed with the Ten Commandments in Hindi and Urdu, died on

the roof of his courthouse, bible in one hand and pistol in the other, having killed a dozen of his assailants. His gravestone read: 'fell at the post of duty 1857, looking unto Jesus'. This was not the story in Simla. Gossip had given the town a brittle temper. On 14 and 15 May, with the commander-in-chief now on his way to Ambala, rumours swirled that at the nearby barracks of Jutogh, the Nasiri battalion of Gurkhas (not one of the Gurkha battalions formed during the war with Nepal but a newer unit) was in a state of mutiny. Rumour had it that the troops had refused General Anson's order to march in support of his move on Delhi. The wife of the army's advocate general Colonel Keith Young wrote to her sister that people believed the Gurkhas

> would attack Simla and loot it instead. Our Commissioner (Lord William Hay) and others said it was merely report, and that the regiment was staunch; however, some of the Goorkhas were seen in the bazaar laughing and talking about the Delhi business, and when an Englishman passed he was hissed at. Another report had spread that they intended to go down as ordered, but would join either Europeans or Natives, whichever was strongest.

Even rumours of a Gurkha mutiny were enough to terrorise Simla's European population. The bank had been designated a safe gathering point under the command of Major General Nicholas Penny, a reportedly experienced officer, but dozens of families were diverted on their way there for fear the Gurkhas had already reached the bazaar. Especially vulnerable were families living in Chhota Simla, an outlying district easily cut off from the security of the town centre. A woman called Emma Young described how she scrambled down into a ravine, or *khud*, near her house, fearing the Gurkhas had already occupied the bazaar. Later, when she arrived at the bank, she found a hundred armed European men and two artillery pieces, enough to stave off an attack.

> But General Penny was quite incapable of maintaining order, and was evidently in the greatest possible fright himself. He allowed many to get intoxicated; and, if the Gurkhas had chosen to come, they could easily have murdered us all. It was a most disgraceful scene and made one ashamed of one's countrymen.

Her opinion was shared by Mrs Keith Young: 'some of the gentlemen, we hear, have behaved so badly, showing shocking cowardice – men who, one would have thought, would have braved anything. People are never known until they are tried.'

That evening, Simla's deputy commissioner Lord William Hay, later the Marquess of Tweeddale, wearily returned from Jutogh, having sought and been given reassurances from the Gurkhas that they would not mutiny, to share the good news with those occupying the bank, some of whom then melted away to their homes. He had seen enough, though, to know it might still go the other way and suggested that the town's women should leave. Colonel Keith Young returned to his house the following morning. 'All quiet. Two sepoys came to the house soon after I got there: very civil, and declared they never intended to alarm any of the "sahib logue" [literally "master race", meaning Europeans]. The scoundrels!' Despite the good humour, he and his wife still quit Simla to sleep at the hilltop palace of the rana, or prince of Keonthal, a state that remained loyal to the British, at the nearby village of Junga. (The rana was promoted to raja for 'good service during the mutiny.' His people may not have seen it that way.) Meanwhile, talk of a massacre at Simla had spread to the plains, and on 17 May Young was writing to a friend reassuring him all was well:

> I write a line to tell you that there is not a word of truth in the reported 'Simla massacre'. F. [his wife] and I and the dear 'babies' are as well as you could wish, enjoying ourselves at this place, some sixteen miles from Simla. We came out here this morning – 'fled', you may say – for fear of the mutineering Nusseree [sic] Battalion at Jutogh rising against us and resorting to deeds of violence.

When the British finally returned to their homes, they were exactly as they left them.

*

During the war in 1814 with the Gorkhalis, the British general Sir David Ochterlony had made an offer to disaffected troops in the Gorkhali army to swap allegiance. Initially, that offer brought a few hundred to the British side. The first 'Gurkha' battalion was raised from these men and was called the Nasiri, commonly translated as 'friends', but more accurately meaning 'helpers': a Mughal term that Ochterlony meant as a mark of deep respect for their useful service. Later, when the fighting in the west was done at the end of the first campaign, some 4,700 troops from Gorkha's western army surrendered to the British. Ochterlony judged that recruiting these men would be preferable to turning them loose to join the other armed bands predating on northern India.

Four battalions were formed and from the start their relationship with their British officers was unusually close, a stark contrast to regiments of the line. Their presence helped stabilise the region after the turmoil of invasion and war and stimulated the local economy. Yet these new battalions were not local irregulars. Around 1,500 were Gorkhalis, as Prithvi Narayan Shah would have judged them: Chhetris, Magars and Gurungs from the heartland of the Gorkha project. The officers and many of the non-commissioned officers would have come from this group. The rest, however, were from regions the Gorkhas had conquered: Kumaon, Garhwal and districts still within Kathmandu's control, including Palpa and Jumla.

Calcutta cautiously welcomed this new source of irregular troops that was cheaper and potentially more reliable than the Bengal Army's core of Brahmins and Rajputs from Bihar and Oudh. A trickle of new recruits, often with links to serving soldiers, continued to arrive from Nepal, despite Kathmandu's determined prohibition on recruitment. Most, however, came from outside Nepal, from the Himalayan hill-states west of the Mahakali river. One battalion, the Kumaon, was stationed near here, to guard against military incursion from Nepal. A second Nasiri battalion was raised and with the Simur these three were tasked with protecting the hills of the Sutlej region from the growing threat of invasion from Ranjit Singh and his Sikh Empire. Ranjit, meanwhile, was also recruiting Gurkhas, as he modernised his army. Some of these men came from within Nepal, but he also tried to tempt those serving the British, whose rates of pay were lower.

Today, after the immense bravery and sacrifice of the Gurkhas in the service of the British through two world wars, it might seem surprising that their intentions and loyalties seemed so opaque to the frightened residents of Simla. But at that time there was a gulf of understanding between the broad mass of colonial servants and those who understood the Himalayan regions the troops called home: British officers who commanded the Gurkhas and the handful of diplomats and political officers from the Foreign and Political Department with deep experience of the region. The 'Simla panic' became part of the rebellion's narrative. When the journalist William Russell described his stay there, he wrote:

> Simla was full of women, and men more timid than the women were, and many bad characters were in the bazaar ready for plunder and outrage if the troops broke out. A revolt on the very border of Punjab might have roused the Sikhs beyond [Sir John] Lawrence's control, and then, indeed history would have had to philosophise over the fall of our empire in India.

A few Gurkhas did rebel. When British troops left the hills for Delhi, a detachment of the Nasiri battalion stationed at nearby Kasauli, under the command of a *subedar* or warrant officer called Bhim Singh, found itself in possession of the garrison's treasure chest, which they promptly broke open to help themselves to arrears in pay. Then they marched towards Simla, coming across General Anson's baggage train, which they destroyed, and a few Englishmen and women, whom they robbed. Anson sent a captain called David Briggs back to talk them round. Briggs was a sensible choice for such a fraught mission. He had been employed for several years supervising construction of the Hindustan–Tibet road, a white elephant dreamed up by the governor general Lord Dalhousie to re-energise Himalayan trade in the aftermath of the Anglo-Sikh wars. Construction relied on corvée labour provided by local chiefs and was bitterly resented. A colleague of Briggs told the House of Commons in 1857 that local people 'detest every one and every thing connected with the road'. The Gorkha occupation of the Sutlej hills had been disastrous, but there was little more affection for the British. Even so, in the course of his work, Briggs had formed strong bonds in the region and these he exploited in cutting a deal with the disaffected Gurkhas. Almost all were pardoned and properly paid, although the Nasiri battalion was disbanded in 1858 soon after the rebellion was suppressed.

Despite this pocket of disaffection, the Gurkhas proved themselves not just bravely capable but also astonishingly loyal to their employers. The Nasiri battalion at Simla was exceptional: it was still quite new, recruited to replace the earlier, more famous battalion of the same name that had been promoted to become a regiment of the line. These established Gurkha regiments would prove wholly trustworthy.

On 14 May, news of the rebellion reached Dehra Dun, in the foothills of the Himalaya between the Ganges and Yamuna rivers, where Major Charles Reid commanded the Simur battalion. Within four hours, his Gurkhas, almost five hundred strong, were marching towards Meerut, where the rebellion had first erupted, their pockets crammed with ammunition and two elephants following behind with more. Along the way they were alternately harried and tempted by rebels, but they never wavered. When Reid learned of the uprising against General Sir Archibald Wilson at Delhi, he pointed his troops there instead, marching forty-three kilometres in one night. As the Gurkhas finally reached Wilson's force, the men of the 60th Rifles opened fire, thinking them the enemy, but cheered when they discovered they were Gurkhas.

Senior officers still had their doubts, as they did about all native troops, and these native reinforcements were stationed near the artillery, which was given orders to open fire if the Gurkhas offered any trouble, although General Wilson himself judged them 'true as steel'. Major Reid he trusted absolutely, unlike some of his other officers. The cheerfulness of the Gurkhas endeared them to the ordinary ranks; the riflemen of the 60th and the Himalayan sepoys were soon calling each other brother. 'They shared their grog,' Reid wrote, 'and smoked their pipes together.' They also carried each other's wounded from the battlefield. More than half the Simur became casualties before Delhi was recaptured in September 1857 but they still ignored the appeals of the rebels to swap sides. Soon the Gurkhas carried the same bounty on their heads as the British did. Their courage was relentless. Reid told a story about finding a wounded Gurkha boy sheltering behind a rock and holding a rifle. The boy explained the rifle was his father's. He had been loading it for him at a forward picket when his father had been killed. After that he had helped an English soldier from the 60th, and then carried him from the battlefield after he was injured. The boy had then returned to fight himself, before being wounded in both legs. 'But

I am not much hurt.' He was fourteen years old. Reid enlisted him on the spot and had him carried to hospital. After Delhi Reid requested and got permission for the Gurkhas to call themselves riflemen rather than sepoys.

Even before 1857, the Gurkhas had their champions, especially after the Anglo-Sikh wars, when the British discovered just how well they could fight. In 1852, before a select committee of the House of Lords in London, Sir Charles Napier, who as commander-in-chief had promoted the original Nasiri battalion, described them as

> very fine soldiers; if we had 30,000 of them in addition to 30,000 of our own Europeans, we should have a force in India that could do what we liked; we should no longer hold India by opinion, but by actual force.

Asked if it would not be better to raise Sikh regiments, Napier replied: 'Yes, but you do not know the Sikhs are true. ... the Sikhs may be good soldiers but the Goorkahs [sic] are as good, and are devoted to us.' The source of that devotion was complex although money was unquestionably at its heart. Napier himself said that 'those people are starving in the hills', and recalled their yell of joy when he told them he had negotiated an increase in pay.

Their wider allegiances seemed less predictable, especially in Calcutta. Northern India had been awash with guns for hire in the eighteenth and first decades of the nineteenth centuries and many British officials saw Gurkhas as just another group of mercenaries who would readily change masters if things went badly. Nepal itself remained hostile forty years on from the Treaty of Sagauli. The logic of these arguments was capped with arrogance: Christian moral superiority among the elite and among younger officers a swelling abscess of casual racism. Napier for one regretted this growing distance between sepoys and officers, who no longer saw advantage in learning Hindustani when it was social connection that won promotion.

> How different this from the spirit which actuated the old men of Indian renown, whom smaller men should take as guides! The desire to converse with the Sepoys would alone have induced me to study their language.

Napier frequently clashed with the governor general Dalhousie, a man half his age. ('Events are rising on the horizon which require the hand of a giant,' he wrote in 1850, 'and a pigmy only is present.') Dalhousie had misgivings about Napier's proposal that the Gurkhas be integrated into the Bengal army:

> I would not have the corps all Goorkhas first because I don't think it expedient to have these corps all foreigners and second because our own hill subjects are as good soldiers and have a claim on us to be employed.

Dalhousie would remain sceptical about those Gurkhas recruited from inside Nepal, though they were only a fraction of their total. In fact, the Gurkha battalions, far from being specifically Nepali, were both ethnically and nationally complex, something British military officers and civil servants often failed to grasp.

Despite his misgivings, Dalhousie did accede to Napier's demands that Gurkha battalions be brought into the regular Bengal Army and paid properly. Towards the end of his term in office he also came to see that Napier's advice to Parliament was right: an increase in Gurkha troops was essential to the security of India. But at the time, Napier's warnings went unheeded; it would be decades after the Indian rebellion before the British were allowed to recruit from within Nepal.

*

When the rebellion began in 1857, an ageing former diplomat living at the new hill station of Darjeeling added a sardonic footnote to an essay he had written a quarter of a century ago: 'On the Origin and Classification of the Military Tribes of Nepal'. Brian Houghton Hodgson, formerly British resident at Kathmandu, had left the Company's service more than thirteen years earlier but there was no one in Calcutta with remotely his understanding of Nepal, and none had pressed so consistently as he had for the expansion of Gurkha regiments. 'Since this paper was written,' he added,

> the value and availability to us of the Gorkhali soldier tribes have been well tested, and it is infinitely to be regretted that the opinions of Sir

H[enry] Fane, Sir C[harles] Napier and of Sir H[enry] Lawrence, as to the high expediency of recruiting from this source were not acted on long ago.

For the past decade, Hodgson had lived on and off at Brianstone, his bungalow at 2,300 metres looking north to the glittering immensity of Kangchenjunga. Soon after he arrived in 1846 the peak had been mistakenly judged the highest on earth and when the mornings were clear he could watch the rising sun touch its summit like a flame. In April 1848, the young botanist Joseph Hooker arrived at Brianstone for what became a prolonged stay of many months. The view of Kangchenjunga entranced him.

> From its vast shoulders the perpetually snowed range I scrutinised east and west for about seventy miles, without the smallest break of the snowline. It is a wonderful panorama, startling in its effect when first revealed by the rising mists on a cloudless morning.

Looking out at this sweeping prospect, Hodgson attempted to process the vast amount of knowledge he had acquired during nearly a quarter of a century spent in Kathmandu. 'My subjects are Ethnology and Zoology and Education,' he wrote to his devoted sister Fanny, '– all ample fields and yet enough untrodden to render intelligent truthful labours permanently valuable.' The events of 1857 were an unexpected interruption to this secluded life of scholarship: the discarded threads of Hodgson's diplomatic career had suddenly reconnected.

A year before the rebellion began in Meerut, Hodgson had received a request from the prime minister of Nepal, the charismatic Jang Bahadur, whose brutal rise to power had ended years of internal strife in the Nepali court and made the king his puppet. Hodgson had left Kathmandu by then, but the two men had once known each other quite well. Hodgson saw in Jang something of his great-uncle, the prime minister Bhimsen Thapa, whose fall from power Hodgson had witnessed. But he shared also the widespread distrust of officials in Calcutta for Jang, who had, more or less, slaughtered his way to the top. Jang now wanted Hodgson to keep an eye on his future son-in-law Gajraj Singh Thapa, from one of Nepal's grandest families, who was coming to Darjeeling to brush up his English, fast becoming the lingua franca of the subcontinent. Then in his mid twenties, Gajraj was so taken with tea and Darjeeling's tea plantations that he introduced the first plantations to Nepal.

Gajraj had been in Darjeeling, staying with Hodgson, for a year when the rebellion began. As he had done in the Sikh wars, Jang Bahadur now offered assistance to Calcutta, putting the whole of Nepal's military at the disposal of the British. For the governor general Lord Canning, the offer was a mixed blessing. If the situation deteriorated further, then the large Gorkhali army might switch sides. The situation deteriorated anyway, with brutal massacres of European women and children at Cawnpore and the ferocious siege of Lucknow. Jang might have taken offence at how Calcutta dragged its heels, but he was above all an opportunist and asked Hodgson to use his influence in his favour. Jang needed a friend of Nepal to reassure Canning he was genuine in his offer of support.

To press Jang's case, in October 1857 Hodgson and his wife Anne went to Calcutta, staying with an old friend, Sir John Colville, chief justice of Bengal. Colville made an introduction to the governor general, whose father Hodgson had met while at the colonial boarding school, Haileybury, the East India Company's training college. 'I could not but be sensible that I had been out of the coach for years,' Hodgson wrote afterwards. 'Moreover that I was liable to be ignored as an avowed friend of the Nepalese, who were then looked upon with much suspicion and dislike.' Lord Canning's wife Charlotte was a favourite of Queen Victoria and a brilliant watercolourist and botanist. She had been to the Kangra valley and painted the famous hill-fort there, so knew the Himalaya. Yet when introduced to Anne Hodgson, she simply swatted away the idea of help from Nepal: 'you praise these Gorkhas like your husband, but I can assure you they are looked on here as being little better than the rebels.' Despite the cool reception, over games of billiards Hodgson talked to Canning about Jang, about his motivation and what he might expect in return for Nepal's help. No one understood Jang's perspective better. Hodgson impressed on Canning that much had happened since the Treaty of Sagauli forty years earlier, events Hodgson had witnessed for himself. Hodgson wasn't simply a retired civil servant offering a relevant and informative briefing. This was a compelling human story with at its heart two very different men: a scholar and a tyrant each learning about the other's world.

Had Hodgson's father, also called Brian, been luckier in business, the fate of his son might have been different. What he did offer were the genes of Methuselah – father and son would live into their nineties – and a passion for hunting. His house, Lower Beech in the Cheshire parish of Prestbury, was full of dogs; one of Hodgson's earliest memories was his father dressed in a scarlet hunt coat standing with his grandfather, who kept the Old Hall hotel at Buxton, freshly returned bloody-handed from a cockfight. But investments in his cousin's Macclesfield bank and an Irish copper mine failed; the family was ruined. Only the support of relatives allowed some semblance of respectability. The Hodgsons left Prestbury for more modest lodgings, first in Macclesfield, then Congleton. Brian started at the grammar school in Macclesfield, where he excelled at cricket and scuffled with boys from the local borough school.

Hodgson's beautiful and charming mother Catherine, matched with an affable but ineffectual husband, did what any woman in her position would: she started networking. Friendship with the Earl of Clarendon secured a government post for Brian senior as warden of a Martello tower in Clacton on the Essex coast, and while his father looked out for Napoleon, Brian junior went to school in Surrey. James Pattison, a former silk manufacturer and a neighbour in Congleton, was also a director of the East India Company, and as such had the right to nominate one civil service candidate each year, a privilege that provoked ferocious lobbying and corruption. James Mill, who published his gigantic *History of India* in 1817, quipped that Britain's empire was 'a vast system of outdoor relief for Britain's upper classes', but in truth to enter the Company as a 'writer' or secretary was to join one of the best-paid commercial entities in the world, like climbing aboard Goldman Sachs, though with a far higher risk of not reaching retirement: the fatality rate among civil servants in India was twice that of those who remained in Britain. Still, Pattison must have liked Catherine and her oldest son, for he bestowed his nomination on Brian. He was less generous to the children who worked in his silk mill.

With Pattison's nomination, Brian Hodgson started at Haileybury a year early, aged fifteen. He was installed in the house of the college's academic star, Thomas Malthus. Here some of the most influential intellectuals and politicians of the early nineteenth century gathered to discuss issues of the day. Hodgson's patron James Pattison, soon to be chairman of the East India Company, visited his young protégé, bringing with him his close friend George Canning, then president of the Board of Control, later prime minister. Canning gave the young Hodgson a seminar on Indian colonial history and 'a brilliant sketch of the career possible for an Indian civilian'. Hodgson was being offered the keys to the kingdom; his family were looking to him to rescue them from debt: he must not fail.

Hodgson excelled at Haileybury, coming top of his year and winning prizes for Bengali, a distinction that put him in the front rank when, aged seventeen, he embarked for Calcutta and his civil service training at Fort William College. The climate almost immediately killed him. Born in the soft, temperate drizzle of the Cheshire plain, the sweltering heat and prodigious rains of the monsoon quickly took their toll. His health broke and never wholly recovered, despite his longevity. His doctor told him: 'Here is your choice – six feet underground, resign the service, or get a hill-appointment.' The advice put Hodgson in a bitter quandary. He had dedicated himself to releasing his family from debt, but there were few opportunities he might survive. In 1819, Darjeeling, a future hub of tea production, remained a forested hill. Simla was still an obscure Himalayan village. There were only two postings available in the mountains: in Kumaon, recently wrested from the Gorkhali kingdom of Nepal, and in the capital of Nepal itself, the residency at Kathmandu. These posts were in the control of the Bengal Civil Service's Foreign and Political Department and were highly prized, their award resting ultimately with the governor general.

Ordinarily, such a post would be out of the question for someone so young and untried but Hodgson's connections in Calcutta rescued him. An aunt was a friend of Lady Elizabeth D'Oyly, wife of Sir Charles D'Oyly, artist and Company man, who held the most entertaining and glamorous salon in Calcutta. Hodgson was hardly a party-goer. His nickname at the Tent Club, dedicated to hunting wildlife, was the 'young philosopher'. Yet he was welcome at D'Oyly's, where the expressed aim was the exclusion of bores, and if he was quieter than some of his fellows, he enjoyed the conversation and company of women, another hint of his mother's influence. So it was, with a word from Eliza D'Oyly to her cousin Flora, wife of the governor general, the Marquess of Hastings, Hodgson secured the post of assistant to George William Traill, commissioner of Kumaon. In

August 1819, Hodgson graduated top of his year, debating publicly at graduation ceremony in both Persian and Bengali. Next day his appointment was made official; he was on his way to the Himalaya.

His new boss George Traill, commissioner of Garhwal and Kumaon, was a no-nonsense frontiersman who would spend twenty-one years roaming the mountains, visiting each inhabited place to catalogue the region's wealth and resources. Kumaon had suffered for generations from a sequence of invasions, first from Afghan Muslims who terror-ised local farmers and moaned about the cold, then from the Gorkhali army. They oppressed Kumaon with such cruelty that it passed into proverb and legend; half of Kumaon's farms had been abandoned. Traill lifted many of the Gorkhali taxes and came up with a more equitable system. The report he eventually produced from these inves-tigations became a model for administrators elsewhere in India. The governor general might have ruled in Calcutta, but Traill was king of the Kumaon. It was under Traill that Hodgson served his apprentice-ship, following his master throughout the winter of 1819 and the first part of 1820, climbing over endless mountain ridges to every remote village where they discussed, with no need of interpreters, everyday problems with the headman. Traill made a point of learning about every aspect of Kumaon life, a habit Hodgson would adopt as his own.

In October 1820, when Hodgson was transferred to Kathmandu as assistant to the resident, the notion he would spend the rest of his career there would have appalled him. The posting was simply another rung on the ladder. Having learned from George Traill, he now had

> another man to form myself upon, a man with all the simplicity and more than the courtesy of Traill – a man who was the perfection of good sense and good temper; who liking the Nepalese and under-standing them, was doing wonders in reconciling a Court of Chinese proclivities to the offensive novelty of responsible international dealing.

This was Edward Gardner, who had taken up his post in the summer of 1816. As we saw earlier, his mission was straightforward: to do as little as possible as politely as possible. Nepal must be calm and China reassured that its western marches were safe from the East India Company. He spent much of his time gardening.

Hodgson had few professional duties to occupy him, beyond acting as Gardner's secretary. He was limited by decree from straying more than half a day's walk from the residency. There was plenty of time to learn Gorkhali, the Khas language now known as Nepali, and Newari, the language of the Kathmandu valley, to go with his Bengali and Persian. Yet ambition gnawed away at him. Hodgson appealed to friends in Calcutta and within two years of his arrival Brian Hodgson was gone, promoted to deputy secretary in the Foreign and Political Department. This was preferment, marking Hodgson as destined for great things, perhaps a seat on the Company's council or government of an Indian province. But once back in the broiling heat of Calcutta, his health collapsed again. Going back to the hills might save Hodgson, but his old job in Kathmandu was taken. He was saved by that rare phenomenon, a powerful but kindly man. William Butterworth Bayley was a senior and trusted figure in the Calcutta secretariat and knew everyone. When Hodgson appealed to him, Bayley sent him back to Kathmandu as the residency's postmaster, a job invented just for Hodgson in order to save his health. 'Go back to Nepal and master the subject in all its phases,' Bayley told him. 'In the present times you can learn little there. But we have had one fierce struggle with Nepal and we shall have another yet.' Mastering Nepal 'in all its phases' would be his life's work.

Hodgson was sustained in Kathmandu by letters from home and his deepening interest in study. He had a long and intense correspondence with his sister Fanny, a detailed and at times moving insight into his isolated life. He poured out his frustrations and hopes to her. Fanny found herself the recipient of despatches from the most exotic posting in the subcontinent. Like his father before him, Hodgson was a keen shot and with his sport came a growing interest in the Kathmandu valley's natural history. He began to make an in-depth study of its birds and animals, its flowers and agriculture.

> I have three native artists always employed in drawing from nature [he told Fanny]. I possess a live tiger, a wild sheep, a wild goat, four bears, three civets, and three score of our beautiful pheasants. A rare menagerie! And my drawings now amount to two thousands.

He worked hard in the residency garden too, planting oats and potatoes and at the cottage given to the resident up in the hills above the
city, he made a little corner of England. 'The sward is emerald,' he
told Fanny, 'and the familiar tokens it displays in its daisies fern, thistle,
and colewort, are dear to the exile.' He showed the same enthusiasm
for his developing interest in Buddhism. Hodgson's collection of
Sanskrit texts was unprecedented for a European. Those he sent the
scholar Eugène Burnouf in Paris helped launch the academic study
of Buddhism in the West. His deep knowledge and appreciation of
Buddhist doctrines earned him the friendship of Tibetan lamas as well
as the court in Kathmandu. Part of his growing influence with Nepal's
rulers stemmed from this cultural sympathy. He gave up alcohol and
meat, partly to protect his weak liver. 'I live,' he told his sister, 'like a
Brahman.'

For his masters in Calcutta Hodgson made a detailed study of the
organisation of the Nepali military – and the possibility of adding to
the Company's Gurkha battalions. In the process, Hodgson judged
that the Company's strengthening grip on northern India, far from
pacifying Nepal's appetite for war, had only sharpened it. British
annexation had damaged Nepal's economic model and left the elite
thirsting for military action and the loot that came with it. Prithvi
Narayan had created a hereditary ruling class whose organising prin-
ciple was military service. 'Soldiers have been and are heads of the
law and finance at Kathmandu, and administrators of the interior.
Soldiers have been and are everything.' Bhimsen Thapa kept those
soldiers in a state of habitual aggression.

> In my humble opinion, [Hodgson told Calcutta, the Gurkhas] are by
> far the best soldiers in India, and if they are made participators of our
> renown in arms, I conceive that their gallant spirit and unadulterated
> military habits might be relied on for fidelity.

Gurkha loyalty, Hodgson added, would be assured by receipt of a
regular pay cheque. By absorbing Nepal's reserve troops, around ten
thousand in number, the British could give the elite in Kathmandu
the cash it needed and dilute Nepal's military frustration. The idea
was sound but when he wrote this, in the early 1830s, India was at

peace. The governor general Lord William Bentinck and the secretariat in Calcutta thanked Hodgson politely for his report and ignored it.

Nine years after his return to Kathmandu and thirteen years since he first saw the city, Hodgson feared he was drifting in a backwater with no influence or importance. Despite being confirmed as resident in 1833, he told his sister: 'I am 33 – the last thirteen years passed in the wilderness without wife, children or the presence of a female. No change, no society!' When his brother Will died, not long after his younger brother Edward, Hodgson told his sister that at least their brothers were spared the disappointments and disillusion of middle age. 'Happy, thrice happy they who quit this troubled scene ere the bloom of their virtuous feelings has been rubbed off!' Hodgson was left to pay off his brother's debts. Despite his growing reputation as an academic, Hodgson felt disappointed, duty-bound to support his ageing parents with no chance of further advancement. It was at this point, just as he had begun to think of his pension, that Hodgson was plunged into the most demanding period of his career.

*

While the Nepali king Rajendra had been a minor, under the regency of Tripura Sundari, her uncle Bhimsen Thapa was able to maintain his tight grip on the army, shutting out the Thapa family's great rivals, the Pandes. Then in 1832 Tripura died of cholera and Rajendra came of age, a man Hodgson described as 'mad, cruel, violent, mean, pusillanimous and weak'. Slowly at first, but then with increasing speed, Nepal's elite imploded in violence and intrigue. Bhimsen was now in his sixties and relied increasingly on his forceful young nephew Mathabar Singh. Hodgson could see his old adversary weakening and took advantage, proposing a new trade agreement. Bhimsen was sympathetic in principle and wasn't strong enough to antagonise Hodgson. Equally he couldn't appear too close to the British in front of the court. So he sent his nephew Mathabar to Calcutta in the winter of 1835 to ask permission to travel to London with letters for William IV, seeking international recognition for his regime. Hodgson blocked that move, which dented Bhimsen's prestige. The stage was being set for Bhimsen's downfall.

Nepal's king Rajendra had two wives, both called Laksmi Devi. The senior queen, Samrajya Laksmi Devi, was a Pande, mother of the crown prince Surendra; the junior queen, Rajya Laksmi Devi, was a Thapa. The king fretted between them, alternately screamed at or ignored. When Samrajya's young infant son Devendra died, rumours spread he had been poisoned. The doctor who attended him was tortured horribly and gave up Bhimsen Thapa as a conspirator, shortly before being crucified. Bhimsen was imprisoned and his nephew Mathabar fled to India.

Bhimsen's replacement was Ranjang Pande, son of Damodar, who had been beheaded in 1804 as Bhimsen came to power. Virulently anti-British and determined to restore his family's fortunes, his rise to power coincided with a worsening political situation for the East India Company which was now embroiling itself in Afghanistan, alarmed at the rise of Russian influence in that region. Ranjit Singh, ruler of the Sikh Empire, was also becoming a threat and had established diplomatic links with Kathmandu. Tension between the British and the Gorkha regime grew so great that the governor general Lord Auckland sent sixteen thousand troops in 1838 to Nepal's southern border. Despite the military presence, Hodgson was horribly exposed.

Luckily for the Company's resident, Ranjang overplayed his hand. Assuming the king would sanction a lucrative war, he had ordered an expensive refit of the military: new cannon, musket balls and gunpowder. But as he raised taxes to pay for it all, opinion in the aristocracy turned against him. So, to secure his position, Ranjang decided to remove once and for all the latent threat posed by Bhimsen and Mathabar. Assassins were sent to India to poison the latter, now living in Simla, albeit uncessfully, while Bhimsen was charged with murdering the previous king Rajendra's father, Girvan Yuddha, an old rumour that was wholly false. More doctors were tortured for information, including a Newari who was impaled in front of the king before having his heart torn out. No evidence was forthcoming, but Bhimsen was thrown back in jail anyway. Exhausted and threatened with torture, Bhimsen was told, falsely, that his wife had been paraded naked through the streets of the city. The old man, burning with shame, committed suicide. At the death of his longstanding adversary, Hodgson told his superiors that apart from Ranjit Singh, there had been no greater native statesman of recent times.

For much of 1840 the situation hung in the balance. The East India Company was stretched, fighting the First Opium War in China while simultaneously occupying Kabul. Rajendra approached the Chinese, on the hunt for allies. In April, a Nepali force seized several villages across the border in India. Hodgson's personal safety was threatened and he sent the residency's head munshi (interpreter) to the palace, warning Rajendra of swift and terrible consequences if he was murdered. The Gorkhali army was on the brink of mutiny, infuriated at cuts in pay and itching to loot Lucknow and Patna across the border. 'True, the English government is great,' a general told Rajendra, who had been summoned to the parade ground to hear the army's grievances, 'but care the wild dogs of Nepal how large is the herd they attack?' They wanted Nepal's old colonies east and west of Nepal's imposed borders returned, and with it Gorkha prestige.

Alerted by Hodgson's warnings, the governor general Lord Auckland promised troops and Hodgson issued an ultimatum, demanding the Nepalis withdraw their forces. As the crisis reached its climax in September he wrote to his parents: 'I steal a moment from official writing to tell you I am well, and that you need entertain no fears for me though war ensue with Nepal, as it probably will immediately.' Instead, the Gorkha show of strength evaporated to nothing. Seventy-five years after Prithvi Narayan Shah consolidated a mosaic of small Himalayan states into a new nation, fear, greed and jealousy had hollowed out its elite and left the economy moribund. Nepal's vaunted martial threat had been shown to be little more than posturing. Nepal paid the East India Company compensation, Ranjang was fired and a chief minister more congenial to the British interest was appointed. Auckland heaped praise on Hodgson's handling of the crisis.

Never again would Nepal pose a serious threat to the British in India. The senior queen Samrajya, outraged by the change in government, continued to resist the East India Company's influence but she died in late 1841, aged just twenty-three. That winter the British army suffered its worst humiliation of the nineteenth century when more than sixteen thousand troops and civilians perished during their retreat from Kabul. Yet Nepal's elite, fatally weakened by court factionalism, was no longer able to take advantage of British vulnerability. In May 1845, Sir Henry Lawrence, Hodgson's successor as resident, could write to Calcutta in reference to this infighting: 'So much blood has been shed in Nepaul, that it must now continue to flow.' He called the rising tide of assassinations and savagery 'sanguinary proceedings', and concluded that because there was 'no chance of domestic peace ...

> I do not therefore augur danger to the British Government. There is not a soldier in Nepaul, scarcely a single man, that has seen a shot fired; and not one that could head an army.

The East India Company judged that only insurrection within India could make Nepal a threat again, a prediction that would come back to haunt them.

Hodgson himself had left Kathmandu in December 1843, evicted by the new governor general Lord Ellenborough, who disliked Hodgson's influence on Nepal's domestic affairs as much as Auckland had been grateful for it. The king Rajendra was distraught. He had known Hodgson for most of his life and at their final audience burst into tears, calling the departing resident, a man he had often wanted dead, the 'saviour of Nepal'. Taking a jewel from his turban, he turned to the new resident, Sir Henry Lawrence, and begged that Hodgson be allowed to accept the gift, for the debt he owed 'Mr Hodgson's prudence and patience under many and great provocations'. The jewel was declined. Ellenborough was not so grateful. He had instructed Lawrence to offer Hodgson the job of sub-commissioner in Simla, a humiliating demotion designed to provoke Hodgson's resignation, which promptly followed.

*

The darbar was now split between three factions: the feeble Rajendra, the psychopathic teenage crown prince Surendra, a man who took pleasure in watching torture, and the previously junior queen Laksmi Devi, a woman no less manipulative and determined than the senior queen Samrajya had been in promoting the interests of her own son. As Lawrence put it: 'Mr Nepal, Master Nepal and Mrs Nepal'. Lawrence stayed in Kathmandu for barely two years, but that was long enough to witness the return, rise and brutal murder of Mathabar Singh, Rajendra's latest *mukhtiyar*, or chief minister, and his replacement by

Jang Bahadur: the potentate whose offer of assistance to the British Hodgson would present to Canning over billiards some fourteen years later, in 1857.

Laksmi Devi had tempted Mathabar home from Simla, where he had been living on a British pension following his uncle Bhimsen Thapa's suicide and the attempt on his own life. To reassure him, Laksmi sent Mathabar's nephew to fetch him: this was Jang Bahadur.

Jang's father was Bal Narsingh Kunwar, a soldier in the bodyguard of Rajendra's grandfather Rana Bahadur. When in 1806 Rana Bahadur was murdered, it had been Bal Narsingh who struck the killer down, earning the gratitude of Bhimsen Thapa. After Bhimsen's putsch, in which he became chief minister and many of his enemies were murdered, Bal Narsingh was promoted to *kazi*, or minister, and later governor of Jumla. Jang's mother was Bhimsen's niece, Ganesh Kumari. When their first son was born, Bal Narsingh wanted to name the boy Bir Narsingh, but the Thapas put their foot down and changed his name to Jang Bahadur: 'brave in war'.

With the Thapas the pre-eminent family in Nepal, Jang's childhood was privileged, but when the queen Samrajya Laksmi Devi sent Bhimsen to prison, Jang, then aged eighteen, disappeared from view. For a time he was quite literally in the wilderness, working as an elephant-tamer in the jungles of the terai to pay off his gambling debts. After a spell in Benares, the family fortunes began to rise again and in 1839, Jang returned to Kathmandu. He came to the attention of Rajendra during an elephant hunt in early 1840. A wild elephant was surrounded but no one could get near it until Jang strode up and lassoed the creature's rear legs. Rajendra was so impressed he promoted Jang to be a captain in the artillery. Later that year, the biggest elephant in the royal stables went wild, trampling its keeper to death. Once again, it was Jang who brought the animal under control. A notorious womaniser, he had to be fetched from a nearby brothel. (Jang claimed to have slept with 1,400 women over the course of his life. His descendants claim he offered any woman twenty thousand rupees if she could make him ejaculate before he was ready. No one ever claimed the prize; it was said Jang's opium addiction was responsible. He also freely admitted to making up stories about himself.)

Once he had been fetched back from Simla at queen Laksmi Devi's behest, Jang's uncle Mathabar was appointed chief minister in late

1843 but soon had cause to regret his homecoming. Jang owed much
to Mathabar, but increasingly the pair clashed. Mathabar was a genuinely impressive man; Lawrence called him 'a hero compared with
the best of them'. Jang, although twenty years younger, was from the
same cloth, only shrewder and more ruthless. Mathabar decided to
take his nephew down a peg or two, transferring him from the *bharadari*, or council of nobles, to prince Surendra's bodyguard, which Jang
resented. Meanwhile, Rajendra, Surendra and Laksmi Devi bickered
incessantly. In contrast to Hodgson's day, the East India Company
maintained a position of icy indifference and with no lead from the
British, Mathabar preferred Surendra as the element of that trio he
could manipulate most easily. This alienated the queen and, when
Laksmi Devi extracted permission from her husband Rajendra to
assassinate Mathabar, it was Jang who was ordered to carry it out.

Summoned to the palace late at night and leaving his bodyguard
behind, Mathabar came before the king and queen, both already in
bed. Jang then stepped out from behind a screen and shot his uncle.
Once he was sure Mathabar was dead, Rajendra leaped out of bed,
kicked Mathabar's corpse and claimed responsibility for the killing.
No one believed him. As the crown prince Surendra observed, Rajendra
couldn't kill a rat, let alone a man like Mathabar. Lawrence told his
superiors: 'The Maharaja may have mangled the corpse; but I must
doubt His Highness having the courage to fire a gun, much more to
face his late Minister.' Even so, he discounted rumours of Jang's
involvement. 'Poor as is my opinion of Jang's moral character, I do
believe him guiltless.' And yet guilty he was.

The crime weighed on Jang, on his conscience and in the knowledge
that if he could do that to his own uncle then Jang would never be
safe himself from anyone, even his own family. Years later, while
showing the colonial official and author Laurence Oliphant around
his house in Kathmandu, he paused before some portraits.

> Jang called our attention to one of these; it was ... of a strikingly
> handsome man, whose keen eye and lofty brow seemed almost to
> entitle him to the position he held between the Duke of Wellington
> and the Queen [Victoria]. 'See,' said Jang, enthusiastically, 'here is the
> Queen of England; and she has not got a more loyal subject than I
> am.' Then turning to the picture of the man with the keen eyes and

high forehead, he remarked, 'That is my poor uncle Mahtiber [sic] Singh, whom I shot; it is very like him.'

The murder of Mathabar Singh prompted a lull, during which the East India Company went to war with the Sikh Empire and Sir Henry Lawrence was recalled from Kathmandu to take up a new post, first assisting the governor general Sir Henry Hardinge and then as agent at Lahore. At Sagauli in January 1846, on their way back to Calcutta, Lawrence's wife Honoria, an adroit and witty observer of Nepali life and politics, wrote to their friend George Clerk, a member of the East India Company's board of directors in London. Likening the factions at court to Kilkenny cats, she was certain the calm mood could not continue:

> Jang Bahadoor, Mathbur's nephew, is likewise a general and called commander-in-chief. He takes no very prominent part just now, and seems to spend his energies in devising uniforms. But he is active and intelligent, and if (perhaps it would be more correct to say, *when*) there is another slaughter in the Durbar, the struggle will probably be between Jang Bahadur and Guggur [Gagan] Singh.

Honoria Lawrence was right. In September that year, late in the evening, the queen's favourite and presumed lover Gagan Singh was 'shot in a chamber of his house', according to the acting resident Captain Ottley, 'while in the performance of his devotions [prayers]'. His son hurried to the palace to tell Laksmi Devi. Incandescent with fury, Laksmi Devi hurried on foot to Gagan's house. When she saw the body she broke down and wept, and for a moment couldn't continue with the rituals she had come to perform, placing gold and basil, and drops of Ganges water, in Gagan's mouth. Then, in a moment of female solidarity, she turned to Gagan's three widows and forbade them to commit *sati* on their husband's funeral pyre. That mercy done, she acted.

Taking a sword from her attendants, Laksmi marched back to the palace and told Jang to summon the *bharadari* to the *kot*, or armoury. While she waited, she cried over and over, as Ottley reported, that 'until the man who had assassinated so faithful a Minister should be discovered and put to death, she would neither take food nor taste water.' Jang complied with her order but took the precaution of bringing three regiments loyal to him to wait outside. He smelt danger but also opportunity. When the courtiers were gathered, Laksmi Devi pointed the finger at the wrong man and ordered him killed. The courtier charged with this task, Abhiman Singh, refused. He knew the man was innocent because he had in fact been one of the conspirators; he said he would kill no one without authorisation from the chief minister, a relative of the king called Fateh Jang Shah. The king Rajendra was sent to fetch him. Night wore on; tempers frayed.

Having fulfilled his mission and told Fateh Jang to go to the *kot*, Rajendra decided to visit the British residency and seek its help. Captain Ottley, a young man uncertain what to do, sent his munshi to temporise. And so it was that the king of Nepal waited at the gates of a foreign power to complain to a man who wouldn't listen about the murder of his wife's lover. The munshi gently suggested Rajendra go home; the king returned to the *kot*. When he got there, the gutters were running with blood and crowds were thronging the entrance, preventing him from entering. He gratefully rushed home and did what he had done before in times of crisis: hid in bed. Rajendra's reign was almost over.

When Fateh Jang Shah had finally arrived that night, Jang had told him they should back the queen and execute Abhiman Singh. Though Fateh refused, Abhiman now feared a plot. He told his bodyguards to load their muskets. Seeing this, Jang climbed up the narrow stairs to warn the queen who was watching from above. She descended to the courtyard, again demanding the man she had accused be killed. When that didn't happen she tried to assault him herself. Fateh Jang Shah and Abhiman restrained her, but while following her back up the stairs, someone, probably one of Jang Bahadur's brothers, opened fire. Given the numbers of troops gathered near the kot supporting various parties inside, a massacre was now inevitable and when the sun rose on 15 September, bodies of soldiers and *bharadari* alike were piled in the courtyard. Fifty-five were judged 'worth having their names preserved', but the true death toll was higher. Jang had his men dig a vast square pit and then shouted up to prince Surendra, who was watching from above: 'Whatever they could do for you, I can do.'

Even before the night was over, the queen had declared Jang prime minister but if she thought she could manage him as she had others, it was a bad miscalculation. Jang had no intention of replacing the malleable Surendra with the queen's son, as she wished. When she replaced him as chief minister, Jang killed his replacement and sent the queen into exile at Benares. Rajendra meekly followed. Although they continued to plot Jang's downfall, there was little loyalty left for them to draw on. Rajendra attempted an invasion but was easily defeated and placed under house arrest, where he remained for the rest of his life, outliving Jang Bahadur by four years. Surendra became king, but was also kept in isolation. Laksmi Devi remained in exile at Benares; a photograph taken years later shows a debauched and prematurely old woman living on a tiny British pension; the date of her death is unknown. The crown of Nepal was now wholly the puppet of Jang Bahadur. With his brothers at his side, Jang felt comparatively secure. He had himself promoted to *pradhan mantri*, a direct translation of the British term 'prime minister'. In time, his family's origins were also massaged. Plain Jang Bahadur Kunwar became Jang Bahadur Kunwar Ranaji. The 'Rana' suffix gave him a princely air, a touch of Mughal swagger with a hint of Rajput class. He even had Surendra 'confirm' the Kunwar's noble Rajasthani origins. Jang Bahadur's Rana clan would dominate Nepal for the next hundred years.

*

Having got a grip of Nepal, Jang's interest turned to the British Empire. He had grown up during a period when British influence in Kathmandu had grown from marginal presence to major influence on court politics. He knew threats to cure the elite's greed and dissatisfaction with an invasion of India would likely end in catastrophe. Better to placate his gigantic neighbour than provoke violence. But his fascination was more than political. What kind of world did the foreigners inhabit? How had they achieved such power?

To answer his own curiosity, on 15 January 1850, seven years before the Indian rebellion and his offer of assistance to Lord Canning, Jang Bahadur left Kathmandu for Britain, or Belait as it is in Nepali, like the Hindustani source for 'Blighty'. Leaving his brother Bam Bahadur in charge, Jang took with him a retinue of around twenty-five, including his two youngest and favourite brothers, an artist, a singer, a doctor – ayurvedic, naturally – and someone to write down the group's impressions of their travels, a document known as the *Belait Yatra*. Accompanying them was Captain Cavenagh of the Bengal Army, who later wrote his own account, and a British Calcutta lawyer called Macleod, who acted as interpreter and private secretary.

First they travelled to Patna, tiger-hunting en route, where the pervasiveness of British influence was faithfully recorded. 'Toasting,' wrote their chronicler, 'is a custom at British banquets.' The Nepalis toured Calcutta, inspecting sewage works and weaving machines, bottle manufacturers and the mint where India's rupees were fashioned. The governor general greeted them with a nineteen-gun salute, not quite the full twenty-one, but more than for other Indian princes. Jang and his retinue, like all good Hindus facing a voyage across the *kala pani*, or 'black water', made a pilgrimage to Puri to prepare their souls for the journey ahead. Then they embarked on the P&O ship *Haddington*. Jang had the boat to himself, which was fortunate given that he became violently seasick. He was quoted as complaining: 'The waves rose high like mountains and people sleeping on the bedsteads were in danger of being rolled down.' The chronicler, whose identity is uncertain, recorded Nepali bewilderment at how efficiently the ship was managed, apparently without violence. And, of course, for a writer who had never seen the ocean, unbroken views of water were compelling. 'There was no mountain, no tree, no bush, no land to be seen. The sun rose out of the water and sank back into it.'

The crew were equally bemused with their illustrious passenger. What was he? A king? A prime minister? Or an ambassador? And what to make of a man wearing clothes of the very finest silks and jewels worth a fortune who nevertheless liked to milk the cows on board ship and strip to his dhoti in public to wash himself. Most intriguingly, he ate alone, to avoid the spiritual pollution of eating with non-Hindus. At Suez the group disembarked and travelled overland to Cairo, where a riverboat took them to Alexandria and the SS *Ripon* whose fore-cabins and saloons had been reserved for Jang and his retinue. Steaming past Gibraltar, which became 'Jivapur' to Jang's chronicler, they reached Southampton – 'Sautanghat' – on 26 May 1850.

Both hosts and visitors were transfixed by each other. The chronicler was overwhelmed by the comparative wealth of ordinary people. 'Not one bad-looking or undernourished individual was to be seen.' There was none of the smallpox victims or disfigured lepers so common in the streets of Kathmandu. Meanwhile British writers were both intrigued and appalled by what they saw. 'The servants of the embassy were evidently of the lowest caste,' observed the *Morning Post*. 'Some were meanly and miserably clad, many of them without shoes, and their clothing formed a striking contrast to the magnificent costume of the chiefs.' The gifts Jang had brought were worth more than £17 million and yet his servants were shabby.

The Nepalis were given digs on Richmond Terrace, or 'Rijavant Karij' as the chronicler transcribed it, a neoclassical block of eight houses completed in 1825 between Downing Street and the Thames. Jang made himself at home, although the Nepalis' habit of slaughtering goats on the premises was met with alarm from their British attendants. Billeted close to the Palace of Westminster, Jang witnessed London approaching the zenith of its imperial splendour. Piped water, hot-air balloons, the theatre, steam engines, parks, railways, ironworks: all of it impressed. Jang said: 'The English have made fire, water and wind their slaves.' The chronicler noticed how everyone in Belait wore a watch. 'Getting dressed, eating, keeping appointments, sleeping, getting up or going out – everything is determined by the clock.' The Nepalis had become explorers in a previously undiscovered land. And as the chronicler observed, it was a land on which Laksmi, the goddess of wealth, had smiled.

Most compelling was the system of government. 'The sovereign,' the chronicler wrote with, you sense, an attitude of incredulity,

cannot confiscate anybody's property, punish anyone, resort to violence or insult, nor hand out and cancel appointments at his own pleasure, as if he were absolute master of his own resources.

Instead, there was a parliament that could dismiss the prime minister should he fail in his duties. Most tellingly, the sovereign was subordinate to the will of the same parliament. That must have pleased Jang. 'A man's rank is of no account if he does wrong,' wrote the chronicler, but he recorded too how the common people had responsibilities to wider society.

For their part, Londoners were enthralled watching the first high-caste Hindu to visit Europe being driven down Piccadilly. The press tried to outdo each other with descriptions of Jang's exoticism. *The*

Times noted how sleek he appeared alongside his 'two short, or rather, fat brothers, who accompany him. His features are of the Tartar cast.' He learned the polka; one enterprising London music publisher was soon selling scores to a dance entitled 'Long Live Jang Bahadur!' Thackeray wrote a ditty about Jang's impact on London society ('Bedad his troat, his belt, his coat / All bleez'd with precious minerals ... ') published in the new satirical magazine *Punch.* Jang and his brothers hated the opera – all that screeching, they complained – but they clapped anyway, so hard in fact, that Queen Victoria, whose box they were sharing, asked why they should be applauding so hard when they hadn't understood a word of it. Jang responded prettily: 'No, Madam, nor do I understand what the nightingales sing.'

The Times also reported that Jang was attempting to pick up a little English, although one writer who met him later in Kathmandu noted he had only three phrases: 'How d'you do?' 'Very well, thank you,' and: 'You are very pretty.' Jang's roving eye and his obvious appeal to English women followed its inevitable if discreet course. The Kunwars adored Cremorne Gardens, with its gigantic dancing platform, modern gaslights and quiet corners where gentlemen could meet the brightly dressed prostitutes. Jang preferred whores and adventurers to noble-born women, because talking them into bed took less effort and had fewer consequences. A shop girl called Laura Bell, born on Lord Hertford's Irish estates and recently arrived from Belfast, caught Jang's eye and he lavished gifts on her, mostly valuable jewellery. Alarmed that adventurous young women were fleecing an honoured guest, ministers of state, anxious to maintain good relations, authorised reimbursement.

When Jang first arrived in Paris on the way home to Nepal, the French rather mocked him for standing off from female company, but his usual habit was soon restored. Jang and his brothers adored the girls at the ballet; after the performance they would nip back-stage to spread some jewellery around. Jang especially wanted to meet a dancer named on the programme as Mme Fanny Cerito, better known in London as Lola Montez and in the narrow lanes of Simla as Eliza James. She had not long been forced out of Bavaria, during Europe's tumultuous summer of revolutions in 1848, after the people of Munich besieged her house, fed up with her fleecing Ludwig, their 'old, adulterous, idiot sovereign'. Now she was dancing again, although she had little skill at it. Her charms lay elsewhere. Having grown up in India she could converse freely with Jang in Hindustani. Neither could believe their luck. The newspaper *L'Illustration* reported how 'there will long be talk of those two splendid diamond bracelets, offered, as they say, from hand to hand by the great Indian prince.'

Among the very best experiences, for the Kunwar boys, was the shopping. They had never seen so much stuff in their lives and they wanted to take home as much as they could manage: jewels from New Burlington Street; guns and rifles from James Purdey & Sons in Mayfair; pianos from Broadwoods, just as good as the one recently supplied to Chopin. Violins. Flutes. Billiard tables. Wolfhounds. An eighteen-foot chandelier. 'The Nepalese Princes,' said *The Times*,

> continue to form one of the most brilliant cynosures of the day. They are, certainly, going through London in style: while, as for diamonds, the brilliant eruption appears to take new forms and still more glittering features every time they appear in public.

Jang and his brothers delighted in clothes. They ordered suits from Savile Row, which they liked to wear as ineffectual disguises at the more risqué venues they visited. But they were also free, in ways that Englishmen were not, to flaunt their wealth in outlandish clothes. At one party, the *Edinburgh News* reported, Jang wore

> a superb oriental costume consisting of a robe or tunic of rich blue cloth or velvet, trimmed with gold lace. His cap, which fitted closely, was of white silk and glittered with pearls and diamonds, loops of emerald coloured stones hanging in front, while a long feather of the Bird of Paradise waved in the air.

The chronicler, however, looked on with distaste at the mixture and familiarity of different classes at the parties the Nepalis attended.

> 'Some officials and their wives danced,' he recorded, 'some walked about and others remained seated. They paid no attention to differences of rank, ignoring all questions of precedence. Such was the entertainment.'

Most important of all, for Jang's future as ruler of Nepal, were his encounters with Queen Victoria and her ministers. Victoria, aged thirty to Jang's thirty-three, had given birth to Prince Arthur, Duke of Connaught, shortly before the Nepali ambassador's arrival. So, for the first few days of his visit, he had to make do with her confidante and adviser, the Duke of Wellington, who was now eighty-one. The Iron Duke was very much the Nepali ruler's kind of man: direct, authoritarian, a soldier, not an intellectual and an isolationist in terms of foreign policy. When Wellington died two years later, Jang ordered an eighty-three-gun salute to be fired from Kathmandu's Tundhikel parade ground: one shot for each year of his life.

When Queen Victoria had sufficiently recovered, she received Jang at an official audience with her family and government officials in attendance. He was as impressed with Victoria as he had been by Wellington. Monarchs, for Jang, had been exclusively querulous, hot-tempered, inconsistent, venal and mad. Queen Victoria was an astonishing contrast. He sat beside her in her drawing room surrounded by her seven children and marvelled that this slight woman should be ruler of such a vast empire. She rewarded him with the Knight Grand Cross of the Order of the Bath, which caused gossip in Kathmandu, where the court assumed that Order of the Bath meant a level of intimacy.

Jang's visits to London and Paris had profound repercussions for his own country. Nepal soon had a modern legal system, the *Muluki Ain*, or 'law of the country', based on the Napoleonic Code, covering in 1,400 pages the administration of the state, revenue collection, criminal and civil law. Unlike the old religious-based system, which had allowed execution or bodily mutilation for a wide range of offenses, the *Muluki Ain* limited corporal punishment. Yet it was Britain's industrial might that impressed Jang the most. When he returned to Kathmandu, he was a changed man. He found his home provincial and dull, his subjects narrow and ill educated. 'Why should I attempt to tell these poor ignorant people what I have seen? It is as ridiculous to suppose that they would believe it as it is hopeless to attempt to make them understand it.'

*

After his return to Nepal, Jang fought a brief war against Tibet, winning new trade concessions from Lhasa, then stepped down as prime minister in favour of his brother, having the king declare him a maharaja. Retirement did not suit him. When his brother died a year later, Jang took up the reins once more, in time for the Indian rebellion. He tightened his family's grip on power, marrying his children into the king's family, including his daughter to the crown prince. The future of his dynasty seemed secure, but Jang was now outwitting opponents he deemed backward and unworthy. The hallmark of his family's rule was indifference to the people they governed. In 1950, when the Ranas finally lost power, the level of public education and health care was pitiful, while the sons of Nepal's elite were being educated in English public schools or their Indian equivalent. In the mid 1960s, when Jang's regime was still fresh in the memory and the artless palaces he built still dominated the city, the Newari scholar Kamal P Malla wrote how the Ranas

> refused to communicate with the rest of society except for money and cheap labour. They turned their backs on the traditional Nepalese arts, crafts and architecture. There is not a single building which shows the regime's patronage of the homespun style. A Rana palace is not only a depressive monument to Western mimicry: it is also convincing evidence of a collective schizophrenia. After all, the Ranas were the rulers; they ought to feel different from the ruled; they must live differently in dream-castles inaccessible to the vulgar herd. But is not all mimicry vulgar particularly the mimicry of a culture only imperfectly understood?

When northern India ignited in rebellion in May 1857, Jang Bahadur had put his entire military at the disposal of the British. And when the governor general hesitated over Jang's offer, he had recruited as advocate Brian Houghton Hodgson, who travelled that autumn to Calcutta to lobby Lord Canning. 'I urged the great value, negative and positive,' Hodgson wrote after their meeting, 'of the proffered aid of Nepal for putting down the Mutiny.' Hodgson was well aware of the suspicion Calcutta felt towards the Nepali maharaja but if Jang

> were fairly trusted and put into the hands of a representative of his Lordship having tact, experience and a liking for the Gurkhas, good faith would be kept with us, some useful military service done for us,

and above all in importance at such a moment, the spectacle exhibited
of the Hindu State *par excellence* in alliance and co-operation with us.

Historians have pored over the reasons for Jang's offer, but it was not
done out of loyalty to Queen Victoria. Material advantage and adventure seem the likeliest explanations: boredom and greed. Hodgson
advised Canning to offer Jang territory in the western terai that Nepal
had lost at the Treaty of Sagauli, the conclusion of its war with the
East India Company, in 1816. Canning reflected and agreed, appointing
Hodgson's friend Sir George MacGregor as Jang's British attaché. In
March of 1858, Jang marched at the head of an army seventeen thousand strong to help Lieutenant General Sir Colin Campbell in the
relief of Lucknow, telling the general that 'had he not visited England
he would now have been fighting against us instead of with us'. Apart
from the land on the terai, Jang's service to the British earned him
four thousand cartloads of loot from Lucknow, ten thousand modern
British rifles, the promise of military training, as well as a substantial
financial pay-off and honours from the British crown.

A few weeks after Lucknow, in the summer of 1858, Brian Houghton
Hodgson left India forever. Aged fifty-seven, he would live another
thirty-six years, dying at his home in Dover Street, London, in 1894.
Jang Bahadur spent his later years living in the ersatz European splendour of his palace in the Kathmandu district of Thapathali. He was
determined to visit Europe for a second time but the British were at
first reluctant; later, in 1874 and with a visit finally arranged, he got
as far as Bombay only to fall from his horse, forcing his return home.
In 1876 he entertained the Prince of Wales, the future Edward VII,
with a fortnight's tiger hunting on the terai. But despite his fascination
with European power, or perhaps because of it, Jang did his best to
keep the British out, resolutely refusing them recruitment of Gurkhas
inside Nepal and stymieing trade between India and Tibet. Almost
exactly a year after the royal visit, in February 1877, Jang Bahadur died,
aged fifty-nine, of cholera.

12

Crossing Borders

The Indian village of Milam sits high in the Johar valley, a few kilo-metres south of the border with Tibet and close to the Milam glacier, from where the headwaters of the Gori Ganga, the 'white river', begin their journey south. These days Milam is a place of ruins. There are roughly four hundred houses in the village but only a dozen are still inhabited. In India's 1901 census, there was a population here of almost eighteen hundred. Now it is down to a handful of shepherds, old men and women who bring their animals north each spring for the rich summer grazing. During winter, bears plunder the surviving homes, ransacking them for anything edible while the bitter wind tears at roofless walls. Look closely, though, and you'll find those walls studded with exquisite hand-carved wooden window frames dating back to the eighteenth century. Milam has been here for a long time and these works of craftsmanship are evidence of more prosperous times. Some of the architecture shows a similar cultural confidence. Ask the locals, and they will show you the *bada ghar*, the 'big house' where their ancestors hid from Gorkha invaders who had heard rumours of the region's wealth. All this decay among the mountains provokes an obvious and overwhelming question: what happened?

The answer usually offered is communist China's occupation of Tibet, the Dalai Lama's flight in 1959 to a sympathetic India and most of all the border war that India and China fought in 1962. Chairman Mao attacked on two fronts, west and east, timing his order to coincide with the Cuban missile crisis, which he knew of in advance from the Soviet premier Khrushchev. India's prime minister Jawaharlal Nehru soon discovered that potential allies were preoccupied with the prospect of nuclear war. He had underestimated China's threat and the Indian army was ill prepared. Over the next few decades, while testing each other's resolve, Beijing and Delhi would bury the Himalayan region's deep history under the aggregate of modern geopolitics. In the aftermath of the 1962 war, patterns of trade and strong cross-border cultural links that had endured for centuries were abruptly severed. A space became a line.

There are half-deserted villages in valleys either side of Milam and across the whole Himalaya that tell a similar story of dereliction and sudden loss of purpose. For many people living close to Tibet, it had always been easier to head north to the Tibetan plateau to travel east or west, rather than tack against the corrugated grain of the mountains, climbing and descending endless ridges: after 1962 that option became either impossible or fraught with regulation. It's also true that people were already drifting south anyway. The village of Milam had been built on trade: salt, borax and wool from Tibet in exchange for grain, a hazardous business with high passes to cross and bandits to fight, but it made the Johar valley the richest in the immediate region. By the twentieth century, cheaper sources of goods from overseas were undermining margins on these trade routes. Reforms brought in after India's independence also changed Himalayan society as land was redistributed. But China's hard new border was a violent *coup de grâce*.

Recognising the economic hardship the conflict provoked, in 1967 the Indian government added the people of Milam and other Himalayan ethnic groups to the list of 'scheduled tribes' established in India's new constitution. This guaranteed political representation and government jobs to marginalised groups. In the aftermath of China's aggression, the Himalaya became more heavily militarised and the Indian army was revamped. A new security force, the Indo-Tibet Border Police, was set up: a few are still stationed in Milam. They have bulldozed a short section of vehicle track downstream to the next village along the valley, Burfu, but porters, many of them poor Nepalis, are still needed to bring food from the closest main road up an ancient drover's road, known as a *khrancha*. Underemployed men in Kumaon and Garhwal took advantage of their new status as scheduled tribes to join the military, often serving in the Indo-Tibet Border Police, mountain troops who train as skiers and mountaineers and are used to the cold and altitiude. In 1962, both Chinese and Indian troops suffered more casualties from the environment than the enemy.

23. A bronze image of Buddha from the late eighth century made in Kashmir or Gilgit. He rests on a stylised interpretation of the cosmic mountain Meru, often identified as Kailas, pictured above.

24. The fabled eleventh-century poet Milarepa, a major figure in the history of the Kagyu school of Buddhism, and associated with Kailas. His life story, as told by his fifteenth-century biographer Tsangnyon Heruka, helped underpin the lineage of Kagyu teachers.

25. A complex series of rock art symbols from Tibet's protohistoric period including a swastika, crescent moon, the sun, trees, a bird of prey, yak and other wild herbivores and possibly a hunter, reflecting the venatic (hunting) lifestyle. Some of these symbols were adopted into the symbolism of Tibetan Buddhism, although hunting was antithetical to it.

26. A stone pendant of malachite and a cylindrical bead of turquoise included on a string of beads dating back to the middle or late Neolithic, some four to five thousand years ago, found at the archaeological site at Kharub, near Chamdo, in eastern Tibet.

27. The Tang dynasty emperor Taizong receives the Tibetan envoy and general Gar Tongtsen, sent in 641 by the Tibetan king Songtsen Gampo, at his capital Chang'an.

28. An image of Padmasambhava, the eighth-century Buddhist master who helped found Tibet's first monastery at Samye. Born in modern Pakistan's Swat valley, he is also known in Tibet as Guru Rinpoche.

29. Tilly Kettle's painting *The Teshu Lama Giving Audience*, painted around 1775. The Scottish explorer George Bogle, emissary of the East India Company and the first Briton to visit Tibet, presents a *kada*, or ceremonial scarf, to Lobsang Palden Yeshe, the sixth Panchen Lama.

30. The great Buddhist teacher Atisa, born into royalty in Bengal, then the focus of the Pala Empire. Brought to the Guge kingdom in western Tibet by its king Yeshe O, Atisa was instrumental in the second diffusion of Buddhism in Tibet in the eleventh century.

31. The fortress of Tsaparang in the upper Sutlej valley, once capital of the Guge kingdom, responsible for a Buddhist renaissance in western Tibet during the eleventh century.

33. The fifteenth-century Tibetan engineer and spiritual master Tangtong Gyalpo, known as Chakzampa, the iron-bridge builder, whose structures can still be seen in Bhutan but who operated across the Himalaya.

32. A thirteenth-century bronze sculpture of the goddess Tara, emblematic of the immense sophistication and skill of the Kathmandu valley's Newari artisans under the Malla kings who ruled the valley for six centuries.

34. The princess Choekyi Dronma, born into the royal family that ruled the small Tibetan kingdom of Mangyul Gungthang, was the consort of Tangtong Gyalpo, who recognised her as the reincarnation of the eleventh-century female tantric adept Machig Labdron. Despite her short life, she established convents and founded the most important female lineage in Tibetan Buddhism: the Samding Dorje Phagmo.

35. Copperplate after George Stubbs' painting *The Yak of Tartary*, modelled on the first yak to reach Britain, a male brought back by the second mission to Tibet led by Samuel Turner. When it perished, the yak was stuffed and exhibited at the Ethnology Court, a kind of anthropological exhibition held at the Crystal Palace in 1854.

JAK DI TARTARIA.

36. One of eight engravings depicting *The Pacification of the Gurkhas*, a collaboration between Chinese artists and Jesuit missionaries in China, with engravings done in Paris. The images commemorate two campaigns to expel Gorkha troops from Tibet, part of the Manchu dynasty's Ten Great Campaigns (including two against Tibetans in Sichuan) that expanded the Qing Empire, but at great financial cost.

37. A miniature watercolour of the Gorkhali prime minister Bhimsen Thapa, who effectively ruled Nepal for over thirty years in the early nineteenth century. Dated 1839, the image was probably painted after his downfall and suicide but portrays him at the height of his powers.

38. This coloured aquatint of Gorkhali soldiers was made from a plate in James Baillie Fraser's *Views in the Himala Mountains*, published in 1820. Fraser wrote admiringly of the Gorkhali army's courage and strength. His brother William had been political agent to Major General Martindell during the Nepal war, leading Gorkhali irregulars who had swapped sides.

39. Major General Sir David Ochterlony, painted in the aftermath of war with Gorkha, where he led the only truly successful British column.

40. The diplomat and scholar Brian Houghton Hodgson aged around sixty, in the aftermath of the Indian rebellion and his lobbying for Gorkhali support of the British.

41. A watercolour showing the artist Hyder Jung Hearsey and William Moorcroft meeting two Tibetan traders in the summer of 1812 as they crossed into Tibet on their way to Manasarovar.

42. *Rhododendron edgeworthii*, still popular in gardens around the world, discovered by Joseph Hooker in Sikkim in 1849 and painted by his father's regular artist Walter Hood Fitch.

43. *Camellia sinensis*, the tea plant, smuggled out from China; its ability to prosper in the eastern Himalaya transformed the region's economy and society.

Recruiting from the hardy mountain communities of the Himalaya made sense.

For the people of Milam, becoming caught up in the dramas of powerful nations was a familiar story. They had found themselves in a similar predicament a century earlier as the British Empire tried to fathom the unknown depths of the country on its northern frontier beyond the Himalaya, Tibet. In 1967 the people of Milam were scheduled as Bhotias, meaning simply people from Bhot, the word used commonly for Tibet by Tibetans. In doing so, the Indian government used a designation that was a legacy of the colonial British, who tended to lump together all ethnic Tibetan groups south of the Himalayan chain as Bhotias. After they acquired Garhwal and the upper part of Kumaon, where Milam is situated, they referred to it as 'Bhotia Mahal', meaning simply 'where the Bhotia live'. As a consequence, there are now 'Bhotia' throughout the Himalaya, from Ladakh in the west all the way to Arunachal Pradesh in the east. Similarly, when Indian diplomats were negotiating with the Chinese to settle their border dispute after the 1962 war, they would use as evidence to support their cause the work of George Traill, the so-called king of the Kumaon, who arrived at Milam after the British defeated the Gorkhas in 1816. As we saw, Traill recognised at once the damage done to the people of the Johar valley by the excessive demands of their Gorkhali masters and lightened their tax burden, in the process creating detailed records of the region's economic activity. In other words, India's argument with the Chinese relied on British India's attempts to administer a group of independent mountain people and define its limits against those of an earlier Chinese empire: the Qing.

At the time of British rule, the people of Milam didn't call themselves Bhotias and they didn't regard themselves as ethnically Tibetan either. Inhabitants of the Johar valley called themselves Shaukas, and also Rawat, the first an ethnic description, the latter more political. They saw their origins in the diaspora of Hindu warrior Rajputs that migrated east through the middle hills of the Himalaya as Muslim control spread from the west. This gloss of aristocratic bearing is reflected in the use of Hindu names like Singh among the people of the valley. There is a story about a seventeenth-century Rawat leader called Hiru Dham Singh, a fighter from Garhwal who helped local Tibetan forces drive out Chinese marauders from the Kailas area, just across the border. As reward, he was given trading privileges by the Tibetans and settled here, in the upper Johar valley. That's one version of Milam's origin. Yet there are stories that are far older, like Kumaoni folk tales that tell of the fearless heroine Ranjuli and her father, the magician trader Sunapati Shauka, whose spells lift him over the mountains. One legend tells how the *chela* or disciples of Sakya Buddha settled the valley first, hence the name Shauka. Archaeological evidence certainly supports a more ancient story; Kumaon was known for its gold smelting as far back as the sixth century, an industry that requires borax as a flux, borax which came from Tibet: Milam most likely existed because of its location on the supply route for this material. By the time of the Chand dynasty, firmly established as rulers of Kumaon by the fifteenth century, we know such trade with Tibet existed because it is recorded in tax records.

The hazy outlines of Milam's past aren't merely coincidental; they are an integral part of its story. Different cultures met and fused here. Just as in western Nepal, close by on the other side of the Mahakali river, Khas migrants to Milam encountered indigenous populations, creating new hierarchies and new ways of living. As trade grew, Tibetan and Turkic raiders saw easy pickings along the Kumaon frontier. Traders needed good relations on both sides of the mountains to defend their business and so the ability to blur cultural allegiances could prove useful. Summers were spent going back and forth across high passes in and out of Tibet, buying borax, salt, wool and gold dust, chiefly at Gartok, the dusty main town of western Tibet, and selling grain and manufactured goods. Rawat women would sometimes join the caravans of sheep, goats, ponies and yaks, crossing the border on pilgrimage to Kailas, in reverence to Shiva and Shakti. Winters were spent at established trade fairs in villages closer to the plains, while families stayed at second homes away from the frozen high valleys.

Religion in Milam is ostensibly Hindu but manages to cover many traditions. The contemporary Indian traveller Chinmoy Chakrabarti observed how the Rawat's

natural surroundings made them pantheist and animist. In most of their temples that I have visited, there are no idols but stones on which rudimentary sketches are made to bring in a resemblance of the Hindu divinities. On my way to the higher valleys, I have also seen prayer flags tied to trees, which are treated as sacred groves. Natural objects like mountain peaks, rocks, rivulets [and] trees also represent deities.

The Johar valley in particular was a favoured route from the south over the mountains to Kailas, another reason the Rawats embraced their Hindu identity so strongly: it brought tolerance from the Chand kings and allowed them to prosper. Yet as the British colonial official Edmund Smyth, who spent many years in Kumaon, observed:

> they have Hindu names, and call themselves Hindus, but they are not recognised as such by the orthodox Hindus of the plains or the hills. While in Tibet they seem glad enough to shake off their Hinduism and become Buddhists, or anything you like.

Cultural versatility was key; the Rawat could fill the different spaces they entered like water in a bowl and yet always be themselves. As traders they were capable linguists, fluent in Tibetan and Hindustani as well as more regional languages like Garhwali. Their own distinct dialects were of Tibetan origin, which gave them an advantage with Tibetan traders, said to do business only with those who would sit down and eat and drink with them. This caused suspicion among higher-caste Hindus in the middle hills who ostracised the Rawat as beef-eaters, ascribing their prosperity not to courage or business acumen but a willingness to compromise caste boundaries. There were immense risks in Tibet as well; the region was infested with bandits. But it was the Milam traders who held the advantage. Each had their own seal, or *thachia*, and a Tibetan counterpart, known as a *mitra*, with whom they dealt directly: the two would split a stone and each kept half. Only Rawat from the Johar valley could sell grain into this corner of Tibet, Ngari Khorsum or the upper Sutlej valley. Only Rawat could dissolve the relationship. They built up immense wealth and used bonded labour to farm their fields. One Rawat trader was said to be so rich that his bags of gold could block the Gori river. There are still a few old stallholders in the town of Munsyari who can remember the thrill of their first caravan, shaking hands with old Tibetan friends arriving at market, sheep laden with salt, gold jewellery flashing in the relentless sun of high altitude.

The British had a relationship with these Rawat, or Bhotias as they called them, even before the East India Company took control in 1816. Eight years earlier the surveyor William Webb, accompanied by Captain Felix Raper and their minder Hyder Jung Hearsey, encountered Bhotias in Garhwal at the village of Mana in the Alaknanda valley, on the west side of the mountain Nanda Devi, during their search for the source of the Ganges. Captain Raper was enchanted with this markedly different ethnic group.

> As soon as we entered the town, all the inhabitants came out to welcome us; and we observed a greater display of female and juvenile beauty, than we recollect to have seen in an Indian village. [He liked the] ruddiness in their complexions, of which the children partook in a very great degree; many of them approaching to the floridness of the European.

Raper also noted how Bhotias 'profess the Hindu religion, and call themselves Rajputs', even though

> they scruple not to perform the most menial offices; and in the article of food are less nice than the lower class of sweepers. Like most inhabitants of cold climates, the *Manah* people are much addicted to drinking; and even consider it necessary for their health.

He described the Bhotias' yaks at length and was, like most travellers since, in terror of their dogs.

> One of them was a remarkably fine animal, as large as a good sized Newfoundland dog, with very long hair, and a head resembling a mastiff's. His tail was of an amazing length, like the brush of a fox, and curled half way over his back. He was however so fierce, that he would allow no stranger to approach him.

As they turned south from the Garhwal towards Kumaon, Webb, Raper and Hearsey found themselves hustled out of what was then Gorkhali territory: the authorities, having got wind the British were asking too many questions, were determined to make sure they left swiftly. There was only enough time to notice that Kumaoni farms were more prosperous than those in Garhwal and to see the mountains from a distance. Otherwise their impressions were fleeting. Yet for much of their journey, the trio, two British and an Anglo-Indian, had enjoyed the company of a man born in Kumaon: a Brahmin called Har-Balam, whom they'd hired as a fixer at the start of their journey. This man had proved his value many times over and left them well disposed towards Kumaonis in general. It was most probably Har-Balam whom Webb meant when he told his superior in Calcutta about an 'intelligent native' who had visited the Tibetan borderlands and described

> two great Lakes, only one of which is laid down in any Map extant, viz. Lake Mansurwar [Manasarovar] ... The other, by far the largest and most important, named Rown Rudh [Rakshas Tal] remains unnoticed.

Webb's information was somewhat awry, but the prospect of these great lakes was irresistible. The source of the Ganges might now be clearer but a new prospect for exploration now arose: what might be discovered on the far side of the mountains?

Crossing these mountains demanded a lot from Europeans who took on the challenge, but they couldn't do it alone. Their efforts would have been wholly in vain without the mediation of a select group of local people, usually traders, who had the skills and access to move between different Himalayan worlds. From the moment the British arrived at the foot of the Himalaya and began investigating Tibet for the purposes of trade and geographic knowledge, they relied heavily on such people, who were as often as not written out or down in published accounts. By the end of the nineteenth century, with the British still kept out of a large proportion of the Himalaya, these quick-witted, courageous intermediaries would be crucial in gathering intelligence on behalf of their imperial masters. The greatest of these would come from the Johar valley.

*

The broad narrative arc of nineteenth century European exploration in Central Asia could be summed up as a process of creeping institutionalisation. In the eighteenth century, the East India Company was

more or less run by adventurers. Forty years later, the free and easy
spirit that had sent George Bogle to Tibet in 1774 had evaporated.
British control of India had expanded rapidly under the governors
general Cornwallis and Wellesley, but the Company was much
reformed and under tighter bureaucratic control. With more to lose,
it moved cautiously and by increments. At the same time, scientific
exploration was becoming hugely popular across Europe. Alexander
von Humboldt was among the most famous men of his day and
Charles Darwin was circling the world in the *Beagle*. Public appetite
for their tales of adventure and discovery sold books and filled lecture
halls. In 1830 the Geographical Society would be founded as a London
dining club, receiving its royal charter in 1859. The reputation of an
explorer could now be made or broken in London committee rooms.
After the 1857 rebellion, alongside Anglican hegemony and racial arrogance, political and institutional control of exploration would also
harden. Yet in the first half of the century there was still enough space
for mercenaries, mavericks and freelancers to prosper.

Hyder Hearsey had certainly been one of these. After the journey
in Garhwal and Kumaon, he had returned to the family estates near
Bareilly. As raids from Gorkhali troops increased through 1811, Hearsey
acted on his own initiative, raising troops and laying in weapons and
ammunition in early 1812 to take the fight to the Nepalis. This infuriated the East India Company agent in Bareilly, as the British were at
this point reluctant to provoke the Gorkha regime. The official had
the governor general revoke that portion of Hearsey's property that
was leased from the Company. Another such character was Alexander
Gardner, known as Gordana Khan, whose adventures and travels in
Central Asia and the Oxus valley in the 1820s were so outlandish that
the Scottish orientalist Henry Yule refused to believe them. Born in
Wisconsin in 1785 to a Scottish father and a Spanish mother, he later
became a mercenary in the Sikh *Khalsa*, or army. But it was another
travelling companion of Hyder Hearsey, a man called William
Moorcroft, who, though not at all romantic himself, led the way in
the wildest, most romantic phase of Europe's encounter with the
Himalaya.

Moorcroft was, in the historian John Keay's phrase, an 'erratic
genius'. 'He still gets described as a horse-dealer, a spy or an adventurer,' Keay wrote, 'each of which possess a grain of truth while sadly

understating his real standing.' The only portrait that exists, assuming that it is in fact of Moorcroft, is poorly done, showing him, in the words of the writer Charles Allen, 'perched uneasily on a rickety chair, a trim, slight man with the face of a spiv – small eyes, long nose, hairline moustache'. He was certainly short and slight, with fair hair and a florid complexion: far from the image of a rugged explorer. But it tells little of the drama of his life, his immense resilience and determination, and more than anything his insatiable curiosity.

The most startling thing about Moorcroft was his age. When he set out with Hearsey for Tibet in May 1812, he was at least forty-five or so, having already worked for several years in India, a country where life expectancy for Europeans was short even for those who didn't stray far from their desks. That made him more a contemporary of Bogle than Webb or Raper. Born around 1765, he had started as a medical student at Liverpool Infirmary when he became involved in battling an epidemic among livestock in his native Lancashire. He then followed the suggestion of pioneering surgeon John Hunter to switch to the new discipline of veterinary science, and the only place to study that was France. Having qualified, he set up practice in London and made a fortune that he then lost after investing in the manufacture of cast-iron horseshoes, an investment that soured over patents. For the rest of his life, it seems, there was always a part of him searching for a scheme that would redeem this failure. In the meantime, he needed a job. Moorcroft had served as a volunteer in the citizen army that was raised to meet the threat of French invasion and in the process had got to know Edward Parry, a director of the East India Company. Parry now offered him the job of improving the military stud in Calcutta. The salary was vast and tax free, but it wasn't simply a question of restoring his fortunes: the older Moorcroft got, the more restless he became.

Arriving in India in 1808, Moorcroft discovered the scale of his task. His job was to provide the Bengal army with eight hundred horses a year. Given the corrupted and feeble stock he inherited, Moorcroft knew immediately he needed better animals, 'an infusion of the bone and blood of the Turkman steed'. During the eighteenth century, India had been plugged into Central Asian horse breeding markets, largely thanks to the Rohilla, ethnic Pashtun tribesmen who had migrated from Afghanistan to serve in the Mughal army, settling in northern

India. The hills of Rohilkhand, the region they inhabited around the towns of Bareilly and Rampur, had just the right grasses for good horse-breeding. The Lavi fair at Rampur, founded in the eighteenth century to boost trade with Tibet, also included a horse market where traders could buy the famous Chamurthi ponies from the Himalayan region of Spiti. With the decline of the Rohillas, access to Central Asian stock became more difficult and the quality of local breeding declined. Moorcroft also needed a different kind of horse. The weight of a Bengal army dragoon with field equipment was 252 lb (115 kilograms), much heavier than a Mughal cavalryman, requiring a bigger, taller horse. He decided he needed to visit the source of the best bloodstock: the horse fairs of Central Asia, particularly that in the Uzbek city of Bukhara. Moorcroft had a second motive. Having sorted out the day-to-day administration of the Company's stud, he was bored and looking for an adventure.

And so, to the annoyance of his employers, William Moorcroft spent much of the cold season of late 1811 sniffing around the horse markets of northern India, which is how he met Hearsey, at Saharanpur, sixty-five kilometres south of the Garhwali town of Dehra Dun, just as the Anglo-Indian was recruiting fighters to clear Gorkhalis off his land. In Hearsey, Moorcroft found someone with the knowledge and contacts to cross the Himalaya, and with the gall too. When this awkward pair sought approval for their journey, the Company agent in Bareilly was glad to be shot of them. They took off for the mountains in search of good horses, as well as Tibet's famous shawl goats, before Calcutta could get wind of the plan and call them back.

Lacking permission from the Gorkhali authorities, the two men went disguised as *gosain*, trader-monks like Purangir, servant of the Panchen Lama, who had accompanied George Bogle to Shigatse almost forty years earlier: the archetype for the sort of intermediary the British would come to rely on. Hearsey, with his Indian blood, looked the part. Moorcroft coloured his skin with walnut juice and the ashes from a fire of cow dung. They took the pseudonyms Hargiri and Mayapuri. With them went an Afghan soldier of fortune called Gholam Hyder Khan, an old friend from Hearsey's mercenary days, and an older Brahman from Kumaon whom Moorcroft named Harballabh – this was the pandit, or 'learned man', who had proved so valuable on Hearsey's earlier journey towards the source of the Ganges and who had spoken of the two lakes beyond the mountains. Moorcroft called Harballabh the 'old pundit' to differentiate him from his nephew Harkh Dev, who also accompanied them. Both these men would help Hearsey and Moorcroft survey their route. Though he lacked a theodolite, Hearsey took a compass and a thermometer to record altitude and Harkh Dev got the tedious job of counting his paces – four feet for two steps – to measure distance. With them went four dozen porters to carry goods they hoped to sell in Tibet.

Hearsey knew the route as far as the junction of the Alaknanda and Dhauli rivers, where they turned east through a deep gorge. This travels up the west side of Nanda Devi, just as the Johar valley follows the east. These days there is a crumbling jeep track; then there was a crumbling footpath. Moorcroft was impressed at the agility of Harballabh, reminding himself that the 'old pundit' had been born in the mountains of Kumaon. But even the pundit had to shelter in a hollow while he summoned up the courage to cross a particularly exposed and dangerous section. Hearsey was almost hit by rocks knocked off the mountainside by bears traversing three hundred feet above him. Moorcroft noted that the path would be much better had not key bridges been washed away, bridges that could be restored for a small investment of no more than a hundred rupees. His account of this journey, published in the *Asiatic Journal* of 1816, is not only brimming with that eighteenth-century impulse for improvement, as though the remote Dhauli valley was an underperforming English estate, but crammed also with observations on every subject: the weather, crops, forestry, fauna and flora, obviously, but in great detail, listing the herbs he found near villages, the fashionable new subject of geology, hydrology and what we would now call anthropology. He saw how the locals wrote receipts on birch bark, examined a yellow snake Hearsey had killed and noted the differences in how sheep and goats, both used for carrying loads from Tibet, negotiated the steep paths.

Moorcroft's powers of observation were remarkable. Across the border in Tibet, he noted the kindness of a Tibetan woman who fetched them water and then described her appearance. Every detail of her dress was recorded, even more so her jewellery, especially that worn on her head:

it was bordered with silver, and from this rim hung seven rows of coral beads, each row consisting of five, which were terminated by seven silver *timashas* [coins] that played upon the forehead. The crown was studded with small pearls distributed in seven rows, and the low part was decorated with green stones something like turquoises but marbled with coral beads, and many bands of silver and of a yellow metal, probably gold, about a finger's breadth.

Moorcroft saw the world with such intensity that he might one day have driven himself mad.

It was certainly typical of him to pay close attention to women. Years later, the French traveller Victor Jacquemont repeated gossip he'd heard in Kashmir about Moorcroft, that 'his chief occupation was making love'. It wasn't altogether true. Moorcroft was also writing a detailed treatise on the shawl-wool trade, and Jacquemont himself was no better in that regard. Moorcroft's interest in women extended far beyond his own sexual appetite. His account of the journey to Tibet is full of telling details about the position of women in the cultures he moved through. He admired the strength and courage of Bhotia women carrying loads. He saw a woman whom he tipped for this service have the coin taken from her by a man he assumed to be her husband; when Moorcroft discovered he wasn't, he chased him for his 'petty tyranny' and recovered the coin for her. He admired women's skill at weaving, 'learned from Tibet', and literally measured how quickly they could produce cloth. He noticed also the widespread practice of slavery, an industry dominated by Gorkhali agents, who sold slaves to rich families of the district. Above all, he noted how women outnumbered men, who were either trading across the border or else had been forcibly recruited into the Gorkhali army, a resentment the British would exploit in their war with Nepal three years later.

When the expedition arrived at Niti, the last village before the pass into Tibet, Hearsey and Moorcroft were forced to stop and negotiate their way across the border. This left the local Bhotias, known as Marchas to Moorcroft and today as Rong-pa, facing a conundrum. Here were wealthy *feringhi* – white foreigners – wanting to spend whatever it took to do something that might annoy officials in Tibet, who could make life difficult for them. Their cover story, that they were pilgrims on the road to Manasarovar, was an obvious sham.

Pilgrims didn't go to Manasarovar this way; certainly not pilgrims this wealthy. The obvious answer was to delay, thus stripping the group of money while at the same time hoping they'd give up and go home.

Moorcroft and Hearsey wrote a letter to the *deba*, or local Tibetan official, explaining they were pilgrims. The headman of the village told them to expect a delay; the route the letter had to take wasn't yet clear of snow and it would be weeks before any messenger could travel. Almost immediately, two Tibetans appeared, coming down from the supposedly blocked pass. The letter was sent. Two days later the locals despatched an ambassador, a man so drunk he fell off the yak he was riding four times before he crested the hillside above the village. There was little cause for optimism. Eight days later the *deba* came back with a firm refusal. There were more meetings, more promises, more rupees spread around to ease concerns. Moorcroft got his medical kit out and used his skills to win friends. Finally a man called Amer Singh, son of the village chief Arjun Singh, told the 'old pundit' Harballabh that he could get the foreigners across the pass to Tibet, or Undes as Moorcroft called it.

Even with Amer Singh's help, Moorcroft and Hearsey were driven to distraction with prevarication and delay; Hearsey resorted to painting a picture of the village, an image now in the British Library. Eventually terms were agreed but both men knew they had been fleeced. The night before departure, the locals held a party and the foreigners donated a bottle of brandy to raise morale. Yet when they rose early the following morning to start, there was no sign of anyone, just the yaks they had hired. Eventually Amer Singh's father Arjun arrived, now doubtful about the wisdom of it all. More rupees were spread around and finally the caravan got underway. Then, after an hour, their guides announced there was a ceremony planned for a villager who had died the year before and they were heading back to the village. Two days later, bored with examining the local rhubarb and observing how easily the sun at high altitude burned his face and lips, Moorcroft sent a messenger to find out what was going on. The messenger reported how the villagers were still sleeping off the party, all piled up in a big heap on the floor of a house. They would be along presently.

In the end, worn down by the foreigners' relentless determination, Amer Singh led Moorcroft and Hearsey across the pass at the head

of the valley and into Tibet. Moorcroft's account of lying awake at
their high camp before the long ascent to the top of the Niti La is
one of the earliest descriptions by an Englishman of altitude sickness
and what is now called Cheyne–Stokes breathing, and one of the best.

> I awoke at a very early hour and was immediately seized with difficulty
> of breathing and great oppression about the heart, which was removed
> for a few seconds by sighing deeply. When on the point of falling asleep,
> the sense of suffocation came on, and the sighing became very frequent
> and distressing: however, as the air became a little warmer, this affec-
> tion [effect] somewhat subsided.

Before they reached the pass the caravan met two Tibetans bringing
salt down to Niti. Amer Singh told Moorcroft that these traders raised
'many objections to our proceeding' and that they should return with
them to the main village thirty kilometres over the pass, a place called
Daba. At the top Moorcroft found them lighting a fire and burning
juniper,

> in the midst of which was a statue having a piece of cloth tied to it,
> and whilst walking, [they] uttered a long prayer. To the East was the
> sacred mountain near the lake of Mansarovar, tipped with snow, and
> called Cailas or Mahadeo ka Ling. Turning his face towards this moun-
> tain, and after raising his hands with the palms joined above his head,
> then touching his forehead, [one of them] suddenly placed them on
> the ground, and going on his knees pressed his forehead to the ground.

It is presumably these two traders that Hearsey later painted in a
jaunty impression of this awkward encounter, smoking their pipes
astride their Chamurthi mountain ponies with their yaks behind them
fully loaded. Hearsey and Moorcroft, wearing their disguise, are riding
their yaks towards the holiest mountain Kailas; in the distance is a
small group of *khyang*, or wild asses.

Two days later the party reached Daba, perched on a rocky prominence that dominates the valley, where Amer Singh incurred the
displeasure of the officials who had earlier sent messages denying the
'pilgrims' access. Moorcroft reports a meeting between the head lama
of the local monastery; the son of the *deba*; the local big landowner;

Amer Singh; the old pandit Harballabh; a man from the Johar valley, whom Moorcroft doesn't name; and another man, also unnamed, described as a sirdar – a chief, or boss. Everybody understood the stakes: the best advantage for the least trouble and not too many questions asked. Amer Singh had the least power and so had to be the most persuasive, picking his way carefully along a treacherous path, meeting the needs of his employers while not causing himself difficulties with local Tibetan officials whose cooperation he needed for future business. Moorcroft and Hearsey were not fools but neither spoke Tibetan so the course of these negotiations was largely obscured from them. They were almost wholly reliant on their intermediary, who led them the following morning into the presence of the lama and the son of the local chief. Having handed over gifts of three yards of scarlet broadcloth, some sugar and spices, the chief's son flourished a letter to the district governor at Gartok that would reassure him that Moorcroft and Hearsey really were *gosain* traders on a pilgrimage and asking for instructions about what to do with them.

A short while later, the governor, or *garpon*, sent word summoning them to visit him. This suited Moorcroft very well. His journey to Tibet in 1812 is best remembered now for his visit to the sacred lake of Manasarovar, the first by an Englishman, and his conviction that it was wholly landlocked, being neither the source of the Indus nor linked, as Harballabh claimed, in any way to its brackish neighbour Rakshas Tal. (In fact, Harballabh was right: there is a link between the two, but it's ephemeral. Moorcroft speculated that an earthquake had interrupted its flow since Harballabh's visit.) But while Moorcroft was intensely curious about the region's geography, it was in fact the possibility of trade – not just horses, but shawl wool too – that was foremost in his mind, and Gartok was the centre of it.

Having left Daba and crossed the Sutlej above the decaying Guge fortress of Tsaparang, their caravan reached the upper Indus and the vast plateau of Gartok in six days. 'The intervening plain,' Moorcroft wrote,

and indeed as far as the eye can reach until it is bounded by a pass to the N.W. is covered by prodigious bodies of sheep, goats and yaks, amongst which is a small number of horses. The number of cattle cannot I think be less than 40000.

Gartok itself was little more than a temporary collection of tents and a rather mean house for the *garpon*. The rolling hills north from here where the sheep and goats grazed had few permanent villages: this was nomad country. Animals were driven here and then shorn, their wool and hair shipped on. It was clear to Moorcroft that a great deal of money was changing hands. When he met the *garpon*, Moorcroft paid close attention to his jewellery and when he asked the Tibetan what he could bring from Hindustan should trade between them prosper he was impressed at the precise and educated list of precious objects the *garpon* requested. The suspicion that they were Gorkhalis or Peling, as the Tibetans called the British, soon wore off, as Moorcroft wryly observed, 'either by the representations of the Deba, or by the weight of our presents'. There was money to be made.

The following day, Moorcroft and Hearsey put the wares they had carried over the Niti La on display. The Kashmiri trade agent of the king of Ladakh, there to buy wool, sent word that he was ready to buy the lot if the *garpon* didn't want them. When they met, Moorcroft pumped him for information about Central Asia's trade routes. He learned that Gartok was a vast temporary marketplace plugging the Chang Tang, the northern region of the Tibetan plateau, and its huge herds of sheep, goats and yaks, into the major trading route between Lhasa and the trade hub of Leh, the capital of Ladakh, which the Kashmiri told him was ten days' journey from there. Kashmir itself, he said, was another ten days beyond Leh. The horse fair at Bukhara, also famous for its carpets, would take a month. The roundabout route to Bukhara from Delhi via Kabul and on to Central Asia 'he represented as very circuitous', in comparison to this route across the Himalaya. Moorcroft also discovered that the sparse population of western Tibet relied on the people of the Johar valley and other Himalayan groups for grain, which they traded for sheep wool. The Kashmiris were most interested in the more valuable shawl wool from goats, a trade they had monopolised thanks to their Mughal overlords, trading saffron in return. Ladakh couldn't produce enough pashmina to satisfy manufacturers in Kashmir so prices in Tibet were high. He also discovered, with some alarm, that trade with Russia was also well established; a Russian trade agent called Mehdi Rafailov, a Persian Jew, had been in Kashmir in 1808. Later a Ladakhi trader showed Moorcroft samples of French woollen cloth and Russian leather that had arrived

from Central Asia, now falling under the shadow of the expanding
Russian Empire. The implications of this would trouble Moorcroft
for the rest of his life, provoking him to fire off prophetic memos to
Calcutta about the Russian threat to India at a time when London
and St Petersburg were allies against Napoleon.

Before leaving for Manasarovar, Moorcroft and Hearsey had themselves done a deal with the *garpon* to buy a quantity of shawl wool.
One morning as they prepared to leave a place called Misar this wool
arrived on horseback, accompanied by the *garpon*'s officer, a man called
Tharchen. The *garpon* had sent more wool than Moorcroft had
requested and would accept only silver rupees in return. Moorcroft
realised this was a test of whether he was in fact a trader or had some
other more nefarious motive for coming to Tibet. It also attracted the
attention of Johari traders in the village 'who were troublesomely
inquisitive as to who we were, what could be our motives for coming,
and why we purchased shawl wool'. The Joharis were at the time the
chief conduit for goods from India and had much to lose.

> The sight of some of our wares seemed to convince them, that we
> were what we appeared to be. I consider this day as the epoch at which
> may be fixed the origin of a traffic which is likely to be extremely
> beneficial to the Honourable Company.

If Moorcroft had gone to the mountains looking for horses, he left
with a grand strategy of Himalayan trade. The final legacy of his
journey would prove to be neither.

* * *

Hearsey and Moorcroft were told to cross back over the Himalaya the
way they had come and when they reached Daba the two had an
encounter whose consequences would stretch out to the end of the
nineteenth century. A Rawat trader called Dev Singh made himself
known to Moorcroft. Singh, the son of a powerful landowner from
the Johar valley, offered to lend the travellers money; their journey
had been unexpectedly expensive and they might need some. Moorcroft
demurred, but instead offered to trade a valuable set of coral beads
for some shawl-wool goats and sheep. He asked they be delivered to

Niti where the 'young pundit' Harkh Dev would be waiting to bring them down to Moorcroft on the plains. The deal was done. Having proved himself useful in this and other ways to Moorcroft, Dev Singh asked Moorcroft for a certificate that would essentially allow him to trade in the East India Company's jurisdiction at the local rate. This Moorcroft was happy to supply.

In providing assistance to Moorcroft, Dev Singh had by chance put his descendants at the heart of one of the great stories of Himalayan exploration, a story that unfolded some fifty years later and hinged on repeated British failures over several decades to gain access to or build relationships with Tibet. In time, the story would add another meaning to the word pundit, more usually spelled in this case 'pundit', one of daring subterfuge and limitless endurance, and its origins are to be found seven years after Moorcroft's journey, with a sudden catastrophic interruption to the flourishing trade Moorcroft had witnessed at the western Tibet settlement of Gartok.

In 1819, Ranjit Singh's Sikh Empire occupied Kashmir and put the valley under the control of loyal Hindu chiefs, Kishore Singh and then his son Gulab, ethnically Dogra Rajputs who had ambitions of their own. Many Kashmiri weavers fled to the plains. Soon after, William Moorcroft embarked on a second, much longer and ultimately fatal journey to explore Central Asia's trade routes. He spent two years in Ladakh, developing a deep respect both for the people and Tibetan Buddhism. The Ladakhis knew that following the Sikh occupation of Kashmir they were likely next and Tsepal Dondup Namgyal, the *chogyal* or king of Ladakh, appealed to Moorcroft, as an East India Company man, for help. Moorcroft drew up a trade agreement that allowed Ladakhis to trade shawl wool directly with India, cutting out the Kashmiri middlemen, and open up Central Asia to the British. This deal not only antagonised the Sikh ruler Ranjit Singh, it also infuriated Moorcroft's masters in Calcutta, who suspended Moorcroft's pay. Calcutta saw no advantage in testing the patience of Ranjit Singh, who was, at least in theory, the Company's ally.

But Tsepal Dondup, the *chogyal* of Ladakh, was right to be anxious about the Sikhs. 'He is said to be rapacious,' Moorcroft wrote of Tsepal, 'but his prevailing qualities are extreme timidity and indolence, and he relinquishes the management of affairs entirely to the Khalun,' essentially the prime minister. The Ladakhi army was undermined by 'the cowardice of the soldiery, and the inefficiency of their equipment'. They had lots of bows and arrows but 'one matchlock for ten men, and one sword for six'. So when, in 1834, the brilliant Dogra general Zorawar Singh, born in the district of Kangra, led an army into Ladakh, Tsepal Dondup was deposed.

Ironically, the consequence of this was to achieve what Moorcroft had proposed. Rather than deal with the aggressive new Dogra regime in Ladakh, traders buying wool at Gartok stopped taking it to the capital Leh, and began instead crossing the mountains further east to sell their wool at Rampur in the Sutlej valley, now under British control following the Treaty of Sagauli. Enraged by the consequent loss of revenue, Gulab Singh sent Zorawar into western Tibet with a few thousand troops to restore his monopoly on the wool trade. In short order Zorawar had marched through Gartok and was at Purang, known in Nepal as Taklakot, close to the Nepali border, scattering a larger but disorganised Tibetan army ahead of him. Dogra troops also occupied hill-states on the other side of the Himalaya north of the Sutlej.

The complexities of this high-altitude aggression were boggling for the East India Company, which at the time was suffering its humiliation in Afghanistan. The British were also trying to negotiate better access to Chinese markets. Tibet was under China's suzerainty and so in theory was Nepal. The Dogras were, at least nominally, the Company's allies. What would happen if any of these parties assumed Gulab Singh's move had the approval of Calcutta? It was, in the words of the Kathmandu resident Brian Houghton Hodgson, 'a most untoward event'. The exiled king of Ladakh sent envoys to Kathmandu seeking support from Rajendra, the pusillanimous Gorkhali king whom Jang Bahadur would shortly depose. Rajendra offered China his support should they wish to intervene but the Daoguang emperor turned him down: Rajendra enjoyed little respect at the Qing court. So Rajendra reversed his position and contemplated an alliance with Gulab Singh instead. This prospect was no less alarming to the British, who were now threatened with an alliance that would span much of the Himalaya.

Luckily for the Company, in December 1841 Tibetan and Chinese troops attacked Zorawar, who, having made a pilgrimage to Kailas, made the fatal mistake of over-wintering in Tibet. His troops were in a miserable state, forced to burn their musket stocks for warmth and succumbing to frostbite and hypothermia. At Toyo, close to Taklakot, Zorawar was utterly defeated and killed; Tibetans were said to have kept scraps of his hair and flesh as talismans. The victorious Qing and Tibetan forces continued on to Ladakh to besiege the citadel of Leh, but Gulab Singh sent reinforcements and after several months of stalemate a treaty was signed at a small village called Chushul that restored the status quo. None of the parties thought it necessary to involve or even inform the British of this arrangement.

By now Ranjit Singh was dead and his Sikh Empire was fracturing as his offspring struggled for control. The East India Company accordingly built up its military presence to face the Sikhs. When war broke out, once more threatening the balance of power in the Himalaya, Rajendra wrote again to the Qing ambans in Lhasa, warning them that

> the Pilings [British] are now fighting with the Sen-pa [Sikhs], and have already defeated the Sen-pa once; that the said nation [Nepal] is connected with the Sen-pa as a neighbour, and if the Pilings have seized the territory of Sen-pa he [Rajendra] fears their victory will cause [them] to covet Tibetan territory.

The Chinese ambans sent a memo to Beijing pouring scorn on Rajendra – 'He is impossible!' – with the implication that as usual the Gorkhali king had his hand out for a donation. They also reassured Beijing that Tibet's borders were being watched closely and the British would remain on the outside.

During this first Sikh war with the British, Gulab Singh steered a clever course that kept him out of the conflict without betraying his former masters, the Sikhs. His reward came in the Treaty of Amritsar, signed in 1846, in which the British recognised Gulab as sovereign ruler of Jammu, Kashmir and Ladakh under the protection of the East India Company: the root of modern Kashmir's suffering. In return Gulab would pay the Company a small tribute, not employ any Europeans or Americans in his military and refer boundary issues to Calcutta. On that basis, two boundary commissioners, Alexander Cunningham and Patrick Vans Agnew, were appointed to establish the frontiers between Ladakh and Tibet. Tibet was expected to reciprocate by sending equivalent officers of their own, but no one arrived from Lhasa to work with the British, who were consequently unable to proceed. Vans Agnew was reassigned and not long after murdered at Multan in the Punjab, an incident that prompted renewed conflict between the British and the Sikhs.

A second commission was established for 1847, again under the command of Alexander Cunningham, a military engineer and later the founding director of the Archaeological Survey of India. With him was Henry Strachey, then a lieutenant in the 13th Bengal Native Infantry. (The year before, Strachey had made his illicit journey to Manasarovar while on sick leave from his posting at Chittagong. Following in the footsteps of Webb and Traill, he had visited the Milam valley and met Moorcroft's old travelling companion Dev Singh, who recommended that to avoid detection he should cross the Lampiya Dhura pass to the east, which Strachey did, disguised like Moorcroft as a pilgrim.) The third member of the boundary commission was the doctor and naturalist Thomas Thomson, who would join the botanist Joseph Hooker on his later explorations in India. They had ambitious plans to explore Ladakh's trade routes and for Strachey to travel to Lhasa but he found himself delayed and obstructed at the village of Hanle, on the historic Ladakhi-Tibetan border some three hundred kilometres south-east of Leh. Tibetan officials at Gartok on the other side of the border continued to ignore the British. Gulab Singh's surveyors came late and grudgingly; those of the Qing never arrived at all. The ambitious plans for Cunningham and his men dwindled almost to nothing.

Another pressing issue for the British was the restoration of the shawl-wool trade from the western Tibetan market at Gartok to their own commercial hub at Rampur, trade that Zorawar Singh's invasion had so rudely interrupted. A land swap was now done with Gulab Singh that brought the Spiti valley under direct British control: Spiti offered fast access to Gartok and was no more than fifty kilometres from Rampur. Trade agents knew the Tibetans were fed up with the high duties Gulab Singh exacted and sensed there was a deal to be done: but how to reach the Tibetans? Given the experience of Cunningham, it was clear officials in western Tibet would refuse to have anything to do with Europeans. So a local man from Kinnaur called Anant Ram who was working for the boundary commission was tasked with translating and delivering a letter from the governor general to Gartok: another local intermediary working both sides of the mountains. He returned with a long story about how unwelcome the letter was and not to expect an answer until the following year. No one could tell if he was telling the truth; no British officials spoke Tibetan even though many areas of the Himalaya now under British control had significant Tibetan populations.

While Anant Ram was (or wasn't) trying to deliver the governor general's letter at Gartok, a copy was on its way to Hong Kong, to be forwarded to the Chinese. This was the first time the British had tried to influence Lhasa in this way, leverage made possible by their success five years earlier in the first of the Opium Wars with China. The resulting Treaty of Nanking in 1842 had given them greater access to Chinese markets. Yet progress from this direction was also very slow. Throughout the nineteenth century, British colonial officials dealing directly with Beijing judged remote Himalayan border disputes as of peripheral concern. Sir John Davis, the second governor of Hong Kong, sent notes via the trading port of Canton, now Guangzhou, to the Daoguang emperor asking for cooperation in settling the border between Ladakh and western Tibet. Beijing promised to send 'proper instructions' to its ambans in Lhasa. These had absolutely no impact. The most influential Chinese official in Lhasa was Qishan, sent to Lhasa in disgrace after mishandling the First Opium War. He had no inclination to ease relations with the hated British. The Tibetan government saw British surveyors as harbingers of invasion. Gulab Singh's proxies in Leh, knowing the British were after their trade in shawl wool, were no less reluctant to settle the border with Tibet. The British remained shut out.

Despite this passive-aggressive resistance, British officials on the Himalayan frontier remained hopeful that access to Tibet would eventually be granted. As things turned out, the priorities and politics of the wider British Empire made this almost impossible. It would take British officials in India more than a decade to realise this; but when they did, they turned to the indigenous inhabitants of the Himalaya to cross the border for them, in particular the people of the Johar valley. The descendants of Dev Singh, Moorcoft's trading partner, would be among them.

*

In 1858, the Second Opium War between Anglo-French forces and the Manchu rulers of China came to a theoretical end with the Treaty of Tianjin. This gave the Europeans more trading ports and more rights of passage, a further blow to the fading prestige of the Qing Empire. Before it was signed, hawks around the Xianfeng emperor encouraged him to resist, prompting renewed hostilities. The fighting ended conclusively in 1860 when the cavalry of the Qing's most trusted Mongol general Sengge Rinchen, a Tibetan name meaning 'lion treasure', was utterly destroyed at the Battle of Baliqiao. The British then marched on Beijing to loot and destroy the emperor's summer palaces. The treaty was signed with yet more concessions forced from the Qing. Included in the Treaty of Tianjin was a new right for foreigners to travel in the interior of China. In theory, this opened the way for British explorers to enter Tibet. Acting on this opportunity, Edmund Smyth, education officer in Kumaon, got support from the Indian government for an official mission to Tibet. Although this expedition never got off the ground, Smyth's involvement would bring the people of the Johar valley to the attention of the British authorities.

Born in Lincolnshire, Smyth was educated at the public school Rugby, his time there immortalised by his contemporary Thomas Hughes in *Tom Brown's School Days*. Smyth was the model for the character Crab Jones,

> sauntering along with a straw in his mouth, the queerest, coolest fish in Rugby. If he were tumbled into the moon this minute, he would just pick himself up without taking his hands out of his pockets or turning a hair.

He had fought in the same regiment as Henry Strachey during the Second Anglo-Sikh War that followed the murder of Vans Agnew. After that he was in Delhi, from where he was able to indulge his great passion for hunting in the Himalaya. Smyth had no interest in leaving behind an account of his life but from what remains it's clear almost no other European travelled so widely in Tibet in the nineteenth century. One of his few surviving letters mentions a four-month hunting trip he made to western Tibet in the 1850s with his friend the future explorer John Speke. Another hunting trip to Tibet, made in

1864 after he'd been refused official permission, is recorded in Thomas
Webber's *The Forests of Upper India*, which makes it clear that Smyth
already had deep experience of the northern Himalaya. Webber also
claimed to have visited the source of the Brahmaputra, although the
Swedish explorer Sven Hedin would later do his best to discredit this.
These journeys were trespassing, illicit and potentially damaging, so
Smyth and those others who indulged kept them quiet: there was no
need to embarrass Calcutta. (Not everyone was so discreet. The
Scottish aristocrat Robert Drummond launched a rubber dinghy on
Manasarovar, which so outraged Buddhist and Hindu pilgrims that
the local governor, according to legend, literally lost his head.)

In 1854, after twenty years of service, Smyth was due his long leave
from India, travelling as far as Aden with his friend Speke, where they
met the young Richard Burton, later among the most famous explorers
in history. These two went off together to Somaliland and their tryst
with the Nile, while Smyth went climbing in the Swiss Alps, where
he made a notable first ascent with his brothers Christopher and James,
both clergymen. We only know this because the alpinist Edward
Whymper wrote Smyth up in a guidebook to Zermatt. 'The natives
used to say that he could climb where birds could not fly, which is
the Oriental equivalent for "Monsieur has the agility of a chamois."'
After that Smyth volunteered for service in the Crimean War, seconded
to the Turkish irregular cavalry known as the Bashi-Bazouks, along
with Burton and Speke, planning with the latter to traverse the
Caucasus, though a lack of passports thwarted them.

By the time his leave was over, Smyth's old regiment had been
disbanded, having suffered appalling casualties defending Lucknow in
the rebellion of 1857. He was appointed 'inspector of public instruction'
– education officer – in Garhwal and Kumaon, with a remit to establish vernacular schools in the hills. This did two things. First, it took
him back to mountains he loved. Second, it put him in close contact
with descendants of Dev Singh, who had helped Moorcroft in Tibet,
in the Johar valley: Bir Singh and Nain Singh, who was a schoolmaster
in Milam, and thus known in the village as 'pandit'. The renewal of
this connection between the Rawats of Johar and British explorers
would soon prove instrumental in British exploration of Tibet.

Smyth's hopes of an official journey to Tibet were raised in the
early 1860s when a Kashmiri merchant working between Lhasa and

Nepal told the British resident in Kathmandu that a Qing imperial
edict had been posted in the Tibetan capital stating that 'if any English
Gentlemen make their appearance there, they are to be treated with
courtesy'. If such an edict ever existed, it made no difference. The
British representative in Beijing in the aftermath of the Second Opium
War was James Bruce, eighth Earl of Elgin, son of the man who
bought the marbles from the Parthenon. It was Elgin who had signed
the Treaty of Tianjin and he wasn't about to jeopardise Sino-British
relations by demanding passports for a speculative adventure in an
obscure corner of China's empire. Smyth's hopes for a passport were
dashed. Without the right papers, Smyth was turned back at the
Tibetan border in 1863 with the suggestion he apply to Beijing, where,
he knew very well, the British representative was not inclined to
support him. It was a diplomatic vicious circle that would repeat itself
for the next quarter of a century.

An officially closed border made little difference to Smyth, who set
off on another illicit hunting adventure inside Tibet the following
year; but it was immensely frustrating to the Great Trigonometrical
Survey, which had arrived at the foot of the Himalaya a few years
earlier to discover that both Nepal and Tibet were off limits. The
superintendent of the Great Trigonometrical Survey, James Walker,
liked the fact that tribes on the North-West Frontier were hostile,
since it allowed for retaliatory military expeditions and an opportunity
to do more surveying. That was much better, he thought, than the
'passive obstruction of the inhabitants of Chinese Tibet'. Walker had
used 'native' surveyors with some success, and now the surveyor in
charge of Kashmir, Thomas Montgomerie, used the same idea as a
way of gaining access to Tibet. In 1862, this skilled political operator,
who 'got his honours and made a name of himself with as little
personal hardship as any man in the Indian Survey', sold a proposal
for sending 'native' surveyors to areas beyond British reach to the
Asiatic Society. Montgomerie could see for himself the ease with which
Indians moved across borders that seemed impermeable to Europeans.
He proposed using 'Mahomedans' to survey Central Asia and sent a
Punjabi surveyor called Abdul Hamid to Yarkand to test the theory,
since the route was partially known already. As for Tibet, Indians
fluent in the language who could pass themselves off as traders or
pilgrims would be required. Montgomerie's only worry was that he

wouldn't find enough reliable local men 'with sufficient nerve'. Thanks to Edmund Smyth he found them.

Knowing that Smyth had crossed the frontier without papers on several occasions and had needed good local men to do so, Montgomerie wrote to Smyth in Kumaon seeking advice. Smyth recommended his friends at Milam in the Johar valley, the descendants of Dev Singh, who had assisted Moorcroft some fifty years earlier. Not only had Smyth hired men from this valley, the Strachey brothers had also taken Joharis on their adventures. Some twenty years later, Smyth recalled why and how he recommended the Joharis to Montgomerie,

> on account of their thorough knowledge of the Tibetan language, and also because they had the entrée into the country. [Montgomerie] asked me to select two, and send them to be trained. I accordingly chose our friend [the teacher, or pandit] Nain Singh, ... and the second man I chose was his cousin Manee or Mau Singh, who was Putwarie or chief native official of Johar. Manee was far superior to Nain Singh in position, wealth, and intellect, and might have done well, but unfortunately he was too well off in his own country to take to the rough life of exploration.

The two cousins left their valley in February 1863 for the Garhwali town of Dehra Dun where James Walker had developed a programme of instruction for these secret surveyors: the use of a sextant, taking bearings with a compass, walking with a disciplined pace so that two thousand steps would equal a mile. In this way they could manage a good route survey. They used a rosary to count off their paces and strips of paper hidden in a prayer wheel to record their observations. To maintain secrecy, they were given code names. Mani Singh was known as 'GM', a reversal of his first and last consonants. Nain Singh was simply called 'the Pundit', for his job as a teacher: it was a name that would extend to all those who entered the service of the British as clandestine travellers.

By December their training was done, but their first attempt to cross into Tibet via a pass near their home valley was thwarted. Perhaps the border guards who turned them back knew their behaviour was erratic for Johari traders. Perhaps they were recognised. They returned to Dehra Dun where Montgomerie agreed to let them try via Kathmandu, using the confiscation of Nepali goods by Tibetan officials as an excuse to enter the country as intermediaries. (You sense the killing of two birds with one stone here.) They tried first via the Kyirong valley where they came under suspicion from Chinese border officials. They thought of appealing to the local governor, but Mani Singh realised he knew the man from Gartok – to do so would blow their cover. Despondent, they returned to Kathmandu where Nain Singh decided to try again, this time alone.

While Mani returned home via north-west Nepal, surveying as he went, Nain Singh, pretending to be a Ladakhi trader, managed to cross the border into Tibet. There he met a group of traders from Rampur, in the old kingdom of Bashahr, on their way to Gartok. He joined them for a while and had his first glimpse of the Yarlung Tsangpo, the river which becomes the Brahmaputra. It earned his immediate respect: as he watched, three men drowned when their coracle over-turned. Feigning illness, he left the traders and doubled back, reaching Lhasa in January 1866, having covered eight hundred kilometres in thirty-seven days. He spent three months in Lhasa, renting a room and teaching when his money ran out. He also had an audience at Sera monastery with the twelfth Dalai Lama Trinley Gyatso, then just nine years of age. Nain Singh left Lhasa in the spring, slowly making his way west along the main trading route to Gartok before crossing the mountains to arrive back in Dehra Dun on 27 October 1866, his mission complete.

*

Nain Singh's report included a survey of nearly two thousand kilo-metres of the trade route to Lhasa, and he defined the course of the Tsangpo to its junction with the Kyi Chu, which flows through the city. The information he provided was a bonanza for the Survey of India, and for the government of India, which released more funds for further journeys. In 1867, Nain and Mani Singh returned to Tibet across the Mana Pass, taking with them Nain's brother Kalian, crossing the Sutlej at Tholing, once more posing as Bashahri traders, selling coral beads for shawl wool. Their targets were the goldfields of Thok Jalong, still in production despite centuries of exploitation, and the sources of the Indus and Sutlej rivers. Kalian was able to reach the headwaters of the Indus, confirming that it rose north of Kailas. Nain would return for a third mission to Tibet and Central Asia, travelling from Yarkand to Leh via Khotan and Pangong Lake. This time he took with him Kalian Singh and his cousin Kishen Singh, also from the Milam valley and already an experienced pundit.

Kishen's codename was A-K; he was also, in the estimation of many, the greatest of them all. In 1878 he left Darjeeling on a four-year mission to survey northern Tibet, an attempt to link what was known of Central Asia with the detailed information the 'pundits' had already acquired of southern and western Tibet. Kishen would spend a year in Lhasa, waiting for a caravan to Mongolia he could join in order to reach the eastern end of the Kun Lun range. While he waited he gathered detailed information on the city and the governance of Tibet. Kishen's record proved useful to the British when they finally did enter Tibet with Francis Younghusband's mission in 1903.

When eventually he travelled north, the caravan Kishen joined was attacked and the Mongolians fled. Kishen was robbed and left almost destitute; his companion then absconded taking what little they had left. Despite it all he kept going, all the way to Dunhuang in northern China where he and his remaining companion Chhumbel were detained for seven months, suspected of being spies. An abbot who was visiting the nearby Cave of a Thousand Buddhas hired the two men as his servants for the journey back home to his monastery, far to the south. This brought Kishen and Chhumbel to the eastern Himalaya and into contact with French missionaries, who relayed a message to Kishen's superiors in India. They had heard nothing from him in three years.

During Kishen and Chhumbel's subsequent journey home through eastern Tibet, they encountered an outburst of smallpox at Litang, and took the opportunity to immunise themselves against it using the Tibetan technique of variolation, snorting dried pustules from the bodies of the infected. When the pair finally reached Darjeeling in November 1882 they were almost destitute, their funds gone, their clothes in rags and, in the words of Kishen's boss James Walker, 'their bodies emaciated with the hardships and deprivations they had undergone'. Kishen Singh discovered his only son had died in his absence and his house had fallen into dereliction. With a price on his head from the Tibetan authorities, his exploring days were done. Although he received no official recognition from the Royal Geographical Society, he was given a pension and kept a chest full of papers, diaries and books about his adventures, as well as medals from societies around the world. He died in 1921, the year the British arrived at Everest.

Rudyard Kipling would use the myth of the pundits in his 1901 novel *Kim*, linking them in his readers' minds inextricably and erroneously with the struggle between Russia and Britain for Central Asia: the 'Great Game'. If any of the pundits was the model for his character Huree Chunder Mookerje it was another man, Sarat Chandra Das. At twenty-five he became headmaster of the new Bhotia Boarding School in Darjeeling, opened in 1874 to teach young Tibetans and Sikkimese boys and provide a cadre of interpreters and geographers who would be of use in the British Empire's dealings with Tibet. Das was much more an intelligence officer, though, born in the port city of Chittagong, a Bengali who learned Tibetan as an adult. By contrast most of the pundits were true mountain people, surveying vast tracts of country, relying wholly on their wits and courage to escape a thousand traps and pitfalls, and more often than not completing their missions without a word of complaint. Michael Ward, part of the successful 1953 Everest expedition, wrote: 'It is difficult to overpraise Kishen Singh's epic final journey.' It seems appropriate that two travellers from the mountains should complete the greatest Himalayan journey of all and grimly typical that they should go under a pseudonym and drift into obscurity.

13

'Forbidden' City

In late 2014, a cache of documents belonging to the first Englishman to visit the holy city of Lhasa was found in a cupboard at the antiquarian booksellers Maggs Brothers. Now in the possession of the Royal Asiatic Society, the find included four hundred letters, diaries, notebooks and ephemera, as well as the manuscript of his travel narrative, and a tiny sketch of the young ninth Dalai Lama, made in December 1811. The largely forgotten and atypical explorer had a brief touch of fame, resurrecting the nineteenth-century myth of Lhasa as a 'forbidden' city, keeping the rapidly changing world at bay.

Thomas Manning was born in the Norfolk village of Broome in 1772, second son of the local rector. A sickly but intelligent child, he was educated at home and in 1790 went up to Cambridge to study mathematics. There he caught the cresting wave of Romanticism, becoming friends with some of the movement's leading lights, notably Charles Lamb. According to Lamb, Manning had an exceptional mind,

> far beyond Coleridge or any other man in power of impressing – when he gets you alone, he can act the wonders of Egypt. Only he is lazy, and does not always put forth all his strength; if he did, I know no man of genius at all comparable to him.

Though others shared Lamb's view, the charge of indolence doesn't seem quite right for this restless, emotionally self-aware man. Disaffection seems nearer the mark. He wrote to a friend about the 'strange power of thought and sentiments that impel me unswervingly to strange things'. He was a rebel too. On the brink of academic glory at Cambridge, he refused to swear an oath of allegiance to the Church of England and so forfeited his degree, leaving his bewildered father in a puddle of anxiety.

China became his great passion and reaching it his obsession, to the amused bafflement of his friends. ('Read no more books of voyages,' Lamb teased him. 'They are nothing but lies.') In 1802 he arrived in Paris, taking advantage of the Treaty of Amiens that brought temporary peace between Britain and France, one of many radicals and Romantics eager to explore the new French republic. Paris was also one of the few places in Europe he could study Chinese. When war broke out again, English travellers in France were detained, but with patient lobbying, Napoleon himself signed Manning's passport and he returned to London, training for six months at Westminster Hospital to equip himself further for his travels. He also won the support of Sir Joseph Banks, then president of the Royal Society, for his plan to explore China disguised in local garb.

In 1806 the East India Company took him up the Pearl river to Canton, then the East India Company's only port in mainland China, now the modern city of Guangzhou. But the tight restrictions then in place on European freedom of movement thwarted Manning's ambition. His fellow countrymen 'with their eyes turned towards their own country, ready to take wing the moment their honey bags are filled', rarely shared his interest in Chinese culture. He drifted for several years doing translation work and practising medicine, grew a formidable beard and developed a reputation for eccentricity although, as someone who knew him after Tibet wrote: 'His eccentricities were quite harmless, and concerned only himself personally.'

After a few years trapped in Canton, Manning decided to enter China via a different route, from Lhasa, and travel east from there. Tibet *per se* was of little interest to him: China was the goal. The governor general of India was then Lord Minto and he promised Canton that Calcutta would help Manning. By this stage, in the early 1810s, the trade imbalance between Canton and Calcutta had eased: opium exports from Bengal to China had turned the Company's trade deficit into surplus, at the expense of the health and economy of the Chinese people. But thirty years earlier, Minto had helped his friend Edmund Burke impeach Warren Hastings; experiments in Tibet were part of Hastings' toxic legacy. Manning got nothing but indifferent tolerance. ('Fools, fools, fools,' he complained to his journal, 'to neglect an opportunity they may never have again.') So at his own expense, he entered Bhutan in September 1811 on a route to the west of that taken by George Bogle, crossing Tangtong Gyalpo's bridge into the fort at Paro. Here Manning was kept in a smoky guardhouse with no windows and banned from the market, bickering more than usual with his Chinese interpreter Zhao Jinxiu. ('A spaniel would be better company.') After they escaped Paro, Manning discovered Zhao Jinxiu had swapped his silver spoons for pewter and pocketed the difference, a new take on debasing currency. Manning sent him back to get them.

At the frontier town of Phari, where the local official was 'vastly civil', he had to quit their lodgings to make way for a Chinese detachment of soldiers. 'The Chinese lord it here like the English in India,' he noted, but Manning was glad of their presence. One of the ambans in Lhasa was a fiercely anti-British Manchu whom Manning knew from Canton: not the sort of man to greet an Englishman with the hand of friendship. Yet thanks to the troops' Chinese commander, whom Manning befriended, he got permission to leave Phari in early November and arrived at Lhasa a month later, the first Englishman to do so and, in all likelihood, the last until Younghusband's bloody expedition of 1904. Only two other Europeans would reach Lhasa throughout the nineteenth century.

On 17 December 1811 Manning had an audience with the young ninth Dalai Lama Lungtok Gyatso, who had just turned six. Manning was utterly charmed.

He had the simple, unaffected manners of a well-educated princely child. His face was, I thought, affectingly beautiful. He was of a gay and cheerful disposition. I was extremely affected by this interview with the lama. I could have wept through strangeness of sensation.

If Manning was aware of the deeply political circumstances of the boy's selection as Dalai Lama, he gives little hint of it. After the Qing had cleared out the Gorkhali army from Tibet in the early 1790s, the Qianlong emperor had tried to insert the Qing Empire into the arcane process of reincarnation; too often, it seemed to the Qianlong, important *tulku*, or reincarnate lamas, were emerging from the same influential families. His plan was instinctively bureaucratic: he demanded lists of important lineages and who held them and promulgated the

'Ordinance for the More Efficient Governing of Tibet'. This featured twenty-nine articles, the first of which was the introduction of the Golden Urn, drawn from the ancient Chinese practice of divination: the Qing ordered the names of likely candidates, written onto slips of ivory, to be put into the urn and for Tibetan lamas and Qing ambans to pick one out. Not for the last time, China was shown to be tone-deaf to the cultural complexities of Tibet. The Panchen Lama had simply ignored this new process when it came to choosing Lungtok Gyatso, and the Qing pretended it was happy about that. The boy would not be Dalai Lama for long, dying at the age of nine having caught a cold during the Monlam festival of 1815. The Golden Urn would and does remain a symbol of Chinese interference: Beijing used it to select its own candidate as Panchen Lama in 1995 after being outwitted by a search party authorised by the Dalai Lama.

Manning's interpreter had warned his master against trying his limited Mandarin in Lhasa so an interpreter with a thick Sichuan accent translated the young ninth Dalai Lama's words into Chinese. The munshi then translated them into Latin, their preferred shared language. This complexity must have added to the sense of disconnection Manning describes often feeling in Tibet. The city was 'dreamy and ghostly' but not in a good way. Like many European travellers fantasising about distant Lhasa, Manning found the reality a disappointment. Apart from the Potala itself, there was 'nothing striking, nothing pleasing in its appearance. The habitations are begrimed with smut and dirt.' In Lhasa's defence, he had said much the same on first acquaintance with Paris. By April 1812, Manning had run out of cash and was on his way back to Calcutta the way he had come, refused permission to enter China.

In the end, Manning did visit Beijing: in 1816 as part of a trade mission led by the future governor general of India Lord Amherst, a mission that went awry when Amherst refused to kowtow to the emperor. Such high-level political positioning would increasingly impact on Tibet's future, which is why British officials in India were forced to use the pundits from Milam to survey the north side of the Himalaya. After Beijing, Manning returned to England, surviving the wreck of the navy frigate *Alceste* and meeting Napoleon in exile on St Helena. He lived for another twenty years, latterly in a barely furnished cottage near Dartford half-hidden from the world, by which

time his milk-white beard reached his waist. He never did visit China
in the way he wanted, to see 'the actual degree of happiness the
people enjoy; their sentiments and opinions'.

The discovery and sale of Manning's papers to the Royal Asiatic
Society in 2014 prompted a rash of newspaper stories about this
'forgotten' explorer: the first Englishman to Lhasa. But he hadn't really
been forgotten, not altogether. In 1876, when Tibet's reputation for
exclusivity was reaching its zenith, the honorary secretary of the Royal
Geographical Society, Clements Markham, published Manning's
journal, along with George Bogle's account, with a detailed introduction and biographical notes.

Markham might have arranged its publication but he didn't like
Manning's account very much; in Markham's opinion, Manning was
'quick-tempered and imprudent'. In the self-satisfied era of imperial
exploration Manning seemed to Markham a dubious sort: he didn't do
geography and wrote far too much about his feelings. Worse, like
Samuel van de Putte, who had been in Lhasa almost a century before
the Englishman, he travelled for the sake of it, to experience and appreciate people who were different. That was no good: risking your skin
should only be done to advance European civilisation. Nor did Manning
court publicity: quite the opposite. He left his story untold. But when
it did emerge, thanks to Markham, it was no longer the right kind of
story. Coleridge would have thrilled to it, but Sir Thomas Holdich,
president of the Royal Geographical Society, dismissed him as 'a bad
traveller and a worse observer' whose journal was 'a monotonous record
of small worries and insignificant details'. Adventure yarns, so crucial
in building the myth of empire and racial superiority, required jeopardy
and a touch of swagger and absolutely no Romantic introspection.

This truth about the purpose of exploration, or at least that
Victorian imperial version of it, reveals another: where these great
adventures took place, at least in the public's mind, was almost
secondary. The location would necessarily be exotic and dangerous.
What the public really responded to was the hero who conquered it.
The story would be full of local colour and observations, but was
most importantly a reflection of the qualities the hero brought to the
challenges he (and quite soon she) faced, qualities people from his
own world aspired to share. Other cultures were simply constructed
for the purposes of the author: an exotic backdrop, a population to

be civilised or converted, contrasted unfavourably with the new colonial world order being fashioned across the globe. The complexities
of Himalayan politics were an irrelevant bore.

For the adventurers themselves, success and the celebrity success
offered could be transformative. Sven Hedin, the Swedish explorer
who surveyed more of Tibet than anyone else, recalled the origin of
his life's calling in his 1926 memoir *My Life as an Explorer*. Growing
up, his 'closest friends were Fenimore Cooper and Jules Verne,
Livingstone and Stanley, Franklin, Payer and Nordenskiöld'. When in
April 1880 Nordenskiöld's ship the *Vega* returned from its epic Arctic
journey, the fifteen-year-old Hedin was there with his family looking
down on Stockholm harbour, lit by 'countless lamps and torches' as
the ship glided into port.

> All my life I shall remember that day. It decided my career. From the
> quays, streets, windows, and roofs, enthusiastic cheers roared like
> thunder. And I thought, 'I, too, would like to return home that way.'

Coming home, for Hedin, was no less important than going out. If
the path was chosen, the destination was only set when he studied at
the Humboldt University of Berlin under the geographer Ferdinand
von Richthofen, uncle of the Red Baron and the man who coined the
term 'Silk Roads'. The mysteries of Central Asia, lost cities in the
desert, ancient trade routes long forgotten, were only now being
pieced together – and the greatest mystery of all was Tibet.

Hedin joined the swelling ranks of explorers, spies, adventurers,
missionaries, plant-hunters and mountaineers from industrialising
nations in Europe and elsewhere trying to pierce the veil that Tibet
had drawn around herself in the middle of the nineteenth century.
In the early decades, explorers like William Moorcroft and numerous
British colonial officials and soldiers had visited remote corners of
Tibet such as Kailas. (Hedin, in the interests of his own reputation,
would do his best to downplay these explorations.) Then the shutters
came down and adventurous British officials probing the southern
borders of Tibet found themselves turned away. This was the moment
the British began using indigenous pundits for information on the far
side of the Himalaya. The myth of 'secret' Tibet, and the 'forbidden'
city of Lhasa was born.

The idea of Tibet as a country determined to keep out the rest of the world was arresting. What was it they wished to preserve or conceal? What were the secrets Tibet held? These questions provoked two responses in the West's imagination, responses that even now continue to frame the outside world's perception of Tibet, as an idea as much as an actual place. First, it provoked a cohort of adventurers willing to accept a perceived challenge and try to lever their way in. They couldn't do that in Nepal, which was no less restrictive, because the British Empire accepted the ruling party's wish that foreigners be kept out. To attempt to go to Nepal would be to risk sanction. That wasn't the case with Tibet, and in particular the city of Lhasa, which is why so many more adventurers tried to go there.

Victorian Britain was primed to the notion of forbidden cities by Richard Burton's bold visit to Mecca in 1853. (The notion of penetrating virginal places speaks for itself.) The impression grew that Lhasa, another holy city, wasn't just currently closed to Europeans but somehow always had been. This was fanciful. For centuries Lhasa had been a hub on trans-Himalayan trade routes with deep religious connections across Asia. It was and remained culturally diverse. Kashmiris, Newars, Mongols, Chinese and Armenians lived permanently in the city. Nor was the Tibetan elite intellectually incurious. As we've seen, the Mongols valued Tibet not just for its spiritual expertise but also for its science, and Jesuit mapmakers relied on Tibetan expertise as well. Yet it was routine for European travellers in the early twentieth century to patronise Tibet's scientific understanding of the world. Tibetans were a simple, otherworldly people who had missed out on the Renaissance. They thought the world was flat and their medicine, known as the Sowa Rigpa, hadn't progressed beyond the equivalent of Europe's medieval humours: *lung*, meaning breath or the air element; *tripa*, the bile or fire element; and *badken*, phelgm or the cold element.

There is another story to set against the cliché of Tibet's superstition and isolation. During the eighteenth century Jesuit missionaries in Beijing had brought European science to the Qing emperors, who saw its value and sponsored the translation of their works into the languages of state, including Mongolian and Tibetan. Throughout the century, Tibetan lamas at the Qing court rubbed shoulders with Jesuit monks and gradually absorbed the value and accuracy of their astro-

nomical calculations. Until this point Tibetans based their own astronomical understanding, like their medicine, on Sanskrit texts imported
from India in the eleventh and twelfth centuries, particularly the
Kalachakra tantra. Now Tibetan scholars at the Yonghe Gong monastery in Beijing engaged fully with the implications of what the Jesuits
were showing them. The Qing court kept tight control of this new
learning and how it was used: Tibetan monks had to acquire this
knowledge for themselves.

Geluk monks from the Tibetan region of Amdo, a place of diverse
cultures and traditions, were, and remain, especially noted for their
intellectual openness. The great monasteries there, Labrang and
Kumbum, adopted new calendars based on Jesuit astronomy, simply
because they were better. And while the *Kalachakra* did say the earth
was flat, by the nineteenth century a monk from Labrang could write
that the 'earth is spherical'; the monastery even had a large spherical
globe painted on the wall. The heliocentric solar system hadn't quite
yet percolated through but the notion that Tibetans refused to accept
physical laws was simply wrong. This myth sprang, ironically enough,
from a newspaper article published in 1938 by Tibet's leading intellectual of that era, Gendun Chopel, famous for his excoriating mockery
of Tibetan backwardness. By then, Tibetan Buddhism really was reluctant to face the modern world. Chopel had been expelled from Labrang
as a young reincarnate lama for his progressive ideas but in this case
underestimated his own institution's historic openness.

Tibetan medicine was not always as conservative as it looked either,
especially when it came to the disease Tibetans dreaded more than
any other: smallpox, known in Tibetan as *drum ne*, 'the disease of
falling scabs'. The Jesuit Ippolito Desideri wrote that, 'Every ten or
twelve years an epidemic of smallpox carries off many people.' The
death from smallpox of the sixth Panchen Lama in Beijing soon after
his encounter with George Bogle was a shock but no surprise. The
panic smallpox provoked was unlike anything else, partly because
Tibetans were unusually susceptible to it and knew they were. The
Lazarist priest Évariste Huc, who reached Lhasa with fellow missionary
Joseph Gabet in early 1846 (the only two Europeans other than
Manning to do so that century), wrote: 'The Tibetan fear of smallpox
was extraordinary. They spoke of it with horror as the greatest scourge
that could attack the human race.' Their visit to the Dalai Lama was

cancelled when there was an outbreak of smallpox that arrived with
the caravan they had joined for the journey to Lhasa. Tibetan officials
weren't averse to using the threat of smallpox as an excuse for keeping
out undesirables. Each year, before allowing trade to resume over the
high passes, local Tibetan officials would check first whether there
was smallpox on the far side of the mountains. In 1869, as the British
Empire's frustration was starting to build, this caution prompted a
mocking article in *The Times* wondering at the 'amusing impudence'
with which Tibetan officials 'gravely inquire and decide every year
whether Her Majesty's Eastern empire is worthy of their patronage
or lofty recognition'.

Despite the fact that Edward Jenner's vaccine, developed in the late
eighteenth century, had arrived at Canton in 1805, shortly before
Thomas Manning, most Tibetans, unlike sarcastic British journalists,
still didn't have access to it decades later, but it wasn't simply a case
of ignoring foreign expertise. Tibetan doctors knew about the Chinese
practice, dating back to at least the fifteenth century, of 'variolation',
a mild infection that gave immunity, which the pundit Kishen Singh
had used during his epic journey. But variolation carried significant
risks of full-blown infection, so the traditional Tibetan response was
most common: to isolate sufferers, usually by leaving them somewhere
remote for several days to see whether or not they recovered. Such
treatment cut against the grain of Buddhist teaching, but it was the
safest strategy on offer.

During his visit in the middle of the nineteenth century, Évariste
Huc told the Dalai Lama's regent about Jenner's vaccine and saw at
once that future missionaries might use it as a Trojan horse, to bring
about 'the fall of lamaism and make possible the establishment of
Christianity in that pagan land'. In the twentieth century, both Britain
and China would also use the smallpox vaccination to win Tibetan
hearts and minds. Yet, even though it was not used in Tibet, the
vaccine was not, as many assumed, unknown there: some Tibetan
scholars had read about Jenner's vaccine in an astonishing book: *The
Treasury of All Precious Instructions*, a compendium of diseases and
their treatments published in Tibet by a Tibetan in the 1830s, more
than a decade before Huc reached Lhasa.

Most of the remedies in the *Treasury* were Indian and Chinese; it
described in detail the process of variolation, essentially inhaling

smallpox scabs up the nose. (Right nostril for men, left nostril for women.) A few, however, were from Europe, including a short section on Jenner's vaccine:

> After the cow has been affected by the virus, fluid from the cowpox is taken and then scratched into the arm of the person who has still not been infected ... This is how the Europeans treat smallpox.

The route this knowledge took to reach Tibet and the author of *The Treasury* is uncertain. It may have come with *gosain* traders, like Bogle's guide Purangir. It may have arrived from southern China or even Siberia, where a vaccination programme was underway in the early 1800s, close to the region of Buryatia, where Tibetan Buddhism was practised. Most probably it arrived from Beijing, where a Russian physician, who had vaccinated a group of Chinese, was friendly with the Tibetan author of the *Treasury*, a man whose achievements – including another book of far greater scope than the *Treasury* – belie the assumption that Tibet was intellectually incurious and closed to foreign influences.

The *Treasury*'s author was Jampel Chokyi Tenzin, fourth in a lineage of reincarnate lamas known as the Tseten Nomonhan, based at the Serkhok monastery in Amdo, far to the north-east of Lhasa. The lineage was politically influential, with seats in Mongolia and Beijing. Following the crushing defeat of the Dzungar Khanate in 1720 and the loss of their Mongolian patrons, the government in Lhasa appointed the second Tseten Nomonhan as ambassador to their new overlords, the imperial Qing court in Beijing. It was a bold decision, because during the war with China the Tseten's monasteries had been burned and his monks killed. For the first time, China had absorbed parts of Amdo within its own borders. Yet despite fears the lama would simply be a hostage, the Tseten instead became a critical link between Lhasa and Beijing and a tutor within the Qing household. He was offered a permanent monastic residence in the Chinese capital.

The fourth Tseten Nomonhan, Jampel Chokyi, was the son of Amdo nomads, born in 1789. The year before, as Tibet's ambassador to China, his predecessor had travelled to Beijing with the sixth Panchen Lama, whom Bogle had known, and died there, soon after the Panchen Lama succumbed to smallpox. Jampel Chokyi was recognised as the reincarnation when he was around two years old and installed at Serkhok, where he studied Buddhism and medicine. In 1806, and not yet eighteen, he travelled to Beijing for the first time. Western explorers might congratulate themselves for making such arduous journeys, but they were a fact of life for Geluk monks like the Tseten. He took up residence in the Yellow Temple, remaining there until an invitation arrived for the enthronement in Lhasa of the ninth Dalai Lama, Lungtok Gyatso. There is no record of their meeting, but Thomas Manning was in Lhasa at the same time as the Tseten, another traveller fascinated by the 'sentiments and opinions' of different cultures. And if Manning was not aware of the young Tibetan, the lama was certainly aware of the *peling*, as Tibetans called the British. He had a reputation for conversation and good humour and given his subsequent career, it seems more than likely the Tseten would have paid Manning close attention.

In 1814 Jampel Chokyi returned to his duties in Beijing where he would remain for the next three years, dividing his time between religious ceremonies for the emperor in the Forbidden City and his own temple, where he taught monks from Tibet and Mongolia. (In 1816, Manning was also in Beijing with Lord Amherst.) Then the Tseten was sent back to Lhasa for ceremonies connected to the death of the Jiaqing emperor. That same year he completed the first version of what eventually become an immense compendium, *The Detailed Description of the World*. This substantial text, much expanded, was published in 1830 in Mongolia at the request of monks there and amounts to an encyclopaedic overview of the regions of the world. In essence, it is a book about how Tibet looked out at the world, rather than how the world looked in.

The Tseten's sources for this immense undertaking are not fully understood. There were European missionaries in Beijing but the evidence is patchy about who contributed. Jampel Chokyi certainly knew the priest Nikita Yakovievich Bichurin, known as Father Iakinf, who led the Russian Orthodox mission in Beijing. Iakinf had seen how a lack of cultural understanding was hampering his mission's work and set about studying Chinese history, geography and literature. Regarded as Russia's first sinologist, he also wrote on Tibet and Mongolia, and likely gleaned knowledge from the Tseten. Russian–Chinese diplomacy was conducted in Mongolian rather than Manchu, so as a fluent Mongolian speaker Tseten's insights were likely useful. This was a time of strengthening ties between the tsar and the Qing emperor and the Tseten had several highly educated Russian missionary friends. He sold them books, some of which were translated into Russian. Another of his sources was the German-speaking doctor and botanist Alexander Georg von Bunge who arrived in the late 1820s and collected plants across Central Asia including Mongolia at the personal request of the great explorer-scientist Alexander von Humboldt. A third was the sinologist Zachar Federovic Leontevsky, who opened the first museum in Russia dedicated to Chinese culture.

The Tseten had to tread carefully in his pursuit of knowledge and what he revealed. European ideas on astronomy flatly contradicted the *Kalachakra*. Other translators concealed the fact that this innovative thinking came from Jesuits so that more conservative lamas wouldn't censor their work. The Tseten didn't do this; he sought instead reassurance in a letter to the seventh Panchen Lama, who agreed there were problems but encouraged the Tseten to continue his work, particularly on the European calendar, which was clearly superior to the Tibetan. Geography at least was less controversial: the Buddhist cosmology, originating in India, that Tibetan monks studied put a great mountain at the centre of the world and four continents around it, a fairly accurate representation of the region. And thanks to guidebooks written to locate sites mentioned in ancient Buddhist texts, better-educated lamas knew the geography of places like Nepal, western China and northern India quite well. The Tseten's text worked from within this tradition.

In a modern context, *The Detailed Description of the World* seems naïve although it has its moments. Britain, the Tseten wrote, was divided into three regions: England, Scotland and Ireland. The 'shape of their faces looks like that of Indians, but they are as white as snow. ... The people are rich, but they like to drink, and they are more dissolute than other Europeans.' Poles on the other hand were 'beautiful, intelligent, and honest. They are especially nice to people from outside their country.' (One of the Tseten's interlocutors was an ethnic Pole.) He also described the North Pole, taking seriously the possibility that part of the earth could be perpetually in darkness, an idea ridiculed by other Tibetan scholars. Africa was 'a big continent, and its shape is like a triangle'. Some African animals had Asian equivalents and were familiar: lions, elephants and rhinoceroses. The giraffe, 'an animal called *da po*', was wholly strange:

> a horse's head with a donkey's tail in different colours such as yellow, brown and green. The animal is very big and its neck is four or three arm spans long.

The continent of Europe was of particular interest, since some Tibetan scholars had identified it as the location for Shambhala, the utopian realm in the west where Buddha had taught crucial initiations to those who lived there. The sixth Panchen Lama, who had written guidebooks himself, had asked George Bogle to look for clues to its location when he went home so the lama could visit. The idea of a mythical land where transformative knowledge lies waiting, so strong within the Tibetan tradition, is reflected in the Tseten's general comments about Europe. The British were a tangible threat just across the border but in magical Europe there was 'no such thing as treating each other badly, accusations, the powerful taking over the weaker, or corruption'. Europe was a wonder house, like Kipling's *ajeeb ghar* in his Himalayan novel *Kim*, with

> lights that have oil and clothing that generates light ... mirrors that recognise thieves, hide one from the enemy, and burn the enemy ... many different stunning things such as celestial and global maps ... There are also machines that are mechanised by fire, water, air and wood.

As the Tibetan historian Lobsang Yongdan writes: 'It is ironic that Western writers created a mysterious land called Shangri-La in Tibet while Tibetan scholars were looking for Shambhala somewhere in Europe.'

Written from a Buddhist perspective, *The Detailed Description of the World* might seem fanciful to European readers but in the 1830s so were the few accounts of Tibet published by Europeans. Most of those that came later either amused or frustrated educated Tibetans. And the Tseten had a much firmer grip than any European on the geography of the north side of the Himalaya, not least that the Yarlung

Tsangpo was the same river as the Brahmaputra, something the British would sweat over for decades to come. Tibetans' knowledge of their own country was extensive, hardly surprising for a culture that had been printing books for a thousand years and liked to travel. The big monasteries drew students from all over Asia and those in Amdo stood at a crossroads of influences from all points of the compass. While the Tseten held a seal from the Manchu ruler in Beijing, he described Tibet as outside the limits of the Qing Empire: a place with its own identity meeting the world on more or less equal terms.

*

Given all that, what was it that made Tibet so reluctant to allow European visitors? Tension between the emerging British Empire and the Qing is one answer, but it ran deeper than that. There are clues in the reception Thomas Manning got when he reached Lhasa in 1811: although he was curious about Tibetan temples, it took him a while, he wrote, to find someone who could show him around them. His interpreter Zhao Jinxiu had asked him a few times whether he intended to visit these temples, and when Manning finally announced that he would, Zhao was relieved. Manning discovered that Chinese mandarins and Tibetan authorities had also been asking about this.

> The mandarins, he said, were aware that the Catholics refused to pay these respects; consequently, if I went it would wipe off their suspicions of my being a missionary.

It had been over sixty years since the Capuchin friars had left Lhasa and yet the memory of their threat retained its potency.

Had Pope Clement XI preferred the Jesuits as missionaries to Tibet over the Capuchins then it's conceivable Tibetan history would have followed a different course. The Jesuit Ippolito Desideri had spent five years in Lhasa from the early spring of 1716. More than any other missionary to Tibet, he was engaged and intelligent enough to pierce the outer layers of Tibetan Buddhism and grasp its core philosophy, learning Tibetan and writing works of real insight. These were left unpublished in a Vatican archive until their rediscovery in the 1870s, and were only finally published in the 1930s. His obscurity lies in the victory of the Capuchins who had been awarded control of the Catholic Church's missionary work by the Vatican in 1703. Over the next four decades they sent three missions to Lhasa. The first had ended in expensive failure, having spent a small fortune to baptise two adults. The second arrived in Lhasa a few months after Desideri in 1716, prompting the protracted long-distance argument with Rome that ended with Desideri's departure. Thereafter the Jesuits would continue to pour scorn on the Capuchin mission's shortcomings and their overly optimistic reports to Rome. They had a shrewder idea than their competitors how things would go in Tibet.

The Capuchins in Lhasa would follow a similar arc of experience as Father Andrade and his Jesuits had in the west Tibetan kingdom of Guge a century before. Both groups saw similarities between the Catholic Church and Tibetan Buddhism, equating the Dalai Lama with the pope and drawing comparisons between monastic institutions. They were also struck by the liberty they were given to practise their faith, wearing their robes in public 'just as in Paris or Rome'. For their part, the Tibetans regarded Christianity as essentially good, showed reverence to Christian symbols and were grateful for the missionaries' medical skills. The Mongol ruler of Tibet at the time of the Capuchin mission to Lhasa, Lajang Khan, was equally curious about western science; he knew what the Jesuits had brought to the Qing court in Beijing and hoped these missionaries would do the same for Lhasa.

The missionaries were encouraged by this tolerance and openness. The Qing state was deeply hierarchical and xenophobic; political relationships were about dominance and subservience. Tibet wasn't like that at all. Tibetan nobles played down their rank to encourage openness, treating the Capuchins as equals. The Christian friars, with their tonsured heads, were even given a nickname: 'the white-headed lamas'. Mindful of the huge expense of their mission, the Capuchins reassured their masters in Rome that progress was good and influential Tibetans were on the brink of converting. It was a fundamental misjudgment.

Lhasa aristocrats valued the concept of *yarab choesang*, being respectful and polite to others, a trope that resonates in modern Tibet just as it did for the eighth-century dharma king Songtsen Gampo, whose sixteen human laws can be characterised as a more affable version of the Ten Commandments. Kindness to neighbours and moderate behaviour are at the heart of this value system. (The fourth Tseten Nomonkhan was a little more cynical. His world encyclopaedia included laconic judgments on Tibetans from different parts of the country: those from Kham were aggressive enemies but loyal friends, too trusting in the view of the Tseten; 'the people of Tsang', meanwhile, referring to the region of Shigatse, 'are honest, polite and cowards. Although smart, they are not deep. ... They love money, but are generous toward the Dharma's purpose.' People in Tsang might judge such wisecracks typical for an Amdo intellectual.) This is why the Capuchins were given residency permits, tax exemptions and allowed to buy property. The prefect of the Capuchin mission Francesco Orazio della Penna, who had joined Desideri in mastering Tibetan at the Sera monastery, was even allowed to conduct masses there. With the invasion of the Dzungars and the death of their patron Lajang in 1717, the missionaries faced a grave setback: Armenian and Russian traders who had given them a sympathetic Christian network fled the city; their hospice was plundered and their funds taken. Yet after the Qing Empire had restored order, the Tibetan elite remained tolerant and welcoming, even when the Capuchins made it clear they wanted to convert Tibetans to Christianity. They were allowed to buy land for a church, and when the local population turned against them, seeing the missionaries as a malign foreign influence disturbing the balance of nature, the Dalai Lama issued a statement saying they must be allowed to continue.

The mistake the Capuchins made was to confuse generosity of spirit with spiritual surrender. They saw tolerance as weakness and opportunity. Yet the Tibetans were not naïve. They liked the Capuchins for their medical skills, respected their faith and had no wish to convert them. (The powerful regent of the seventh Dalai Lama, Polhane Sonam Topgay, wrote to the Capuchins at the end of their second mission that 'despite the fact that we do not know [your] religion, we give credence and pay respect to all religions, ours and yours; moreover, in the past we have not slandered it and we do not slander it now.') They were interested in the knowledge and technology the foreigners might offer and were disappointed when it didn't materialise. Mostly the Tibetan state was too busy with a continuing storm of political unrest to pay much attention. The Capuchins on the other hand saw the Tibetans as backward heathens; it was their job to bring them to Christ. Unlike the Jesuit Desideri, they saw little value in studying the complexities of Buddhist metaphysics. They took from Tibet only what they needed to undermine what they regarded as its central defining feature: Buddhism.

During their third mission, beginning in 1741, the Capuchins finally managed to convert some Tibetans to Christianity. It was a sign confirming that God wanted Buddhism destroyed. The Dalai Lama, the missionaries claimed, was not the embodiment of Chenrezig, the *bodhisattva* of compassion, after all. They demanded a special regulation so their converts could celebrate Christian holidays. The converts refused to perform *u lag*, a much-resented tax in the form of labour levied by monastic institutions. They also refused to receive blessings from the Dalai Lama. The Tibetans might have been tolerant of other faiths but this was now about more than freedom of religious expression: it was regarded as disloyalty to the Tibetan state. At the insistence of the religious establishment, legal charges were made not against the Capuchins but against the converts. They in turn refused to respect the legitimacy of the court since its authority rested on false religion. The secular and the religious had become so intertwined in Tibet that to pull at the threads of one was to unravel the other. Five converts, two women and three men, were convicted and publicly flogged.

The Capuchins were advised in future to confine their preaching to foreigners. They replied that their only purpose in Tibet was to preach the gospel and demanded freedom of conscience. The Dalai Lama's regent Polhane was incredulous:

Kashmiri, Newari, Azaras [meaning Indians], Chinese, Turkish, Kazakhs, Kirghiz and other peoples living in Tibet adhere to their own religions and are supported as much as possible and not harmed. But you have spoken evil of the Tibetan religion. If any of us were to go to your country and preach our religion to you in the same manner as you have done with us, would you punish him? Destroying other religions implies nobody may follow his own religion. We have to defend our religion as you are defending yours. You came here of your own accord, we did not call you; as a consequence it is up to you to decide where to go and what to do.

Orazio della Penna and the rest of the mission withdrew from Lhasa in the spring of 1745. He died at Patan, in the Kathmandu valley, that June and was buried in a grave now lost. Soon after came news from Lhasa that their church had been levelled to the ground. All that survived of the Capuchin mission was the small bell the friars had cast in the Newari city of Bhaktapur, which still hangs in the Jokhang temple. They also left behind a sour taste, a suspicion not only of Christian missionaries but also their political intent.

When Huc and Gabet, 'the lamas of the western heavens', arrived a century later, just as keen as the Capuchins to provoke the fall of Buddhism, Lhasa was in Huc's words still 'the rendezvous of all Asiatic peoples ... with an astonishing variety of features, costumes and languages'. The political map of Asia, on the other hand, had changed dramatically. Tibet had for centuries triangulated itself between the Mongols and China, nurturing patron–priest relationships that allowed its people to maintain their identity and a deep measure of cultural independence. The arrival of British armies and missionaries on Tibet's southern border was regarded as a new and uncertain threat. According to Huc, a Kashmiri merchant in Lhasa told him how 'Pelings', meaning the British,

> are the most cunning of men. They are getting control of all parts of India, but it is always by trickery rather than by open force. Instead of overturning the authorities, they cleverly try to win them over to their side and share the spoils with them. In Kashmir there is a saying: 'The world is Allah's, the land is the Pasha's, but the East India Company rules.'

The Tibetan elite, from the Dalai Lama down, shared that view and Huc was at pains to reassure anyone who mistook him as British that he was in fact French. 'The Tibetans have got it into their heads, for some reason, that the British are an aggressive people of whom they had best beware.' That fear was heightened in 1864 when Calcutta sent troops into Bhutan and took control of Bhutan's territory on the plains. The Tibetans had every right to be anxious.

Évariste Huc and Joseph Gabet faced an accelerated version of the fate of the Capuchins. The Tibetans were friendly and allowed them to open a chapel; the Qing amban, Qishan, was far less tolerant. Qishan was a Mongol who had enjoyed a meteoric rise in the Qing hierarchy and then been humiliated for his negotiations with the British to settle the First Opium War. A death sentence had been commuted to a posting in Lhasa. The French had arrived from Mongolia via Amdo, spending time at Kumbum, but they planned to leave Tibet for India, in the footsteps of the legendary Chinese Buddhist traveller Xuanzang. Yet that would have left the impression that the marches of the Qing Empire were becoming a free-for-all. Furthermore, should the Qing seem to act in support of Christian missionaries whose intention was to subvert Tibetan Buddhism, then Chinese power in Lhasa would be weakened. Qishan wasn't about to make the same mistake twice and expelled Huc and Gabet back to China via Sichuan with an escort to see them off the premises. By the time Huc reached Canton, his death had already been reported in the newspapers. He remained there for three years writing an account of his travels. When it was published in Paris in 1850 the book was an instant bestseller. Neither Bogle nor Manning had published anything and Desideri's writings on Tibet were languishing in Rome. Huc's account was the first time many Europeans and Americans had read much of significance about the mysterious land north of the Himalaya.

Huc's intention had been to produce something brimming with missionary zeal but he couldn't resist packing it with wonders and narrative drive. It was more a religious adventure story; a simplified version was given to French schoolchildren much as the works of Alexandre Dumas would be. William Hazlitt, son of the essayist and radical, translated Huc's account into English and it was published in London a year after the French edition. Other European editions soon followed. Suffering a breakdown in health, Huc returned to a hero's welcome in Paris, where Napoleon III gave him the *Légion d' honneur*. But he fell out with his order, which judged his narrative as too sympathetic to the Tibetans and placed it on the Catholic index of prohibited books. His health never recovered from his years in China and he died in 1860, aged just forty-seven.

★

Death saved Huc from watching as his reputation took a battering in the later decades of the century, principally at the hands of the explorer Nikolay Przhevalsky, a Russian imperialist whose judgment concerning Asians frequently tipped into racism. (Suggesting Moscow should annex Mongolia and Qinghai, he said: 'A thousand of our soldiers would be enough to subdue all Asia from Lake Baykal to the Himalayas.') Przhevalsky denounced Huc as a fraud, partly because he had been thwarted in his own desire to visit Lhasa. Luckily the Frenchman had his champions too, particularly the American diplomat William Woodville Rockhill, who read Huc's book as a teenager in the 1860s, and in doing so set the course of his life. Rockhill would help rescue Huc's reputation and become involved in Tibetan affairs himself just as the United States became politically engaged in the region for the first time.

French missionary interest in Tibet didn't end after Huc and Gabet's epic journey. In 1846, the year they reached Lhasa, the Capuchins finally gave up their missionary interest in Tibet, which the Vatican then awarded not to the Lazarists, who were in Mongolia, but to the Paris-based Société des Missions Étrangères. One of their priests in China, Charles Renou, almost immediately visited Kham, despite a prohibition on travel to the Tibetan interior under the terms of China's trade agreements at that time with France. In 1854 Renou established a small mission in a remote village near the border of Kham and began translating Christian texts into Tibetan and growing food, introducing new plants to the area, including the potato. Yet as in Lhasa, when local Tibetan Buddhist authorities began to understand what Renou and his fellow priests were doing, hostility grew. They had to abandon their first mission and while the Missions Étrangères remained on the fringes of Tibet for a century, they were never able to settle in areas where Lhasa's influence was strong. After the Treaty of Tianjin was signed in 1860, and freedom of movement for Europeans markedly improved, Renou was still not able to visit Lhasa. In theory the treaty gave them the right to do so, but as with Edmund Smyth, the change in rules didn't make any difference in Tibet. The Manchu dynasty was struggling to extinguish the Taiping Rebellion, the bloodiest civil war in history: Qing officials weren't going to enforce passports for missionaries to the remote western provinces. The French had the support of their government, and the British asked the Gorkhali strongman Jang Bahadur to send a letter to Lhasa requesting the French passports be honoured, but the Missions Étrangères never got there.

As the nineteenth century wore on, Christian missionary efforts gathered strength. Protestants began to arrive, including Hudson Taylor's China Inland Mission, founded in 1865, which sent nineteen missionaries to eastern Tibet before 1900. Among them was Cecil Polhill, an Eton and Cambridge-educated Pentecostal, whose missionary work featured in a book by his sister-in-law Annie Westland Marston that she titled *The Great Closed Land: A Plea for Tibet*. A Moravian missionary called Benjamin La Trobe wrote the preface, reflecting the evangelical excitement at opening up Tibet:

> A cordon of missionary posts is being drawn around Tibet. Already it extends westward from Kashmir along the northern frontier of India and Burmah, and reaches up to the north of China. True, it is thin and weak as yet, and there are long gaps in the ranks. Yet, if the missionaries be 'few and far between,' each occupies his post in the name and at the bidding of an omnipotent Prince and Saviour, with whom there is no restraint to save by many or by few.

The arrival of Protestant missionaries created opportunities for adventurous women to bring the word of the Lord to the roof of the world. Isabella Bird was the daughter of a curate who travelled to Ladakh in 1889 and wrote *Among the Tibetans*. She was also the first woman to lecture to the Royal Geographical Society in London. Like a surprising number of the first Western women to travel to the Himalaya, Bird had suffered from chronic poor health as a child but seemed much healthier riding a pony across the plateau of Tibet. The first Western woman to reach Tibet proper was Hannah or 'Annie' Royle Taylor. Born in Cheshire in 1855, she was the daughter of a shipping company director. Like Bird she suffered poor health as a child; aged seven, doctors diagnosed a heart problem that would likely prove fatal before she reached adulthood. She thus escaped formal education and her rebellious instincts went unchecked. Aged thirteen Annie declared herself an evangelical Christian and at sixteen, having heard a missionary lecturing about his work, discovered her life's calling.

Against the wishes of her family, Taylor had medical training in London and then in her late twenties joined Hudson Taylor's China Inland Mission. Posted to Lanzhou in the modern province of Gansu she found herself on the fringes of the Tibetan world.

Taylor described herself as a 'lone wolf' who struggled to work well in a group; it was hardly surprising she didn't fit in with her colleagues in Lanzhou. So instead she used her family's money to launch her own one-woman mission to Tibet. She moved to Darjeeling, where a young Tibetan called Puntso was brought to her house for treatment on his damaged feet. Born in Lhasa, Puntso would be her connection to Tibet for almost two decades. Having moved to Sikkim in 1890 to study Tibetan at a monastery, she and Puntso, by now a Christian (at least nominally), travelled to Gansu where she shaved her head and adopted Tibetan dress. Trekking for weeks over the high plains of Amdo, she slipped unnoticed past Gyegu, a hub for the tea trade from China, but was then intercepted outside Nagchu, just three days from Lhasa. Forced out of Tibet, Taylor became briefly famous on her return to London and leveraged her fame – 'God's little woman' as one journalist dubbed her – to launch another mission to Tibet. The China Inland Mission weren't prepared to support a project based in India or a woman leading men in the field, so Taylor once more set up her own, establishing the Tibetan Pioneer Mission in Sikkim and recruiting thirteen missionaries from Britain and Scandinavia, but the project soon foundered on the shoals of her abrasive personality.

Determined to remain in the Tibetan world, Taylor discovered a rather clever loophole. The British had recently signed the Convention of Calcutta with the Qing authorities and in 1893 were allowed to install a trade agent just across the border at Yatung. Using the terms of this treaty, Annie Taylor moved there with Puntso and his wife Sigu and opened a shop, selling Tibetan objects to museums in Scotland to keep her head above water. The locals called her *ani*, meaning nun; the British customs officer there, Captain McDonnell Parr, thought her a 'perfect nuisance'. She was still at Yatung in late 1903 when Younghusband reached the village at the start of his campaign in Tibet, intercepting him at the stone arch at the entrance of the village, dressed as a Tibetan: 'Is this Colonel Younghusband?' she demanded before interviewing him at length about his religious views. Initially supportive of Younghusband's campaign, she offered her medical skills at Younghusband's base in the Chumbi valley but the disruption and violence seems to have upended her mental health, often fragile, and she ended her days in an asylum.

In contrast to Taylor, a missionary who sought medical training, Susie Carson was a doctor who became a missionary. She was born in Ontario to Methodist parents in 1868; her father, a superintendent of schools, encouraged her to go to medical school. She practised as a doctor with her sister Jennie until her mid twenties, and then in 1894 heard a Dutch-born missionary called Petrus Rijnhart lecturing about China where he had recently been working with the China Inland Mission. It's unclear whether Susie knew his whole story: that he'd worked for the Salvation Army in the Netherlands and then been sent abroad to Canada after allegations of sexual misconduct. His initial application to join the China Inland Mission had been turned down, but he spent three years working for them in Lanzhou before being thrown out. He was back in Canada raising funds to lead a mission to Tibet when he met Susie, who as a girl had dreamt of missionary work. They soon married and within a year were in China at Lusar, the village of the vast Geluk monastery of Kumbum, close to the city of Xining, treating victims of the Dungan Revolt, a largely forgotten Sufi Muslim uprising that was brutally suppressed by Qing and Tibetan troops with the deaths of a hundred thousand men, women and children.

Soon after, the Rijnharts moved to Tankar, also in the Tibetan province of Amdo, and opened a dispensary, hosting the British cavalry officer and explorer Montagu Wellby who had just crossed northern Tibet from Ladakh, been refused access to Lhasa and was now almost penniless. (His book, *Through Unknown Tibet*, was prefaced with the honest suggestion that it was written 'that some future traveller may learn, not so much what he ought to do, as what he ought not to do'.) Wellby was not the only explorer who dropped in. While Petrus Rijnhart was guiding him to Beijing, Sven Hedin arrived in Tankar. Susie was able to correct his impression of the caravans passing through Tankar from the monasteries of the Dalai and Panchen Lamas: they were not carrying tribute for Beijing, as Hedin believed, but goods to trade.

Although popular in Tankar, the Rijnharts had always intended to reach Tibet's capital. 'We knew that if ever the Gospel were proclaimed in Lhasa,' Susie wrote, conveniently putting to one side the Catholics who had already been there, 'someone would have to be the first to undertake the journey, to meet the difficulties, to preach the first sermon and perhaps never return to tell the tale – who knew?' In June 1897, Susie had given birth to a son, Charles, and so they delayed until the following summer. Their journey started well but after two months and just north of Nagchu everything began to fall apart. Charles died suddenly and was buried in their emptied drugs case, wrapped in 'white Japanese flannel'. Then Tibetan soldiers blocked their path. At Nagchu, just a hundred and sixty kilometres short of Lhasa, they were told to go no further and put on the caravan route to Kangding, a thousand kilometres to the east. At this point, their reliable guide Rahim headed home to Ladakh. Attacked and robbed by bandits, the rest of their crew fled. Ten days later, Petrus Rijnhart forded a river to seek information from a band of nomads they had seen nearby and was never seen again. Two months later, without husband or child, Susie Carson staggered into Kangding penniless and dressed in rags to be greeted by a missionary called James Moyes who years before had been part of Annie Taylor's mission. Moyes and Carson later married and had a child, but Susie died only days after the birth. Her account of her travels, *With the Tibetans in Tent and Temple*, is well observed but heartbreaking.

Not all the women travelling to Tibet were missionaries. The remarkable Teresa Littledale, like Susie Carson born in Canada, came closer to Lhasa than any western woman before the French-Belgian spiritualist and explorer Alexandra David-Néel reached the city in 1924. Unlike these others, she had no need or compulsion to write about her adventures; she wasn't spreading the gospel or filling lecture halls. Born in London, Ontario in 1839, Teresa met her second husband St George Littledale in Japan in 1874, when he was twenty-two, thirteen years her junior. At the time, she was still married to an older man, a Scottish landowner called Willie Scott, whom Teresa's mother once described as 'the reverse of handsome'. St George, on the other hand, was young and rather beautiful, the son of a much respected mayor of Liverpool. Like his father, St George was also noted for being affable, self-effacing and hugely determined. On his majority he inherited his father's wealth and took off to travel the world and indulge his passion for hunting. Having befriended the Scotts in Japan, he travelled with them through Kashmir, by which time he and Teresa were having an affair. With consumate and generous timing, Willie Scott died of typhoid on the voyage home leaving St George and Teresa free to marry.

For the next thirty years they explored the world together, most usually collecting specimens for the Natural History Museum or plants for the Royal Botanic Gardens at Kew. Their greatest journey was crossing Tibet in 1895 when they came closer than any European since Huc to reaching Lhasa. It was, St George wrote in a rare article for the *Geographical Journal*, 'the same party as usual': he and Teresa, now aged fifty-five, and their plucky fox terrier Tanny, but also St George's muscular nephew Willie Fletcher, who had rowed stroke for the Oxford boat in the early 1890s. (He was gassed at Passchendaele in the summer of 1917 and never recovered, dying of pneumonia two years later.) 'My scheme,' St George wrote,

> was to strain every nerve to reach Tibet, and, if possible, Lhasa, with plenty of food and animals to carry it. Most of the other expeditions had failed owing to their arriving in a more or less destitute condition, and then, of course, the Tibetans could dictate their own terms. We also relied upon bribery, and went well prepared with the sinews of war for wholesale corruption.

They reached Kashgar in western China in January 1895, where they entertained the ubiquitous Sven Hedin, then in the middle of his first four-year expedition, and were relieved to see the handful of Pathan bodyguards they had requested 'in case of a scrimmage' finally arrive after a snowy crossing of the Karakoram. The expedition then headed south to Yarkand and east to Cherchen before crossing the high passes of the Arka Tagh mountains – 'the most absolute of frontiers' – in bitter conditions in order to reach the northern fringes of the Chang Tang on the Tibetan plateau. Here things got even worse. Their pack animals died like flies: only eight of 170 would make it through to the other side of the Himalaya. One night the small flock of sheep they brought for food was allowed to wander; wolves tore out the throats of every one. Teresa suffered from dysentery, confessing to her diary that 'I feel afraid to look at the future of this trip. It is not bright for me.' To St George she said not a word of complaint. The wind was almost constant and bitterly cold. Her husband, now responsible for shooting their food, found his aim put off by his heavy breathing in the thin air. Only Tanny was happy, nestling in Teresa's thick coat for warmth.

By mid summer they had crossed the Chang Tang and were in striking distance of the Himalaya. Yet below the Goring La, just eighty kilometres short of Lhasa, they were blocked by a hundred or so Tibetans armed with matchlocks. St George waved their Chinese passport, which luckily the Tibetans couldn't read, since it prohibited travel through Tibet. He tried threats, promising that if any of them were hurt three thousand Indian sepoys would march on Lhasa, a shadowy prefiguring of the British invasion nine years later. He tried 'the golden key' of 'wholesale corruption'. Nothing worked. The religious official responsible for keeping them out was almost in tears as he told the Littledales he would be executed if he let them through. Teresa, who had just turned fifty-six, demanded St George's Mannlicher rifle and presented it to the lama, asking him to shoot her rather than send her back across the Chang Tang. It was finally agreed they would be escorted west to Ladakh and return home from there.

Back in London, St George was feted. 'My greatest traveller,' Edward VII called him, conveniently forgetting about Teresa. The Royal Geographical Society awarded him their patron's medal, but again, excluded Teresa. In 1893, two years before Teresa was in Tibet, the Royal Geographical Society had been at war with itself over female membership; *Punch* magazine had run this satirical doggerel:

> A lady an explorer? A traveller in skirts?
> The notion's just a trifle too seraphic:
> Let them stay and mind the babies, or hem our ragged shirts.
> But they mustn't, can't and shan't be geographic.

The publisher Edward Arnold offered St George a good advance to write up their adventures but the article had been enough; Littledale didn't care much who knew what they had done and he slipped quietly beyond the reach of bibliographers. Teresa went on a final expedition to Mongolia and then retired from the expedition life. In January 1928, a few months before she died at the age of eighty-nine, the elderly couple had a small house party for Tibetan friends old and new: Francis Younghusband, who by then had solved the problem of entering Lhasa by kicking down the door, and Sir Charles Bell, the former special ambassador who had lived a year in the city and steered British policy in a more constructive direction. Younghusband also brought two Tibetan friends to meet the Littledales, one of them part of the Lhasa government thirty-three years earlier when St George and Teresa had come so close.

> He knew all about us. He said that he thought the risk was too great for any of them to have taken a bribe. It meant forfeiture of land & banishment if discovered. How Willy would have enjoyed it hearing the other side.

The Littledales were exceptional in leaving their story untold. Almost everyone else visiting Tibet in the late nineteenth century published books. The stories they brought back, taken at face value by the public, were often compromised: by a lack of Tibetan, the difficulties of functioning at high altitude in a hostile environment, and often just naked prejudice. Henry Savage Landor's *In Forbidden Tibet* was one particularly egregious example: in its excoriation of Tibetans and their way of life, not much more than fantasy. ('The Lamas are said to have a great craving for human blood, which, they say, gives them strength, genius and vigour.') Needless to say, the reviewers loved it. 'Why should people write falsehoods about us,' wrote the Tibetan emigré Rinchen Lhamo in the 1920s, fed up with the steady flow of twisted perspectives on her country; 'why should they write at all of things they do not know?'

In the absence of Tibetan voices, and with proper scholarship on the Himalaya still emerging, it was these versions of Tibet that would have primacy in the public imagination, skewing the world's understanding even now. For some, Tibet was a mystical blank on the map, a place about which you could say almost anything because there was almost no one to contradict you. Tibet became an otherworldly place that promised ancient, esoteric answers to a spiritual dislocation provoked in Europe by rapid industrialisation. As Martin Brauen put it in *Dreamworld Tibet*:

> In the late nineteenth century, in non-missionary literature Tibet was able more and more to signify a mountain towering above the sorrows and problems of the world, an island of seekers.

The woman who did more than anyone else to foster this image of Tibet was Helena Blavatsky, the Russian-born occultist and chief spiritual architect of the Theosophical Society, a synthesis of 'science, religion and philosophy' that would revive a lost and ancient system of knowledge. Essentially an occultist, Blavatsky started her esoteric travels in Egyptology and then moved on to Tibet which appeared to be a much less crowded field. Central to her arcane belief system, which had some rather dark notions about evolution, were the Masters of Ancient Wisdom, also known as the Mahatmas. She claimed to have been instructed by two of them, called Mourya and Koot Humi, in the monastery of Tashilhunpo in Tibet, although neither of them was Tibetan. There isn't a shred of evidence that Blavatsky ever went to Tibet, although she did travel in the Himalaya, causing a minor sensation in Simla. Rudyard Kipling's father Lockwood described her as among 'the most interesting and unscrupulous impostors' he had ever met.

Her genius, if that's the right word, was blending together disparate ingredients, some fact, many others fiction, into a chimera of spiritual feeling that would comfort isolated and anxious individuals with the promise of redemption, that modern life was not as mundane and meaningless as it seemed. Take for example the concept of 'vril', an 'all-permeating fluid' which first appears in Edward Bulwer-Lytton's proto-science-fiction novel *The Coming Race*, published in 1871. At the time Bulwer-Lytton was a hugely popular novelist and a politician, the man who coined the phrase, 'the pen is mightier than the sword'. Vril was a kind of power or strength, and it briefly caught on. A Scottish butcher called John Lawson Johnston used the name to market his nutritious beef stock: Bovril. Blavatsky cheerfully scooped up vril and wove it into the complex spiritual fantasy-world she created. 'The name vril may be a fiction;' she wrote. '[But] the Force itself is a fact doubted as little in India as the existence itself of their Rishis, since it is mentioned in all the secret works.'

Unlike Savage Landor's portrayal of Tibet, full of cannibalistic monks and sexual depravity, Mahatma Koot Hoomi showed Blavatsky a very different Tibetan world:

> For centuries we have had in Thibet a moral, pure hearted, simple people, unblest with civilization, hence – untainted by its vices. For ages has been Thibet the last corner of the globe not so entirely corrupted as to preclude the mingling together of the two atmospheres – the physical and the spiritual.

This was the Tibet that would fix itself in the Western imagination and remains influential, as though we were still to assess modern Africa through the prism of the Tarzan legend. When Arthur Conan Doyle wanted to resurrect Sherlock Holmes following his apparent death at the Reichenbach Falls, it was only natural that he should emerge from mystical Tibet; the Tibetan novelist Jamyang Norbu wrote a pastiche of what the detective got up to in *The Mandala of Sherlock Holmes*.

Blavatsky was not the only fantasist to weave Tibet into her story. George Gurdjieff, the mystical 'man of the fourth dimension' who came to prominence in the early 1920s, also claimed to have lived in Tibet, although there's no evidence that he did either. Neither did the Hungarian-born con man and former Liberal member of parliament Ignaz Trebitsch-Lincoln, who founded his own Geluk-pa monastery in Shanghai and promised to help the Nazis turn Asia's Buddhists against the British. Nor had Cyril Hoskin, a plumber from Devon who under the name Lobsang Rampa wrote *The Third Eye*, a wholly fictitious account of growing up as a monk in Tibet, which became an international bestseller following publication in 1956 despite being quickly unmasked as a fraud. Hoskin simply said that like Blavatsky he had been inhabited with the spirit of Lobsang Rampa. It was these fictional versions of Tibet that filled the vacuum, tilting the world's understanding at significant cost.

The myth of the 'forbidden' city of Lhasa and the fantasies invented around its 'secrets' would have dangerous consequences. As the Tibetan historian Tsering Shakya wrote:

> The Western perception of Tibet and the images that have clustered around Tibet have hampered the Tibetan political cause. The constant mythologisation of Tibet has obscured and confused the real nature of the Tibetan political struggle.

When the Tibetan state finally threw off the last shreds of Qing hegemony, those misconceptions would skew western engagement with an old nation resuming its place on the world stage.

14

The Plant Hunters

At the Chelsea Flower Show in the spring of 1926, delayed for a week by the General Strike, the British public was riveted by a sensational new flower that seemed like the stuff of legend. It came from south-eastern Tibet, country as strange and remote as the moon, and yet here it was in England, apparently prospering as though it were native. In the history of horticulture, few plants achieved such popularity so rapidly as the Tibetan blue poppy. Strictly speaking, it wasn't a poppy at all but a *meconopsis*, from the Greek meaning 'like a poppy' but the distinction was too fine for many to care. For the American gardener and biographer Eleanor Perenyi, they were the 'color of a summer day, with golden anthers'. The familiar red poppy had been adopted in 1921 by Field Marshal Alexander Haig as a remembrance of the sacrifice of the Great War; the blue poppy was both an echo of that sacrifice and a fresh start. Blue flowers had been a powerful motif in Romanticism, a symbol of love, but also of the infinite and the unreachable. And where else would this ideal originate but mysterious, spiritual Tibet?

The following year, seedlings of the blue poppy went on sale at Chelsea for a guinea each: three days' wages for a labourer. Thomas Hay, superintendent of the Royal Parks in London bedded out massed displays of the new flower in Hyde Park, delighting the public and inspiring amateur gardeners to try for themselves. Alas, blue poppies proved fiendishly difficult to grow: Perenyi dubbed them her 'abominable snowman' so conspicuous were they by their absence, despite repeated attempts.

I have never seen it – not the tiniest shoot having come up from repeated sowings. ... I would give anything for a glimpse of it even in somebody else's garden.

In his memoirs, Russell Page, the impossibly tall designer of gardens
for everyone from the Duchess of Windsor to Oscar de la Renta,
judged the blue poppy 'as difficult to succeed with as the philosopher's
stone'. (Always tuned to the infinite, Page married as his first wife
Lida, niece of the mystic George Gurdjieff; his second was the widow
of poet René Daumal, author of *Mount Analogue*.)

Such judgments, not quite deserved, were a disappointment for the
slight, taciturn man who more than anyone was responsible for the
sensation the blue poppy made in 1926. Frank Kingdon-Ward was not
the first European to discover or even collect the blue poppy; that
distinction went to a French missionary forty years earlier. Kingdon-
Ward wasn't even the first Briton: that was the enigmatic explorer,
spy and diplomat Eric Bailey, recorded in the Latin name for one of
the handful of species of blue poppy, *Meconopsis baileyi*. Bailey had
discovered the flower before the Great War in south-east Tibet while
exploring the secrets of the Tsangpo gorges. Yet it was Kingdon-Ward,
a gifted plant collector, who was able to collect viable seed and bring
the plant to market, a landmark in his long career.

The son of Harry Marshall Ward, professor of botany at Cambridge
University, Frank had once heard a friend of his father say: 'There are
places up the Brahmaputra where no white man has ever been.' As a
boy, the notion of discovery thrilled him. In 1924 he was 'up the
Brahmaputra' himself, three hundred kilometres east of Lhasa and
following in the footsteps of his hero Eric Bailey, gazing at the flower
that would make him famous. 'Never,' he wrote in *The Riddle of the
Tsangpo Gorges*,

> have I seen a blue poppy which held out such high hopes of being
> hardy, and of easy cultivation in Britain. Being a woodland plant it will
> suffer less from the tricks of our uncertain climate; coming from a
> moderate elevation, it is accustomed to that featureless average of
> weather which we know so well how to provide it with; and being
> perennial, it will not exasperate gardeners.

It did exasperate gardeners, but Kingdon-Ward's description reveals
his genius as a plant hunter, perhaps the last of the great collectors
who with immense courage and expertise travelled the Himalaya. In
relocating the valuable species they found there around the world,

they enriched the gardens of Europe and North America and transformed economies. Just as the growing awareness of Buddhism, from
the patient scholarship of Eugène Burnouf and Sylvain Lévi to the
wild imaginings of Helena Blavatsky, changed the philosophical and
spiritual landscape of Europe, botany's exploration of the intensely
biodiverse eastern Himalaya would alter its physical landscape too.
But gardeners at horticultural shows on both side of the Atlantic were
not the only beneficiaries of this exchange: plants travelled in the
opposite direction too, into the Himalaya, in some cases a catalyst for
social, economic and demographic upheaval with long-term political
consequences that still ripple outwards today.

★

There was nothing new about plant hunting. Our species has been
relocating other species for pleasure and profit since we began. Ancient
Egyptians sent out expeditions to find the trees that produced the resin
they burned in their temples. What changed in the eighteenth century
was epistemological: Sweden's Carl Linnaeus, the 'prince of botanists',
founder of modern ecology, created a workable system of binomial
classification for every species on earth. With a reliable intellectual
structure in place to study the earth's plants and creatures, exploration
had a powerful new tool with which to approach the undiscovered.
In 1768 Linnaeus' pupil and fellow Swede Daniel Solander took leave
from his job cataloguing the collection at the British Museum to join
the wealthy naturalist Joseph Banks on board James Cook's *Endeavour*
for its famous three-year voyage, first to Tahiti to witness the transit
of Venus, then in search of Antarctica. When *Endeavour* reached home
in July 1771, it was Banks, not Cook, whom London applauded loudest.
George III gave him great influence at the Royal Botanic Gardens at
Kew and the energetic Banks used the opportunity to encourage more
botanists to go exploring. He had brought home an extensive plant
collection – or *herbarium* – from his voyage round the world but little
that would grow. What he wanted were living specimens, bulbs, roots
and seeds, shipped home as quickly as possible.

The first professional collector he sent into the field was Francis
Masson in 1772 and to the place that had most inspired Banks on his
travels: South Africa. Much later in life and confined to a wheelchair

by gout, Banks suggested to a young Norfolk-born botanist called William Jackson Hooker that he go to Iceland. It was the first collecting trip of what would turn out to be a remarkable career. Although a second expedition to Ceylon had to be shelved, at great personal expense, Hooker made further collecting trips in Europe and built a reputation as a botanic writer and collector, partly to pay his debts. In 1820, he was appointed professor of botany at Glasgow University, where he helped establish the Royal Botanic Institution of Glasgow to supply the university with medicinal plants; later he persuaded the British government to include scientists on official expeditions. In 1841, by then in his mid fifties, he took over as director of the Royal Botanic Gardens at Kew. It was an auspicious moment. Botany was playing an increasingly important role in the economic development of the British Empire and Kew, along with the Royal Botanic Gardens in Edinburgh, was central to that, breeding viable commercial species for the various colonies' particular climates and locations. The abolition of tax on glass, 'that absurd impost on light' as *The Lancet* described it, also allowed a rapid expansion of commercial greenhouses. Technology was catching up with aspiration and Kew and Edinburgh became the engines of what was known as 'economic botany'.

All plant hunters faced challenges, but the deep gorges and steep slopes of the Himalaya were remote and their geography poorly known. And while an experienced collector could scan a mountainside for the unfamiliar, they still faced the challenge of reaching their target and assessing its potential, be it aesthetic or commercial, or both. They also had to do this twice, first when the plant was flowering and then again when it produced seed, meaning the collector would have to know its precise location often in areas that hadn't yet been mapped. And of course there was always the risk that by the time they returned the plant might have been eaten or crushed. If it was intact, then the collector faced hours of painstaking work each evening, preparing herbarium specimens, writing up detailed notes, drying and cleaning seeds and packing everything so that the seeds remained viable.

One great advantage that Edwardian collectors like Kingdon-Ward enjoyed was access to a terrarium, a sealable glass container. The terrarium, known at first as a Wardian case after its inventor Nathaniel Bagshaw Ward, is one of those inventions that most people have never heard of even though it radically changed the world. Before Ward,

specimens collected by plant hunters had only a narrow chance of
making it home in a viable state. Many plants travelled badly, especially
at sea, exposed to salt spray on deck or else hidden in the dark below,
and sailors were disinclined to share valuable drinking water with a
plant if it began to run low. The problem was recognised as a major
hurdle preventing the spread of valuable crops around the world.
Ward's invention would overcome this problem, another chain in the
link of our hyperconnected world.

Born in 1791 and raised in the Essex town of Plaistow, Nathaniel
Ward was the son of a doctor who followed his father's example,
plying his trade from 'dingy dwellings' in Wellclose Square in London's
docklands, very much a Dickensian scene, wreathed in smog that
poisoned Ward's garden and his collection of ferns. (Joseph Conrad
lived there too, as a young sailor a few years after Ward's death.) As
a boy he would get up at three in the morning to go botanising in
the Essex countryside and his deep knowledge and medical background
put him at the heart of London's scientific society. Most early botanists
were medical men, since the remedies, syrups, powders and ointments
they gave their patients grew in gardens or wild in the countryside:
materia medica, as it was known. Most of the botanic gardens founded
in the era were linked to hospitals.

Ward was an entomologist as well as a gardener, and in the late
1820s, looking into a sealed glass bottle that contained the pupa of a
moth and some leaf mould, he noticed that seeds trapped in the bottle
were germinating. He put the jar on a window ledge and over the
next few months watched them grow into common species of grass
and fern. It was only when the bottle top failed – four years later –
that the plants died. Through the 1830s Ward experimented with sealed
glass containers, proving beyond doubt that plants could thrive in a
well-lit closed environment without the need for watering. Moisture
could be recycled almost indefinitely, condensing out of the air at
night to soak the soil once more. Two prototypes were sent to Australia
with British plants that happily survived the journey. Then the boxes
were cleaned out and returned to Ward with the Australian fern
Gleichenia microphylla growing inside. Despite a trip around Cape Horn,
the fern was alive and well when it reached London.

Among the first people Ward told about his long and patient research
was William Hooker, whose son Joseph Dalton Hooker became one

of the first plant collectors to use the invention in the field. Joseph, William's second son, is most widely known now as the friend and correspondent of Charles Darwin but his career as a botanist was even more glittering than his father's. Towards the end of his life, during a speech to the Royal Society, he described himself as a 'puppet of natural selection', growing up in a household steeped in botany and exploration. He was identifying mosses as a small boy and sitting on his grandfather's knee reading Cook's *Voyages*. Although in his youth he suffered from croup – his mother dubbed him 'croaky Joe' – any infirmity disappeared as he grew. He worked hard and became phys-ically strong. His father recalled how Joseph once walked the forty kilometres home from Helensburgh rather than wait for the steamer back to Glasgow. In a firmament of heroes peopled by James Cook and Joseph Banks, the idea of exploration was always in his mind. In 1837, he enrolled in an astronomy class to get the practical and theo-retical knowledge he needed to survey. It was time well spent. Sixty-six years later, when Hooker was eighty-six, he received a telegram from British officers of the Sikkim-Tibet Boundary Commission, including Francis Younghusband and David Prain, who would succeed him at Kew, congratulating Hooker on his surveying efforts there.

William was always on the lookout for his son's interests, so when at a friend's house he met Captain James Clark Ross, commander of a proposed Antarctic voyage, he suggested Joseph be included in the party as a naturalist. Ross agreed, but only if the young man had completed his medical training and served in the Royal Navy. The expedition left Chatham Dockyard in September 1839 and would last almost exactly four years. It remains among the most significant voyages in the history of British exploration. It also made Joseph Hooker's reputation, not just as a capable and thoughtful botanist, especially on plant distribution, but also as a hugely entertaining correspondent; his letters are among the best of any explorer, shining with energy and interest.

Much had changed by the time the expedition's two boats *Erebus* and *Terror* finally returned, dropping anchor at Folkestone in September 1843. Hooker's father had achieved a long-held ambition to become director of Kew and was transforming an institution only recently threatened with closure. Joseph, who learned of his father's promotion while in Australia, had sent home a stream of exciting new discoveries.

In the Antarctic, Hooker learned his older brother Willy had died in Jamaica of yellow fever and his sister Mary Harriette of consumption.

In the aftermath of Hooker's epic adventure, he developed a friendship with Darwin that provided one of the most significant correspondences in the history of science. He had met Darwin for the first time in 1839, shortly before he left for Antarctica, walking through Charing Cross with Robert McCormick, who had served on the *Beagle* and was surgeon on Ross's ship *Erebus*. Hooker was now returned from Antarctica 'well salted', having shed a little of the Puritan strictness that had characterised his upbringing. Darwin felt increasingly confident in testing his ideas of natural selection on the young botanist. Both had travelled to remote places, like Tierra del Fuego, and Darwin was supportive of Hooker's *Flora Antarctica*, his classic work on the expedition's botanical discoveries.

Despite recently getting engaged and starting a new job, Hooker was restless. He wanted to travel again and botanise somewhere new and exciting, perhaps in the tropics but certainly in India. He had good contacts there: Hugh Falconer, superintendent of the Botanic Garden at Saharanpur in northern India, was one; Falconer suggested the kingdom of Sikkim as somewhere new to investigate. Another was a botanist friend from student days in Glasgow. Thomas Thomson had served as a doctor during the Anglo-Sikh wars of the 1840s and then been appointed to the commission aimed at settling the border between Ladakh and Tibet. The commission was largely thwarted in its aims, so Thomson had spent much of his time botanising in Ladakh and Zanskar. With the quickening march of economic botany, the transforming technology of Wardian cases and his father's new position at Kew it seemed the perfect moment for Hooker to explore new frontiers in the world's highest mountains.

Europeans had been plant collecting in the Himalaya for more than half a century before Hooker arrived. Collection had been part of George Bogle's mission to Tibet of 1774, and in 1796 the naturalist Thomas Hardwicke had been part of a collecting mission to Garhwal. Ten years earlier, the Calcutta Botanical Garden had been founded, initially to identify and develop plants of commercial value. By the 1830s the garden had developed a strong scientific foundation, first through William Roxburgh, who introduced mahogany to India, and then the Danish-born surgeon Nathaniel Wallich, whose catalogue of

Indian plants exceeded eight thousand. Few went plant hunting in India without consulting Wallich and sending him new species. The Himalaya was now part of this expanding body of botanical knowledge: Edward Gardner sent him plants from the garden of the Kathmandu residency and William Moorcroft from the western Himalaya. Wallich himself had spent the whole of 1821 in Nepal collecting plants and published a short monograph on Nepali botany, *Tentamen Florae Napalensis Illustratae*. John Forbes Royle, another medical man, was in 1823 made director of the botanic garden at Saharanpur, founded in an old Pashtun palace at the foot of the Himalaya. He worked on the medicinal value of Himalayan plants, publishing *Illustrations of the botany and other branches of natural history of the Himalayan mountains and of the flora of Cashmere* in 1839. Royle was among the first botanists to suggest that the cinchona tree, the source of the anti-malarial quinine, might be grown in India.

One of the earliest British interventions in Himalayan horticulture was the humble potato. Warren Hastings had encouraged his Tibet envoy George Bogle to conduct an experiment on his journey through Bhutan, planting potatoes on each stage of his route to see if they would flourish. 'Don't return without something to shew where you have been,' Hastings told him,

> though it be but a contraband Walnutt, a pilfered Slip of Sweet Briar, or the Seeds of a Bootea Turnip taken in *Payment* for the Potatoes you have given them *gratis*.

Samuel Turner, following in Bogle's footsteps nine years later, judged the experiment a failure having been shown 'a small specimen of potatoes' that had been grown in Bhutan, 'not bigger than boys' marbles'. Turner concluded that 'either from ignorance or idleness', the people of Bhutan had 'failed in the cultivation of this valuable root'.

A decade after Samuel Turner's journey to Tibet, William Kirkpatrick arrived in Kathmandu on his stillborn mission to mediate between the Gorkhalis and the Qing.

> I had heard, before my visit ... that our most esteemed kitchen vegetables did not only grow there in much higher perfection than in Bengal,

but that the propagation of them was annually continued from their own seed ... My disappointment, therefore, was very great on finding the fact otherwise, and on being assured that they could not raise even potatoes, without procuring every year from Patna fresh roots for sowing; I think it extremely probable, however, that their failure in this respect has been occasioned solely by want of attention or skill, having no doubt ... that with proper management, there are few of our hortulan productions, whether fruit, flower, or herb, which might not be successfully reared, and abundantly multiplied ... in the valley of Nepaul.

Potatoes had been in India for over a century by that point, introduced by the Portuguese not long after arriving in Europe. They now spread through the Himalaya along with seasonal labourers returning home from British hill stations. Frederick Young, the Irish officer who had commanded the Sirmur batallion in the war with Gorkha, planted potatoes at Mussoorie, the hill station he founded. Kathmandu's potatoes almost certainly came from Patna. Those in western Nepal arrived from Simla or Naini Tal and in the east from Darjeeling. Francis Buchanan-Hamilton, later briefly the superintendent at the Calcutta Botanic Garden, visited Nepal a decade after Kirkpatrick and in one brief comment managed to report that the people of the Himalaya were getting to grips with the potato while at the same time maintaining a prejudice against them:

In the hilly parts of the country *Solanum tuberosum* [the potato] has been introduced, and grows tolerably; but it does not thrive so well as at Patna, owing probably to a want of care.

Buchanan-Hamilton had made a typically arrogant assumption about the competence of Nepali farmers. In fact, over the next few decades, the introduction of the potato and the success of its cultivation by local farmers would lead to a Himalayan population boom, just as it had in Europe, as experimentation yielded results and subsistence farmers benefitted from more easily won calories. Monasteries in the Himalaya were among the potato's greatest champions, since its cultivation wasn't as labour-intensive, and so freed up time for religious duties. Potatoes made the biggest impact at higher altitudes, strengthening the resilience of highland communities like the Sherpa and allowing them to occupy higher habitations through the winter. The crop was so productive that Sherpas didn't have to commit so much land to get a substantial reward. They learned how to store potatoes in pits, or by drying them in the cold dry air of high altitude for use in stews or trade with Tibet, or else turned them to powder. Even today, potatoes grown in the Everest region are appreciated elsewhere in the country for their taste. The wider Himalayan region has proved astonishingly inventive with the humble *alu*, as it is known there. As the Nepali writer Ramyata Limbu put it:

> People in Palpa are proud of their *aloo chukauni* [dressed in yoghurt], plains Nepalis enjoy *aloo bhujia* [spicy potatoes] with roti [flatbread], those living in the highlands salivate over *aloo bhat* [with rice] and *aloo daal* [with lentils]. Sometimes even better on a cold, dark winter's day is plain *usineko aloo*, boiled potatoes with marcha chillies pounded with salt and garlic. In the realm of the spud, Nepal might well be tops.

The crop that most exercised the East India Company was not potatoes, however, but tea, *Camellia sinensis*. From the middle of the eighteenth century it had been the most popular drink in Britain, outselling even beer. The British drank a fifth of what the Chinese could grow. Light and easy to transport, tea and the trade in it with China were the foundation of the Company's fate and consequently part of Britain's strategic interest: ten per cent of British tax revenues came from the sale of tea, and the East India Company's tea trade with China was worth as much as all its other business there – from silk to porcelain – put together. Yet in the populist, anti-mercantilist atmosphere of the 1830s, the days of the Company's monopoly on Asian trade were numbered. In 1834 it lost its monopoly in China and the need to end its reliance on Chinese tea intensified.

It was not that tea didn't grow in India. Earlier in the nineteenth century, the Scot Robert Bruce had discovered a plant that looked like tea growing at sea level in Assam. The local Singpho people he met were drinking a brew made from the plant and he tried some: it tasted a bit like tea. In the 1830s, a few years after Robert Bruce's death, his brother Charles sent the plant to Calcutta to be examined. Bruce had been right: it was tea, but a different variety. Hugh Falconer, Hooker's contact in India, was by the 1830s superintendent of the botanical gardens at Saharanpur in the modern state of Uttar Pradesh. Falconer's time there is famous for the fossil hunting he did in the Siwalik hills, finding the first fossilised monkey skull at the foot of the Himalaya, and for his subsequent correspondence with Darwin. But he also conceived the idea of growing Chinese tea in the Himalaya, persuading the Company to explore the idea. A committee was set up and in the *Journal of the Asiatic Society*, Falconer laid out in magisterial detail the growing conditions found in China and the problems of replicating them on the plains of India. 'In the Himalaya mountains', on the other hand,

> the case is widely different: excepting periodical rains, all the conditions of a temperate climate are here found, and here above all parts of India, we may look for the successful cultivation of tea.

Part of Falconer's plan was to acquire tea seeds from China. These duly arrived in 1835 and were dispersed to several sites throughout India to be grown experimentally. George William Traill, in one of his last acts as the commissioner of Kumaon, helped select sites there that would within a few years have expanded to several acres and thousands of tea bushes under Falconer's watchful eye. A plant collector was also despatched to locate the tea bushes the Bruce brothers had discovered, and Nathaniel Wallich was commissioned to investigate the possibility of growing this indigenous tea in north-east India. At the age of forty-nine, in poor health, Wallich set out for the leech-filled forests of the north-east. With him went John McClelland, 'a persevering Scotchman, without much ability' according to Hooker, and William Griffith, a brilliant botanist and capable artist who was far more highly regarded. Wallich couldn't hide his jealousy of his more able and much younger colleague and had the unfortunate habit of bursting into tears. Eventually he returned to Calcutta and Griffith continued to the Mishmi hills and Lohit valley in the modern state of Arunachal Pradesh.

That year the Company also began growing the indigenous plant in the highlands of Assam. Falconer insisted that Chinese tea processors were hired to offer their expertise. Unluckily for the East India Company, the men came from a low-quality green tea area and over the years proved mediocre workers and reluctant teachers. Worse, the

Assam leaves had a strong, malty flavour, and though there was a flurry of interest when the first cases arrived in London, it didn't suit a British taste matured on more subtle Chinese tea. The Assam plant's low productivity also made it uneconomic. Even so, the experiment was not a total failure. The Company was acquiring experience of growing tea in India at a commercial scale, laying the foundation for eventual success.

Since the eighteenth century, the East India Company had been selling opium to China and buying tea with the proceeds. Not only had this pernicious trade generated colossal revenues for the British government, it was still financing expansion in India, culminating in the mid 1840s with expensive wars against the Sikh Empire on the North-West Frontier. But it was a trade that was growing ever more vulnerable. In 1839 the Qing emperor had cracked down on opium, culminating with the destruction of hundreds of tonnes held by foreign merchants at Canton. At a stroke, foreign merchants lost, in today's terms, hundreds of millions of dollars. Britain sent gunboats, and despite Qing defiance, China's feeble navy was overcome. The British used this, the First Opium War, to gain greater access to more Chinese ports in the Treaty of Nanking of 1842, forcing a resentful China to open a little more to foreign influence.

This new relationship was clearly unstable. China's humiliation, a raw nerve even now, made for a volatile situation. In 1844, Henry Hardinge, an old soldier who had fought Napoleon, arrived in India as governor general. His time in office was marked by victory over the Sikhs and the Treaty of Amritsar but he also warned of the dangers a wounded China might hold.

It is in my opinion by no means improbable that in a few years the Government of Pekin [Beijing], by legalising the cultivation of Opium in China, where the soil has been already proved equally well adapted with India to the growth of the plant, may deprive this Government of one of its present chief sources of revenue.

In which case, Hardinge argued, it was 'most desirable to afford every encouragement to the cultivation of Tea in India'. More money and land was made available to speed up the development of India's tea industry.

The place for this cultivation had now been firmly established. The middle hills of the eastern Himalaya offered the equivalent of China's best tea-growing regions: high in altitude, its soils richly nutritious and sufficiently wet, often clouded in dampness and in winter frosty enough to add complexity, sweetness and flavour. While British growers still had no access to China's tea plantations, the experiments with Chinese seed were starting to bear fruit. Hardinge had given authorisation to commercial plantations at Kangra, in modern Himachal Pradesh, and the new hill station of Darjeeling. The tea was processed, packed and shipped to England, arriving at the Company's offices on Leadenhall Street in the City of London on 12 January 1848. The tea was sent out to the most important brokers: the House of Twinings, Miller and Lowcock, Gibbs and Peek Brothers. Their verdict, when it came, was hugely encouraging. The tea was a far better proposition than the Assam variety. In fact, it was almost as good as the best from China: almost, but not quite. The only stumbling block was the seed available to Canton wasn't a patch on that from the best tea-growing areas and the manufacturers lacked the finesse of their Chinese counterparts.

*

British imperial wealth rested heavily on botanical knowledge. From spices and dyes to cotton and opium, knowing what plants grew where was the first step in exploiting them. But Joseph Hooker's ambitions were intellectually wider than commercial exploitation. He wanted to know *why* plants grew where they did. Understanding the principles – climate, altitude, soil chemistry and so on – that underpinned the geographic distribution of plants meant a greater chance of them thriving elsewhere. That was what he wanted to study in Sikkim. He travelled to India on the navy ship *Sidon*, docking at Calcutta on the very day that the first batch of Indian-cultivated Chinese tea arrived in Leadenhall. Also on board was the Earl of Dalhousie, Hardinge's replacement as governor general. Dalhousie was a workaholic widely blamed for the disaster of the 1857 rebellion but someone who also brought the advances of Victorian Britain – the railways and telegraph – to India, tying its disparate regions together just as a national movement sparked into life. Hooker and Dalhousie got on famously, although the botanist's attempts to interest his distinguished new friend in his subject were hopeless. On the voyage out, stopping briefly in the Middle East, they took a trip into the desert. Hooker found some gum arabic, a significant export from British colonies in Africa, and so perhaps of interest to a former president of the Board of Trade. But Dalhousie 'chucked it out of the carriage window; and the Rose of Jericho, with an interest about it of a totally different character, met with no better fate'. Tea was another matter.

> The Governor-General [Hooker wrote to his father at Kew] hints to me that he would like reports on the Tea districts of India ... I need not say that I shall lay myself out to attend to his wishes in India.

While in Calcutta, Hooker spent much time at the botanic gardens where Hugh Falconer had recently been appointed superintendent. Until he arrived, John McClelland was in charge. Hooker found McLelland preparing William Griffith's journals for publication following Griffith's death at Malacca three years earlier of a liver parasite, aged just thirty-four. The clash between Griffith and Wallich had caused real damage to the gardens. While Wallich was away on sick leave, Griffith had completely remodelled their layout to better suit a scientific institution and in doing so caused many plants to fail. McLelland had tried to improve things but with only mixed success. 'The Library is in dreadful confusion, just as Wallich left it, and the Herbarium worse,' Hooker told his father. He wrote a long letter to Falconer with his recommendations for the future, laying the ground-work for closer cooperation between Kew and Calcutta in the coming years.

In April 1848 the young botanist arrived at Darjeeling, where he would spend much of the next two years in its 'Greenock-like climate'. (Darjeeling gets a lot of rain. The diabolist and mountaineer Aleister Crowley, en route for Kangchenjunga, complained: 'The whole town stinks of mildew.') Hooker met Brian Houghton Hodgson soon afterwards, in the garden of Hodgson's bungalow where the former resident of Kathmandu was 'talking Tibetan to a Chinese-looking man' about the geography of Central Asia. Hodgson had retired to a forest clearing in the new hill station of Darjeeling, having returned to the Himalaya after an awkward period at home. Despite the concern and love of his family, particularly his sister Fanny, now married to a Dutch district court judge and living in Arnhem, Hodgson had realised he was 'alienated entirely from European ways from the first to last'. Since returning, he had developed a new interest to set alongside his passion for the birdlife and mammals of the Himalaya: the region's ethnically and culturally diverse human population. As a kind of proto-anthropologist, he was determined to describe in detail 'the Aborigines of the frontier in its Mountains and its Tarai'.

Hooker was thirty-one and Hodgson forty-eight but the difference seemed even greater. Hodgson declared he was plagued with insomnia and Hooker judged his new friend 'ill & nervous to such a degree that he fancies the Darjeeling doctors want to kill him'. Yet although Hooker told his father that Hodgson was 'said to quarrel with every one, and in truth is as proud a man as I ever met', they became firm friends and during the monsoon Hooker came to live with his reclusive mentor. He told his family that they had become like brothers and that he would always regard Hodgson 'as one of my dearest friends on earth'. Excited to have someone as knowledgeable as Hooker interested in his life's work, Hodgson was happy to share his knowledge of Himalayan natural history, which Hooker saw as 'the very best chance for me that could have occurred'. Later, out of gratitude, Hooker would name a species of rhododendron after his friend, despite Hodgson's protestations.

The young botanist was blessed in having such powerful contacts. Dalhousie could open political doors and Hodgson furnished him with the knowledge he needed to make the most of his time in Sikkim. Getting permission for his visit was more problematic. The tiny kingdom of Sikkim and its indigenous Lepcha population, with smaller numbers of Limbus and Magars, had been ruled since the mid seventeenth century by the Namgyal family, which originated in eastern Tibet. Rulers were called *chogyal,* dharma kings, but the geographic space they occupied was vulnerable, surrounded by more aggressive powers: Hooker likened it to Poland, despite its small size. Bhutan had invaded in the early eighteenth century and Sikkim was prey to frequent raids from the Gorkhali regime in Kathmandu. Squeezed from all sides, when the Gorkhas captured the capital at Rabdentse and the *chogyal* fled to Tibet, Sikkim found support from the Qing, who in 1793 pushed back the Gorkhas and restored the *chogyal*'s young

son to the throne. This was the ruler Hooker would meet as a weakened old man.

As Qing power waned and the British arrived, the *chogyal* Tsugphud
Namgyal found a new ally against the Gorkha regime. In 1814 the
Gorkhalis once again overran Sikkim's eastern territory, but the East
India Company restored the *chogyal* and in 1817 he signed a treaty with
the British. Hooker thought this treaty feeble, since, as he told his
mother in a letter that June,

> we did not demand even a nominal tribute from the Rajah, who at
> once fell under the influence of China, whose policy it is to rule the
> Councils and hearts, but not the people, of these three Border powers;
> and by teaching them a wholesome dread of the English, they exclude
> the latter from these several States and prevent our interfering with
> the Chinese Trade from the East into Thibet.

This was disingenuous on Hooker's part. The British had gained plenty.
That portion of Sikkim occupied by the Gorkhalis was ceded to the
East India Company and in 1835, when the Company decided it also
wanted Darjeeling and its district, 2,500 square kilometres of territiory,
the *chogyal* had little option but to accept the terms offered: an annual
pension of three thousand rupees. The written contract was short
and ambiguous. In the *chogyal*'s mind, he was being paid rent for
Darjeeling; the British regarded the territory as theirs for good.

The man who made Darjeeling was Archibald Campbell. Born on
the Scottish island of Islay, he had studied medicine at Glasgow and
Edinburgh and joined the Bengal Medical Service, serving as surgeon
under Hodgson in Kathmandu before his appointment as superintendent of the new hill station in 1839. When he arrived in Darjeeling it
was 'an inaccessible tract of forest, with a very scanty population' but
in little more than a decade the energetic Scot had overseen the
construction of not just the sanatorium that had inspired its acquisition but a small town as well. A road was built, scores of European
houses, a bazaar and jail. A local militia was formed and the practice
of forced labour ended. Campbell also experimented with the introduction of new crops, including in 1841 tea acquired from gardens in
Kumaon that had planted Chinese seed. (Twenty years later one of
these bushes was twenty feet high and fifty feet in circumference.) By

1852, the year the first commercial tea garden was planted, the station was already generating revenues of fifty thousand rupees from farming and forestry, substantially more than the few hundred rupees it had earned the *chogyal*.

As political agent or officer for Sikkim, Archie Campbell was a necessary ally for Hooker in getting permission to enter the kingdom. But Campbell had fallen out with Calcutta and was at first reluctant to push the request, much to Hooker's frustration. 'The Govt. won't order Campbell to send me without the Rajah's consent for fear of a war with China; Campbell won't run the risk of committing himself without an order!' Even so, as Campbell was an old friend of Hodgson it was almost inevitable that the two men would get to know each other well during Hooker's stay in Darjeeling. Campbell's young children adored Hooker who returned the compliment by naming a rhododendron for their mother, just as he had for Hodgson. While negotiations continued, Hooker explored the hills first around Darjeeling and then further north along the Rangit river, moving beyond British jurisdiction to where it met the Tista. He collected several magnolias, three of which Falconer confirmed were new to science, and three new rhododendrons, 'one, the most lovely thing you can imagine, a parasite on gigantic trees, three yards high, with whorls of branches, and 3–6 immense white, deliciously sweet-scented flowers at the apex of each branch'. This he named *Rhododendron dalhousiae* for his patron in Calcutta.

Hooker's attitude to the indigenous population was often arrogantly dismissive, typically so for his race and class, even among men of science. Like Falconer, he regarded the people of India as incapable of ruling themselves. If politics were threatening to thwart his ambitions then why shouldn't he get involved himself? The *chogyal*'s ambassadors, Hooker wrote, had been chosen 'for their insolence and incapacity'. The key figure blocking his progress was Tokhan Namgyal, the new chief minister, a Tibetan married to the *chogyal*'s illegitimate daughter. In Darjeeling he was called the Pagla Dewan: the 'crazy minister'. He was certainly anti-British, anxious about the reaction of the Qing envoys in Lhasa to a visit from the neighbouring empire. His conduct Hooker described as 'Indo-Chinese': 'assuming, insolent, aggressive, never perpetrating open violence, but by petty insults effectually preventing all good understanding'. Hooker railed against the Sikkim government for harbouring 'notorious offenders' even though the administration at Darjeeling did the same: both authorities were short of labour and took whomever they could get. 'The Cis-Himalayan Bhoteas,' he wrote to his father, 'whether of Sikkim or, worse still, of Bhotan [Bhutan], are as uncouth a race as I ever beheld.' He wrote more sympathetically of the Lepchas, as most travellers did, and the affection was apparently reciprocated. Henry John Elwes, the next plant hunter to visit Sikkim twenty-two years later said the older Lepchas he met didn't just remember Hooker but almost worshipped him 'as an incarnation of high wisdom and kindly strength'.

Thanks to Hodgson's links to the durbar at Kathmandu, where Jang Bahadur was now in charge, Hooker got permission in the autumn of 1848 to extend his explorations into eastern Nepal and travel via the Tamur valley as far as the Tibetan border to the west of the vast peak of Kangchenjunga. He left in late October with a retinue of fifty-five and on 26 November reached the Tipta La on the border 'where he could see nothing of Thibet but had no strength to crawl farther'. He was suffering 'an excruciating headache'. There had been huge numbers of new plants to collect, including the rhododendron he named for Hodgson, and because of Darwin's interest, he was also paying close attention to the breeding of yaks. Returning south from the Ghunsa valley on 5 December, at a place Hooker called the 'Choonjerma pass', he paused to sketch a view of distant mountains that included Everest, which had been measured that year. Quite where Choonjerma is remains uncertain. The 'pundit' Chandra Das believed it was a balcony or terrace close to a pass called on modern maps the Mirgin La. Wherever Hooker stopped, it's likely he made the first recognisable image of the world's highest mountain. The setting sun reminded Hooker of the work of Turner, and as it set

the Nepal peaks to the right assumed more definite darker and gigantic forms, and floods of light shot across the misty ocean, bathing the landscape around me in the most wonderful and indescribable changing tints.

On his way back to Darjeeling, Hooker and Campbell had an audience with the ageing *chogyal* Tsugphud Namgyal and despite his continuing reluctance Hooker was finally granted access to Sikkim. The following May he set out again to explore the country east of Kangchenjunga and the headwaters of the Tista. Hooker's presence in Sikkim exposed the fault-lines among the *chogyal*'s ministers. The minister, or *dewan*, Tokhan Namgyal opposed foreign interference and did what he could to impede Hooker, but the *dewan* had a rival: Tsepa Adan, known to the British as Chebu Lama, whose clan had its origins in eastern Tibet but had over the generations intermarried with Lepchas. Because of this, Chebu was more popular within Sikkim but had, rather like Thomas Wolsey, got into trouble trying to fix the *chogyal*'s lack of an heir. He wanted an accommodation with the British, and worked in Hooker's interest, accompanying him and intervening at critical moments. This jostling for position reached its climax in early November, as Hooker and Campbell tried to cross the Cho La, a pass of over fifteen thousand feet on the Tibetan border. The *dewan* saw their actions as a provocation too far and had his men arrest Campbell, keeping him bound. By twisting the ropes that tied him, his captors compelled Campbell to write to the governor general with their demands. Back in Darjeeling, Hodgson wrote to Hooker's parents to reassure them their son was not involved, but he lost much of his collection, and equipment was stolen or damaged.

Campbell was not imprisoned for long. When the East India Company promised 'a severe retribution' Hooker and his party were delivered back to Darjeeling just in time for Christmas. The *dewan*, thinking the whole matter closed, even came with them to do some pony trading. The government in Calcutta had little sympathy for Campbell; he was judged the architect of his own misfortune. One official thought Campbell's actions 'a grave indiscretion' likely to antagonise the Chinese. A senior army officer thought it perfectly understandable that hill people would be suspicious of a European surveying their territory. Predictably, Dalhousie promoted him. Hooker, now realising the consequences of his pressure on Campbell to force their way into Sikkim, was a little chastened. Even so, for reasons of prestige Dalhousie ordered a response that was swift and stern. A powerful military force took up positions on the north bank of the Rangit against a small Buddhist nation with no army worth the name. The annual payment to Sikkim was stopped. Hundreds of square kilometres of Sikkim's terai, its most productive land, was annexed and put under the jurisdiction of Darjeeling. As the official in Calcutta noted: 'A weak power between great powers must doubly suffer.'

Even before Hooker arrived back in Britain, the field sketches, dried plants and descriptions he sent home to Kew allowed his father to publish *The Rhododendrons of Sikkim-Himalaya*, with illustrations worked up by the Scot, Walter Hood Fitch. This talented botanical artist had worked for William Hooker in Glasgow and then followed him to Kew, where he illustrated more or less everything they published. The rhododendrons were planted in Kew's hollow way, which became known as 'rhododendron dell', or else shared with botanical gardens across Europe. Rhododendrons had been known in Europe since the sixteenth century and Linnaeus had classified a small number of species in the mid eighteenth, but Hooker's publication and their presence at Kew helped spark a fascination for the plants. They fitted neatly into a changing fashion in British gardens for hardier, more naturalistic planting and proved popular on shooting estates, where they offered game birds cover.

In 1855 Hooker, whose *Himalayan Journals* and rhododendron book had received critical acclaim, was appointed assistant to his father at Kew. Over the next few years he became one of the great figures in economic botany, actively involved in transplanting some of the world's most valuable plants around the globe in Wardian cases and remaking how the world did business. The plant hunter Richard Spruce and Clements Markham, who later ran the Royal Geographical Society and launched the career of the Antarctic explorer Robert Falcon Scott, brought the cinchona tree, source of the anti-malarial quinine, back to Kew from the Andes. Thousands of seedlings were grown and distributed to experimental sites including Darjeeling, where, against Hooker's expectations, it flourished. The cost of quinine plummeted, becoming affordable even for the poor. Cork oaks went to the Punjab, chocolate to Ceylon, Liberian coffee to the West Indies. There were crazes for rhododendrons and orchids. But the greatest prize, in economic terms at least, was rubber. Hooker persuaded the government to back expeditions to acquire seeds of the tree, *Hevea brasiliensis*, from the Amazon to grow them at Kew. After years of effort, seedlings were shipped to Malaya and Sri Lanka, establishing a lucrative colonial industry that materially affected Britain's ability to fight two world wars. (Years later, a tea planter ruefully told Hooker that at the start of his working life he had failed to follow Hooker's advice to go into rubber and had consequently missed out on a fortune.)

The tea industry would be among the first to benefit from the rapid advances in botanical knowledge and technology. In May 1848, as Joseph Hooker explored the hills of Darjeeling, the former superintendent of Saharanpur's botanical garden John Forbes Royle paid a visit to the Chelsea Physic Garden in London. The verdict of the famous tea brokers on Indian-grown Chinese tea had just arrived: it was good, but not quite good enough. Now the East India Company had a new strategy: go to China and acquire samples from the best plants and everything else deemed necessary to finish the task of establishing viable commercial tea plantations in India. As the Company's chief botanist, Royle's task in Chelsea was to persuade the man best qualified for that job, one that would likely prove almost impossibly difficult and no less dangerous.

Not all early Victorian plant hunters were doctor–botanists. Some of the greatest were working-class gardeners who had served long apprenticeships. They were intelligent and knowledgeable but had no formal scientific education. Among these, Robert Fortune was the shining example. Born in the tiny Berwickshire village of Edrom, his father was a farm worker and his formal education began and ended at the local parish school. He was apprenticed to a local nurseryman, moved to the Royal Botanic Gardens at Edinburgh under head gardener William McNab and then to the Horticultural Society's garden at Chiswick, where he took charge of the indoor plants. He was cool-headed, ambitious and deeply skilled, so when the Horticultural Society decided to take advantage of easier access in China, following the Treaty of Nanking, they knew just the man to send. Fortune arrived in Hong Kong in May 1843 and spent the next three years collecting in northern China, bringing back to Europe the winter-flowering jasmine, the kumquat, a fan-palm presented to Victoria for her thirty-second birthday and best of all, the legendary double yellow rose, stolen from a mandarin's garden. Despite such riches, the public might never have heard of him were it not for his hugely entertaining travelogue *Three Years' Wandering*, with its show-stopping account of how he took on a fleet of pirates single-handed to protect his specimens. The East India Company was more interested in his two chapters about the Chinese tea industry. No European had seen or knew more of Chinese tea.

Fortune's first expedition had not helped him live up to his name. His pay had been a miserly £100 per annum and the Horticultural Society had been reluctant to provide firearms for him to defend himself as he travelled. They were more used to gentlemen who came with their own guns and didn't rely on being paid. Yet his immense success did win him the directorship of the Chelsea Physic Garden, which he proceeded to improve wholesale. The job wasn't lucrative but it came with a house and other benefits and more importantly didn't involve risking his life. The notion of intellectual property barely existed in 1848 but Fortune knew very well that what he was being asked to do by John Forbes Royle wasn't so much plant collecting as industrial espionage. He also knew what could happen if he were caught. The East India Company would have to offer a much better deal to persuade him back to China – and it did: five times his previous salary, free passage and Fortune could keep whatever else he collected to sell to the growing market of wealthy gardeners, who already knew China as a treasure trove. All he had to do was deliver what the Company needed.

Disguising himself as a merchant and masking his indifferent Chinese accent by claiming to be from whatever region was furthest from where he was, Fortune completed his mission. Even when the East India Company killed the vast majority of the thousands of tea plants he sent in his first batch, he didn't give up. Told that all the seeds he sent had proved unviable, Fortune developed an ingenious method of transporting them in the soil of a mulberry bush inside a Wardian case so that when Falconer received them more than twelve thousand plants had germinated. Despite the setbacks and the subterfuge, he not only delivered viable plants, he also sourced all the best equipment necessary and hired Chinese tea growers who not only knew what they were doing but were prepared to teach others. The Indian tea industry, thanks to Fortune, finally reached critical mass and exploded into life. The Himalaya would never be the same again.

In little more than a decade, ten thousand acres around Darjeeling were planted with tea in thirty-nine gardens. Some of Darjeeling's most famous tea gardens were founded in this period: Happy Valley, formerly the Wilson Tea Estate, founded by the Englishman David

Wilson in 1854; Glenburn, named by the Scot Kimble Murray, its first manager; Makaibari, in the Bengali Banerjee family for four generations. (Narendra Modi presented Queen Elizabeth with a packet of Makaibari tea when they met in 2018.) In the rush to plant tea, tree cover in the region largely disappeared. What had been largely undisturbed forest thirty years before was simply gone. Yet the impact on the people of the Himalaya was even greater. More trees could be planted, and were; Darjeeling's hunger for workers, on the other hand, would uproot communities in ways that would change society and politics for good. In 1839, when Archie Campbell arrived, there were around a hundred people in the district of Darjeeling. Ten years later, when Hooker was in Sikkim, the population was ten thousand. In 1871, when the first official census was done, it had climbed to 94,712. Ten years later, the year the railway arrived in Darjeeling, a more reliable census recorded 155,179. Ten years after that, in 1891, the figure had risen to 223,314. The town of Darjeeling itself was by then more than sixteen thousand strong and had been made Calcutta's summer capital, home to some of India's best private schools: St Paul's and the Jesuit college St Joseph's, where kings of Nepal and Bhutanese nobles went to school, as well as the novelist Lawrence Durrell.

This spiralling population growth was driven largely by the expansion of the tea industry. At the time of the 1891 census forty-five thousand acres were under tea in 177 gardens and they all needed large workforces. These came from all the neighbouring countries but by far the greatest proportion came from Nepal, often with the assistance of Nepali leaders who were rewarded with parcels of land. In the 1891 census, eighty-eight thousand were recorded as Nepali, almost certainly an underestimation. The majority were Rais, Tamangs and Limbus, and some Newari merchants as well, Tibeto-Burmese ethnic groups with their own religious traditions disadvantaged by a stratified society that favoured the dominant Khas. There were migrants from Sikkim and Bhutan, and from across the mountains in Tibet. The district of Darjeeling had become a new frontier, once sparsely populated, now a polyglot, multicultural experiment. You could escape debts, bad marriages or the boredom of village life in Darjeeling. It became a magnet, a new centre of gravity in the eastern Himalaya. In the British imagination, Darjeeling is about colonial life, like an extended episode of *The Jewel in the Crown*. Yet the European population was tiny in comparison to the tens of thousands of migrants starting new lives in a world where the rules of home were powerfully changed. It's hardly surprising that Darjeeling became a Himalayan cultural and literary melting pot, though when independence came in 1947 this Nepali population would find itself fighting for political space.

*

If tea changed the landscape of the Himalaya, then the Himalaya also changed the landscape of Europe and North America, or at least their gardens. In 1866 the now Royal Horticultural Society organised the most expensive international plant show in history. Despite the cold London weather, it was a smash, so popular in fact that it managed to turn a profit. The exhibition was sponsored and organised in part by the prominent Victorian plant nursery James Veitch & Sons, which had made a fortune furnishing the gardens of the aristocracy. Through the 1860s, Veitch had sponsored plant hunters to travel the world looking for new species for its wealthy clients, particularly South America and Japan, where John Gould Veitch had climbed Mount Fuji before bringing back the largest collection of Japanese conifers yet collected and important new maples as well. (He shared the voyage home with Robert Fortune, who had been on a similar mission.) This was still the era of Joseph Paxton, Victorian Britain's head gardener, who had died the year before: huge formal gardens adorned with hugely expensive and finicky bedding plants grown under glass. The philosophy of this extravagance was clear from the Lord Mayor of London's speech at the 1866 exhibition banquet:

> It has been said that Nature, so fair and bounteous in herself, needs not the hand of man to train and cultivate her; but Nature in every shape requires cultivation.

Resistance to such unnatural extravagance came from an Irish gardener called William Robinson, who founded what the biographer Nicola Shulman has dubbed 'the horticultural lodge of the Arts and Crafts movement'. In 1870 he published *The Wild Garden*, which advocated more naturalistic planting and an end to labour-intensive and expensive 'bedding out'. Nature should lead the way, he argued, and that meant relying on plants more suited to Britain's temperate climate. He championed herbaceous borders, planted with shrubs and perennials to lighten the workload for ordinary gardeners, but while he spoke out for native plants, he also saw a role for other parts of the world that were suited to the northern European climate. That's where the Himalaya came in, since altitude acts in many ways like latitude. Unlike tropical species from South America, Himalayan plants were much more the 'natural, hardy species' Robinson had in mind, like the rhododendron, which flowered beautifully but resisted frost.

This growing fashion for hardy plants and more naturalistic planting offered a final glorious flourish to a world of Himalayan plant hunting that was now facing decline. In 1906 Joseph Hooker wrote to a colleague deploring the decline of botany in India in comparison to other parts of the British Empire. There were exceptions. Inspired by Hooker, the British Association organised an expedition to Sikkim that included the gigantic Henry John Elwes, botanist, butterfly collector and former Scots Guard, whose booming voice was best experienced from a distance. And in 1906, the same year Hooker complained of the parlous state of Indian botany – 'Excuse my growl. I do love Indian Botany. I long to see another Griffith' – the Kew botanist Isaac Henry Burkill also visited Sikkim. The following year he was in Nepal, the first trained botanist to visit the Kathmandu valley since Wallich more than eighty years earlier, collecting some four hundred species. Later Burkill was attached as botanist to a punitive security operation in the Abor Hills of modern Arunachal Pradesh against the Adi people, ethnic Tibetans who resented British control. This was country both Griffith and Hooker had explored, the latter, after his expedition to Sikkim, in the company of his friend Thomas Thomson. Yet Hooker was right when he wrote how 'the contrast between India and China in this respect is deplorable, especially as I am sure that many of the new Chinese plants will be found in the E Himal'.

For several decades, the botanists discovering those plants in the eastern Himalaya weren't British but French. The Lazarist missionary Armand David, known as Père David, is well known for the colossal study he made of China's natural history. That work included botanising along the eastern fringes of the Himalaya in what is now western Sichuan during his second collecting expedition, which began in the spring of 1868 and lasted over two years. His most famous discoveries were the giant panda and the handkerchief tree, whose whole genus, now named *Davidia* in his honour, was new to western science. Yet the breadth of the herbarium he collected was no less impressive. A native of the Pyrenees, he had as a father a doctor with a broad interest in natural history, who taught his son well. David was a brilliant naturalist. He sent 676 plant specimens from Sichuan to the natural history museum in Paris where the botanist Adrien Franchet discovered among them a hundred and fifty new species: a dozen rhododendrons, including *Rhododendron aureum*, primulas, violets, cotoneasters and willow. Despite suffering 'more fatigues, pains, privations, and diseases, than it is advisable to say', Père David reached Beijing via the Qinghai plateau just so he could see for himself the turquoise waters of Kokonor, the largest lake in China.

Other French missionaries followed David's example, the most remarkable being Jean-Marie Delavay, who like David grew up in mountains but on the other side of France in Haute-Savoie, where he developed a lifelong passion for alpine flowers. He arrived in Canton in 1867 and, to begin with, gave whatever he collected to the British consul Henry Hance, who shared his passion for botany. During a trip home in 1881, he met Père David who persuaded him to collect instead for the Paris natural history museum's Adrien Franchet and *la patrie*. The change galvanised Delavay and when he returned to China in 1882 he based himself in north-west Yunnan, possibly the first European to visit the deep gorges of what was then a remote region of the far eastern Himalaya. He worked alone, like David, amassing a vast collection of dried specimens, the finest, Franchet said, he had ever seen, comprising four thousand species of largely alpine flora, of which fifteen hundred were new discoveries. Among these was the blue poppy, *Meconopsis betonicifolia*, which Franchet described. Seeds from this were grown at the botanic gardens in Edinburgh, then enjoying a golden period under the directorship of Isaac Bayley Balfour. (Whether this meconopsis and *Meconopsis baileyi* are the same species is a matter of debate; *betonicifolia* was on display in London in 1926.)

Without the retinue of helpers other plant hunters relied on to carry equipment and specimens, the amount of material Delavay collected from each species was small and as a result only a few of his discoveries were successfully introduced into Europe. That task fell to the next generation of plant hunters in the eastern Himalaya:

the Dutch-born American Frank N Meyer, working for the US Department of Agriculture, a new entrant to the world of Himalayan exploration; Ernest Henry Wilson, who went to Yunnan for James Veitch & Sons to find the fabled dove tree, *Davidia involucrata*, and later worked for the Arnold Arboretum in Boston; and George Forrest, a Scot recruited by Bayley Balfour, who was the most successful collector in Yunnan, one of the most biodiverse regions on earth. Forrest got help along the way from the French missionary Jules Dubernard who had by then lived in the upper Mekong valley for forty years, converting former slaves to Christianity. On his first collecting expedition to Yunnan in 1905, Forrest witnessed the aftermath of a violent insurrection by Tibetan monks, triggered in part by the British invasion of Tibet the year before, against Christian missionaries and Qing officials. Having fled the rebel monks, Forrest returned to discover that Dubernard had been decapitated and he was himself a hunted man.

As the Qing dynasty began its death spiral, China's Tibetan marches became increasingly dangerous for plant hunters. William Purdom, the tall and likeable son of a Northumberland gardener, had steadily worked his way up from garden boy to the post of junior foreman at Kew. Having been fired, apparently without reasonable cause, he went to work for Veitch and the Arnold Arboretum, collecting in Gansu, the province bordering the north-west Tibetan plateau. Though the collecting was mixed, Purdom proved a talented photographer, capturing some of the only images of the 'old dance' festival at Chone monastery, when the spirits of the dead return. Chone sat at the heart of an independent Tibetan enclave with its own lineage of rulers dating back to its founding in the late thirteenth century as a Sakya monastery under the patronage of Kublai Khan. Purdom showed an ethnographer's eye, catching echoes of this deep history in his photographs.

Purdom was back in Gansu in 1914 with Reginald Farrer, the man who inspired the rage for rock gardens, a fashion more recently back in favour. Farrer was short, almost dwarfish, and was born with a cleft lip, which he later concealed behind a moustache, although the psychological scars of so many painful operations and the pity of strangers would never leave him. Educated at home in Yorkshire, where his family owned Ingleborough Hall, and then Balliol College, Oxford, he was after making as big a mark as possible and fretted against his conventionally prosperous family. What he wanted, according to his biographer Nicola Shulman, 'was to be a literary figure of grand repute'; what he became was a lively, endearing gardening writer, whose tendency, more than usual, was 'to write about himself, no matter what the ostensible subject'.

Hunting for plants in the Himalaya had been a lifetime's ambition for Farrer and with the public profile he acquired in championing rock gardens it became possible. His original intention had been Yunnan but when he put out feelers for financial backing he discovered from Isaac Bayley Balfour at the Royal Botanic Gardens in Edinburgh that not only would he not give the amateur Farrer any money but Frank Kingdon-Ward and George Forrest were already hard at work in Yunnan scooping up anything and everything of value. He should go to Gansu instead. Farrer was tougher than he looked, but even so, it was his great good fortune that Purdom also signed up for the adventure. He had been to Gansu before, was tough and brave, knew photography and was happy to let Farrer beat their drum.

Farrer and Purdom discovered Gansu – always bandit country – in the grip of a rebellion that had tipped northern China into chaos. Its insurgent leader, Bai Lang, had been trained in Japan to undermine the new Chinese republic that had replaced the last Qing emperor. His name sounds similar to the Mandarin for 'white wolf', which is how Farrer and Purdom termed their adversary. Purdom found himself ambushed by two hundred of Bai Lang's men who shot dead two of his ponies. He returned fire and then scarpered. In his account of their journey, *On the Eaves of the World*, Farrer included a photograph of a rakish Purdom, dressed as a local bandit. The pair also found themselves in trouble when a storm destroyed the crops of local villages. The powerful head lama of the local monastery ordered retribution and Purdom and Farrer were confronted by an angry mob brandishing matchlocks. Purdom was able to charm their way out.

If the risks were great, the rewards were magical: *Viburnum fragans*, also known as *V. farreri*, still hugely popular in British gardens, its pink-tinged white flowers described by Farrer as 'blushing stars'; a new buddleia with lavender flowers and the scent of raspberries that 'hugs only the very hottest and driest crevices, cliffs, walls, and banks down the most arid and torrid aspects of the Ha Shin Fang'; and the tree peony, *Paeonia rockii*, with its 'single, enormous blossom, waved and crimped into the boldest grace of line, of absolutely pure white, with featherings of deepest maroon radiating at the base of the petals from the boss of golden fluff at the flower's heart'. Farrer didn't collect any of its seeds and the explorer and botanist Joseph Rock has been credited with its introduction, although it's debated whether what Farrer saw and what Rock collected were the same plants. Rock's peony was collected in 1926, the year of the blue poppy craze, from the garden of Chone monastery, which Purdom had photographed years before. There was, however, no way for Farrer and Rock to compare notes: Reginald Farrer was already dead, aged forty, in the mountains of Upper Burma, succumbing in the autumn of 1920 to infection and heavy drinking. As though her son had fallen on the horticultural equivalent of the Western Front, Farrer's mother dedicated a small fountain to him in the gardens of Ingleborough Hall with the inscription: 'He died for love and duty, in search of rare plants.'

Frank Kingdon-Ward's 1924 expedition to Tibet's mysterious Tsangpo gorges, accompanied by the young aristocrat John Campbell, fifth Earl Cawdor, was a coda to the Romantic age of Himalayan plant hunting. Along with sober commissions from Kew and the Natural History Museum, he also agreed to collect seeds for the thirteenth Dalai Lama to grow in the gardens of his summer palace, the Norbulingka, sending primula and meconopsis seeds: 'showy plants' that 'could be easily raised'. When Kingdon-Ward first saw the blue poppy, flowering among bushes some three hundred kilometres east of Lhasa, he thought at first he'd seen the plumage of some fabulous bird. 'The flowers,' he wrote, 'flutter out from amongst the sea-green leaves like blue-and-gold butterflies.' Although he would spend the rest of his life exploring the highlands of Asia, and Himalayan botany is no less relevant today, in the public's imagination there would never be another moment quite like Kingdon-Ward's discovery. The blue poppy proved the perfect emblem of the Himalaya as a remote Eden, and the bloom of that vision was never as strong.

15

The First Mountaineers

On a summer's evening in 1895, a young Welshman, piggy-eyed and burly, sat on a wall in a remote shepherd's enclosure on the west side of Nanga Parbat, the world's ninth highest peak, watching the slaughter of a sheep. The Honourable Charles Granville Bruce was a man of gargantuan appetites and having been on the go for more than thirty hours, the young Gurkha officer was ravenous. The night before, spent at 5,800 metres on the south side of the mountain, had been bitterly cold and sleepless. Bruce had travelled to Nanga Parbat in haste; his warm mountaineering clothes were still in his trunk in Kashmir. Not yet recovered from a bout of mumps, he had shivered through the night in a sweater and light flannel suit, one of his puttees wrapped around his middle, legs stuffed in a rucksack. But as the sheep's liver went on the fire, Charlie Bruce was feeling more like his usual boisterous self. 'Nothing rejoices me so much as the prospect of food,' he wrote of that moment, 'especially under such conditions.'

Forty years later, and a retired brigadier, Bruce was famous as the leader of the first attempts to climb Everest. To young mountaineers of the 1930s, he was a figure from legend. The Everest climber Raymond Greene, older brother of the novelist Graham, was Bruce's doctor in his later years and had served in Bruce's first regiment, the 'Ox and Bucks'. They were still telling stories about the old general four decades after he left. Bruce's father, Lord Aberdare, had served as William Gladstone's home secretary, passing licensing laws making it an offence to be drunk in public. His youngest son met that challenge in spectacular fashion. Bruce once wagered he could run from London to Brighton in a day stopping for a drink at every pub he passed. He could swear without repetition for minutes on end, an ability that left his fellow climber Tom Longstaff 'transfixed with envy'. His appetite for physical activity in the Alps earned him the nickname the 'Mad Mountain Machine'.

Bruce is now categorised as supporting cast in the imperial drama of Everest, a boisterous cartoon of a man, a high-altitude roisterer. He was shrewder than that. His Himalayan career spanned the rich but little known period from the 1890s to the years immediately after the Great War. In the popular imagination, Everest was a step into the unknown, but mountaineering in the Himalaya did not start with Everest. By 1922, leading the first full attempt on Everest, Charlie Bruce had thirty years' experience of the world's highest mountains and the challenges peculiar to them: their scale and extreme altitude. There had been decades of thought and debate about the pros and cons on a host of issues: the problems of hypoxia, diet and equipment, the debate over enlisting guides from the Alps or relying on local men, something Bruce favoured. As a soldier stationed in the Himalaya and a member of the Alpine Club, Bruce was in the right place at the right time. As a consequence, he came to know almost all the small cast of unusual characters who set the stage for Everest.

He took up climbing as a young officer in the mid 1880s, when the ethical framework that underpins mountaineering emerged for the first time in its modern form. Put simply, climbers needed to address a fundamental question: what was mountaineering for? Should it serve some wider, moral or scientific purpose or was it simply an end in itself? The activity had emerged in the late eighteenth century on a wave of Romanticism, scientific enquiry and an adventurous extension to the grand tour. Men, and women too, could make a name for themselves by scrambling up a peak: Victorian 'selfie' culture. This self-regard dismayed someone like John Ruskin, who felt the aesthetic glory of mountains was compromised by the antics of tourists. When the Alpine Club was formed in 1857, staking an interest in the world of science, Charles Dickens mocked its pretensions:

> the scaling of such heights as the Schreckhorn, the Eiger, and the Matterhorn contributed about as much to the advancement of science as would a club of young gentlemen who should undertake to bestride all the weather-cocks of all the cathedral spires in the United Kingdom.

The scientist John Tyndall, whose work on radiant heat is one of the cornerstones of our understanding of climate science, was also a leading mountaineer, in 1861 making the first ascent of the much-prized Weisshorn, a peak near Zermatt in the Swiss Alps. He was also an early member of the Alpine Club but a year after the Weisshorn, having just become vice president, he resigned his membership, infuriated by a light-hearted paper by the young Leslie Stephen, father of Virginia Woolf and Vanessa Bell, who joked how science was merely an adjunct to the serious business of mountaineering. After the Matterhorn disaster of 1865, when four men, including the son of the Marquess of Queensbury, fell to their deaths while descending from the summit, the air of disapproval became a storm of protest. It wasn't just an accident; 'it was *the* accident', in the words of an editor of the *Alpine Journal*, after which alpinists 'went about under a sort of dark shade, looked on with scarcely disguised contempt by the world of ordinary travellers'.

The impact on the leader of that Matterhorn climb, Edward Whymper, was no less profound. Alpinism had, almost by chance, lifted him out of humble social origins, just as science did for John Tyndall. After the Matterhorn, his excitement and energy for mountaineering congealed; he couldn't see any value in the innovations and developments within the sport that followed his glory years. After the Matterhorn, his adventures were freighted with heavy purposes: scientific expeditions to Greenland and then Peru, where he made the first ascent of Chimborazo. That mountain is still closely associated with Alexander von Humboldt, who was the inspiration for almost every significant figure in nineteenth-century scientific exploration, including Charles Darwin. If mountaineering had a purpose, it surely lay, for Edward Whymper, within the learned and socially prestigious circumference of Humboldt. The bonus, for a man who spent his working life in publishing, was the prospect of a hefty and indispensable book at the end of it.

After exploring the Arctic, the Himalaya would have been a logical next step for Whymper, not least because of his strong family ties there. His brother Henry trained as a brewer and then left for India to work at the new Murree Brewery in the Pir Panjal mountains north of Rawalpindi, on the road to Kashmir. Edward had a shareholding in the company, and Henry found jobs in Murree for their brothers

Joseph and Samuel. Another brother, Frank, worked for the post office, finishing his career as postmaster general in Mumbai. Joseph later moved to Mussoorie, the hill station where George Everest had built his house, some thirty kilometres north of Dehra Dun and the head-quarters of the Indian Survey Department. Here he founded the Crown Brewery, where Samuel also worked for a while, before moving on to do similar work at Naini Tal, within sight of some of the Garhwal's grandest mountains: Kamet, Trisul and Nanda Devi. All three of these peaks, made available as the East India Company spread north, were early objectives for Himalayan pioneers, but Whymper was not among them. His nephew Robert later said that Whymper had contemplated an attempt on Everest, whose primacy suited his ambition, but such notions were 'abandoned as far too expensive'. Whymper had little of the romantic in him: an expedition to Chimborazo made more economic sense. Despite building up a large collection of material on India, and despite his sisters travelling there to visit their brothers, Whymper, the most famous climber of his age, never even saw the Himalaya.

For Humboldt himself, the opening up of the Himalaya came too late, despite his fervent ambition to travel there, and perhaps emulate his attempt on Chimborazo: 'nothing in my life has filled me with a more intense regret,' he wrote towards the end of his life, which came in 1859. His ambitions were transferred to the small army of young explorers he supported, an ageing spider at the centre of a web of correspondents feeding him data as he struggled to finish *Cosmos*, his colossal work on the natural world. In the 1840s, he had helped his friend Joseph Dalton Hooker, using his London contacts to generate financial support for Hooker's travels in the eastern Himalaya. By the mid 1850s, Kashmir, and the southern approaches to Nanga Parbat, had also come under the control of the East India Company, and it would fall to further protégés of Humboldt to make the first attempt on a significant Himalayan peak just for the sake of it, in the course of a remarkable but ultimately tragic three-year expedition.

Humboldt called them the 'shamrock', three – of five – Bavarian brothers, Hermann, Adolf and Robert Schlagintweit, sons of a Munich ophthalmologist, Joseph Schlagintweit. Hermann was the oldest, born in 1826, but still only in his late 20s when the three of them left for India in 1854. The three had published works on the geography and geology of the Alps and in their Alpine travels come close to making the first ascent of Monte Rosa, second highest mountain in Western Europe. These were mountaineers from alpinism's Golden Age, the only ones from that era to make it to the Himalaya. They did so with Humboldt's support and his contacts with the East India Company. Their stated mission was the magnetic survey of India, the earth's magnetic field being a subject close to Humboldt's heart. They would bring home with them a vast treasure of geological, zoological and botanical specimens, theories on glaciology, capable watercolours of the mountains, as well as a great deal of ethnographic material, enough to launch their youngest brother, Emil Schlagintweit, on a lifelong career as a Tibet scholar. Charles Darwin later wrote to them seeking knowledge on the breeding patterns of the yak, after the brothers spoke at the annual meeting of the British Association for the Advancement of Science, held in Dublin in September 1857.

The brothers travelled widely in the Himalaya, often independently of each other. In the spring of 1855, Hermann left Calcutta alone, headed for Darjeeling, hoping to follow the Singalila ridge towards Kangchenjunga, a mountain firmly planted in the Western imagination, like the craze for rhododendrons, by Hooker. Adolf and Robert, meanwhile, set off for Kumaon. While Robert waited in the Johar valley, Adolf travelled up the Pindari glacier. Although capable and adventurous travellers, the Schlagintweits were often following in a pioneer's footsteps: to be reunited with his brother, Adolf made the second crossing of Traill's Pass, linking the Pindari glacier to the village of Milam – not the first, but no less challenging for that. At Milam they hired the future pundits Nain and Mani Singh before crossing the border into Tibet (disguised as Buddhist pilgrims to escape arrest), to reach Gartok, the trading encampment on the banks of the Indus, the first Europeans to do so since William Moorcroft in 1812. British naturalists had passed through the region more recently, taking advantage of the greater access won with the conclusion of the Sikh Wars; Richard Strachey, brother of Henry and John, for example, after collecting specimens in Kumoan, crossed into Tibet and visited the sacred Lake Manasarovar.

Where Adolf and Robert Schlagintweit were truly innovative was in their quixotic tilt at a summit on their way back south from Tibet, having been rumbled by the authorities in Gartok and expelled.

From above the Sutlej valley, the northern view of Garhwal is dominated by the triangular mass of Kamet, 7,756 metres high, a massif,
then commonly known as Ibi Garmin, identified and crudely measured by Strachey in 1848. Adolf and Robert decided to explore this
group while returning to India and spent over two weeks camped
at 5,200 metres under the mountain. They made one determined
attempt on the summit from a camp at around 6,000 metres and
reached a point some 800 metres higher. As the twentieth-century
mountaineer Charles Meade showed during his own exploration of
Kamet, the brothers had in fact been on the wrong mountain,
attempting Kamet's near neighbour, which rises on the other side
of what is known as Meade's Col. Anyone without a map, which
didn't exist in 1855, setting off for Kamet from the north, might
make the same mistake. This second peak, known today as Abi
Garmin, flattens itself against its higher, southerly neighbour Kamet,
merging altogether in the middle of the day. The brothers took a
barometric reading to calculate their high point at 6,778 metres, an
altitude regarded for many years as a comfortable record. The
discovery in 1999 of haunting and well-preserved mummies of Inca
child sacrifices left five hundred years before on the summit of
Llullaillaco, on the border between Chile and Argentina at an altitude
of over 6,700 metres, has prompted a reconsideration of such records.
While there is no physical evidence of humans reaching the summit
of the higher Andean peak of Aconcagua, 6,961 metres, it's a distinct
possibility. Given that Tibetan yak herders routinely take their
animals above 6,000 metres, it's logical that Andean people reached
similar altitudes.

The scale of the Schlagintweits' work in the Himalaya, in the pattern
of Humboldt, won them many admirers on their return. The fate of
Adolf, who disappeared after electing to travel home overland and
separately from his brothers, only added spice to their reputation. The
Indian authorities, including Richard Strachey's brother Henry, took
great trouble to discover Adolf's fate: he had been beheaded without
trial in Kashgar, accused of being a Chinese spy. His head was eventually recovered in 1859 by a Kazakh soldier and scholar, Shoqan
Walikhanov, inspiration for Rudyard Kipling in his short story 'The
Man Who Would Be King'. While their work was published in important British journals, the multivolume record of their travels was not

translated, and the Schlagintweits faded from view in the English-speaking world, their mountaineering exploit a spontaneous adventure hidden behind a forest of academic detail.

In the years after, the Survey of India expanded its work across the Himalaya and Karakoram, as we have seen, claiming a number of summits along the way, but just as in the Alps or the Caucasus, where military surveyors reached high vantage points, the purpose was information, not sport. The first Himalayan expedition dedicated purely to mountaineering had to wait for another twenty-five years. The Indian Rebellion of 1857 was cited by contemporary alpinists as one explanation for the pause; there were also many exploratory challenges remaining in the Alps in the 1860s. As rail networks robbed the Alps of their wildness, alpinists began visiting more remote ranges, like the Caucasus, which provided a useful laboratory for the Himalaya. With Britain's grip on India extending deeper into the mountains, access to the Himalaya became easier.

In February 1883, a freshly minted barrister called William Woodman Graham arrived in Mumbai with the Swiss guide Josef Imboden. It's somehow appropriate that this progenitor of Himalayan climbing should be such an enigma, a man whose reputation hovers between adventurer, maverick and fraud. Graham's Alpine experience was deep, despite his years, and yet the Alpine Club had, the previous December, blackballed him. This was surprisingly common at the time, and often personal, but in this case, the vote against was overwhelming. The explanation remains uncertain, but that summer Graham had bagged the first ascent of a dramatic and much prized granite tower above the mountain town of Chamonix called the Dent du Géant. In doing so, he relied on some shameful ironmongery and fixed ropes placed by an Italian team. Graham hadn't quite shot the fox, but he'd stood on the shoulders of men who had.

Others might have taken it personally, but Graham didn't hesitate to offer the *Alpine Journal* a full account of his Himalayan expedition, which he read to an audience at the Royal Geographical Society. The story he told was impressive, a sustained campaign over several months that saw him start in the Kangchenjunga region north of Darjeeling, move on to Garhwal for the summer and then return to Sikkim in the autumn. His guide Imboden returned after the first leg feverish and homesick, finding the mountains too wintry for climbing. In his

place came Emil Boss, proprietor of the Bear Hotel in the Swiss village
of Grindelwald, famous for its proximity to the Eiger, with the guide
Ulrich Kaufmann. The two men had almost climbed Mount Cook in
New Zealand the year before and were a formidable pair. In Garhwal,
travelling in the monsoon, they were plagued with leeches, from which
a French member of the Alpine Club they picked up on their travels,
a Monsieur Décle, fled in horror. The plan was to climb Nanda Devi,
highest mountain wholly within India, but after a spirited effort at
accessing the formidable Rishiganga Gorge, Graham had to settle for
a strong attempt on Dunagiri, reaching a height of almost 7,000 metres,
some 150 metres short of the summit, before worsening weather drove
him and Boss down. He also claimed a mountain that surveyors had
dubbed A21, later known as Changabang. The idea Graham might
have climbed this notoriously difficult peak was laughed out of court;
it was finally done in 1974, with all the advantages of modern equipment and techniques. It was likely a case of mistaken identity, as
Graham tried to square an indifferent map with the country as he
experienced it.

Back in Darjeeling, he reunited with his 'sirdar', meaning 'boss', a
'sturdy, honest Tibetan' called Gaga, who had organised his porters
that spring, and in early October, from a camp at around 5,600 metres,
Graham said he came within ten or twelve metres of the summit of
Kabru, one of Kangchenjunga's mightier neighbours. Kauffman, 'one
of the fastest step-cutters living', had managed to climb its final steep
ice slope only because it was covered with a skin of frozen snow. The
summit itself was 'little more than a pillar of ice', but too hard and
steep to overcome. They were back in camp late in the evening having,
on the face of it, come within a hair's breadth of climbing a peak of
7,412 metres, almost certainly the highest any human had been before.

Graham's lecture on his experiences to the Royal Geographical
Society was full of incident but laconic; Joseph Hooker, now in his
late sixties and in the audience, didn't much care for this young upstart
and challenged Graham's claim that the altitude hadn't bothered him
much. Hooker was sceptical, having himself been unable to move at
such heights without 'a hoop of iron' around his heart. Graham also
included some sharp observations about the quality of maps being
produced by the Survey of India. It pained him, allowing for the
hospitality he'd received, 'but what can I say when we found one

whole range omitted, glaciers portrayed where trees of 4 ft. thickness are growing ... ' He had come across another traveller near Nanda Devi who described the map they were both using as 'beautifully inaccurate'. His fellow climber Emil Boss wasn't just an hotelier; he was a captain in the Swiss army, which produced maps of Switzerland that were second to none. The day after Graham's lecture, Boss spoke at the Alpine Club. While the Survey's latest map of Sikkim was admirable, he said, that of Garhwal was a work of the imagination. There had been a long collaboration between mountaineers and military authorities in the preparation of accurate mountain maps. The offer was there for officers of the Indian Survey Department to come to Switzerland to get some Alpine training. Douglas Freshfield, a leading member of the Alpine Club and one of those alpinists spreading the gospel of mountaineering beyond Europe, then spoke in support of William Henry Johnson, a humbly born surveyor whose idea of a Himalayan Club similar to the Alpine Club had been dismissed by complacent Indian authorities.

If the criticism was meant to be constructive, the Indian Survey Department didn't take it that way. An anonymous correspondent, describing himself as 'for nearly 30 years a wanderer in the Himalayas', wrote a damning dismissal of Graham's claim to have almost climbed Kabru, which was published in the Allahabad newspaper the *Pioneer*, where Rudyard Kipling would shortly be working. Letters to the paper quickly followed, from the 'Indian school of mountaineers', speaking up for the Survey of India and pouring scorn on Graham. If doughty Tibetans and Sherpas at Darjeeling said it was impossible, then so it must be. Graham, they claimed, had probably confused Kabru with Kabur, a foothill on the approach march, a suggestion designed to insult. Freshfield dismantled the *Pioneer's* arguments, reiterated that offers of help were well meant and, in a nod to the Great Game, drew unfavourable comparisons between the nanny-like attitudes of the Indian authorities and the cheerful laissez-faire of the Russians. Graham himself remained silent and soon slipped from view. A rumour surfaced that having suffered some kind of financial disaster he had left for America to become, some said, a cowboy. In 1910 he resurfaced as vice consul in the Mexican city of Durango, a blurry face captured in a few faded cuttings from Mexican newspapers, like a character from a Graham Greene novel, the veneer of his position barely concealing what must have been quite a story, and one we will likely never know.

It's sometimes claimed the mountaineering 'establishment' turned its back on Graham, but this was far from the case. Douglas Freshfield maintained his support, joined by almost all those alpinists who made their way to Sikkim in the years before the Great War. Those mountaineers who did dismiss Graham's claims usually had a dog in the fight, like William Hunter Workman, husband of the indomitable New England heiress and explorer, Fanny Bullock Workman. His own, rather creaky claim to the world altitude record, set in 1903 in the Karakoram, relied on Graham's being discounted. One of the few members of the Alpine Club to express doubts about Graham's climb, in public at least, was the illustrious Sir Martin Conway: art historian, writer and like the Workmans a dedicated self-promoter. Conway also had a claim to the altitude record, having reached 6,904 metres on Baltoro Kangri during his 1892 expedition to the Karakoram. He dismissed Graham's ascent while promoting his own record in an entry he wrote on mountaineering for the 1908 *Encyclopaedia of Sport*. Douglas Freshfield, by then an old-stager of Himalayan exploration himself, locked horns with Conway in the pages of the *Alpine Journal*, and in the 1911 edition Conway recanted.

Perhaps Graham's most potent detractor was Kenneth Mason, decorated soldier and celebrated geographer, a Survey of India man to his fingertips and later professor of geography at Oxford. His history of Himalayan exploration and mountaineering, first published in 1955, some seventy years after Graham's expedition, was the Everest of its type and remains influential even now. Mason's dismissal of William Woodman Graham from the record books was made with the indulgent patience of a parent removing a precious heirloom from their toddler's sticky fingers. Mason had been inspired as a boy by the exploratory travels of Francis Younghusband, 'the last imperial adventurer', who, in 1893, had cooked up the notion of attempting Everest with Charlie Bruce on a polo field in Chitral. (Or at least, that was the yarn. Younghusband had forgotten all about it when Bruce reminded him decades later. That didn't stop them using the story in a *Daily Telegraph* puff piece about Everest: 'if it brings in another twenty quid to the Expedition funds that is all to the good'.) To Mason, and the long sequence of surveyors before him, mountaineering ought to be well organised, productive and useful. It should advance knowledge and fill libraries with maps and catalogues. Mountaineering was not a game, to be played for its own sake; blanks on the map were there to be filled, not relished.

Mason's perspective was philosophically different from that of many mountaineers, reflecting a schism, begun in the 1880s, whose consequences would percolate through to attempts on Everest, even up to its ascent in 1953. At its extreme, these differences became polar opposites. One side put result ahead of method; the other did precisely the reverse: *how* you climbed was more important than reaching a summit. This alternative view saw mountaineering as its own reward, the game for its own sake, producing a more whimsical and slighter literary output. Some in authority found this self-indulgent, believing that risking your neck required a higher purpose, especially a patriotic one. They preferred large expeditions with heavy financial backing, invested with the prestige of institutions, with purposes beyond mountaineering: scientific and geographical. They delighted in packed lecture halls and weighty books, the sort of expedition to advance a career.

That was certainly true for Martin Conway. He was a strong alpinist, once climbing the Matterhorn from Zermatt and still getting back in time for afternoon tea, but, like most things, climbing eventually bored him. His 1892 expedition to the Karakoram was modelled on Whymper's Peruvian adventure after the viceroy of India, Lord Lansdowne, suggested he delete the phrase 'mountaineering party' from his request for a permit and replace it with 'a party of exploration', since 'mountaineering is a sport and couldn't be taken official notice of, at any rate in my case'. He took with him Matthias Zurbriggen, the great guide from the Swiss village of Saas-Fee, later hired by William and Fanny Workman, as well as the young Charles Bruce as transport officer, and the fiery socialist Oscar Eckenstein, an exceptional climber, who introduced Conway to crampons, then rather frowned on. Together, Conway, Bruce and Eckenstein explored the Hispar and Biafo glaciers, which together make the longest glacier passage, 120 kilometres, outside the Arctic regions. Eckenstein then left the expedition after one political argument too many, starting an enduring feud. Conway moved on to the Baltoro glacier, where he attempted a peak he dubbed Golden Throne, now known as Baltoro Kangri. Knighted in 1895, ostensibly for his efforts in mapping the

Karakoram, he later became Slade Professor of Fine Art at Cambridge and a 'coalition coupon' member of parliament in the 1918 general election. When his peerage was announced, *Punch* carried a cartoon of 'The Climber', and Conway weaved an ice axe into his coat of arms. But he never went to the Himalaya again.

'There are three great Himalayan views familiar to English dwellers in India', Bruce wrote. 'Kangchenjunga from Darjeeling, Nanda Devi and Trisul from Naini Tal, and Nanga Parbat from the Murree hills.' The contrast between Conway's expedition in the Karakoram and Fred Mummery's attempt on Nanga Parbat in the summer of 1895 could not have been starker. This was the first time anyone had tried a mountain of such scale and great height, and it happened almost at the start of Himalayan mountaineering, as though the Wright brothers had set off across the Atlantic a week after Kitty Hawk.

From the Deosai plateau, south-east of the mountain, the impression is even starker; the south face, rising above the Rupal valley, is a vast white shining wall. One of the first Europeans to view Nanga Parbat was the traveller Godfrey Thomas Vigne, welcomed there in the late 1830s by the raja of Baltistan, Ahmed Shah, as the first Englishman he had met. Vigne's book, the first comprehensive Western account of the region and an instant classic, described the peak from this angle as 'the most awful and magnificent sight in all the Himalaya'. The Schlagintweits passed Nanga Parbat on their travels in the mid 1850s, translating its Sanskrit name as 'naked mountain', capturing in a watercolour how its powerful bulk dominates Kashmir. Many famous Himalayan peaks are concealed from view by intervening ranges: Nanga Parbat is not one of them. From the banks of the Indus, which flows close by, to its summit is a height gain of seven kilometres.

To call it an expedition is too grand. It was a climbing party, a collection of friends from the Alps. In camp with Charlie Bruce, watching the sheep being butchered, was the Yorkshireman Geoffrey Hastings, strong, quietly determined, the trusty lieutenant type. He ran a worsted business in Bradford. In the Alps, he was famous for producing welcome delicacies from his rucksack, like bacon or champagne, at the most opportune moments. Having injured his foot a few days before, Hastings spent much of this expedition roaming bandit country trying to buy food. Last into camp were Norman Collie and Fred Mummery. Collie was tall and distinguished, a chemist at University College, London working with his boss, the future Nobel Prizewinner William Ramsay, to discover the noble gases. Some mountaineering contemporaries thought him austere, but students loved him, appreciating his quietly sarcastic wit and profitable racing tips. He had wide-ranging tastes, loved claret, was an expert on Japanese carving and could blow his own glass flasks without removing his pipe from his mouth. In Norway, where he did a great deal of exploratory mountaineering, the combination of pipe and deerstalker meant Collie was often mistaken for Sherlock Holmes.

The mountaineering star of this group was undoubtedly Albert Frederick Mummery. Approaching his fortieth birthday, Mummery came from Dover where his father owned a tannery and served as mayor. Although his reputation has endured into the twenty-first century, we know little about his early life: family papers were lost in a German bombing raid. We do know he developed a perinatal weakness of the spine and was badly short-sighted. Classed as a sickly child, he was kept at home rather than sent away to school like most of his contemporaries. Bruce had been to Harrow, where he set a record for the number of times he was beaten, Collie to Charterhouse. Mummery never forged the connections they made, or left a paper trail. Generally indifferent to posterity, he was self-conscious about his appearance and hated having his picture taken. Yet Collie did get a snap of Mummery on Nanga Parbat, sitting next to Bruce. Bruce, nicknamed 'Bruiser', sits with legs splayed, arms resting on his knees, his neck, swollen with mumps, adding to the general impression of a bulldog in a pith helmet. ('I think,' he once wrote, 'I have run away from every tribe on the Frontier at one time or another.') Mummery, cunningly, wears two floppy hats, with snow sandwiched between them, a solution to the stifling heat of a Himalayan summer's day. His thin limbs are gathered to his body like those of a wary spider, thick spectacles balanced on a beaky nose, his chin arrow-shaped, the overall impression that of an attenuated Mr Magoo.

As a sixteen-year-old, on a family holiday to Switzerland, Mummery had seen the Matterhorn 'shining in all the calm majesty of a September moon' and instantly fallen in love. He served a patient apprenticeship, learned his craft and discovered how to cope with the limits of his physical ability. Eight years later, climbing with his guide and great friend Alexander Burgener, he made the first ascent of the Matterhorn's Zmutt ridge, the first of many important new routes in the Alps that provoked admiration but also jealousy. His first application to the Alpine Club, supported by Douglas Freshfield, was black-balled anonymously at the sly instigation of a Foreign Office civil servant called William Edward Davidson. Mummery was plunged into a spiral of self-doubt and almost quit climbing alogether.

In the 1880s, during this mountain furlough, he developed what was clearly an original intellectual life. His friends, highly regarded academics like Collie, thought Mummery an incisive thinker. He had, according to Martin Conway, 'the same original, unfettered freshness of mind, with which he approached a mountain'. His great passion, beyond mountains, was economics. Many climbing historians have judged this aspect of Mummery's life as an interesting aside. In fact, his ideas were more than merely interesting: they were influential. With John Atkinson Hobson, he co-authored a treatise on the negative impact of under-consumption, *The Physiology of Industry*, a work that influenced John Maynard Keynes. Mummery wasn't Hobson's sounding board; it was Mummery who convinced Hobson of the dangers of austerity. (There's no evidence Mummery shared Hobson's antisemitism.)

Mummery's fascination with unpicking complex human behaviour extended to mountaineering. When he returned to the mountains, he applied his curious mind to unravelling his sport's multifaceted appeal. No one before Mummery, in his book *My Climbs in the Alps and Caucasus*, had articulated so shrewdly how the sport's core principles might best be practised. While equipment and knowledge have developed exponentially since Mummery's era, leading modern climbers still draw on these ideals. Reinhold Messner, the first person to climb Everest alone and without bottled oxygen, with his own deep relationship with Nanga Parbat, the place where his brother Günther died and where he did his hardest climb, once described Fred Mummery as perhaps the most important climber in history.

Mummery's key insight was the importance of self-reliance, 'the great truth' of alpinists 'trusting exclusively to their own skill and knowledge'. He stopped climbing with guides and refused those aids that diminished the challenge. He upended the status quo, climbing difficult routes with women, to the annoyance of more conservative elements in the Alpine Club. 'The essence of the sport,' Mummery wrote, 'lies not in ascending a peak, but in struggling with and over-coming difficulties.' Theodolites bored him. Large-scale expeditions didn't interest Mummery either; he turned down the offer of going to the Karakoram with Martin Conway. Climbing was supposed to be fun: 'unmixed play' is Mummery's phrase. One of his friends wrote: 'He was always happy on a mountain, and that is what made him such a delightful companion.' It's not surprising that a hard-bitten professional like Edward Whymper, for whom climbing was business, despised him. Davidson, Mummery's Foreign Office nemesis, was equally dismissive, writing to Whymper:

> I don't fancy either that Mummery can spare the time or the money requisite for success in such a difficult and distant field of exploration and therefore do not anticipate any results of importance from it.

Mummery chose Nanga Parbat for its size and accessibility; he and his friends didn't have the time or funds for a longer campaign. He wrote to Bruce, already an expert in Himalayan travel, to supply a couple of Gurkhas, strong lads to support the climbers in their efforts, 'who can speak English and the native lingo'. Then, in his good-natured, spur-of-the-moment way, he invited Bruce along when they met in Kashmir. There were no learned institutions offering grants or commercial sponsorship. They were simply on holiday. The letters Mummery sent to his wife – 'I think we are bound to have the summit,' he told her, 'as it is merely a matter of steady training to get our wind in order' – are full of his breezy optimism, prompting the charge of naïvety from historians. Yet that was the point for Mummery: to find out things that weren't known, and test limits so far not reached. There was no point being disheartened.

The team, however, was undoubtedly depleted. Hastings was injured. Collie was ill. Bruce had recovered from his mumps, but his leave was over and he was obliged to return to his regiment. Undaunted, Mummery made a final attempt with one of Bruce's Gurkhas, Raghubir Thapa, climbing a series of difficult pillars of rock in the middle of Nanga Parbat's colossal Diamir face. They reached over 6,000 metres before Raghubir called a halt. When in 1939, an

Austrian party that included one of the first people to climb the Eiger's famous north face, Heinrich Harrer, tried the same route, they found a piece of firewood at the top of the first rock rib Mummery climbed. They described the climbing as continuously difficult; Mummery had not set an altitude record on Nanga Parbat but he and Raghubir had done the hardest climbing achieved in the Himalaya for decades to come.

A few days later, while Collie and Hastings took the long way round with the bulk of the expedition's equipment, Mummery set off to find a short cut to the Rakhiot valley, below Nanga Parbat's northern flank, the only face of the mountain they hadn't yet seen. With him went the two Gurkhas, Raghubir and Goman Singh. They never arrived and were never seen again, most likely buried in an avalanche. Mummery had reassured Collie that he wouldn't risk anything for the sake of a pass, but he had risked everything – and lost. These were the first climbing deaths in the Himalaya; it was grimly prophetic that two Asian men suborned into the enterprise should be among the casualties. Douglas Freshfield told the Alpine Club: Mummery's 'untimely death is a grievous loss to the Club'. Edward Whymper underlined these words in his copy of the *Alpine Journal* and wrote in the margin: 'I do not agree.' There were difficulties with the Indian authorities after the expedition and Geoffrey Hastings felt obliged to resign from the Alpine Club. Norman Collie never went to the Himalaya again. In 1929, an English army officer who crossed the Mazeno pass, as Mummery had done, met an old man from the nearby village of Chilas who remembered the impressive feats of the English 'lat', or lord, a distant echo of an enterprise years ahead of its time. Whatever Whymper thought, it would be Mummery's legacy, and not his, that inspired the future.

*

It's widely held that the Nanga Parbat catastrophe turned mountaineers against the lightweight style of Himalayan expedition, certainly until the 1930s. That simply isn't true. Lightweight ventures continued without pause alongside larger, more expensive 'national' expeditions, with as much if not greater success. Of these less formal ventures, historians have been drawn, moth-like, to the more garish flames that

lit up Himalayan expeditions after Mummery's, like that of Aleister
Crowley, the self-styled 'wickedest man in the world' and a good friend
of Oscar Eckenstein. They climbed together in the Alps, and Crowley
was even proposed as a member of the Alpine Club, nominated by
Norman Collie, who liked a joke, and Sir Martin Conway, whose
support is simply baffling. His application disappeared before a vote
was held, and in later years Crowley roundly mocked the Alpine Club,
complacent and conservative in comparison to a man like Eckenstein.
He and Crowley put together an attempt on K2 in 1902, which included
the talented Austrian Heinrich Pfannl. Although some useful exploration was done, and the mountain attempted, the expedition was ill
fated. Eckenstein was briefly arrested as a spy, possibly at the instigation of Conway, while Crowley brandished his pistol at another expedition member, forcing him to quit. A second expedition, to
Kangchenjunga in 1905, destroyed Crowley's reputation as a mountaineer. There was an argument at 6,400 metres over whether to camp
or retreat late in the day. Among those who foolishly chose the latter
option, three local men died in an avalanche. Crowley, meanwhile,
remained in his tent sipping tea, technically correct in his judgment,
but callously indifferent to the fate of his companions. In 1923, when
Raoul Loveday, an Oxford friend of Raymond Greene's, died at
Crowley's occult 'anti-monastery' on Sicily, Greene went there to track
Crowley down for an explanation, finding a corpulent, peevish man;
he thought him rather silly. Greene expected exciting stories of drugs
and sex; all Crowley wanted to discuss was rock climbing.

The contrast between Crowley and Eckenstein's expedition and that
of Prince Luigi Amedeo di Savoia-Aosta, Duke of the Abruzzi, could
not have been greater. Abruzzi, grandson of the first king of Italy,
had immense wealth and had used it in lavishly funded expeditions
to Mount St Elias, on the border of Alaska and the Yukon, the Arctic
and the Ruwenzori. The hallmark of these expeditions was their scale,
and Abruzzi's attempt on K2 in 1909 was no exception; it began an
enduring fascination with K2 in Italy that reached its climax with the
first ascent in 1954. Abruzzi brought with him seven Italian guides and
porters, the guides all having Himalayan experience, six tonnes of
equipment requiring five hundred local porters, all of which allowed
his team to spend months in the field. 'What Whymper and Conway
had shaped,' wrote the mountaineering historian Walt Unsworth, 'the

Duke brought to perfection.' Abruzzi's team made a spirited effort on what would become the route of first ascent, the south-east ridge, known more commonly as the Abruzzi spur, reaching 6,710 metres; his deep pockets meant the expedition was beautifully recorded. Doctor and researcher Filippo de Filippi, who worked in London during the Great War, wrote the official account, moving hurriedly past Eckenstein's earlier attempt, but catching the almost incomprehensible scale of the Karakoram, 'so vast that one cannot get an impression of the whole at any one moment; the eye can take in only single portions.' Luckily for Abruzzi, he had with him an exceptional eye, that of Vittorio Sella, who had been round Kangchenjunga with Douglas Freshfield as well as travelling with Abruzzi on his other expeditions. Sella remains one of the very best mountain photographers in history, capturing images that recorded the architectural structure of the mountains but also something ineffable, something of their spiritual power. His photographs would inform and inspire generations of mountaineers to come. Nor was Sella the only Italian photographing the Himalaya; the Piedmontese climber Mario Piacenza made the first ascent of the Kashmiri 7,000-metre peak Kun in 1913, in the same year touring Sikkim with his camera. But Sella was the master.

While Abruzzi was on K2 with his expensive pantechnicon, a very different kind of venture was unfolding eighty kilometres to the south-east. Three English mountain explorers crossed the Saltoro Pass for the first time and looked down on what would become known as the Siachen glacier, Siachen meaning 'abundance of roses', for which the Saltoro region is famous. Given the continuing and bloody high-altitude conflict between India and Pakistan for this glacier, it's a melancholy name, but likely the invention of one of those Englishmen, Tom Longstaff, whose piratical red beard became a common sight in the Himalaya in the years before the Great War. Longstaff was the son of Llewellyn Longstaff, a wealthy businessman who paid for the *Discovery*, the boat Robert Falcon Scott and his crew sailed to Antarctica. Free of the need to work and inspired by William Graham, Longstaff dedicated himself to mountain exploration, explaining that his medical degree was simply a way to make himself more useful on expeditions. A dedicated botanist, he taught himself a working

knowledge of the languages he would need and often travelled only
in the company of locals.

Longstaff's approach was the antithesis of Abruzzi's. His first expedition to the Himalaya lasted six months, to start with exploring and
climbing in Garhwal, attempting Nanda Devi East and Nanda Kot
with the brothers Alexis and Henri Brocherel, mountain guides from
Courmayeur, on the Italian side of Mont Blanc. Then he took advantage of an invitation from Charles Sherring, deputy commissioner at
Almora, to join him on a journey through Tibet, near the north-west
corner of Nepal, including a daring attempt on Gurla Mandhata, the
mountain that towers above the southern shore of the lake Manasarovar.

> We were like Cortez, [he wrote,] seeing the Pacific for the first time;
> for no other eyes had seen these peaks from such a height spread as a
> continuous range.

He and the Brocherels reached 7,300 metres before turning back. All
this he accomplished on a budget of less than a hundred pounds.
Longstaff would be the inspiration for the famous names of lightweight mountaineering from the 1930s: Eric Shipton and H W Tilman
chief among them.

Longstaff's great year in the Himalaya was 1907, the fiftieth anniversary of the Alpine Club's formation. He had hoped to join a reconnaissance of Everest, with Charles Bruce and the publisher Arnold
Mumm, enjoying, like Younghusband, the patronage of Lord Curzon.
Alas, the secretary of state for India Lord Morley disapproved of
Curzon in general and Younghusband's invasion of Tibet in particular,
and vetoed the enterprise. Instead, the three men hired the two
Brocherel brothers, Alexis and Henri, and travelled to Garhwal, where
they failed, as Graham had done, to find a way through the Rishiganga
gorge to Nanda Devi. With the Gurkha Karbir Budhathoki, Longstaff
and the Brocherels did, however, climb Trisul, which was, for a few
years at least, the highest mountain yet climbed, at 7,120 metres. On
the day he reached the summit, Longstaff had managed to climb 1,800
metres from his top camp, a prodigious act of stamina.

In Sikkim that same year, two twenty-year-old Norwegian students,
Carl Wilhelm Rubenson and Ingvald Monrad-Aas, came close to

reaching the summit of Kabru, just as Graham claimed to have done in 1883. Rubenson had some climbing experience, his partner Monrad-Aas none whatsoever. The energy of youth was enough, but strong autumn winds turned them back short of the top. When they outlined their experiences to the Alpine Club in London, they expressed their admiration for their Sherpa 'coolies', using the term of the era, who had supported them so well. Taking careful note was a thin man, 'stooping and narrow chested', according to the Everest climber George Mallory, his appearance 'made grotesque by veritable gig-lamps of spectacles and a long pointed moustache'. His name was Alexander Kellas, and he contributed more than anyone before the Great War to our understanding of human physiology at altitude.

That Kellas remains unsung is not surprising. Like Mummery, he wasn't overly concerned about posterity, not for himself anyway. Unlike Mummery, he was shy, essentially a loner, and published little on his own account. He could write that 'mountaineering, in its widest adaptation, is the most philosophical sport in the world', and leave almost no trace of his own. He was born in Aberdeen in 1868; there are clues in his childhood to some underlying psychological illness that would trouble him most in his last years with auditory, paranoiac hallucinations. Perhaps it's not surprising that he lived alone. He trained as a chemist and worked in the same laboratory as Norman Collie, but he was never a leading climber as Collie was, let alone Mummery. He was considered reliable rather than inspired at work and, feeling thwarted, took a job lecturing medical students at Middlesex Hospital. His mountain experience accreted slowly and then suddenly burst into flame when he travelled to Sikkim in 1907, the same year as Rubenson and Monrad-Aas. He took with him two Swiss guides, but on subsequent expeditions, and there were several, he took Sherpas instead, the Tibetan ethnic group who had arrived as migrants in the high mountains of eastern Nepal, including the Everest region of Khumbu, centuries earlier. Often climbing without a European partner, Kellas developed a deep affection for his Sherpa friends, equipped them well and became fascinated not only by their physiology but their culture too. If Kellas was not the first to admire the Sherpas, he became their most influential advocate. The biologist J B S Haldane knew Kellas, who was a friend of his father, J S Haldane, like Kellas another great self-experimenter. Haldane junior told a high-altitude symposium in Darjeeling in 1962:

some people hear voices at high altitudes. Dr Kellas also heard them at sea level . . . He said that in the mountains, when no other Europeans were there, he answered these voices, and his Sherpas had great confidence in a man who had long conversations with spirits at night.

He remained always sympathetic to local sensibilities, arguing publicly that Everest should be known by its local name: Chomolungma.

Alec Kellas's greatest mountaineering achievement was his ascent in 1911 of Pauhunri in Sikkim. By then, he knew this stretch of the Himalaya as well as the hills of his native Scotland, having travelled back and forth across it several times in much the same way as the locals did, without a trace of the pomp or comfort imported with larger expeditions. Thanks to an error by the Survey of India, he never knew Pauhunri's true height was 7,128 metres, a few metres higher than Trisul, meaning Kellas and not Longstaff once held the altitude record. The omission is almost irrelevant: it was his ideas that made Kellas a true pioneer. He recorded and measured as much as he could, trained local men as photographers and sent them to Everest. The use of guides was, he argued, unethical. He theorised about rates of ascent. Kellas believed that a human without supplementary oxygen could only climb three hundred feet (ninety metres) an hour near the summit of Everest, a figure largely proven when Reinhold Messner finally managed the feat in 1978. Arthur Hinks, the dry and often irritable secretary of the Mount Everest Committee wrote to Kellas: 'no one perhaps in the world combines your enterprise as a mountaineer and your knowledge of physiology'.

As his researches deepened, he became increasingly obsessive and unstable, as though he knew his time was short. He quit his job to focus on Everest. His final winter and spring were spent in frenzied activity, to the extent that when, in the summer of 1921, he joined a reconnaissance expedition in advance of the first attempt on Everest, he was already exhausted. The expedition's food was poorly managed and several in the team came down with stomach problems that proved fatal for Kellas, who died on the high Tibetan plateau with none of his teammates near him. The expedition's leader, the austere and disagreeable soldier Charles Howard-Bury, wrote: 'It does not pay to send middle-aged men out to this country.' John Noel, who filmed the 1924 expedition, when George Mallory was lost, had shared with Kellas the dream of reaching Everest. The British might have had a chance, he wrote, with 'the combination of Kellas' Himalayan knowledge and Mallory's dash'. It was Mallory's dash that would achieve immortality; the useful intelligence and open-mindedness of Alexander Kellas would slide from view.

16

Everest Diplomacy

'I sometimes think of this expedition,' George Mallory wrote from under the shadow of Everest in the summer of 1921,

> as a fraud from beginning to end, invented by the wild enthusiasm of one man, Younghusband; puffed up by the would-be wisdom of certain pundits in the A[lpine] C[lub]; and imposed upon the youthful ardour of your humble servant.

If climbing Everest was a fraud, then it was one Mallory paid for with his life. Three years later, in early June 1924, he disappeared while attempting to reach the mist-shrouded summit, leaving behind one of the enduring legends of exploration and a mystery too: did he reach the summit before he perished? That question will likely remain unanswered; even the discovery of his body in 1999 failed to produce definitive evidence. That most expert opinion concludes Mallory didn't reach the top only adds to the enduring image, as potent now as it was then, of a human striving against all odds to realise a seemingly unattainable dream. His friend and mentor Geoffrey Winthrop Young, in a letter to the recently widowed Ruth Mallory, called it 'that magnificent courage and endurance, that joyous and supreme triumph of a human spirit over all circumstances, all mortal resistance'. Mallory himself recognised such talk as a kind of propaganda. In his letter from 1921, he wrote with cynical weariness:

> The prospect of ascent in any direction is almost nil, and our present job is to rub our noses against the impossible in such a way as to persuade mankind that some noble heroism has failed again.

There were three expeditions to Everest in the early 1920s, a drama in three acts with Mallory the star. Born in Cheshire, the son of a clergyman, his mother the daughter of a clergyman, he was, in author Patrick French's words, a 'public schoolmaster and minor Bloomsbury groupie'. Mallory balanced his restless streak of self-absorbtion with bourgeois respectability. As a Cambridge undergraduate Lytton Strachey lusted after him. ('Mon Dieu! – George Mallory! – When that's been written, what more need be said?') But beyond some unsatisfactory fumbling with Strachey's brother James, Mallory generally stuck to the rails. As the decade of flappers and modernism dawned, he was a married teacher in his mid thirties with three young children, not quite matching the dazzling brilliance of his more famous friends at Cambridge; the 'label of Everest', as Geoffrey Winthrop Young called it when persuading him to go, was an opportunity to stoke the embers of his early promise.

Sir Francis Younghusband, imperialist, mystic and president of the Royal Geographical Society, had as a young man forty years earlier thrilled the British public with his daring traverse of the Mustagh Pass. Climbing Everest was a chance for him to rekindle that youthful fire, if only by proxy. He needed an arrow to aim at the mountain, and Mallory was the best available in a quiver half-emptied by the Great War. (Or as Tom Longstaff put it in a note to the editor of the *Alpine Journal*: 'Owing to the War the supply of young climbers is less than formerly.') Younghusband thought Mallory 'good-looking, with a sensible, cultivated air'. Later, after Mallory's death, he was more critical, complaining that Mallory had never grasped the scale of Younghusband's vision, judging it all to be 'a bit of sensationalism'. Mallory, prone to striking arch poses in letters to friends, wrote how Younghusband 'amuses and delights me'. The Everest reconnaissance planned for 1921 had 'become a sort of religious pilgrimage in his eyes. I expect I shall end by sitting at his feet, hearing tales of Lhasa and Chitral.' That quasi-mystical strand remains a key flavour in Mallory's enduring myth, a narrative deliberately frothed up by Younghusband, who had a flair for publicity and was helped in that side of things by the novelist John Buchan and Geoffrey Winthrop Young, who dubbed Mallory the Galahad of Everest.

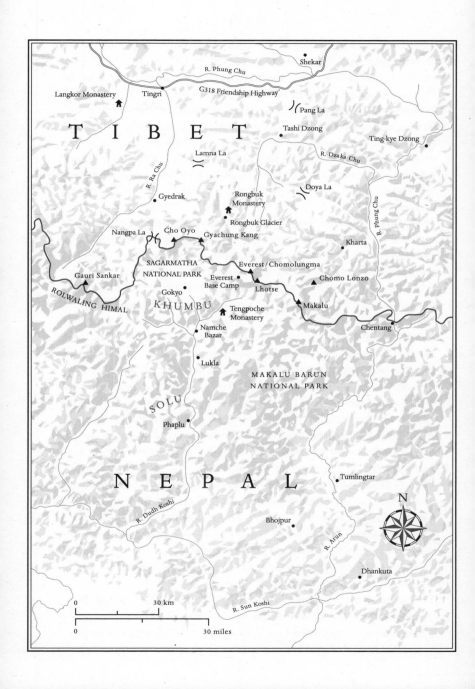

The Everest expeditions of the 1920s, the first in 1921 an exploratory reconnaissance and then two full attempts in 1922 and 1924, have been characterised as a coda to the horrors of the Great War. Many of those involved had fought, including Mallory. Yet the cultural inspiration was not the sorrow of war and its modernist aftermath; it was instead an attempt to recapture the self-assurance of the Edwardian era. Naturally enough, those, like Younghusband, who drove the project, were older, but the average age of those who went on the 1921 reconnaissance was forty and the average for the specialist climbers was even higher. They may have fought in the war but they weren't formed in it.

This atmosphere of late imperialism was meshed in Younghusband's mind with an ill-defined spiritual yearning that preoccupied him throughout the 1920s, years the old soldier spent writing increasingly self-indulgent mystical tracts. Such apparent contradictions were his hallmark. In 1904, just before he marched into Tibet at the head of a potent military force to wage war on a hopelessly outgunned Tibetan army, he had read a book by the Theosophist and political campaigner Annie Besant, whom he had recently met, called *Cosmic Consciousness*. It offered, Younghusband told his wife Helen, 'a most intensely beautiful and peaceful idea of the Universe'. It was typical of Younghusband to hold inside his head two potent but contradictory myths about Tibet, as a lost spiritual haven and the imperial adventurer's blank canvas. In fact, the early Everest expeditions as a whole can be understood both as mystical feats of tragi-heroic mountaineering and part of a decades-long campaign of military and diplomatic intervention by the British in Tibet.

Younghusband wasn't the only powerful Victorian adventurer with an interest in Tibet. His predecessor as president of the Royal Geographical Society was the more prosaic surveyor Sir Thomas Holdich. In 1906 Holdich had published *Tibet the Mysterious*, one of several such books published in the aftermath of Younghusband's invasion. Holdich's Tibet was in fact not at all mysterious.

Now that our mission to Tibet has returned to the Indian border, [he wrote,] we know how very little there is in Lhasa to justify that mystic fascination ... The veil has been torn aside and the naked city has been revealed in all its weird barbarity.

Yet it was on Holdich's watch that pre-war dreams of an attempt on Everest were resuscitated. Before Holdich was the Himalayan explorer Douglas Freshfield, president during the Great War, whose grandfather's fortune had been made working for the East India Company. Before Freshfield was the political titan Lord Curzon, who as viceroy not only sent Younghusband into Tibet but offered early and powerful support to the Everest adventure. 'It has always seemed to me,' Curzon wrote to Freshfield in 1905,

> a reproach that with the second highest mountain in the world [Kangchenjunga] for the most part in British territory and with the highest in a neighbouring and friendly state we, the mountaineers and pioneers par excellence of the universe, make no sustained and scientific attempt to climb to the top of either of them.

When the British did finally make their first visit to Everest in 1921, the enterprise was not only launched from within the imperial worldview these men shared, it followed a physical route made viable by Curzon's aggressive policy and the 1904 invasion. Permission for the expeditions required considerable diplomatic effort, bringing into play high-ranking political officers. While the climbers got the headlines, it was the intervention of these singularly placed diplomats that gained them access to the mountain. After Mallory's death, there would be no further attempts in the 1920s. Ostensibly, this was because of offence caused to the Tibetan government. The true reasons for this rupture went far deeper, revealing a structural faultline in the British Empire's strategy on its Himalayan frontier, a strategy whose origins emerged from the smouldering wreckage of the rebellion of 1857.

*

On 1 November 1858, Queen Victoria's proclamation appointing Lord Canning as her first viceroy in India was published at Allahabad, formalising the transfer of power from the East India Company to the British crown. Victoria promised toleration of race and creed and acknowledged herself bound by 'obligations of Duty' to her new Indian subjects, a new contract built on justice, an attempt to turn

the page on the horror of civil war. Another commitment was aimed
at India's elite.

> We desire no extension of Our present territorial Possessions; and while
> We will permit no aggression upon Our Dominions or Our Rights, to
> be attempted with impunity, We shall sanction no encroachment on
> those of others.

That pledge reassured Indian princes anxious about their future status.
It also signalled a shift in perspective. The Company's violent struggle
for control of India was ended, beginning a period of consolidation
under the aegis of a just and protective monarch. This didn't prevent
millions of Indians dying miserably in a sequence of famines, particularly those of the late 1870s, when laissez-faire economics devastated
southern India. The then viceroy Lord Lytton was more anxious about
external threats, particularly the Russian Empire: the Great Game,
although the term hardly existed before Kipling popularised it in 1901
with the publication of *Kim*. The bulk of this confrontation took place
in Central Asia, to the north-west of India, but as years passed and
British policy developed the Himalaya was drawn in. Victoria's promise
to avoid the acquisition of new territory wouldn't prevent the British
Raj from consolidating its influence in the hodgepodge of states along
its Himalayan marches, whether they liked it or not.

Viewed from Lhasa, the British arrival in the Himalaya in the early
nineteenth century must have looked like a wildfire spreading out of
control. The Dalai Lama, whom the Qing had made temporal head
of state in 1750, was boxed in by China's ambans in Lhasa, the demands
of an ancient and often fractious aristocracy and the immense
power of Tibet's enormous monastic institutions, which controlled
much of the economy. Buddhist Tibet's instinct was simply not to
engage with the belligerent power occupying the holy land where the
Buddha had preached. And with the East India Company anxious not
to antagonise the Qing, British dealings with Tibet had been almost
non-existent in the first part of the nineteenth century. By the 1850s
it was a different story. War with Nepal had given the Company control
of Kumaon and Garhwal. The bullish militaristic regime in Kathmandu
might have dragged the Company into further damaging and expensive wars. Instead, a combination of geography, internal rivalries and

diplomacy meant Nepal, unlike Afghanistan, became a model frontier state, at least from the British point of view.

Things looked different from Tibet. Far from being pacified, Nepal's charismatic leader Jang Bahadur sought to recover lost prestige elsewhere. In the early 1850s, with the Qing Empire embroiled in its devastating civil war with the Christian millenarian Taiping Heavenly Kingdom and Tibet distracted by the death of the eleventh Dalai Lama, Jang invaded Tibet, swiftly occupying the familiar mountain trade routes through the Kyirong and Bhote Kosi valleys. Thousands of Tibetan troops retreated to the desolate plain of Tingri, so familiar to early Everest climbers, to defend the approaches to Lhasa. Although Jang faced stiffer resistance than anticipated, he forced the Tibetans to sign the Treaty of Thapathali, restoring a good proportion of Nepal's old trading privileges and returning a Nepali ambassador or *vakil* to Lhasa, a diplomatic presence that would become immensely beneficial to the British.

Fears about Jang's reaction to the 1857 rebellion were eased after his intervention on behalf of the British at the siege of Lucknow; in subsequent decades, dynastic struggle among his successors gave the British a useful lever. In 1885 Jang's younger brother and successor Ranodip was assassinated. It was, as so often, a family affair. Four of the seventeen sons, the *satra bhai*, of Jang's youngest brother Dhir, entered the palace on the false pretext of delivering a message from the governor general in Calcutta. Bir Shamsher, the eldest, remained a floor below, where the king had his apartments; the others, including another future prime minister Chandra Shamsher, continued upstairs. Here, in the words of the campaigning journalist William Digby, he 'requited his uncle's confidence by basely murdering him'. The first bullet grazed Ranodip's forehead. The second hit him squarely. Digby had written a passionate exposé of British failures during the famines of the late 1870s and was a powerful critic of the Raj who worked for a while for the Indian National Congress. He wrote an account of Anglo-Nepali relations criticising Calcutta for doing nothing in this crisis to help Ranodip's dynasty, despite his support during the 1857 rebellion.

No public department in any country, despotically or constitutionally ruled, ever had so short a memory, or one more oblivious to history and the claims of justice, than the Calcutta Foreign Office.

For Calcutta's foreign office, it was simply a question of expediency. For generations the British had wanted to recruit Gurkha troops inside Nepal, something Jang Bahadur and his brother Ranodip had resisted. Bir's bloody coup gave the British the necessary leverage to negotiate that access.

As far as Tibet was concerned, the British were looking through a glass, darkly. The East India Company had brilliant scholars at its disposal but none of them spoke Tibetan. The Company had invested precious little in studying the vast country to the north. Years before it had given a small allowance to the Hungarian philologist Sándor Csoma de Kőrös, who had met William Moorcroft in Kashmir in July 1822. The two men, both prodigious travellers, became friends: the ever-curious and bullish Englishman and the quiet Hungarian, a born scholar, shy but dedicated. Moorcroft suggested Csoma de Kőrös travel with him to Ladakh to study and translate manuscripts in the Buddhist monasteries there. With Moorcroft's introductions, the Hungarian became the first European to visit Zanskar, the hauntingly wild region south of the Ladakhi capital Leh, studying with a lama called Sangey Phuntsog at the palace of Zangla on the banks of the Zanskar river. Sangey Phuntsog wasn't a monk, but an *amchi*, a medical practitioner and also an astrologer. The two men sat on a sheepskin rug huddled against the cold in the Hungarian's tiny cell, ploughing through the great encyclopaedias of Tibetan Buddhism.

Csoma de Kőrös also visited Zongkhul monastery where he learned more about the practice of Buddhism from the abbot Kunga Choeleg. The abbot wrote a book based on the questions the Hungarian asked him: *The Questions of European Skandar*, Sándor being the Hungarian version of Alexander. After years of study and intense labour, latterly in Kinnaur on the banks of the Sutlej at the Buddhist centre of Kanam, Csoma de Kőrös travelled to Calcutta where in 1834, he published the first Tibetan grammar in English. He was welcomed into the Asiatic Society of Bengal, working as their librarian for several years before setting out for Lhasa in 1842 at the age of fifty-eight. Crossing the terai on his way to the mountains, he contracted malaria and died at Darjeeling, where he is buried.

Work like that of Sándor Csoma de Kőrös might have seemed peripheral to the business of government but what Calcutta lacked in its dealings with Tibet during the later years of the nineteenth century were precisely his soft skills. The focus in Calcutta for dealings with princely states and foreign powers was the Indian Political Department. Reformed by Lord Ellenborough in 1843, its officers, known as 'politicals', were responsible for managing relationships with the leaders of princely states loyal to the British and with regional foreign countries such as Tibet, Bhutan and Nepal. Men like Traill in Kumaon and Hodgson in Kathmandu had proved immensely effective in these roles but building the personal networks required to broker deals and read the complexities of each political crisis, as they had done, required years of dedicated service. George Bogle in Tibet had understood this very clearly and built a good working relationship with the Panchen Lama. Had both men lived, British relations with Tibet might have developed in a more constructive direction. A handful of more perceptive diplomats consulted Bogle's account of his journey both in manuscript and after it was published in 1876. Yet it took British officialdom until the early years of the twentieth century to appreciate its message. By that time a century had passed and great damage had been done.

A clearer understanding of Tibetan culture might also have answered one of the questions the government in Calcutta found most perplexing: the relationship between China and Tibet. Even as late as the 1890s there were few informed European views of contemporary Tibet, and opinion as to the status of the Chinese there was contradictory. Many of the observers were Christian missionaries who took a dim view of Tibetan Buddhism, a spiritual practice they were attempting to subvert. As a teenage boy in the mid 1860s the US diplomat William Woodville Rockhill had read Évariste Huc's account of his 1846 expedition to Lhasa and been inspired to learn Tibetan, the first American to do so, using inherited wealth to explore western China and eastern Tibet while working at the legation in Beijing. 'Whenever China sees the necessity of doing so,' he wrote in his account of those travels,

it can effectually assert its supremacy in Tibet, for it is absurd to say that China is not the sovereign power there and that Chinese officials are only there to manage their own people, and are tolerated, as it were, in the country.

Yet there were opposite views. General Sir Hamilton Bower had, as a young cavalry officer, performed a number of intelligence missions in Central Asia in the late 1880s and early 1890s. He had looked for the killer of a Scottish trader, Andrew Dalgleish, murdered on the road between Leh and Yarkand, and bought the ancient Sanskrit text, written on birch bark, that had galvanised interest in the lost Buddhist culture of the Silk Roads in eastern Turkestan. After that, Bower crossed Tibet from west to east, without attempting to visit Lhasa. 'My own impression,' he wrote in his account of that journey,

> is that the Chinese suzerainty is very shadowy, though the Tibetans in exclusiveness are quite willing to take shelter behind the Chinese in negotiations with foreign powers. If China really has power in Tibet, and if it is a part of China then by the treaty of Tien-tsin [Tianjin], Englishmen can go there on passport, but every one knows that the Chinese are not in a position to issue a passport which the Tibetans would consider valid.

By 1858 and the end of the Indian rebellion, there were several reasons for Tibetans to mistrust and dislike the British. Tibet's powerful monastic institutions dominated trade, especially the import of tea from China, and didn't want their revenue streams interrupted by interfering foreigners. Nor did they wish to offer a route in for European missionaries gathering on Tibet's borders. French Lazarist priests in Tibet's eastern fringes would prove expert in winding up international opinion for a more open Tibet. More urgently, the British were perceived as allies of the Gorkha regime in Kathmandu, which since its inception had been at odds with Lhasa. Tibet feared Gorkha's military aggression and resented the Treaty of Thapathali they had signed with Nepal following Jang Bahadur's invasion of 1854, involving not just the restoration of a Nepali resident to Lhasa but also the payment of tribute. True, in the early nineteenth century Nepal had been an enemy of British India but the relationship had over the decades altered dramatically. In the minds of Tibet's rulers, Gorkhali support for the East India Company during the 1857 rebellion completed the picture.

In that context, when in the 1860s the British began building roads in India close to the Tibetan border, particularly in Sikkim, Tibet considered such activity a security threat. Tibet also feared any strengthening of the relationship between Kathmandu and Beijing. Jang Bahadur had resumed Gorkha's tribute missions to Beijing in 1866, although more for trade than an expression of obedience. In return Beijing sent ambassadors to Kathmandu, but this apparently cosier arrangement provoked anti-Nepali riots in Lhasa. China's ambans were swift to reassure the Dalai Lama's government, and as a gesture of support instructed their troops to use the Nepali resident's house for musket practice. Relations between Beijing and Kathmandu soured further when China helped Tibet fortify its border with Nepal; by 1873 war between the two small neighbours seemed almost inevitable. That it didn't happen says a great deal about the relative weakness of all concerned. Nepal feared a repeat of 1792, when Chinese troops came close to Kathmandu. China knew that while it still had a couple of thousand troops in Tibet, it could no longer attempt that kind of boldness. Tibet was almost paralysed, its leaders invested in a theocratic system that seemed unwilling and incapable of facing the immense political and cultural changes that industrialisation and global trade had brought.

Britain was at the forefront of both and looked with interest at how it might exploit this conflict. The Indian army officer and administrator Owen Tudor Burne wrote in 1874 that tension among India's Himalayan neighbours

cannot but be productive of advantage to ourselves, as whatever the issue, it must tend to improve our relations with Nepal and Tibet which are now closed doors, and will ever remain so as long as we rely on Mr Wade and Sir Jang Bahadur.

Mr Wade was Thomas Francis Wade, 'Envoy Extraordinary and Minister Plenipotentiary and Chief Superintendent of British Trade in China', and as such was not inclined to push the almost negligible issue of trans-Himalayan trade at the cost of good relations with the Qing. To Wade, Tibet was picturesque but unprofitable and consequently not worth the bother. British officials in Darjeeling were left to make educated guesses about the political situation across the border from the frequent interruptions to trade between Tibet and India.

Pressure to improve this trade nevertheless remained strong, a weight of opinion galvanised by the self-styled 'pioneer of commerce' Thomas Thornville Cooper. The eighth son of a ship-owner from County Durham, Cooper was a sickly teenager who on medical advice escaped Britain for the sunshine of Australia. At nineteen he was working for the Arbuthnot bank in Madras, then travelled throughout India before embarking for Shanghai, where he became mixed up in the hugely destructive Taiping rebellion. With that ended, he set out to travel to India via Tibet with support from European traders in the city. Cooper considered joining the Nepali tribute mission as it returned home to Kathmandu, but was denied permission to enter Tibet even before he'd left Shanghai. So in early 1868 he set out on his own. Reaching Batang in China's Sichuan province on the main trade route between Chengdu and Lhasa, he met the town's Lazarist missionaries, who, sensing an opportunity, offered their help. They persuaded the governor of Sichuan to give Cooper a passport for Tibet, hoping that Cooper would be arrested by the Tibetans, forcing the British to act and so open up Tibet to missionaries, including them. Cooper played along but when he reached the border his passport was simply refused: the pioneer of commerce was forced to turn south and approach India across the Hengduan mountains, again unsuccessfully and he returned to Shanghai. Cooper later attempted the same journey but in reverse: reaching China from the Indian state of Assam. Once again he was turned back.

Despite these reversals, Cooper became a champion of trade between India and western China. He read a lengthy memorandum on the subject to the Calcutta chamber of commerce after returning from his second attempt, describing the state of trade running between Chengdu and Lhasa via the border town of Kangding, historically known as Tachienlu. At the heart of this trade was tea. Cooper estimated that Tibet consumed annually more than two thousand tons of the stuff, largely imported from Sichuan. Why should that tea not come from the gardens of Darjeeling instead? Cooper knew Tibet's monasteries held a near monopoly on this trade and took a cut of the taxes paid on it. They weren't about to give up that interest without some kind of intervention. As far as Cooper was concerned, nothing would change until a 'British Minister resides in Lhasa and the Lamas have been taught their utter helplessness when actually brought into

contact with a British force'. In 1873, as Tibet and Nepal came close
to war, Cooper helped put together a powerful lobbying group of old
Himalayan stagers that included Brian Houghton Hodgson and Joseph
Hooker. Their proposals for improved roads, trade fairs and British
representation inside Tibet would become the policy of the Indian
government. Pressure came too from chambers of commerce in
northern English industrial towns, which even before Cooper's entry
on the scene had petitioned the India Office to do something about
access to western China's markets. The prolific author Demetrius
Charles Boulger, an imperial cheerleader writing in the 1880s, looked
forward to the day when 'the people of Szechuen [Sichuan] wear
Manchester goods and use Sheffield cutlery'.

The conduit for such trade was to be via Sikkim's Chumbi valley
into Tibet, which Younghusband would call 'the only strategical point
of value in the whole north-eastern frontier from Kashmir to Burma'.
In March 1860, Archie Campbell, still smarting a decade on from his
humiliating imprisonment, took a company of native troops into
Sikkim to protest against infringements of British jurisdiction but was
himself attacked and forced to retreat so hastily that the baggage of
his small force was abandoned. Once again clearing up Campbell's
mess to maintain British prestige, Calcutta retaliated with a much
larger force led by John Cox Gawler. With him went the political
officer Ashley Eden who on conclusion of a swift campaign signed
the Treaty of Tumlong with the *chogyal*. Restrictions on trade were
lifted and the British were given the right to build roads inside Sikkim.

Some of Calcutta's enemies in Sikkim fled to Bhutan, the catalyst
for an escalation of tension that had been brewing for decades. Eden
was despatched to reach some kind of settlement but was treated
rather like Campbell had been in Sikkim. This time Calcutta didn't
hesitate in sending troops. Bhutan was destabilised by civil war and
its military was armed with antiquated matchlocks and bows and
arrows. Some of its soldiers still wore chain mail. Yet they offered
stiff resistance and British Indian forces suffered embarrassing reversals.
When they eventually prevailed in 1865, Bhutan ceded the *duars*, the
plains at the foot of the mountains, to the British in return for rent.
Calcutta concluded that buying Bhutan's cooperation would be easier
than enforcing it. The violent civil unrest that plagued Bhutan for the
next two decades offered the British little hope of using the country

as a route to Tibet. With western Tibet closed, Nepal off limits and a proposed railway to China through Assam little more than a distant dream, the focus for liberalising trade across the Himalaya really did fall squarely on Sikkim.

The assumption remained throughout this period that the riddle of Tibet would be solved in Beijing. And at times it seemed as though progress was being made. In 1875, the British translator Augustus Raymond Margary was murdered returning through Yunnan to Shanghai from a mission to explore trade routes between China and Burma. (Violent death was an occupational hazard for colonial serv-ants in such remote locations: three years later, the trade lobbyist Thomas Cooper, by then serving as political agent in Burma, was also murdered.) Thomas Wade, Elgin's successor in Beijing, used Margary's death to win more concessions on freedom of movement from the Chinese, in the Chefoo Convention of 1876, making sure Tibet was covered too. It didn't make any difference. Trade across the border at Sikkim was no easier and Tibet remained forbidden ground, whatever passports were issued in Beijing.

In 1883, the Bhutanese, buoyed with British subsidies and resentful of Lhasa's suzerainty, looted the Tibetan frontier town of Phari, close to the Sikkimese border. That interrupted trade across the Jelep La, the pass separating Tibet from Sikkim, which in turn was noticed in the bazaar at Darjeeling. An official called Colman Macaulay, financial secretary of the government in Calcutta, was despatched to Tibet to investigate. An Ulsterman with a Protestant father and Catholic mother, Macaulay sensed an opportunity. At Khamba Dzong, an administrative centre on the road to Shigatse, a local official told him of pent-up demand in Tibet for European goods and how 'whenever a man gets an article of English manufacture, a hundred people come to look at it'. It was the conservatism of the great Lhasa monasteries that stood in the way: a sizable chunk of the laity would welcome warmer relations. The Panchen Lama at Shigatse, he hinted, might offer a route in. Macaulay had read George Bogle and adopted his strategy: the Indian government should offer the Panchen Lama a piece of land in Calcutta, as Bogle had done. The monasteries at Lhasa, which he described as 'the national party in permanent oppo-sition to the Chinese', could be paid off. The Panchen Lama for one seemed delighted at this prospect, sending Calcutta a long shopping list that included English–Tibetan dictionaries and photographic equipment. The prospect of exporting Indian tea and English manufactured goods to Tibet and western China seemed within reach.

Not everyone was so optimistic. The chargé d'affaires in Beijing was another Irishman, Nicholas O'Conor from County Roscommon. O'Conor warned London that the Qing still regarded Tibet as an integral part of its empire but could not impose its wishes on the Dalai Lama, or at least his government, since the Dalai Lama was then a boy of nine. There was the real risk of a violent reception for any British mission, especially if it went armed. Macaulay pressed ahead, winning the approval of Randolph Churchill, then secretary of state for India, while on leave in London. Churchill sent Macaulay to Beijing to get the necessary Tibetan passports. With him went Sarat Chandra Das, counted among the pundits for his secret journeys within Tibet. In Beijing he stayed at the Yellow Temple, where the Tseten Nomonhan, Tibet's ambassador, had his residence, and from where the Tibetans kept a close eye on Macaulay's negotiations. Das realised the Tibetan establishment was determined to block Macaulay, that the Panchen Lama had simply been looking for leverage against Lhasa and that the Chinese were anxious to avoid a repeat of the Margary affair. Should something happen to Macaulay, they reasoned, the British would have an excuse to annex Tibet much as they were doing in Burma. Nor was there much enthusiasm for Macaulay's plan in Calcutta. The viceroy Lord Dufferin was acutely aware of public hostility at home to the Burmese campaign and only too happy to cancel Macaulay's mission in exchange for China recognising the British position in Burma. A more astute diplomat than Macaulay or Churchill, the last thing he needed was another unpopular and expensive war on the fringes of the empire.

Dufferin's decision came a shade too late. Some within the Tibetan government were reluctant to antagonise the British but the monastic power behind the Dalai Lama thought otherwise. The Nechung, Tibet's state oracle, advocated military action and in the summer of 1886 Tibetan troops crossed the Jelep La into Sikkim where they fortified themselves against attack. This wasn't an isolated show of strength. For years and all along its Himalayan frontier, Tibet had been asserting itself, as much to show its independence from China as in defiance of British India. Two years later, with Calcutta's patience at an end,

a British force finally cleared the Tibetans out of Sikkim and a
protracted series of negotiations began. In 1890 a new treaty was
signed with the Qing dynasty that tightened Britain's grip on Sikkim.
John Claude White became the first British political agent at the
Sikkimese capital Gangtok and a trade agent was stationed at Yatung
close to Sikkim's border with Tibet. Trade talks continued and further
regulations were agreed in 1893. A year later the scholar Herbert Hope
Risley, author of the *Sikkim Gazetteer*, wrote that Tibet 'lies on the
other side of a great wall, which we, as rulers of India, have not the
slightest ambition to climb'. Any attempt to make that climb would
be, Risley concluded, 'a piece of surpassing folly'.

Despite Risley's warning, within a decade the Indian government
would send Francis Younghusband and a military expedition across
that great wall to occupy Lhasa.

*

For half a century the British had tried to regulate its Himalayan
border with Tibet through China but Tibet's invasion and brief occupation of Sikkim had now made it clear that China could no longer
guarantee the terms of any treaty it signed with relation to Tibet. In
1895, the Qing were defeated at the hands of imperial Japan. It was
now starkly obvious that the balance of power in East Asia was shifting
towards Japan and away from the Western European powers, a process
accelerated by the Boxer Rebellion, the anti-imperialist and anti-Christian uprising that began in 1899. In the tiny world of Sikkim, less than
a rounding error in the business of empire, John Claude White discovered the Tibetans reluctant to adhere to the agreement signed in 1890;
trade remained paltry and border disputes continued. Two men, both
charismatic and ambitious, now emerged to galvanise this uncertain
scene: Lord Curzon and the thirteenth Dalai Lama. Antagonists who
never met, both men can be judged to have failed, but only one of
those failures, that of the Dalai Lama in his attempts to modernise
his country, would prove a tragedy.

Lord Curzon of Kedleston became Queen Victoria's last viceroy of
India in January 1899, at the apogee of the British Raj, fulfilling an
ambition he had held throughout his adult life. Talented, industrious
and widely disliked, Curzon's name is almost shorthand for the

dismissive arrogance of the British upper classes. At Balliol College, Oxford, the doggerel written for him stuck:

> My name is George Nathaniel Curzon,
> I am a most superior person.
> My cheeks are pink, my hair is sleek,
> I dine at Blenheim twice a week.

His second wife recalled how in the Curzon household, foot servants were chosen for the elegance of their wrists while holding a plate. Even as a young man his friends predicted he would be foreign secretary; before he entered politics he had a passion for exploratory travel, despite a chronically injured back, that would echo in his enthusiasm for the Everest adventure. The fact that in 1919 he realised his friends' prediction by actually becoming foreign secretary also helped the prospects of an Everest expedition.

There is a photograph taken in 1901 that captures Curzon, his brilliance and his vanity, and the world he moved through. He stands in neatly creased plus fours, pith helmet in his right hand, among a group of British staff officers and officials, Nepali colonels and turbaned bearers proudly looking down at the corpse of the gigantic tiger he has just shot. Hunting, or *shikar*, was the imperial equivalent of a businessman's round of golf, beloved of British aristocrats and Indian potentates alike. It was a chance to do business, and Curzon had an agenda.

The viceroy wasn't altogether welcome in Nepal. Bir Shamsher Rana, nephew of Jang Bahadur and still maharaja following the assassination of his uncle Ranodip in 1885, had been unwell when Curzon requested an invitation to visit Nepal and was initially reluctant to accede. Then, after the invitation had been made but before Curzon arrived in March 1901, Bir Shamsher died, to be replaced by his younger brother Dev. Among the *satra bhai*, the seventeen brothers, Dev had been closest to the marginalised sons of Jang Bahadur and was consequently distrusted. Worse, he had reforming instincts. Dev wanted universal primary education for Nepali children and wider engagement in politics. So Curzon's visit, a fortnight after Bir Shamsher's death, was inconvenient. Dev's younger brother Chandra, head of the army, volunteered to take Curzon hunting but from what happened next it seems unlikely they talked only of tigers. Three months later, in June 1901, Chandra deposed Dev in a coup and with lightning speed Calcutta recognised his government, congratulating him on how it had been achieved without the usual bloodletting. Queen Victoria might have promised the British would not acquire more territory in the subcontinent but that didn't exclude regime change.

What Curzon got from Chandra in return was support for his Tibet policy. Nepal, under the terms of its 1856 treaty with Tibet, was technically obliged to come to Lhasa's aid if attacked by a foreign power. Curzon needed to anchor Nepal firmly to his side before moving forward. He was determined to end the drift on the border with Tibet where agreements signed in good faith were being ignored and his letters to the Dalai Lama were returned unopened. More importantly, Curzon was determined to stop what he perceived as a Russian threat to absorb Tibet into its empire as China's power waned. It was true that Russia had benefitted from the collapse of the Qing Empire by taking territory in Manchuria. And the British had known for a century that Russian influence could be felt in the Himalaya: George Bogle and William Moorcroft had both seen it. What Curzon feared was altogether different. He believed that the other great figure in this drama, the thirteenth Dalai Lama, was falling under the political control of St Petersburg. Yet while there was some mutual interest between Russia and Tibet, it wasn't remotely sufficient to justify military intervention. As with the weapons of mass destruction not found in Iraq in 2003, serious politicians were convinced a Russian threat existed, but it was more or less fiction.

For most of the nineteenth century, the Dalai Lamas were little more than political pawns, boys whom the progressively more conservative religious establishment could control and who died shortly before or after they reached their majority, not always of natural causes. Trinley Gyatso, the twelfth Dalai Lama, had been enthroned in 1873 at the age of sixteen but died of a 'mysterious illness' two years later. This sequence of underage national leaders meant the Panchen Lama at Tashilhunpo and senior monks in the great lamaseries at Lhasa kept a tight if not always harmonious grip on the political helm under the watchful eyes of China's ambans. The thirteenth Dalai Lama, Thubten Gyatso, was different. First, the Panchen Lama at this time was a child too. Second, as Chinese influence waned, Thubten Gyatso had been presented as the only candidate for Dalai Lama to the Qing, signalling Lhasa's growing confidence to act independently of the Golden Urn. As a boy he survived an outbreak of smallpox, leaving him with a mildly pitted complexion, and he grew up in an atmosphere of spiritual seclusion, insulated from the growing tension with British India. While most Dalai Lamas assumed political control by the age of eighteen, Thubten Gyatso requested he continue his studies for two more years. Even then he remained anxious that he was too inexperienced to face the growing crisis developing across the mountains and was persuaded to take up the reins of power only after consulting the Nechung Oracle. He also faced threats from within, surviving an assassination attempt by his former regent.

What worried Curzon was the Dalai Lama's long-standing friendship with a Buryat Mongol monk called Agvan Dorzhiev. More than twenty years his senior, Dorzhiev was a teacher and debating partner of the young Thubten Gyatso. He told him about his homeland and the growing influence of Russia. With China signing treaties with the British that the Tibetans neither wanted nor approved, and increasingly incapable of securing Tibet's borders, the Dalai Lama used Dorzhiev as a contact with the imperial capital of St Petersburg, explicitly requesting the support of Russia as a diplomatic counterweight to the increasing British pressure. As much as this shocked the British, it was an obvious move. As the Russian Empire established itself in Siberia, the tsars treated those of their subjects that practised Tibetan Buddhism relatively well, whereas the British appeared hostile to Buddhism and supportive of Christian missionaries. The notion of Russia sending an army to Tibet was fanciful, but Curzon used Dorzhiev's mission as the foundation on which to stack every half-baked rumour of Russian influence that emerged from the bazaars of Simla and Darjeeling. He was aided in this by his friend the maharaja of Nepal, Chandra Shamsher, who relayed to Calcutta any anti-Russian gossip that arrived from Kathmandu's representative in Lhasa: passing on news of Russian arms shipments arriving in the Tibetan capital spurred the British to supply the Nepali army. Chandra promised Curzon when they met at the Delhi coronation durbar in 1903 – the 'Curzonation' – that Nepal would disregard any obligations to Tibet but only in return for compensation.

The point man for Curzon's policy in Tibet was his loyal friend Francis Younghusband. They had met when Younghusband returned on leave to Britain in 1892 and again in Chitral, in modern-day Pakistan, two years later. Having been something of one himself, Curzon took a shine to explorers, and frontiers obsessed him. Younghusband could see Curzon's faults but knew he was on the fast track to greatness and admired his assurance and drive. He would have no better friend, at least professionally. When Curzon arrived in India as viceroy, Younghusband's glittering early promise had rather stalled. He was a colonial administrator in Rajasthan dealing with a horrifying famine and had witnessed desperate Indians eating roots and leaves, or else 'seizing burnt remains from the funeral pyres and gnawing at them'. Curzon invited him to Simla for a rest and gave him a more prestigious posting, reassuring Younghusband he was still regarded 'as an old friend and fellow-traveller'. When Curzon decided to force Tibet's hand he had already singled out Younghusband as the perfect man for the job.

In July 1903 Younghusband crossed the Tibetan border at the head of a diplomatic mission to make clear to the Tibetans that Curzon was determined to resolve the situation. With him went the political officer Claude White, 'a little god' in Sikkim, according to Younghusband, but 'worse than useless in dealing with high officials of an independent nation'. Younghusband himself got almost nowhere. The Tibetans maintained their stony indifference to British demands. Camped uselessly outside the fort at Khamba Dzong, Younghusband in desperation passed on rumours to Calcutta from Annie Taylor, the missionary at Yatung, that twenty thousand Russians were marching on Lhasa. 'We have merely to burst the bloated bubble of monkish power,' he wrote to Curzon, 'and we shall have the people with us, and be able to oust that Russian influence which has already done us so much damage.' As a misreading of the situation in Tibet it was hard to beat.

In late December, as winter settled its bitter grip on the high Tibetan plateau, Younghusband set out once more for Tibet, this time at the front of a column of a thousand troops, mostly Gurkhas and Sikhs, with a vast baggage train featuring thousands of yaks, mules, bullocks and ponies most of which would perish in the harsh conditions of a Tibetan campaign. The military force was commanded by Major General James Macdonald, a seasoned if rather dull engineer with long experience of Africa. More recently he had been building roads in Sikkim and was the senior officer on the spot when Curzon ordered military intervention. Macdonald fretted about supply lines and constantly urged caution. In frustration, Younghusband turned to the younger officers around him, especially Captain Frank O'Connor, born in County Longford, who had arrived in Darjeeling as a young artillery officer and fallen in love with the high, unexplored country to the north. O'Connor was the first and at the time only British officer in the whole of the Indian army capable of holding a conversation in Tibetan and had been appointed to Younghusband's mission as interpreter. O'Connor's presence in British Himalayan diplomacy would be understated but seemingly ubiquitous for the next twenty years. Another was Frederick Marshman Bailey, discoverer of the blue poppy. Known as Eric and then in his early twenties, Bailey was born in Lahore, the son of a lieutenant colonel in the Indian army and a friend of O'Connor who followed his example in learning Tibetan. He caught Younghusband's eye as just the sort of man the empire needed on the frontier.

The Tibetan winter was no less brutal for the British than it had been for Zorowar Singh's Dogra army sixty years earlier. At the British encampment at Tuna, marooned five kilometres high on the windblasted plateau, troops huddled round yak-dung fires; a dozen Sikh Pioneers died of pneumonia. Lieutenant Arthur Hadow of the Norfolk Regiment, who commanded the column's pair of Maxim guns, used rum and kerosene to keep their cooling system from freezing up in temperatures that sank to minus 30 °C. (It was the Maxim guns that revealed the bullying nature of the British mission in Tibet.)

Near the hot springs of Chumi Shengo on the last day of March 1904, as the British column resumed its march towards the important town of Gyantse, their path was blocked by two thousand Tibetan troops, many of them *dob-dob*, monks who kept order in the sometimes turbulent monasteries. There was a brief meeting between the Tibetan general Lhading and British commanders; then British troops outflanked their opponents to make surrender inevitable. Not a shot had been fired. As Sikh Pioneers began disarming the Tibetans, British officers had time to photograph their exotic-looking enemies with their matchlocks and swords. Then a moment's misunderstanding and the shooting began. A Sikh was hit in the jaw and the Maxim guns opened up. Macdonald reported to Curzon the following morning that his men had used fourteen hundred machine-gun rounds and over fourteen thousand rounds of rifle ammunition, as well as fifty shrapnel shells from the column's artillery. A dozen on the British side had been injured, mostly from swords and slingshots, while Campbell counted the Tibetan dead at 628. Many had been shot in the back, walking away. The *Daily Mail* journalist who witnessed this slaughter asked, 'Why, in the name of all their Bodhisats and Munis [sic], did they not run?' As for modern Russian weapons: almost nothing, just a handful of old breech-loaders and later some hunting rifles likely traded decades before.

Younghusband himself was appalled by what he told his father was 'pure butchery'. The blame, however, he shifted elsewhere, to the Tibetan general Lhading for his 'crass stupidity and childishness' and the Tibetan troops themselves for their 'inability, even when our troops absolutely surrounded them, to take in the seriousness of the situation'. He blamed the Dalai Lama too, who was, ultimately, 'at the bottom of all the trouble and deserves to be well kicked'. Such excuses were Younghusband's myth creation at its most grotesque. He had no comprehension of the struggles within the outmoded Tibetan political system: the rising tide of nationalism and unwillingness to compromise that beset its leaders. All he wanted was to 'smash those selfish filthy lecherous Lamas'. Such naked prejudice was rooted in a particular strand of English evangelical anti-Catholicism, which saw in Lhasa echoes of Rome. Younghusband's argument, shared by Curzon, had been that Tibetans were a religiously oppressed people gasping for liberty, but this was simply a fiction, and one used to justify the use of modern weaponry against troops who genuinely believed that magic amulets would ward off bullets. Even after the slaughter of Chumi Shengo, the naïve courage and sacrifice of the Tibetans continued, impressing the urgently needed British reinforcements who witnessed it. That didn't stop them looting and shopping their way to Lhasa, sending back four hundred mule-loads' worth of artworks and souvenirs, some of these still in British museums and private collections. What was supposed to have been a demonstration of British authority had become a rather squalid smash and grab.

As Younghusband neared Lhasa in triumph, 'the greatest success of my life', Curzon was in London, defending the mission against an

increasingly hostile British cabinet. A day before the city fell, the Dalai
Lama, the physical and spiritual embodiment of Tibetan identity, fled
with Dorzhiev to the Mongolian capital Ulaanbaatar, at that time
called Urga. The choice had political significance: in avoiding China,
he made an expression of independence; there was also a Russian
consulate he could consult. (The presence of the Dalai Lama alienated
Mongolia's spiritual leader, the eighth Jebtsundamba Khutuktu,
himself a Tibetan, being the son of a steward in the Dalai Lama's
retinue, and Mongolia's most senior Geluk monk. He was an equivocal
figure, described by the doughty British traveller Beatrix Bulstrode in
1919 as 'a man of middle age, already decrepit, in appearance bloated,
dissipated, uninspiring'. The Polish traveller Ferdynand Ossendowski
thought him 'clever, penetrating and energetic'. The monk's blindness
in old age has been ascribed to both syphilis and alcoholism.) In
September 1904, Younghusband signed a treaty at Lhasa in the absence
of the Dalai Lama. It would be abandoned at the end of the following
year by Britain's newly formed Liberal government amid distaste at
imperial meddling. (This was less to do with human rights and more
that foreign meddling was expensive.) By that time, Curzon had
resigned as viceroy. The missionary Annie Taylor, although snidely
dismissed by British officers, put the outcome rather neatly:

> far from being strengthened, the prestige of Britain has been weakened
> all along the border between Tibet and India, the only gain in this
> respect being on the part of China.

Russia and Britain effectively ended their rivalry in Tibet with the
Anglo-Russian Convention of 1907, agreeing to deal with Tibet only
through China. The Dalai Lama now had little choice but to deal
with Beijing. He moved back to Amdo for a while and then decided
to travel to Beijing, despite fears that he might be detained there. On
the way, he paused at the Wutaishan monastery, where he sent invita-
tions to foreign diplomats to visit, including the British. It was part
of a deliberate effort to change Tibet's course of determined isolation
to one of engagement. He told the American diplomat William
Woodville Rockhill about his struggles against the Chinese and how
Tibet had 'no friends abroad'. Rockhill told the Dalai Lama he was
wrong, that Tibet had around the world many well-wishers who

wanted to see Tibetans prosper. Rockhill wrote to his friend Theodore
Roosevelt, then serving his second term as president, that the meeting
was 'the most unique experience of my life'. The Dalai Lama was a
man 'of quick understanding and of force of character'.

A day later, the Dalai Lama met the future president of Finland
and Russian imperial army officer Gustaf Mannerheim while the
Lama's attendants ensured that the Chinese agent watching the Finn
was kept out of the room. Mannerheim, ostensibly travelling but in
reality a spy, was keeping notes in Swedish of his travels through
Central Asia for his masters in St Petersburg. The Dalai Lama asked
if Mannerheim had a message for him from the tsar, which he didn't,
but gave him his pistol for protection – a Browning, not a Russian
weapon – and showed him how to load it. He also noted the lively
intelligence Tibet's exiled leader showed in foreign affairs, writing that
he

> does not look like a man resigned to play the part the Chinese
> Government wishes him to, but rather like one who is only waiting
> for an opportunity of confusing his adversary.

When the Dalai Lama finally arrived in Beijing in September 1908, he
refused to kowtow to the Guangxu emperor and the dowager empress
Cixi, who nevertheless made it clear he must return to Lhasa and
obey the ambans there.

Both the emperor and Cixi were dead within days, the Guangxu
emperor poisoned at the age of thirty-seven. The Dalai Lama was
forced to remain for the obligatory period of mourning but his presence in Beijing made him available to European diplomats for the first
time. By chance Frank O'Connor was there, accompanying the young
prince of Sikkim on a world tour. He thus became the first British
government representative to meet the leader of Tibet, as well as his
Buryat adviser Agvan Dorzhiev. The meeting was cordial, even friendly;
it helped that the British had by then almost completely withdrawn
from Tibet. The Dalai Lama, aided behind the scenes by the American
Rockhill, also managed to see Japan's ambassador, despite Chinese
objections. Fascination in Japan for Tibet had been sparked with the
publication of *Three Years in Tibet*, the experiences of the traveller Ekai
Kawaguchi who had met the thirteenth Dalai Lama in Lhasa while

posing as a Chinese monk. When the Dalai Lama finally returned to Lhasa, Japanese military advisers arrived to help modernise the Tibetan army. It was too little, far too late.

*

Not long before Curzon quit as viceroy he had set the ball rolling for an expedition to Everest with his letter to Douglas Freshfield. During the Younghusband mission, two army captains Cecil Rawling and Charles Ryder, later surveyor general of India, had got clear views of Everest from around a hundred kilometres away, which had put the issue firmly in Curzon's mind. There are two approaches to Everest, from the north through Tibet and from the south through Nepal. Curiously, in his letter Curzon explicitly suggested approaching the maharaja of Nepal Chandra Shamsher to request access to the southern route and made no mention of Tibet. He may have felt that despite Britain's military intervention, access from that direction would be unlikely and they were better off asking his friend Chandra.

The Alpine Club were delighted at such powerful support and began putting together an expedition for 1907 in time for their golden jubilee, banking on the Tibetan route since it seemed more practical and better known. The wealthy publisher and Alpine Club member Arnold Mumm offered to underwrite the attempt if he and his Swiss guide could be part of the team. With him would go the Himalayan veterans Tom Longstaff and Charlie 'Bruiser' Bruce with two Alpine guides and nine of Bruce's Gurkhas. Alas, the alpinists had hitched their wagon to a political faction that almost immediately came off the rails. The new secretary of state for India was the dry and bookish John Morley, not a man sympathetic to romantic adventure; even his own prime minister Henry Campbell-Bannerman once described him as a 'petulant spinster'. Negotiations with the Russians were continuing and Morley wasn't prepared to allow a mountaineering expedition to muddy the waters. Sir George Goldie, the Cecil Rhodes of Nigeria, then president of the Royal Geographical Society, wrote a caustic letter to *The Times* but there was no shifting Morley; a leader in *The Times* rather took his side.

Morley also blocked Curzon's suggestion of trying from Nepal. In 1908, while the Dalai Lama was heading to Beijing, Chandra Shamsher arrived in Britain, where he was given an honorary degree at Oxford, awarded personally by the university's vice chancellor Lord Curzon, now in the political wilderness. Chandra also got an honorary award from the Royal Geographical Society, but when he met privately with Morley, the secretary of state told him that 'a very important society, the Geographical Society demanded a pass from me to explore Everest. I refused it. Is it not as you wish me to do?' Chandra concurred. Nepal's isolation maintained the good reputation of the British among ordinary Nepalis flocking to join its army. If mountaineers were allowed in, then others would follow. And 'all Englishmen, Your Lordship, cannot be expected to be gentlemen'. With Chandra's consent, however, the India Office did allow one concession, a sop to Curzon: in 1907 Nathu Singh from the Survey of India became the first outsider to explore the south side of the Everest region in Nepal, including the Dudh Kosi, the 'milk river' that flowed from its glaciers. Mumm, Bruce and Longstaff went not to Everest but the Garhwal and made their creditable first ascent of Trisul.

In the face of official disapproval, approaches to Everest became a clandestine affair. Alexander Kellas, the Scottish chemist who would perish on the 1921 reconnaissance, had a secret plan to try from the north and in 1913 Captain John Noel of the Machine Gun Corps made a clandestine journey across the border from Sikkim that got a little closer than Rawling had. It was a lecture on this enterprising adventure in March 1919 that Younghusband, soon to take over from Holdich as the new president of the Royal Geographical Society, used as a springboard for the attempts of the 1920s. In October, Curzon was made foreign secretary, just the sort of ally in government to get things moving. Yet it was ironically another invasion of Tibet that would prove to be the key in unlocking the gates of Everest and which would send British policy in Tibet in a new and wholly more constructive direction under the expert guidance of one man: Charles Bell. It would be Bell's presence in Lhasa that would bring the necessary permission for Younghusband's adventure to move forward.

*

Soon after the British left Lhasa in late 1904, the Qing magistrate Zhao Erfeng had arrived in western Kham where the Qing had been trying to establish Chinese farming colonies among indigenous Tibetans. This had led to riots and the murder of the official responsible for implementing the policy. Zhao had begun a vicious campaign to reassert China's control, provoking further retaliation. A group of rebellious monks had taken refuge behind the stout walls of the monastery at Chaktreng but Zhao had finally tricked them into opening the doors in the belief reinforcements had arrived. He then executed the survivors. Zhao's success in pacifying Kham won him promotion and in 1909 he repeated his tactic in the formerly independent kingdom of Derge, 'the land of mercy', a significant polity in the Kham region, destroying the historically important Drakyap monastery in the process. The atrocities his troops committed earned him the soubriquet 'Butcher Zhao'; the destruction of Tibetan culture prefigured the far darker shadow of the Cultural Revolution. In February 1910, only weeks after the Dalai Lama's return, Zhao arrived in Lhasa with two thousand men. The official reason was to police trade marts established by the British under the terms of a new treaty signed in 1908, but the Tibetans read it as an aggressive statement of intent. The sight of Halley's Comet burning through the night sky was taken as an ill omen. The Dalai Lama, now in his mid thirties, was forced to flee once again, this time heading for Sikkim, beyond the reach of China.

The British trade agent at Yatung, on Tibet's border with Sikkim, was David Macdonald, a civilian veteran of the 1904 Tibet mission who had taken over as interpreter when Frank O'Connor fell ill. Macdonald's father had been a Scottish tea planter who abandoned his mother, a local Lepcha woman, when David – born Dorje – was small. Macdonald had been warned by telegraph that the Dalai Lama was coming and had orders to help him while remaining ostensibly neutral. Chinese officials in Yatung, waiting for the arrival of Zhao's troops, demanded that the Dalai Lama be handed over. That night in the midst of a winter snowstorm, he escaped across the Jelep La into Sikkim. From there he went on to Darjeeling where the urbane and sympathetic political agent Charles Bell welcomed him. Bell accompanied his new guest to Calcutta where the viceroy Lord Minto greeted the Dalai Lama with deep respect and listened to his pleas for help. The secretary of state John Morley, back in London, wasn't the least interested. Echoing Younghusband, he dismissed the Dalai

Lama as nothing more than a 'pestilent animal' and one who 'should be left to stew in his own juice'. Morley assessed China's invasion as simply the natural assertion of its sovereignty. There was no question of British support, not least because it contravened the Anglo-Russian Convention of 1907. Morley told Minto to maintain a position of strict neutrality. Given the surprisingly warm welcome the Dalai Lama had enjoyed so far, this sudden reversal of his hopes was a bitter blow. Bell recalled how the news left the Dalai Lama 'so surprised and distressed that for a minute or two he lost the power of speech'.

With a brutal Qing army occupying Lhasa and the British apparently indifferent, the Dalai Lama approached the Russians, but the political winds had changed and he got a polite rebuff. He considered travelling from India to Beijing to make a direct appeal but the situation in China was fast deteriorating and he had little option but to remain under British protection, going on pilgrimage to Kapilavastu, where the Buddha had lived as a child, and Bodhgaya, where he achieved enlightenment, before settling at Kalimpong, just east of Darjeeling.

One of those who joined the Dalai Lama in exile was the diplomat and military leader Dasang Damdul, who had held up Chinese troops at the Chaksam river crossing as the Dalai Lama fled through Tibet, killing around seventy of them. Then in his mid twenties, the humbly born Dasang Damdul would later marry into the powerful Tsarong family, taking the name and the titles that went with it, particularly that of Shap-pe. He rapidly became the most influential political figure in early twentieth-century Tibet. The Dalai Lama called him 'Chensel', meaning visible, because he was always there. More than anyone, Tsarong Shap-pe as he became known, shared the Dalai Lama's vision of a modernising nation more able to face down foreign threats. He would become Britain's best friend in Tibet, 'the one man who is really wide-awake in Lhasa', according to the Gyantse-based teacher Frank Ludlow. In the autumn of 1911 he was sent to Shigatse to lead a rebellion against the Qing as the centre in Beijing crumbled, opening the way for the Dalai Lama's return.

While exiled in Kalimpong, the Dalai Lama developed a real friendship with Charles Bell. Unlike so many of his contemporaries, Bell was deeply sympathetic to Tibetan culture. He understood as well as the Chinese that the Dalai Lama was, as the incarnation of Chenrezig, Tibet's protective deity, the crucial figure in Tibetan politics, no matter what his boss Lord Morley might think. Born in Calcutta in 1870, Bell was educated at Winchester and New College, Oxford before following his father Henry into the Indian Civil Service. As such he was one of the minority of 'politicals' drawn from civilian ranks and regarded by military colleagues as a 'babu', a pen-pusher, not the sort of daring fellow the frontier demanded. He had previously been in Bihar and Orissa but the galvanising moment of his career was his posting to Darjeeling, where he was wholly captivated by the Tibetan world. Bell not only became fluent in the language, he wrote a book about it: *A Manual of Colloquial Tibetan*. When under the terms of the treaty signed by Younghusband the Chumbi valley came under British control, Bell was put in charge before taking over as political agent for Sikkim, Bhutan and Tibet from Claude White, who was more interested in his pension than the political fate of the Himalaya. The Dalai Lama's exile in 1910 was a moment of serendipity for all concerned. Bell would become the sympathetic architect of a new British policy in Tibet.

In September 1913, Bell arrived in Simla to advise the Indian foreign secretary Sir Henry McMahon as he oversaw the latest attempt to delineate the boundaries between India and Tibet. Negotiations were tortuous and China ultimately refused to sign, but Tibet did, and the agreement bore the hallmarks of Bell's ideas. The trade agencies the British had fought for were retained. Bell also persuaded the Tibetan chief negotiator Longchen Shatra, a veteran diplomat with long and sometimes bitter experience of the British, to cede the strategic town of Tawang, previously acknowledged as part of Tibet, to the government of India. Although the Tibetan government got rifles and ammunition as compensation, officials in Lhasa were outraged. The Tibetans continued to administer the town, but the status of Tawang, now in the Indian state of Arunachal Pradesh, has remained a flashpoint ever since, and was one of the causes of the conflict between China and an independent India in 1962. It also reveals that while Bell was pro-Tibetan, 'Tibetanised' was his word, he still worked for the Raj. After Simla, he continued to support the Dalai Lama's attempt to modernise Tibet and its army, although the Great War put constraints on further military support. A more effective army with British backing was a threat to the monastic establishment: a harbinger of the modern world and an alternative powerbase.

What Bell really wanted was to visit Lhasa, something no British officer had done since Younghusband's mission. When he retired in 1918 to focus on his Tibetan studies, it seemed he had missed his chance. The Dalai Lama was on a lengthy retreat and the Simla Convention, signed in 1914, seemed to have neutralised British concern in the region. Then the implications of the Russian Revolution became clearer. The Bolsheviks tore up Tsarist treaties, opening the door once again to another British visit. Bell's replacement as political agent stepped down unexpectedly and Bell, who had remained in the region, was reappointed. Best of all for the Everest expedition, Curzon was made foreign secretary in October 1919 and Bell's patient and carefully thought-out arguments for a mission to Lhasa were given a sympathetic hearing. Then, while Bell was waiting in the wooded surroundings of Yatung to hear if he had been granted his wish, a representative for the proposed 1921 Everest reconnaissance expedition arrived to press the case for the mountaineers.

Charles Howard-Bury was a wealthy Irish landowner and senior British army officer and consequently had the money and prestige for a successful lobbying campaign. Having served on the Somme and then been captured in the German spring offensive of 1918, Howard-Bury had been free for barely three months when he wrote to Arthur Hinks, secretary of the Everest committee, offering his services – at his own expense. A year later, as Younghusband pushed the issue, he had been approached to take up the challenge of changing minds in India. Things did not start well. When Howard-Bury arrived at Simla in July 1920 to confer with the British Indian authorities, he sensed a great decision was pending and that Everest was a distraction. It was clear also that Charles Bell, preoccupied with his own mission to Lhasa, held the key to Tibet but was unsympathetic. 'The more I hear of Bell, the less I fear he will help us,' Howard-Bury reported to Younghusband. 'They all say he is a most tiresome man to deal with because he is very slow and cautious and does not make any mistakes.' By the end of July, the India Office in London had formally denied permission, but Younghusband instructed Howard-Bury to visit Bell in Yatung anyway.

It was the question of weapons that had made the issue so tense. As Howard-Bury understood it, the Tibetans were anxious for the British to sell them more guns for its army. In fact, the issue of weapons was desirable but not critical. Bell understood very well how to get what he wanted from the system, using requests like this as bargaining chips, to be discarded when required. When Howard-Bury joined Bell for lunch,

> he said that he could ask the Tibetan government today and he was quite certain that they would allow the expedition, but that he did not think that it would be advisable at the present time.

Bell was quite possibly using Howard-Bury to send a message via Younghusband to Curzon, who had publicly supported the Everest project, that if His Majesty's Government wanted British climbers in Tibet then it should send Bell to Lhasa. In mid October Bell got his permission and on 17 November 1920, a day carefully chosen as auspicious according to Tibetan astrology, he arrived in the holy city, fulfilling an ambition he had worked towards for more than a decade.

Within a month, the mountaineers had their permission for Everest. The leader of the 1921 reconnaissance would be Howard-Bury rather than the mountaineer Charles Bruce, a more obvious candidate, reward for Howard-Bury's patient efforts and acknowledgment that there might be a diplomatic angle to the exploration: Bruce was no diplomat. Mallory now entered the scene and the legend of those early Everest expeditions was born. 'The accomplishment of such a feat,' Younghusband had told the world in his inaugural address to the Royal Geographical Society,

> will elevate the human spirit. It will give men a feeling that we really are getting the upper hand on the Earth, that we are acquiring a true mastery of our surroundings.

In the aftermath of the bloodiest war in human history and against a rising modernist tide of alienation and urbanism, his message seemed like an echo from another world.

*

Charles Bell remained in Lhasa for a year, long after the footnote of
permission to attempt Everest was dealt with and against the expectations of his superiors. In that time he reframed relations between
Britain and Tibet, cementing his friendship with the Dalai Lama. Bell
would always stress how he inhabited the Tibetan world to advance
his agenda, quoting a monastic official as saying:

> When a European is with us Tibetans I feel he is a European and we
> are Tibetans; but when Lönchen Bell is with us, I feel that we are all
> Tibetans together.

That did not mean that Bell went unchallenged. Conservatives associated him with the modernising influence of Tsarong Shap-pe, the
head of the army. At the great prayer festival, Monlam Chenmo,
during the Tibetan new year in early 1921, Bell saw placards demanding
his assassination. Bell's sly acquisition of Tawang for British India
under the terms of the Simla Accord had also annoyed monks from
the powerful Drepung monastery who lost an outpost that earned
them revenue. As Britain developed a closer relationship with Tibet,
it found ways to put money into the monasteries and buy off some
of this opposition. The army, and later a new police force, remained
targets for discontent. Yet these were the very institutions Bell felt
necessary for Tibet to secure its status as a nation independent of
China.

Education was another source of friction. The Indian government,
at the request of the Dalai Lama, had experimented with introducing
British public school values to Tibet. In 1913, four Tibetan boys, all
from powerful families, had been sent to Rugby School and each was
trained in practical skills that would prove useful in the process of
modernisation at home. One, Khyenrab Kunzang Mondo, studied
mine engineering at the pit village of Grimethorpe in South Yorkshire,
but later as a local governor in western Tibet was notorious for
exploiting the local population. Rigzin Dorje Ringang stayed in Britain
the longest, studying electrical engineering, and returned home with
sufficient equipment to build a small hydroelectric scheme that brought
electric light to the Dalai Lama's summer palace, the Norbulingka.
Ten years later and as a consequence of Bell's visit, a new approach
was taken, this time inside Tibet. A teacher called Frank Ludlow from

the Indian Education Service arrived at the trade agency in Gyantse to open a small English school.

Ludlow was a sensitive and capable man, a trained naturalist who studied under the father of the plant hunter Frank Kingdon-Ward at Cambridge. He would spend his life on the frontier, mixing diplomatic service, natural history and exploration. He arrived in Gyantse in August 1923 full of optimism, but it took patient persuasion to attract sufficient pupils to such a foreign innovation; the school finally opened that December with thirteen boys, a number that would eventually double. One introduction that did catch on was football. Ludlow had brought a few balls with him from India but the boys soon wore them out and he had to send for more. He also bought them a football strip in the monastic colours of yellow and maroon, since the long Tibetan coat, or *chuba*, wasn't practical for running around. Ludlow himself stuck to refereeing, finding that in the high altitude 'I couldn't run more than twenty yards without getting hopelessly out of breath.'

Ludlow's school would fall victim to a souring in the relationship between British India and Tibet that would stall the progress Charles Bell had made and interrupt access to Everest for several years. As we shall see, the 1924 expedition would be blamed for this break in rela-tions but its true cause ran far deeper. While the deaths of George Mallory and his climbing partner Andrew Irvine caught the public's attention, 1924 was unusually dramatic in other respects. At the start of the year, the Panchen Lama, so often a rival to the Dalai Lama's authority, fled the Tashilhunpo monastery at Shigatse for exile in China. Then conflict broke out in Lhasa between the modernising faction, associated with the British, and the Lhasa monastic establish-ment, increasingly resistant to the growth in military capability that the British wanted in order to make Tibet an effective buffer state. And at the heart of this intricate struggle for control was the new British political officer in Sikkim, a man steeped in intelligence work and political manipulation: Frederick Marshman Bailey.

Eric Bailey, known as 'Hatter' to his friends, had little time for Charles Bell's method of 'Tibetanising' himself to advance British interests. Although softly spoken, Bailey was a military man, who maintained an unyielding dignity, one of Younghusband's young officers during the campaign of 1904, and an explorer too, making a celebrated journey to the upper reaches of the Brahmaputra. During

the war he'd been badly wounded on the Western Front, served with
the Gurkhas at Gallipoli and was then sent on an intelligence mission
to Tashkent to assess the intentions of Moscow's new Bolshevik
government in Central Asia. When Bailey needed to get home, he
posed as an Albanian army clerk and persuaded the Cheka, the
Bolshevik secret service, to help him look for British spies in Bukhara.
En route, he received a telegram from his handler requesting he keep
a look out for a notorious British agent called Bailey.

Bell had dismissed the idea of Soviet influence in Tibet, but Bailey
and his former boss and ally Frank O'Connor were convinced the new
Soviet Union would seek to undermine British interests in the region:
the Russians certainly had their spies in Lhasa. They were both propo-
nents of a more aggressive 'forward' policy, like their old patron
Younghusband. Perhaps Bell feared what impact this would have on
his painstaking efforts at closer relations; when Bailey arrived in Sikkim
in 1921 anxious to visit Tibet, Bell, who was still in Lhasa, kept him
out. This snub provoked a deep loathing in Bailey, one that he largely
kept to himself but revealed in a letter to his mother: Bell, he wrote,

> is a hopeless fraud and has got on entirely by writing himself up. He
> did all he could to make the work for me here difficult – as he was
> jealous of giving it up after 15 years. I wanted to go to Lhasa in 1921
> and for him to introduce me to the Dalai Lama and others in Lhasa
> but he would not let me go there ... after retiring he has been trying
> to continue his correspondence with the Dalai Lama which makes
> things difficult for me here as they hardly realise that when a man has
> retired he is finished.

Bailey was writing in November 1924, soon after returning from Lhasa
himself and at the start of a sudden cooling in diplomatic relations
between Tibet and the government of India, a process that scuppered
the good work done by the despised Bell. This reversal would result
in a pause in the British attempts on Everest, but its cause lay in
Bailey's efforts at steering the Tibetan elite towards British imperial
interests and away from the threat of communism. At the centre of
those efforts was Tibet's security apparatus, which Bailey was keen
to assess and influence. Unlike Bell, he lacked the necessary permission from his superiors to visit Tibet for himself. To influence Tibetan

policy from a distance was difficult and Bailey had to be creative, just as he had been in Tashkent.

In October 1922, George Pereira, a former British army general, arrived in Lhasa having crossed China and the Tibetan plateau. Pereira, known as 'Hoppy' because of a childhood riding accident, had been military attaché in Beijing before the war and was fluent in Chinese, but the old soldier had taken a shine to Tibet on his way to the capital.

> I have seen the children running about, playing games, and heard the laughter of the elders, and there seemed to be a freedom of care about the Tibetan peasantry, very different from village life in China.

Officially termed a 'private traveller', Pereira was in fact an old friend of Bailey, who had arranged Pereira's journey personally, without informing his superiors in Calcutta. Pereira was doing his old job of military attaché, reporting back to Bailey on the state of the Tibetan military and meeting with the head of the army Tsarong Shap-pe. The day after Pereira left Lhasa, on a return journey that proved fatal, the Tibetan government requested help from the government of India in establishing a modern police force, an idea Bell had planted but hadn't seen bear fruit. Bailey's policy, on the other hand, seemed to be making progress.

A few weeks later, however, another white man arrived in Lhasa, this one uninvited. This man's presence would reveal how tenuous British influence in Lhasa remained. William McGovern was a young American lecturer teaching at the School of Oriental Studies in London. He had been part of an official research group that had arrived at Gyantse but was then refused permission to continue to Lhasa, largely at Eric Bailey's insistence. The India Office in London had cabled Bailey to warn him that although the party comprised Oxford University graduates, they 'clearly show the cloven hoof', meaning they were sympathetic to communism. Bailey wasn't going to stand for that and the group were recalled to India. McGovern refused to accept this decision and later recrossed the border without permission and in disguise, reaching Lhasa in February 1923. When monks got wind of his presence in the city, they stoned his accommodation and McGovern was soon escorted back to India. Bailey and other political officers, including Bell, were furious when the

American published an account of his journey, an account that revealed the existence of a pro-China faction in Lhasa. Bailey asked the secretary of the Everest committee, Arthur Hinks, for help, in rubbishing McGovern's reputation through the journal of the Royal Geographical Society, a 'quid pro quo' for supporting the Everest expeditions.

The person charged by the Indian government with helping the Tibetans establish a modern police force was another veteran of the Younghusband mission of 1904. Sonam Wangfel Laden La, now forty-six, had grown up in the intelligence world of the British in the Himalaya. The nephew of a famous pundit, his first job, aged eighteen, had been for another one: Sarat Chandra Das, who was compiling his Tibetan dictionary. After that Laden La joined the Darjeeling police and performed a number of sensitive tasks, like keeping an eye on the Panchen Lama as he made a pilgrimage to India, at a time when the British were contemplating support for a breakaway state based on the Panchen Lama's seat at Shigatse. Later Laden La was security officer for the Dalai Lama during his period in exile and one of those chosen to accompany the four Tibetan boys to Rugby School. When Laden La arrived in Lhasa in August 1923, the factionalism McGovern had witnessed was coming to the boil and Bailey must have hoped the policeman's presence in the city would strengthen the British position.

Laden La soon built an embryonic police force and developed a bond with the head of the army Tsarong Shap-pe. Quite what that involved is controversial but there is some evidence that either early in the summer of 1924, while Mallory was on Everest, or a few weeks later, the two agreed to topple the established religious government in favour of a more progressive secular version, with the Dalai Lama remaining as a national figurehead running the monasteries. Although he claimed ignorance, it seems likely Eric Bailey, a deeply experienced intelligence officer expert in the region, knew of this plan. He arrived in Lhasa himself later that summer and held meetings with both Tsarong and Laden La. Whether he knew about what Tsarong and Laden La were contemplating in advance is another matter. But years later, when a version of what happened finally leaked into the British press, Bailey defended Laden La to his superiors, something he might not have done had the policeman acted alone.

When Bailey left Lhasa, Tsarong did so too. But when he returned that autumn, Tsarong found he had been dismissed as head of the army and his favoured junior officers dispersed to remote corners of Tibet. He had been replaced by a shrewdly political aristocrat called Lungshar, who was already a senior treasury minister, or *tsipon*. Lungshar and Laden La had history; Lungshar had been to Europe with the Rugby schoolboys and without Lhasa's approval had met China's ambassador, which Laden La had reported to his superiors. Understanding the fragility of his position, Laden La now returned to India, where it was said he suffered a nervous breakdown. As the purge of the Tibetan army got underway, a Bhutanese monk called Pema Chandra, who had been working for Laden La in Lhasa, also fled. Tibetan soldiers caught him before the border; his head was brought back to Lhasa and put on public display, together with a note accusing him of embezzlement and speaking ill of the Dalai Lama. Frank Ludlow, still teaching in Gyantse, now began hearing rumours that his school would be closed. The axe finally fell in 1926, partly because of what Ludlow described as the 'tom-foolery on the part of Laden La, Tsarong and others in Lhasa in 1924'. Whether or not Tsarong and Laden La's talk of a coup had been serious, it had been enough to turn the conservative Tibetan establishment against British support for the modernisers. Bailey's efforts had been in vain and he was now out in the cold.

The unwitting victim of this frost in the diplomatic air was the Everest adventure. In November 1924, Arthur Hinks wrote to Bailey asking for his help in securing permission from the Tibetans for another try in 1926. Having helped Bailey out by denigrating the American academic McGovern, he would have hoped for a positive response. But Bailey cabled back saying permission for Everest was unlikely. He claimed offence had been taken in Lhasa from John Noel's film of the expedition, *The Epic of Everest*, in particular a sequence of an old Tibetan eating lice from a child's head. He followed this with a letter explaining that Lhasa was also upset at Noel hiring a group of lamas from the monastery at Gyantse. Noel had then brought them to Britain to perform dances, an attempt to add an exotic human dimension to screenings of a film that seemed austere and harsh. The sight of lamas using thighbone trumpets at cinemas in the British provinces was hardly the stuff of diplomatic nightmares – they regularly did such tours in India – but Bailey insisted that what became known as the 'affair of the dancing lamas' had made things impossible. When he realised that the lamas hadn't been given the correct passports, despite Noel's insistence, Bailey saw his chance. He had the India Office in London fall on the Mount Everest Committee with icy fury. There would be no more Everest expeditions in the foreseeable future.

John Noel knew perfectly well it was Eric Bailey who had blocked the Everest application and not the Tibetans. What he didn't understand was why. Bailey had been Younghusband's protégé and Everest was Younghusband's dream. His friend Henry Morshead, with whom he'd shared the Tsangpo gorge adventure, had been part of the Everest reconnaissance in 1921. Bailey was usually so helpful to fellow explorers, no matter what he thought of them privately. In the summer of 1924 he had supported Frank Kingdon-Ward and Lord Cawdor as they prepared to follow in Bailey's footsteps and solve the riddle of the Tsangpo gorge. He had welcomed the mystical French-Belgian traveller Alexandra David-Néel to the residency at Gangtok after her clandestine journey to Lhasa. No one understood that the affair of the dancing lamas was the best excuse available for the real story: that Bailey's policy had failed and relations with Tibet had almost collapsed.

It would be another two years before any news of the alleged coup attempt that summer reached the outside world and by then Bailey was nearing the end of his posting. In October 1928 his replacement arrived at Gangtok. Leslie Weir had been trade agent at Gyantse when the Dalai Lama was in exile and knew Tibet. He was also an admirer of Charles Bell, describing him as 'his guru'. Settling into his new job, Weir discovered that 'our prestige ... has gone back woefully since I was last here'. By then, Eric Bailey, a man with many secrets, had moved on: to the plum posting of Kashmir and then his final job, as the British envoy in Kathmandu.

17

Utopias

On 16 August 1936, the German-born mountaineer Günter Dyhrenfurth arrived at Albert Speer's Olympic Stadium in Berlin to receive the International Olympic Committee's alpinism prize, a gold medal for mountaineering. Recognising the best climb done in the years before each Olympics was a passion for the founder and president of the modern games, the Baron de Coubertin (as were hunting and aviation). Others on the committee were lukewarm: the medal was first awarded at the inaugural winter Olympics in 1924, held at Chamonix in the French Alps, twenty-eight years after the revival of the summer games. That year Edward Lisle Strutt, climbing leader of the 1922 Everest expedition, collected medals on behalf of the British and Sherpas, seven of whom had died on the mountain in an avalanche. The alpinism prize stuttered on thereafter. Dyhrenfurth and his wife Hettie were chosen in 1936 for a successful expedition to the Karakoram two years earlier. Hettie was among the climbers who made the first ascent of Sia Kangri, breaking the female altitude record Fanny Bullock Workman claimed in 1905.

Dyhrenfurth barely made the closing ceremony, which featured a parade of standard-bearers lowering their national flags under the watchful gaze of Adolf Hitler, his arm raised in the Nazi salute. (This was so similar to the Olympic salute that the latter didn't survive the comparison.) While he had known about the award for some time, an official invitation, sent by telegram, hadn't arrived at Dyhrenfurth's new home in Switzerland until the day before. This was no oversight. Dyhrenfurth was a *Mischling*, of mixed Aryan and Jewish blood, who had in 1933 quit his post as geology professor at Breslau (now Wrocław) University, as a protest at Hitler's rise to power. Hettie herself was from a notable Jewish family of Silesian industrialists, a former tennis champion who despite her slight frame was courageous in the mountains. She also hated convention. In 1930, on the boat out to India to take part in her husband's expedition to Kangchenjunga, Hettie got a ticking off from the British mountaineer Frank Smythe for dancing with Indians, something he deemed 'impossible for a lady'. She smiled politely and kept on dancing.

Hettie Dyhrenfurth chose not to join her husband in Berlin, partly out of disgust at German antisemitism. Her son Norman, still a teenager, had faced harassment earlier in 1936 working as an assistant on the film being made of the winter Olympics in Garmisch-Partenkirchen, summer and winter games being held in the same year until 1994. The cameraman on that film was the other reason Hettie stayed away. Hans Ertl, an ambitious young climber turned filmmaker, had also been part of her husband's Karakoram expedition. Ertl had been there to get high-altitude footage for the production company underwriting the venture. (Their route to the Karakoram led them through Kashmir and past the dramatic Tibetan Buddhist monastery at Lamayuru in Ladakh but despite such vivid locations, the film, *Der Dämon des Himalaya*, was roundly panned. This didn't stop the Hungarian-born director Andrew Marton remaking the movie in Hollywood after the war as *Storm over Tibet*, using the original footage. 'See the roof of the world cave in ... in a billion tons of ice!') During the expedition, Hettie and Ertl had become lovers but he was mortified at this betrayal of team spirit and decided to confess. Günter Dyhrenfurth, substantially taller than Ertl, clasped the shoulders of his wife's lover and then reassured him: 'These things happen, my young friend.' Dyhrenfurth liked everything to be open: marriages, mountains, borders. That was not how things were in Europe anymore. Now Ertl was in Berlin working for Leni Riefenstahl, another former lover, on her technically dazzling paean to fascism *Olympia*. Hettie had no wish to run into either of them. A year later, and now separated from Günter, she left for the United States; her son Norman would soon follow.

As the rise of right-wing nationalism permeated every aspect of European life, even mountain climbing, in India a different kind of political storm was gathering. Gandhi's movement of peaceful disobedience and other strands of the independence movement were coiling themselves around a weakening British Empire, a struggle that already included political hotspots in the Himalaya like Darjeeling. Change came more slowly elsewhere in the mountains. In Nepal, the Rana dynasty's iron grip on power had begun to fracture following the death in 1929 of Curzon's ally Chandra Shamsher, but the absence of a large, educated middle class meant challenging the status quo was both desperately difficult and dangerous.

In Tibet, the political class were wholly absorbed in the search for a new Dalai Lama following the death in late 1933 of the energetic Thubten Gyatso. Tibet was still reeling from a disastrous border war with the army of China's nationalist party, the Kuomintang, under the command of Muslim warlord Ma Bufang. Since the collapse of the Qing dynasty in 1911 and the declaration of a Chinese republic a year later, China had been mired in civil war and warlordism. The Kuomintang, under the leadership of Chiang Kai-shek, had spent the 1920s reunifying the country and was now attempting to regain influence in its more distant colonies like Tibet. More border wars followed and the souring of relations between Tibet and China encouraged a thaw between the Indian government and Lhasa – leading in turn to the first Everest climbing permit in nine years.

Despite this, conservative opinion remained powerful. Beyond political changes in Europe that followed the Great War, the end of empires and the rise of nations, technological advances were making the world a faster, smaller and more materialistic place. When George Mallory went to Everest for the first time, aircraft were made of canvas and travel was expensive. Radio stations were new and rare. Films, like John Noel's *The Epic of Everest*, were silent. In ten years all that had changed. If the Wall Street Crash had made the lives of many ordinary working people miserable, modernity carried on creating new futures that seemed alienating and almost inhuman. For a moment, the Himalaya seemed to the West somewhere suspended in time, a lost world of light above dark clouds threatening war. The 1930s would be the golden years of Himalayan mountain travel: a last glance at an old world before the storm broke and it disappeared for ever. To the people who lived there, they were also the last years of outmoded regimes that had held the people of the Himalaya back for far too long.

*

A few weeks after Günter Dyhrenfurth received his award for alpinism at the Berlin Olympics, Tom Longstaff was on Shetland when a laconic telegram reached him: 'two reached the top August 29'. The veteran mountaineer, whose career stretched back almost to the beginning of Himalayan climbing, was now in his early sixties, his famous red beard fading to grey, but he was as interested and enthusiastic as ever, and knew exactly what the message meant. Nanda Devi had been climbed. No mountain meant more to him: it had been his ambition 'years before I set foot in the Himalaya'. Even after a lifetime's mountain travel, and an expedition to Everest in 1922, he still believed Garhwal, where Nanda Devi was located, to be 'the most beautiful country of all High Asia', a 'sum of delight unsurpassed elsewhere'. The prospect of Nanda Devi being climbed filled him with dread, 'a sacrilege too horrible to contemplate'. Yet somehow the terseness of the telegram reassured him. No names were mentioned, no conquering heroes identified: 'here was humility not pride'.

In some ways, Longstaff was typical of his era and class, an Eton and Christ Church man. On his way to Everest in 1922, for example, he was delighted at Gandhi's arrest for sedition, 'which was greeted joyfully by everybody'. Yet when it came to alpinism, he was as thoughtfully progressive as anyone. The juggernaut of the Everest expedition was far less appealing than a small group of friends moving as lightly among the mountains as possible. It was almost an article of faith. In 1905 he had climbed from the Johar valley east of Nanda Devi to reach a ridgeline, from where he could look down into a stupendous hidden valley, a sanctuary as enticing as it was difficult to reach. Longstaff returned in 1907 for another try. He climbed the neighbouring peak of Trisul, believed to be the highest summit reached for the next twenty-one years, but Nanda Devi's sanctuary remained untouched. There were more attempts in the 1920s but only in 1934 did a party manage to scramble through the difficult Rishi gorge and reach the foot of the peak: two English climbers, Eric Shipton and Bill Tilman, and three porters, 'blokes' as Tilman liked to call them: Ang Tharkay, Pasang Bhotia and a cousin of Ang Tharkay's, Kusang.

Shipton and Tilman: their names as readily connected for a mountaineer as Lennon and McCartney, shorthand for a method of adventure that was lightweight but ambitious, a paradoxical combination of the expansive and the understated. Nanda Devi was Shipton's idea.

In 1933 he had been on Everest, the first expedition following the thaw in relations with Tibet. Its leader was a self-effacing former Indian civil servant called Hugh Ruttledge who while stationed in Almora had mounted two expeditions of his own to Nanda Devi. Inspired by Ruttledge, Shipton looked around in vain for a companion to go with him. He had resigned himself to travelling as the only European with Ang Tharkay and the others when a letter turned up from an old climbing acquaintance from his years as a coffee planter in Kenya. Bill Tilman was ten years his senior and had recently returned home after crossing Africa from east to west on a bicycle. He was proposing a fortnight in the Lake District. Shipton's counter-proposal was an expedition of seven months in Garhwal. A photograph of the pair embarking at Liverpool shows them smartly dressed in the 1930s fashion: wide ties, high collars and fat lapels. Shipton, the taller man, has an overcoat on, his wavy hair at odds with his sharp cheekbones. Tilman has a crisp, military moustache, his hair oiled and scraped flat, his dimpled cheeks offering a glimpse of the humour beneath the terse manner he presented to the world. He had fought in the Great War, turning eighteen during the Battle of the Somme. Unlike the generation of climbers before him, the war had been his formative experience: a burden he carried with him in near silence for the rest of his life.

Shipton was far more affable but in his way even more enigmatic. His father was a Ceylon tea planter who died when Eric was three. To escape her grief, his emotionally distant mother travelled before settling in the cool relief of Southern India's Nilgiri hills, a way of life that appealed hugely to an adventurous boy. That freedom ended when his mother remarried and returned to London and a flat in Kensington Gardens. Eric was sent to an uncongenial preparatory school where his slowness to read alienated him further. Although he portrayed himself as dreamy and rather lonely, Shipton had a talent for friendship and unlike Tilman, who is often marked down as a misogynist, he charmed women his whole life. Beatrice Weir, daughter of the political officer who replaced Eric Bailey and negotiated the 1933 Everest permit, met Shipton in 1938 at a garden party in Kashmir when she was seventeen. 'He had blazing blue eyes everyone used to talk about; he just sat and looked. It was indefinable. I melted like an ice cube.' They took walks together in the Shalimar Gardens but her mother knew better and squashed the liaison. 'This man's a dreamer and just lives on a glacier.'

Shipton had certainly found a way of life that set little store by position or career, a philosophy that would cost him the leadership of the Everest expedition that made history in 1953. Around the time of his first expedition to Everest in 1933, he realised there was no reason to curtail the things that made him happy: freedom, mountains, exploration. 'Why not spend the rest of my life doing this sort of thing?' The obvious answer was money, but while hardly cheap, Himalayan travel, especially the Spartan version Shipton and Tilman practised, was becoming more affordable. Their seven-month expedition in 1934 cost less than £300, including the voyage from England: perhaps £9,000 each in today's terms. The future war hero Freddy Spencer Chapman and his five-man team of two Europeans and three Sherpas managed to climb the gorgeous peak of Jomolhari for £39 5s: little more than £2,600 now. (This was the peak Sir William Jones had spotted from the plains in 1784; it's rarely been climbed since Chapman's day.) Most frugal of all was the Austrian Herbert Tichy, later a reluctant Nazi propagandist, who in 1935 rode a Puch motorcycle to India. Disguised as a pilgrim, he crossed the Lipu Lekh, just beyond Nepal's western border into Tibet where he made a circumambulation of holy Kailas before attempting the first ascent of Gurla Mandhata. As Shipton wrote during the war, so far as wealth was concerned,

> There are few treasures of more lasting worth than the experience of a way of life that is in itself wholly satisfying. Such, after all, are the only possessions of which no fate, no cosmic catastrophe can deprive us; nothing can alter the fact if for one moment in eternity we have really lived.

Tilman felt roughly the same but was cured with irony, like an old leather boot, and would never articulate such ideas out loud: he was better on weather than emotion, his eye most usually on the horizon. Human judgments in his writing were rare and often came from the most oblique angle. He praised Shipton for being 'one of the first to doubt that in mountaineering the great and the good are necessarily the same,' by 'great' meaning famous. Both men viewed self-promotion

by climbers with distaste. Anything that diluted the richness of imme-
diate experience – publicity or reputation – was ditched from their
rucksacks. Anything extraneous was cast aside: 'bagging and scrapping'
Tilman called it. Both preferred lentils and flatbread to hampers from
Fortnum's. Even their friendship was carefully rationed. Tilman was,
Shipton once said, 'astringent company'.

Solving the problem of the Rishi gorge and gaining access to Nanda
Devi's inner sanctum, which he and Tilman achieved in the summer
of 1934, was among the sweetest moments of Eric Shipton's life. The
appeal of a secret or hidden valley like the Rishi gorge is a common
trope: for Tibetans, *beyul*, as they were known, had been part of how
they conceptualised their sacred landscapes for centuries. Shipton
found in them a kind of psychological relief.

> My most blissful dream as a child was to be in some such valley, free
> to wander where I liked, and discover for myself some hitherto unre-
> vealed glory of Nature. Now the reality was no less wonderful than
> that half-forgotten dream; and of how many childish fancies can that
> be said, in this age of disillusionment?

With access to the valley impossible for local herdsmen, Shipton had
stumbled into a lost world of botanical riches:

> the giant cliffs of Nanda Devi rose sheer and forbidding in true
> Himalayan style; but, bounding the glacier on the right-hand side,
> beyond a well-defined lateral moraine, an expanse of undulating grass-
> land stretched for miles, in lovely contrast ... Now this pasturage is a
> sanctuary where thousands of wild animals live unmolested. Long may
> it remain so!

It did not remain so for very long at all. In the aftermath of China's
border war with India in 1962, Indian and American climbers, with
Sherpa support and backing from the CIA, secretly attempted to place
an atomic-powered sensing device near the summit of Nanda Devi
but had to abandon it in bad weather. The device subsequently disappeared in an avalanche, much to the embarrassment of both governments when the story, if not the radioactive material, leaked out in
the mid 1970s. Climbers and trekkers had a more obvious impact,

leaving behind so much trash that in 1982 the Indian government banned access altogether. The impacts of climate change can now be added to that list.

Perhaps such degradation was what Tilman had in mind when he reached the summit of Nanda Devi – not with Shipton but with the geologist Noel Odell – in the summer of 1936. It was late in the day and afternoon cloud hid many of the surrounding peaks, but to the north the brown, sunlit Tibetan plateau stretched far into the distance.

> After the first joy in victory, [he wrote,] came a feeling of sadness that the mountain had succumbed, that the proud head of the goddess was bowed.

This was as close as Tilman came to opening a door to his emotional world. Behind it you can make out a world-weariness born in the shadow of war. The expedition itself had been a great success, an energising mix of enthusiastic young Americans and veteran British climbers, brought together almost by chance. Charlie Houston, then a young Harvard medical student, would have stood on the summit instead of Tilman had he not eaten some spoiled tinned meat at their top camp.

> The Brits didn't know what to make of us Yanks, [Houston recalled,] and had some difficulty understanding our form of the language we were supposed to share.

Yet despite their differences, their climbing philosophy was similar, a far more potent connection in the mountains than a shared passport. Nanda Devi, the thirtieth highest peak in the Himalaya, was the highest summit to be reached before the Second World War.

Shipton kicked himself for not being there with Tilman instead of wasting time 'on that ridiculous Everest business': that same summer, there had been a fourth attempt to reach the summit. But despite any private envy, Shipton publicly acknowledged the achievement as 'the first of the really difficult Himalayan giants to be conquered'. This latest Everest expedition had been another colossal enterprise costing half a million pounds in today's terms, lavishly equipped and expertly planned. Yet it didn't come close to matching progress made on the previous three tries. Bad weather and frequent heavy snowfalls shut the climbers down before the expedition could properly begin. In late May Shipton and Frank Smythe had shepherded forty-one porters, an almost grotesque number, to the north col when, in Smythe's words, 'the heaviest snowstorm I've ever experienced in the Himalayas' began.

> Two feet came down. The camp was half-buried. There was nothing to do but lie up for two whole days in our sleeping bags with the Primus stove between us cooking hot drinks to keep warm.

The team had the latest radio equipment and Smythe was able to talk to base camp and seek advice. He decided to descend despite the avalanche risk. 'It was a big responsibility – 41 men's lives – and one I hope I never have to face again.'

The miseries of base camp, pitched in the stony wasteland above the Rongbuk monastery, preyed on Smythe. 'So intensely dry is the air that we all suffer from congested throats. Otherwise I'm O.K. and can smoke a pipe all day long.' His nose, blasted by the sun of high altitude was 'blotchy red, cracked, raw and covered with congealed blood'. What kept him going were dreams of the English countryside and his newly built Surrey home.

> I can picture that very well – the fruit trees out in bloom and Tenningshook wood in vivid green, with a carpet of bluebells drifting beneath the trees. What a contrast to this utter desolation. There is nothing so beautiful as an English countryside.

There was something of the little Englander about Smythe: bristling at the German Hettie Dyhrenfurth dancing with an Indian man or talking loftily of Himalayan cultures he marched past but barely understood. Much of this was insecurity. Raymond Greene had known Smythe at Berkhamsted School where Greene's father was headmaster and Tilman had been a pupil ten years earlier. Berkhamsted was where Smythe started climbing, 'a rather frail fair-headed boy who was said to have a weak heart and was not allowed to play football because of a murmur in the chest'. When they went to Everest together in 1933, Greene, by then a doctor, could still hear it through his stethoscope. Smythe may have looked frail but was arguably the best alpinist Britain had between the wars. 'At great altitudes a new force seemed to enter Frank,' Greene wrote in his memoirs.

> His mind, too, took on a different colour. At sea-level the mistaken sense of inferiority so unfairly implanted by his early experiences rendered him sometimes irritable, a little tactless and rather easily offended.

And despite his Everest dreams of English gardens, Smythe never could quite relax at home. He felt trapped by domesticity and was a remote father.

Smythe found a different sort of sanctuary in the upper Bhyundar valley of Garhwal, a place so botanically rich he called it the Valley of Flowers, a name the Indian authorities used when they designated the area a national park. Smythe had discovered its riches with Eric Shipton while climbing Kamet in 1931, a peak not far from Nanda Devi and one of the landmark ascents of Himalayan mountaineering. Frustrated at the dismal failure on Everest in 1936, Smythe chose to spend the following summer in what he called his Shangri-La, alone with a small crew of Sherpas.

> For the first time in my life I was able to think [he wrote]. I do not mean to think objectively or analytically, but rather to surrender thought to my surroundings. This is a power of which we know little in the West but which is a basic of abstract thought in the East. It is allowing the mind to receive rather than to seek impressions, and it is gained by expurgating extraneous thought. ... When this happens the human mind escapes from the bondage of its own feeble imaginings and becomes as one with its Creator.

Smythe was a prolific writer, although as Raymond Greene observed he 'was always trying to be "literary" and somehow never brought it off because he was trying too hard'. (The old Everester Edward Strutt, by then a vituperative editor of the *Alpine Journal* and member of the Mount Everest Committee, called it 'psychological bilge'.) Smythe's writing has few admirers these days, unlike that of Tilman, yet despite the straining for effect, it's touching to consider this self-absorbed and scratchy man momentarily at ease with himself in one of the most beautiful valleys on earth.

Tilman might himself have been on Everest with Smythe and Shipton in 1936 but he acclimatised badly the year before, during a reconnaissance put together at the last minute when permission from Tibet arrived unexpectedly. Little new had been learned from that trip, even though the weather remained settled and fine deep into July, more than a month after the monsoon was expected. (Had the weather in 1936 been anything like as good, it's quite possible Everest would have been climbed before the war.) Instead a large number of lesser peaks were climbed during the reconnaissance of 1935, twenty-six over 20,000 feet (6,096 metres), 'a veritable orgy' as Shipton described it. Michael Spender, brother of the poet Stephen, did much surveying work and the expedition also gave work to a young Tibetan-born high-altitude porter called Tenzing Bhotia, better known to the public after 1953 as Tenzing Norgay, or Sherpa Tenzing. It was his first job as a mountain porter, selected at the last moment by Eric Shipton on the basis of his warm smile. At least the 1935 venture had been cheap to organise.

While the team was at Everest, a bleak discovery exposed the raw and questionable motivation behind their venture. Charles Warren, the expedition's doctor and later a well-regarded paediatrician, had the shock of finding the body of the adventurer Maurice Wilson, a veteran of the Great War. Wilson had won the Military Cross at the fourth Battle of Ypres but was later wounded by machine-gun fire that struck his chest and left him with a chronic injury in his left arm. Too mentally fractured to continue his old life he emigrated from his native Bradford: first to the United States, then New Zealand, searching for some kind of resolution or purpose. He was in no way a sad or pathetic figure: tall and physically fit despite his chronic injuries, he prospered well enough, but couldn't settle anywhere for long. On a boat back to England in 1932 he got to know some Indian yogis and discovered a little about fasting and their spiritual practice. When he fell ill after his return and conventional medicine failed him, he used this knowledge to heal, melding it into his strong Christian beliefs. Galvanised by this experience, and wanting to demonstrate his powerful new tool of faith and fasting, he settled on climbing Everest: 'faith – only faith: the thing that moves mountains you know.'

Wilson had the idea of flying to the foot of the mountain and so joined the London Aero Club. Despite a lack of aptitude he got his pilot's licence and bought a second-hand Gypsy Moth, which he dubbed *Ever Wrest*. When the press got wind of his plans, Wilson became a minor sensation, attracting the disapproval of authorities from Whitehall to Delhi and all points between. Despite this, Wilson persevered and finally reached India only to be denied permission to fly over Nepal. Undaunted, he sold his aircraft and in the spring of 1934, disguised as a monk, trekked through Sikkim and Tibet with three experienced Bhotias to base camp. The monks at Rongbuk were a little surprised to see a lone British climber but he told them he was one of the team from 1933 returning to the mountain. The monks handed over food Ruttledge had stored with them for a future attempt. Sadly, Wilson had not prepared himself as a mountaineer as thoroughly as he had an aviator, and he perished in his tent after several attempts to reach the north col. Warren concluded that a combination of hunger, exposure and exhaustion had done for him. The final entry in his diary read: 'Off again. Gorgeous day.'

Wilson's fate drew no censure from the men who discovered his windblown corpse. Charles Warren recalled how after burying him in a crevasse,

> We all raised our hats ... and I think that every one was rather upset at the business. I thought I had grown immune to the sight of the dead; but somehow or other, in the circumstances, and because of the fact that he was, after all, doing much the same as ourselves, his tragedy seemed to have been brought a little too near home for us.

As fat flakes of snow fell outside the tent, Edwin Kempson, a brilliant mathematician and schoolmaster known as 'G', read extracts from Wilson's diary to Shipton and Warren. Shipton said: 'it was as if the man himself was speaking to us, revealing his secret thoughts'. He had no doubts about Wilson's sincerity, even if 'it was clear that he had little liking for the mountains, and he certainly claimed no spiritual uplift in their presence'. There were plenty in Britain who saw climbing Everest as some kind of metaphysical struggle or a matter of national prestige. The climbers actually on Everest in the 1930s were more sceptical, not least Raymond Greene:

I think a lot too much has been said in the past about the spiritual and mystical significance of climbing Everest and about its possible effects on British prestige. ... we go to Everest not for those reasons at all, but either simply because it is fun or in order to satisfy some purely personal and selfish psychological urge.

★

Some of the inspiration for Wilson's daring plan to use an aircraft to reach Everest came from the dazzling and ultimately successful attempt to fly an aircraft over the summit the year before. Balloons had risen higher than Everest before the Great War and in 1919 the French fighter ace Jean Casale had flown a plane at over nine thousand metres. Using an aircraft to survey the approaches to Everest seemed plausible; the scientist Alexander Kellas had written a paper on the subject. The year before he led the Everest reconnaisance of 1921, Charles Howard-Bury, on his mission to India to acquire an Everest permit, approached the Royal Air Force in India to sound them out. While initially indifferent, an offer was eventually made of an aircraft and pilot with the necessary photographic equipment. Nothing came of it, which was probably for the best, since the aircraft in question, an Airco DH9a, had a ceiling of little more than three thousand metres. In the mid 1920s, the American 'barnstormer' pilot Roscoe Turner contacted the Mount Everest Committee. Turner later became famous for buying a lion cub, bred in captivity for Hollywood. He named him Gilmore, for his sponsor, and flew Gilmore around the West Coast in his Sikorsky S29A, at least until Gilmore got too big for his parachute harness. Stunts of that nature were far beneath the Mount Everest Committee's dignity.

Unfortunately for the committee, aviation had become a lot more fashionable than mountain climbing. This was the era of world-famous pioneering aviators such as Charles Lindbergh, Amelia Earhart and Amy Johnson. In 1931, five British Westland Wapitis had flown past Nanga Parbat shooting spectacular film footage along the way. Why shouldn't the same be done over Everest, if the Nepali government would give permission? Stewart Blacker was a weapons designer and Great War pilot who had survived being shot down three times. He was also a descendant of Valentine Blacker, a predecessor of George

Everest as surveyor general of India. In March 1932 he set up offices
at the College of Aeronautical Engineering in order to prosecute this
mission. Almost immediately he had the backing of the Royal
Geographical Society and a host of aristocratic supporters, both Indian
and British, including the novelist and politician John Buchan. Knowing
precisely the sort of hero a project like this required, he sought out
the dashing young pilot Douglas Douglas-Hamilton, Marquess of
Douglas and Clydesdale and eldest son of the Duke of Hamilton.
Aged twenty-nine, Clydesdale was the youngest squadron leader in
the Royal Air Force and a member of parliament for the Scottish
constituency of East Renfrewshire. When the economy worsened that
summer and several backers pulled out, he approached his friend Lucy,
Lady Houston, known as 'Poppy', once a wasp-waisted chorus girl
and now the colossally wealthy widow of shipping magnate Sir Robert
Houston, her third husband. She was sceptical, considering it dangerous
and not wanting anything to happen to this attractive young man. 'I
told him I did not want to help him commit suicide.' Clydesdale reassured her that flying over Everest was safer than a walk around
Hampstead Heath on a foggy evening. Lady Houston wrote a cheque
for £10,000 with the promise of more if required.

It wasn't just Clydesdale's aristocratic charm that persuaded her.
The year before, Houston had given ten times that amount to the
aircraft manufacturer Supermarine Aviation where the engineer
Reginald Mitchell was developing what would become the Spitfire,
after Ramsay MacDonald's national government had cut funding to
the project. This cash allowed the company to continue competing in
aviation's Schneider Trophy, established to boost aircraft innovation,
and was part of a determined publicity campaign against MacDonald,
whom she regarded as a traitor for leaving the skies above London
defenceless. A suffragist in her salad days, Poppy had since galloped
to the right and was now a supporter of the fascist Oswald Mosley.
Flying over Everest would be another opportunity to advertise British
prestige and remind Indians what the mother country could still accom-
plish. Not surprisingly, the Indian National Congress thought the
project an outrage. Along with Lady Houston's support came new and
highly effective management in the form of Air Commodore Peregrine
Fellowes whose expert military planning saw the project delivered on
time. Clydesdale flew the prototype Westland Wallace with its super-

charged Bristol Pegasus engine over the summit on 3 April 1933 with Blacker as observer, craning his neck for any sign of Mallory and Irvine. David McIntyre, an impossibly handsome Scot who later founded Prestwick Airport, piloted a second aircraft with a Gaumont British Films cameraman on board who filmed dramatic footage of the mountains before collapsing when his oxygen tube fractured in the cold. A handkerchief fixed that. *The Times* celebrated the breathtaking achievement on its front page, illustrating the story with a picture, taken from the cockpit, of Makalu: the wrong mountain.

That such an exciting feat had been managed in so short a time made the Mount Everest Committee look rather threadbare. Peregrine Fellowes had a genius for planning and achieved in a few months what had taken the committee a decade. The film of this adventure was another matter. *Wings over Everest* was co-directed by Ivor Montagu, a Jewish communist, Russian intelligence asset and ping-pong champion. (His brother Ewen worked for MI6 during the war, devising Operation Mincemeat ahead of the invasion of Sicily in 1943.) Montagu's political affiliations can be seen in the cutaway shots of impoverished Indian farm boys looking up from their paddy fields as the gleaming British machines fly overhead on another spurious imperial adventure. With only a very few minutes of footage from the mountains, the film certainly needed padding out. The vituperative Strutt wrote an acid review for the *Alpine Journal*, barely hiding his resentment that so much attention had been paid to a public-relations stunt, once more missing the point that the public didn't care about fine detail, just glorious headlines. 'The films,' he wrote,

> give mostly the appearance of having been taken through a keyhole covered with sheep netting. For this the hopeless construction of the otherwise excellent machines seems responsible. With few exceptions, the successful shots are ruined by wing and stay obstruction.

None of this bothered the Academy of Motion Pictures, which gave *Wings over Everest* an Oscar in March 1936. That summer, Lord Clydesdale flew his own private aircraft to Berlin, joining a parliamentary group invited by the Third Reich to attend the Olympics.

*

Less than a century before the Berlin Olympics, Joseph Hooker had sketched the first image of Everest by a European. In Hooker's world, the European imagination conceived mountains either in the Romantic context of the sublime, or else as somewhere to explore the scientific values of the Enlightenment, as Humboldt had done. With the advent of photography, especially the development just before and after the Great War of lighter, portable cameras, like the Vest Pocket Kodak carried by the British on Everest in the 1920s, the thrilling nature of extreme mountain landscapes was suddenly available to the public in a way it had never been before. This radical new mountain imagery shifted perspectives in a way that photos of the Moon landings would half a century later. Moving pictures only emphasised this impression. Creative artists and thinkers drew on this dramatic new palette to pursue philosophical ends very different to those of Hooker's era.

In her documentary *Olympia*, Leni Riefenstahl and her cameraman Hans Ertl applied lessons they had learned making *Bergfilme*, 'mountain films': Germany's version of the Western. Her vision of alpinism offered a useful metaphor for Nazi propaganda. The opportunity to capture images of powerful young Aryans conquering nature's harshest challenges was intoxicating. Climbing itself was drawn inside this philosophy, nowhere better illustrated than attempts by Germans and Austrians to climb Nanga Parbat, the world's ninth highest mountain, where Fred Mummery had met his end in 1895. As the British struggled on Everest, the Germans mounted five expeditions to Nanga Parbat during the 1930s, a sustained campaign that caused the deaths of twenty-six climbers and Sherpas through a combination of personal arrogance and political ideology. It also tore apart Germany's sizable mountaineering community as the Nazis fought to take control of a powerful sporting lobby, part of Hitler's grand strategy of *Gleichschaltung*, or coordination, the Nazification of every aspect of German life. That struggle would put the very ethos of mountaineering under the microscope.

The Deutscher und Österreichischer Alpenverein, the German and Austrian Alpine Club, had its origins in the 1860s, when the first Austrian section was set up in imitation of the original Alpine Club in London. Unlike the Alpine Club, which was limited to dedicated alpinists and socially elitist, the German and Austrian version was open to all, regardless of ability or class. As a consequence, by the early 1930s the Alpenverein had a membership of 240,000 compared to several hundred in the Alpine Club. Divisions within the German and Austrian club predated the rise of Hitler but shared common themes. A number of Austrian sections banned Jews in the early 1920s, to the disgust of the Munich-based *Neue Deutsche Alpenzeitung*.

> You search for heritage and the shape of a skull and overlook the beating of the heart and the sound of the soul. What is the point and how will things end?

Not all Munich climbers felt the same way, including the lawyer Paul Bauer, who would direct Hitler's process of *Gleichschaltung* in German mountaineering and extend those fractures into the Himalaya, with deadly consequences. Bauer had joined the German army at the outbreak of the Great War and been captured by the British in 1917. After the war, bitter at what he perceived as the betrayal of ordinary fighting men, he joined the Freikorps and latched onto the idea that climbing could help restore German pride. 'When the rifle was taken from us,' he once said, 'our orphaned hands reached for an ice axe.' Such revisionist nationalistic rhetoric had inevitable consequences as the fatality rate among the self-styled *Bergkamaraden*, 'mountain-comrades', spiralled on challenges like the north face of the Eiger. Bauer despised the woolly internationalist values of Günter Dyhrenfurth, who invited foreign climbers, including Frank Smythe, on his expedition to Kangchenjunga in 1930. Bauer too was obsessed with Kangchenjunga but his teams would be German only. For Bauer, the team, the *Mannschaft*, was everything. The Akademischer Alpenverein München, the student club in Munich, had for Bauer been a focus of sanity in the chaos and confusion of post-war Munich, when the things Bauer held most dear were ridiculed. Climbing for Bauer was a way to return to the comradeship of war and

> test those qualities which had become superfluous in everyday life but which to us were still the highest qualities in the world: unshakeable courage, comradeship and self-sacrifice.

Although he was a nationalist, Bauer was also an Anglophile who had joined the Alpine Club. 'One effect of the geographical situation of the Himalaya,' he wrote in the *Himalayan Journal*, is that it brings us into contact with English mountaineers and other people of England and the British Empire; and we thus come, again and again, to enjoy their help and hospitality.

In 1931, Bauer tangled with the rising star of German alpinism Willo Welzenbach over their competing interests in the Himalaya. Bauer wanted the British to give him permission for Kangchenjunga, which lay within their imperial Indian borders. Welzenbach thought Bauer's plans on the world's third highest mountain were a pipe dream, and decided to lead his own expedition to Nanga Parbat, where he felt there was a better chance of success, much to Bauer's fury. But Bauer knew how to handle the British and it was he, with his superior contacts in India, who got permission for that year. In 1932, the International Olympic Committee gave Bauer's published account of his expedition to Kangchenjunga a medal and after Hitler's rise to power his position within the German mountaineering establishment grew ever stronger. The Nazi sports minister Hans von Tschammer und Osten wanted the Alpenverein to ban Jews, and he set up a rival organisation with Bauer in charge. German mountaineers wanting to visit the Himalaya now had to accede to the prevailing political climate. Dyhrenfurth left for Switzerland with his wife Hettie because, as the liberal Austrian climber Erwin Schneider put it, 'the accident of his birth means he will no longer be able to win a flower pot in the Third Reich'.

There were a very few exceptions. In 1934 another expedition to Nanga Parbat was planned and alongside the climbers a scientific team was brought together to study the mountain's geology. Hans Peter Misch, a major figure in the discovery of how granite is formed, was among them. Born in Berlin, Misch was the grandson of the influential philosopher Wilhelm Dilthey and had just earned his doctorate studying the petrology of the central Pyrenees. Yet his father had been born Jewish, which disqualified Misch from the expedition, under the antisemitic Law for the Restoration of the Civil Service. The leader of the expedition's scientific team, Richard Finsterwalder, appealed against Misch's exclusion all the way up to Rudolf Hess, Hitler's deputy, arguing that 'an otherwise healthy law had here been applied to a guiltless man'. Misch was allowed to go. Finsterwalder and his team did useful work, and achieved an impressive circumnavigation of the mountain, producing a highly accurate and detailed topographic map. The climbing itself was a disaster. The route selected on Nanga Parbat was not up the Rupal or Diamir faces Mummery had explored but on the vast, sprawling northern slopes of the peak, the Rakhiot face. The climbing wasn't difficult but the risks were great. In early June, the climber Alfred Drexler died quite suddenly, probably of high-altitude pulmonary oedema. Expedition leader Willy Merkl took photographs and footage of Drexler's corpse wrapped in a giant swastika, being dragged down the mountain, photographs that were printed in newspapers at home. The Nazi symbolism enraged Erwin Schneider, who was part of the team, but in response to his objections, Merkl threatened to ban him from climbing. Willo Welzenbach wrote of his fears about Merkl's leadership.

> Merkl increasingly acts like a dictator who allows no criticism. He appears to really believe that a stern and uncompromising demeanour serves to establish his authority.

It wasn't the best atmosphere in which to attempt such an immense enterprise.

In early July an unwieldy group of sixteen climbers and Sherpas from Merkl's expedition were caught in a savage storm at an exposed camp, the eighth above base and located just below the summit. That so many were so high was part of Merkl's plan: the sanctity of the group. Nine of the sixteen would perish in the maelstrom while attempting to descend in what was the worst Himalayan climbing tragedy thus far. The frozen bodies of Merkl and the Sherpa Gaylay who had loyally remained with him were found four years later. Von Tschammer und Osten had told Merkl when he left, 'The conquest of the peak is expected for the glory of Germany.' But with the high death toll and expense, with little to show for it that would thrill ordinary Germans, the expedition had become an embarrassment, especially when the traitor Dyhrenfurth was awarded a gold medal at the Berlin Olympics. Bauer distanced himself from the enterprise, accusing Schneider and his fellow Austrian Peter Aschenbrenner of abandoning Sherpas; they were made the subject of a spurious enquiry. He even criticised Willo Welzenbach, one of the 'fallen', as someone interested only in personal glory, unlike Bauer, who was an 'old soldier', a favoured term among early Nazis. Bauer told von Tschammer und Osten: 'For us, Adolf Hitler was already, in 1923, a man we would not impugn.' Nazi officials ordered the racially suspect Peter Misch, who had acted bravely in desperate rescue attempts, to hand over his research material. Misch refused and fled the country, teaching first in China before war with Japan forced him to emigrate once more. He settled finally in Seattle at the University of Washington where he enjoyed a long and distinguished academic career. Erwin Schneider didn't return to the Himalaya until after the war, when this brilliant cartographer drew the first maps of Nepal's mountains, including Everest.

In 1936, a new Nazi-backed Himalayan exploratory organisation, the Deutsche Himalaja-Stiftung, was founded, with Bauer pulling its strings. That year he led an expedition to Sikkim, where his team made the first ascent of a peak called Siniolchu. One of the successful pair to reach the top was his trusted lieutenant Karl Wien, who was given the task of leading another expedition to Nanga Parbat the following year. But on 15 June 1937 a cornice broke off above Wien's camp, triggering a massive avalanche that dumped snow ten feet thick on their tents. Seven climbers and nine Sherpas were killed. Bauer rushed to Nanga Parbat from Germany and despite contracting malaria managed to reach the site of the tragedy a month later. When they dug the bodies out, they found the wristwatches the men were wearing had stopped at 12.10 a.m.

After the war, when Bauer had been through the process of denazification, he applied to rejoin the Alpine Club, having been thrown out after war was declared. This was a quandary for the Alpine Club. In the immediate, chaotic aftermath of war, the Allies had appointed Bauer to run Munich; he wasn't judged a war criminal. The committee decided to seek opinion from the members. Charles Houston was appalled.

> His letters to me during and after the German invasion of Poland so sickened me, and evidenced such a callous attitude towards human rights, that I must strongly protest.

Bill Tilman, who had spent the war fighting with partisans behind enemy lines, first in Albania and later in Italy, disagreed. It was Tilman's argument that won the day. Bauer died in 1990, at the age of ninety-four.

*

Just as Himalayan climbing was co-opted for dark political ends, Himalayan mythology offered an otherworldly metaphor to set against the spiritual dislocation of modern life. In the summer of 1936, on the other side of the world, the Himalaya was being recreated in Hollywood, as filming of James Hilton's novel *Lost Horizon* got underway. The director was the bankable Frank Capra, whose movie *Mr Deeds Goes to Town* had just opened and would win him his second Oscar, swept along on the same emotional tide that saw Franklin D Roosevelt re-elected in a landslide. *Lost Horizon*, on the other hand, would be an expensive failure that could have sunk Columbia Pictures. Later in life, Capra would claim credit for turning the project around, explaining how he threw the first two reels in the studio's incinerator after a test audience found the movie long-winded. In fact, it was studio boss Harry Cohn who painstakingly cut Capra's sprawling mess into something that had a chance at the box office. Even so, *Lost Horizon* was a dud compared to Capra's earlier work, for reasons that Graham Greene caught perfectly in his review for the *Spectator*.

> Nothing reveals men's characters more than their Utopias. This Utopia closely resembles a film star's luxurious estate in Beverly Hills; flirtatious pursuits through grape arbours, splashing and divings in blossomy pools under improbable waterfalls, and rich and enormous meals.

In conclusion, Greene thought it 'a very long picture ... and a very dull one as soon as the opening scenes are over'.

Greene had put his finger on a flaw shared by the novel: Shangri-La, the lost Himalayan world portrayed, was an idealised version of the West. The set designer at Columbia Pictures, Stephen Goosson produced a late art deco Tibetan monastery for Capra that won him an Oscar but was more stylised Hollywood real-estate fantasy than anything drawn from the immense architectural heritage of the Himalaya. Shangri-La itself was simply mindful consumerism. Capra did hire a consultant on all things Tibetan, the National Geographic journalist Harrison Forman, who had in 1932 interviewed Thubten Choekyi Nyima, the ninth Panchen Lama, when the latter was in exile at Labrang monastery in north-west Tibet. Little of this shows in the film. Beyond its vague Orientalist mysticism, Shangri-La is a colonialist fantasy, with simple 'Tibetan' farmers overseen by a cultured and tasteful European elite who guide them like children.

The spiritual philosophy behind *Lost Horizon* was rooted more in Theosophy than Tibet. The self-absorbed ramblings of Helena Blavatsky had almost nothing to do with Tibetan Buddhism as it's practised in the Himalaya, but in the early 1890s, after the publication of Blavatsky's *The Secret Doctrine* and before Sigmund Freud became a more persuasive draw, Theosophy became fashionable soul food in Europe and North America. The literary hostess Elizabeth Burke-Plunkett, Countess of Fingall, recalled her excitement at meeting Jiddu Krishnamurti, the Theosophist Society's 'world teacher'. Her friend W B Yeats described Blavatsky as 'the most living person alive'. Later in life he was more circumspect:

> They had no scholarship and they spoke and wrote badly, but they discussed great problems ardently and simply and unconventionally as men, perhaps, discussed great problems in the medieval universities.

Theosophy was successful as a catalyst, however. When Yeats visited Stanford University in 1904, he inspired a young student and Theosophist called Walter Evans-Wentz to study Celtic mythology at Oxford. There Evans-Wentz met the young T E Lawrence who recommended he go east. In India Evans-Wentz met Theosophy's leading figures, including Annie Besant and Krishnamurti, and worked on his famous translation of what is known in English as *The Tibetan Book of the Dead*. Everyone from Carl Jung to Hermann Hesse to Jawaharlal Nehru took an interest in Theosophy. Its ideas about cosmic geometry, the universe rippling out from a single point to infinite complexity, was also an inspiration for generations of abstract artists, including Piet Mondrian, who searched for the utopian and universal in his work, and the Russian Wassily Kandinsky.

Another Russian artist immersed in Theosophy would become firmly rooted in the actual Himalaya. Nicholas Roerich was born in St Petersburg in 1874, a polymath who studied art at the city's university and became part of the group orbiting the impresario Sergei Diaghilev. Roerich's early work focussed not on abstract geometrical shapes but Russia's mythical past and he became famous designing sets for Diaghilev's Ballets Russes, including Igor Stravinsky's *Rite of Spring*. In 1901 he married Elena Ivanovna Shaposhnikova, who introduced him to Hindu mystics and writers like Rabindranath Tagore. She also translated Blavatsky's *The Secret Doctrine* into Russian.

Following the Russian Revolution, the politically moderate Roerichs left Russia for Europe, arriving in London in 1919, where they joined the local branch of the Theosophy Society and befriended the young Christmas Humphreys, a barrister and formidable prosecutor who later founded the Buddhism Society and wrote widely on the subject for the rest of his sometimes controversial life. The civil war in Russia had for the Roerichs a millenarian dimension, as would their interest in Tibetan mythology: both believed that the king of Shambhala would eventually return to destroy the wicked and reignite mankind's creative spirit. Nicholas continued to work as a set designer in London for the conductor and impresario Sir Thomas Beecham and later in the United States, but what he and Helena (as his wife was now known) really wanted was to travel in the Himalaya and find Shambhala: ambassadors for Western Buddhism returning to the root of the mystical teachings that enriched them. He also offered to do a little light spying for the Soviet Union if the Bolsheviks covered some of his costs on what would be an expensive expedition. The savage suppression of Buddhism in Russia's eastern provinces was not yet underway, but the Soviets were still suspicious of Roerich's utopian mission. Nonetheless, they did support him logistically when he came within their sphere of influence.

The journey, which included Helena and their adult son George, a famous Tibet scholar who studied at the Sorbonne under Paul Pelliot – he of the Dunhuang Caves – and the Indologist Sylvain Lévi, began in Sikkim where Eric Bailey was still political officer. (He called them 'my Russian artist friends', but confessed he 'did not like [Nicholas'] pictures very much'.) Because of the lull in relations between Tibet and British India, news of the Roerichs' progress on this epic adventure was often patchy; in the summer of 1927 they fell out of contact altogether and remained so for almost a year: they were thought to be dead. In fact, they were merely in prison, detained by the Tibetan

authorities despite their passports and passion for Buddhism. After
their release in March 1928, the Roerichs hastened to India where they
established the Himalayan Research Institute, or *Urusvati*, the 'light
of the morning star', first in Darjeeling and then permanently in the
Kullu valley in the far north-west of India.

After the Second World War, Helena Blavatsky's more occultist
ideas resurfaced in a rash of books exploring National Socialism's
esoteric interest in Tibet. The French writer Louis Pauwels claimed
communities of Tibetan Geluk monks were living in Germany from
the 1920s at the invitation of Karl Haushofer, a German soldier and
professor of geopolitics who had taught Rudolf Hess and remained
on good terms with him. Haushofer was also the supposed founder
of the Vril Society and a friend of the mystic George Gurdjieff. The
truth in such stories is almost indiscernible. A few of those at the
heart of the Nazi project were intrigued by occultist myths and racial
theories involving Tibet. Others were demonstrably hostile. Alfred
Rosenberg, for example, was a racial ideologue close to Hitler, a rival
of Heinrich Himmler, executed for crimes against humanity. For
Rosenberg, Tibetan Buddhism had been a malign influence like
Catholicism. If it hadn't been for the Protestant Reformation, he
believed,

> Europe today would have reached the condition of holy men of India
> and Tibet, thick with dirt, a condition of the most complete stultifica-
> tion.

The adoption of the swastika as a Nazi emblem didn't arise from its
ubiquity in the Himalaya. Its status there is more good-luck charm
than sacred symbol and was used in Europe before the Great War:
Kipling put it on the cover of his books. (In fact, it was the swastika's
discovery at Troy by the German archaeologist Heinrich Schliemann
that intrigued Nazi racial theorists: if the swastika represented a link
to an ancient past, it was this one.)

Beyond the propaganda value of German mountaineering, Nazi
interest in the Himalaya was restricted to *Reichsführer-SS* Heinrich
Himmler's 'research' group the Ahnenerbe, meaning 'ancestral
heritage'. Himmler himself took an interest in Indian philosophy and
was said to read the *Bhagavad Gita*. His interest in Tibet was likely

sparked by his acolyte Karl Maria Wiligut, whose passion for esoteric paganism was matched with mental instability: Wiligut fell from favour when Himmler discovered he had once been committed to an asylum by his own wife. Among Wiligut's fantasies was a supposed journey he had made to a Tibetan Buddhist monastery and a complex network of energy beams linking ancient sites across Eurasia, including Tibet, a geomantic worldview that chimed with Himmler's own. While scientifically spurious, the purpose of the Ahnenerbe, founded in 1935, was to dress the darkest Nazi policies, including the eventual exter-mination of the Jews, with some kind of academic respectability. In 1938, it withdrew its backing for a scientific expedition to Tibet because the expedition leader thought the Ahnenerbe's work bogus. But the scientists still travelled with the support of Himmler, who made a personal appeal to the Foreign Office in London and the intervention of the pro-Hitler British admiral Sir Barry Domvile.

The leader of this expedition was the naturalist Ernst Schäfer, whose fascination with Tibet had been inspired by his boyhood hero Sven Hedin. When Schäfer joined the SS in 1936, he had just returned from his second expedition to eastern Tibet with the American academic Brooke Dolan. (Dolan would visit Lhasa in 1942 on behalf of the American intelligence services along with Ilya Tolstoy, grandson of Leo.) Much of the work Schäfer's team undertook was recognisably scientific: natural history, geophysics and meteorology. Himmler was particularly interested in the meteorological work, since independent reliable weather forecasts were essential preparation for war; his interest extended, for the same reason, to horse-breeding, echoing William Moorcroft's journey in the early nineteenth century. The exception to all this was the spurious anthropology performed during the expedition by Bruno Beger, a former student of the eugenicist Hans Friedrich Günther, who in the late 1930s was teaching Nazi racial theories at the University of Berlin. (Hitler had four copies of his influential book *Racial Science of the German People* and put it on his recommended reading list for party members.) Günther held that the ideal of the Nordic type, the *Herrenrasse* or 'master race', would be found most readily among society's elite. This is why Beger paid most attention to Lhasa aristocrats as the most likely stratum of Tibetan society in which to find evidence of a common Aryan ancestor. Unfortunately for him, Lhasa's aristocrats all refused to let him take

measurements of their heads in the way that he did with hundreds
of ordinary Tibetans. (During the war, Beger worked with the SS
anatomist August Hirt, selecting victims from various ethnic groups
at Auschwitz. They were then gassed and defleshed for the Jewish
skeleton collection, a gruesome attempt to display Jewish racial degen-
eracy. Beger was convicted of war crimes in 1971 and sentenced to
three years in prison, reduced to probation on appeal. He died in 2009,
aged ninety-eight.)

*

The murderous racial theories of the Third Reich meant about as
much in pre-war Lhasa as Hollywood's version of Shangri-La, or the
fertile imaginings of the Theosophists. These were simply orientalist
fantasies projected onto the Himalaya. The rise of the nation state on
the other hand, in its way another kind of utopia, was a burning issue.
It was nationalism that would drive the coming storm and have a
lasting impact on the people of the Himalaya.

The thirteenth Dalai Lama and his Buryat follower Agvan Dorzhiev
had once had a vision of a pan-Central Asian Tibetan Buddhist stronghold. Now Stalin's purges were underway and Buddhism was being
supressed in Mongolia. Dorzhiev himself died at the hands of Soviet
torturers. The Dalai Lama, prematurely aged, saw the same fate
engulfing Tibet itself.

> In the future, this system will certainly be forced either from within
> or without on this land that cherishes the joint spiritual and temporal
> system. If in such an event we fail to defend our land, the holy lamas,
> including their triumphant father and son [the Dalai and Panchen Lama]
> will be eliminated without a trace of their names remaining ... my
> people, subjected to fear and misery will be unable to endure day or
> night.

After the Dalai Lama's death in 1933, China sensed an opportunity and
the nationalist government in Beijing sent a mission of condolence to
Lhasa under the command of General Huang Mu-sung, a member
of president Chiang Kai-shek's National Military Council. He was
welcomed with far more ceremony than any British official ever had

been and the Tibetan government allowed the Chinese to establish a wireless transmitter, obviating the need for China to use British telegraph wires, which were easily monitored for intelligence. Huang was patient but his aim was clear: to have the Tibetans declare their country a republic and themselves as one of the 'five races' and so part of China. He brought with him a large cash reserve to bribe important officials, but despite this the Tibetan leadership politely told him that they had been ruled by thirteen Dalai Lamas and weren't about to change. Tibet was an independent nation and would remain that way. They also asked about the return of the Panchen Lama, who had been in exile since Eric Bailey's time as political officer, but without the large escort of Chinese troops that the Kuomintang insisted he bring with him. This show of unity and resolve disheartened Huang Mu-sung and he returned home without achieving China's overall aim. Yet the direction of travel was clear: since their expulsion in 1912, the Chinese had been trying to reassert their power in Lhasa, no longer as the Qing Empire but as the republic of China. It was only a matter of time before they tried again.

The permanent presence of Chinese officials in Lhasa triggered alarm in India. Charles Bell had reasoned that the British didn't need a legation in Lhasa unless China returned: now they had. Huang Mu-sung's mission, monitored on behalf of India's foreign service by the long-serving political agent Norbu Dhondup, prompted a new British mission to Lhasa. Like the one from China, it would become a permanent feature without ever admitting that this was its intention. Basil Gould arrived in Lhasa on 24 August 1936, a week after the Berlin Olympics closed and a week before Bill Tilman climbed Nanda Devi. Gould had been political officer in Sikkim since the start of the year and was cut from the same cloth as Charles Bell, under whom Gould had served twenty years previously. Bell had been a presence on the frontier in the mid 1930s, warning the Tibetan government that 'bit by bit, Britain is giving more power to India, who will hardly show the same friendship ... or have the same power to help Tibet'.

Gould now had the opportunity to reignite relations with Tibet and offer reassurance in the face of increasing Chinese pressure. With him came two telegraph operators, a medical officer and the mountaineer Freddy Spencer Chapman, whom Gould had encountered by chance and invited as his personal secretary. Chapman had with him the latest Dufaycolor film stock and he made a stunning colour record of Lhasa, capturing the city as it was, little more than a decade before the Chinese invasion of 1950 changed everything. The final member of Gould's team was Hugh Richardson, the new trade official based at Gyantse, halfway between Lhasa and Gangtok, a tall Scot from St Andrews who had developed an interest in Tibet at Oxford. He would spend eight of the next fourteen years in Lhasa, first for the British and then the Indian governments, in the process becoming a valuable and scholarly expert on Tibet as well as a potent champion for its independent status in the maelstrom that was to come. It was Richardson who would monitor the activities of the Schäfer expedition two years later, relieved when Tibetan opinion turned against the Germans for their careless intrusions with cameras and hunting of animals for their zoological collection. Luckily for him, Himmler's idea for a high-altitude insurgency force, led by Schäfer, aimed at disrupting the British in Central Asia, came to nothing.

As a way to build bridges, Gould encouraged football matches between the British, the 'Mission Marmots', and anyone who wanted to join in. They played a team from the Nepali embassy, another from Lhasa's longstanding Muslim community and a team of Tibetan soldiers, who offered the toughest opposition, drawing two matches. 'The Tibetans play [a] hard clean sporting game,' Gould reported. The teacher Frank Ludlow's influence had clearly survived. The season only came to an end that November when the goalposts were used for firewood. Jampal Yeshe Gyaltsen, the *tulku* or reincarnate lama of Reting monastery who, aged just twenty-three, had been appointed regent of Tibet, asked Chapman if he could borrow the football, which Chapman took as a good sign of the mission's progress. (The resumption of football in Tibet proved popular and there were more than a dozen teams playing regularly in Lhasa when Tibet's conservative monastic elite blew the final whistle in 1944 and banned it. The fourteenth Dalai Lama's younger brother Gyalo Thondup recalled ruefully how he was beaten at school along with the rest of his team for playing illicitly.)

Gould's mission arrived at a hugely sensitive time as the search for the new Dalai Lama got underway. The period following the thirteenth Dalai Lama's death in 1933 had been predictably traumatic. The most powerful minister at the time was Thubten Kunphel, known as

Kunphela, a strong man who had entered the Dalai Lama's service as a servant and risen through force of personality to lead the most effective military unit in Tibet. He was regarded as sympathetic to the Kuomintang. His enemies, particularly Lungshar, one of four *tsipon*, state treasury ministers, and who was Tsarong's rival in the 1920s, used the Dalai Lama's sudden death to build a coalition against him. Kunphela's power base melted away and he was imprisoned. His fall provoked rebellion in the eastern Tibetan province of Kham from his allies, the powerful and wealthy Pandatsang family. These rebels, small in number, also fought China's communists as they struggled through the grinding horror of the Long March, their flight from Kuomintang forces deep into the interior of China and the eastern marches of Tibet. Kunphela and the Pandatsang would soon start an opposition movement in exile: the Tibet Improvement Party.

Lungshar didn't enjoy his ascendancy for long. Like Kunphela he was a moderniser. It was Lungshar who had accompanied the four young Tibetan aristocrats to Rugby school and understood that Tibet must change. Yet his attempt to increase state revenues at the cost of Lhasa's aristocracy and monastic establishment left him vulnerable and he was accused of communist leanings, something Laden La had warned about following their trip to Europe. The ultra-conservative leader of the cabinet – or *kashag* – Trimon Shap-pe outmanoeuvred Lungshar, who was arrested and suffered the archaic torture of having his eyes put out. No one alive had performed this punishment and it was botched. Soon afterwards Trimon Shap-pe himself resigned from public service, giving up his role in selecting the new Dalai Lama. This process was as usual a fraught enterprise, with divinations vulnerable to political influence. The head of the thirteenth Dalai Lama, lying in state, was seen to turn to the north-west. Reting Rinpoche, the regent, saw a vision in a sacred lake of two letters: 'A' and 'K', suggesting Amdo and the monastery of Kumbum, far to the north-east of Lhasa in modern Qinghai, at the time under the control of the Kuomintang warlord Ma Bufang. Hugh Richardson reported suspicions in Lhasa that such visions were conveniently helpful for Reting, a deeply controversial figure in this crucial moment of Tibetan history. Tibet's monastic elite was still vulnerable to sectarian conflict, between the dominant Geluk institutions and those of the Nyingma school. Reting, although Geluk, was seen as too sympathetic to the Nyingma

side, which had found protection under China's rule. Reting may have
been indicating that a Dalai Lama from the periphery was needed to
challenge the great monasteries of the centre.

In theory, the Panchen Lama also had to be involved in the search
for the little boy, but negotiations for the Panchen Lama's return from
exile had stalled and he remained under China's control in eastern
Kham, on the periphery of the Tibetan cultural world. Kewtsang
Rinpoche, the lama from Sera monastery who led the search for the
fourteenth Dalai Lama, went to the monastery at Jyekundu, where
the Panchen Lama was living, to seek his opinion. The Panchen Lama
offered three names, including that of a 'fearless' young boy in the
village of Taktser, not far from Kumbum. A year later, at the start of
December 1937, the Panchen Lama died unexpectedly. At first, the
Chinese tried to use the return of the Panchen Lama's corpse as a
bargaining chip in much the same way as they had with the living
version. Then the situation changed. As Hugh Richardson put it:
'Chinese interest in a dead [Panchen] Lama soon gave way to the
more promising prospect of a live Dalai Lama.' That same year,
Kewtsang became convinced that the fearless boy from Taktser, called
Lhamo Thondup, was indeed the next Dalai Lama.

For a while Kewtsang was forced to remain silent. Taktser and the
nearby monastery at Kumbum were still under the control of the
Muslim warlord Ma Bufang. It had been Ma Bufang who had smashed
the Tibetan army in the early 1930s, just before the death of the thirteenth Dalai Lama, and annexed portions of Amdo to Qinghai,
including Kumbum. Ma Bufang was on the rise and, like his father
Ma Qi before him, had a ferocious reputation, especially among
Tibetans. He had conducted a campaign of ethnic cleansing against
the Ngoloks, a Tibetan tribe that resisted his rule, sacking and looting
monasteries along the way. Though strongly Islamic, Ma Bufang, now
governor of the Chinese province of Qinghai, was a dedicated Chinese
nationalist and virulently anti-communist. Should the boy's identity
be announced while under Ma Bufang's control, there was the grave
risk he might arrive in Lhasa with a large Chinese military escort.

Ma Bufang knew Kewtsang had met with several candidates in his
province and knew that if the infant Dalai Lama was declared in his
jurisdiction, it would boost his leverage with central government in
Beijing and increase his power locally. So he kept three-year-old Lhamo

44. Charles Bruce and Fred Mummery on their way to Nanga Parbat in 1895. Mummery would wear two soft hats, with snow packed between them, to keep his head cool in the hot sun.

45. Frank Smythe's portrait of the irrepressible Charles Bruce, Himalayan climbing pioneer and leader of the first full expedition to Everest in 1922.

46. The summit of Trisul on 12 June 1907, the first peak over seven thousand metres to be climbed. The successful party included Tom Longstaff, Courmayeur guides Henri and Alexis Brocherel, and a Gurkha, Karbir Budhathoki, who succeeded despite frostbite.

47. The Canadian doctor and Protestant missionary Susie Carson Rijnhart, whose infant son Charles perished on the Tibetan plateau.

48. Albert Shelton's photograph of a baptism in the Kham town of Batang, now in China's Sichuan province. Also a medical doctor, Shelton, born in Indianapolis, ran a mission at Batang between 1908 and 1922 for the Foreign Christian Missionary Society. He was murdered in 1922.

49. Teresa Littledale, the woman who came closest to Lhasa before Alexandra David-Néel. She travelled widely though Central Asia with her husband St George Littledale, but the couple published little and were largely forgotten.

50. The French-Belgian explorer, mystic and anarchist Alexandra David-Néel, in 1924 the first European woman to reach Lhasa, at the age of fifty-five. A Theosophist who influenced the beat generation, she died in 1969 at a hundred years old.

51. Eric Shipton and Bill Tilman became the first mountain explorers to reach the Nanda Devi Sanctuary in 1934, supported by the legendary Sherpa Ang Tharkay, Pasang Bhotia and Ang Tharkay's cousin Kusang.

52. The anthropologist Bruno Beger measuring a Tibetan woman's head during the 1938–9 Schäfer expedition. Beger was convicted in 1971 for his role in the Jewish skeleton collection.

53. The Nechung Oracle, photographed by the Schäfer expedition. The oracle had been institutionalised under the fifth Dalai Lama, a protector for the new Ganden Phodrang system of government. In 1947 the oracle warned of great danger facing Tibet in the next Year of the Tiger: 1950.

54. Archibald Steele's 1939 photograph of the young fourteenth Dalai Lama, taken during his assignment to visit the child at the Kumbum monastery in Amdo.

55. The capable Tsarong Dzasa, who despite his humble birth became a major force in Tibetan politics, and the gifted Italian anthropologist Giuseppe Tucci, pictured in 1948 at Tsarong's home. Tucci was consulting his library.

56. King Tribhuvan stands with Nehru and leading figures in Nepal's interim government of early 1951, including the new home minister B P Koirala, looking over their shoulders, and Mohan Shamsher to Nehru's left, the last of the Rana prime ministers.

57. Mao Zedong with the fourteenth Dalai Lama and tenth Panchen Lama in Beijing in 1956.

58. The tenth Panchen Lama meets with the Dalai Lama's fact-finding delegation of 1979, with Phuntsok Wangyal standing right, a year after his release from prison.

59. The tenth Demo Rinpoche and his wife during a *thamzing* or struggle session on the streets of Lhasa in 1966. A keen photographer, the *tulku's* camera is hung around his neck as a sarcastic admonishment. His work was largely destroyed.

60. The political activist
Ngawang Sangdrol.

61. Queen Elizabeth II and Prince
Philip, the Duke of Edinburgh,
tiger hunting in Nepal in March
1961, weeks after King Mahendra
had seized power from
a democratically elected
government and put the prime
minister B P Koirala in jail.

62. The young journalist Liz Hawley.

63. The former Russian ballet dancer, club manager, hotelier and entrepreneur Boris Lissanevitch and his second wife Inger. With his flair for theatricality, Lissanevitch had stage-managed Mahendra's coronation and the visit of the British royal family.

64. The crown prince of Nepal Birendra and his bride Aishwarya at Frankfurt airport in July 1970. Having acceded to the throne in 1972, Birendra, facing huge popular demonstrations, restored democracy in 1990. He, his wife and two of their three children were murdered by Prince Dipendra on 1 June 2001.

65. Nepali Congress leader Ganesh Man Singh meeting President George H W Bush at the White House in 1990. That year, co-operating with Nepal's communists, he was at the forefront of the *jana andolan* movement to restore democracy. Born in 1915, Singh had a reputation for integrity and was arrested with B P Koirala in 1960, spending eight years in jail without trial.

Thondup and his family close at hand. At first, Lhasa temporised, keeping their selection hazy as they negotiated with the Chinese for the terms of the new Dalai Lama's arrival in Lhasa. Luckily the Kuomintang government was now at war with Japan, a situation of far greater consequence than any problem in Tibet could be. When the Tibetans sent a high-level delegation to fetch the boy from Qinghai there was a deal to be done. Tibet was forced to pay Ma Bufang four hundred thousand Chinese silver dollars as compensation, money the Indian government helped source.

In July 1939, two years after his discovery and now four years old, Lhamo Thondup and his retinue, together with a small escort of Ma Bufang's troops, left Kumbum monastery for southern Tibet. As they crossed the border of Ma Bufang's territory, all vagueness over the identity of the Dalai Lama was abandoned: officials announced that Lhamo Thondup was and always had been the one true candidate. At Lhasa, Reting Rinpoche ordained the boy a monk, giving him the new name Tenzin Gyatso, fourteenth Dalai Lama, embodiment of Chenrezig, *bodhisattva* of compassion, known to Tibetans as Kundun: 'presence'. By then the world was at war. Tibetans and all the peoples of the Himalaya stood on the brink of profound and sometimes violent change that would threaten their identity even as it brought the modern world crashing in.

18

Summit Fever

Sunrise on the Kalindi glacier, high in the mountains of Garhwal: six men prepare to leave camp, shouldering rucksacks as the white summits flare into light above valleys still sunk in blue shadow. Yesterday they prepared a trail of steps, kicked into soft snow, and after last night's frost these are now firm, like a staircase, crusty with ice whose crystals dazzle with refracted light as the men plod north-east. Above them is the Kalindi *khal*, a snowy pass almost six thousand metres above sea level linking the sacred Gangotri region behind them with the Arwa valley that cuts east towards the village of Ghastoli, a day's walk north of the pilgrim town of Badrinath. At the crest of the pass, the group pauses. In front of them is a new horizon of spectacular mountains, including, to the north-east, the sentinel summit of Kamet, looking down on the forgotten world of the Guge kingdom and the bone-dry expanse of western Tibet. It is 15 August 1947.

There can have been few better places to welcome India's independence day, in this throne room of the mountain gods, at least until monsoon clouds rolled up the valley and snow started falling. The night before, as the clock ticked toward midnight and these men took shelter from the bitter cold inside their tents, Jawaharlal Nehru, India's first prime minister, had delivered his 'tryst with destiny' speech in the central hall of the Indian parliament.

> It is a fateful moment for us in India, for all Asia and for the world. A new star rises, the star of freedom in the east, a new hope comes into being, a vision long cherished materialises.

That vision held immense implications for the people of the Himalaya.

One of the six standing on the Kalindi pass that independence morning would meet Nehru six years later in his own tryst with destiny. Tenzing Norgay was now thirty-three years of age, recently a widower with two young daughters, Pem Pem and Nima, living back in Darjeeling. He carried their pictures with him in a frame. Tenzing had marked time through the war as an orderly for the Indian army in Chitral, far to the north-west. Now he was back working for a climbing expedition as a 'Sherpa' (the ethnic identity of Sherpa had by the 1940s become confused with the job description of a high-altitude porter). This trip would prove pivotal in his long journey to the summit of Everest with Edmund Hillary six years later. The expedition leader, not present on the pass that day, was the Swiss mountain guide André Roch. Among the most successful Himalayan climbers before the war, he had climbed in the Karakoram with Günter and Hettie Dyhrenfurth. Now, after the war, Roch was returning to the Himalaya at the age of forty to start again. A glaciologist, on rest days he would spend his afternoons painting landscapes. Among his team was René Dittert, a good-natured, self-effacing Genevois and an integral member of the Androsace Club, which included many of the best Swiss mountaineers. These two would both be part of the first Swiss attempt on Everest five years later, when Tenzing and Raymond Lambert came close to the top. Roch had just made Tenzing *sirdar*, leader of the expedition's small team of Sherpas, after the man he first selected was injured. The other Sherpas seemed indifferent to reaching summits, but not Tenzing. There was, as one of the climbers put it, 'a gleam of determination in Tenzing's eyes'. André Roch judged him 'our best man'. It was Tenzing who had led the way on the first ascent of a seven thousand-metre peak called Kedarnath, with highly trained and fit Swiss guides in his wake.

Tenzing found working for the Swiss a warmer experience than he had the pre-war British expeditions to Everest. After their ascent of Kedarnath, there had been a party. One of the expedition recalled how that evening,

> when we all came down to base camp, and we all sat down, he sat down with us and drank a glass of wine. This was something unheard of. Shipton and Tilman wouldn't have thought it odd but I can think of plenty of English climbers who would have done.

That expedition member was Trevor Braham, not Swiss but British, born in Calcutta in 1922. It was Braham that Tenzing and a team of five Sherpas was accompanying to the Kalindi pass that independence morning, where three turned back to camp, leaving Braham and two of the Sherpas to continue downhill towards Badrinath.

Braham had accepted a general invitation from the Swiss to the Himalayan Club for one of their number to join the Gangotri expedition: a gesture of goodwill. In the 1920s and 1930s the club had been first port of call for anyone exploring the mountains. Now, hollowed out by the war, it had stalled. Chaos and austerity in Europe had slowed the stream of climbers to a trickle. Braham, educated at St Joseph's in Darjeeling, where his parents escaped the hot summer months in Calcutta, had only been climbing for a short while and only in Sikkim; his nine-week trip to Garhwal in the company of leading European alpinists was a test and an education.

That day, 15 August 1947, Braham was returning home ahead of the main group, wanting to visit the Bhyundar valley, Frank Smythe's valley of flowers. Sixty years later he could still recall the scent of freshly cut pine filling the air as he rattled down the trail to Badrinath, new wooden homes going up as men returned from military service. When he reached the temple, two days' walking from the Kalindi pass, bunting for India's independence day was still up and the mood was still buoyant. Yet on the train to Delhi, the horror of Partition was evident. He shared a compartment with a Sikh,

> such a quiet man; we talked a lot. Then we stopped at a station. He got out and was transformed into some kind of fierce warrior. He shouted: 'Kill them! I've seen what they've done to our people.'

At Delhi there were corpses laid out on the platform and the police tried to confiscate Braham's ice axe.

Much of the violence was focussed on the Punjab, but it spilled over into the Himalaya. On their return to the small town of Joshimath, the Swiss were put on an army truck back to Delhi for their safety, leaving the Sherpas to fend for themselves. After a fortnight spent hanging around, Tenzing and his crew got a lift to Dehra Dun, where civil order was unravelling. One young Sikh recalled how the town's Muslim enclave was torched and the next day watching the bodies of fifteen Muslim girls being loaded onto a truck. Tenzing had a good friend in Dehra Dun, Jack Gibson, headmaster of the Doon School, who had hired him for a climbing holiday just after the war. Gibson had established a small refugee camp within the school grounds for Muslims escaping the chaos, and the Sherpas stayed in this oasis of peace until Gibson could find them transport home.

Not all foreigners were as lucky as the Swiss. Theos Bernard was an American traveller and yoga celebrity who grew up in Tombstone, Arizona in a family obsessed with eastern religions: his uncle was Pierre Bernard, 'Oom the Magnificent', who was an early American proponent of yoga and a spiritual snake-oil merchant. Like Oom, Theos was a relentless self-promoter. Before the war he had travelled in Tibet, upsetting monks with his intrusive photography. Back home he appeared on the cover of *Family Circle* magazine dressed in tailor-made monk's robes next to a Hollywood starlet and wrote about his experiences in his travel memoir *Penthouse of the Gods*. He had spent the war studying for a doctorate on Hatha yoga and after the war travelled to Spiti on the hunt for lost manuscripts. Caught with Muslim porters on his way to Kye monastery during the violence of partition, Theos Bernard and his third wife Helen were murdered, their bodies presumed thrown in the Spiti river.

The impact of independence was felt in every Himalayan nation, not just India. On 15 August, as Trevor Braham was saying goodbye to Tenzing Norgay on the Kalindi pass, a Nepali political leader, among the most admired the country has seen, was being freed from a Kathmandu jail, a shrewd attempt to quell spiralling public discontent against the Rana dynasty. Bishweshwar Prasad Koirala, known simply as B P, had been born in Benares in India in 1914. His father was a *bahun*, a hill Brahmin called Krishna Prasad, who had migrated from his home east of Kathmandu to the then small village of Biratnagar near the Indian border. He prospered, both as a businessman and a government tax collector; he had two wives who between them had five surviving sons and four daughters, the makings of a political dynasty. Three of the sons would be prime ministers of Nepal. Krishna Prasad Koirala had seen the poverty around him and began to take action, opening a school at his own expense, but even these mild attempts at social reform earned him the displeasure of the Rana regime and he fled to Benares. The Ranas confiscated his properties and the extended family and retinue was plunged into poverty. Krishna Prasad joined the Indian National Congress, on the basis that nothing in Nepal would change until the Ranas lost their protective ally, the British Raj. One of B P's earliest memories was seeing his father receiving garlands in the early 1920s from his Nepali political supporters in Benares. When Gandhi called for a campaign of civil disobedience in 1929, B P responded by standing up at his school desk and saying: 'I leave my school.' Three years later he was arrested on suspicion of helping 'terrorists' conspiring against British authority and imprisoned for the first time in his young life. It would not be the last.

Krishna Prasad had gone into exile during the First World War, when Chandra Shamsher, the close ally of Curzon, was Nepal's prime minister. Uncharacteristically for the sprawling Rana family, Chandra was an austere man, teetotal and monogamous and not prone to smiling. (It was said that when he did, it boded ill for those he smiled at.) He gave substantial assistance to the British war effort, sending some fifty-five thousand recruits for the Indian army's Gurkha regiments and releasing eighteen thousand troops from the Nepal army for garrison duties in India. Taking into account Nepali subjects in other Indian military or policing roles, the country's contribution had been around a hundred thousand men, with ten thousand fatalities, from a total population of five million.

In June 1915, during the disastrous invasion of Gallipoli in modern-day Turkey by Allied troops, Himalayan explorer Charlie Bruce had been reunited with his old battalion, the 1/5th Gurkhas, and an old friend from his climbing days, Subardar Major Harkabir Thapa. (In the summer of 1899, Harkabir had bewildered local people on the Isle of Skye with his speed in the mountains, running barefoot to the summit of Glamaig, and doing it again when they didn't believe his time.) It was Bruce's task to show his old comrades their route of advance for a planned attack on the heights of Achi Baba, overlooking the Gallipoli peninsula. Bruce knew this was asking 'the impossible with quite inadequate means'. It was, he recalled, 'a practical certainty that I was saying goodbye to my best friends'. Seven officers and 129 men lost their lives on the day of the attack. Harkabir Thapa was wounded but survived.

This level of sacrifice couldn't help but galvanise Nepali society. Before the war, recruitment into the Gurkha regiments stood at around a thousand men a year. After it tens of thousands of Nepali soldiers who had seen the world outside returned home, or else preferred Nepali communities inside British India, where work was easier to find and political debate was giving way to direct action. The new king Tribhuvan was not content to be a mere figurehead for the Ranas. Having ascended to the throne in 1911 aged eight, as he grew to adulthood in the 1920s he began exploring routes back to power. Even some younger members of the Rana family saw the need for change, a group that became far more engaged when Chandra tried to limit the immense cost of this sprawling family by classifying them into three streams: 'A', 'B' and 'C'. Those in the 'C' bracket were cut loose from the Rana payroll to agitate on the periphery. Many of them had studied in India and could see how Nepal was being left further and further behind.

Chandra's loyalty to the Raj did have its rewards. Before the war the British had begun to regard Nepal more as a princely state than a fully independent nation. In 1923, the Raj had formally recognised Nepali independence. The British also doubled Chandra's subsidy, money he used to resume Nepal's token development programme, building suspension bridges and beginning work on a road and ropeway that linked Birgunj on the Indian border to the Kathmandu valley 130 kilometres to the north. He outlawed the practice of *sati*, widows immolating themselves on the funeral pyres of their husbands, and attempted to deal with the far more widespread curse of slavery: more than sixty thousand slaves were freed thanks to this initiative. Yet these were really only expediencies in the face of pressure from outside Nepal. Chandra's main interest was maintaining his family's grip on power, even at the expense of ordinary Nepalis, supposedly telling George V that the British were in trouble in India because they had made the mistake of educating ordinary Indians.

The most important reform Chandra agreed with the British was the right to import goods from third countries without paying duty taxes to the Raj. Up to this point, the Nepal economy had run a surplus, selling rice to India. Now, thanks to this deal, there was a flood of cheap imports, particularly from Japan, where rapid industrialisation was undercutting the cost of British goods. (After the war, this duty-free privilege encouraged widespread smuggling back across the border into India, with a wink from politicians and sometimes their active involvement.) This new trade deal prompted a consumer boom that quickly soaked up the savings of ex-servicemen. Domestic textile production collapsed. Chandra of course charged duty of his own on this glut of imports, further enriching the Rana dynasty, which now enjoyed a moment of flamboyant excess. The politician Pashupati Rana, born in 1941 and a great-grandson of Chandra, recalled the extravagant fashions his mother's generation wore:

> block-printed Dhaka layered with fine muslin, velvet embroidered with heavy pure gold thread interspersed with pearls, exquisitely worked saris with beautiful borders, diamonds and jewelled tiaras.

It was a life of boggling luxury. Pashupati recalled hundreds of servants at his father's home: 'as a child I had four maid-servants and a wet-nurse to look after me indoors and four men-servants to attend to me out of doors.'

As a revenue collector, a position the Ranas auctioned off to the highest bidder, Krishna Prasad Koirala had been acutely aware of his position in a society of such dire inequality. The story of precisely why he was forced into exile is a famous one, recounted by his son and political heir B P Koirala:

> It was winter and [a] large number of his men, very poor and in rags, were migrating to India in search of employment. He asked one of them for his clothes and himself fished the rags out of the man's bag. And he had them sent to the Prime Minister with a covering letter saying that this was the usual clothing that 'your subject wears in winter and compare this with what you are wearing. I hope it will not be interpreted as disrespect on my part to have sent these dirty rags to Your Highness.'

Chandra was already suspicious of Krishna Prasad; bringing rebellious Bengalis to the safety of Nepal to teach in a school for ordinary people was verging on sedition itself. This package of rags was the last straw. The Koirala clan fled arrest into the arms of India's independence movement, planting seeds that would bear fruit after the war.

When Chandra died in 1929, his brother Bhim Shamsher had taken over, who survived just long enough to demand the British do something about the growing bands of anti-Rana Nepalis living in India. After him came Juddha Shamsher, the last of the seventeen sons of Dhir, Jang Bahadur's youngest brother, to rule as maharaja. Juddha was far more autocratic, a competent and energetic military man who performed well in the devastating earthquake that shook Kathmandu almost to pieces in 1934. Politics however baffled him. There was a constant drip of corrosive anti-Rana stories in Indian newspapers and gossip in Kathmandu's bazaars that king Tribhuvan would soon take back power. Even the army became dissatisfied. In 1936, an activist called Shukra Raj Shastri organised public meetings, which quickly landed him in jail. Shastri was part of a renaissance in Newari culture, the first stirrings of a political consciousness among Nepal's ethnic minorities. An opposition party took shape, called the Praja Parishad or People's Council, and when it called for an uprising the Rana regime arrested scores of activists and executed four of them, including Shastri, who was still in jail following his earlier conviction. The freedom movement had its first martyrs.

By then the world was at war again. Juddha showed the same commitment to the British as Chandra had but many Ranas were dismayed as German forces swept across Western Europe. British India's once impressive façade was also crumbling. In August 1942, Indian National Congress party activists cut the telegraph wires linking Nepal with the outside world, tore up railway tracks and burned police stations and post offices, cutting the British off from their ally in Kathmandu. It took weeks for the Indian authorities to restore links with the city, providing a moment of clarity for Juddha's government. The slow response showed Nepal exactly where it stood in the eyes of the British, despite the country's loyal sacrifice. (Of 282 Victoria Crosses awarded during the Second World War, thirteen went to Gurkha regiments.) Wanting more from the relationship, Juddha requested British help in building factories that would compete on favourable terms with those in India. The British preferred a plan to fund hydroelectric plants to raise Nepali living standards.

Neither party could do much to protect Nepal from Indian inflation. The collapse of the Indian rupee during the war cut the value of Gurkha pensions, a significant benefit to the Nepali economy, by a third. In Indian hill stations like Darjeeling, the spiralling cost of living ate into the savings of those least able to cope, including Tenzing

Norgay, who recalled relying on his second wife Ang Lhamu working
as an *ayah*, or nanny, to keep their heads above water: 'there seemed
to be no ups – only downs.' He bought a couple of horses to carry
tourists, mostly visiting American troops, up Tiger Hill for its spectacular view of Kangchenjunga. As Nepali soldiers flooded home,
bringing with them millions of Indian rupees, there was a currency
crisis: Nepal simply didn't have enough coins in circulation to exchange
all that Indian paper money. The government in Delhi wasn't prepared
to sell silver on acceptable terms so a Nepali diplomat in London
toured the capital's silver dealers and bought a million ounces on the
open market, enough to stabilise the currency.

Ordinary Nepalis were resilient and resourceful but growing
numbers wanted change: their children had no schools and their ageing
parents no health care. The Nepali state, meaning the Rana family,
didn't have the technical capacity or sufficient political will to develop
the country. Juddha Shamsher, a father of twenty sons and twenty
daughters, feared he was nearing his end and retired in late 1945 to
go on pilgrimage. His replacement was Padma Shamsher Rana, the
son of Juddha's elder brother Bhir, a low-key pragmatist who clashed
with the sons of Juddha and Chandra, particularly Chandra's outspoken
eldest son Mohan. This political vulnerability hampered Padma's
sensible programme of reform: more schools, more electricity and
more roads, including a start on an east–west highway. Yet development had to materialise promptly to save the Rana dynasty and the
winds of history were already against them. Nepal needed heavy
equipment to build roads but Britain, exhausted and almost bankrupt
from war, was slow to deliver it. Padma showed real acumen in looking
elsewhere. If the British were broke and quitting India, then the Rana
dynasty needed to make new and preferably rich friends. Japan had
provided Nepal with a taste of consumerism before the war but now
lay in ruins. America was clearly the new power. And so Padma
instructed Nepali leaders attending the Allies' victory parade in London
in June 1946 to continue on to Washington for talks with Harry
Truman. Nepal, with an eye on American development aid, invited
the United States to establish diplomatic relations.

On the day the American mission arrived in the spring of 1947 a
Gandhi-style *satyagraha*, or peaceful demonstration, began nationwide,
organised by a new political party called the Nepali National Congress.

This had coalesced from Nepali communities based in the Indian cities of Benares and Calcutta, with the tacit approval of the king. Tribhuvan, who had a history of heart disease, had used his health as an excuse to visit Calcutta, where he held talks with opposition leaders. By the time the Americans arrived, B P Koirala was already under arrest for helping to organise a strike at a jute mill in Biratnagar to demand fairer wages, and was now being force-marched back to Kathmandu. There he was jailed, attracting sympathy and support from the Indian independence movement's most famous leaders, including Gandhi, who wrote to Padma demanding his release.

Again, Padma showed himself an adroit politician. Anxious not to encourage an equivalent movement within Nepal, he promised a new constitution and invited Indian constitutional lawyers to help write it. He announced an independent judiciary, the introduction of female education and municipal elections. Although autocratic, the Ranas could present themselves as conservative Hindu champions of the *pahadis*, the dominant Brahmin–Chhetri caste of the middle hills. This was enough to persuade Nehru that there need not be a coup in Nepal to bring change, at least under Padma's leadership. And on the day India became independent, Padma ordered the release of B P Koirala, who immediately went back to India and exile.

The people Padma most needed to convince of the need for reform, but couldn't, were his own extended family. His cousin Mohan saw in Padma's constitutional reform an end to Rana dominance. One or other of them would have to go and Padma blinked first, resigning his position in early 1948, soon after Nepal's new constitution was promulgated. On taking power, Mohan didn't revoke it, but it remained largely inoperative. Instead, he cracked down on freedom of speech and assembly, and banned the Nepali National Congress, earning the contempt of ordinary Nepalis who had liked their taste of freedom. Banning the Nepali Congress also proved a tactical disaster in his dealings with Nehru, who played on Mohan's fear of how India might respond in order to screw concessions out of Nepal's government: on trade and the use of Nepali troops now serving in the Indian army. And when that was accomplished, Nehru offered his support to a skilfully managed coup that levered the Ranas out of power.

Tribhuvan's position, meanwhile, had become increasingly difficult. The focus for opposition hopes, the king remained under the Rana family's tight control. Early one morning in November 1950, he left the palace with most of his family for a hunting trip, his sons at the wheel of their motorcade. As it passed the Indian embassy, they simply turned through the open gates, which were locked behind them. Tribhuvan's young grandson Gyanendra had been left behind to reassure the Ranas nothing was afoot, so Mohan had the child declared king and allowed Tribhuvan to fly into exile in India. The British were prepared to continue their support for Mohan, partly because the Nepali Congress were hostile to Gurkha recruitment, but it was Nehru and not Britain who was now calling the shots. He could turn armed Nepali insurgents on and off at will and used the threat of insurrection to build pressure against Mohan, who finally capitulated in early 1951. Tribhuvan returned at the head of a new government that Nehru had carefully calibrated to include some of the old regime alongside his allies in the Nepali Congress. A century after Jang Bahadur murdered his way to power, the nation seemed poised on the slipway of democracy.

*

What Mohan hadn't done as he tried in vain to turn back the tide of reform was to return Nepal to its former isolation. Apart from British diplomats, few Europeans had visited Nepal in the first half of the twentieth century, fewer than visited the supposedly exclusive Tibet. Family members living abroad brought back news of India's burgeoning independence movement, but otherwise ordinary Nepalis continued their lives as they had for centuries. A few journalists were allowed in. Penelope Chetwode wrote an article titled *The Sequestered Kingdom* for National Geographic in 1935. Chetwode, still only twenty-five and recently married to the poet John Betjeman, was the only daughter of Field Marshal Lord Chetwode and not someone likely to challenge Nepal's unusually static *status quo*. Likewise Edward Alexander Powell, an American adventure-travel journalist who applied for a visa on a whim in 1927 while staying in Calcutta and got lucky. His book was *The Last Home of Mystery: Adventures in Nepal*. Like Chetwode he portrayed the Ranas as 'distinctly progressive', while overlooking the fact that attempts at modernisation were for the benefit of Nepal's rulers, not its people.

The European most capable of burrowing under the surface of Nepal at this time was the Italian scholar Giuseppe Tucci, who spent four months in the Kathmandu valley in the summer of 1929, the first Italian to do so since the missionaries of the eighteenth century. There was no greater European scholar of the Himalaya before the war. Few adventurers travelled as far or wide, but this brilliant, cynical and ambitious opportunist never hesitated to apply political expediency if it took him closer to his academic goals: the past was his kingdom, not the present, and the Ranas would have nothing to fear from Tucci. He was born in 1894, the son of a tax officer in the provincial backwater of Macerata, whose most famous son was the Jesuit missionary Matteo Ricci. At the age of seventeen Tucci published his first paper, on Latin inscriptions in the countryside around his hometown, in a prestigious German archaeological journal and barely stopped writing for the rest of his life. At university in Rome he came under the influence of the fascist philosopher Giovanni Gentile and by extension Gentile's patron Mussolini, and developed a lasting passion for Chinese philosophy, in particular Taoism and the semi-mythical teacher Laozi. His interest in Buddhism, he once told an Indian journalist, was born in an earlier life. The joke neatly sidestepped a paradox: no European scholar before Tucci came as close to unravelling the myriad complexities of Tibetan Buddhism, but Tucci took for himself only its core philosophy: the use of detachment as a protection, a transparent bubble, against the mediocre or tiresome. For a while, fascism held the same appeal. Tucci was, in the early 1920s, friendly with the fascist intellectual Julius Evola, author of *Revolt against the Modern World*: they met at the Italian branch of the Theosophical Society. Long after the war and in his early sixties, Tucci could still write that, 'In Tibet man had not yet disintegrated: he still sank his roots fully into the collective subconscious, which knows no difference between past and present.' He was, like so many Westerners in the Himalaya, a 'seeker'.

In late 1925 Tucci and his Sanskrit professor Carlo Formichi arrived in India at the invitation of Rabindranath Tagore, India's first and so far only winner of the Nobel Prize for literature, who had been touring the world seeking support for his experimental Visva-Bharati college in the sleepy Bengali town of Shantiniketan, dedicated to outdoor learning and Indian nationalism. Formichi had been Tagore's interpreter when he visited Italy earlier that year and had written to

Mussolini begging financial support for an Italian teacher to accompany Tagore home for a return visit. Il Duce hadn't given India much political thought until that point, but looking to counter negative publicity about a fascist Italy in the rest of Europe, he saw an opening. He ordered an extravagant library of Italian literature be sent to Visva-Bharati and paid the fare for a teacher: Giuseppe Tucci. When Tagore returned to Italy a year later, the poet was bamboozled by Mussolini's blunt charm, telling Formichi: 'There is such a massive vigour in that head that it reminds one of Michael Angelo's chisel.' Flattered by his warm reception, he told an Italian newspaper: 'Let me dream that from the fire-bath the immortal soul of Italy will come out clothed in quenchless light.' Tagore's more liberal European friends were aghast, and once out of Italy the poet soon backtracked. There would be no more generous gifts from Mussolini, although the dictator later welcomed a semi-admiring Gandhi to Rome.

The months in between Tagore's visits to Italy were a delicious interlude for Tucci, reading and studying in the warm seclusion of Shantiniketan, walking with Formichi in the gardens of Tagore's college. Formichi was full of admiration for the younger man.

> In addition to Sanskrit and the literary dialects of India, he knows Chinese, Tibetan, and has delved into the study of Iranian and the languages of Central Asia.

He was, Formichi said, the 'future prince of Oriental scholarship', and he regarded him as a son. Tucci, when he was famous, would keep a cool distance from Formichi, describing himself as an 'auto-didact' who as a young scholar had felt stifled in Italy's dreary academic scene. Sharing credit was never easy for him. Never much of a photographer, he relied on his companions for making a visual record, including his second wife Giulia Nuvolini, whom he took to India in 1925. Her photos were rarely credited. Such ingratitude was typical of Tucci, according to his student Pio Filippani-Ronconi, himself a fascist of the Gentile school. Filippani saw Tucci as by turns charming and cruel, a man who could swiftly calculate the use of another person.

That charm was nowhere better applied than in his dealings with British colonial officials in the Himalaya. His first trek there had been with Tagore in the hills beyond Darjeeling, but he soon focussed his interest on western Tibet and the second diffusion of Buddhism that had taken place there between the tenth and eleventh centuries. He earned his keep teaching in Dacca, Calcutta and Benares, and made research trips to Ladakh and Zanskar, learning the system of permissions he would need for more extensive explorations in Tibet. Returning to Italy in 1931 as professor of Chinese in the Oriental Institute of Naples, he organised two long expeditions to western Tibet of immense ambition that took him to those places he had identified as crucial to his studies of the second diffusion: the monasteries of Tabo, in the Spiti valley, and nearby Nako, built in a similar style, as well as Tholing, across the modern border in the west Tibet region of Ngari, and the nearby citadel of Tsaparang. In western Tibet in particular, he felt as though a vast spiritual enterprise had crumbled away almost to dust and squalor and showed no compunction in removing whatever he could from the crumbling monuments he found, including an entire wall painting.

This didn't go unnoticed. The Anglo-Greek mountaineer and Buddhist Marco Pallis was another exceptional traveller, and his passion for the Himalaya wasn't confined to its past. He and his companions spent months travelling in Ladakh wearing the *chuba*, the long sheepskin coat beloved of Tibetan nomads, as a deliberate reversal of the attitude among most British that Western dress maintained a safe distance from the natives. Pallis had climbed near Nako and when he became aware of what Tucci was doing, Pallis wrote to the authorities about it. Tucci rather disingenuously suggested the Indian authorities should have a museum for such antiquities and would keep his collection safe and sound until they did. He wasn't the only academic to bring Himalayan treasures home with him.

Tucci made two more journeys before the war, this time to central Tibet, the second, in 1939, being the more productive, in which he visited the monastery at Sakya and made a detailed record of everything that would be ruined in the Cultural Revolution. On his first visit, in 1937, he took with him the photographer, anthropologist, writer and mountaineer Fosco Maraini, whose warm character glows like coals from his travel books on the Himalaya and Japan. He liked Tibetans for the way they lived and contemplated writing a book, which he would call *Secret Tibet*.

The secret will be, not the strange things that it will reveal, but the normal things in it – real people, flesh and blood, love, desire, repentance, pride and cowardice.

The images Maraini brought back from his first Tibet expedition were among the best to emerge from Tibet before the war and stand as an enticing historical record. Maraini had been born in Florence in 1912 to a half-Englishwoman, Cornelia 'Yoï' Crosse, joking that his exposure to bad food thanks to her was excellent preparation for expedition life. His father was the sculptor Antonio Maraini, whose career flourished under Mussolini. When he signed the whole family up as fascists, Fosco tore up his party card in front of his father. Tucci, on the other hand, went to Japan as Mussolini's representative in 1937. Maraini would spend two years in a Japanese concentration camp during the war, along with his wife, the beautiful Sicilian Topazia Alliata, and their three daughters, having refused to support the Republic of Salò, Mussolini's rump of a fascist state.

After the war, despite Tucci's support for Mussolini, which cost him his chair at Rome University, he wasted no time in attempting a return to Tibet, in 1946 writing to the government of India's representative in Lhasa Hugh Richardson to request permission. Tucci could shed allegiances like a snake does its skin. 'To the vanity, inconsistency and double-dealing of politicians, I have opposed the saints and the heroes, the poets and scientists,' he wrote. It speaks to Tucci's charm that he was one of very few Europeans the British welcomed in Tibet. Technically, Britain and Italy were still at war, but Richardson offered circumspect support. The Chinese had recently funded a library in Lhasa, and the British, to keep up, had done likewise. Richardson suggested Tucci send some copies of his latest book to important officials in the city to prepare the ground.

Tucci's journey took place in 1948, by which time a peace treaty had been signed with Italy and the violence of Partition was over, but the visas for his travelling companions, including Fosco Maraini, were delayed. Tucci went on ahead, taking with him Tenzing Norgay as his factotum. Tucci admired Tenzing's efficiency and with his fluent Tibetan could discuss anything with the climber, from obscure Tibetan saints to his friend, the new Indian prime minister Jawaharlal Nehru. Tucci promised Tenzing an introduction. In Lhasa they met the

Austrians Heinrich Harrer and Peter Aufschnaiter, who had been detained in 1939 following another German attempt on Nanga Parbat. Having escaped their prisoner-of-war camp at Dehra Dun towards the end of the war, they had crossed into Tibet and to avoid detection reached Lhasa via a bitter winter crossing of the Chang Tang. Harrer, whose first wife Hanna Charlotte was the daughter of geologist Alfred Wegener, was astonished to hear Tucci agreeing with their Tibetan hosts that the world was flat, but Tucci would argue black was white to get what or where he wanted. He visited the three great monasteries of Lhasa – Drepung, Sera and Ganden – and sat with Eric Bailey's old friend Tsarong Shap-pe, looking through the veteran politician's personal library. There were long conversations with the fourteenth Dalai Lama, now a teenager taking an active interest in the outside world. Civil war in China and the rise of Mao Zedong were preoccupying Tibet's cautious and conservative political leadership. It was dawning on them, too slowly and too late, that what the rest of the world knew and thought about Tibet would have implications for the country's survival as an independent entity. Tucci's record of Tibet's treasures came just as they reached the brink of destruction.

*

For decades, Western writers – missionaries, explorers and mystics – had said pretty much what they liked about life in Tibet, sometimes without even going there. In the late 1940s, as Mao's communists fought toward the founding of the People's Republic of China on 1 October 1949, there was an urgent need to raise public interest in contemporary Tibet, both at home and abroad, to help defend Tibet's integrity from Mao's likely ambitions there. Following the lead of his mentor Charles Bell, the Sikkim political officer Basil Gould fostered the notion of an independent Tibet by subsidising the only newspaper yet published in Tibetan, the *Melong* or *Mirror*, edited not at Lhasa but in neighbouring Sikkim by a Tibetan-speaking Christian called Gergan 'Khunu' Tharchin. (He was nicknamed 'Khunu' after the corner of Spiti he was born in. A convert of Moravian missionaries, Tharchin was a teacher in the early part of his career, developing connections that permeated the Himalaya.) Foreign coverage was more difficult, not least because communists in China were trying to get their line across as well. The British resident in Lhasa Hugh Richardson had been posted during the war to Chongqing as liaison officer with Chiang Kai-shek's national government, where China's communists also had a liaison officer, Zhou Enlai. Richardson would have been aware of Enlai's ability to charm foreign correspondents into parroting the party line. One of these was the British journalist Stuart Gelder, a leftist who had been a minor figure in the Bloomsbury group and whose pro-communist sympathies would in 1962 get him access to Tibet, just as the process of collectivisation was at its height. In Chongqing Richardson had recruited an enterprising Canadian-born journalist called Archibald Trojan Steele to Tibet's cause. Steele had scooped the world with his reporting on the Nanjing Massacre in 1938. Richardson arranged for him to travel to Lhasa to interview the young Dalai Lama in 1944 for the *Chicago Daily News*, an assignment Archie Steele regarded forever after as the most exciting of his long career. Even so, when Steele asked an official why there were no newspapers in Lhasa, he was told: 'nothing ever happens in this country'. By the end of the decade, that attitude had given way to near desperate urgency, as Mao's intentions for Tibet became clearer.

The prospect of China's inevitable invasion gripped the handful of Europeans living in Tibet. Peter Aufschnaiter wrote to his old friend the Munich climber Paul Bauer that

> my fate hangs once more in the balance, after I had begun to settle very strongly for staying here forever, because somehow I prefer life here to anywhere else. A fixed job in Europe or any other part of the world no longer interests me in the least. This half-wild country is just right, and as I wrote to you before, no European willingly leaves it. How terrible that is, you can picture for yourself, because the Tibetans do not know starvation and live better than their neighbours.

Although Aufschnaiter had arrived in Tibet with Heinrich Harrer, they were different sorts of men. He had mastered Tibetan before he left his prison camp at Dehra Dun, something Harrer relied on heavily as they travelled to Lhasa. Later, Harrer wrote his bestseller *Seven Years in Tibet* and achieved a large measure of fame. Aufschnaiter preferred to live simply and continue his work in the Himalaya. As an agricultural scientist, he was in a good position to do so, working on seed stocks and Tibet's first irrigation project, although he never underestimated the knowledge and resilience of the people he worked for. His skills were unusually diverse: he produced a town plan of Lhasa and worked on the electricity project that General Electric wanted to build. He was also a deeply astute observer of Tibetan culture, calibrating the difference between Lhasa's Buddhism and the more culturally fluid version that permeated the Himalaya. Giuseppe Tucci for one was impressed by Aufschnaiter's discoveries of early Buddhist art. His guiding inspiration was the eleventh-century teacher and poet Milarepa, another lover of nature and solitude.

In October 1950, little more than a year after declaring the People's Republic of China, Mao sent troops into Tibet. Aufschnaiter clung on as long as he could. He spent the next year in southern Tibet, mapping the Kyirong region close to the immense peak of Shisha Pangma and trekking up the East Rongbuk glacier to the slopes of Everest. Eventually, the proximity of the Chinese became too perilous. Communist officials sent word he would be welcome to stay and continue his development work but, sensing what was to come, Aufschnaiter preferred to leave: he wanted the life of a Tibetan estate owner, not an apparatchik with propaganda value. In January 1952, he joined a Kyirong friend and landowner making a pilgrimage to Bodhgaya in India, descending the Trisuli valley towards Kathmandu.

At this precise moment one of Nepal's more famous agitators was going in the opposite direction, fleeing up valley towards Tibet, although so far as we know the two men never actually encountered one another. Kunwar Inderjit 'K I' Singh was a doctor and Nepali Congress fighter who made his name ('Robin Hood of the Himalaya') doling out grants of land he'd confiscated in the western terai. In February 1951, as Tribhuvan returned from asylum in India at the head of the first post-Rana government, Singh had refused to lay down his arms, and the new cabinet summoned the Indian army to arrest him. It was not a propitious start to Tribhuvan's reign and some ordinary Nepalis questioned what kind of change had just occurred. This was compounded when Tribhuvan had the task of appointing a replacement for Mohan Shamsher as prime minister later that year in November. He ignored the popular choice, B P Koirala, preferring instead B P's older half-brother Matrika Prasad 'M P' Koirala, a conservative figure whom the Indians trusted more. In early 1952, as

Aufschnaiter was preparing to leave Tibet, a radical Nepali Congress militia called the Raksha Dal, fed up with Nepal's direction of travel, staged a revolt in Kathmandu. Hot-headed activists drove around Kathmandu announcing the dictatorship of the proletariat and sprang K I Singh from jail. Singh was invited to lead this coup attempt but promptly declined and set off instead for the People's Republic of China, now just across the Tibetan border, destroying the bridge at Shabru so no pursuing Indians could nab him again.

In this world of rapid change, the future suddenly seemed up for grabs. At Trisuli Bazar, Aufschnaiter heard talk among local Newars about re-establishing their former kingdom, turning back the clock to the days of the Malla kings. Minorities in Nepal could already see how Brahmin hill-men, the *pahadis*, were getting a grip on power. For two centuries, the Shahs and then the Ranas had treated the terai like a colony; it looked like the new government might do the same. When Aufschnaiter got to Kathmandu he stayed for a few days in a grimy lodge in the district of Asan Tol, right in the heart of the city, a place used by Kyirong people passing through. Almost immediately he was interrogated by Indian soldiers, who grilled him for information about Chinese troop deployments. Having brokered the change of government the year before, India was exerting immense influence in Nepal. The British ambassador at the time noted how often Tribhuvan was in India, which was denting his popularity, and reported that the Indian ambassador to Nepal had direct lines to both Tribhuvan and B P Koirala.

India's great anxiety was security. In late 1950, Nehru made a speech to the Indian Parliament pointing out that 'we have had from imme-morial times a magnificent frontier, that is to say the Himalayas.' Part of that 'magnificent frontier' now lay in theoretically independent states. Nehru's government had already signed a treaty with Bhutan, effectively continuing colonial India's control of Bhutan's foreign policy under the terms of the Treaty of Punakha, signed with the British in 1910. Now he warned that

as much as we appreciate the independence of Nepal, we cannot risk our own security by anything going wrong in Nepal which either permits that barrier to be crossed or otherwise weakens our frontier.

At the heart of Nehru's concerns was uncertainty about what China would do. As far as India was concerned, the Himalayan frontier had been settled during the colonial era, including the McMahon Line separating north-east India from Tibet, signed off at the Simla Convention in 1914. China had refused to recognise these borders and India was anxious what Mao would do when the People's Liberation Army reached them. To that end, the Indian army sent small detachments of troops with radios to remote points within Nepal to monitor the border. (The young journalist James – later Jan – Morris, would later use one of these radio posts, located at Namche Bazar in the Everest region, to report that Tenzing Norgay and Edmund Hillary had reached the summit.) Concern about China may also explain why India was so reluctant to allow Peter Aufschnaiter to remain in Nepal, despite the patronage of his friend Kaiser Shamsher Rana and the fact he was needed by the UN's Food and Agriculture Organisation, then setting up shop in Kathmandu. Instead, Aufschnaiter wound up in Delhi, drawing maps of Tibet. Nepal had little choice in any of this and Nepali politicians grew increasingly resentful at Delhi's taking them for granted.

Maharaja Krishna Rasgotra, later India's high commissioner in London, began his diplomatic career in Nepal at this time, working on aid projects in the terai. He noted the cynical way M P Koirala's party workers manipulated Indian aid efforts for political ends, telling local people that the aid was either American, or else part of an Indian plot to alienate the terai from Nepal: 'simple, credulous folk, who had nothing but goodwill for India, were being misled by a government that Nehru had gone out of his way to help.' In the summer of 1954, a delegation of Indian politicians on a goodwill mission was met at Kathmandu's airfield by anti-Indian protestors throwing stones. Nehru was furious and wrote an aggrieved letter to M P Koirala:

> We go all out to help the Nepal government, financially and otherwise, and yet our people are subjected to insults there and intrigues against India continue.

Koirala, who had by then split from Nepali Congress to form his own party, blamed the Rana family for the trouble. Indian diplomats weren't fooled. Nehru had found M P Koirala a big disappointment, someone who asked for advice and then ignored it, while encouraging his party workers to stir up anti-Indian sentiment.

For their part, Nepali politicians were in a quandary. Nepal's isolation had ended and the modern world was crashing in. The country had been administered as a fiefdom under the Ranas, without any of the institutions a democracy needed. Nepal's leaders had to fill that gap while maintaining whatever sense of national identity the Rana dynasty had fostered. They were constantly promising things they didn't know how to deliver and were struggling with each other for ascendancy, with parties fracturing accordingly. Needing technical help for everything from healthcare to schools to policing, they also needed some kind of counterweight against their enormous neighbour to the south, before it overwhelmed them.

Once again, the obvious candidate was America. Harry Truman used American aid as a way to turn the world's poor away from communism, and the State Department saw strategic interest in the Himalaya. The Delhi embassy's chargé d'affaires George Merrell had argued as early as 1947 that Tibet might make a handy rocket-launching pad against the Soviets. Tribhuvan had signed an agreement for technical assistance with the US while he was still in exile in Delhi but he died suddenly in 1955, aged only forty-eight, while receiving medical treatment in Switzerland, the family having a history of weak hearts. It was his autocratic son Mahendra who fully realised the potential. Far less sympathetic to democratic experiments, Mahendra saw opportunity in playing the aid budgets of competing powers against each other. His greatest coup was a no-strings grant from China of $126 million, at a time when Mao was proving the miracle of communism by handing over the people's wealth. Along with the money coming from America, Nepal literally had more cash than it was able to spend. In 1959, Mahendra would quash Nepal's first democratically elected government when it tried to institute a taxation system that included Nepal's elite families: 'Why,' the king wondered, 'should we pay taxes when we can always get more money from the Americans?'

*

Throughout these long and tortuous political upheavals, Nepal's competing factions had all courted foreign support. While getting visas was still difficult, for those with the right credentials – at first diplomats and scientists, then mountaineers and more general tourists – access to its 'sequestered kingdom', so long denied, was suddenly possible. At George Merrell's suggestion, the ornithologist Sidney Dillon Ripley, who later ran the Smithsonian to great effect, got permission for expeditions in the pre-monsoon of 1947 and the post-monsoon of 1948 to start cataloguing Nepal's birds. Ripley had worked for the Office of Strategic Services, a predecessor of the CIA, during the war and while stationed in Asia had cultivated a relationship with the last viceroy of India, Lord Mountbatten. The joke about Ripley was that while spies often used science as a cover, he used intelligence work to continue his birdwatching. Even if his mission was innocent, there was no shortage of spies at work in the Himalaya. The Smithsonian, the national museum and archive of the USA, later acknowledged that one of its researchers had done work on the side for the CIA interviewing Tibetan refugees. The Welsh mountaineer Sydney Wignall, planning an expedition to far western Nepal in 1955, recounted decades later how he had been approached by a member of Indian intelligence ('Call me Singh') to spy on Chinese troop deployments in the old strategic border town of Taklakot and survived an uncomfortable return journey in winter across the Himalaya after they were caught and imprisoned.

Mountaineers were not initially welcome in Nepal and only allowed in if accompanied by scientists. In this way, Bill Tilman spent almost four months in the summer of 1949 exploring the Langtang massif north of Kathmandu, the border crossing at Rasuwagadhi, where the Qing army had once invaded, the rugged peaks of Ganesh and finally the Jugal massif to the east. With him was the climber Peter Lloyd, who had shared the adventure of Nanda Devi, and two men of science, Hamish Scott, an undergraduate geologist and former Scottish rugby international, and the botanist and botanical writer Oleg Polunin, brother of the environmentalist Nicholas, who wrote a plant collector's addendum to Tilman's 1952 book *Nepal Himalaya*. Tilman hired his old friend Tenzing Norgay to manage arrangements and heard all about Tenzing's adventures with Tucci the year before:

he told me they had brought away forty *maunds* [around a tonne] of books. Tensing [sic], who gets on well with everyone and handles the local people well has a charming smile, great steadiness on a mountain, and a deft hand for omelettes which he turns out nicely sloppy and firm.

Tilman entered into the spirit of things, deciding he would collect beetles – in fact any beetles, although happily one of these turned out to be new to science. Yet the complexity of sometimes competing interests wasn't to his liking. 'The killing of two birds with one stone, however desirable, is seldom achieved intentionally and never by aiming consciously at both.'

The improvement in Nepal's diplomatic ties with western countries was beyond exciting for mountaineers around the world. There are fourteen mountains over eight thousand metres in the Himalaya and Karakoram ranges and eight of them are either partly or wholly in Nepal. While a number of climbers had gone above that altitude, no summit had been reached before 1950 and all the Nepali peaks had been off limits. By 1960 only one remained unclimbed. Seven of the eight in Nepal had been polished off by 1956: a mountain-climbing feeding frenzy. A number of Himalayan climbers both before and after the war had expressed the hope that climbers from many nations could come together to climb these giants. It didn't happen. An international team was responsible for only one of the eight-thousanders, Dhaulagiri, the seventh highest. Individuals could not afford to climb these mountains – it took national sporting organisations to raise the finance and deal with the diplomatic difficulties of getting official permission – and the opportunities for European countries rebuilding national prestige after the war were too important to waste.

The French were the first to profit from the new openness. When Tilman got back to Kathmandu in 1949, he buttonholed the maharaja Mohan Shamsher, pointed to the Annapurna massif on a map of west Nepal and asked for Mohan's permission to go there; but by the time permission had been granted, a French expedition was already in the field that would eclipse anything Tilman's expedition could do: a dazzling ascent of Annapurna, one of the great achievements in exploratory mountaineering as the first and only eight-thousander to be climbed first try. There were two obvious reasons for this: French mountaineering had arguably the strongest cadre of young alpinists in its history, men like Louis Lachenal, Lionel Terray and Gaston

Rébuffat; and all the important French national climbing organisations, including the Club Alpin Français, were run by the same man, a domineering autocrat called Lucien Devies who drove the project with relentless energy.

The third advantage the French held, something largely ignored since, was diplomatic. Working in the French embassy in Delhi was a young alpinist and resistance hero called Francis de Noyelle. Knowing that France had just appointed Daniel Levi to be its first ambassador in Kathmandu, de Noyelle asked Levi to help put the case to Mohan Shamsher's government for the first attempt on a Nepali eight-thousander to be French. Noyelle's reward for his success was to be made liaison officer on the expedition; in later life de Noyelle also served as ambassador to Nepal. Permission was granted for two mountains, Dhaulagiri and Annapurna, which rise five kilometres and more on either side of the Kali Gandaki gorge. Dhaulagiri, in expedition member Lionel Terray's phrase, proved 'fiendishly difficult' and so they turned their attention to Annapurna, so far unseen. Just getting a view of it would prove surprisingly elusive. By mid May and with time running out before the monsoon, the team still hadn't made much progress, so Maurice Herzog, their intensely ambitious leader, called a council of war at their base camp in the village of Tukche. Working at extraordinary speed, the climbers first tried the peak's north-west spur before coming to a dead end. Then in rapid order they pushed a route and a series of camps up the north face. Eric Shipton's old friend Ang Tharkay had led the Sherpas and in a spirit of equality was offered a place on the summit team, which he politely declined. Terray and Herzog had proved the strongest and best acclimatised, but when the supply chain stalled, Terray gave up his chance for the summit to bring supplies to a high camp. Fellow member Louis Lachenal took his place at their top camp for the push on the summit.

Lachenal and Herzog were wearing leather boots that offered insufficient insulation and Lachenal, who earned his living as a mountain guide, was anxious about his feet. What would Herzog do, he asked, if he turned around? 'I should go on by myself,' he told Lachenal. 'Then I'll follow you,' Lachenal replied. They reached the top at 2 p.m. on 3 June, although whether they were at the very top of Annapurna has proved a matter of controversy in recent years. The descent would become an unquestionable nightmare as Herzog lost

his gloves and suffered appalling frostbite. It would take six weeks for
Herzog to make it home, suffering agonies in his hands, by which
time his blackened feet were riddled with maggots. Yet the image of
him on the summit holding the tricolour sold more copies of *Paris
Match* than any in its history: they called him 'our number one hero'.
The French president Vincent Auriol was at the premiere of the expedition film and when it ended Herzog held up his ruined hands to
acknowledge the applause. The book Herzog wrote sold eleven million
copies, far more than any other mountaineering book in history. By
the end of the decade he was a government minister married to the
daughter of the duc de Brissac. Lachenal also suffered badly but his
life after Annapurna was more troubled, and he died aged thirty-four
falling into a crevasse while skiing the Vallée Blanche above Chamonix.

The success of the French concentrated minds among other
climbing nations. The Swiss also had a strong cadre of experienced
mountaineers, like the climbers who had taken Tenzing Norgay to
Garhwal, André Roch and René Dittert, who had more experience of
the Himalaya than the French. The Swiss had their own diplomatic
secret weapon as well, the travel writer Ella Maillart who was in
Kathmandu and able to press the case for the Swiss to be given permission ahead of the British for a first try at Everest.They also had an
organisation, the Schweizerische Stiftung für Alpine Forschung,
capable of supporting not one but two attempts on Everest in 1952,
before and after the monsoon. On their first attempt, the Swiss solved
what was widely regarded as the critical problem of reaching the
upper slopes of Everest from the south side: the Icefall. This jumble
of vast ice blocks is the consequence of the Khumbu glacier flowing
over a steep drop and fracturing, presenting climbers with what
amounts to a lethal maze. A number of climbers had speculated that
there might not be a route through it and if there was, had doubted
whether the risk was worth it. Once above this barrier, the climbers
reached the Western Cwm, the vast hanging valley that George
Mallory had looked down into during the reconnaissance from the
north side in 1921. The Swiss climbed the steep slope above this to
reach the South Col, giving access to the last eight hundred metres.
During the spring attempt, Raymond Lambert and Tenzing Norgay
attempted to reach the summit from a camp on the south-east ridge
above the South Col but their oxygen equipment was barely worth

its weight and after five hours they gained only two hundred metres; they were still three hundred metres below the top, at roughly the same height Edward Norton reached on the 1924 Everest expedition, the previous known high point.

The Himalayan Committee that replaced the Mount Everest Committee had been aghast when M P Koirala's government preferred the Swiss; it was a clear signal that British influence had faded, along with the Ranas. It was also true that the British weren't quite ready. While the Swiss were on Everest, Eric Shipton led an expedition to the nearby peak of Cho Oyu, sixth highest in the world. Although unsuccessful, the team did important research work under the maverick eye of physiologist Griffith Pugh. It also galvanised the Himalayan Committee into a moment of ruthless pragmatism, sacking Eric Shipton as leader of the planned 1953 Everest attempt and replacing him with John Hunt, dubbed 'Thruster John' for his ambition and drive. Politically Hunt was to the left of most of his predecessors, a bit more social democrat than imperial adventurer, in tune with Britain's Commonwealth era. The choice of the successful summit team, the New Zealander Ed Hillary and Tenzing Norgay from the locality itself, reflected that.

Once M P Koirala's government had granted its permission, a small army of porters – hundreds of them – left Kathmandu in stages with supplies and equipment for the dozen foreign climbers and twenty-eight Sherpas Hunt had planned to hire. Hillary and Norgay had not climbed together, just the two of them, until the expedition reached the Western Cwm, Hillary having led the route through the Icefall. Both men had their eyes on the summit and Hillary calculated that Hunt might not want to see the expedition's two Kiwis, himself and George Lowe, partnered for the top. Hillary was curious about Tenzing, who at that stage had more experience of the mountain than anyone else.

> Although not perhaps technically outstanding in ice-craft, he was very strong and determined and an excellent acclimatizer. Best of all, as far as I was concerned, he was prepared to go fast and hard.

He soon had reason to thank Tenzing. Racing down to base camp from the Western Cwm, as much for a bet with George Lowe as anything, Hillary went into a crevasse. As the New Zealander attempted to brace himself between its walls, Tenzing whipped the rope around his ice axe behind his boot and held his partner in exemplary fashion. Again and again, the two men went out of their way to illustrate their strength at altitude; it was clear from events that Hunt regarded the pair as his best card in beating Everest's formidable hand. When progress to the South Col stalled and the expedition seemed in jeopardy, Hunt sent the pair up to boost morale and get things moving. The fact that Hunt's team was able to lift far more supplies of oxygen, fuel, equipment and supplies than the Swiss to the South Col was the key difference.

The British pair of Charles Evans and Tom Bourdillon had first crack on 26 May, using an experimental 'closed' oxygen apparatus that was more efficient and effective than the 'open' system but prone to breakdown. Although they made rapid progress, when they paused to change cylinders, Evans' set began acting up and it was already one o'clock when they reached the mountain's south summit, the highest anyone had ever been on Everest. To push on would have been reckless, so they turned around and descended safely. Thanks to the immense supply effort to the South Col, a second summit attempt now began, with Hillary and Tenzing using the more reliable 'open' oxygen gear. A team of support climbers helped the pair establish an intermediary camp between the South Col and the summit, increasing their chance of success. Leaving camp at 6.30 a.m. on 29 May, and despite snow conditions that left Hillary anxious with worry, they reached the top in good order five hours later. 'My first sensation was one of relief,' Hillary wrote, 'relief that the long grind was over.' That soon gave way to satisfaction. 'I turned and looked at Tenzing. Even beneath his oxygen mask and the icicles hanging from his hair, I could see his infectious grin of sheer delight.' Hillary offered his hand, but that wasn't enough for Tenzing, who threw an arm around Hillary's shoulders and the two 'thumped each other on the back in mutual congratulations'.

Thanks to Hunt's leadership, Pugh's science, strong logistics and two highly ambitious climbers, Everest was finally climbed, the news arriving just in time for the coronation of Elizabeth II. As in France, the nature and scale of the achievement somehow matched a new mood of hope in Europe that followed post-war austerity. In the

Himalaya, the political consequences of Tenzing Norgay being one of the successful pair were huge, and hugely complicated. A humbly born Asian had become globally famous almost overnight. Some Indian journalists called for the mountain to be renamed in his honour. In Darjeeling, when All India Radio broadcast news of Tenzing's success, his friend Rabindrinath Mitra had pictures of him put up all over town. Mitra was a Bengali born in Calcutta but from a local family who had taken over a failing tea plantation and started a Nepali-language newspaper *Sathi*, meaning 'friend'. He had run articles on the Sherpa community, feeling their contribution to mountaineering had been overlooked. He also encouraged them to organise for themselves and stop relying on the colonial-era Himalayan Club. It was Mitra who gave Tenzing an Indian flag to take to the summit. Stories began appearing in the Indian press, quoting 'sources close to the expedition', that Tenzing had reached the summit first and led Hillary to the top. This idea hadn't come from Tenzing; he was still walking back from the mountain, but the notion chimed in postcolonial India. Inder Malhotra, then a young journalist but later editor of *The Times of India*, recalled:

> The idea that white man is the leading one, oh no rubbish, this time, we have done it, our people have done it, Tenzing has done it and why should this credit be misappropriated by others. This was the feeling.

The problem was, who were 'our people'? Tenzing had been born in Tibet, spent time in Khumbu and lived in Darjeeling for the last twenty years. In that time an empire had crumbled and new nations risen. Nepal, deeply sensitised to Indian interference, was no less keen to claim Tenzing as one of 'our people'. Nepal's newspaper *Gorkhapatra* picked up the Indian story that Tenzing had reached the summit first. Dharma Raj Thapa, a poet who worked as a radio producer in Nepal, was with Mitra in Darjeeling when they heard the news and set to work on a lyric that began 'Hamro Tenzing Sherpa le', 'our Sherpa Tenzing', later going to Calcutta to record it to music. The song was a huge hit and it carried the same message, that Tenzing had guided Hillary, only this time it wasn't an expression of Indian nationalism but Nepali nationalism. The publisher Kamal Mani Dixit, a student in 1953, recalled 'Wherever Nepalese were, they were singing this song.

Nepalese songs on 78 rpm records were new. The idea of Nepalese nationality was new.' More than that, Tenzing had been born poor and yet almost overnight had become globally famous. In a place as hierarchical as Kathmandu, where caste and class defined you, that was truly revolutionary. 'For those of poor birth,' Dixit said, 'Tenzing's success was a big impetus. At one time he was more popular than King Tribhuvan.' The mood in Kathmandu when the expedition returned was, as Jan Morris put it, 'a cross between a circus and a hustings'. Tenzing would leave the city on Tribhuvan's own private aircraft and into the embrace of Pandit Jawaharlal Nehru.

> From the very first, Panditji was like a father to me [Tenzing said]. He was warm and kind, and, unlike so many others, was not thinking of what use he could make of me.

If that was naïve, Nehru did take a genuine personal interest in Tenzing, whose success reflected what Nehru hoped for his country: that ordinary people could thrive. The glow of Nehru's attention would give Tenzing an Indian passport and a sense of mission – 'If Nehru had told me I was Indian,' Ed Hillary said, 'I would have believed him' – but when Tenzing next came to Kathmandu, in the late 1950s, his reception was cooler.

The immense global coverage of the 1953 Everest expedition and the avalanche of articles, books and films that followed it fixed in the public mind that how this mountain had been climbed was how all mountains must be climbed: with fixed camps and huge teams. On the day the newly titled Sir John Hunt and his team arrived in London, the Austrian climber Hermann Buhl reached the summit of Nanga Parbat. Buhl had toasted the British success with a can of Munich beer when he heard about it almost three weeks later, camped at six thousand metres on Nanga Parbat's Rakhiot face. The expedition leader was Karl Herrligkoffer, half-brother of Willy Merkl, whose own expedition in 1934 had ended in such disaster. Herrligkoffer, in the mould of Paul Bauer, despised the 'zeal of individuals', and preferred 'the collaborative expedition that didn't reach the summit'. On the other hand, he wasn't much of a climber, while Hermann Buhl was one of the best in the world. When Herrligkoffer ordered Buhl to descend following a poor weather forecast, Buhl ignored him, making a bravura dash for the summit from his top camp, some four thousand feet below, twice the height Hillary and Tenzing had needed to cover, fuelled by *Panzerschokolade*, the chocolate methamphetamine used by the German military in the Second World War. (Buhl was far from the only climber to rely on speed to keep him going on a tough ascent. It was on the British equipment list in 1953.) After a forty-one hour round-trip he was back at his top camp in a state of frostbitten exhaustion but triumphant. Herrligkoffer never forgave him and the two ended up mired in legal proceedings. Buhl would make another lightweight first ascent of an eight-thousander in 1957, Broad Peak in the Karakoram, but died soon after, stepping through a cornice on the summit ridge of a nearby peak on yet another alpine-style climb.

This golden era of mountain climbing added lustre to the Himalaya as a fashionable and exotic tourist destination. The man who drove that fashion more than anyone was a Russian emigré called Boris Lissanevitch. Previously a dancer with Sergei Diaghilev's Ballets Russes whose career came to end with Daighilev's death in 1929, Lissanevitch met his first wife Kira Stcherbatcheva in Monte Carlo, and the pair earned their living dancing the tango in smart hotels and clubs from Shanghai to Bombay. When the marriage failed, Boris became the inspiration, manager and frontman of the 300 Club in Calcutta, an exclusive 'mixed' venue where Europeans and Indians could get a drink together at any time of day or night, assuming they could afford it. The club was a favourite of King Tribhuvan, and in 1951, after restrictive licensing laws killed his business, Boris took up the king's invitation to move to Kathmandu. With his new Danish wife Inger Pheiffer and backing from Tribhuvan's alcoholic younger son Basundhara, he opened Nepal's first successful European-style hotel in the wing of a royal palace. The Royal Hotel was considered the only place in town for diplomats, spies, aid workers, mountain climbers, yeti hunters, celebrity guests – from the movie stars Ingrid Bergman and Cary Grant to the economist and diplomat Kenneth Galbraith – and the trickle of wealthy tourists Boris managed to attract through his contacts at the travel agency Thomas Cook. The hotel was, as one visitor put it, 'an exhibit hall of some Victorian museum', its lobby full of stuffed crocodiles, chandeliers and gilt-framed oil paintings of Rana princes, a kind of Raj fantasy of tiger shoots and derring-do. Inger's mother, who lived at the Royal, kept a pet red panda – called Pandaji – given to her by regular guest Ed Hillary. The standard was often ropey. Guests would spot enormous rats in their rooms and there was a pig living in the kitchen. But stays were always memorable.

Among Nepalis, there was scepticism and disquiet at the prospect of tourism. Ritual pollution from contact with foreigners made inter-action awkward at first for those from higher castes and many in Nepal's elite couldn't understand why foreigners would want to come anyway. What was so special about a few old temples? With his patron King Tribhuvan undergoing treatment in Switzerland, Boris sought permission from the crown prince Mahendra to bring in as many rich Americans as he could fit in a Dakota aircraft to stay at his new hotel. Mahendra indulged him but couldn't see much in the idea until he watched the Americans vacuuming up every trinket on offer in the hotel's gift shop. When Tribhuvan died in March 1955, Mahendra told Boris he wanted him to organise his coronation the following year. This became a shop front for Nepal, both as a tourism destination and a development aid project. Hundreds of foreign dignitaries were invited and scores of western reporters. The journalist Lowell Thomas was among them, arriving in a convoy of jeeps along Kathmandu's first road to the outside world. His enormous cameras were set up in front of the royal dais and Thomas could be heard shouting instruc-tions – 'Hold it, king!' – to Mahendra during the ceremony.

Another of the foreign reporters was the Eurasian novelist Han Suyin, born Rosalie Matilde Kuanghu Chou in the Chinese province of Henan; her novel *A Many-Splendoured Thing* had appeared as a Hollywood blockbuster the year before. Han Suyin captured fragments of Kathmandu's coming-out party and the boozy world of Boris Lissanevitch in her barely fictionalised story *The Mountain is Young*. ('They do say that there is a thing called mountain exhilaration,' she wrote, 'that when in the high places a strange elation seizes one; akin to ecstasy or madness.') It was in Kathmandu that she met her third husband, an Indian army colonel called Vincent Ratnaswamy, providing the novel's love story. Han Suyin had studied in Brussels before the war and was a friend of the Belgian cartoonist Hergé, who in 1956 was casting around for a new location for his fictional reporter Tintin's next adventure. Their friendship may have been an influence on his choice of the Himalaya, although Hergé had used Tibet as a setting for Tintin as early as the 1940s. The new story appeared under the title *Tintin in Tibet*, which had tested well with the publisher's sales force, but it takes place as much in Nepal as Tibet and features drawings of Kathmandu's temples that are both charming and accurate. The story also features a yeti, the mythical abominable snowman, then at the height of its fame. The self-styled cryptozoologist Bernard Heuvelmans was Hergé's 'expert' advisor on this creature, and he talked too with the French mountaineer Maurice Herzog, who claimed to have seen the creature's footprints.

But the deeper inspiration for *Tintin in Tibet* was the psychological torment Hergé was experiencing as he wrote the story, torn between two women, searching for an exotic dream-world of innocence and hope. That would be the version of the Himalaya the new King Mahendra would peddle as he ruthlessly put Boris Lissanevitch out of business and invested himself in the tourism business, even as he crushed Nepal's first attempt at democracy.

19

Songs from a Dark Cell

A few weeks after Saddam Hussein's regime fell to American-led coalition forces, I interviewed a Tibetan prisoner of conscience called Ngawang Sangdrol. At the time she was still only twenty-five but had spent almost half her life behind bars. She was the best known of a small group of nuns imprisoned for protesting against China's continuing occupation of Tibet, so I knew a little about the beatings and torture she had suffered at the hands of her guards. What I hadn't been prepared for was her size. Sangdrol was barely five feet tall and slight: too slight. I could see the bones of her shoulders under her thin cardigan. What a man armed with an iron bar could do to her didn't take much imagination. As she answered my questions in her soft voice, Sangdrol unconsciously massaged her head; migraines were a long-term consequence of the sustained violence she suffered, along with damaged kidneys and a malfunctioning digestive tract. It seemed a miracle she had survived. Only when I asked her why she thought she had been singled out for particularly harsh treatment did I get a glimpse of her resolve. Her eyes hardened and she gave a wry half-smile: 'Maybe they didn't like me.'

The Himalaya overflows with stories of courage and resilience but few compare with that of Ngawang Sangdrol. She was born in Lhasa in 1977 with the lay name Rigchog, the name her guards would use to strip her of her spiritual identity. Her family was poor but close, and dedicated to the cause of freedom and to Tibetan Buddhism as an expression of their culture. Her father, Namgyal Tashi, had fought in the Lhasa Uprising of March 1959, when Tibetans rose up against China's occupation amid fears about the safety of the fourteenth Dalai Lama, who fled into exile. Through the early 1960s and 1970s, years of collectivisation and the disaster of the Cultural Revolution, he had been in and out of prison and detention camps. Namgyal Tashi would tell Sangdrol and her brothers and sisters about Tibet before communism changed everything. Her mother, Jampa Choezom, described how during the Cultural Revolution their father would be carried home unconscious from political 'struggle' sessions, known in Tibet as *thamzing*, in which party cadres publicly humiliated and beat those deemed politically untrustworthy. He suffered more persecution when he refused to sign a letter expressing support for China's policies in Tibet. Sangdrol admired these stories of resistance and shared her parents' strength of feeling for their identity as Tibetans.

At the age of twelve, Sangdrol joined the Garu nunnery just north of Lhasa. The nunnery's foundation myth tells how Guru Rinpoche, founder of the Nyingma tradition, saw its location as propitious but couldn't decide if it should become a monastery or a nunnery. He then had a vision of three female spirits, *khandroma* in Tibetan, *dakini* in Sanskrit, dancing in front of him. He went with the nunnery. Guru Rinpoche, known also by his Sanskrit name Padmasambhava, had as his consorts two *dakini*, Mandarava and Yeshe Tsogyel, both teachers in their own right, both adepts in tantric Buddhism. Yeshe Tsogyel in particular remains a popular figure in Tibetan mythology and there are many sites across the Himalaya associated with her name. She's unusual to have had biographies dedicated to her, Tibetan Buddhism being as capable of misogyny as other religions; women are routinely characterised as intellectually incapable of fully grasping the *dharma*. An exception was the bridge-builder Tangtong Gyalpo, whose partner, in life as well as in *dharma* practice, was a woman called Choekyi Dronma: she was recognised by Tangtong as a female *tulku*, or reincarnate lama, one of the few female reincarnate lineages, and the most important: the Samding Dorje Phagmo. (The East India Company's man George Bogle would, three centuries after her death, meet Choekyi Dronma's reincarnation.) Yeshe Tsogyel was no sidekick either. In a reversal of the usual scenario she took consorts for herself, an inspirational exception, which is why she has such currency today among progressive feminist Buddhists. In one story, Yeshe Tsogyel and her followers find Guru Rinpoche meditating in the caves at Taktsang in the upper Paro valley of Bhutan. (She has carried him there earlier in the guise of a tigress.) Yeshe Tsogyel prostrates herself and he calls her *heruka*, meaning here an adept who has fully realised the true nature of existence. Guru Rinpoche tells her:

> Oh yogini who has accomplished the secret mantra, the human body is the basis for attaining enlightenment. Male or female, inferior body – it makes no difference. If possessed of the aspiration to enlightenment, a female body is actually superior.

In Tibetan, the name for a female spirit, *khandro*, means something like space-dancer; there's a playful or joyful quality in the term: a fully realised mind with the psychological space to express itself. There was little of this in Sangdrol's experience. At Garu she discovered that her father's suffering wasn't exceptional; many of the older women could tell similar stories. In August 1990, when Sangdrol was still only thirteen, she went on her first demonstration with twelve other nuns, shouting slogans – 'Long live the Dalai Lama!' – at the Sho Dun festival held each summer in the Norbulingka park on the edge of Lhasa to mark the end of a traditional period of retreat for Geluk monks. There was a heavy security presence. Tibet was still tense after a sequence of major public demonstrations against Chinese rule in the late 1980s that had frequently ended in violence and the deaths of scores of protestors. Martial law had only ended three months earlier. Almost immediately, police, uniformed and plainclothes, dragged the nuns away and put them in a truck. They were taken to the Public Security Bureau's Gutsa detention centre east of the city, interrogated and beaten. Neither Sangdrol's age nor her small size made any difference. She recalled being thrown around the room like a doll. The authorities wanted confessions and names of other protestors but the nuns refused, which earned them more abuse. There was never enough food and it was common at Gutsa for prisoners to be forced to give blood as payment for their rations. Sangdrol told me how when it rained she would stick her cup out of her cell window to collect water but was so small she could barely reach.

Her mother Jampa Choezom found out where she was being held and was allowed a visit. Sangdrol forced herself not to cry; her mother was too upset to speak and didn't want to in front of the guards. When she was released after nine months Sangdrol discovered her father and one of her brothers, Tenzin Sherab, had been imprisoned following a demonstration at Samye monastery; her mother was dead, aged fifty-two, from a heart attack. As a former political prisoner, Sangdrol was banned from returning to her nunnery so she lived at home with her brothers and sisters, watched by police, and kept away from her friends in case she incriminated them by association. She said prayers for her mother but all the time thought of those still in prison and of returning to political action. In June 1992, less than two years after her first demonstration and imprisonment, she joined other Garu nuns and monks from Ganden monastery in a peaceful demonstration of support for the Dalai Lama and Tibetan freedom in the Barkhor, the circular thoroughfare and pilgrimage route that surrounds the Jokhang, the temple that stands at – and for – the heart of Lhasa and by extension Tibet. It had hardly begun before Sangdrol and the others were dragged away. She was sentenced to three years in prison 'for incitement to subversive and separatist activities'. Still only fifteen years old, Sangdrol was one of the youngest political prisoners in the world.

This time she was incarcerated at Drapchi, the prison complex that took its name from an old Tibetan army regiment whose barracks once occupied the site. The People's Liberation Army had taken it over to house prisoners following the Lhasa Uprising in 1959. As a form of political quarantine, two new units, or *rukhag*, were opened to house the surge in dissidents being incarcerated following this new wave of unrest. Men, often monks, were put in Rukhag 5; her father was being held here. The women went in Rukhag 3. Although the men always outnumbered the women, the authorities were forced to expand Rukhag 3 to cope as nuns continued to protest. Life in Rukhag 3 was brutally hard. Sangdrol was put to work in the prison's carpet factory and given a daily quota. If she didn't meet it, she was beaten or had her rations withheld. Yet even in this atmosphere, protest continued. One of the prisoners smuggled in a tape recorder and fourteen nuns collaborated in writing and recording songs about their lives in prison and their resistance to the occupation. Each of them gave their names and dedicated a song or poem to friends and supporters who had not forgotten them in jail, telling of the beatings they had suffered and their commitment to Tibetan independence. The recordings were smuggled out of Drapchi and released abroad as an album. In October 1993, little more than a year after her original three-year sentence, Sangdrol was given another six years for her role in 'spreading counter-revolutionary propaganda'.

The head of Rukhag 3 was a Tibetan in her forties called Pema Butri, a woman who after work would go to a chapel nearby to say her prayers. She called the nuns *dumo*, she-devil, and if they didn't pay sufficient respect, she made them suffer. Pema Butri singled out Ngawang Sangdrol as a ringleader for her small acts of defiance. In March 1996, Sangdrol was sitting outside her cell block. It was snowing. Pema Butri arrived with a small group of guards and seeing Sangdrol sitting there told her to stand. Sangdrol refused. A guard dragged her upright and the others began beating her. Sangdrol broke free and began shouting political slogans. Chaos reigned for a moment until armed police arrived and demanded to know who had started it. Pema Butri pointed out Sangdrol but the nearest policeman thought she meant another woman, Pema Phuntsog, and kicked her in the stomach. Not *her*, Pema Butri shouted, that one, Sangdrol. Although Phuntsog had done nothing wrong, both women were dragged off to solitary confinement, what the Tibetan prisoners referred to as a 'dark cell' with no window or light. Phuntsog was put in the next cell but one to Sangdrol's: the one in between was left empty.

There was a metal grill in the ceiling of Sangdrol's cell, through which a male prisoner, convicted of criminal offences, could look down on her. Some of the light from his cell filtered into hers. If she stretched out her arms, she could touch both its walls. When she rolled out her mattress, it more or less filled the floor. In one corner was a hole in the floor where she could defecate. The smell was so bad that guards were loath to step through the door. Sometimes, as she slept, a rat would come up through the hole and one winter's night it crawled up the sleeve of her prison uniform, looking for the warmth in her armpit. There was no heating, even in the depths of the Tibetan winter. At night the water in her tap froze. Sangdrol suffered constant back pains from sleeping on a thin mattress on a cold floor; sometimes the guards would shout at her in the night to check she was still alive.

Sangdrol spent her days praying, looking through a gap in the cell door's hatch at a shadow in the corridor outside. If the dark edges of the shadow flickered, she knew a prison guard was approaching. If she were caught praying, she would be beaten. Under her prison uniform she wore a thin red sweater and Sangdrol unpicked a thread from its hem to make a *mala*, a rosary. She used this to count off her prayers for the Dalai Lama, for saints like Tsongkhapa, guiding inspiration for the Geluk tradition, for liberation from the psychological torment she suffered. She regretted she had been banned from her nunnery so young; she hadn't had time to study Buddhism properly. The older nuns seemed to her stronger, less angry. Each evening, as long as the guards weren't around, she and Pema would call to each other, keep each other going. Eventually the other women in Rukhag 3 went on hunger strike in protest at their treatment and after six months the pair were released. When they were finally able to speak freely, Sangdrol asked Phuntsog why she had admitted to shouting slogans when she hadn't. Phuntsog smiled. 'To support you.' Sangdrol was taken back to court and sentenced to a further eight years, on top of the nine she was already serving. She'd just turned nineteen.

The beating that almost killed Ngawang Sangdrol happened in the spring of 1998. On 1 May, Labour Day in China, prison officials arranged a ceremonial parade for the raising of the Chinese flag. Two criminal inmates began shouting for Tibetan independence and political prisoners joined in. There was pandemonium. Armed police grabbed prisoners and dragged them away. When order was finally restored, the authorities announced another Labour Day parade for 4 May, but this time long-standing political prisoners like Sangdrol would not be allowed to attend. Despite this, inmates still shouted support for the Dalai Lama. Sangdrol and the other nuns were watching through the windows of their block and smashed the glass, so their shouts of support could be heard. Monks prevented from attending now rushed the gate of the prison courtyard and armed police opened fire, hitting one of them. After half an hour, Pema Butri arrived in the nun's block with more armed police and dragged Sangdrol outside, where they beat her with batons so badly that she quickly lost consciousness. A nun who saw it described how blood ran from her head like water. Pema Butri then stepped forward and hit her with her belt buckle, something Red Guards did habitually during the Cultural Revolution, as though Pema Butri were quoting from a familiar script. Sangdrol woke up at this blow and Pema Butri shouted at her: 'I thought you had died, but you still didn't die.' Sangdrol didn't die, but in the violent aftermath of this demonstration five other nuns did. Prison authorities claimed they had committed suicide although witnesses who saw the bodies claimed they had been beaten beyond recognition. Sangdrol was given a further extension of her sentence for her role in the 1998 demonstration but increasing attention from international human rights organisations prompted the authorities to reduce her sentence and she was released in October 2002, just in time to be reunited with her father before his death. She is now an American citizen and a human rights campaigner.

Although Ngawang Sangdrol has a higher profile than many Tibetan prisoners of conscience, her story is not exceptional among Tibetan dissidents of that era, and certainly not in the context of the previous fifty years of China's occupation. Nuns had at times played a notable role in resisting Chinese oppression, and unlike Ngawang Sangdrol's, that resistance wasn't always peaceful. In the late 1960s, as the Chinese authorities began to restore some measure of control after the chaos of the Cultural Revolution, a young nun called Thrinley Choedron led a ferociously violent rebellion from her home county of Nyemo, west of Lhasa. During this campaign Choedron and her followers stormed into county headquarters armed with swords and spears and slaughtered party cadres who worked there. Some of the Chinese victims were set on fire and Tibetan collaborators had their hands chopped off. The massacre sparked a popular uprising that spread quickly to other counties. This being Tibet, Thrinley Choedron claimed she was an emanation of Labja Gongmo, a holy bird from the *Gesar* epic, giving her magical powers. No bullet could harm her. Yet when the Chinese finally deployed the People's Liberation Army (PLA) to crush the rebellion, she and fifteen of her followers were caught hiding out in the mountains, brought to Lhasa and executed.

The meaning of what's euphemistically called the 'Nyemo incident' is contested, as you might expect in this drawn-out and one-sided confrontation. At first, authorities in Lhasa assumed Thrinley Choedron's group was another expression of the brutal factionalism the Cultural Revolution had unleashed, something Mao had relished and Beijing was now trying to contain. Most of rural Tibet followed the line of the Lhasa communist establishment; Nyemo on the other hand was a known radical hotspot. At second glance, they concluded Choedron was not in fact some rogue Red Guard but a self-styled holy warrior targeting the 'enemies of faith'. When they caught her, she was simply assumed to be a Dalai-clique 'splittist' and executed, reasserting the all-embracing control of the party. Her execution was an instinctive reflex, the spasm of a struck nerve; there was no open-minded inquiry into why an ordinary woman should act in this way. And while the party's tactics have become more sophisticated in the last fifty years, China's leaders still have little idea or interest in how Tibetans conceive the world, as you would expect from a colonial power. You can see this in how communist authorities sell Tibetan tourism, promoting, without irony, a culture they had once tried to erase, but as a brand rather than a philosophical world view.

The Tibetan historian Tsering Shakya has called the Nyemo revolt a 'millenarian movement', which captures the crazed despair of 1960s Tibet and the desperate rage many Tibetans felt as every aspect of their lives came under attack. China's occupation wasn't just spatial, a strategic acquisition of territory, although that was important: Tibet was perceived as China's back door and it needed shutting before India or the Soviet Union could wander in. The occupation was also psychological. China's invasion was of minds, an assault on every aspect of Tibetan identity as all the old institutions and traditions that had created those minds were systematically attacked. Not only that: during the Cultural Revolution, Tibetans were required to assist in this destruction. The process created a kind of mental dissonance; people who lived through the Cultural Revolution in Tibet described it as when the sky fell to earth. There are countless stories of people simply losing their minds in the face of this violent attack on their own selves. Twenty years ago, in a village near Everest, I was told how, during the Cultural Revolution, party cadres had instructed local people to destroy the treasures in their monastery, a process then underway right across the plateau. One of the villagers took these treasures and buried them secretly on the mountainside across the valley. Only he knew their location. He was later taken away to a re-education camp and beaten so badly he lost his mind. Villagers spent years digging in likely places but without success. The treasures remain hidden where he left them.

Maoism believed human nature is a blank slate. Tibetan minds could simply be scraped clean and the party's wishes written over the past. It didn't work out like that. Ngawang Sangdrol's defiance, more than two decades after that of Thrinley Choedron, has been followed by two more decades of protest. This has culminated in the last decade with a horrific campaign of self-immolation, mostly in areas outside central Tibet, in historically Tibetan areas now absorbed into Chinese provinces. Many of those committing suicide have been current or former monks and nuns. One of these was a nun called Palden Choetso, the eleventh of around a hundred and fifty Tibetans who have now sacrificed themselves in this way and the second woman to do so. She was thirty-five years old and had been a nun since the age of twenty. Choetso's nunnery was Geden Choeling, near Tawu in Sichuan. A number of Geden Choeling's nuns had been involved in the widespread demonstrations that erupted in March 2008 in the run-up to the Beijing Olympics. On 3 November 2011, Choetso walked into the centre of town, poured petrol over her head and set herself on fire. Unlike the first female self-immolation, twenty-year-old Tenzin Wangmo, the death of Palden Choetso was filmed. Witnesses reported hearing her shouting slogans in support of the Dalai Lama but it's the screams of onlookers that dominate the footage. Choetso stands ramrod straight for more than twenty seconds as she is wholly engulfed in flames. As she finally collapses on the ground, a woman steps forward with a *kada*, the white silk ceremonial scarf, and throws it towards her.

In 1975, Han Suyin, the China-born novelist who had put the coronation of Mahendra in her novel *The Mountain is Young*, was granted permission to tour Tibet. A feminist and admirer of the Chinese Communist Party, she zeroed in on what communism had done for Tibetan women:

> the Tibetan woman appears to me more 'revolutionary', ready to revolt, because her exploitation has been so great. Since she was kept out of religious ritual though not free from religious extortion, once she realised that her labour was a strength, her repudiation of that system was all the more forceful.

So what does the long sequence of women prepared to suffer unimaginable physical agonies tell us? China argues that such protests are orchestrated externally, the culprits being those who wish to split the motherland, the Dalai Lama chief amongst them, and damage China. Yet the perseverance of such visceral and extreme opposition after seventy years suggests powerful misjudgments on the part of Beijing.

Ordinary Chinese, even when they know about the self-immolations, manage to disconnect the agony of Tibetans from the picture postcard appeal of Tibet. The Tibetan-born poet and essayist Tsering Woeser recalled discussing the issue with Chinese tourists on the train to Lhasa but they soon lost interest.

> I wanted to say more, to tell them about the last words uttered by self-immolators. But at that point most people don't want to listen anymore. Going to Tibet on holiday is a dream for many Chinese people, and my fellow travelers that day just wanted to carry on with their journeys and make good use of their hard-earned vacation.

At Lhasa, as the Chinese tourists streamed out of the station excited to visit the city, Woeser and the handful of Tibetan passengers were held behind to have their identity cards scanned and suffer further questioning.

In recent years, China has made colossal investments in the Tibetan region. In 2011, a few months before Palden Choetso set herself on fire, Beijing announced a package of 226 infrastructure projects – airports, roads, railways and hydropower – worth $21 billion. The consequent rise in living standards among Tibetans is obvious. And yet Tibetan people continue to make their dissatisfaction clear, to the bewilderment and anger of Han Chinese, who are sensitised to react to criticism of China's policy in Tibet as foreign meddling. Despite the most intrusive and sophisticated state surveillance anywhere in the world, despite myriad layers of informants and subsidies, Tibetans continue to find enough space to maintain their identity: to remain space-dancers. The gap between China's rhetoric and reality suggests that in some profound way China's occupation has failed. And the obvious question is why.

*

Tibet was not wholly and immediately opposed to China's intervention in 1950. The Chinese behaved with considerable restraint after their brief military campaign, leaving the aristocratic and monastic power structures in place in the short term. Within four years, two roads had been constructed to link Tibet with China, a stunning achievement that employed thirty thousand grateful Tibetans. With Tibet's Indian border now closed because of China's occupation, the wool trade suffered, so China simply bought up all the wool, to the delight of rich trading families. Health care improved and opportunities for education in China were welcomed. When the Dalai Lama went to Beijing and met Mao in 1954, he wrote a poem in which he called China's intervention the 'timely rain'. The Dalai Lama himself told the writer Patrick French how he

> had enthusiasm that Tibet could transform itself under Communist leadership. Chairman Mao made a lot of promises. ... The reason I left Tibet was not because I was against reform in principle.

Indeed, the need for reform in Tibet had been glaringly obvious throughout the first half of the twentieth century. The thirteenth Dalai Lama had wanted in a modest way to usher Tibet towards the modern world but resistance to change was deeply entrenched. Tibet was a theocracy and monasteries controlled much of its economic activity, relying on landholdings and trade to maintain huge numbers of monks, like much of Europe in the fourteenth century. Pull one strand, and the whole tapestry would fall apart. Government was not something ordinary Tibetans did; political consciousness amounted to a visceral trust in the Dalai Lama. Running the country was left to senior lamas and Tibet's aristocratic families, who would often compete for influence when the Dalai Lama was in his minority. Ordinary Tibetans outside Lhasa had little or no idea of how a modern country was run; that was confined to those wealthier individuals educated in India. It was this class that was agitating most strongly for change.

Much of that agitation happened outside Tibet. The Indian town of Kalimpong in Sikkim, high above the Tista valley east of Darjeeling, was in the 1930s the focus of the wool trade with eastern Tibet and consequently a centre of intrigue; it was here, in fact, that Gergan Tharchin ran the *Mirror*, the only Tibetan-language newspaper, with support from the British. In 1939, it was also where a number of dissidents founded the opposition Tibet Improvement Party, although its activities remained piecemeal and clandestine. The new party's most influential figures were Thubten Kunphela, the thirteenth Dalai Lama's strongman in the early 1930s but banished after his death, and Pandatsang Rapga, one of the hugely rich Pandatsang clan from Kham, which more or less controlled Kham's wool trade, much of which was now exported through the town. Rapga was an ardent admirer of the Chinese nationalist Sun Yat-sen and his 'three principles': nationalism, democracy and the people's welfare. The ninth Panchen Lama, in exile on the western fringes of nationalist China, was another who favoured Sun Yat-sen's political philosophy. Rapga envisaged a future for Tibet as an autonomous republic within China, and sought the help of Chiang Kai-shek and the Kuomintang in support of a Kham militia that would defeat the Tibetan army, overthrow the *kashag* government in Lhasa and liberate the people from the rule of the monastic elite.

Caught up in this proto-revolutionary movement was the influential Tibetan writer Gendun Chopel, a man whose complicated life reveals far more about pre-invasion Tibet than either Kunphela or Rapga. To what extent he committed himself to the cause of these Tibetan political exiles is, like so much about Chopel's life, hard to pin down. A maverick former monk, Chopel was the Tibetan intellectual star of the early twentieth century, expelled from his monastery in Amdo for asking all the right wrong questions. In 1927, aged twenty-four, he travelled to Lhasa and studied at Drepung monastery, debating with its best young scholar, Sherab Gyatso, who became so infuriated that he gave up using Chopel's name and began referring to him simply as 'madman'. In 1934 Sherab Gyatso introduced Chopel to the Indian Sanskrit scholar Rahul Sankrityayan, a Buddhist and independence campaigner, whom the British had once jailed. (Sankrityayan later became an atheist Marxist teaching Buddhism in Leningrad.) At the time of their meeting, Sankrityayan was on his second trip to Tibet, hunting original Sanskrit versions of the ancient Buddhist scriptures that the *lotsawa* had translated into Tibetan at the start of the millennium. He had identified two monasteries near Shigatse, Ngor and Shalu, as likely sources but needed an expert translator to help him look. Knowing Sherab Gyatso's reputation, he asked him; Sherab Gyatso instead put him in touch with his most quarrelsome student, Gendun Chopel. Sankrityayan and Chopel found what they were looking for, written in faded ink on crumbling palm leaves, and continued south to Kathmandu, where they spent five months studying them. They seem to have got on well: Sankrityayan introduced Chopel to the Maha Bodhi society, the most important Buddhist organisation in India, leading the campaign to restore Buddhism's most sacred sites. When Sankrityayan was done in Kathmandu, he headed to Japan, leaving Chopel to fend for himself, first in Darjeeling, later in Kalimpong, where he became friends with the newspaper editor Gergan Tharchin.

Chopel was able to help Tharchin with a translation problem, one that would have significant political impact. Tharchin had in his possession some documents from the Dunhuang Caves, left to him by the French scholar Jacques Bacot. Translating them from archaic to modern Tibetan had so far proved too difficult. As Chopel made progress, a new way of seeing his country began to emerge. Chopel had read translations of the Tang annals, which offered a view of Tibet's early history from the end of the first millennium, albeit from the perspective of an imperial Chinese dynasty. But this was the first time a Tibetan historian had access to Tibetan sources illustrating the scope of Tibet's old empire. In the flowing tide of Indian nation-alism, swollen by the prospect of independence, these fresh perspec-tives inspired him to write a new history of Tibet, called the *White Annals*, 'To measure the dominion and power of the first Tibetan kingdom'. He was still working on it at his death, more than a decade later.

In all Chopel spent twelve years in India during the late 1930s and 1940s, living the life of a *dharma* bum, a drifter with a razor mind; he kept himself fed with translation work, spending years working for the wealthy Russian Tibetologist George Roerich on a translation of the fifteenth-century Tibetan history, the *Blue Annals*. (Chopel wrote that in taking such work 'the lion is made servant to the dog' and fretted he wasn't given due credit.) He drank heavily, smoked opium and drew on his visits to brothels in Calcutta to produce a book of erotica, written entirely in verse: the *Treatise on Passion*. (He recom-mends reciting multiplication tables to men wanting to delay ejacula-tion and hopes, rather generously, his former lovers 'Continue on the path, from bliss to bliss / To arrive at great bliss, the place of the *dharamakaya*.') Chopel remarked acidly how as a young monk he had kept his vows of celibacy when so many monks around him hadn't – and yet he was the one expelled. The three main monasteries at Lhasa had around five thousand monks each, which must have made them intimidating places for young *getsul*, or novice monks. The Tibetan historian Tashi Tsering, press-ganged as a boy into joining the Dalai Lama's dance troupe in 1942, described the dangers of being captured by senior monks on the look-out for a new catamite. Chopel made fun of this in his poetry, which is more accessible and much more fun than his philosopy: sly but warm. 'Everyone pretends to dislike sex, / But in the mind sex is the only thing everyone likes.' During this time he also wrote *Grains of Gold*, an encyclopaedic account of the modern world and how it was made, with a shrewd take on the evils of colonialism, as well as newspaper articles in which he lambasted the Tibetan establishment for its backwardness.

In 1937, hearing that his old sparring partner Sherab Gyatso was leaving Lhasa to travel by sea to China, Gendun Chopel went to Calcutta to see him off. They had a fiery argument in a hotel room about whether or not the world was flat. Sherab Gyatso thumped the table and said: 'I will make it flat.' Chopel, who had studied some Western astronomy in India, warned his friend he wouldn't be taken seriously in China if he carried on like that. Sherab Gyatso slapped him round the head, startling those who had gathered in the room to witness the conversation of these great Buddhist scholars. Chopel wrote up the argument for Gergan Tharchin's *Mirror* the following year.

While waiting for the boat, a mutual friend from Lhasa introduced the pair to Francis Younghusband, now in his seventies, who had arrived in India a few days before to meet Charles Lindbergh. America's famous aviator had written to Younghusband out of the blue with the ambition to explore the mysteries of the universe and 'squat with a yogi'. They had dinner together with Lindbergh's wife Anne, as well as David Macdonald, the long-serving 'political' and trade agent, and the American Theos Bernard, the self-styled 'white lama', just back from Tibet, where Tharchin had been showing him around. Bernard took a shine to Gendun Chopel and would have brought him to America if Chopel had not been refused a visa. Next day, Younghusband gave a short speech on the Calcutta dockside as Sherab Gyatso embarked for China. Gyatso would later work with the Chinese, becoming deputy chairman of the new communist Qinghai provincial government even before China took over central Tibet.

There is no record of Gendun Chopel's response to the irony of the imperialist adventurer Younghusband wishing safe travels to a Tibetan scholar. We do know that under the influence of his Indian friend Sankrityayan, Chopel was excoriating on the subject of British colonialism and the British themselves. 'Beware the race of golden-haired monkeys,' he wrote in a poem that condemned the British for 'Lacking the oil of compassion that benefits others'. Chopel's last years in India were spent in political intrigue back in Kalimpong. While the depth of his commitment to the Tibet Improvement Party is unclear, he did design its logo, which featured its name in Tibetan and Chinese. (The Chinese name was more upfront, translating as Tibet Revolutionary Party.) Pandatsang Rapga commissioned Gendun Chopel to return to Lhasa via a roundabout route and along the way make maps and notes of the border with British India, information that would be passed on to the Kuomintang. That may be what landed Chopel in hot water.

Hugh Richardson also knew what was happening; an informant told him that Rapga had put in a print order for party membership cards. The Tibetans demanded Ragpa be extradited, but Chiang Kai-shek had given him a Chinese passport and he fled to Shanghai. The unlikely charge the Tibetan authorities made against Gendun Chopel, meanwhile, was distributing counterfeit money; he was inter-rogated, lashed, given a three-year sentence and thrown in the grim Shol prison at the foot of the Potala. Even then, the lamas still wanted his scholarship, giving him writing materials so he could continue working. While in Lhasa he produced his most famous work, the *Adornment for Nagarjuna's Thought*, a treatise on *madhyamaka*, or 'middle way', philosophy, although only those with a working knowledge of the Geluk school of Buddhism can properly appreciate its brilliance. His sense of humour never left him, though, nor his love of verse. On the wall of the cell he left an impish poem:

> May the wise regard as an object of compassion
> The small truthful child left all alone
> In the wilderness where the frightening roar resounds
> Of the stubborn tiger drunk on the blood of envy.

When the People's Liberation Army came he advised Tibet's youth to go to China for a decent education and then modernise the country. Chopel died of alcoholism in 1951.

*

If the Tibet Improvement Party was tinged with the half-bored resentment of the aristocrat in exile, Tibet's communists proved much more direct. The central figure in the party was Baba Phuntsok Wangyal, his name often abbreviated to Phunwang, born in the eastern Kham town of Batang in 1922, a place beyond the political reach of the *kashag* government in Lhasa but very much part of the ethnic Tibetan world. He grew up a tall, bearish man, though highly intelligent and cultured, and was educated at a special academy in Nanjing in China, run by the Kuomintang's Mongolian and Tibetan Affairs Commission. In 1934, after war broke out between China and Japan, the school moved to the provisional Kuomintang capital at Chongqing and there he came into contact with communism. Chiang Kai-shek personally expelled Phunwang from the academy when his political affiliation was discovered. Aged eighteen and already mobilising Tibetan communists, he met Zhou Enlai, later the first prime minister of communist China under Chairman Mao. Phunwang's ambition was vast. While Gendun Chopel had been impressed at the scale of old Tibet's power, Phunwang envisaged recreating it: reuniting all the different parts of the Tibetan world, including Ladakh, and transforming its anachronistic feudal system into a modern socialist state.

Through much of the 1940s he was living in Lhasa, his house a talking shop for left-wing intellectuals and those aristocrats who wanted modernisation. At the same time he was running a guerrilla campaign against the Sichuan warlord Liu Wenhui, a thorn in the side of Tibetans in Kham since he allied with Ma Bufang in the 1930s to defeat the Tibetan army. (In fact, Liu Wenhui's alignment with the Kuomintang was nominal: he had given the communists an easy ride during the Long March, when they retreated into the interior from their bases in Jiangxi province, and would prove more than ready to switch sides when the communists took power.) The problem was nobody took Phunwang that seriously. When he went to Kalimpong to drum up British support for the Tibetan army against Liu Wenhui he had little success: the British were too busy planning their exit strategy to pay any attention. When his communist activities eventually got him expelled from Lhasa in 1949, the year that the communist party took control of China, he wrote to the editor of the *Mirror*, Gergan Tharchin, whom he had befriended while in Kalimpong: 'If the Tibetan government does not listen, I shall bring the [communist] Chinese Army to Tibet. Then I shall write to you.' That October, communists in eastern Kham held a public meeting in Phunwang's hometown of Batang to celebrate the founding of the People's Republic of China: Mao had triumphed in the civil war and his opponent Chiang Kai-shek was on the verge of fleeing to Taiwan. Phunwang made a speech and had the moment recorded on camera as he allied his small band of communists to the might of the Communist Party of China.

Early in 1950, a few weeks after his speech, Phunwang got a telegram from Zhu De, commander-in-chief of the People's Liberation Army, inviting him to Chongqing to discuss the 'practical questions of peacefully liberating Tibet'. Later that year he met Deng Xiaoping, then the party's secretary general, later Mao's successor as leader of the People's Republic from 1978, who described him as a

> very able man, has connections with upper class Tibetans, united a group of outstanding youths. An open communist in the Kham–Tibet region, fluent in Chinese, can read English books. Has basic knowledge of Marxism–Leninism and great power of understanding. Rare cadre among Tibetan nationalities. ... [We] have decided to order him to go with the PLA entering Tibet.

During the night of 6 and 7 October, the People's Liberation Army crossed the Jinsha river, the upper Yangtze, and moved with dazzling speed to isolate the main strength of the Tibetan army, poorly dug in around the border town of Chamdo. The Tibetan commander, Ngabo Ngawang Jigme, a deeply equivocal figure for many Tibetans, did not think his troops had any kind of chance against the Chinese. Some units fought bravely, but this limited engagement, at the cost of a few hundred lives, far from the capital Lhasa, constituted the extent of Tibet's military opposition. On 19 October Ngabo surrendered and negotiations for the wider surrender began. When the

Chinese marched into Lhasa in 1951 Phunwang sent Tharchin a telegram: 'Safely arrived in Lhasa Phuntsok Wangyal.'

Not surprisingly, many Tibetans came to regard Phunwang as a traitor but his role and eventual fate would reveal him as a patriot, one who would pay dearly for his commitment to the Tibetan people's cause. In 1957, during Mao's short-lived Hundred Flowers Campaign, a neat trick to flush out his enemies by inviting them to express their complaints and suggestions, Phunwang had suggested administrative changes in Kham that would address resentments there that were fuelling the Tibetan guerrilla war against communist rule then underway; it was a way of addressing the discrimination meted out against those who were not ethnically Han Chinese, chauvinism that Mao said he was keen to attack. The following summer Phunwang got a call from his boss ordering him to Beijing. There he was denounced. Han chauvinism, it transpired, had given way to a new evil: local nationalism. Phunwang had been a loyal senior cadre with the ear of the Dalai Lama. He had been the Dalai Lama's interpreter in Beijing and before that had worked on the Seventeen-Point Agreement that had followed the 1950 invasion. But like any bureaucracy, the communist party was a career path best suited to those who kept their heads down. In 1960, this experienced and capable man was put in solitary confinement in Beijing's notorious Qincheng prison (where the Tiananmen Square leaders were later incarcerated) for eighteen years. When Phunwang was finally released, several years after Mao's death, his daughter recalled her father drooling from the side of his mouth. In his mid eighties he wrote a series of powerful essays, including open letters to the Chinese president Hu Jintao, detailing China's flawed policies in Tibet and calling for the return of the Dalai Lama.

Phuntsok Wangyal and Gendun Chopel were both punished for their opposition to Tibet's *kashag* government: Chopel with imprisonment and Phunwang with banishment. Tibet's theocratic regime saw itself as synonymous with the state. Reform had been difficult enough before the war, when China was weak; it was impossible to contemplate structural change during a period of existential crisis. During 1949, as the Kuomintang faced defeat, the *kashag* took steps to distance itself from all brands of Chinese hegemony. A list was drawn up of communist sympathisers, among them Phunwang, who were expelled.

At the same time, the Kuomintang's representatives, who had arrived in 1934 under the pretext of the death of the thirteenth Dalai Lama, were told to pack their bags and leave. There was justified concern that elements of this group would happily switch sides when the communists won, giving Mao a de facto presence in Lhasa from the start.

An editorial in China's *Xinhua Daily* dismissed the move as 'a plot undertaken by local Tibetan authorities at the instigation of the British imperialists and their lackey, the Nehru administration of India'. As the editorial continued, rooting out the Kuomintang was 'the business of the Chinese people in their revolutionary struggle under the leadership of the Chinese Communist Party'. It was no business of foreign countries. Accusations of foreign interference have remained an unbroken thread in China's narrative about Tibet, a spectre from the Opium Wars and China's colonial humiliation, useful in generating a shared sense of national outrage. It was true that Hugh Richardson stayed on in Lhasa as an employee of the Indian government and likely had some influence on the *kashag*'s action. And it is undeniable that, like the Rana dynasty in Nepal, Tibet turned, with increasing desperation, to the international community as an answer to the new realities of postcolonial Asia. But this was done by force of circumstance, not least the rise of an anti-religious communist party in China, rather than because Tibet had been duped into self-harm by a Western imperial puppet-master.

*

In 1949, India's political officer in Sikkim was Harishwar Dayal, a rising diplomatic talent in his mid thirties married to the former Indian tennis star Leela Row. (He would later serve as India's ambassador to Nepal but collapsed and died there while trekking in the Everest region.) Dayal was regarded as sympathetic to the Tibetans. His predecessor, the last British political officer of Sikkim Arthur Hopkinson, had written to Eric Bailey, now in retirement at Stiffkey in Norfolk, birdwatching and writing up his life's adventures: 'At first the [Indian National] Congress were showing signs of completely selling out the Tibs [sic], but we persistently combated this.' Dayal promised to supplement arms and ammunition deliveries already made by the government of India to Tibet but stressed the importance of training. Little had changed since Basil Gould's mission in 1936, when Brigadier Philip Neame, the only man ever to earn a Victoria Cross *and* an Olympic gold medal, gave a devastating indictment of Tibetan military capability:

> The Tibetan Government has absolutely no idea of military organisation, administration or training. The military authorities, even if they had the knowledge, have no power to apply it. The troops are untrained, unreliable, and unpopular with the country. ... In fact, it is justifiable to say that, except for the fact that they possess a certain number of modern weapons, which few of them know how to use, the army has advanced but little from its condition in 1904.

When Neame attended a drill exhibition staged for him in Lhasa, he discovered that none of the soldiers on parade had fired their guns for six years. He drew up a list of proposals to modernise the army. By the summer of 1949, Heinrich Harrer reported, the 'flat pasture lands around Lhasa were transformed into training grounds', but it was far too late to be fixing the roof: the storm was upon them.

With Tibet's military ill prepared to deal with the battled-hardened People's Liberation Army, the best hope for an independent Tibet lay with diplomacy and an appeal to the outside world. In 1948 a trade mission was sent to Britain and the United States. (This gave the delegates foreign visa stamps in Tibetan passports, which were held up as naïvely hopeful evidence of Tibet's independent status.) As we have seen, the sudden rush towards a world that had for so long been kept at arm's length was startling – and not just for the world's mountaineers. The Tibetan government asked Heinrich Harrer to monitor foreign news stations for references to Tibet, and in January 1950 Radio Lhasa made its first broadcast, a half-hour news bulletin in Tibetan, Chinese and English, the latter read by Reginald Fox, one of two British radio engineers working for the Tibetan government on equipment donated by the United States. The other British operator was an ex-air force engineer from Burton-on-Trent called Robert Ford. In the summer of 1949 he left Lhasa to establish a radio link with the eastern province of Kham and help train the Tibetan army for the coming invasion. He was still there when the People's Liberation Army arrived, and spent the next five years in a Chinese prison in fear of his life, an illustration of how Britain's former influence in the region had crumbled to nothing.

In the autumn of 1949, an engineer from General Electric called J E Reid spent seven weeks in Lhasa to assess the potential for a new hydroelectric scheme. He reported the Tibetan government 'had suddenly awoken to the reality of the dangers which threatened it and is now regretting its past policy of keeping aloof'. The Lhasa government now wanted 'full world publicity' and to that end had hosted the journalist Lowell Thomas, who seven years later was in Kathmandu for Mahendra's coronation. He came bearing inappropriate gifts for the Dalai Lama: an ivory cigarette holder and a wastepaper basket made from an elephant's foot. When Thomas left, he was given a letter to forward to president Harry Truman expressing friendship and seeking recognition.

Tibet knew of the growing influence of the United States: the thirteenth Dalai Lama had met US ambassador William Rockhill while in exile following the British invasion of 1904. War with Japan had galvanised that relationship. The loss in 1942 of the Burma Road, linking modern Myanmar with south-west China, meant the Allies had to resupply their forces in China by air from India, flying to Kunming in Yunnan over the eastern Himalaya, which pilots dubbed the 'Hump'. This was dangerous and costly of material, so the Office of Strategic Services mooted the idea of a motor road across Tibet. Despite the State Department's misgivings, the OSS got permission to send two intelligence officers from India to survey a potential route to Lhasa. They would then continue via Jyekundu in Kham to General 'Vinegar Joe' Stilwell's command in Chongqing.

In December 1942, the two OSS officers reached Lhasa: Captain Ilya Tolstoy, grandson of the novelist, and Lieutenant Brooke Dolan, who had visited Tibet as a naturalist before the war with the German ornithologist and future SS officer Ernst Schäfer. They carried with them a letter from Franklin D Roosevelt dated 3 July, which explained how 'the United Nations are fighting today in defense of and for preservation of freedom'. (The United Nations Declaration had been signed on New Year's Day that year by the 'four policemen': the US, the UK, the Soviet Union and nationalist China.) Tolstoy made a good impression on the Tibetan leadership. When he discovered they wanted communications equipment, he arranged for it to be delivered; it was these transmitters that began broadcasting Radio Lhasa in early 1950. Tolstoy also suggested that Tibet might like to attend the peace conference planned for the end of the war. The head of the British mission in Lhasa in late 1942 was the former Gyantse schoolteacher and naturalist Frank Ludlow, through long association a deep Tibetophile: on behalf of the government of India, he promised the Tibetans to 'do all in my power to help'. Neither man had the authority to make such promises and Tolstoy realised he had overstepped the mark. Roosevelt's letter had only been written with the express proviso that it didn't recognise Tibetan independence. With the war far from won, the Americans didn't want to annoy their Chinese allies.

However ill founded the promises, the Tibetan Foreign Affairs Bureau leapt at the prospect of attending a post-war peace conference. The foreign minister was an aristocrat called Surkhang Wangchen Gelek, who told his visitors that

> Tibet owed her present independence entirely to Great Britain [and that the] Tibetan Government had always placed implicit trust in Britain's good faith and had never found this trust misplaced.

This was disingenuous; many Tibetan aristocrats were Anglophile but they weren't fools. Even so, they must have been disheartened at how quickly the colonial administration in Delhi disowned the suggestion. Ludlow was instructed to tell the Tibetan government that this idea was his own and not the policy of the government of India. Then he was replaced. An official in London noted: 'I hope that the Tibetans' childlike trust in Britain's good faith will not prove to be misplaced – but I do not feel too much confidence.'

The British government did consider openly supporting Tibetan independence. Contemplating a postcolonial world, a Foreign Office report written in the spring of 1943 was blunt about how China would spin a future occupation of Tibet:

> The Chinese are the least sentimental and altruistic of nations but they are shrewd propagandists and have been clever enough to present their aspirations as an unselfish desire to secure for their neighbours the same freedom from foreign imperialism that they themselves desire.

Some kind of obligation, the report suggested, could be handed on to a future independent government of India to secure Tibet's borders against China. In the end, it was deemed prudent not to antagonise China, an ally against Japan. The assumption was made that 'China is bound to absorb Tibet at the end of the war if not before,' and in the event of Indian independence, Britain could do little for Tibet. It would be 'a poor service to the Tibetans to encourage them against the Chinese now'. When the communists announced their intention to invade, Clement Attlee's government sat on its hands. More than forty years later, in 1987, Robert Barnett, later a noted Tibet activist and academic, watched the anti-China demonstrations that tore through Lhasa that year, the first witnessed by Westerners. He was taken to meet a senior monk and asked the monk if he had a message that Barnett could deliver to his government.

> 'Which government is that?' he asked.
> 'The British,' I explained.

> He wasn't crying anymore and he seemed composed. He thought a little and then, almost imperceptibly, he shook his head. And then he said, 'The British betrayed us in the past and will betray us in the future.'

They had and they would. In 2008, with the Beijing Olympics fast approaching, Tibet erupted into violence once again, four days after 10 March, the anniversary of the 1959 uprising. The death toll is disputed, but dozens died, Han and Tibetan. (Chinese media, wanting to highlight innocent Chinese victims, called them the 3/14 riots, an echo of 9/11.) Thousands of Tibetans were detained and by June Amnesty International reported a thousand were still being held, their whereabouts unknown. Four Tibetans were eventually executed for their role in the rioting. That November, as talks between the Dalai Lama's envoys and Beijing to calm the situation concluded, the British foreign secretary David Miliband announced that Britain was changing its policy towards Tibet. It no longer regarded China as merely having suzerainty over Tibet, a fossil from the Simla Accord of 1914, but instead recognised Tibet as part of China. The word 'sovereignty' wasn't used, but that was the implication. The only weapon of value left from Britain's colonial war chest was tossed away for no discernible gain.

★

In 1947, when Nehru became the first prime minister of an independent India, he was uncertain how to deal with Tibet. There was antipathy to the regime in Lhasa, which was viewed as out of date and socially restrictive. The notion of 'buffer states' was part of the fast-receding tide of British imperialism. Zhou Enlai told India's new ambassador Madhava Panikkar that the 'liberation' of Tibet was China's 'sacred duty', as though Tibet was a little Asian brother in need of a helping hand. Compared to Beijing's focussed resolve, Delhi seemed distracted. Although in 1949 Harishwar Dayal had been supportive during his time as political officer of Sikkim, he was pessimistic that India would do anything meaningful to stop China absorbing Tibet. When China did invade the following year he sent a despairing memo suggesting India occupy the Chumbi valley north of Sikkim, a smart idea that was wholly ignored.

Given that China's ally the Soviet Union was a member of the UN Security Council, Lhasa's ambition to join the United Nations could get nowhere. Krishna Menon, India's ambassador at the UN and high commissioner to the United Kingdom, told the British that Panikkar had advised India to 'wash her hands completely of Tibet'. Lhasa continued to look hopefully towards the United States, where fear of communism was now driving foreign policy. The Americans were sympathetic, but were guided by India and Britain, and needed the Tibetans to declare themselves anti-communist. That was something the *kashag* was reluctant to do with a communist army of some forty thousand gathering strength on Tibet's eastern border. Only later, as insurgent opposition to China's occupation grew from the mid 1950s, did America provide covert funding for the rebel group Chushi Gangdruk, meaning Four Rivers, Six Ranges, the historic name for its region of origin, Kham.

China, watching these attempts at international legitimacy, proved adept at exploiting dissension within Tibet. In January 1950, the Xinhua News Agency released a telegram sent to Mao in the name of the Panchen Lama, then at Kumbum monastery in Qinghai, asking for Chinese troops 'to liberate Tibet, to wipe out reactionaries, expel the imperialists'. The tenth Panchen Lama was not yet twelve; his 'statement' reflected long-standing friction between his followers in Shigatse and the government in Lhasa. The scholar Sherab Gyatso, also in Qinghai, warned Tibetans during a broadcast in June not to trust 'British and American imperialist slander aimed at sowing discord between nationalities'. China under the Qing had at times proved a useful lever in Tibetan politics. Why shouldn't Mao?

When the Dalai Lama fled to India in 1959, the Panchen Lama became the most senior religious leader still in Tibet and a useful ally for China. But in 1962, having toured Tibet and seen how communisation was tearing apart the monastic system and the practice of Buddhism itself, the Panchen Lama delivered a devastating indictment of the party's policies in Tibet, known as the 'Seventy Thousand Character Petition'. He warned that poverty had worsened, the population was decreasing and communist reform was failing. Zhou Enlai, China's prime minister, was sympathetic, but as the situation across China deteriorated, attitudes within the party hardened. Mao dubbed the Panchen Lama's petition a 'poisoned arrow' and he was denounced and imprisoned in Qincheng – with the communist Phuntsok Wangyal. At least the Panchen was hidden away in the relative safety of a jail cell when the Cultural Revolution began. In 1968, Mao's Red Guards smashed Sherab Gyatso's leg so badly he died of the injury.

In September 1950, Hugh Richardson left Lhasa for the last time.

That was the season of the annual parties that are held there; everybody was taking it easy, and they had their eyes only on the course of negotiations which had just begun between their representatives and the new Chinese ambassador. At all events, no one was prepared – apparently not even the Chinese ambassador in India – for the invasion of Tibet by Chinese troops about 7 October 1950.

Six days later, Mao sent two hundred thousand troops into Korea, and Tibet's plight was lost in the shadows of that titanic confrontation.

*

Sixty-six years after China's invasion, I stood on a terrace in the Jokhang, Tibet's most sacred temple, looking down on pilgrims prostrating themselves on flagstones at the temple's door, polished to a bright sheen by countless generations before them. During the Cultural

Revolution the courtyard beneath my feet had been converted into a pigsty and later a guest house before being rather haphazardly restored following Mao's death. It is, though, one of the few parts of the city of Lhasa that Hugh Richardson would still recognise. When he lived there, the city had a population of around thirty thousand. Now it's home to something like ten times that number. Lhasa as Richardson knew it, or at least its street plan, is now its central kernel: the old city, dominated by Tibetans. The rest is pretty much like any other big Han Chinese town. He would, I imagine, be gratified to see so many geraniums, a flower he introduced, being nurtured by the city's gardeners. And to see so many trees in the city, shading new wide boulevards in areas that were pasture when he was here, although they hardly compensate for the unregulated plundering of southern Tibet's forests for China's construction industry.

When I first came to Lhasa, more than twenty years ago, the old Tibetan houses round the Barkhor, the street that circles the Jokhang, were being torn down. It was agonising to watch. Han Suyin had boasted in 1975 that 'beautiful old houses belonging to Tibetan nobility are being kept, cleaned and repaired'. The opposite was true. Houses were left to rot and become unsafe, easing their eventual demolition in favour of modern concrete. Tibet had almost no industry when I first arrived but cement was an exception. In the 1990s Lhasa was still dominated by vast cement factories that poisoned their workers. People, admittedly mostly children, still defecated in the street. Now it's much cleaner, a modern and far more prosperous town than it had been under Mao. There's a hi-tech, high-altitude railway bringing millions of Chinese tourists. The Barkhor is no longer a demolition site, but a smart arcade of shops, which often surprises Western tourists, some of whom may wonder if that's appropriate in *Lha sa*, the place of the gods. In fact, commerce was always part of the pilgrim's experience. It was how the monks made their money.

Walking the circuit at dusk, the smell of juniper smoke hanging in the air, you are still surrounded by Tibetans muttering prayers and spinning prayer wheels. It's rather special to share in what feels like an intense community spirit, although it is always rash to make assumptions in this contested city. As the activist–academic Robert Barnett put it:

A foreigner always has limited access to the associations that hover around the streets and buildings of another people's city, but in Tibet even visitors fluent in the language are left to guess whether their more political conceptions are shared by local people.

Ordinary Tibetans at the entrances to the Barkhor seemed fairly resigned to being searched for lighters, a consequence of the self-immolation campaign, and having their bags put through X-ray machines. But I couldn't tell how they really felt and I wasn't about to ask. Among the biggest changes between my first visit to Tibet in 1995 and my last in 2016 was the breadth and depth of surveillance the state has managed to achieve. The vehicle I travelled in was required to download its satellite-tracking data to the police. Far from Lhasa, I'd watched new security cameras being installed on gantries across the highway. I revisited remote villages where twenty years ago there had been little evidence of the state. Now there was a small police station. The tendrils of the state reach ever deeper and further. Cash machines have been installed with face-recognition software and there are plans to do the same with Lhasa's taxis. In the future, China will surveille how Tibetans walk, using gait-recognition software, a more accurate system even than reading their faces.

Technologies like this might have something to offer citizens whose rights are protected by independent judiciaries. In China, they look like paranoia: the tools of a colossal polity anxious about the limits of its control. As an issue, Tibet has become a useful resource for Chinese nationalists. No government call for national unity against the Dalai Lama's splittist intrigues goes unheeded, as posts from ordinary citizens on China's social media testify. Chinese people are welcome to express their outrage when former colonial powers lecture China on internal matters. No communist party cadre prospers arguing for a more tolerant line. In the West, Tibet is almost synonymous with Buddhism, a philosophically rich alternative to the environmentally destructive consumerism China has used to transform its economy. In China, the Dalai Lama and Tibet's government in exile are inflammatory reminders of China's humiliation at the hands of greedy imperialists.

There are around six million Tibetans living in the Tibet Autonomous Region and the various autonomous prefectures with Tibetan populations. That's some 0.4 per cent of China's population, in a quarter of its territory. In the last seventy years China has starved, murdered, tortured, imprisoned, bribed, and marginalised Tibetans. This systematic hostility hasn't stopped them from wanting to remain Tibetan, just as the Chinese feel no less Chinese for having also endured the horrors of Mao's famine and the Cultural Revolution. Identity, it turns out, is not, as Mao believed, a tap; you cannot reach inside someone else's mind and turn it off. In the letters Baba Phuntsok Wangyal wrote to the former president of China Hu Jintao, in which he made a cogent socialist argument for real autonomy for Tibet within a sovereign China and the return of the Dalai Lama, he finished with a warning: 'Comrade Jintao, a single matchstick is enough for the arsonist, but putting out the fire would take a great effort.' Baba Phuntsok died aged ninety-two at the end of March 2014. That month three more young Tibetans had burned themselves to death.

20

Claiming Chomolungma

It was gloomy in Liz Hawley's Kathmandu apartment but nicely so, a drowsy refuge from the hot pre-monsoon sun and the chaos outside in Dilli Bazar. Everything was precisely arranged, the papers on her desk and the cushions on chairs that looked severe but were surprisingly comfortable. This was in 2015, when Liz was ninety-one. When I met her first in the mid 1990s, she was like one of the city's sparrows, flitting busily between hotels to meet the leader of every climbing expedition in town, recording what they planned to do and afterwards what they had or had not done, before jumping in her sky-blue Volkswagen to move on to the next one. And like the city's sparrows, crowded out these days by construction and pollution, Liz was nearing the end. She was frail, and cross about it, but pushed this unwelcome development aside with a wry twist of her mouth. When she sank onto a small sofa across from me, her face became lost in the shadows but her voice was as firm as ever. I closed my eyes and listened.

Liz was reminiscing about B P Koirala, the Nepali prime minister whom King Mahendra had arrested and imprisoned in December 1960, not long after she settled in Kathmandu and began stringing for American news outlets. She had planned to go trekking with B P that month to write him up for *Life* magazine: Nepal's democratic visionary in the mountains of his homeland. Her story about him had had to wait more than twenty years. In July 1982 she was at Bangkok airport for her flight to Kathmandu, heading home from her annual trip to see her mother, when she spotted B P's brother Girija at the airline's desk. B P, she discovered, had been told his throat cancer was out of control and Girija was taking him back to Nepal to die. He was laid on the floor in business class and Liz spent the flight making notes for an article, going forward to check facts with both of them. B P died that night, even before Liz had finished her piece, which she filed with Reuters. At the age of fifty-eight, she'd made the front page of the *New York Times*.

Despite half a century in Nepal, you could still hear New England in her voice, an accent her mother had been determined Liz acquire after her years as a young girl in the Midwest. Her manner was direct and rather grand and could topple into rudeness. I liked to imagine Liz in 1950s Manhattan, on her way from her Midtown apartment up Fifth Avenue to the Rockefeller Center, where she worked for eleven years as a researcher for *Fortune* magazine: a formidable background in the sanctity of facts but also the glass ceiling for a woman in that era. Realising this and becoming a little bored, in her mid thirties she elected to travel for a while and do some reporting. Nepal was at first one more stop on a long itinerary that began with observing communism in Eastern Europe and the Soviet Union, then afterwards Beirut, where she met the double agent Kim Philby and his father John, who had known her hero, the great Middle East explorer Gertrude Bell. In Cairo, she climbed the Great Pyramid by moonlight. Karachi was just another ugly South Asian city that had grown too fast; Kathmandu, when she arrived in February 1959, was a peaceful contrast, green and beautiful, 'a kind of fairy-tale mirage' as Liz described it, the myth of 'timeless Asia'.

In Delhi she had picked up an assignment from *Time* magazine's bureau to cover Nepal's first general election, which B P Koirala won handsomely. Mahendra had agreed to the vote reluctantly and only because he was sure it would result in a divided parliament he could easily dominate. Liz moved among Nepal's political elite with Cyril Dunn of *The Observer* and Elie Abel, a friend from the *New York Times* who as Delhi correspondent would cover the Lhasa Uprising that spring. It all seemed so much more exciting than researching other peoples' stories in the archives of *Fortune*. When she got back to New York, she wandered round Union Square eating a chocolate sundae and watching the crowds. 'This is great,' she told herself, 'but it's not the real world.' She imagined herself instead in Nepal, 'a place where you can see what the world is becoming'. A place also where she could live cheaply and still employ staff: stretch out a little. Eighteen months after her first visit, and with a couple of freelance contracts in her pocket, Hawley was back in Kathmandu, this time for good.

She had chosen an auspicious moment to set up as a journalist and researcher in the Himalaya. During her absence, following China's ruthless crackdown in the aftermath of the Lhasa Uprising of March 1959, tension had risen steadily. Nehru had offered shelter to the Dalai Lama but not much else – certainly negligible political support – believing as a consequence he could ride out China's annoyance without damaging his strategic interests. He was wrong about this. Beijing was infuriated when the Dalai Lama was allowed to give a press conference from his Indian exile. Despite his youth, he was showing himself to be a capable political leader and began to attract positive global media attention. Mao was struggling in the spring of 1959 with the negative consequences of the Great Leap Forward; Nehru had pressed on an open wound, pain that was reflected in aggressive anti-Nehru articles in the *People's Daily*, personally overseen by Mao: 'The Indian big bourgeoisie maintains innumerable links with imperialism,' the paper warned. Any goodwill generated from India's acceptance in 1954 of China's rule of Tibet evaporated. Nehru's response was that of a disappointed teacher:

> I have been greatly distressed at the tone of the comments and the charges made against India by responsible people in China. They have used the language of the cold war regardless of truth and propriety.

Such loftiness annoyed China; Zhou Enlai told Henry Kissinger in 1973 that China wanted 'to keep down his [Nehru's] cockiness'. The joke in India was how the optimistic slogan *Hindi-Chini bhai bhai*, the 'Indians and Chinese are brothers', had been replaced with 'Hindi-Chini bye-bye'.

If Tibet provoked this tension, as Mao later told Nepali diplomats, the Himalayan border between China and India was the trigger for conflict. After the communists came to power in 1950, Chinese maps started showing large tracts of the Himalaya, whose borders had been regarded as settled for generations, now belonging to the People's Republic. In south-west Xinjiang, cadres who met inhabitants of Ladakh, until then an Indian region, told them their home was now also part of China. In 1953, to link the remote western province of Xinjiang with Tibet, China began driving a road across the Aksai Chin, desolate country north-east of Ladakh that Delhi regarded as within the Indian state of Jammu and Kashmir. The following year, India and China had signed a treaty legitimising China's position in Tibet, the preamble of which is famous for articulating Nehru's 'five virtues', the basis for India's peaceful coexistence with foreign powers. Mao read this as complacency, a gift China could exploit, and the communists continued with their plans: the road was completed in 1957. In fact, American and presumably Indian intelligence had known about it from the start, thanks to spy networks in Kashgar, but Nehru, mindful of his earlier pronouncements about socialism and the rise of Asia, kept the road's existence a secret from the Indian people; as late as April 1959, even after the Lhasa Uprising, Nehru was still denying the Aksai Chin road crossed Indian territory.

Although after 1950 there were Chinese troops in Gartok in western Tibet, many regions of the Tibetan Himalaya, including Dingri, north of Everest, saw little of the communists in the following years. That changed after the Lhasa Uprising, as units of the People's Liberation Army arrived to restore order. Facing them in India were lightly armed border forces. With gathering speed, China's true intentions in the Himalaya were revealed. On 26 August 1959 there was an exchange of fire between Chinese and Indian troops at Longju on the McMahon Line in the eastern Himalaya and an Indian soldier was captured. Chinese troops had made incursions across the border before but the Indian public got to hear about this one, raising the political temperature. Then a letter arrived in Delhi from Zhou Enlai laying claim to 130,000 square kilometres of Indian territory in the Himalaya. ('I must frankly say,' Nehru replied, 'that your letter of 8 September has come as a great shock to us.') Indian patrols were ordered along the Ladakh frontier, even though Nehru had explicitly prohibited them, and a group of Indian reserve police officers were ambushed near the Kongka La, roughly a hundred and sixty kilometres east of Leh. There was a brief, dramatic stand-off, as the Indian officer Karam Singh stooped to pick up a handful of dirt and let it fall from his hand, implying this was Indian soil. The Chinese officer did the same. (The irony was that this territory had once been part of a greater Tibet and was still culturally Tibetan.) Then Chinese heavy machine guns opened up from the hillside opposite, catching the Indians in a deadly crossfire. Eleven policemen died, one from untreated wounds; others were captured, including Karam Singh, who was tortured into signing a confession that the Indians had been on Chinese territory and were consequently responsible for the violence.

The impact of these killings on Indian public opinion was immense; crowds of protestors demanded that the defence minister Krishna Menon, a pro-China influence, should resign. Nehru ordered that the Indian army take over responsibility for the border, authorising outposts north of the McMahon Line, bullishly staking India's claim without committing the forces necessary to discourage an attack. The Chinese would cleverly spin this 'forward policy', with its echoes of Curzon and the British, into a hostile act: previously, they argued, colonial-era borders in Ladakh to the west and Tawang in the east had robbed China of its possessions; now China simply wanted what already belonged to her.

Throughout the summer of 1962, skirmishes and encounters raised the temperature but until the last moment Indian strategists discounted a full-blown conflict. Even so, on 20 October 1962, with negotiations stalled and using the Cuban missile crisis as cover, the PLA attacked on two fronts, east and west: Indian positions north of the disputed town of Tawang were overrun and the inhabitants evacuated. The Indian army dug in around the pass of Se La. At the other end of the Himalaya, Chinese troops drove out those Indian troops still in the Aksai Chin and swept into eastern Ladakh, surrounding army posts that were insufficiently manned or supported to resist. After four days, China had secured its objectives in what appeared to British observers to be a limited border skirmish. There was no declaration of war and negotiations for a settlement were soon underway as Zhou Enlai wrote to Nehru offering terms.

President Kennedy was alive to the dangers of China's invasion, wondering aloud 'which crisis [the Indian or the Cuban] would be the more significant in the long run'. In the immediate aftermath, however, the existential threat to the United States meant it was left to Kenneth Galbraith, American ambassador in Delhi, and the National Security Council staffer Robert Komer to develop US policy in regard to the Sino-Indian war. When fighting resumed, on Nehru's birthday, with an Indian attack on Chinese positions at Walong in eastern Arunachal Pradesh, the Chinese retaliated with an assault on the Indians at Se La and in Ladakh at Chushul, where huge superiority in numbers resulted in heavy Indian losses. Galbraith was amazed the following day when news of these reversals reached a panicked Delhi, 'the first time I have ever witnessed the disintegration of public morale'. Nehru appealed to the Americans for a dozen squadrons of jet fighters to drive back what was looking for a moment like a full-scale Chinese invasion, one that threatened 'not merely the survival of India, but the survival of free and independent governments in the whole of the sub-continent'. Despite Nehru's panic, China soon called a halt, happy with consolidating its position in the Aksai Chin and thus securing its new road. The Indian defence minister Krishna Menon quit and the Indian military began a period of rapid modernisation. The Americans tried to use the military aid they were now providing to India as leverage, hoping to force India into a resolution of the dispute with Pakistan over Kashmir. Delhi resented this, but soon afterwards China signed a deal with Pakistan recognising their mutual border, which undermined the Americans' strategy. This brief conflict, which cost a few thousand lives, many of them through the bitter conditions of the Himalaya, traumatised Sino-Indian relations for decades to come.

Galbraith, ignorant of the famine then unfolding in China, had been an admirer of Mao's economic reforms. He also considered the Tibetan resistance movement, Chushi Gangdruk, to be little more than 'dissident and deeply unhygienic tribesmen'; America's support for them was for Galbraith 'a particularly insane enterprise', a view shared by the CIA's Indian station chief Harry Rositzke. Discovery of American involvement would enrage Nehru and damage relations with India. It certainly annoyed Mao and Zhou, who assumed Nehru knew the CIA was training Tibetans to fight the Chinese. As it was, the supply of arms was insufficient and far below expectations. (The Dalai Lama's brother Gyalo Thondup, the link between Tibetan resistance fighters and the CIA, later wrote: 'Mao was not the only one to cheat the Tibetans. The CIA did, too.' This was true, but dodged Gyalo Thondup's own responsibility.) When China invaded India, Galbraith could come clean about the CIA's support for Tibetan rebels and fall in line with the strategy of the White House and Langley.

Even by the start of 1960, two years before China attacked India, Tibetan armed resistance to China's occupation had been in disarray. In the wake of the Dalai Lama's flight to India, the Chinese had cracked down on it with brutal intensity. Chushi Gangdruk's base at Lokha had been overwhelmed; fighters, including those trained by the CIA, had been killed or else fled, many to Kalimpong and Darjeeling, swelling the region's reputation as a crossroads for agitators and spies. Many of these men were put to work building roads in Sikkim. In Darjeeling, the leader of Chushi Gangdruk, Gonbo Tashi, a wealthy trader from the historically important Kham town of Litang, now in western Sichuan, called a meeting of his senior cohorts to discuss setting up a new base. Who it was that chose Mustang, a region in northern Nepal, as its location is disputed. Some historians believe it was the CIA's idea; they could lean on King Mahendra to turn a blind eye. Given the Americans were more interested in intelligence on China than liberating Tibet, Mustang had the advantage to the CIA of being within striking distance of the road the Chinese had built across southern Tibet, now designated the G219. If that was the case, it proved a shrewd choice; the following year, Chushi Gangdruk fighters captured highly sensitive information after a raid on this road from their Mustang base revealing plans for new troop deployments in Tibet as well as the rift in Sino-Soviet relations. For Tibetan fighters, although Mustang was inconveniently distant from Lhasa, it had advantages for them, too. The local Mustangis, essentially ethnic Tibetans, were supportive. Lhamo Tsering, deputy to the Dalai Lama's brother Gyalo Thondup and one of those the CIA had trained abroad, was put in charge of organising a base there. Gonbo Tashi, meanwhile, got on with recruitment and it didn't take Delhi long to figure out why hundreds of Tibetan road-workers in Sikkim were suddenly quitting their jobs. Yet even before this new Tibetan force arrived, tiny Mustang was the cause of an international incident that would embroil Nepal's young democracy.

*

The threats facing Nepal's new prime minister B P Koirala and his elected government were mostly domestic: principally, the king's faction and communist opponents. Yet China also worried him. Although he abstained from the vote at the United Nations in the autumn of 1959 that censured Beijing for its actions in Tibet, Koirala was instinctively pro-India and saw Nepal's future as closer to its southern neighbour. India, he said, should support Nepal's democratic experiment lest it wake up one day and find China in its backyard;

Beijing was already leaning on Koirala to allow them to extend Tibet's road network over the border to Kathmandu. The same Chinese maps worrying Delhi with their implied claim to large chunks of the Himalaya had alarmed the Nepali government as well. Among these were the entire Everest massif and the district of Khumbu, in which the Nepali portion of Everest is located. This affront to national dignity prompted demonstrations in Kathmandu, where many believed the whole peak, not just the south side, was Nepal's. A mountain no one in the capital had heard of a century earlier was now a piece on Asia's strategic chessboard.

By 1960, China understood the political value of Everest very well, thanks in large part to mountaineers from the Soviet Union. Climbing had been an elite pastime in Tsarist Russia and after the Revolution in 1917 mountaineers had needed to work hard to create a proletarian framework strong enough to convince the Soviet authorities. During the 1920s, alpinism became a kind of socialist ideal, a team without individuals prepared to face anything to succeed. After the Second World War, as competitive sport became a cultural front in the Cold War, climbing was made more conventionally competitive, garnering not only the state's permission but its funds. Despite this conformity, Russian mountaineers weren't trusted to travel abroad and remained isolated within the mountains of the Soviet Union.

That began to change in 1953 with the death of Stalin and the ascent of Everest. At first, the Soviet Union ignored the success of Ed Hillary and Tenzing Norgay, but ordinary Russians were interested and journalists had eventually to find an acceptable line on this imperialist success. In 1954, the sports journalist Evgeny Simonov solved the problem by showering praise on the Sherpas: 'Innocent and honest, enduring and fulfilling their deed to the last! Such are these sons of the mountains.' Tenzing had shown 'what new powers are maturing among the people of rising Asia'. Tenzing's role allowed Simonov to stress a timely political message, of how the Soviet Union was helping Asia throw off the shackles of colonialism. Despite the word 'Everest' having been in common usage throughout the 1930s, Russian writers began using the indigenous 'Chomolungma', the name preferred by China in its Sinicised form 'Qomolangma'. Khrushchev had authorised a colossal aid effort to China, building industrial and military capacity, and sport was part of the relationship.

In 1955, Russian climbers introduced the Chinese to mountaineering on Soviet turf, first in the Caucasus and then at high altitude in the Pamirs of Central Asia. A year later the two countries organised an expedition to the Chinese province of Xinjiang, climbing Muztagh Ata and Kongur Tiube, both over seven and a half thousand metres. The encounter between these two groups is instructive. In theory, they had the same political ideology but it was clear to the Russians that they were at different stages of their journey. 'When I looked at them more closely,' one of the Soviet climbers recalled, almost forty years later,

> I understood that our brothers were not only no mountaineers, but no sportsmen at all. The party had directed them to this work front, strength and mountain experience had been replaced by political conviction and literacy by devotion to the party.

In May 1958, the All-Chinese Committee of Physical Culture and Sport extended an official invitation to Soviet alpinists to join them in an attempt on the north ridge of Everest, the same route taken by George Mallory and all the other British mountaineers before the war. At a meeting in Beijing it was agreed to try in the pre-monsoon season of the following year. The Russians, cautious about what they might find, suggested a reconnaissance that autumn. The Chinese promised to think about it and preparations got underway. With such a prize on offer, both governments threw considerable resources behind the project. Russian engineers began developing oxygen equipment and the People's Liberation Army started work on an unpaved road so trucks could bring supplies to base camp. In early October Beijing told the Russians that the reconnaissance was on.

On 23 October, Evgeny Beletsky, who had become famous climbing in the Pamirs before the war, and two colleagues, Lev Filimonov and Anatoly Kovyrkov, arrived in Lhasa, where unrest was building. The Russians reported meeting the deputy chair of China's Preparatory Committee of the Autonomous Region of Tibet, Zhang Guohua, who told them: 'The people here do not understand us.' They were warned of clashes between Chinese and Tibetans and instructed not to tell anyone they met what they were doing there. Even the expedition's Tibetan porters were hand picked from the communist youth league. The fear something might happen to their Russian guests was palpable. A very secret Everest team – three Russians, ten Chinese climbers, three meteorologists, four topographers, four radio operators and the ten porters – set off for Shigatse with a substantial military escort armed with mortars and grenades. The Chinese told the Russians that the Tibetans particularly feared the mortars since a soul leaving a body torn to pieces would not find peace.

At Shigatse they switched to pack animals, since the promised road was still under construction. Frustrated at the slow pace and with winter approaching, Beletsky raced ahead of the main column, to reach Rongbuk monastery at the foot of the mountain, where seventy monks were still in residence, on the brink of China's brutal suppression of monastic life. In just twelve days, Beletsky's small team was able to explore both approaches to the North Col; having photographed the key sections to the North Col himself, Beletsky began to descend and almost immediately discovered the body of one of the seven Sherpa and Tibetan porters who had died in 1922. Like many of the Russians, Beletsky didn't think much of using large numbers of porters in the mountains and didn't like the vast expedition the Chinese were proposing. Even so, as they left Rongbuk optimism was high about the prospects of the full attempt the following spring.

After a winter training camp, the Russian Everest team gathered in March at a leaving party in Moscow only to see their leader Kirill Kuzmin arrive, head bent, his eyes filled with tears. The Chinese had cancelled. No explanation was given and only later did the rest of the expedition learn of the Lhasa Uprising and the chaos in Tibet. China would extend another invitation to the Soviet climbers for the spring of 1960 but by then relations between Mao and Khrushchev were souring. Compounding the blow, that spring, the Chinese reported they had climbed Everest on their own.

According to their account, they struggled for hours to overcome the vertical cliff of the Second Step, the climber Qu Yinhua even taking off his boots and socks to try, all to no avail.

What was to be done? Turn back like the British climbers had done before? No! Certainly not! The whole Chinese people and the Party were watching us. The moment we thought of the big send-off we got at the Base Camp with the beating gongs and drums and loud

cheers, the solemn pledge we had taken before we started out, and the
national flag and the plaster bust of Chairman Mao which we took
along, we felt all powerful again.

Qu, still barefoot, stood on the shoulders of his companion Liu
Lianman, banged in a piton and hauled himself up, pulling his three
companions after him. Liu, now exhausted, remained behind while
Qu continued on with Wang Fuzhou and a Tibetan called Gonbu
leading the way into the gathering dark. It would take another eleven
hours to reach the summit, at 4.20 a.m. on 25 May. There were no
photographs – it was still dark – and the Maoist rhetoric, praising 'the
unrivalled superiority of the socialist system of our country' (as
opposed to that of the Soviet Union), undermined the plausibility of
official accounts; their former Russian climbing partners wouldn't
believe it. The frostbite was real enough, though: Qu lost all his toes
and six of his fingers. He received a hero's welcome in Beijing. Thirty
years later, when the former Soviet climber Evgeny Gippenreiter met
Gonbu, by then a sport official in the Tibet Autonomous Region, any
lingering scepticism was gone.

In March 1960, as Chinese and Tibetan climbers were beginning
their climb on Everest, B P Koirala travelled to Beijing for talks about
the border and China's claim on what the Nepalis regarded as their
territory. The Chinese were reasonably sympathetic. Both sides agreed
they would not allow troops within twenty kilometres of the border
and a boundary agreement was signed that was mutually acceptable.
Mao had not shown much concern about where the border ran, except
when it came to Everest. Mao wanted the summit to be common
ground, 'a friendship summit', but Koirala demurred, claiming the
whole mountain for Nepal. Mao pointed out that Nepal didn't even
have a name for Everest. In fact, a Nepali name did exist: Sagarmatha,
meaning 'one whose brow touches the sky'. The name had been offered
to the world in 1939 by the historian Baburam Acharya, who wrote an
article for the Nepali paper *Sharada* explaining that he had consulted
various locals and porters. That story was a fig leaf; Sagarmatha is a
deeply Sanskrit term and one coined to annoy the Ranas, which it did,
as being anti-British. Koirala struggled to recall the name 'Sagarmatha',
so pointed out to Mao that the Chinese didn't have a name either,
since 'Chomolungma' was Tibetan. Mao said: 'Tibet is China.'

In the end, Mao and Koirala agreed to split the mountain down the middle, although Koirala kept this news to himself when he returned to Kathmandu, knowing it would be unpopular. Only when Zhou Enlai returned the visit a few weeks later did the agreement to split Everest become clear. Soon after Zhou's visit came the news that Chinese climbers had reached the summit, infuriating Koirala: it was clear that even before negotiations were complete China had pressed ahead. In a news briefing, Koirala tried to reverse his position and claim the whole mountain for Nepal but it was too late. The new reality – that China could and would do as it pleased – was unanswerable, stoking fears of Chinese hegemony.

Then, a few weeks later at the end of June, the Indian military radio post in Mustang, part of the network of such stations that Nehru had demanded from Nepal after independence, sent a message from the local raja that a large group of Chinese troops was gathering across the border. China's ambassador in Delhi told the Nepali military they were on the hunt for Tibetan rebels. The Nepali officer attached to the Indian radio post sent an unarmed patrol, out of uniform, to assess the situation; a soldier was shot dead by Chinese troops and Kathmandu erupted in nationalistic anger.

*

These two events, the expedition to Everest and the fatal shooting in Mustang, coming as they did within weeks of each other, became linked in the minds of several historians. Was it simply coincidence or were they part of a pattern illustrating China's ability to control Nepal's borders as it saw fit? ('You cry murder even when we do nothing,' Mao had told Koirala, 'and no one believes our protestations. Everybody prefers to believe you, the smaller states.') Koirala responded to the crisis with calm authority, impressing the British ambassador with his leadership, while at the same time milking the situation for any political advantage over his opponents, the nationalist Gorkha Parishad party and the communists, who tended to side with China. Koirala had been regularly accused of being weak in foreign affairs, so his strong performance now was welcomed. In assessing Nepal's situation that year, the Foreign Office concluded: 'There is little doubt that this Government represents Nepal's best hope for the future.'

Koirala's administration certainly had its problems – a level of corruption, splits in his party and threats to public order – but Koirala had shown 'a welcome determination to tackle the difficult problems with which they are faced'. Unfortunately, his government proved short-lived. Koirala met regularly with Mahendra, who had a fascination with his prime minister's popularity as well as a fear of his agenda. 'Once,' Koirala wrote,

the king asked me to explain my aspiration. I told him they were to provide a standard of middle-class living, such as that of my family, for all the people. 'How long will that take?' he asked, and I replied that it would require me to win elections three times, and that I would work towards that.

Mahendra didn't give him the chance: in December 1960, only months after the shooting in Mustang, he had Koirala and his cabinet arrested, chopping down Nepal's democracy before it had spread its leaves.

Koirala, back in a prison cell, couldn't complain he hadn't been warned. In the early 1950s Mahendra had fallen out with his father Tribhuvan over whom to marry after the death of his first wife Indra. (This was more like a squabble between brothers than between father and son since both Mahendra's parents were only thirteen when he was born.) Indra had been a granddaughter of Juddha Shamsher, the autocratic maharaja who had done his best to smash political opposition and humiliate Tribhuvan into the bargain. Rather than choose, say, a royal princess from India's former princely states as his new wife, Mahendra chose to marry Indra's sister Ratna. He was aligning himself once more with the influential Rana dynasty from which Tribhuvan had wrested control of the country and which still dominated the army. Tribhuvan knew what this meant and refused to attend the wedding, so Mahendra had sent B P Koirala to persuade him. Tribhuvan was having none of it, telling Koirala that the royal family should sever all links with the Ranas. Later, when Koirala had left, Tribhuvan warned those around him: 'mark my words this crown prince will make you all sob; he will make you weep. I know him, and he will make you weep.'

In the weeks before he ousted Koirala, Mahendra had been in Britain. He and Queen Ratna stayed at Buckingham Palace for a lavish four-day state visit and then toured the country on Queen Elizabeth's royal train. His son Birendra, the fifteen-year-old crown prince, then at Eton, was given leave to accompany him. There were aircraft factories to inspect and agricultural centres, but the highlight was a visit to Oxford. Mahendra was angling for an honorary degree just like the one Chandra Shamsher had been given half a century before. Alas, Oxford was no longer so pliable and there was no Lord Curzon as chancellor to square things. To rub salt in the wound, the university invited Mahendra to inspect the collection of Sanskrit manuscripts Chandra had donated to the Bodleian Library and then take tea with Chandra's great-grandson Pashupati Shamsher. The Foreign Office thought this would be nice, since Pashupati and Queen Ratna were cousins, but there was a sour rivalry between the descendants of the two brothers Chandra and Juddha. (This rivalry would prove toxic. In June 2001, when the crown prince Dipendra massacred ten of his family, including his father Birendra and his mother Aishwarya, ordinary Nepalis knew the history: Aishwarya was a granddaughter of Juddha while Dipendra's girlfriend Devyani, whom he wanted to marry, was the daughter of Pashupati and thus a descendant of Chandra.)

Just before he left London in early November 1960, Mahendra had lunch at 10 Downing Street with the prime minister Harold Macmillan, at Queen Elizabeth's personal request. If Mahendra offered any clue to what he was planning when he got home there is no recorded hint of it. Those Nepali politicians he confided in warned Mahendra he might face a backlash from abroad; he should at least delay in case his grab for power jeopardised Queen Elizabeth's return visit planned for late February. As things turned out, almost no one, at home or abroad, turned a hair. The Nepali writer C K Lal noted how

> Not a dog barked in Kathmandu when Prime Minister B P Koirala, commanding a two-third majority in the parliament, was whisked away by the military from a public program of the youth wing of his party in the centre of the city.

The British were indifferent. Harold Macmillan loftily waved away concerns about Her Majesty visiting a king who had recently locked up a competent democratic government.

Queen Elizabeth's four-day visit was one of the first big stories Liz Hawley covered. Looking for a local human-interest angle, she wrote about a heavily pregnant Sherpa woman who had walked from Khumbu to Kathmandu to see the queen; she had stopped for a couple of hours along the way to give birth. (It was a boy, named Philip, after the Duke of Edinburgh.) Having made such a success of Mahendra's coronation, it was left to Boris Lissanevitch of the Royal Hotel to manage things: the horse-drawn carriages, the picnics and parades, and the tiger hunt. The latter involved more than three hundred elephants – 'nobody thought on the same scale as Boris' – which raised their trunks in salute one by one as the queen departed. Prince Philip, soon to become a founder member of the World Wide Fund for Nature, got round the expectation that he would personally kill a tiger by feigning a trigger-finger injury. (That didn't stop his aide Rear Admiral Christopher Bonham-Carter from bagging one, the foreign secretary Alec Douglas-Home having missed twice.) Newsreels showed Mahendra in his trademark dark sunglasses, like a despotic Roy Orbison, greeting the young queen; narrators revelled in the exotic clichés of Kathmandu – 'crossroads of Asia', 'land of contrasts' – but failed to mention how the vast crowds had so recently been denied their government. Newsreels showed the queen cruising in an open-top limousine through the fresh, unpolluted streets of Kathmandu waving at thousands of recently disenfranchised voters.

The people of Nepal had not forgotten their brief taste of democracy. If opposition to Mahendra's coup had been muted, it soon began to build. As the US ambassador Henry Stebbins pointed out, in getting rid of B P Koirala and the Nepali Congress, Mahendra had 'created a new set of problems' and had no real idea about how he might solve them. In October 1961, Mahendra was in China to sign the completed border agreement that Koirala had negotiated. Mahendra had a reputation for playing his vast neighbours off against each other, a policy he dubbed 'positive neutralism', but he went out of his way to avoid saying anything that might annoy the Indians further. Then, right at the end of the visit, Mahendra found himself bounced into agreeing to China's request to link Kathmandu and Tibet with a motor road: no road, no border agreement. If this was 'positive neutralism', Delhi didn't much like it. That same month an armed insurgency against Mahendra's regime was launched from inside India, formed from Nepali opposition parties that had joined forces to restore democracy. Mahendra was already contemplating compromise when India began an unofficial economic blockade in late September. He told his advisers he was prepared to release B P Koirala; they told him to wait for a couple of weeks.

Lucky Mahendra. On 20 October 1962 China launched its full military offensive on India's borders and in the aftermath of India's humiliation, Nehru suddenly needed a compliant Nepal. He switched off the insurgency and ended the blockade. Mahendra was free to promulgate his new constitution based on the ancient South Asian Panchayat system, 'the assembly of five': a system that left him entirely in control. Indian aid continued to flow into the country. B P was left to rot in jail.

To keep the Americans sweet, Mahendra burnished his anti-communist credentials by allowing Tibet's resistance fighters to maintain their base in Mustang, even travelling by helicopter to meet their leader Baba Yeshi. Kennedy reciprocated by making Nepal one of the first countries to receive Peace Corps workers. But while Chushi Gandruk managed a handful of raids inside Tibet, they were never enough of a threat to rupture Nepali relations with China. In early 1964, the *New York Times* reported that twelve thousand 'Nepalese farmhands' were hard at work carving out the Nepali side of the road to Lhasa, backed with Chinese money and expertise. There were two traditional trade routes through the Himalaya from Kathmandu, one up the Trisuli valley and through Kyirong, the other to the east, up the Bhote Kosi to the village of Kodari. When China asked Mahendra which of these they should survey, he chose the Bhote Kosi route, since the country was more difficult and the road would take longer to build. Chinese engineers moved at lightning speed, finishing their side of the road by 1963. Vehicles were using the road later that year and the whole of it was fully operational by the spring of 1967.

For the rest of his reign, which ended unexpectedly in early 1972 with a fatal heart attack, Mahendra was able to feed off the residual tension created by China's move against India. By 1968 he was confident enough of his position to release B P Koirala and his ally Ganesh Man Singh from prison, although B P soon escaped into exile when his political campaigning went too far. Mahendra's son Birendra was a milder king: his Nepal was a 'zone of peace', a gentler version of 'positive neutrality'. That didn't save his kingdom from the shifting tectonic plates of geopolitics. In 1972 President Nixon went to China to meet Mao and restore relations between their two countries. American support for Tibet was turned off like a tap. The following year, India's prime minister Indira Gandhi sent troops into Sikkim, at the invitation of the ethnically Nepali prime minister, to quell a rebellion there; the semi-independent kingdom was swallowed whole. The three-century rule of the *chogyal*, Sikkim's Tibetan monarchy that had once enraged the British Raj by capturing Joseph Hooker, was ended. Neighbouring dynasties in Bhutan and Nepal took careful note. Soon after, in June 1975, India itself was plunged into its own autocratic darkness, with Indira Gandhi's state of emergency, which allowed her to rule by decree and saw widespread human rights abuses. Dissidents like B P Koirala found they were no longer welcome, and he was forced to return to Kathmandu and face arrest.

Despite such setbacks, Nepal's course was a steady if slow return to democracy. Rapid population growth was filling the country with young people eager for change. The convulsive events of 1989, when Eastern Europe shrugged off decades of Soviet repression, galvanised Nepali opposition to the Panchayat rule imposed by Mahendra. Facing an Indian economic blockade and an irresistible popular uprising, the *jana andolan*, or 'people's movement', Birendra agreed to restore multi-party democracy. By then B P Koirala had been dead for eight years.

Liz Hawley was a great admirer of B P: 'one of the few remarkable men that we had in Nepal and one political leader who stuck to his beliefs'. In Liz's eyes, the lost opportunity of his 1959 government cast a long shadow over the democratic administrations of the 1990s, which saw the Nepali Congress and various communist factions mired in infighting and corruption; frustration among Nepal's poorest communities grew. In 1996, a small splinter group of Maoist political leaders began a People's War, using Mao's *On Guerilla Warfare* as its textbook. Nepal's leaders, political and military, stewed together unhappily in the introverted bowl of the Kathmandu valley as the Maoists spread their influence over the rest of the country. The crown prince's massacre of his family in 2001 seemed symptomatic of a nation being hollowed out from the inside. The new king, Birendra's brother Gyanendra, was much more like Mahendra. In 2005, he repeated his father's bold decision to take power away from democratically elected

politicians and faced a similar backlash. This time there was no international crisis to save him. When Gyanendra returned power to Nepal's
politicians, among them B P's younger brother Girija Prasad 'G P'
Koirala, they had the backing of the people to do away with the
monarchy altogether. Mahendra might have got away with betraying
democracy; his dynasty did not.

★

As well as stringing for Time Inc. and then Reuters, Liz had made
ends meet working in Nepal's embryonic tourist industry, doing administrative tasks for an ex-Gurkha called Jimmy Roberts, sometimes
called the father of the trekking industry, and his company Mountain
Travel. Both of them had a reputation for being at once shy and rather
waspish, but she learned a great deal from him about recent mountaineering history. She did a similar job for John Coapman, the burly,
charismatic, unreliable and widely disliked founder of the Tiger Tops
wildlife lodge in western Nepal, modelled on African safari camps and
their equivalents in India established after the Great War by the big-
game hunter turned naturalist Jim Corbett. Coapman had bonded
with Mahendra over big-game hunting and been with the king when
he suffered his fatal heart attack. Foreigners couldn't get far working
in tourism without some kind of royal patronage. The 1960s was when
Nepal's tourism industry really caught fire and Liz had been a shrewd
witness to it all. She was there when the first jetliner landed in 1967,
watched the hippies come and go: the Harvard psychologist Richard
Alpert tripping on mescaline, learning to 'be here now', the title of
his book; Cat Stevens smoking hash at the Cabin Restaurant and
writing three albums' worth of material. She was there for the boom
in adventure travel that followed, enduring the huge and sudden
growth of the city that buried its gem-like temple squares in concrete
and tangles of telephone wires.

Although Liz had tried to learn Nepali when she first arrived, she
concluded that anyone she needed to speak to already spoke English.
She was certainly well connected to the elite, the royals and Ranas
she met at the Royal Hotel, where she quickly became part of the
scene around Boris Lissanevitch. Her introduction to the mountaineering world came on her first New Year's Eve in Kathmandu when

she met Ed Hillary for the first time. Two years earlier, almost to the day, Hillary had reached the South Pole in a converted Massey Ferguson tractor, the third party to do so after Amundsen and Scott, ignoring the furious demands of his expedition leader Vivian Fuchs, approaching from the other side, that he slow down. Hillary's behaviour, politely ignored in Britain, had earned him a reputation elsewhere for arrogance. The French journalist Raymond Cartier, a columnist at *Paris Match*, wrote: 'Few men have come into contact with [Hillary] without having reason to complain of his egocentricity.'

Rather bruised, Hillary had retreated to New Zealand and resumed his old occupation of beekeeping, until ambition and restlessness drove him from home again. When Liz met him he was in the middle of a landmark medical research expedition based in the Khumbu region of Nepal on the slopes of Ama Dablam. The scientific leader was the physiologist Griffith Pugh, from the 1953 Everest expedition, but Hillary had got crucial funding from a Chicago encyclopaedia company who wanted him to find the yeti. Scouting around the high valleys of Khumbu for mythical beasts, he had visited the desperate refugee camp below the village of Thami sheltering thousands of Tibetans who had fled the Lhasa Uprising and the security crackdown that followed. Back in Kathmandu he was helping a Swiss pilot deliver relief aid to the refugees; in return the pilot had promised to fly in materials for a school building in the village of Khumjung. The idea of helping the Sherpas had come to him sitting around a campfire with his *sirdar*, or lead porter, Urkein. Hillary had wondered aloud what the future held for the people of Everest. Urkein had told him they suffered from the absence of schooling. 'Our children have eyes but they cannot see,' he said. The school was the first project in what would become a lifelong mission for Hillary: the development of Khumbu through the charity he founded, the Himalayan Trust. Liz was one of many friends he brought in as collaborators and as the years passed they developed a strong bond. When Hillary's first wife Louise and their daughter Belinda were killed in an air crash at the end of May 1975, it was Liz who flew to where Hillary was working in the mountains to give him the news.

It was her friendship with Hillary that also sparked her interest in mountaineering as a subject. Politics had featured heavily in foreign news coverage of the Himalaya in the post-war period, with China's occupation of Tibet and the postcolonial optimism of Indian independence. By the 1960s that interest was fading; adventure was a much easier sell to editors than confusing local politics, especially with the Americans trying Everest in 1963. But there wasn't much to report after their success, at least not for a while, not least because in March 1965, a few days before an official visit by China's foreign minister Chen Yi, Nepal announced a ban on climbing that lasted for the next four years.

Why they did so is not altogether certain. A Chinese engineer working on the Friendship Highway to Lhasa had recently defected to Taiwan, claiming the road's Nepali bridges were designed to bear the weight of Chinese tanks. Tensions were also high in Kashmir as India and Pakistan drifted towards war. A more likely reason was an unauthorised television documentary shot in 1964 focusing on a group of fighters based in Tsum in Nepal, not far from the main force of four thousand in Mustang. The man responsible was George Patterson, a Scottish missionary dedicated for many years to the cause of Tibet, who reported on the Lhasa Uprising for the *Daily Telegraph*. By the mid 1960s he was a well-respected journalist based in Hong Kong and in 1964 he travelled to Nepal with a film crew to meet the Tibetan rebels based there, persuading a small group of Tibetan resistance fighters based in the Tsum valley to mount a raid on Chinese forces for Patterson to document. Once the footage was safely out of Nepal, he had confessed all to the British ambassador, Antony Duff, a former submarine captain and later head of the British intelligence service MI5. He in turn passed the news to Mahendra. Up until that point, Nepal's government had chosen to deny the presence of the Tibetan fighters and China had chosen to believe it. Mahendra now warned Duff the film would be 'a big headache for us and for you'. Although the documentary itself wouldn't be aired until 1966, Patterson published an article shortly before China's Foreign Minister, Chen Yi, was due to visit Kathmandu, describing what had happened, which was quickly picked up by Indian newspapers. It seems likely Mahendra imposed the mountaineering ban to placate China and prevent anything similar recurring.

When mountaineering did resume in 1969 a new generation of climbers arrived, with new ideas and huge ambitions: Reinhold Messner, Chris Bonington and the charismatic Polish expedition leader

Andrzej Zawada, whose team were first to climb Everest in winter. These were the sorts of mountaineers Liz admired, larger than life, the kinds of people who could dominate a press conference. Under the force of these personalities, her record of mountaineering in the region gathered momentum, becoming a database of human achievement, suffering and loss unparalleled in the history of adventure. It occurred to me soon after meeting Liz for the first time in the mid 1990s that, having arrived in 1960 at the tail end of the fashionable, moneyed era of Nepali tourism, she now found herself in a less attractive, more demotic age. She seemed a little bored with it all. Commercial expeditions, with paying clients on familiar routes, were becoming more and more common and there wasn't so much juice there. Her wry sense of humour and the integrity of her record keeping kept her going. Given the often self-admiring but brittle nature of elite mountaineers, I took her lack of personal interest as a positive advantage. She could be imperious and beady, staring impatiently over the frames of her glasses. It was no surprise to discover her accountant grandfather had been part of the fight against organised crime in Chicago in the 1930s.

Liz was laughing when the phone rang. We'd been talking about the assault of three European climbers the year before at camp two on Everest, among them the Swiss Ueli Steck, then one of the stars of world mountaineering. When a team of Sherpas fixing ropes had kicked ice onto them, Steck's Italian companion Simone Moro had called them 'motherfuckers' in Nepali. The cell-phone footage of Sherpas striking a European climber had gone round the world. Liz rolled her eyes and then struggled to her feet to get the phone. I half-listened to the conversation at first, and then more keenly. 'Eleven dead,' she said. Then: 'At least eleven.' In fact the number was sixteen: sixteen high-altitude workers, most of them Sherpa, buried in ice that had fallen from high on the shoulder of Everest as they carried loads to camp two in Everest's Western Cwm. In all her long career this was the worst climbing disaster Liz had ever encountered. An hour later, once Liz had generously shared all she'd learned, I left to organise a flight to Lukla, the closest airport to Everest, for the following morning and start the trek to base camp. That was the last time I saw her.

*

Five days later I was at Everest, much too quickly for an unacclimatised journalist with a story to write. Nursing a headache, I took in the sprawling village of tents staked out on the shifting ice of the Khumbu glacier. Each time I returned to Khumbu I was amazed at the changes tourism had brought. In 1964, the psychologist Jim Lester, who had done fieldwork during the American Everest expedition the year before, had spotted the first advertisement Jimmy Roberts had run for his new trekking business. He mentioned it in a letter to the American mountaineer and writer James Ramsey Ullman, who had covered the climb for *National Geographic*. 'All the jokes we made about the lemonade concession at Namche etc etc, may yet turn out to be prophetic.' And how. Namche Bazar, the largest town in Khumbu, now has an Irish pub and a German bakery serving the sixty thousand or so trekkers who now pass through each year. Cell-phone reception at base camp is better than many mountain towns in Britain or the United States. Helicopters were coming and going with astonishing frequency, ferrying climbers back to Kathmandu over country that had once taken weeks to traverse. Huge mule trains clog the trails, bringing food supplies for the tourist lodges, creating another waste problem that adds to the environmental pressure.

The narrative the year before, when the fight on Everest had been reported, was either that arrogant Westerners had abused Sherpas or that Sherpas had lost their cheerful naïvety in a rush for business. (The businessman Tashi Sherpa, who owns a famous clothing brand named Sherpa, employing fourteen hundred local Nepalis, mostly women, snorted at that one: 'Do you still want the Sherpas to be the same, uneducated, simple folk? No. We want our children to be educated, to go out into the world.') This year it was simpler: the selfish ambition of pampered foreign climbers, 'blithe cretins' as one British columnist put it, had cost sixteen fathers and sons their lives. The same columnist also claimed that Everest was becoming more dangerous for Sherpas. This wasn't quite true. Liz Hawley's statistics, tabulated with Richard Salisbury, showed that since 1950 the death rate among high-altitude workers in the dangerous Icefall had more than halved. Yet it was absolutely the case that local staff, mostly Sherpas, faced a much higher risk than foreign clients, who make very few trips through this dangerous terrain. It seemed grotesque that men and occasionally women should risk their lives in this way to meet the overambitious aspirations of foreigners, who mostly couldn't cope without their support.

It was a confused scene at base camp, as you would expect following a tragedy of that scale. I had watched footage of a spreadeagled body slung beneath a helicopter being flown out of the Icefall, like a darker version of the opening scene in *La Dolce Vita*. Groups of Sherpas hung around looking angry or bereft; many foreign climbers were deeply sympathetic while a few wondered if they would still get a chance to climb. Most had spent many tens of thousands of dollars to get there. There had been demonstrations and even a few threats of violence against any Sherpa continuing with the climbing season, threats that were exaggerated in the media but passed around base camp by those reading news online. Some climbers were shocked at this, still believing in the romantic portrayal of Sherpa culture they had read in books by their heroes.

Change had come quickly to Khumbu. Tashi Sherpa's grandfather Gyalzen recalled in later life how before the expeditions began most of them led lives of extreme poverty. 'There were few houses. Most Sherpas worked as coolies transporting loads for the few rich traders that lived here. The expeditions changed that.' Ed Hillary's schools, the boom in tourism and the soaring value of real estate in Khumbu gave the Sherpas who were born there an opportunity they took with both hands. The Austrian-born Christoph von Fürer-Haimendorf was the first anthropologist to visit Khumbu in 1953 and got to know the important village of Khumjung well. He returned in the 1980s to research a second study he called *The Sherpas Transformed*. By then the closure of the Tibetan border had wholly disrupted ancient trading patterns and the economy was now driven by tourism. Revisiting every house in Khumjung, he tracked how pervasive trekking and climbing work had become. The rate of change only accelerated after that and Khumbu experienced a construction boom. Sherpas used the cash from climbing to build trekking lodges or open restaurants. The next generation went to private schools in Kathmandu and to college in Australia or the United States. This generation chose to live in Kathmandu for much of the year, or else migrated abroad. There are now as many Sherpas in New York City as Khumbu.

Media coverage of Everest leaves an impression that climbing is all Sherpas do, but for most of them, Everest had simply been a springboard for their kids to do something safer: becoming businesspeople, pilots or doctors. They don't have to farm their fields any more: they can use migrant labour to do that, providing fresh food for their trekking lodges. In the late 2000s, following Nepal's civil war – when Maoists were busy pulling down statues of the old Shah royal dynasty – tourism began to recover and has since been booming. Sherpas comprise just half of one per cent of the Nepali population but their economic impact has grown out of all proportion to their numbers. Namche Bazar is among the very wealthiest parts of the whole country, despite not having a road. Yet for every pilot or doctor, there are still a hundred more Sherpas, not born on the trekking route to Everest, desperate to get their foot on the first rung of the tourism ladder, even if that ladder is bridging a crevasse.

Out of the confusion at base camp, two themes emerged that I soon realised applied across much of the Himalaya and not just to this small group living in the shadow of Everest, and not only now but through history. Western media tended to focus on the rich people who pay for the Everest industry but paid little attention to what was in effect an industrial accident. Much more could have been done to keep workers safe. Some victims recovered from the Icefall were found to have been carrying loads far above the legal limit. Some weren't sufficiently trained to deal with the challenges of the job. It isn't hard to imagine the panic, struggling under a monstrous weight, hearing the ice crack and the rumble above your head, the rush of adrenalin, and all this for twenty dollars a day. Yet those asking high-altitude workers to carry more than they should or accept more danger than necessary were Nepali, not foreigners. The Nepali regulatory system is weak and riddled with corruption, which is as true for construction workers or truck drivers as those working on Everest. A week after the accident in the Icefall, another sixteen men were buried, this time in a landslide at a hydropower construction site north-east of the tourist town of Pokhara. This time there was a happier outcome: thirteen men, including three Chinese engineers, survived. But police had to cordon off the site when the families of the dead and injured staged a protest demanding compensation. Unions called on the government to punish construction companies not following the law: the same case could have been made on Everest. It was a cruel irony that Dorje Khatri, one of the most effective and honest union leaders in the trekking and climbing industry, was killed on Everest that day.

For centuries, lack of opportunity had driven Nepalis abroad to look for work, as soldiers, porters, tea-garden workers and labourers. The rapid growth of Darjeeling was predicated on their labour. Not much has changed in the twenty-first century. Population growth and a stagnant manufacturing sector means there's a ready supply of people. In the decade before 2018 the Nepali government issued three and a half million permits for its citizens to go abroad to work. That's around ten per cent of the population. The remittances these workers send home make up a third of Nepal's economy; half of the population of Nepal relies on them. Foreigners often assume tourism is Nepal's most important industry but it accounts for only 4.3 per cent of the nation's economy, well below the world average of 5.2, a minnow compared to migrant labour. Indeed, one of the few areas to see rapid growth within Nepal is the banking sector, thanks to all that cash flowing into the country. But migrant labour has been tainted with corruption, since ordinary Nepalis are often desperate to get the necessary papers. Nor have politicians always stood up for the interests of its citizens abroad, since the nation's economy is at stake. The deaths of Nepali migrant workers building stadia for football's world cup in Qatar in 2022 have attracted headlines, but those workers are at risk wherever they go because they are seen as less powerful than migrants from elsewhere. As a Nepali friend told me when I got back to Kathmandu: 'Forget Everest, there are three body bags a day arriving back at the airport. People should write about that.' I assumed by 'people' he meant me.

Something else struck me about the protests on Everest that spring, something harder to analyse or define but which sprang from a combination of identity and sovereignty. Put simply, I was left with a question: who owns Everest? In 1960 B P Koirala and Mao Zedong had discussed this issue, Koirala claiming the whole mountain for Nepal, Mao archly pointing out that Nepal didn't even know what to call it. The people living either side of the mountain, more or less the same in terms of language and culture, weren't invited to that meeting. Now, more than fifty years later, Sherpas were expressing their anger that while the government in Kathmandu collected millions of dollars in tax revenues, it was Sherpas taking the risks. A government minister was flown in, breathing bottled oxygen to keep him upright, as he nervously reassured protestors their grievances would be answered; the Sherpas looked at him sceptically. They had heard it all before.

A quarter of a century earlier, shortly before the Maoist rebellion began in 1996, a leading Nepali journalist had told me how encouraged he felt that Nepal had not split along ethnic lines. Yet as they whipped up support for their insurgency, the Maoists had zeroed in precisely on ethnic differences, hoping they could energise the grievances of minorities, the so-called *janjati* groups, like Tamang and Rai, and those on the plains like the Tharu and Madhesi, people marginalised by the Brahmin–Chhetri majority of the middle hills who continue to dominate the government. Over the course of the civil war, the expectations of these minority groups had been raised and then disappointed as the Maoists failed to deliver on their promises. Their leaders proved no less corrupt than other Nepali politicians. Having been the largest party at elections held in 2008, the first since the declaration of the republic, they sank to third at the next vote in 2013. The concerns of minorities, however, were not going away; the idea of identity, as in so much of the world, had become a potent factor in Nepal's febrile political discourse. It was a great irony that one of those at Everest base camp in the spring of 2014 taking political advantage of the tragedy was Prakash Dahal, son of the Maoist guerrilla leader and former prime minister Pushpa Kamal Dahal. Here was the chance for a few populist headlines to remind voters that the Maoists still cared about ethnic rights.

Many Westerners thought it sad that Everest, a symbol of our shared humanity, a physical challenge to the boundaries of our minds, should have been mired in this way, struggling under a weight of human excrement, both real and metaphorical. Life on the roof of the world had once seemed above all that kind of confusion and mess, a better place where we could find ourselves. The familiar welcoming smiles on the faces of local people had been replaced by angry scowls. There was, however, another perspective on the Sherpa protests that spring: they reminded the world that although empires and distant populations had often treated its peoples with indifference or hostility, the Himalaya is a real place with its own history and cultures. Look where we come from, the Sherpas seemed to be saying from their place in the mountains: see what made us.

Acknowledgements

Given that the gestation of this book stretches back 25 years, it's hardly surprising that I am indebted to a large number of individuals and organisations throughout the region, ranging from yak men and farmers to government ministers and reincarnate lamas. It seems unnecessary to list them, and even invidious, since I'm liable to forget someone important or else identify someone who would rather not be. Some of those I most wish to thank are people whose name I never learned, including those who offered shelter and food when I needed them even though they had little enough of their own. This impulse of generosity among the region's poorest is one of the most humbling aspects of travel in the Himalaya. I do however want to thank my agent David Godwin for being supportive and brilliant, and Will Hammond, my editor at The Bodley Head for backing the idea and being so deeply engaged in the editing process, as well as Henry Howard for his close and knowledgeable attention to detail. I must also thank my family for putting up with my long absences and for sometimes coming with me.

All maps © Bill Donohoe 2020. The following images in the picture sections are © the following organisations and individuals and/or reproduced with their permission: 1: Image courtesy of the Earth Science and Remote Sensing Unit, NASA Johnson Space Center • 2: with thanks to Mike Searle / Colliding Continents • 3: Dongju Zhang, Lanzhou University • 4: blickwinkel / Alamy Stock Photo • 5, 8, 11, 12, 15, 18, 21, 38 and 41: British Library Board. All Rights Reserved / Bridgeman Images • 6: Freddy Spencer Chapman • 7: Bundesarchiv, Bild 135-KA-06-039 / reproduced under the Creative Commons Attribution-Share Alike 3.0 Germany licence • 9: Xinhua / Alamy Stock

Photo • 10: Crawford, Charles. (1819, December 14). Kathmandu, Nepal. Map of Charles Crawford, 1802-03. Zenodo. http://doi.org/10.5281/zenodo.2245205 • 13: Pictorial Press Ltd / Alamy • 17: National Portrait Gallery, London • 19: President and Fellows of Harvard College. Arnold Arboretum Archives • 20 and 51: Royal Geographical Society / Getty • 22: Bridgeman Images • 23 (bronze), 32 and 33: Art Institute of Chicago • 23 (Kailas) and 31: Ed Douglas • 24: Asian Purchase Campaign Endowment and Robert Ross Fund • 25 and 26: with thanks to John V. Bellezza • 28: Everett and Ann McNear Collection • 29: Royal Collection Trust / © Her Majesty Queen Elizabeth II 2020 • 34: Hildegard Diemberger • 35: Florilegius / Alamy • 36: Ethnological Museum of Berlin • 37: IndianMiniaturePaintings / Peter Blohm • 39: National Army Museum • 40: Art Collection 2 / Alamy • 42 and 43: Biodiversity Heritage Library. Contributed by Missouri Botanical Garden, Peter H. Raven Library. www.biodiversitylibrary.org • 44 and 46: Alpine Club Photo Library, London • 49: Archives and Special Collections, Western Libraries, Western University • 50: Preus Museum • 52: Ernst Krause, Federal Archives • 53: Ernst Schäfer / Bundesarchiv • 54: Archibald Steele • 55: Courtesy of Istituto Italiano per l'Africa e l'Oriente (Is.I.A.O.) in l.c.a. and Ministero Degli Affari Esteri e della Cooperazione Internazionale • 60: Nick Gulotta • 61 and 64: Keystone Press / Alamy Stock Photo • 62: Courtesy of Michael Leonard • 65: George Bush Presidential Library and Museum

A Note on Sources

During the long gestation of this book, I found myself at dinner with a former Conservative cabinet minister. He was graceful enough to take an interest, and seemed delighted with some of what I told him about the Himalaya. And then, to conclude the conversation, he said: 'Of course, no strategic interest.' This seemed to me a revealing comment. Not because it's true, because it isn't: just ask political scientists in Delhi, Beijing or Kathmandu. Rather, it opened a window on how the British imperial project – from which, however self-ironically, he was drawn – saw India's northern border. Ultimately, the British Empire regarded the Himalaya as peripheral, somewhere exotic, a place for yarns, or adventure, not resources or policy, a place to recruit troops, not send them. Moreover, he had no inkling about how British interest in the relationship between China and Tibet made that relationship more combustible.

One consequence of this perspective is a lacuna in how the Himalayan region has been mediated by outsiders. It is not that the Himalaya is an intellectual blank on the map: there's a wealth of scholarship on every aspect of life there. It's more that myths and legends about the Himalaya continue to dominate popular culture, insulating the West from using that scholarship to create a wider understanding of the region. In a small way, this book is an attempt to bridge that gap. It is, for better or worse, an attempt to write something of popular appeal to those with an interest who want to know more, using the insights of a long interest and much reading in Himalayan studies. That's why I've deliberately not included endnotes, which would make a big subject even more unwieldy. Most scholars specialising in the region will recognise where most of what's written here comes from. The bibliography below sets out the sources and offers a starting point for those who wish to read more wildly and more deeply. I draw particular attention to bibliographies from John Whelpton on Nepali history and Julie Marshall's magisterial work on Tibet.

Largely missing from this list are the myriad media outlets that I've relied on over the years, the *Nepali Times*, the *Kathmandu Post*, *Himal* and its successor *Himal South Asian*, *The Record*, *Phayul*, the *Tibet Sun* and *Tibet Post* and the Nepali literary magazine *La.Lit*. There are many Himalayan bloggers at work today but I enjoy particularly Jamyang Norbu's 'Shadow Tibet' and Tim Chamberlain's 'Waymarks'. John Vincent Bellezza's 'Flight of the Khyung' is referenced in the bibliography. The work of the Tibetan activist and writer Woeser appears on the website 'High Peaks Pure Earth'. Other online resources I found useful included the website 'Treasury of Lives', which offers a useful guide to the complex world of Tibetan Buddhism and 'Himalayan Art Resources', art being perhaps one of the most accessible ways of appreciating the range and depth of Himalayan culture. Also missing, necessarily, is the Himalayan fiction that has deepened my appreciation and knowledge of the region. Manjushree Thapa's non-fiction is referenced, but not her novels *The Tutor of History* and *Each of Us in Our Own Lives*. She and the outstanding short-story writer Prawin Adhikari have both translated works by the major Darjeeling author Indra Bahadur Rai, whose haunting work is consequently now available to non-Nepali speakers. Rai had such a particular voice and his writing catches a world that non-fiction, especially from an outsider, could never hope to match. Shradha Ghale is another Nepali writer who bridges non-fiction and fiction: her novel *The Wayward Daughter* is a beautifully written insight into the trials of growing up a young woman in modern Nepal, as well as revealing how Kathmandu is changing in the age of identity. There are many others: Rabi Thapa, Pranaya S J B Rana, Samrat Upadhyay and the Sikkimese architect and author Chetan Raj Shrestha. Himalayan writers deserve much more attention than they get, living as they do in the shadow of India. I've also benefitted from the work of Himalayan film-makers, particularly Kesang Tseten but also Ngawang Choephel, Khyentse Norbu, Deepak Rauniyar and Lu Chuan, to name but a few.

Of the works listed below, I want to pick out a very few that the general reader will enjoy. Apart from the Himalayan writers already mentioned, Kate Teltscher's book on George Bogle, *The High Road to China*, is a delight. So, for different reasons, is Nicola Shulman's sharp-witted portrait of the self-absorbed plant collector Reginald Farrer, *A Rage for Rock Gardening*. Thomas Bell's layered and shifting *Kathmandu* catches not only the complexities of this ancient city but those of modern Nepali politics as well. Robbie Barnett's *Lhasa: Streets with Memories* does something similar for Tibet's capital, capturing something of the old city before it was remade. Sam Cowan's *Essays on Nepal* have all the insight you'd expect from a former Colonel Commandant of the Brigade of Gurkhas but are accessible and full of energy. I would also want to draw attention to the collections of academic essays included in the bibliography, for their variety of voices and the tight focus of subjects.

Finally, although there was almost no original research in the writing of this book, I did explore the papers of F M Bailey in the British Library, where I found evidence of his antipathy towards Charles Bell, and made use of one or two gems I came across in the Alpine Club's archive, and wish to thank the Alpine Club's archivist Glyn Hughes and the librarian Nigel Buckley.

Bibliography

ARTICLES AND PAPERS

Akasoy, Anna, and Yoeli-Tlalim, Ronit, 'Along the Musk Routes: Exchanges between Tibet and the Islamic World', *Asian Medicine* 3, 2007.

Amatya, Shaphalya, 'British Diplomacy and its Various Missions in Nepal from 1767–1799', *Ancient Nepal* 6, 1969.

———, 'The Failure of Captain Knox's Mission in Nepal', *Ancient Nepal* 46–48, 1978.

Anon., 'Obituary: Colonel Edmund Smyth', *The Geographical Journal* 39, 1912.

———, 'Dr McGovern's Visit to Lhasa', *The Geographical Journal* 63, 1924.

———, 'Obituary: Professor Augusto Gansser', *Daily Telegraph*, 9 August 2017.

Bajracharya, Manik, and Michaels, Axel, 'On the Historiography of Nepal: The 'Wright' Chronicle Reconsidered', *European Bulletin of Himalayan Research* 40, 2012.

Batten, J H, 'Notes and Recollections on Tea Cultivation in Kumaon and Garhwál', *Journal of the Royal Asiatic Society* 10, 1878.

Beall, C M, et al., 'Natural selection on EPAS1 (HIF2a) Associated with Low Hemoglobin Concentration in Tibetan Highlanders', *Proceedings of the National Academy of Sciences* 107, 2010.

Beckwith, Christopher I, 'Tibetan Sciences at the Court of the Great Khans', *Journal of the Tibet Society* 7, 1987.

Bell, Tom, 'What Happened to Kinloch's Expedition to Kathmandu', *European Bulletin of Himalayan Research* 51, 2018.

Bellezza, John Vincent, 'Review: "Earliest Tea as Evidence for One Branch of the Silk Road across the Tibetan Plateau"', *Flight of the Khyung* (tibetarchaeology.com), April 2016.

———, 'A Mirror of Cultural History on the Roof of the World: The Swastika in the Rock Art of Upper Tibet', *Flight of the Khyung* (tibetarchaeology.com), May and June 2016.

Bharati, A, 'Fictitious Tibet: The Origin and Persistence of Rampaism', *Tibet Society Bulletin* 7, 1974.

Bidari, Keshav, 'Halji Monastery: A Hidden Heritage in North-West Nepal', *Ancient Nepal* 155, 2004.

Bilham, Roger, 'Location and Magnitude of the 1833 Nepal Earthquake and its Relation to the Rupture Zones of Contiguous Great Himalayan Earthquakes', *Current Science* 69, 1995.

Black, C E, 'The Trade and Resources of Tibet', *Asian Review* 26, 1908.

Blakeney, T S, 'Whymper and Mummery', *Alpine Journal* 57, 1957.

Blaser, Willy, and Hughes, Glyn, 'Kabru 1883: A Reassessment', *Alpine Journal* 114, 2009.

Bonapace, Caterina, and Sestini, Valerio, 'Traditional Materials and Construction Technologies Used in the Kathmandu Valley', UNESCO (unesdoc.unesco.org), 2003.

Boulnois, L, 'Chinese Maps and Prints on the Tibet–Gorkha War of 1788–92', *Kailash* 15, 1989.

Bray, John, 'A History of the Moravian Church', *The Himalayan Mission*, 1985.

———, 'The Lapchak Mission from Ladakh to Lhasa in British Foreign Policy', *Tibet Journal* 15, 1990.

———, 'Ladakhi History and Indian Nationhood', *South Asia Research* 11, 1991.

———, 'Christian Missionaries and the Politics of Tibet 1850–1950', in Wagner, Wilfried (ed.), *Kolonien und Missionen*, Bremen, 1993.

———, 'French Catholic Missions and the Politics of China and Tibet 1846–1865', in Krasser, H., et al., *Tibetan Studies: Proceedings of the 7th Seminar of the International Association for Tibetan Studies, Graz, 1995*, Vienna, 1995.

———, 'Captain Barré Latter and British Engagement with Sikkim during the 1814–1816 Nepal War', in McKay, Alex, and Balikci-Denjongpa, Anna (eds), *Buddhist Himalaya: Studies in Religion, History and Culture. Volume II*, Gangtok, 2012.

———, 'Stumbling on the Threshold: Annie Taylor's Tibetan Pioneer Mission, 1893–1907', *Bulletin of Tibetology* 91, 2014.

——— and Gonkatsang, Tsering D, 'Three 19th Century Documents from Tibet and the Lo Phyag Mission from Leh to Lhasa', Supplement 2 to *Rivista Studi Orientali* 80 (n.s.), 2009.

Brown, C W, '"What we Call 'Bhotias' are in Reality not Bhotiyas": Perspective of British Colonial Conceptions', *Himalaya Past and Present* 2, 1991–2.

———, 'Salt, Barley, Pashmina and Tincal: Contexts of being Bhotiya in Traill's Kumaon', *Himalayan Past and Present* 3, 1992–3.

Burke, Jason, 'First Englishman in Lhasa: Intimate Letters Reveal Story of Unsung Explorer', *The Guardian*, 13 October 2015.

Cammann, Schuyler, 'New Light on Huc and Gabet: Their Expulsion from Lhasa in 1846', *Far Eastern Quarterly* 1, 1942.

Chakrabarti, Chinmoy, 'Bhotias of the Bhotia Mahal', *Himalayan Journal* 62, 2006.

Chamberlain, Tim, 'Edge of Empires', *British Museum Magazine*, 2010.

Chatterjee, Bishwa B, 'The Bhotias of Uttarakhand', *India International Centre Quarterly* 3, 1976.

Chinn, B, 'Rulers, Reconstructions and Responses: Kumaon under British Rule', *Himalaya Past and Present* 4, 1993–4.

Choegyal, Lisa, 'Hiking with Jimmy [Roberts]', *Nepali Times*, 8 June 2018.

Christie, Clive, 'Great Britain, China and the Status of Tibet 1914-21', *Modern Asian Studies* 10, 1976.

Church, Mimi, and Wiebenga, Mariette, 'A Four-fold Variocana in the Rinchen Zangpo Tradition at Halji in Nepal', *Asian Art*, 21 October 2008.

Cohn, Bernard S, 'The Role of Gosains in the Economy of Eighteenth and Nineteenth Century Upper India', *Indian Economic and Social History Review* 1, 1963–4.

Corbett, Geoffrey, 'The Word Himalaya', *Himalayan Journal* 1, 1929.

Dabaral, S P, 'Gorkhali Rule in Garhwal', *Regmi Research Series* 20, 1987.

Datta, C L, 'The Simla Hill States under British Rule 1816–1856; and Construction of Roads and the Begar', *Proceedings Punjab History Conference* 10, 1976.

Davis, Richard, 'Davis on Burnouf, *Introduction to the History of Indian Buddhism*', H-Asia (networks.h-net.org/h-asia), 2011.

Devereux, David R, 'The Sino-Indian War of 1962 in Anglo-American Relations', *Journal of Contemporary History* 44, 2009.

Douglas, Ed, 'I was Ready to Die in Tibet', *The Observer*, 29 June 2003.

———, 'Out of Thin Air: Discovering how Climbers and People who Live at Altitude Cope with Limited Oxygen Could Bring Big Advances in Medicine', *New Scientist*, 15 June 2013.

Dyhrenfurth, Günther O, 'The International Himalayan Expedition, 1930', *Himalayan Journal* 3, 1931.

Engelhardt, Isrun, 'Between Tolerance and Dogmatism: Tibetan Reactions to the Capuchin Missionairies in Lhasa, 1707–1745', *Zentralasiatische Studien* 34, 2005.

En-Lai, Chou, et al., '59. Memorandum of Conversation: Beijing, November 13, 1973', *Foreign Relations of the United States, 1969–1976, XVIII: China, 1973–76*.

Fleetwood, Lachlan, '"No Former Travellers Having Attained Such a Height on the Earth's Surface": Instruments, Inscriptions, and Bodies in the Himalaya, 1800–1830', *History of Science* 56, 2018.

Free Tibet, 'Eleventh Tibetan – Second Nun – Dies After Setting Fire to Herself', 3 Nov 2011.

French, Patrick, 'Mad, Bad and Dangerous', *Telegraph Magazine*, 2001.

Gardner, Kyle J, 'The Ready Materials for Another World: Frontier, Security, and the Hindustan-Tibet Road in the 19th Century Northwestern Himalaya', *Himalaya* 33, 2013.

Gellner, David N, 'Hodgson's Blind Alley? On the So-Called Four Schools of Nepalese Buddhism', *Journal of International Association of Buddhist Studies*, 12, 1989.

——, 'The Emergence of Conversion in a Hindu-Buddhist Polytropy: The Kathmandu Valley, Nepal *c.*1600–1995', *Comparative Studies in Society and History* 47, Oct 2005.

——, 'The Idea of Nepal', Mahesh Chandra Regmi Lecture, 2016.

—— and LeVine, Sarah, 'All in the Family: Money, Kinship and Theravada Monasticism in Nepal', *Occasional Papers in Sociology and Anthropology* 10, 2007.

Gettelman, Nancy M, 'Letter of First Westerner to Visit Bhutan, Tibet, Nepal (Joao Cabral, 1599-1669)', *Kailash* 9, 1982.

Gippenreiter, Yevgeniy B, 'Mount Everest and the Russians 1952 and 1958', *Alpine Journal* 99, 1994.

Giri, Anil, 'Kathmandu-Kerung Railway Project "Complicated and Arduous", Report Says', *Kathmandu Post*, 16 Aug 2018.

Gittings, John, 'Han Suyin Obituary', *The Guardian*, 4 Nov 2012.

Gommans, Jos, 'The Horse Trade in Eighteenth-Century South Asia', *Journal of the Economic and Social History of the Orient* 37, 1994.

Goodwin, Stephen, 'Everest Revealed?', *Alpine Journal* 115, 2011.

Graafen, Rainer, and Seeber, Christian, 'Important Trade Routes in Nepal and their Importance in the Settlement Process', *Ancient Nepal* 130–33, 1992–3.

Grey-Wilson, Christopher, 'Bailey's Blue Poppy Restored', *The Alpine Gardener*, Jun 2009.

Griffith, William, 'Journal of the Mission which visited Bootan in 1837–38, under Captain R Boileau Pemberton', *Journal of the Asiatic Society* VIII, 1839.

Gurdon, E M, 'Obituary: Brigadier-General the Hon Charles Granville Bruce MVO CB', *The Geographical Journal* 96, Oct 1940.

Hansen, Peter H, 'The Dancing Lamas of Everest: Cinema, Orientalism, and Anglo-Tibetan Relations in the 1920s', *American Historical Review* 101, 1996.

Hay, W C, 'Report on the Valley of Spiti; and Facts Collected with a View to a Future Revenue Settlement', *Journal of the Asiatic Society* 19, Calcutta, 1850.

Heller, Amy, 'The Silver Jug of the Lhasa Jokhang: Some Observations on Silver Objects and Costumes from the Tibetan Empire', *Asian Art*, 2002.

Heller, Amy, 'Tibetan Inscriptions on Ancient Silver and Gold Vessels and Artefacts', *Journal of the International Association for Bon Research* 1, 2013.

Hilton, Isabel, 'Royal Blood', *New Yorker*, 2001.

Hodgson, Brian Houghton, 'Notices of the Languages, Literature and Religion of the Bauddhas of Nepal and Bhot', *Asiatick Resarches*, XVI, 1828, updated in 1841 and 1874.

——, 'On Three New Species of Musk (Moschus) Inhabiting the Himalayan Districts', *Journal of the Asiatic Society* 8, 1839.

Hodgson, J A, 'Journal of a Survey to the Heads of the Rivers Ganges and Jumna', *Asiatic Researches* 14, 1822.

Höfer, András, 'On Re-Reading *Le Népal*: What We Social Scientists Owe Sylvain Lévi', *Kailash* 7, 1979.

Howard, Neil F, 'Military Aspects of the Dogra Conquest of Ladakh 1834–1839', *Proceedings of the Fourth and Fifth International Colloquia on Ladakh*, Delhi, 1995.

Howgego, Raymond J, 'Edmund Smyth: English Explorer (1823–1911)', *International League of Antiquarian Booksellers* (ilab.org), 30 May 2011.

Huerta-Sánchez, Emilia, et al., 'Altitude Adaptation in Tibetans Caused by Introgression of Denisovan-like DNA', *Nature* 512, 2014.

Huntingdon, John, and Bangdel, Dina, 'A Case Study in Religious Continuity: The Nepal–Bengal Connection', *Orientations* 32, 2001.

Jing, Anning, 'The Portraits of Khubilai Khan and Chabi by Anige (1245–1306), a Nepali Artist in the Yuan Court', *Artibus Asiae* 54, 1994.

Jinpan, Nawang, 'Why Did Tibet and Ladakh Clash in the 17th Century? Rethinking the Background to the "Mongol War" in Ngari (1679–1684)', *Tibet Journal*, 2015.

Joshi, Maheshwar P, and Brown, C W, 'Some Dynamics of Indo-Tibetan Trade through Uttarakhanda', *Journal of the Economic and Social History of the Orient* 30, 1987.

Kak, Manju, 'Indo-Tibet Trade Routes as Public Sphere', in Muthukumaraswamy, M D, and Kashaul, Molly (eds), *Folklore, Public Sphere and Civil Society*, New Delhi and Chennai, 2004.

Kalmus, Marek, 'Remarks on Selected Bridges of Thangtong Gyalpo', *Journal of Comparative Cultural Studies in Architecture*, 2015.

Kathayat, Gayatri, et al., 'The Indian Monsoon Variability and Civilization Changes in the Indian Subcontinent', *Science Advances* 3, 2017.

Kellas, Alexander M, 'A Fourth Visit to the Sikkim Himalaya, with Ascent of Kangchenjhau', *Alpine Journal* 27, 1913.

———, 'A Consideration of the Possibility of Ascending the Loftier Himalaya', *Geographical Journal* 49, 1917.

———, 'The Possibility of Aerial Reconnaissance in the Himalaya', *Geographical Journal* 51, 1918.

———, 'The Nomenclature of Himalaya Peaks', *Geographical Journal* 52, 1918.

———, 'A Consideration of the Possibility of Ascending Mount Everest' [1920], *High Altitude Medicine and Biology* 2, 2001.

Khachikian, Levon, 'The Ledger of the Merchant Hovhannes of Joughayetsi', *Journal of the Asiatic Society* 8, 1966.

Khan, D S, 'Nepal's Relations with British India', *Regional Studies* 5, 1987.

Kingdon-Ward, Frank, 'Blue Poppies', *Blackwood's Magazine*, 1946.

Kobayashi, Ryosuke, 'Tibet in the Era of 1911 Revolution', *Journal of Contemporary East Asia Studies* 3, 2014.

Kuleshov, Nikolai, 'Agvan Dorjiev, the Dalai Lama's Ambassador', *Asian Affairs*, 1992.

Kunwar, Mayura Jang, 'China and War in the Himalayas 1792–1793', *English Historical Review* 77, 1962.

Lama, Tsewang, '"It's Difficult to Govern a Place if You Don't Understand its Ecology", Tsewang Lama Discusses Life and Governance in Humla', *The Record*, 4 Nov 2018.

Lange, Diana, 'Decoding Mid-19th Century Maps of the Border Area between Western Tibet, Ladakh, and Spiti', *Revue d'Etudes Tibétaines*, 2017.

Le Calloc'h, Bernard, 'Historical Background of Csoma de Körös' Soujourn in Ladakh (Zanskar) between 1822 and 1826', *Proceedings of the Fourth and Fifth International Colloquia on Ladakh*, Delhi, 1995.

Lecomte-Tilouine, Marie, 'On Francis Buchanan Hamilton's Account of the Kingdom of Nepal', *European Bulletin of Himalayan Research* 14, 1994.

Lee, Peter, 'The British Forgery at the Heart of India and China's Border Dispute', *South China Morning Post*, 1 Nov 2016.

Leland, John, 'Sherpas of Elmhurst', *New York Times*, 14 July 2017.

Lohani, S C, 'The Birth of Rana Feudalism in Nepal', *Ancient Nepal* 8, 1969.

Losty, J P, 'Clarence Comyn Taylor (1830–79): The First Photographer in Udaipur and Nepal', *History of Photography* 16, 1992.

Lu, Houyuan, et al., 'Earliest Tea as Evidence for One Branch of the Silk Road across the Tibetan Plateau', *Scientific Reports* 6, 2016.

Luczanits, Christian, 'From Kashmir to Western Tibet: The Many Faces of a Regional Style', in Linrothe, Rob (ed.), *Collecting Paradise. Buddhist Art of Kashmir and Its Legacies*, New York, 2014.

Malla, Kamal P., 'Epigraphy and Society in Ancient Nepal: A Critique of Regmi', *Contributions to Nepalese Studies* 13, 1985.

Manandhar, Tri Ratna, 'Crisis with Tibet (1883–84)', *Voice of History* 3, 1977.

———, '"Note on our Position with Regard to Nepal": A Report by H Wylie Dated 19 March 1894', *Voice of History* 4–6, 1978–80.

———, 'A New Light on the Kot Massacre', *Rolamba* 4, 1984.

———, 'Some Documents on Nepal–Tibet War (1855–56)', *Rolamba*, 1985.

———, 'British Residents in the Court of Nepal during the 19th Century', *Voice of History* 20, 2005.

Marpeau, Benoît, 'Gustave Le Bon et les universitaires. Fragments de correspondance', *Mil neuf cent* 16, 1998.

Martin, Dan, 'On the Cultural Ecology of Sky Burial on the Himalayan Plateau', *East and West* 46, 1996.

Mason, Kenneth, 'Frederick Williamson 1891–1935', *Himalayan Journal* 8, 1936.

———, 'Great Figures of Nineteenth Century Himalayan Exploration', *Journal of Royal Central Asian Society* 43, 1956.

Maurer, Eva, 'Cold War, "Thaw" and "Everlasting Friendship": Soviet Mountaineers and Mount Everest, 1953–1960', *International Journal of Sport* 26, 2009.

McGranahan, Carole, 'The CIA and the Chushi Gangdruk Resistance, 1956–1974', *Journal of Cold War Studies* 8, 2006.

———, 'From Simla to Rongbatsa: The British and the "Modern" Boundaries of Tibet', *The Tibet Journal* 28, 2003.

McKay, Alex, 'The Establishment of the British Trade Agencies in Tibet: A Survey', *Journal of the Royal Asiatic Society* 3, 1992.

———, 'David Macdonald: The Early Years', *Tibet Society Newsletter* 4, 1992.

———, 'Tibet 1924: A Very British Coup Attempt', *Journal of the Royal Asiatic Society* 7, 1997.

———, 'Hitler and the Himalayas: The SS Mission to Tibet 1938–39', *Tricycle* 10, 2001.

———, '19th Century British Expansion on the Indo-Tibetan Frontier: A Forward Perspective', *Tibet Journal* 28, 2003.

———, '"A Difficult Country, A Hostile Chief, and a Still More Hostile Minister": The Anglo-Sikkim War of 1861', *Bulletin of Tibetology* 45, 2010.

Mirsky, Jonathan, 'Destroying the Dharma', *New York Review of Books*, 2 December 2004.

Mojumdar, Kanchanmoy, 'Nepal–Tibet War 1855–56', *Journal of the United Service Institution of India* 94, 1964.

———, 'Nepal and the Indian Mutiny 1857–58', *Bengal Past and Present* 85, 1966.

Molenaar, Dee, 'Hans Peter Misch 1909–1987', *American Alpine Journal*, 1988.

Monika, Chansoria, 'Reaching Tibet in July 1900 via British India and Nepal: Journey of the First Japanese, Ekai Kawaguchi', Policy Brief, Japan Institute of International Affairs (www.jiia-jic.jp/en), 2019.

Moorcroft, William, 'A Journey to Lake Mánasaróvara in Ún-dés, a Province of Little Tibet', *Asiatick Researches* 12, 1816.

Moore, L G, et al., 'Maternal Adaptation to High-Altitude Pregnancy: An Experiment of Nature – A Review', *Placenta* 25, 2004.

Mulmi, Amish Raj, 'The Making of the Gorkha Empire', *The Record* (recordnepal.com), Aug 2017.

———, 'Using Shikhar Diplomacy in 19th-Century Nepal', *The Wire* (thewire.in), 19 Aug 2017.

———, 'Momo: The One Dumpling that Rules them All', *LiveMint* (livemint.com), 22 Sep 2017.

Nalesini, Oscar, 'A Short History of the Tibet Explorations of Giuseppe Tucci', in Seccaroni, C, et al. (eds), *Visibilia Invisibilium*, Rome, 2011.

Neame, Philip, 'Tibet and the 1936 Lhasa Mission', *Journal of the Royal Central Asian Society* 26, 1939.

Norbu, Dawa, 'The Europeanization of Sino-Tibetan Relations, 1775–1907', *Tibet Journal* 15, 1990.

Norbu, Jamyang, 'The Incredible Weariness of Hope: Review of *Tibet, Tibet* by Patrick French', *Phayul* (phayul.com), 2003.

———, 'Untangling a Mess of Petrified Noodles: Reflections on Gyalo Thondup and Modern Tibetan History', *Shadow Tibet* (www.jamyangnorbu.com/blog), 29 June 2016.

Pathak, Sunitikumar, 'British Activities in India during the Gorkha–Tibet War II (1854–56)', *Proceedings of the Indian History Congress* 23, 1960.

Pearse, Hugh, 'Moorcroft and Hearsey's Visit to Lake Mansarowar in 1812', *The Geographical Journal* 26, 1905.

Peng, Y, et al., 'Genetic Variations in Tibetan Populations and High-Altitude Adaptation at the Himalayas', *Molecular Biology Evolution* 28, 2011.

Pereira, George, 'Peking to Lhasa (from the Diaries of the Late Brigadier-General George Pereira)', *Geographical Journal* 64, 1924.

Pradhan, Kamal, 'The Myth of Chinese Suzerainty', *Voice of Tibet* 1, 1967.

Qiu, Jane, 'Tibetan Plateau Gets Wired up for Monsoon Prediction', *Nature* 524, 2014.

———, 'Listening for Landslides: A Year after a Devastating Earthquake Triggered Killer Avalanches and Rock Falls in Nepal, Scientists are Wiring up Mountainsides to Forecast Hazards', *Nature* 532, 2016.

———, 'Tibetan Plateau Discovery Shows Humans May Be Tougher Than We Thought', *Scientific American*, December 2016.

———, 'The Surprisingly Early Settlement of the Tibetan Plateau', *Scientific American*, March 2017.

Rana, R, 'B H Hodgson as a Factor in the Fall of Bhimsen Thapa', *Ancient Nepal* 105, 1988.

Raper, F V, 'Narrative of a Survey for the Purpose of Discovering the Sources of the Ganges', *Asiatick Researches* 11, 1810.

Rawlinson, H G, 'A Forgotten Hero; Some Notes on the Life and Work of Csoma de Körös', *Journal of Indian History* 8, 1929.

Regmi Research (Private) Ltd, 'The Salt Trade during the Nepal-Tibet War', *Regmi Research Series* 16, 1984.

Richardson, Hugh, 'George Bogle and his Children', *Scottish Genealogist* 29, 1982.

Riccardi, Theodore (trans.), 'Sylvain Lévi: The History of Nepal. Part I', *Kailash* 3, 1975.

Romolo, Gandolfo, 'Bhutan and Tibet in European Cartography (1597–1800)', in *The Spider and the Piglet: Proceedings of the First Seminar on Bhutan Studies*, Centre for Bhutan Studies, Thimphu, 2004.

Rovato, Giuseppe de, 'An Account of the Kingdom of Nepal', trans. John Shore, *Asiatick Researches* 2, 1790.

Rubenson, Carl W, 'An Ascent of Kabru', *Alpine Journal* 24, 1908.

Sakya, Tsering, 'Tibet and the League of Nations with Reference to Letters Found in the India Office Library, under Sir Charles Bell's Collections', *Tibet Journal* 10, 1985.

———, 'Making of the Great Game Players: Tibetan Students in Britain between 1913 and 1917', *Tibetan Review* 21, 1986.

———, 'Interview: Beyond Development and Diversity', *Himal Southasian* (himalmag.com), 25 June 2018.

Sankararaman, Sriram, et al., 'The Combined Landscape of Denisovan and Neanderthal Ancestry in Present-Day Humans', *Current Biology* 26, 2016.

Santoli, Ali, and Getachew, Mahlet, '"The Tibetan People Seek Dignity, Freedom and Respect": An Interview with Former Tibetan Political Prisoner, Ms Ngawang Sangdrol', 2003.

Sarkar, Swatahsiddha, 'Obituary: Kumar Pradhan (1937–2013)', *Himalaya* 34, 2014.

Schaik, Sam van, 'Review: *The Gathering of Intentions: A History of Tibetan Buddhist Tantra*, by Jacob P Dalton', *Buddhist Studies Review* 35, 2018.

Selin, Eva, 'Carl Rubenson, Kabru and the Birth of the Norwegian AC', *Alpine Journal* 113, 2008.

Sen, Jahar, 'India's Trade with Central Asia via Nepal', *Bulletin of Tibetology* 8, 1971.

———, 'Arms Deal between India and Nepal: Genesis of Gurkha Recruitment in the British Army', *Calcutta History Journal* 4, 1980.

Shakya, Min Bahadur, 'Nepalese Buddhist Artist Arniko and his Contribution to Buddhist Heritage of China', Nagarjuna Institute, n. d.

Sharma, Prayag Raj, 'Kirkpatrick's An Account of the Kingdom of Nepal', *Contributions to Nepalese Studies* 1, 1973.

Shivram, Balkrishan, 'Reflections on 1857 Revolt: A Study of Himachal Pradesh', *The Punjab Past and Present* 37, 2006.

Shrestha, Bal Gopal, 'Ritual and Identity in the Diaspora: The Newars of Sikkim', *Bulletin of Tibetology* 25, 2011.

Shuttleworth, H Lee, 'A Wool Mart of the Indo-Tibetan Borderland', *Geographical Review* 13, 1923.

Slusser, Mary S, 'The Lhasa gTsug lag khang: Further Observations on the Ancient Wood Carvings', *Asian Art* (asianart.com), 7 February 2006.

Smyth, Edmund, 'Obituary: The Pundit Nain Singh', *Proceedings of the Royal Geographical Society* 4, 1882.

Snelling, John, 'Agvan Dorjiev: Eminence Grise of Cental Asian Politics', *Asian Affairs* 21, 1990.

Spear, Percival, 'Morley and India, 1906–1910 by Stanley A Wolpert', *Modern Asian Studies* 3, 1969.

Toffin, Gérard, 'Royal Images and Ceremonies of Power in Nepal (17th–21st Centuries)', *Rivista di Studi Sudasiatici*, 2008.

Traill, G W, 'Statistical Report on the Bhotia Mehals of Kamaon', *Asiatic Researches* 17, 1832.

Truschke, Audrey, 'The Power of the Islamic Sword in Narrating the Death of Indian Buddhism', *History of Religions* 57, 2018.

Wade, Nicholas, 'Scientists Cite Fastest Case of Human Evolution', *New York Times*, 1 July 2010.

Wang, B, et al., 'On the Origin of Tibetans and their Genetic Basis in Adapting High-Altitude Environments', *PLoS ONE* 6, 2011.

Wang, Y, et al., 'The Effect of Low Density over the "Roof of the World" Tibetan Plateau on the Triggering of Convection', *Atmospheric Chemistry and Physics*, July 2019.

Ward, Michael, 'The Survey of India and the Pundits', *Alpine Journal* 103, 1998.

West, John B, 'A M Kellas: Pioneer Himalayan Physiologist Mountaineer', *Alpine Journal* 94, 1989.

———, 'Alexander M Kellas and the Physiological Challenge of Mount Everest', *Journal of Applied Physiology* 63, 1987.

Whelpton, John, 'A Reading Guide to Nepalese History', *Himalaya* 25, 2005.

Witzel, Michael, 'The Coronation Rituals of Nepal: With Special Reference to the Coronation of King Birendra (1975)', in Gutschow, Niels, and Michaels, Alex (eds), *Heritage of the Kathmandu Valley. Proceedings of an International Conference in Lübeck, June 1985*, Sankt Augustin, 1987.

Wong, Edward, 'Printing the Ancient Way Keeps Buddhist Texts Alive in Tibet', *New York Times*, 21 March 2017.

Xu, S, et al., 'A Genome-Wide Search for Signals of High-Altitude Adaptation in Tibetans', *Molecular Biology Evolution* 28, 2011.

Yamamoto, Carl, 'Review of *Crazy for Wisdom: The Making of a Mad Yogin in Fifteenth Century Tibet* by Stefan Larsson', *Himalaya* 32, 2013.

Yi, X, et al., 'Sequencing of 50 Human Exomes Reveals Adaptation to High Altitude', *Science* 329, 2010.

Yongdan Lobsang, 'Tibet Charts the World: The Btsan po No mon han's Detailed Description of the World, an Early Major Scientific Work in Tibet', in Tuttle, Gray (ed.), *Mapping the Modern in Tibet*, [Andiast,] 2011.

———, 'The Translation of European Astronomical Works into Tibetan in the Early Eighteenth Century', *Inner Asia* 17, 2015.

———, 'The Introduction of Edward Jenner's Smallpox Vaccination to Tibet in the Early 19th Century', *Archiv Orientální* 84, 2016.

———, 'A Scholarly Imprint: How Tibetan Astronomers Brought Jesuit Astronomy to Tibet', *East Asian Science, Technology, and Medicine* 45, 2017.

Zhao, Yang, et al., 'Effects of the Tibetan Plateau and its Second Staircase Terrain on Rainstorms over North China: From the Perspective of Water Vapour Transport', *International Journal of Climatology* 39, 2019.

BOOKS AND LONGER WORKS

Acharya, Baburam, *The Blood Stained Throne: Struggles for Power in Nepal 1775–1914*, trans. Acharya, Madhav, New Delhi, 2013.

Adhikari, Aditya, *The Bullet and the Ballot Box: The Story of Nepal's Maoist Revolution*, London, 2014.

Adhikari, Krishna Kant, *Nepal under Jang Bahadur 1847–1877*, 2 vols, Kathmandu, 1984.

Aitken, Bill, *Touching upon the Himalaya*, New Delhi, 2004.

Akbar, M J, *Nehru: The Making of India*, London, 1988.

Alder, Garry J, *Beyond Bokhara: The Life of William Moorcroft*, London, 1985.

Allen, Charles, *The Search for Shangri-La: A Journey into Tibetan History*, London, 1999.

———, *The Buddha and the Sahibs*, London, 2002.

———, *A Mountain in Tibet: The Search for Mount Kailas and the Sources of the Great Rivers of India*, London, [1982,] 2003.

———, *Duel in the Snows: The True Story of the Younghusband Mission to Lhasa*, London, 2004.

———, *The Prisoner of Kathmandu: Brian Houghton Hodgson in Nepal 1820–43*, London, 2015.

Anderson, J R L, *High Mountains and Cold Seas: A Biography of H W Tilman*, London, 1980.

Anderson, James A, and Whitmore, John K (eds), *China's Encounters on the South and Southwest: Reforging the Fiery Frontier Over Two Millennia*, Leiden, 2014.

Andreyev, Alexandre, et al., *The Quest for Forbidden Lands: Nikolai Przhevalskii and his Followers on Inner Asian Tracks*, Leiden, 2018.

Archer, Mildred, and Falk, Toby, *India Revealed: The Art and Adventures of James and William Fraser 1801–35*, London, 1989.

Aris, Michael, *Bhutan: The Early History of a Himalayan Kingdom*, Warminster, 1979.

———, *Views of Mediaeval Bhutan: The Diary and Drawings of Samuel Davis, 1783*, London, 1982.

——— and Aung San Suu Kyi, *Tibetan Studies in Honour of Hugh Richardson*, Warminster, 1979.

Astill, Tony, *Mount Everest: The Reconnaissance 1935*, [Ashurst,] 2005.

Atkinson, Edwin Thomas, *Gazetteer of the Himalayan Districts of the North-Western Provinces of India*, 3 vols, Allahabad, 1884.

Aufschnaiter, Peter, and Brauen, Martin (eds), *Peter Aufschnaiter's Eight Years in Tibet*, Bangkok, 2002.

Avedon, John F, *In Exile from the Land of Snows*, London, 1984.

Aziz, Barbara Nimri, *Tibetan Frontier Families*, Delhi, 1978.

Baker, Ian A, *The Dalai Lama's Secret Temple*, London, 2000.

Bailey, Frederick Marshman, *China, Tibet, Assam: A Journey*, London, 1911.

————, *Mission to Tashkent*, London, 1946.

————, *No Passport to Tibet*, 1957.

Bajpai, S C, *Kinnaur in the Himalayas*, Delhi, 1981.

Bajwa, Fauja Singh, *Military System of the Sikhs During the Period 1799–1849*, Delhi, 1964.

Bamzai, P N K, *A History of Kashmir; Political, Social, Cultural, from the Earliest Times to the Present Day*, Delhi, 1962.

Banskota, Purushottam, *The Gurkha Connection: A History of the Gurkha Recruitment in the British Indian Army*, Jaipur, 1994.

Barnett, Robert, *Cutting Off the Serpent's Head: Tightening Control in Tibet, 1994–1995*, New York, 1996.

————, *Lhasa: Streets with Memories*, New York, 2006.

———— and Akiner S (eds), *Resistance and Reform in Tibet*, London, 1994.

Bates, C E, *A Gazetteer of Kashmir, and the Adjacent Districts of Kishtwár, Badrawár, Jamú, Naoshera, Púnch, and the Valley of Kishen Ganga*, Calcutta, 1873.

Bauer, Paul, *Himalayan Quest*, London, 1938.

Baumgartner, Ruedi, *Farewell to Yak and Yeti? The Sherpas of Rolwaling Facing a Globalised World*, Kathmandu, 2015.

Bell, Charles, *Tibet Past and Present*, Oxford, 1924.

————, *The People of Tibet*, Oxford, 1928.

————, *The Religion of Tibet*, Oxford, 1931.

————, *Portrait of a Dalai Lama*, London, 1946.

Bellezza, John Vincent, *The Dawn of Tibet: The Ancient Civilization on the Roof of the World*, Lanham, 2014.

Bernard, Theos Casimir, *Penthouse of the Gods: A Pilgrimage into the Heart of Tibet and the Sacred City of Lhasa*, New York, 1939.

Bernstein, Jeremy, *In the Himalayas: Journeys through Nepal, Tibet, and Bhutan*, New York, 1996.

Berry, Scott, *Monks, Spies, and a Soldier of Fortune: The Japanese in Tibet*, London, 1995.

Bishop, Peter, *The Myth of Shangri-La: Tibet, Travel Writing and the Western Creation of Sacred Landscape*, London, 1991.

Bista, Dor Bahadur, *People of Nepal*, Kathmandu, 1967.

————, *Fatalism and Development: Nepal's Struggle for Modernisation*, Kathmandu, 1991.

Boileau, Digby W, et al., 'The Chronicles of the Family of Boileau', unpublished, n.d.

Braham, Trevor, *Himalayan Playground: Adventures on the Roof of the World 1942–72*, Glasgow, 2008.

Brauen, Martin, *Dreamworld Tibet: Western Illusions*, Bangkok, 2004.

Bruce, Charles G, *Kulu and Lahoul*, London, 1914.

————, *The Assault on Mount Everest 1922*, London, 1922.

————, *Himalayan Wanderer*, London, 1934.

Buckley, Michael, *Meltdown in Tibet: China's Reckless Destruction of Ecosystems from the Highlands of Tibet to the Deltas of Asia*, New York, 2014.

Buhl, Hermann, *Nanga Parbat Pilgrimage*, London, 1956.

Bulwer-Lytton, Edward, *Vril, the Power of the Coming Race*, London, 1871.

Byron, Robert, *First Russia, Then Tibet*, London, 1933.

Cams, Mario, *Companions in Geography: East–West Collaboration in the Mapping of Qing China (c.1685–1735)*, Leiden, 2017.

Chan, Victor, *Tibet Handbook*, Chico, 1994.

Chapman, Frederick Spencer, *Lhasa: The Holy City*, London, 1938.

————, *From Helvellyn to Himalaya*, London, 1940.

Chapple, John, *The Lineages and Composition of Gurkha Regiments in British Service*, 2nd ed., Winchester, 2013.

Chopel, Gendun, *In the Forest of Faded Wisdom: 104 Poems*, ed. and trans. Lopez, Donald S, Chicago, 2009.

———, *Grains of Gold: Tales of a Cosmopolitan Traveler*, trans. Jinpa, Thupten, and Lopez, Donald S, Chicago, 2014.

Clinch, Elizabeth, and Nicholas, *Through a Land of Extremes: The Littledales of Central Asia*, Stroud, 2008.

Cocker, Mark, and Inskipp, Carol, *A Himalayan Ornithologist: Life and Work of Brian Houghton Hodgson*, Oxford, 1988.

Coleman, A P, *A Special Corps: The Beginning of Gorkha Service with the British*, Edinburgh, 1999.

Collie, Norman, *Climbing on the Himalaya and Other Mountain Ranges*, Edinburgh, 1902.

Collister, Peter, *Bhutan and the British*, London, 1987.

Conefrey, Mick, *Everest 1953: The Epic Story of the First Ascent*, London, 2013.

Conner, Victoria, and Barnett, Robert, *Leaders in Tibet: A Directory*, London, 1997.

Cooper, Thomas Thornville, *Journal of an Overland Journey from China towards India*, Calcutta, 1869.

Cowan, Sam, *Essays on Nepal: Past and Present*, Kathmandu, 2018.

Craig, Mary, *Tears of Blood: A Cry for Tibet*, London, 1992.

———, *Kundun: A Biography of the Family of the Dalai Lama*, London, 1997.

Cranston, Sylvia, *H P B: The Extraordinary Life of Madame Helena Petrovna Blavatsky, Founder of the Modern Theosophical Movement*, New York, 1994.

Cunningham, Alexander, *Ladak, Physical, Statistical, and Historical; With Notices of the Surrounding Countries*, London, 1854.

Dahal, Pushpa Kamal, *Problems and Prospects of Revolution in Nepal*, Kathmandu, 2004.

Dalrymple, William, *City of Djinns: A Year in Delhi*, London, 1993.

———, *White Mughals: Love and Betrayal in Eighteenth-Century India*, London, 2002.

———, *The Last Mughal: The Fall of a Dynasty: Delhi, 1857*, London, 2006.

Danielli, Giotto, and Spranger, J A, *Storia della Spedizione Scientifica Italiana nel Himàlaia, Caracorùm e Turchestàn Cinese (1913–1914)*, Bologna, 1924.

Dasgupta, Atis K, *The Fakir and the Sannyasi Uprisings*, Calcutta, 1992.

Datta, C L, *Ladakh and Western Himalayan Politics: 1819–1848*, New Delhi, 1973.

Dattaray, Sunanda K, *Smash and Grab: Annexation of Sikkim*, revised ed., Chennai, 2013.

David-Néel, Alexandra, *My Journey to Lhasa*, London, 1927.

Davis, Wade, *Into the Silence: The Great War, Mallory and the Conquest of Everest*, London, 2011.

Desideri, Ippolito, *An Account of Tibet: The Travels of Ippolito Desideri of Pistoia*, London, 1932.

Dhondup, Kelsang, *The Water-Horse and Other Years: A History of 17th and 18th Century Tibet*, Dharamsala, 1984

———, *The Water-Bird and Other Years: A History of the 13th Dalai Lama and After*, New Delhi, 1986.

Diemberger, Hildegard, *When a Woman Becomes a Religious Dynasty: The Samding Dorje Phagmo of Tibet*, New York, 2007.

Digby, William, *A Friend in Need, 1857, Friendship Forgotten, 1887: An Episode in Indian Foreign Office Administration*, London, 1890.

Dikötter, Frank, *The Tragedy of Liberation: A History of the Chinese Revolution 1945–1957*, New York, 2013.

DiValerio, David M, *The Holy Madmen of Tibet*, Oxford, 2015.

Dixit, Kanak Mani, *Peace Politics of Nepal: An Opinion From Within*, Kathmandu, 2011.

——— & Ramachandaran, Shastri (eds), *State of Nepal*, Lalitpur, 2002.

Dodin, Thierry, and Räther, Heinz (eds), *Imagining Tibet: Perceptions, Projections, And Fantasies*, Somerville, 2001.

Douglas, Ed, *Chomolungma Sings the Blues*, Constable, 1997.

———, *Tenzing: Hero of Everest*, National Geographic, 2003.

Duff, Andrew, *Sikkim: Requiem for a Himalayan Kingdom*, Edinburgh, 2015.

Duka, Theodore, *Life and Works of Alexander Csoma de Kőrös*, London, 1885.

Dunham, Mikel, *Buddha's Warriors*, New York, 2004.

Evans, Charles, *Kangchenjunga: The Untrodden Peak*, London, 1956.

Evans-Wentz, Walter Y, *The Tibetan Book of the Dead*, London, 1927.

Farrer, Reginald, *On the Eaves of the World*, 2 vols, London, 1917.

Farwell, Byron, *The Gurkhas: A History of the Finest Infantrymen in the World*, London, 1984.

Feigon, Lee, *Demystifying Tibet: Unlocking the Secrets of the Land of the Snows*, London, 1999.

Fisher, James F (ed.), *Himalayan Anthropology: The Indo-Tibetan Interface*, The Hague, 1978.

————, *Sherpas: Reflections on Change in Himalayan Nepal*, Berkeley, 1990.

Fisher, Margaret W, Rose, Leo E, and Huttenback, Robert A, *Himalayan Battleground: Sino-Indian Rivalry in Ladakh*, London, 1963.

Fleming, Peter, *Bayonets to Lhasa*, London, 1961.

Ford, Robert, *Captured in Tibet*, London, 1957.

Foster, Barbara and Michael W, *The Secret Lives of Alexandra David-Néel*, New York, 2002.

Francke, August Hermann, *A History of Western Tibet, One of the Unknown Empires*, London, 1907.

————, *Antiquities of Indian Tibet*, 2 vols, Calcutta, 1914–26.

Fraser, James, *Journal of a Tour through Part of the Snowy Range of the Himala Mountains and to the Sources of the Rivers Jumna and Ganges*, London, 1820.

French, Patrick, *Younghusband: The Last Great Imperial Adventurer*, London, 1994.

————, *Tibet, Tibet: A Personal History of a Lost Land*, London, 2003.

Fürer-Haimendorf, Christoph von, *The Sherpas of Nepal*, Berkeley, 1964.

————, *Himalayan Traders*, London, 1975.

———— (ed.), *Asian Highland Societies: In Anthropological Perspective*, Michigan, 1981.

————, *The Sherpas Transformed: Social Change in a Buddhist Society of Nepal*, Delhi, 1984.

Gamble, Ruth, *Reincarnation in Tibetan Buddhism: The Third Karmapa and the Invention of a Tradition*, Oxford, 2018.

Garzilli, Enrica, *Il Duce's Explorer: The Adventures of Giuseppe Tucci and Italian Policy in the Orient from Mussolini to Andreotti*, Milan, 2015.

Gellner, David N, *Monk, Householder and Tantric Priest: Newar Buddhism and its Hierarchy of Ritual*, Cambridge, 1992.

————, Pfaff-Czarnecka, Joanna, and Whelpton, John (eds), *Nationalism and Ethnicity in a Hindu Kingdom: The Politics of Culture in Contemporary Nepal*, Abingdon, 1997.

Ghosh, Durba, *Sex and the Family in Colonial India*, Cambridge, 2006.

Ghosh, Jamin Mohan, *Sannyasi and Fakir Raiders in Bengal*, Calcutta, 1930.

Gibson, J T M, *As I Saw It*, Delhi, 1976.

Gillman, Peter and Leni, *The Wildest Dream: Mallory, His Life and Conflicting Passions*, London, 2000

Gilmour, David, *Curzon*, London, 1994.

————, *The Long Recessional: The Imperial Life of Rudyard Kipling*, London, 2002.

————, *The British in India*, London, 2018.

Goldstein, Melvyn, *A History of Modern Tibet, Volume 1: The Demise of the Lamaist State, 1913–1951*, London, 1989.

————, *The Snow Lion and the Dragon: China, Tibet and the Dalai Lama*, Berkeley, 1994.

————, *A History of Modern Tibet, Volume 2: The Calm Before the Storm, 1951–1955*, Berkeley, 2007.

————, *A History of Modern Tibet, Volume 3: The Storm Clouds Descend, 1955–1957*, Berkeley, 2013.

————, Sherap, Dawei, and Siebenschuh, William R, *A Tibetan Revolutionary: The Political Life and Times of Bapa Phüntso Wangye*, Berkeley, 2004.

————, Jiao, Ben, and Lhundrup, Tanzen, *On the Cultural Revolution in Tibet: The Nyemo Incident of 1969*, Berkeley, 2009.

Greene, Raymond, *Moments of Being*, London, 1974.

Gregson, Jonathan, *Blood Against the Snows: The Tragic Story of Nepal's Royal Dynasty*, London, 2002.

Gurung, Harka, *Maps of Nepal: Inventory and Evaluation*, Bangkok, 1983.

Gutschow, Niels, *Architecture of the Newars: A History of Building Typologies and Details in Nepal*, 3 vols, Chicago, 2011.

Gyatso, Palden, *Fire Under the Snow: Testimony of a Tibetan Prisoner*, London, 1997.

Gyatso, Tenzin, HH The Dalai Lama, *Freedom in Exile*, London, 1990.

——, *Awakening the Mind, Lightening the Heart*, New York, 1995.

——, *Tibet and the Tibetan People's Struggle: 10 March Statements (1961–2005)*, Dharamsala, 2005.

——, *The Essential Dalai Lama*, London, 2005.

Gyawali, Surya Bikram, *Amar Singh Thapa 1748–1816*, Darjeeling, 1943.

Hackett, Paul G, *Theos Bernard, the White Lama: Tibet, Yoga, and American Religious Life*, New York, 2012

Hagen, Toni, *Nepal*, Bern, 1960.

Hamilton, Francis Buchanan, *An Account of the Kingdom of Nepaul, and of the Territories Annexed to this Dominion by the House of Gurkha*, Edinburgh, 1819.

Harcourt, Alfred Frederick Pollock, *The Himalayan Districts of Kooloo, Lahoul and Spiti*, London, 1871.

Harrer, Heinrich, *Seven Years in Tibet*, London, 1954.

Harris, Clare E, *The Museum on the Roof of the World: Art, Politics, and the Representation of Tibet*, Chicago, 2012.

Harris, Clare E, *Photography and Tibet*, London, 2016.

Harris, Georgina Maria, *A Lady's Diary of the Siege of Lucknow*, London, 1858.

Harvey, Andrew, *A Journey in Ladakh*, London, 1983.

Hasrat, Bikrama Jit, *History of Nepal, as Told by its Own and Contemporary Chroniclers*, Hoshiarpur, 1971.

Hedin, Sven, *Transhimalaya*, London, 4 vols, 1909.

Heruka, Tsangnyön, *The Life of Milarepa*, trans. Quintman, Andrew, London, 2010.

Hibbert, Christopher, *The Great Mutiny: India 1857*, London, 1978.

Hillary, Edmund, *High Adventure*, London, 1955.

——, *View from the Summit*, London, 1999.

Hilton, James, *Lost Horizon*, London, 1933.

Ham, Peter van, *Guge: Ages of Gold: The West Tibetan Masterpieces*, Munich, 2016.

——, *Alchi: Treasure of the Himalayas*, Munich, 2019.

Herzog, Maurice, *Annapurna*, London, 1952.

Hilton, Isabel, *The Search for the Panchen Lama*, London, 1999.

Hobson, John Atkinson, and Mummery, Albert Frederick, *The Physiology of Industry: Being an Exposure of Certain Fallacies in Existing Theories of Economics*, London, 1889.

Hodgson, Brian Houghton, *Essays on the Languages, Literature, and Religion of Nepál and Tibet; Together with Further Papers on the Geography, Ethnology and Commerce of those Countries'*, London, 1874.

Hoerlin, Bettina, *Steps of Courage: My Parents' Journey from Nazi Germany to America*, Bloomington, 2011.

Höfer, András, *The Caste Hierarchy and the State in Nepal: A Study of the Muluki Ain of 1854*, Kathmandu, 2004.

Hoftun, Martin, Raeper, William, and Whelpton, John, *People, Politics and Ideology: Democracy and Social Change in Nepal*, Kathmandu, 1999.

Holdich, Thomas Hungerford, *Tibet the Mysterious*, London, 1904.

Hooker, Joseph Dalton, *The Rhododendrons of Sikkim-Himalaya*, London, 1849

——, *Himalayan Journals: Or, Notes of a Naturalist in Bengal, the Sikkim and Nepal Himalayas, the Khasia Mountains, etc*, London, 1854.

Hopkirk, Peter, *Trespassers on the Roof of the World: The Race for Lhasa*, London, 1982.

——, *The Great Game: On Secret Service in High Asia*, London, 1990.

Hopkirk, Peter, *Quest for Kim: In Search of Kipling's Great Game*, London, 1996.

Howard-Bury, Charles, Leigh-Mallory, George H, and Wollaston, A F R, *Mount Everest: The Reconnaissance, 1921*, London, 1922.

Huc, Régis-Evariste, and Gabet, Joseph, *Travels in Tartary, Thibet and China 1844–1846*, trans. William Hazlitt, 2 vols, London, 1852.

Hunt, John, *The Ascent of Everest*, London, 1953.

Hunter, William Wilson, *Life of Brian Houghton Hodgson*, London, 1896.

Hussain, Asad, *British India's Relations with the Kingdom of Nepal 1857–1947*, London, 1970.

Hutt, Michael, *Nepal in the Nineties*, Delhi, 1994.

——, *Modern Literary Nepali: An Introductory Reader*, Oxford, 1997.

—— (ed.), *Himalayan People's War: Nepal's Maoist Rebellion*, London, 2003.

——, *The Life of Bhupi Sherchan: Poetry and Politics in Post-Rana Nepal*, Delhi, 2010.

—— et al., *Nepal: A Guide to the Art and Architecture of the Kathmandu Valley*, Singapore, 1994.

Huxley, Leonard (ed.), *Life and Letters of Sir Joseph Dalton Hooker*, 2 vols, London, 1918.

Isserman, Maurice, and Weaver, Stewart, *Fallen Giants: A History of Himalayan Mountaineering*, New Haven, 2008.

Ives, Jack D, and Messerli, Bruno, *The Himalayan Dilemma: Reconciling Development and Conservation*, London, 1989.

Jha, Pranab Kumar, *History of Sikkim (1817–1904): Analysis of British Policy and Activities*, Calcutta, 1985.

Jha, Prashant, *Battles of the New Republic: A Contemporary History of Nepal*, London, 2014.

Kapadia, Harish, *Exploring the Hidden Himalaya*, London, 1990.

Kawaguchi, Ekai, *Three Years in Tibet*, Adyar, 1909.

Keay, John, *Explorers of the Western Himalayas*, London, 1977.

——, *The Honourable Company: A History of the English East India Company*, London, 1991.

——, *The Great Arc: The Dramatic Tale of How India Was Mapped and Everest Was Named*, London, 2000.

Khan, Sulmaan Wasif, *Muslim, Trader, Nomad, Spy: China's Cold War and the People of the Tibetan Borderlands*, Chapel Hill, 2015.

Kimura, Hisao, and Berry, Scott, *Japanese Agent in Tibet: My Ten Years of Travel in Disguise*, London, 1990.

Kingdon-Ward, Frank, *The Land of the Blue Poppy*, Cambridge, 1913.

——, *The Mystery Rivers of Tibet*, London, 1923.

——, *The Riddle of the Tsango Gorges*, London, 1926.

——, *A Plant-Hunter in Tibet*, London, 1941.

Kinloch, George, 'Journal of Capt George Kinloch on the Expedition to Nepal', 1767. Unpublished MS, British Library.

Kircher, Athanasius, *China Illustrata*, Amsterdam, 1667.

Kirkpatrick, William, *An Account of the Kingdom of Nepaul, being the Substance of Observations made during a Mission to that Country in the Year 1793*, London, 1811.

Klimburg-Salter, Deborah E, *Tabo: A Lamp for the Kingdom*, London, 1998.

Knaus, John Kenneth, *Orphans of the Cold War: America and the Tibetan Struggle for Survival*, New York, 1999.

Koehler, Jeff, *Darjeeling: A History of the World's Greatest Tea*, London, 2015.

Kohli, M S, and Conboy, Kenneth, *Spies in the Himalayas: Secret Missions and Perilous Climbs*, Lawrence, 2002.

Koirala, B P, *Atmabrittanta: Late Life Reminiscences*, trans. Kanak Mani Dixit, Kathmandu, 2001.

Korn, Wolfgang, *Traditional Architecture of the Kathmandu Valley*, Kathmandu, 1976.

Lach, Donald F, and Van Kley, Edwin J, *Asia in the Making of Europe, Volume III*, Chicago, 1998.

Lall, John, *Aksaichin and Sino-Indian Conflict*, Ahmedabad, 1989.

Lamb, Alastair, *British India and Tibet, 1766–1910*, London, [1960,] 1986.

———, *The China–India Border: The Origins of the Disputed Boundaries*, London, 1964.

———, *The McMahon Line: A Study in the Relations Between, India, China and Tibet, 1904 to 1914*, 2 vols, Abingdon, 1966.

———, *Tibet, China and India 1914–1950*, Hertingfordbury, 1989.

Landon, Perceval, *Lhasa*, 2 vols, London, 1905.

———, *Nepal*, 2 vols, London, 1928.

Larsson, Stefan, *Crazy for Wisdom: The Making of a Mad Yogin In Fifteenth Century Tibet*, Leiden, 2012.

Lawrence, John, *Lawrence of Lucknow: A Biography*, London, 1990.

Le Bon, Gustave, *Voyage to Nepal*, Bangkok, 1986.

Legassie, Shayne Aaron, *The Medieval Invention of Travel*, Chicago, 2017.

Lévi, Sylvain, *Le Népal, étude historique d'un royaume hindou*, 3 vols, Paris, 1905–8.

Lhamo, Rinchen, *We Tibetans*, London, 1926.

Liechty, Mark, *Far Out: Countercultural Seekers and the Tourist Encounter in Nepal*, Chicago, 2017.

Lopez, Donald S, *Prisoners of Shangri-La: Buddhism and the West*, Chicago, 1998.

———, *The Madman's Middle Way: Reflections on Reality of the Tibetan Monk Gendun Chopel*, Chicago, 2006.

———, *The Tibetan Book of the Dead: A Biography*, Princeton, 2011.

———, *From Stone to Flesh: A Short History of the Buddha*, Chicago, 2013.

———, *Gendun Chopel: Tibet's Modern Visionary*, Boulder, 2013.

——— and Jinpa, Thubten, *Dispelling the Darkness: A Jesuit's Quest for the Soul of Tibet*, Harvard, 2017.

——— and Bloom, Rebecca, *Assembly of the Exalted: The Tibetan Shrine Room from the Alice S. Kandell Collection*, Milan, 2018.

Lyte, Charles, *The Plant Hunters*, London, 1983.

———, *Frank Kingdon-Ward: The Last of the Great Plant Hunters*, London, 1989.

Macaulay, Colman, 'Report of a Mission to Sikkim and the Tibetan Frontier with a Memorandum on our Relations with Tibet', Calcutta, 1885.

Macdonald, David, *Twenty Years in Tibet*, Delhi, 2008.

Mailänder, Nicholas, *Er ging voraus nach Lhasa: Peter Aufschnaiter, Die Biographie*, Innsbruck, 2019.

Malla, Kamal P, *The Road to Nowhere: A Selection of Writings 1966–1977*, Lalitpur, [1979,] 2015.

Manandhar, Tri Ratna, *Some Aspects of Rana Rule in Nepal*, Kathmandu, 1983.

Manandhar, V K, *Cultural and Political Aspects of Nepal–China Relations*, Delhi, 1999.

Maraini, Fosco, *Secret Tibet*, London, 1952.

Markham, Clements R, *Narratives of the Mission of George Bogle to Tibet, and of the Journey of Thomas Manning to Lhasa*, London, 1876.

———, *Major James Rennell and the Rise of Modern English Geography*, London, 1895.

Markus-Gansser, Ursula, and Eichenberger, Ursula, *Augusto Gansser: From the Life of a World Explorer*, Zürich, 2012.

Marshall, Julie G, *Britain and Tibet 1765–1947: A Selected Annotated Bibliography of British Relations with Tibet and the Himalayan States Including Nepal, Sikkim and Bhutan*, Abingdon, 2005.

Marshall, Steven D, *Hostile Elements: A Study of Political Imprisonment in Tibet, 1987–1998*, London, 1999.

———, *Rukhag 3: The Nuns of Drapchi Prison*, London, 2000.

———, *Suppressing Dissent: Hostile Elements II, Political Imprisonment in Tibet, 1987–2000*, London, 2001

Mason, Kenneth, *Abode of Snow*, London, 1955.

Maxwell, Neville, *India's China War*, New York, 1970.

McDonald, Bernadette, *I'll Call You in Kathmandu: The Elizabeth Hawley Story*, Seattle, 2005.

McKay, Alex, *Tibet and the British Raj: The Frontier Cadre 1904–1947*, London, 1997.

———— (ed.), *Tibet and Her Neighbours: A History*, London, 2003.

————, *Kailas Histories: Renunciate Traditions and the Construction of Himalayan Sacred Geography*, Leiden, 2015.

Mill, Christine, *Norman Collie: A Life in Two Worlds*, Aberdeen, 1987.

Mishra, Kiran, *B P Koirala: Life and Times*, New Delhi, 1994.

Mitchell, Ian R, and Rodway, George W, *Prelude to Everest*, Edinburgh, 2011.

Mojumdar, K, *Political Relations between India and Nepal 1877–1923*, New Delhi, 1973.

Montgomerie, Thomas George, *Routes in the Western-Himalayas, Kashmir etc with Additions from Major C E Bates's Gazetteer and other Sources*, 3rd ed., Dehra Dun, 1909.

Moorcroft, William, and Trebeck, George, *Travels in the Himalayan Provinces of Hindustan and the Panjab in Ladakh and Kashmir; in Peshawar, Kabul, Kunduz and Bokhara*, ed. Wilson, Horace Hayman, 2 vols, London, 1841.

Morris, Jan, *Coronation Everest*, London, 1958.

Mullik, B N, *The Chinese Betrayal: My Years with Nehru*, Delhi, 1971.

Mummery, Albert Frederick, *My Climbs in the Alps and Caucasus*, London, 1895.

Muthukumaraswamy, M D & Kaushal, Molly (eds), *Folklore, Public Sphere and Civil Society*, Chennai, 2004.

Noel, John B L, *Through Tibet to Everest*, London, 1927.

Norbu, Jamyang, *Warriors of Tibet: The Story of Aten and the Khampas' Fight for the Freedom of Their Country*, London, 1987.

————, *The Mandala of Sherlock Holmes*, New York, 2003.

Norbu, Thubten Jigme, *Tibet is my Country*, London, 1960.

Northey, William Brook, and Morris, Charles John, *The Gurkhas: Their Manners, Customs and Country*, London, 1928.

Norton, Edward F, *The Fight for Everest: 1924*, London, 1925.

Nugent, Maria, *A Journal from the Year 1811 to the Year 1815, Including a Journey to and Residence in India*, 2 vols, London, 1839.

Ogura, Kiyoko, *Kathmandu Spring: The People's Movement of 1990*, Lalitpur, 2001.

Oidtmann, Max, *Forging the Golden Urn: The Qing Empire and the Politics of Reincarnation in Tibet*, New York, 2018.

Oldfield, Henry Ambrose, *Sketches from Nipal*, 2 vols, London, 1880.

Oliphant, Laurence, *A Journey to Katmandu (The Capital of Nepaul), with the Camp of Jung Bahadur; Including a Sketch of the Nepaulese Ambassador at Home*, London, 1852.

O'Malley, L S S, *Bengal District Gazetteers: Darjeeling*, Calcutta, 1907.

Ortner, Sherry, *Sherpas through their Rituals*, New York, 1978.

————, *High Religion: A Cultural and Political History of Sherpa Religion*, Princeton, 1989.

————, *Life and Death on Mount Everest: Sherpas and Himalayan Mountaineering*, Princeton, 2011.

Osmaston, Henry, and Denwood, Philip (eds), *Proceedings of the Fourth and Fifth International Colloquia on Ladakh*, London, 1995.

Pal, Pratapaditya, et al., *Himalayas: An Aesthetic Adventure*, Chicago, 2003.

Pallis, Marco, *Peaks and Lamas*, London, 1939.

————, *The Way and the Mountain*, London, 1960.

Patt, David, *A Strange Liberation: Tibetan Lives in Chinese Hands*, New York, 1992.

Pearse, Hugh, *The Hearseys: Five Generations of an Anglo-Indian Family*, Edinburgh, 1905.

Peissel, Michel, *Tiger for Breakfast: The Story of Boris of Katmandu*, New York, 1966.

————, *Mustang: A Lost Tibetan Kingdom*, New York, 1967.

Pemble, John, *The Invasion of Nepal: John Company at War*, Oxford, 1871.

Perrin, Jim, *Shipton and Tilman*, London, 2013.

Petech, Luciano, *Mediaeval History of Nepal c.750–1482*, Rome, 1958.

————, *The Kingdom of Ladakh: c.950–1842*, Rome, 1977.

————, *China and Tibet in the Early 18th Century*, Leiden, 1978.

Pomplun, Trent, *Jesuit on the Roof of the World: Ippolito Desideri's Mission to Tibet*, New York, 2010.

Pradhan, K L, *Brian Hodgson at the Kathmandu Residency 1825–1843*, Guwahati, 2001.

Pradhan, Kamal, *A History of Nepali Literature*, Delhi, 1984.

———, *Gorkha Conquest: The Process and Consequences of the Unification of Nepal, with Particular Reference to Eastern Nepal*, Calcutta, 1991, reprinted Lalitpur, 2009.

Pranavananda, Swami, *Kailas-Mansarovar*, Calcutta, 1949.

Praval, K C, *Valour Triumphs: A History of the Kumaon Regiment*, Faridabad, 1976.

Prinsep, Henry Thoby, *History of the Political and Military Transactions in India during the Administration of the Marquess of Hastings 1813–1823*, 2 vols, London, 1825.

Pye-Smith, Charlie, *Travels in Nepal: The Sequestered Kingdom*, London, 1988.

Raeper, William, and Hoftun, Martin, *Spring Awakening: An Account of the 1990 Revolution in Nepal*, New Delhi, 1992.

Ramble, Charles, *The Navel of the Demoness: Tibetan Buddhism and Civil Religion in Highland Nepal*, Oxford, 2008.

Raj, Prakash A, *'Kay Gardeko?': The Royal Massacre in Nepal*, Delhi, 2001.

Rana, Prabakhar S J B, Pashupati S J B, and Gautam S J B, *The Ranas of Nepal*, Geneva, 2002.

Rasgotra, Maharajakrishna, *A Life in Diplomacy*, Delhi, 2016.

Rathaur, Kamal Raj Singh, *The British and the Brave: A History of the Gurkha Recruitment in the British Army*, Jaipur, 1987.

Rawling, Cecil G, *The Great Plateau*, London, 1905.

Ray, Desmond, *Sir Joseph Dalton Hooker: Traveller and Plant Collector*, London, 1999.

Regmi, Dilli Rahman, *A Century of Family Autocracy in Nepal*, Kathmandu, 1958.

———, *Modern Nepal: Rise and Growth in the Eighteenth Century*, Calcutta, 1961.

———, *Medieval Nepal*, Calcutta, 1965.

———, *Inscriptions of Ancient Nepal*, 3 vols, New Delhi, 1983.

Regmi, Mahesh Chandra, *A Study in Nepali Economic History 1768–1846*, New Delhi, 1972.

———, *Land Ownership in Nepal*, Berkeley, 1976.

———, *Thatched Huts and Stucco Palaces: Peasants and Landlords in Nineteenth Century Nepal*, New Delhi, 1978.

———, *An Economic History of Nepal 1846-1901*, Varanasi, 1988.

———, *Imperial Gorkha: An Account of Gorkhali Rule in Kumaun (1791-1815)*, New Delhi, 1999.

Richardson, Hugh E, *Tibet and its History*, London, 1962.

———, *High Peaks, Pure Earth: Collected Writings on Tibetan History and Culture*, London, 1998.

Rijnhart, Susie Carson, *With the Tibetans in Tent and Temple*, Edinburgh, 1901.

Risley, Herbert Hope (ed.), *The Gazetteer of Sikkim*, Calcutta, 1894.

Roberts, David, *True Summit: What Really Happened on Maurice Herzog's First Legendary Ascent of Annapurna*, New York, 2000.

Roch, André, *Garwhal Himalaya: Expedition Suisse*, Neuchâtel, 1947.

Rocher, Rosane, and Ludo, *The Making of Western Indology: Henry Thomas Colebrooke and the East India Company*, Abingdon, 2012.

Roerich, George, *The Blue Annals*, 2 vols, London, 1949–1953.

Rose, Leo E, *Nepal: Strategy for Survival*, Berkeley, 1971.

——— and Fisher, Margaret W, *The Politics of Nepal: Persistence and Change in an Asian Monarchy*, Cornell, 1970.

Rose, Sarah, *For All the Tea in China: Espionage, Empire and the Secret Formula for the World's Favourite Drink*, London, 2010.

Russell, W H, *My Diary in India*, London, 1859.

Ruttledge, Hugh, *Everest 1933*, London, 1934.

Sandberg, Graham, *The Exploration of Tibet: Its History and Particulars from 1623 to 1904*, Caluctta, 1904.

Sangharakshita, *Facing Mount Kangchenjunga: An English Buddhist in the Eastern Himalayas*, Glasgow, 1991.

Sawerthal, Anna, 'A Newspaper for Tibet: Babu Tharchin and the "Tibet Mirror" (Yul phyogs so so'i gsar 'gyur me long, 1925–1963) from Kalimpong', doctoral dissertation, Heidelburg University, 2018.

Schaeffer, Kurtis R, Kapstein, Matthew T, and Tuttle, Gray (eds), *Sources of Tibetan Tradition*, New York, 2013.

Schaik, Sam van, *Tibet: A History*, London, 2011.

Schlagintweit, Hermann and Robert, *Official Reports on the Last Journeys and the Death of Adolphe Schlagintweit in Turkistán*, Berlin, 1859.

Schlagintweit, Hermann, Adolphe and Robert, *Results of a Scientific Mission to India and High Asia*, 4 vols, Leipzig, 1861–6.

Schneider, Hermann G, *Working and Waiting for Tibet: A Sketch of the Moravia Mission in the Western Himalayas*, London, 1891.

Schwieger, Peter, *The Dalai Lama and the Emperor of China: A Political History of the Tibetan Institution of Reincarnation*, New York, 2015.

Searle, Mike, *Colliding Continents: A Geological Exploration of the Himalaya, Karakoram, and Tibet*, Oxford, 2013.

Sen, Jahar, *Essays in Indo-Nepal Trade: A Nineteenth Century Study*, Calcutta, 1991.

Sever, Adrian, *Nepal under the Ranas*, New Delhi, 1972.

Shaha, Rishikesh, *Jung Bahadur: The Strongman of Nepal*, Kathmandu, 1978.

——, *Modern Nepal: A Political History 1769–1955*, 2 vols, New Delhi, 1990.

Shakabpa, W D, *Tibet: A Political History*, New York, 1984.

Sharma, Prayag Raj, *Preliminary Account of the Art and Architecture of the Karnali Region*, Paris, 1972.

Sharma, Shivaprasad, Vaidya, Tulsiram, and Manandhar, Triratna (eds), *Military History of Nepal*, Kathmandu, 1992.

Sherring, Charles A, *Western Tibet and the British Borderland*, London, 1906.

Shipp, John, *Memoirs of the Extraordinary Military Career of John Shipp, Late a Lieutenant in His Majesty's 87th Regiment*, London, 1829.

Shipton, Eric, *Nanda Devi*, London, 1936.

——, *That Untravelled World*, London, 1969.

Shokdung, *The Division of Heaven and Earth: On Tibet's Peaceful Revolution*, trans. Akester, Matthew, London, 2016.

Shulman, Nicola, *A Rage for Rock Gardening: The Story of Reginald Farrer, Gardener, Writer and Plant Collector*, London, 2002.

Shaha, Rishikesh, *Modern Nepal: A Political History, 1769–1955*, New Delhi, 2001.

——, *Politics in Nepal 1980–1991*, New Delhi, 1992.

Shakya, Tsering, *The Dragon in the Land of Snows: A History of Modern Tibet Since 1947*, London, 1999.

Shrestha, Bal Gopal, *The Sacred Town of Sankhu: The Anthropology of Newar Ritual, Religion and Society in Nepal*, Newcastle upon Tyne, 2012.

Singh, Amar Kaur Jasmir, *Himalayan Triangle: Historical Survey of British India's Relations with Tibet, Sikkim and Bhutan, 1765–1950*, London, 1988.

Slusser, Mary S, *Nepal Mandala*, Princeton, 1982.

Smythe, Frank S, *Kangchenjunga Adventure*, London, 1932.

——, *Kamet Conquered*, London, 1932.

——, *The Valley of Flowers*, London, 1938.

Snellgrove, David L, *Himalayan Pilgrimage: A Study of Tibetan Religion by a Traveller through Western Nepal*, Oxford, 1961.

—— and Richardson, Hugh, *A Cultural History of Tibet*, London, 1968.

Snelling, John, *The Sacred Mountain: Travellers and Pilgrims at Mount Kailas in Western Tibet, and the Great Universal System of the Sacred Mountain*, London, 1983.

——, *Buddhism in Russia: The Story of Agvan Dorzhiev*, Shaftesbury, 1993.

Sperling, Elliott, *Tibet Since 1950: Silence, Prison, or Exile*, New York, 2000.

Steele, Peter, *Eric Shipton: Everest and Beyond*, London, 1998.

Stein, Rolf A, *Tibetan Civilization*, London, 1972.

Stevens, Stanley F, *Claiming the High Ground: Sherpas, Subsistence and Environmental Change in the Highest Himalaya*, Berkeley, 1993.

Stiller, Ludwig F, *Prithvinarayan Shah in the Light of Dibya Upadesh*, Kathmandu, 1968.

———, *The Rise of the House of Gorkha: A Study in the Unification of Nepal, 1768–1816*, Kathmandu, 1973.

———, *The Silent Cry, the People of Nepal 1816–39*, Kathmandu, 1973.

———, *Letters From Kathmandu: The Kot Massacre*, Kathmandu, 1981.

———, *Nepal: Growth of a Nation*, Kathmandu, 1993.

Suyin, Han, *The Mountain is Young*, London, 1958.

———, *Lhasa: The Open City*, London, 1977.

Swinson, Arthur, *Beyond the Frontiers: The Biography of Colonel F M Bailey, Explorer and Secret Agent*, London, 1971.

Tapovanam, Swami, *Wanderings in the Himalayas*, Mumbai, 1960.

Taylor, Annie R, *Pioneering in Tibet*, London, 1898.

Teltscher, Kate, *The High Road to China: George Bogle, the Panchen Lama and the First British Expedition to Tibet*, London, 2006.

Tenzing, Judy and Tashi, *Tenzing and the Sherpas of Everest*, Sydney, 2001.

Thapa, Deepak, *A Kingdom Under Siege: Nepal's Maoist Insurgency 1996–2004*, Kathmandu, 2004.

Thapa, Manjushree, *Forget Kathmandu: An Elegy for Democracy*, Delhi, 2005.

———, *The Lives We Have Lost: Essays and Opinions on Nepal*, New Delhi, 2011.

Thapa, Rabi, *Thamel: Dark Star of Kathmandu*, New Delhi, 2016.

Tharkay, Ang, *Mémoires d'un Sherpa*, Paris, 1956.

Thomas, Lowell, *Out of this World: Across the Himalayas to Tibet*, New York, 1950.

Thondup, Gyalo, *The Noodle Maker of Kalimpong: My Untold Story of the Struggle of Tibet*, London, 2015.

Thubron, Colin, *To a Mountain in Tibet*, London, 2010.

Tibet Information Network, *A Poisoned Arrow: The Secret Report of the 10th Panchen Lama*, London, 1997.

Tilman, H W, *The Ascent of Nanda Devi*, Cambridge, 1937.

———, *Everest, 1938*, London, 1948.

———, *Nepal Himalaya*, London, 1952.

Tladhar-Douglas, Will, *Remaking Buddhism for Medieval Nepal: The Fifteenth-Century Reformation of Newar Buddhism*, Abingdon, 2005.

Toffin, Gérard (ed.), *Man and his House in the Himalayas*, Delhi, 1991.

———, *From Monarchy to Republic*, 2013.

Troelstra, Anne S, *Bibliography of Natural History Travel Narratives*, Leiden, 2016.

Tucci, Giuseppe, *To Lhasa and Beyond*, Rome, 1956.

———, *Nepal: The Discovery of the Mallas*, London, 1962.

———, *Tibet: Land of Snows*, London, 1967.

———, *Transhimalaya*, London, 1973.

Tuckey, Harriet, *Everest: The First Ascent*, London, 2013.

Tuladhar, Kamal Ratna, *Caravan to Lhasa: A Merchant of Kathmandu in Traditional Tibet*, Kathmandu, 2011.

Turner, Samuel, *An Account of an Embassy to the Court of the Teshoo Lama in Tibet*, London, 1800.

Tuttle, Gray, and Schaeffer, Kurtis R (eds), *The Tibetan History Reader*, New York, 2013.

Unsworth, Walt, *Tiger in the Snow: The Life and Adventures of A F Mummery*, London, 1967.

———, *Everest: The Ultimate Book of the Ultimate Mountain*, Oxford, 1989.

Upadhya, Sanjay, *Nepal and the Geo-Strategic Rivalry between China and India*, Abingdon, 2012.

Uprety, Prem R, *Nepal: A Small Nation in the Vortex of International Conflicts*, Kathmandu, 1984.

Vitali, Roberto, *Records of Tho.ling: A Literary and Visual Reconstruction of the 'Mother' Monastery in Guge*, Dharamsala, 1999.

——, *A Short History of Mustang (10th–15th Century)*, Dharamsala, 2013.

Waddell, Laurence A, *The Buddhism of Tibet, or Lamaism, with its Mystic Cults, Symbolism and Mythology, and in its Relation to Indian Buddhism*, London, 1895.

——, *Among the Himalayas*, London, 1899.

——, *Lhasa and its Mysteries*, London, 1905.

Waller, Derek, *The Pundits: British Exploration of Tibet and Central Asia*, Lexington, 1990.

Wangyal, Phuntsok, *Witness to Tibet's History*, New Delhi, 2007.

Ward, Michael, *Everest: A Thousand Years of Exploration*, Glasgow, 2003.

Wasserstein, Bernard, *The Secret Lives of Trebitsch Lincoln*, London, 1988.

Waterhouse, David, *The Origins of Himalayan Studies: Brian Houghton Hodgson in Nepal and Darjeeling*, London, 2004.

Webber, Thomas W, *The Forests of Upper India and Their Inhabitants*, London, 1902.

West, John B, *High Life: A History of High Altitude Medicine and Exploration*, Oxford, 1998.

Wheeler, James Talboys, *Summary of Affairs of the Government of India in the Foreign Department from 1864 to 1869*, Calcutta, 1868.

Whelpton, John, *Jang Bahadur in Europe: The First Nepalese Mission to the West*, Kathmandu, 1983.

Whelpton, John, *A History of Nepal*, Cambridge, 2005.

White, John Claud, *Sikhim and Bhutan: Twenty-One Years on the North-East Frontier 1887–1908*, London, 1909.

Wignall, Sydney, *Spy on the Roof of the World*, Edinburgh, 1996.

Williamson, Margaret D, *Memoirs of a Political Officer's Wife in Tibet, Sikkim and Bhutan*, London, 1987.

Woeser, Tsering, *Tibet on Fire: Self-Immolations Against Chinese Rule*, London, 2016.

Wolpert, Stanley, *Morley and India: 1906–1910*, Berkeley, 1967.

Wright, Daniel (ed.), *History of Nepal, Translated from the Parbatiya by Munshi Shew Shunker Singh and Pandit Shri Gurunand*, Cambridge, 1877.

Wulf, Andrea, *The Invention of Nature: The Adventures of Alexander von Humboldt, the Lost Hero of Science*, London, 2016.

Young, Keith, *Delhi 1857: The Siege, Assault, and Capture as Given in the Diary and Correspondence of the Late Colonel Keith Young*, London, 1902.

Younghusband, Francis, *The Epic of Mount Everest*, London, 1926.

Zurick, David, and Pacheco, Julsun, *Illustrated Atlas of the Himalaya*, Lexington, 2006.

Index